The European Banking Regulation Handbook, Volume I

Christos V. Gortsos

The European Banking Regulation Handbook, Volume I

Theory of Banking Regulation, International Standards, Evolution and Institutional Aspects of European Banking Law

Christos V. Gortsos
Law School
National and Kapodistrian University
of Athens
Athens, Greece

ISBN 978-3-031-32858-9   ISBN 978-3-031-32859-6 (eBook)
https://doi.org/10.1007/978-3-031-32859-6

© The Editor(s) (if applicable) and The Author(s), under exclusive license to Springer Nature Switzerland AG 2023

This work is subject to copyright. All rights are solely and exclusively licensed by the Publisher, whether the whole or part of the material is concerned, specifically the rights of translation, reprinting, reuse of illustrations, recitation, broadcasting, reproduction on microfilms or in any other physical way, and transmission or information storage and retrieval, electronic adaptation, computer software, or by similar or dissimilar methodology now known or hereafter developed. The use of general descriptive names, registered names, trademarks, service marks, etc. in this publication does not imply, even in the absence of a specific statement, that such names are exempt from the relevant protective laws and regulations and therefore free for general use.
The publisher, the authors, and the editors are safe to assume that the advice and information in this book are believed to be true and accurate at the date of publication. Neither the publisher nor the authors or the editors give a warranty, expressed or implied, with respect to the material contained herein or for any errors or omissions that may have been made. The publisher remains neutral with regard to jurisdictional claims in published maps and institutional affiliations.

This Palgrave Macmillan imprint is published by the registered company Springer Nature Switzerland AG
The registered company address is: Gewerbestrasse 11, 6330 Cham, Switzerland

To Christina

Preface

A. The present book is the first volume of my handbook on European Union (EU) banking regulation (law), to be followed by a second volume in 2024. As one can imagine, keeping the length of such handbook under control was a demanding exercise, considering the plethora and, to a certain extent at least, great length and detail of EU legislative and delegated (not to mention, implementing) acts of the EU legislators that constitute the sources of such a vast field, as well as a quite extensive relevant case-law of the Court of Justice (CJEU). Furthermore, several books and commentaries and hundreds of articles (most of them referred to herein) have already covered most of the building blocks of this branch of EU economic law in a comprehensive manner. The purpose of this work is thus to provide a comprehensive synthesis, by systematically presenting and analysing the key concepts, institutions and substantive rules, which could serve as a "gateway" to those who are keenly interested in this field.

The cut-off date for information contained in this first volume, which deals with the evolution and key institutional aspects of EU banking law (through the lens of the theory of banking regulation and under the influence of international financial standards), is 31 December 2022. The second volume, pertaining to the substantive aspects of EU banking law, will follow in 2024. The reason behind the decision to defer the completion of the second volume, in agreement with the publisher, is that a very important amendment of certain key sources of EU banking law is pending and is reasonably expected to be finalised by mid-2023. Hence, it would not be appropriate to produce a handbook that would need to be *substantially* modified a short while after its publication. I am of course well aware that EU banking law is a "moving target" and that amendments thereto are continual. However, I regard this as inescapable and a mere signal to the dire need for subsequent periodical updates of this handbook (if conditions allow).

B. The book is structured in three parts, each containing three chapters. **Part I**, titled "Theory of Banking Regulation and International Financial Standards" deals, firstly, with the case for banking regulation (**Chapter** 1). This chapter briefly discusses the functions of the financial system, and the role(s) of banks therein, and then focuses on the policy objectives and the instruments of financial and (in particular) banking regulation (under 1.1). The various instruments of banking regulation, which constitute the "bank safety net", are then discussed in more detail, with a distinction between prudential measures in banking, as well as crisis prevention and management measures in banking (under 1.2 and 1.3, respectively). In Chapters 2–3, the discussion turns to the international financial architecture and to public international financial law, which exerts a significant influence on the shaping of EU banking and, in general, financial law. **Chapter** 2 presents the key aspects of this law, including its definition and evolution (under 2.1 and 2.2), and systematically elaborates on the four levels of its making and enforcement and on the role of international financial institutions and international financial fora therein (under 2.3), as well as its key sources, which are encompassed in soft law instruments (under 2.4). The key institutional aspects of the international financial fora, such as the Basel Committee on Banking Supervision (BCBS) and the International Association of Deposit Insurers (IADI), which are of importance for international banking law, the international fora in the field of capital markets law and other international financial for a, are examined in **Chapter** 3 (under 3.1–3.4, respectively), which concludes with a brief interim assessment (under 3.5).

Parts II and III contain the key elements of European (EU) Banking Law. The first chapter in **Part II** ("European Banking Regulation (Law): Definition, Evolution and Sources"), **Chapter** 4, gives the definition of EU banking law and its position within the system of EU economic law (under 4.1), then discusses the first three periods in its evolution and the (current) fourth period, until the creation of the (European) Banking Union (under 4.2–4.3) and, finally, elaborates on the creation of the Banking Union (BU), and in particular on its two key pillars in place, namely the Single Supervisory Mechanism (SSM) and the Single Resolution Mechanism (SRM) (under 4.4). Developments after the establishment of the Banking Union are discussed in **Chapter** 5, including the Commission's 2016–2017 reform agenda and its (partial) implementation, the creation of the Capital Markets Union (CMU), the impact of the COVID-19 pandemic crisis and current developments relating, *inter alia*, to sustainable and digital finance (5.1–5.4, respectively). The last Chapter in this part, **Chapter** 6, briefly overviews the seven legislative acts which constitute the sources of EU banking law (under 6.1–6.7) and concludes with an *Excursus* on the Emergency Liquidity Assistance (ELA) mechanism.

Part III, titled "European Banking Regulation (Law): Key Institutional Elements", contains, as its title suggests, the key institutional aspects of the

European Banking Authority (EBA), and its (significant) role in the law-making process, as well as those of the SSM and the SRM. In **Chapter 7**, the EBA is, firstly, examined as part of the European Supervisory Authorities (ESAs), which constitute the first pillar of the European System of Financial Supervision (ESFS) (under 7.1–7.2). Sections 7.2–7.4 expand on EBA's founding regulation, legal status, scope of action, objective, and bodies, its tasks and powers, as well as its integration within the EU institutional framework. The law-making process and EBA's role therein are also discussed in some detail (under 7.5), followed by an *Excursus* on the Comitology procedure. **Chapter 8**, on the SSM, is structured in six sections (8.1–8.6), dealing with the European Central Bank (ECB) as a supervisory authority within the SSM, which is the hub within that mechanism, the division of tasks within the SSM and cooperation arrangements, the powers of the ECB and the NCAs, aspects of independence and accountability, the Administrative Board of Review (ABoR) and the Mediation Panel, and, finally, the institutional safeguards and liability. Similar (and in some cases identical) is the structure in **Chapter 9**, on the SRM. The Single Resolution Board (SRB), which is the hub within that mechanism, the general principles governing the operation of the SRM, division of tasks within the SRM and cooperation arrangements, the SRB's investigatory powers, and its power to impose fines and periodic penalty payments, aspects of independence and accountability, the Appeal Panel, as well the institutional safeguards and liability are dealt with in turn (under 9.1–9.6).

C. All primary sources are duly referenced in footnotes. A list thereof at the end, albeit practical for readers, was deemed too vast; it was thus decided not to include such a list in the Annex. On the other hand, the book contains, without any claim to exhaustiveness, an extensive list of secondary sources in every chapter, all of which are referenced in the footnotes, as appropriate. All related web references were last accessed on 31 December 2022.

D. The book has benefited from ongoing discussions with the most demanding of audiences, my students. It has also mostly benefited from comments by a great number of colleagues and friends, including Bart Joosen, David Ramos Muñoz, Filippo Annunziata, Concetta Brescia Morra, Matthias Lehmann and Edgar Löw. I want to thank them all most cordially. Special thanks are extended to three younger colleagues and friends: Lukas Böffel for specific accurate suggestions, Dimitri Kyriazis for his thorough comments and remarks on Parts II and III, as well as to Katerina Lagaria for her own very useful comments and remarks, as well as for the outstanding linguistic editing of the text (once again). I also wish to thank Athina Papadatou for her valuable administrative support. Any errors or omissions are my sole responsibility. Last but not least, special thanks are extended to my publisher, Palgrave Macmillan, for including this book in its Series of "Studies in Banking and Financial Institutions", as well as to Tula Weiss, Executive Editor, Scholarly & Professional Finance, for our excellent cooperation.

E. This book is dedicated to my beloved partner Christina Livada for her unfailing support over so many years.

Athens, Greece Christos V. Gortsos
December 2022

TABLE OF EU JUDGEMENTS AND ORDERS

Judgment of the Court of 13 June 1958 in joint **Cases C-9/56** and **C-10/56**, *Meroni & Co., Industrie Metallurgische, SpA v High Authority of the European Coal and Steel Community*, ECLI:EU:C:1958:7

Judgment of the Court of 14 May 1981 in **Case 98/90**, *Giuseppe Romano v Institut National d'assurance Maladie*, ECLI:EU:C:1981:104

Judgment of the Court (Second Chamber) of 13 December 1989 in **Case C-322/88**, *Salvatore Grimaldi v Fonds des maladies professionnelles*, ECLI:EU:C:1989:646

Judgment of the Court of 19 November 1991 in joint **Cases C-6/90** and **C-9/90**, *Andrea Francovich and Danila Bonifaci and others v Italian Republic*, ECLI:EU:C:1991:428

Judgment of the Court of 10 July 2003 in **Case C-11/00**, *Commission of the European Communities v European Central Bank*, ECLI:EU:C:2003:395

Judgment of the Court (sitting as a full Court) of 12 October 2004 in **Case C-222/02**, *Peter Paul, Cornelia Sonnen-Lütte, Christel Mörkens v Bundesrepublik Deutschland*, ECLI:EU:C:2004:606

Judgment of the Court (sitting as a full Court) of 27 November 2012 in **Case C-370/12**, *Thomas Pringle v Government of Ireland and Others*, ECLI:EU:C:2012:756

Judgment of the Court (Grand Chamber) of 26 February 2013 in **Case C-617/10**, *Åklagaren v Hans Åkerberg Fransson*, ECLI: EU:C:2013:105

Judgment of the Court (Grand Chamber) of 22 January 2014 in **Case 270/12**, *United Kingdom of Great Britain and Northern Ireland v European Parliament and Council of the European Union*, ECLI:EU:C:2014:18

Judgment of the General Court (Third Chamber) of 9 September 2015 in **Case T-660/14**, *SV Capital OÜ v European Banking Authority (EBA)*, ECLI:EU:T:2015:608

Judgment of the Court (Grand Chamber) of 19 July 2016 in **Case C526/14**, *Tadej Kotnik and Others v Državni zbor Republike Slovenije*, ECLI:EU:C:2016:570

Rectification Order of 30 September 2016 in **Case C526/14**, *Tadej Kotnik and Others v Državni zbor Republike Slovenije*, ECLI:EU:C:2016:767

Judgment of the Court (First Chamber) of 14 December 2016 in **Case C-577/15 P**, *SV Capital OÜ v European Banking Authority (EBA)*, ECLI:EU:C:2016:947

Judgment of the General Court of 16 May 2017 in **Case T-122/15**, *Landeskreditbank Baden-Württemberg – Förderbank v European Central Bank*, ECLI:EU:T:2017:337

Judgment of the Court (Fifth Chamber) of 4 October 2018 in **Case C-571/16**, *Nikalay Kantarev v Balgarska Narodna Banka*, ECLI:EU:C:2018:807

Judgment of the Court (Grand Chamber) of 19 December 2018 in **Case C-219/17**, *Silvio Berlusconi and Finanziaria d'investimento Fininvest SpA (Fininvest) v Banca d'Italia and Istituto per la Vigilanza Sulle Assicurazioni (IVASS)*, ECLI:EU:C:2018:1023

Judgement of the Court (Grand Chamber) of 26 February 2019 in joined **Cases C202/18**, *Ilmārs Rimšēvičs v Republic of Latvia* and **C238/18**, *European Central Bank v Republic of Latvia*, ECLI:EU:C:2019:139

Judgment of the General Court of 19 March 2019 in Joined **Cases T-98/16**, *Italian Republic v Commission*, **T-196/16**, *Banca Popolare di Bari v Commission*, and **T-198/16**, *Fondo Interbancario di Tutela dei Depositi v Commission*, ECLI:EU:T:2019:167

Judgment of the Court (First Chamber) of 8 May 2019 in **Case C450/17 P** on the appeal brought by *Landeskreditbank Baden-Württemberg Förderbank*, ECLI:EU:C:2019:372

Judgment of the Court (Grand Chamber) of 17 December 2020 in **Case C316/19**, *European Commission v Republic of Slovenia*, ECLI:EU:C:2020:1030

Judgment of the Court (Grand Chamber) of 2 March 2021 in **Case C-425/19 P**, *European Commission v Italian Republic, Banca Popolare* *di Bari, Banca d'Italia and Fondo Interbancario di Tutela dei Depositi*, ECLI:EU:C:2021:154

Opinion of Advocate General Bobek of 15 April 2021 in **Case C-911/19**, *Fédération bancaire française (FBF) v Autorité de contrôle prudentiel et de résolution (ACPR)*, ECLI:EU:C:2021:294

Judgment of the Court (Grand Chamber) of 15 July 2021 in **Case C-911/19**, *Fédération bancaire française (FBF) v Autorité de contrôle prudentiel et de résolution (ACPR)*, ECLI:EU:C:2021:599

Order of the General Court of 10 August 2021 in **Case T-760/20**, *Stasys Jakeliūnas v. ESMA*, ECLI:EU:T:2021:512

Judgment of the General Court (Third Chamber) of 9 February 2022 in **Case T-868/16**, *QI and Others v European Commission and European Central Bank*, ECLI:EU:T:2022:28

Judgment of the Court (Grand Chamber) of 13 September 2022 in **Case C45/21**, *Banka Slovenije* (Central Bank of Slovenia), ECLI:EU:C:2022:670

Contents

Part I Theory of Banking Regulation and International Financial Standards

1 The Case for Banking Regulation — 3
 1.1 Banking Regulation: Policy Objectives and Instruments — 3
  1.1.1 Setting the Scene: Functions of the Financial System and the Importance of Banking Intermediation — 3
  1.1.2 The Case for Financial Regulation in Economically Developed Countries (Advanced Economies) — 10
  1.1.3 Instruments to Achieve the Policy Objective of Ensuring Banking Stability: The 'Bank Safety Net' — 19
 1.2 Prudential Measures in Banking — 26
  1.2.1 Risks to Which Banks May Be Exposed as the Key Driver for Adopting Prudential Measures — 26
  1.2.2 Authorisation Requirements — 32
  1.2.3 Microprudential Banking Regulation — 32
  1.2.4 Microprudential Banking Supervision — 36
  1.2.5 Macroprudential Policies — 40
 1.3 Crisis Prevention and Management Measures in Banking — 45
  1.3.1 Crisis Prevention Measures — 45
  1.3.2 Lending of Last Resort (LLR) by the Central Bank — 48
  1.3.3 Banking Resolution — 51
  1.3.4 Deposit Guarantee — 56
  1.3.5 Institutional Relationship Among 'Bank Safety Net' Institutions—Relation with Macroeconomic Policies — 63
 Secondary Sources — 64

2 Key Aspects of Public International Financial Law: International Financial Standards — 85
 2.1 Definition, Branches and Delimitation — 85

		2.1.1	Definition	85

      2.1.1   Definition   85
      2.1.2   Branches   86
      2.1.3   Delimitations   88
  2.2 Evolution   91
      2.2.1   Introductory Remarks   91
      2.2.2   The Period from the Abolition of the Bretton Woods System Until the 'Asian Crisis' (1997–1998)   92
      2.2.3   The Period from the 'Asian Crisis' Until the Global Financial Crisis (2007–2009)   96
      2.2.4   The Period Since the Global Financial Crisis (GFC)   97
  2.3 The Four Levels of Making and Enforcement of Law and Policy   105
      2.3.1   Introduction   105
      2.3.2   The Level of Political Decision-Making   105
      2.3.3   The Level of Adoption of the Rules of Public International Financial Law   108
      2.3.4   The Level of Coordination: The Financial Stability Board (FSB)   116
      2.3.5   The Level of Indirect Enforcement of the Rules of Public International Financial Law   122
  2.4 Key Sources   131
      2.4.1   Introductory Remarks   131
      2.4.2   The Legal Nature of International Financial Standards   138
      2.4.3   Key Sources of Public International Banking Law Included in the Compendium   140
      2.4.4   The Other FSB "Key Standards for Sound Financial Systems"   146
  Secondary Sources   150

3 Key Institutional Aspects of the International Financial Architecture and an Interim Assessment   161
  3.1 The Basel Committee on Banking Supervision (BCBS)   161
      3.1.1   Establishment, Seat and Charter   161
      3.1.2   Mandate and Legal Status   164
      3.1.3   Activities   164
      3.1.4   Membership   168
      3.1.5   Oversight—The Group of Governors and Heads of Supervision (GHOS)   173
      3.1.6   Organisation   173
      3.1.7   Standards, Guidelines and Sound Practices   176
      3.1.8   Consultation with Non-member Authorities   180
      3.1.9   International Cooperation   181
  3.2 The International Association of Deposit Insurers (IADI)   181

	3.2.1	Establishment, Seat, Membership, Legal Personality and Governance	181
	3.2.2	Objectives	183
3.3	International Fora in the Field of Capital Markets Law		184
	3.3.1	The International Organisation of Securities Commissions (IOSCO)	184
	3.3.2	The International Accounting Standards Board (IASB)	186
	3.3.3	The International Federation of Accountants (IFAC)	188
	3.3.4	The Committee on Payments and Market Infrastructures (CPMI)	188
3.4	Other International Financial Fora		190
	3.4.1	The International Association of Insurance Supervisors (IAIS) in the Field of Public International Insurance Law	190
	3.4.2	The Joint Forum in the Field of Public International Financial Conglomerates Law	191
	3.4.3	The Financial Action Task Force (FATF) in the Field of Combatting the Use of the Financial System for the Commitment of Economic Crimes	192
	3.4.4	The Committee on the Global Financial System (CGFS)	193
3.5	An Interim Assessment and the Link to Parts II and III of This Study		196
Secondary Sources			197

Part II European Banking Regulation (Law): Definition, Evolution and Sources

4 Definition and Evolution up to the Creation of the Banking Union 201

4.1	General Introduction		201
	4.1.1	Financial Integration as the Conceptual Basis of European (EU) Financial Law	201
	4.1.2	A Definition of European (EU) Financial Law	204
	4.1.3	The Branches of European (EU) Financial Law	205
	4.1.4	Delimitation vis-à-vis European Monetary Law	209
	4.1.5	Delimitation vis-à-vis Other Branches of European Economic Law	214
	4.1.6	Evolution of European (EU) Banking Law Within the System of European (EU) Financial Law	214
4.2	The First Three Periods		216
	4.2.1	The First Period	216
	4.2.2	The Second Period	217
	4.2.3	The Third Period	220

	4.3	The (Current) Fourth Period, Until the Creation of the Banking Union	227
		4.3.1 Institutional Development: Creation of the European System of Financial Supervision (ESFS)	227
		4.3.2 Regulatory Developments	233
	4.4	Creation of the Banking Union (BU)	241
		4.4.1 The BU in a Historical Perspective	241
		4.4.2 The New Institutional and Regulatory Framework of 2013–2014	245
		4.4.3 Authorisation, Prudential Supervision and Prudential Regulation of Credit Institutions	246
		4.4.4 Resolution of Credit Institutions	248
		4.4.5 Deposit Guarantee Schemes	250
	Secondary Sources		253
5	Developments After the Establishment of the Banking Union		269
	5.1	The Commission's 2016–2017 Reform Agenda and Its (Partial) Implementation	269
		5.1.1 General Overview	269
		5.1.2 Finalisation of the 2016 "Legislative Banking Package"	270
		5.1.3 Introduction of Sovereign Bond-Backed Securities	272
		5.1.4 The NPL Problem and Measures Taken to Address It	273
		5.1.5 The 'Common Backstop' to the Single Resolution Board (SRB) for the Single Resolution Fund (SRF)	275
		5.1.6 Creation of the EDIS	280
	5.2	Creation of the Capital Markets Union (CMU)	281
		5.2.1 The Initial Phase	281
		5.2.2 The Full Implementation of the 2015 CMU Action Plan	284
		5.2.3 In Particular: The Sustainable Finance Agenda	287
	5.3	The Impact of the Pandemic Crisis	290
		5.3.1 Introductory Remarks	290
		5.3.2 Macroprudential Measures—Buffers	292
		5.3.3 Microprudential Measures	293
		5.3.4 Temporary Ban on the Payment of Dividends by Credit Institutions	294
		5.3.5 Resolution Planning	295
		5.3.6 The Contribution of the ESRB	296
		5.3.7 The Commission's 2020 NPL Action Plan	297
		5.3.8 Measures in Relation to Capital Markets Law	298
	5.4	Current Developments	299
		5.4.1 Further Amendment of Key Legislative Acts Relating to the BU	299

	5.4.2	Developments in Relation to Sustainable Finance	301
	5.4.3	The Commission's 2020 Digital Finance Package	304
Secondary Sources			306

6 The Legislative Acts Which Constitute the Sources of EU Banking Law — 317

6.1 The Capital Requirements Regulation (CRR) — 317
    6.1.1 General Aspects — 317
    6.1.2 Objective and Field of Application — 319
    6.1.3 The System of Rules — 323
    6.1.4 Other Aspects — 324
6.2 The Capital Requirements Directive No IV (CRD IV) — 324
    6.2.1 General Aspects — 324
    6.2.2 Objective and Field of Application — 325
    6.2.3 The System of Rules — 326
    6.2.4 Other Aspects — 327
6.3 The SSM Regulation (SSMR) — 327
    6.3.1 General Aspects — 327
    6.3.2 Objective and Field of Application — 331
    6.3.3 The System of Rules — 331
    6.3.4 Review by the Commission — 332
    6.3.5 Other Related Legal Acts and Agreements — 333
6.4 The Bank Recovery and Resolution Directive (BRRD) — 336
    6.4.1 General Aspects — 336
    6.4.2 Objective and Field of Application — 336
    6.4.3 The System of Rules — 338
    6.4.4 Other Aspects — 339
6.5 The SRM Regulation (SRMR) — 340
    6.5.1 General Aspects — 340
    6.5.2 Objective and Field of Application — 341
    6.5.3 The System of Rules — 342
    6.5.4 Relation to the BRRD—Applicable EU and National Law — 342
    6.5.5 The SRF Agreement — 344
6.6 The Deposit Guarantee Schemes Directive (DGSD) — 348
    6.6.1 General Aspects — 348
    6.6.2 Objective and Field of Application — 349
    6.6.3 DGSs and Credit Institutions Covered by the Field of Application — 350
    6.6.4 The System of Rules — 353
    6.6.5 Other Aspects: Commission and EBA Reports — 354
6.7 The Directive on the Reorganisation and Winding-Up of Credit Institutions — 356
    6.7.1 General Aspects — 356
    6.7.2 Objective and Field of Application — 356

	6.7.3 Other Key Provisions	357
Secondary Sources		371

Part III European Banking Regulation (Law): Key Institutional Elements

7 The European Banking Authority (EBA) and Its (Significant) Role in the Law-Making Process — 383

7.1 The European Supervisory Authorities (ESAs) as the First Pillar of the ESFS and Their Joint Committee — 383
    7.1.1 The ESAs as Mainly Regulatory Authorities and the Asymmetry in EU Financial Supervision — 383
    7.1.2 The Joint Committee — 387

7.2 Founding Regulation, Legal Status, Scope of Action, Objective and Bodies of the EBA — 388
    7.2.1 Founding Regulation, Legal Status, Scope of Action and Objective — 388
    7.2.2 Objective — 390
    7.2.3 Bodies — 391

7.3 Tasks and Powers of the EBA — 395
    7.3.1 The Structure of Chapter II of the EBA Regulation — 395
    7.3.2 The EBA's Tasks According to Article 8(1) EBA Regulation — 396
    7.3.3 The EBA's Powers Under Article 8(2) EBA Regulation — 403
    7.3.4 The EBA's Task and Powers Relating to Consumer Protection and Financial Activities Under Article 9 EBA Regulation — 405

7.4 The EBA's Integration Within the EU Institutional Framework — 407
    7.4.1 Introductory Remarks — 407
    7.4.2 Independence — 407
    7.4.3 Accountability — 408
    7.4.4 Appeals—Judicial Review of EBA Decisions — 410
    7.4.5 Liability — 412

7.5 The Law-Making Process and EBA's Role Therein — 413
    7.5.1 The TFEU Provisions and Their Application to EU Financial Law — 413
    7.5.2 Delegated Acts and Regulatory Technical Standards (RTSs) — 416
    7.5.3 Implementing Acts and Implementing Technical Standards (ITSs) — 418
    7.5.4 EBA Recommendations and Guidelines — 419
    7.5.5 Concluding Remarks — 422

Secondary Sources — 430

8	**The Single Supervisory Mechanism (SSM)**		**437**
	8.1 The European Central Bank (ECB) as a Supervisory Authority Within the SSM		437
		8.1.1 The Specific Supervisory Tasks Conferred on the ECB	437
		8.1.2 Organisational Principles: The New Governance Structure	439
	8.2 Division of Tasks Within the SSM and Cooperation Arrangements		447
		8.2.1 The Two Components of the SSM	447
		8.2.2 The Regulatory Perimeter	448
		8.2.3 Cooperation Arrangements	455
	8.3 Powers of the ECB and the NCAs		460
		8.3.1 Regulatory Powers	460
		8.3.2 Investigatory Powers	464
		8.3.3 Supervisory Powers	469
		8.3.4 Powers of Host Authorities and Cooperation on Consolidated Supervision	469
		8.3.5 Administrative Penalties	470
	8.4 Independence and Accountability		474
		8.4.1 Aspects of Independence	474
		8.4.2 Accountability of the ECB vis-à-vis EU Institutions and National Parliaments	478
	8.5 The Administrative Board of Review (ABoR) and the Mediation Panel		481
		8.5.1 The ABoR	481
		8.5.2 Creation of 'Chinese Walls'—The Mediation Panel	484
	8.6 Institutional Safeguards and Liability		486
		8.6.1 Institutional Safeguards	486
		8.6.2 Liability	487
	Secondary Sources		491
9	**The Single Resolution Mechanism (SRM)**		**499**
	9.1 The Single Resolution Board		499
		9.1.1 Legal Status	499
		9.1.2 Seat—Headquarters Agreement and Operating Conditions	500
		9.1.3 Composition and Governance	500
	9.2 General Principles Governing the Operation of the SRM, Division of Tasks Within the SRM and Cooperation Arrangements		511
		9.2.1 General Principles Governing the Operation of the SRM	511
		9.2.2 Division of Tasks Within the SRM	512
		9.2.3 Cooperation Arrangements	514
	9.3 Powers of the SRB and the NRAs		520

	9.3.1	*Investigatory Powers*	520
	9.3.2	*Power to Impose Fines and Periodic Penalty Payments*	522
9.4	*Independence and Accountability*		526
	9.4.1	*Independence*	526
	9.4.2	*Accountability*	530
9.5	*The Appeal Panel*		534
9.6	*Institutional Safeguards and Liability*		535
	9.6.1	*Institutional Safeguards*	535
	9.6.2	*Liability*	537
Secondary Sources			539

Index   545

List of Abbreviations

ABoR	Administrative Board of Review *(ECB – SSM)*
ACPR	Autorité de Contrôle Prudentiel et de Résolution *(France)*
AEUV	Vertrag über die Arbeitsweise der Europäischen Union
AI	Artificial Intelligence
AIF	Alternative Investment Fund
AIFM	Alternative Investment Fund Manager
AIFMD	Alternative Investment Fund Managers Directive *(2011/61/EU)*
AIG	American International Group Inc.
AMC	Asset Management Company
AML	Anti-Money Laundering
AMLSC	Anti-Money Laundering Standing Committee *(EBA)*
APG	Asia/Pacific Group on Money Laundering
BaFin	Bundesanstalt für Finanzdienstleistungsaufsicht *(Germany)*
BCBS	Basel Committee on Banking Supervision
BCCI	Bank of Commerce and Credit International
BCG	Basel Consultative Group *(Basel Committee)*
BIS	Bank for International Settlements
BoA	Board of Appeal *(ESAs)*
BoE	Bank of England
BoS	Board of Supervisors *(EBA)*
BPdB	Banca Popolare di Bari
BRRD	Bank Recovery and Resolution Directive *(2014/59/EU)*
BRRD II	Bank Recovery and Resolution Directive No II *(2019/879)*
BSC	Banking Supervision Committee
BSG	Banking Stakeholder Group *(EBA)*
BU	Banking Union
BVerfG	Bundesverfassungsgericht *(Germany)*
CAD	Capital Adequacy Directive *(93/6/EEC)*
CASs	Country Assistance Strategies
CBDC	Central Bank Digital Currency
CCB	Capital Conservation Buffer
CCPs	Central CounterParties

xxiii

CCR	Counterparty Credit Risk
CCyB	Countercyclical Capital Buffer
CDIC	Canada Deposit Insurance Corporation
CEBS	Committee of European Banking Supervisors
CEIOPS	Committee of European Insurance and Occupational Pensions Supervisors
CESEE	Central, Eastern and Southeastern Europe
CESR	Committee of European Securities Regulators
CET1	Common Equity Tier 1
CFATF	Caribbean Financial Action Task Force
CFR	Charter of Fundamental Rights *(EU)*
CGFS	Committee on the Global Financial System
CIS	Conference of Insurance Supervisors
CIWUD	Credit Institutions Winding-Up Directive *(2001/24/EC)*
CJEU	Court of Justice of the European Union
CLOs	Collateralised Loan Obligations
CMGs	Crisis Management Groups
CMU	Capital Markets Union
COB	Conduct of Business
COFRA	Cooperation Framework Agreement
CPs	Core Principles
CPMI	Committee on Payments and Markets Infrastructures
CPSS	Committee on Payment and Settlement Systems
CRA	Credit Rating Agency
CRD I	Capital Requirements Directive No I *(2006/48/EC and 2006/49/EC)*
CRD IV	Capital Requirements Directive No IV *(2013/36/EU)*
CRD V	Capital Requirements Directive No V *(2019/878)*
CRR	Capital Requirements Regulation *(575/2013)*
CRR II	Capital Requirements Regulation no. II *(2019/876)*
CSD	Central Securities Depository
CSDR	Central Securities Depositories Regulation *(909/2014)*
CSRD	Corporate Sustainability Reporting Directive *(2022/2464)*
CVA	Credit Valuation Adjustment
DAR	Detailed Assessments Report *(IMF and World Bank)*
DEFI	Decentralised Finance
DGS	Deposit Guarantee Scheme
DGSD	Deposit Guarantee Schemes Directive *(2014/49/EU)*
DIS	Deposit Insurance Scheme *(IADI)*
DLT	Distributed Ledger Technology
DLTR	Distributed Ledger Technology Regulation *(2022/858)*
DORA	Digital Operational Resilience Act *(Regulation (EU) 2022/2554)*
DRI	Direct Recapitalisation Instrument
D-SIB	Domestic Systemically Important Bank
DSP	Digital Stored-value Product
EAD	Exposure at Default
EAG	EurAsian Group
EBA	European Banking Authority
EBAR	European Banking Authority Regulation *(1093/2010)*
EBC	European Banking Committee

EBI	European Banking Institute
EBRD	European Bank for Reconstruction and Development
EC	European Community
ECA	European Court of Auditors
ECB	European Central Bank
ECC	Economic Consultative Committee
ECL	Expected Credit Loss
ECLI	European Case-Law Identifier
ECOFIN	Economic and Financial Affairs Council
ECON	Economic and Monetary Affairs Committee (European Parliament)
ECSC	European Coal and Steel Community
ECSPR	European Crowdfunding Service Providers Regulation *(2020/1503)*
EDIF	European Deposit Insurance Fund
EDIRA	European Deposit Insurance and Resolution Authority
EDIS	European Deposit Insurance Scheme
EEA	European Economic Area
EEC	European Economic Community
EFDI	European Forum of Deposit Insurers
EFSF	European Financial Stability Facility
EFTA	European Free Trade Association
e-GDDS	enhanced General Data Dissemination Standard
EIB	European Investment Bank
EIOPA	European Insurance and Occupational Pensions Authority
EIOPAR	European Insurance and Occupational Pensions Authority Regulation *(1094/2010)*
EIOPC	European Insurance and Occupational Pensions Committee
ELA	Emergency Liquidity Assistance
ELTIFR	European Long-Term Investment Funds Regulation *(2015/760/EU)*
EMEs	Emerging Market Economies
EMF	European Monetary Fund
EMIR	European Market Infrastructure Regulation *(648/2012)*
EMU	Economic and Monetary Union
EP	European Parliament
EREP	European Resolution Examination Programme *(EBA)*
ESAAMLG	Eastern and Southern Africa Anti-Money Laundering Group
ESA	EFTA Surveillance Authority
ESAs	European Supervisory Authorities
ESC	European Securities Committee
ESCB	European System of Central Banks
ESEP	European Supervisory Examination Programme *(EBA)*
ESFS	European System of Financial Supervision
ESG	Environmental, Social and Governance
ESM	European Stability Mechanism
ESMA	European Securities and Markets Authority
ESMAR	European Securities and Markets Authority Regulation *(1095/2010)*
ESRB	European Systemic Risk Board
ESRBR	European Systemic Risk Board Regulation *(1092/2010)*
EU	European Union
EUGBS	EU Green Bond Standard

EuSEFR	European Social Entrepreneurship Funds Regulation *(346/2013)*
EUV	Vertrag über die Europäische Union
EuVeCaR	European Venture Capital Funds Regulation *(345/2013)*
FATF	Financial Action Task Force
FBEs	Forborne Exposures
FBF	Fédération Bancaire Française
FCA	Financial Conduct Authority *(United Kingdom)*
FCC	Federal Constitutional Court *(Germany)*
FDIC	Federal Deposit Insurance Corporation *(United States)*
FESCO	Forum of European Securities Commissions
FICOD I	Financial Conglomerates Directive No I *(2002/87/EC)*
FICOD II	Financial Conglomerates Directive No II *(2011/89/EU)*
FinfraG	FinanzmarktinfrastrukturGesetz *(Switzerland)*
FINMA	Swiss Financial Market Supervisory Authority
FinTech	Financial Technology
FITD	Fondo Interbancario di Tutela dei Depositi *(Italy)*
FIU	Financial Intelligence Unit
FMIs	Financial Market Infrastructures
FOLF	Failing Or Likely to Fail
FPC	Financial Policy Committee *(United Kingdom)*
FSA	Financial Sector Assessment *(World Bank)*
FSAP	Financial Sector Assessment Program *(IMF and World Bank)*
FSAP	Financial Services Action Plan *(EU)*
FSB	Financial Stability Board
FSF	Financial Stability Forum
FSI	Financial Stability Institute
FSMA	Financial Services and Markets Act *(United Kingdom)*
FSRB	FATF-Style Regional Body
FSSA	Financial System Stability Assessment *(IMF)*
G7FE-TLPT	G7 Fundamental Elements for Threat-Led Penetration Testing
G-SIB	Global Systemically Important Bank *(FSB)*
G-SIFI	Global Systemically Important Financial Institution *(FSB)*
G-SII	Global Systemically Important Institution *(EU)*
GAAP	Generally Accepted Accounting Principles *(US)*
GAB	General Arrangements to Borrow
GAFISUD	Financial Action Task Force on Money Laundering in South America
GATS	General Agreement on Trade in Services
GATT	General Agreement on Trade and Tariffs
GC	Governing Council *(ECB)*
GCC	Gulf Cooperation Council
GdC	Groupe de Contact
GDP	Gross Domestic Product
GDPR	General Data Protection Regulation *(2016/679)*
GEM	Global Economy Meeting *(BIS)*
GEMC	Growth and Emerging Markets Committee *(IOSCO)*
GFC	Global Financial Crisis
GFSTs	Government Financial Stabilisation Tools
GHOS	Group of Governors and Heads of Supervision
GIABA	Inter-Governmental Action Group against Money Laundering in West Africa

GLRA	Group-Level Resolution Authority
GPFI	Global Partnership for Financial Inclusion
GRC	Charta der Grundrechte der Europäischen Union
GST	Global (bank) Stress Test *(IMF)*
HLEG	High—Level Expert Group on Sustainable Finance
HLSSC	High Level Securities Supervisors Committee
HQLA	High-Quality Liquid Assets
IADI	International Association of Deposit Insurers
IAIS	International Association of Insurance Supervisors
IASB	International Accounting Standards Board
IBOR	Interbank Offered Rates
ICAAP	Internal Capital Adequacy Assessment Process
ICBS	International Conferences of Banking Supervisors
ICC	International Chamber of Commerce
ICR	Insolvency and Creditor Rights' (Standard) *(UNCITRAL)*
ICSD	Investor Compensation Schemes Directive *(97/9/EC)*
ICS	Investor Compensation Scheme/System
ICT	Information and Communication Technology
IDD	Insurance Distribution Directive *(2016/97)*
IFAC	International Federation of Accountants
IFD	Investment Firms Directive *(2019/2034)*
IFR	Investment Firms Regulation *(2019/2033)*
IFRS	International Financial Reporting Standard
IFSB	Islamic Financial Services Board
ILAAP	Internal Liquidity Adequacy Assessment Process
IMD	Insurance Mediation Directive *(2002/92/EC)*
IMF	International Monetary Fund
INFE	International Network on Financial Education *(OECD)*
IORP	Institutions for Occupational Retirement Provisions
IORPD I	Institutions for Occupational Retirement Provision Directive No I *(2003/41/EC)*
IORPD II	Institutions for Occupational Retirement Provision Directive No II *(2016/2341)*
IOSCO	International Organisation of Securities Commissions
IPS	Institutional Protection Scheme
ISA	International Standards of Auditing
ISD	Investment Services Directive *(93/22/EEC)*
ISDA	International Swaps and Derivatives Association
ISSB	International Sustainability Standards Board
ITSs	Implementing Technical Standards
IVASS	Istituto per la Vigilanza Sulle Assicurazioni *(Italy)*
JST	Joint Supervisory Team
KID	Key Information Document
LAA	Loss Absorption Amount
LCR	Liquidity Coverage Ratio
LGD	Loss Given Default
LIBOR	London InterBank Offer Rate
LLR	Lending of Last Resort
LTF	Legal Theory of Finance

MAD II	Markets Abuse Directive No II *(2014/57/EU)*
MAR	Markets Abuse Regulation *(5962014)*
MENAFATF	Middle East and North Africa Financial Action Task Force
MiCAR	Markets in Crypto-Assets Regulation *(not yet published)*
MiFID I	Markets in Financial Instruments Directive No I *(2004/39/EC)*
MiFID II	Markets in Financial Instruments Directive No II *(2014/65/EU)*
MiFIR	Markets in Financial Instruments Regulation *(600/2014)*
MMF	Money Market Fund
MMFR	Money Market Funds Regulation *(2017/1131)*
MMLR	Market Maker of Last Resort
MMoU	Multilateral Memorandum of Understanding
MONEYVAL	Council of Europe Committee of Experts on the Evaluation of Anti-Money Laundering Measures and the Financing of Terrorism
MoU	Memorandum of Understanding
MPI	Macro Prudential Indicator
MREL	Minimum Requirement (for own funds and) Eligible Liabilities
MSME	Managers of Micro, Small and Medium-sized Enterprises
MTF	Multilateral Trading Facility
NAB	New Arrangements to Borrow
NBFI	Non-Bank Financial Intermediation
NCWO	No Creditor Worse Off (principle)
NCA	National Competent Authority
NCB	National Central Bank
NDA	National Designated Authority
NFCI	Net Fee and Commission Income
NFRD	Non-Financial Reporting Directive *(2014/95/EU)*
NGFS	Network for Greening the Financial System
NIFA	New International Financial Architecture
NJA	National Judicial Authority
NPE	Non-Performing Exposure
NPL	Non-Performing Loan
NRA	National Resolution Authority
NSFR	Net Stable Funding Ratio
O-SII	Other Systemically Important Institution *(EU)*
OECD	Organisation for Economic Co-operation and Development
OJ	Official Journal (of the European Union)
OLAF	Office Européen de Lutte Antifraude (European Anti-Fraud Office)
OTC	Over-The-Counter
P2G	Pillar 2 Guidance
P2R	Pillar 2 Requirements
PAO	Professional Accountancy Organisation
PD	Probability of Default
PDG	Policy Development Group *(Basel Committee)*
PEPP	Pan-European Personal Pension Product
PRA	Prudential Regulation Authority *(United Kingdom)*
PRIIP	Packaged Retail and Insurance-based Investment Product
PSD	Payment Services Directive *(2007/64/EC)*
PSD II	Payment Services Directive No II *(2015/2366)*
PSG	Policy and Standards Group *(Basel Committee)*

PSI	Private Sector Involvement
Q&As	Questions and Answers
RCA	ReCapitalisation Amount
RCAP	Regulatory Consistency Assessment Programme *(Basel Committee)*
REFIT	Regulatory Fitness and Performance Programme
ResCo	Standing Committee on Resolution
ROSCs	Reports on the Observance of Standards and Codes
RPC	Resolution Planning Cycle
RRF	Recovery and Resilience Facility
RTGS	Real-Time Gross Settlement (system)
RTSs	Regulatory Technical Standards
RVG	Risks and Vulnerabilities Assessment Group *(Basel Committee)*
RWAs	Risk-Weighted Assets
SASB	Sustainability Accounting Standards Board
SBBSs	Sovereign Bond-Backed Securities
SCAV	Standing Committee on Assessment of Vulnerabilities *(FSB)*
SCBR	Standing Committee on Budget and Resources *(FSB)*
SCG	Supervisory Cooperation Group *(Basel Committee)*
SCSI	Standing Committee on Standards Implementation *(FSB)*
SCSRC	Standing Committee on Supervisory and Regulatory Cooperation *(FSB)*
SDDS	Special Data Dissemination Standard
SDGs	Sustainable Development Goals
SEA	Single European Act
SEC	Securities and Exchange Commission *(US)*
SEPA	Single Euro Payments Area
SFDR	Sustainable Finance Disclosure Regulation *(2019/2088)*
SFR	Supervisory Fess Regulation *(ECB/2014/41)*
SFT	Securities Financing Transaction
SFTR	Securities Financing Transactions Regulation *(2015/2365)*
SGP	Stability and Growth Pact
SIBs	Systemically Important Banks
SIFI	Systemically Important Financial Institution
SIFS	Systemically Important Financial Sectors *(IMF)*
SIG	Supervision and Implementation Group *(Basel Committee)*
SME	Small-Medium Enterprise
SNDO	Swedish National Debt Office
SPV	Special Purpose Vehicle
SREP	Supervisory Review and Evaluation Process
SRB	Single Resolution Board
SRF	Single Resolution Fund
SRM	Single Resolution Mechanism
SRMR	Single Resolution Mechanism Regulation *(806/2014)*
SRMR II	Single Resolution Mechanism Regulation no. II *(2019/877)*
SRR	Special Resolution Regime
SSFIs	Systemically Significant Financial Institutions
SSM	Single Supervisory Mechanism
SSMR	Single Supervisory Mechanism Regulation *(1024/2013)*
SSM-FR	SSM Framework Regulation *(468/2014)*

SSRs	Social and Structural Reviews
STF	Securities Financing Transaction
STS	Simple, Transparent and Standardised (securitisation)
TARGET	Trans-European Automated Real-Time Gross Settlement Express Transfer (system)
TBTF	Too-Big-To-Fail
TCBU	Training and Capacity Building Unit *(IADI)*
TCFD	Task Force on Climate-related Financial Disclosures
TEC	Treaty (establishing the) European Community
TEU	Treaty on European Union
TFCR	Task Force on Climate-related Financial Risks *(Basel Committee)*
TFE	Task Force on Evaluations *(Basel Committee)*
TFEU	Treaty on the Functioning of the European Union
TLAC	Total Loss Absorbing Capital
TR	Taxonomy Regulation *(2020/852)*
TSC	Technical Screening Criteria
UCITS	Undertakings for Collective Investment in Transferable Securities
UCITS I	UCITS Directives no. I *(2001/107/EC and 2001/108/EC)*
UCITS IV	UCITS Directive No IV *(2009/65/EC)*
UCITS V	UCITS Directive No V *(2014/91/EU)*
UK	United Kingdom
UN	United Nations
UNCITRAL	United Nations Commission on International Trade Law
UNEP	United Nations Environment Programme
UNIDROIT	International Institute for the Unification of Private Law
UNODC	United Nations Office on Drugs and Crime
US	United States (of America)
VASP	Virtual Asset Service Provider
WTO	World Trade Organization

LIST OF TABLES

Table 1.1	Financial policy objective: instruments for safeguarding the stability of the banking system—the 'bank safety net'	25
Table 2.1	The work of the Financial Stability Board (FSB) and the Basel Committee (BCBS) amidst the first phases of the pandemic crisis	103
Table 2.2	G20 members	108
Table 2.3	International fora (in chronological order of establishment)	111
Table 2.4	Governance of the 'Basel process'	114
Table 2.5	Members of the Financial Stability Board (FSB)	118
Table 2.6	Institutions of public international financial law	132
Table 2.7	States' participation in the institutional structure of the international architecture of the financial system following the G20 Summit in London	132
Table 2.8	The evolution of the BCBS' capital adequacy and (since 2010) regulatory frameworks	135
Table 2.9	The Compendium of Standards of the Financial Stability Board (FSB): *Key Standards for Sound Financial Systems*	139
Table 3.1	Members of the Basel Committee	170
Table 3.2	Classification of members of the Basel Committee according to their competences in microprudential banking (financial) supervision	172
Table 4.1	Cooperation of national banking supervisory authorities at European level: from informal *fora* to 'European (*quasi-*)Supervisory Authorities'	230
Table 4.2	The key legal sources of the three main pillars of the Banking Union (BU) for credit institutions	253
Table 6.1	Addressees of and date by which the main provisions of the key legal sources pertaining to the Banking Union (BU) are applicable	355
Table 6.2	The legal basis of the legislative acts which constitute the sources of EU banking law	358
Table 6.3	Definition of regulated/supervised entities and groups	359

Table 6.4	Definition of national supervisory and resolution authorities	361
Table 6.5	The partial Europeanisation of the 'bank safety net' (even) within the Banking Union (BU)	371
Table 7.1	The asymmetry in EU institutional architecture in relation to prudential supervision in the three main sectors of the financial system	387
Table 7.2	The relation between Article 8(1) EBAR (on the EBA's tasks) and other provisions of the EBAR	402
Table 7.3	Equivalence between Articles in Decision 1999/648/EC and in Regulation 182/2011	429
Table 7.4	Procedure for the adoption of legal acts which constitute the sources of European financial law after the entry into operation of the ESFS	429
Table 7.5	The four levels of the making and enforcement of public international and European financial law: a comparative view	430
Table 8.1	National competent authorities (NCAs)—members of the Single Supervisory Mechanism (SSM)	449
Table 8.2	The powers of the ECB and NCAs to impose administrative penalties	471
Table 8.3	ECB Legal acts on the Single Supervisory Mechanism (SSM)—other than the SSM-FR	489
Table 9.1	National resolution authorities (NRAs)—members of the Single Resolution Mechanism (SRM)	515

LIST OF BOXES

Box 1.1	Categories of markets for debt instruments and equities	5
Box 1.2	Problems relating to the operation of TBTF financial firms/ SIFIs (1)	12
Box 1.3	Theories of banking panics	20
Box 1.4	Approaches to the institutional structure of microprudential supervision	37
Box 1.5	The two dimensions of systemic risk	41
Box 1.6	Definition of Various Buffers	44
Box 1.7	Problems relating to the operation of TBTF financial firms/ SIFIs (2)	61
Box 2.1	The SRB's Standing Committees	120
Box 2.2	The three key methodological tools in the FSAP	126
Box 3.1	The Herstatt Bank crisis	162
Box 3.2	The six key pillars of the Basel Committee's initial perimeter of activities	165
Box 3.3	The current structure and mandates of BCBS Groups	175
Box 3.4	The modules of the Regulatory Consistency Assessment Program (RCAP)	179
Box 3.5	Differences in terminology	182
Box 3.6	Key CGFS publications since 2007	194
Box 4.1	Definition of the terms credit institution and financial institution	206
Box 4.2	The three key pillars of the 1999 Financial Services Action Plan (FSAP)	224
Box 4.3	Two significant SSMR recitals	246
Box 4.4	Two significant BRRD recitals	249
Box 4.5	The three phases in the evolution of the EDIS in accordance with the 2015 Commission's legislative proposal	251
Box 5.1	The three pillars of the 2016 "legislative banking package"	270
Box 5.2	The Direct Recapitalisation Instrument (DRI)	276
Box 5.3	The three legislative acts on the Capital Markets Union (CMU) adopted in 2017	283
Box 5.4	Key elements of the Taxonomy Regulation (TR)	288

Box 5.5	The Four Pillars of the 2021 "Legislative Banking Package"	299
Box 5.6	Two related aspects—not further discussed but quite significant	303
Box 6.1	Definition of G-SIIs (and O-SIIs)	320
Box 6.2	The new definition of the terms credit institution and institution	322
Box 6.3	Some remarks on Article 127(6) TFEU	329
Box 6.4	The structure of the SSM Framework Regulation (SSM-FR)	333
Box 6.5	The Conditions Set Out in Article 113(7) CRR in Relation to IPSs	350
Box 6.6	The Tercas case	351
Box 7.1	The short selling case	384
Box 7.2	The EBA methodology for its 2023 EU-wide stress test	399
Box 7.3	The *FBF v ACPR* case	421
Box 8.1	Essential definitions regarding 'significant' and 'less significant' supervised entities	450
Box 8.2	The *Landeskreditbank Baden-Württemberg—Förderbank v ECB* case	452
Box 8.3	The application of other provisions of the SSM-FR on close cooperation	457
Box 9.1	Tasks of the SRB in its Plenary Session	502
Box 9.2	Composition of the two formats of the SRB Executive Session	506
Box 9.3	Tasks of the SRB in its Executive Session	507
Box 9.4	Aggravating and mitigating factors—adjustment coefficients	523

PART I

Theory of Banking Regulation and International Financial Standards

CHAPTER 1

The Case for Banking Regulation

1.1 Banking Regulation: Policy Objectives and Instruments

1.1.1 Setting the Scene: Functions of the Financial System and the Importance of Banking Intermediation

1.1.1.1 Introductory Remarks

(1) The financial system and notably its banking sector[1] is one of the branches of the economy that are subject, in almost every country of the world, to heavy **'sector-specific'** regulation (and supervision). According to Kane (1987):

> On average, across the world, the financial sector (and in particular the banking industry) is probably more closely regulated than any other segment of the private economy.[2]

Financial firms are also subject to regulatory intervention for reasons that equally apply to other categories of providers of services, as reflected (indicative) in the **'horizontal'** provisions of the following areas: company, competition, data protection, taxation and labour law; however, this is not considered to be part of financial regulation.

---

[1] Even though the use of the term 'banking system' is common, it is more accurate to label it as 'banking sector' since it is one sector of a broader system, as discussed below; in this study, both terms are used as synonymous.

[2] See Kane (1987), p. 111. A notable exception is 'offshore financial centres', which are characterised by a substantial lack of financial regulation, coupled with favourable corporate taxation ('tax havens').

© The Author(s), under exclusive license to Springer Nature Switzerland AG 2023
C. V. Gortsos, *The European Banking Regulation Handbook, Volume I*,
https://doi.org/10.1007/978-3-031-32859-6_1

(2) Financial regulation applies to the financial system, which is one of the systems set up for the performance of two functions through a (in certain cases complex) nexus of service providers (financial firms) and markets: the *first function* is channelling funds from the economy's positive savers to the negative savers[3]; the *second* consists in enabling natural and legal persons (including positive and negative savers) to make payments without using cash, namely coins and banknotes.[4] For the implementation of these functions, two infrastructures are necessary: payment, clearing and settlement systems, as well as clearing and settlement systems for transactions in transferable securities.[5] The first function of the financial system is performed *via* two channels: direct financing and indirect financing (or financial intermediation), which are discussed in turn below.[6]

One of the most important technological evolutions in financial systems is "decentralised finance" ('**DeFi**'), a term used to describe services in crypto-asset markets that aim to replicate some functions of the traditional financial system in a widely variable decentralised manner; hence, the processes for providing services are usually novel. However, in terms of the functions it performs and the vulnerabilities to which it is exposed, DeFi does not substantially differ from traditional finance.[7]

1.1.1.2 Direct Financing

(1) The channel of direct financing from positive to negative savers is activated through financial markets, defined as the markets where debt instruments and equities are issued and traded, and derivatives are traded. Financial markets are

---

[3] The term 'channelling funds' comprises both borrowed and own funds. In every economy, the amount of funds channelled through the financial system is a subset of the funds generally channelled from positive to negative savers, since borrowed funds are also channelled to negative savers through private lending, while a large part of own funds of non-listed, public limited liability companies and funds of other corporate forms is drawn from natural and legal persons outside the financial system. The latter can bring added value to the economy by, *inter alia*, offering businesses the opportunity to draw own and/or borrowed funds from a pool of positive savers to which they either have no access or they have access at a disproportionately high cost.

[4] On the functions of the financial system, see, by means of mere indication, Armour et al. (2016), pp. 22–50, with extensive further references. On the function of contributing to cashless payments as an integral part of the financial system, see details in Stillhart (2002), pp. 105–121 and Kokkola (2010), pp. 25–37.

[5] From the relatively limited literature on this subject, see de Haan, Oosterloo, and Schoenmaker (2009), pp. 136–163 and Kokkola (2010), pp. 37–47.

[6] During the last decade, a new type of funds' channelling has emerged, namely 'crowdfunding': this consists in getting as many people as possible to each provide a specific amount of money to finance a business. Typically, crowdfunding services are offered over the internet and are classified in two groups: 'crowdlending' and 'crowdinvesting'. For a literature review, see Baumann (2014) and Moritz and Block (2014).

[7] See also below, under 1.1.2 (at the discussion of financial stability considerations).

also referred to as money and capital markets.⁸ The markets for debt instruments (such as bonds and bills) and equities are divided into categories (as briefly discussed in **Box 1.1 below**). Derivative financial instruments are also available in financial markets allowing on the one hand, to hedge the risks that economic units assume in their commercial (and also financial) transactions, given the price volatility of various parameters (e.g., interest rates, bonds, equities, foreign exchange rates), and on the other hand, to take advantage of speculative opportunities regarding the future price fluctuation of those parameters.⁹

Box 1.1 Categories of markets for debt instruments and equities

(1) Depending on the function performed, debt instruments and equities markets are divided into primary and secondary markets: a **'primary market'** is a financial market to which certain classes of negative savers¹⁰ can turn to draw either borrowed and/or own funds from positive savers through the issuance of debt instruments and equities, respectively.¹¹ Debt instruments and equities can be sold to positive savers either by private placement, or by a public offer procedure; a **'secondary market'** is a financial market where debt instruments and equities issued by negative savers are traded and where the current market value of financial instruments is fixed to ensure, *inter alia*, their liquidity.

---

⁸ The distinction between money markets and capital markets is based on the maturity of financial instruments traded therein: 'short-term debt instruments' (with an initial term of up to one year), issued by businesses and governments, are traded in money markets; 'long-term debt instruments' (with an initial term of more than one year), issued by businesses and governments, are traded in capital markets along with equities of listed companies. For the sake of brevity, the terms 'financial markets' or 'capital markets' will be used in this study to describe both money and capital markets—unless otherwise specified.

⁹ They are divided into two categories, depending on the organisation of the markets in which they are traded: the *first* includes instruments traded in regulated markets ('exchange-traded derivative instruments'), such as futures and options contracts; the *second* category includes instruments developed and valued outside regulated markets and, as a rule, through the banking system (over-the-counter ('OTC')), such as forwards, options and swaps. For more details on these financial instruments, see the seminal work of Cox and Rubinstein (1985), as well as Hull (1997), Benjamin (2007), pp. 64–79, McKnight (2008), pp. 559–572 and Murphy (2022), pp. 9–46.

¹⁰ Typically, access to capital markets is limited to governments when issuing debt instruments and to public limited liability companies drawing funds through the issuance of equities and debt instruments.

¹¹ For enterprises/negative savers, issuing debt instruments in the markets is an alternative to borrowing funds through the banking system. On the contrary, choosing between a loan and the issuance of equities depends on the amount of leverage they wish to be exposed to.

> **(2)** Depending on the way in which they are organised, debt instrument and equity financial markets are divided into regulated markets and non-regulated markets (**OTC**) markets[12]: a **'regulated market'** is a financial market authorised in a state by the competent supervisory authorities of the capital markets and operating in accordance with the specific rules laid down by national legislation; stock exchanges are a typical example of this[13]; a **'non-regulated market'** is initially a financial market that does not meet the above-mentioned conditions and in which investment services providers buy and sell financial instruments in the name and on behalf of their clients at prices fixed according to the given demand and supply; hence, this market also has a price fixing mechanism (albeit often inadequate, especially in terms of transparency), which is a condition determining the liquid nature of financial instruments traded therein. At the same time, in the past few years, rapid technological advances and novel applications have made it possible for banks, investment firms and the markets themselves, *inter alia*, to develop alternative trading mechanisms enabling the execution of buy/sell orders for debt instruments and equities outside regulated markets, in particular through multilateral systems operated by a bank, an investment firm or a market operator (called multilateral trading facilities (**'MTFs'**)) and internally within the bank or investment firm ('internalisation').[14]

(2) Various categories of financial firms operate in direct financing and can, in principle, be categorised from a systematic point of view as follows[15]: The *first category* includes those providing on a professional basis 'investment services' to both positive and negative savers on an individual basis. These are cumulatively called 'investment firms' (or 'market intermediaries') and include: 'securities firms' (or 'investment firms'), which are allowed by law to provide investment services, including the execution of orders for the purchase or

---

[12] Traditionally, regulated markets were known as 'organised markets', a term falling gradually out of use.

[13] Traditionally, stock exchanges were either bodies managed by their members ('mutualisation') or legal persons of public law. Currently, as a rule, they are being managed and operated by public limited liability companies, which may themselves be listed in regulated markets and are known as 'market operators'. On the 'demutualisation' process, see Aggarwal (2002) and Steil (2002).

[14] For a precise definition of the terms 'multilateral trading facility' and 'internalisation' and their distinction from the term 'regulated market', see Binning and Willey (2008), pp. 73–100.

[15] The extent of the investment services provided in each state, the mix of providers that can professionally provide them and the terms applicable to the provision of such services and are determined by the legislation in force. More often than not, it is legally stipulated that these providers must be authorised and be subject to micro- and macroprudential regulation and supervision (see below, under 1.1.2).

sale of financial instruments in the name, and on behalf, of their clients; and banks, to the extent that they are also allowed by law to provide investment services. The *second category* of market intermediaries includes the managers of 'undertakings for collective investment in transferable securities' ('**UCITS**', e.g., mutual funds and (portfolio) investment companies); despite the name undertakings for collective investment in *transferable securities* (i.e., equities and bonds), these also make placements in financial derivative instruments. As a rule, UCITS used to have the monopoly by law to provide financial portfolio management services on a collective basis, without being precluded from providing at least certain investment services on an individual basis as well. A type of investment vehicle, the 'alternative investment funds' ('**AIFs**'), including '**hedge funds**', has also emerged over the last decades. However, their operation has been subject to prudential regulation and supervision after the (2007–2009) global (or great) financial crisis[16] ('**GFC**').[17]

1.1.1.3 Indirect Financing

General considerations: According to financial theory, financial intermediation has emerged because of the (relatively high) cost of transactions in financial markets; the (relatively high) credit risk that investments in debt instruments and equities entail for positive savers (**'risk sharing'**); and information asymmetries arising in the relationship between positive and negative savers in the context of direct financing.[18] Even though these arguments are strong from a theoretical-systemic point of view, it should be noted that banks historically operated before financial markets developed. *Furthermore*, banks and other categories of financial intermediaries offer the possibility to draw borrowed funds to many categories of negative savers (mainly households and various categories of enterprises) with no access to financial markets, as already mentioned. Indeed, in most jurisdictions, indirect financing mainly through banks (**'bank-based' systems**) is more extensive than direct financing, even in the United States ('**US**') which traditionally has deeper and more liquid financial markets (**'market-based' system**).

---

[16] On this crisis, see Chapter 2 below, under 2.2.4. AIFs are an asset pool consisting of funds raised from (usually high net worth) private and institutional investors, placed in various financial instruments, primarily derivatives, with a view to capitalising on the imperfections of the markets and operating at high leverage. On the operation of hedge funds and the policy objective to regulate and supervise them, see Garbaravicius and Dierick (2005), Chan, Getmansky, Haas and Andrew (2006), Crocket (2007), Ferguson, Hartmann, Panetta and Portes (2007), pp. 119–130, and Athanassiou (2012). 'Private equity funds' are different from AIFs, since their investment strategy consists in buying *equity participations* of non-listed companies, restructuring such companies and re-selling them at a higher price (usually also aiming at listing them on a regulated market).

[17] For a comprehensive overview of the theory of financial markets, the role of information intermediaries therein and the market structure, see, by means of mere indication out of a vast existing literature, Armour *et al.* (2016), pp. 101–159, with extensive further references.

[18] On information asymmetries, see under 1.1.2 below.

Financial intermediaries operate in the market to address the above problems.[19] Systematically, these can be classified into three categories: banks (discussed just below), non-banking credit providers[20] and insurance undertakings and pension funds.[21] To the extent that credit intermediation is provided by non-bank entities, which are not subject to regulation and supervision, reference is made to the **"shadow banking" system**, which is defined as *"credit intermediation involving entities and activities outside the regular banking system"*.[22] In practice, shadow banking entities and activities raise funding with deposit-like characteristics, perform maturity or liquidity transformation, allow credit risk transfer or use direct or indirect leverage.[23]

Banking intermediation: As just noted, banks are prevailing among financial intermediaries.[24] In the course of this intermediation, positive savers offer their lent funds in the form of deposits—a **monopoly by law** in almost all jurisdictions,[25] and subsequently, banks provide loans and other credit facilities to negative savers acting as **'delegated monitors'**.[26] The indirect nature

---

[19] The term 'financial intermediaries' covers all categories of financial firms providing services in the context of indirect intermediation. For a detailed presentation of their functions in the financial system, see Allen and Santomero (1999), Allen (2001), Allen and Gale (2001) and Gorton and Winton (2002).

[20] Even though taking deposits from the public is a legal monopoly of the banks, the service of providing credit on a professional basis may also be offered by other companies financing this activity by drawing own or borrowed funds from the financial system or outside of it, such as leasing, factoring and credit companies.

[21] Insurance undertakings and pension funds deal directly only with positive and not with negative savers but invest their available funds in financial instruments and deposits. See analytically Dionne, G. (2013, editor).

[22] Financial Stability Board (2011): "Shadow Banking: Strengthening Oversight and Regulation, Recommendations", 27 October, Section 1 (at: https://www.financialstabilityboard.org/2011/10/r_111027a).

[23] On shadow banking, see, by means of indication, Gorton and Metrick (2010), Pozsar et al. (2010), Financial Stability Board (2011), Gerding (2011), Nijskens and Wagner (2011), Adrian and Ashcraft (2012), Claessens et al. (2012), European Commission (2012), Kane (2014), Schwarcz (2015), Armour et al. (2016), pp. 433–448, Pacces and Nabilou (2017), and Alexander (2019), pp. 300–306.

[24] The most characteristic (and in most states the larger in terms of size) category of banks is commercial banks. However, in various economies, there are also special bank categories, such as cooperative, mortgage, development and savings banks (often called 'special credit organisations'), whose enactment is usually the result of regulatory intervention, notably (but not exclusively) in developing or less developed economies. On the various banks' business models (such as investment banking, wholesale banking, focused retail banking, and diversified retail banking) in the contemporary financial system, see, by means of mere indication, Ayadi et al. (2012) (on the EU), Wehinger (2013) and contributions in de Haan and Bruinshhofd (2014, editors).

[25] A deposit is not just a loan to the bank, but also a consignment. The level of its interest rate is the best indicator of the prevailing element (obviously, a higher interest rate reflects a bank's need to attract deposits).

[26] See on this the seminal paper of Diamond (1984).

of this form of financing consists in the fact that no legal or economic relationships develop between depositors and negative savers. The former obtain receivables against banks and, for their part, banks obtain receivables against the latter.[27] Four remarks deserve attention in this respect:

> *First*, positive savers resorting to bank intermediation services include households, enterprises and governments. On the contrary, negative savers include, as a rule, households and (private and state-owned) companies alone, because in developed economies governments draw borrowed funds exclusively from capital markets (unless they are 'excluded' from these markets as a result of credit rating downgrades, as recently in the case of several countries in the European Union ('**EU**') as a result of the euro area fiscal crisis).[28] However, in many less developed economies regulations are applied imposing on banks to place an (often quite significant) share of their deposits on government bonds not placed in the primary market. On the contrary, banks are free to buy government bonds on the secondary market in the context of their asset management.
> *Second*, given their function, banks are one of the most highly leveraged categories of companies, since their borrowed funds are significantly higher than their own funds (typically, share capital).
> *Third*, banks draw borrowed funds not only from depositors, but also from their central bank, from other banks as part of interbank market operations and also through the issuance of debt securities in financial markets.
> *Finally*, banks do not channel the entirety of their deposits into loans or other credit facilities. Apart from retaining liquid and promptly cashable assets to meet depositors' demand for cash withdrawals, banks also invest in financial instruments traded in financial markets in the context of their portfolio management either long-term (included in the '**banking book**') or aimed at capitalising on the short-term market conditions (included in the '**trading book**').[29]

(2) In their capacity as financial intermediaries, banks perform a set of transformations: '**credit risk transformation**' by assuming the credit risk of the economic units they finance, transferring the risk of their own solvency to positive savers; '**size transformation**' by converting liabilities of usually small

---

[27] For an overview of theoretical models on why banks can offer such services and make the transformations mentioned below, see Allen and Santomero (1999) and Gorton and Winton (2002), pp. 5–20; see also Armour *et al.* (2016), pp. 275–289.

[28] On this crisis, see Chapter 4 below, under 4.4.1.

[29] While in the former case banks are primarily exposed to the credit risk of the issuer of the financial instrument, in the second case they are also exposed to position risk; see below, under 1.2.1.

nominal value (e.g., retail deposits) to large-value receivables (e.g., industrial loans); and **'maturity transformation'** by converting short-term liabilities (e.g., sight/demand deposits) into long-term receivables (e.g., housing loans). Their ability to perform these transformations is, concurrently, the main cause of their (in some cases, structural) exposure to financial risks and, hence, the main reason behind the need for prudential regulation in order to ensure the stability of the banking system.[30]

1.1.2 *The Case for Financial Regulation in Economically Developed Countries (Advanced Economies)*

1.1.2.1 Introductory Remarks

(1) According to economic theory, regulatory intervention is always necessary to mitigate **market failures**. The main market failures observed in the financial system concern the existence of information asymmetry between various actors and conditions favouring negative externalities.[31] By contrast, the financial system is not a natural monopoly.[32] Hence, the case for financial regulation is mainly linked (but not confined) to the financial (and other) risks to which financial firms may be exposed and the negative spill-over effects from the eventuality of their failure for the operation of the financial system or the real economy, as further discussed below.[33] At this point, it is important to precisely define four terms which are the main subject of our discussion:

> **'Financial regulation'** means the legislative or (by delegation) administrative provisions, which prescribe or prohibit behaviour on the part of financial firms in order to achieve specific financial policy objectives. The outcome of this intervention is the adoption of **'financial regulations'**, which comprise the 'regulatory (or normative) framework' and constitute administrative law (hard or soft). Depending on their specific scope, these

---

[30] See below, under 1.2.1.

[31] On these market failures, see Mercuro and Medema (2006), pp. 60–67, Stiglitz and Walsh (2006), pp. 239–255, and in more detail Ippolito (2005), pp. 153–379. Specifically, regarding the meaning of information asymmetry and the problems that it causes to transactions, see Rasmusen (1989), pp. 181–203 as to 'adverse selection', and pp. 133–179 as to 'moral hazard'.

[32] See Gorton (1988b), pp. 5–7.

[33] It is also noted that, from a comparative point of view, the financial system may be regulated for various other reasons; hence, on account of policy objectives, the extent of regulatory intervention is graduated, and typically, there are significant differences between economically less developed and developing countries (states), those with emerging market economies ('EMEs'), and economically developed countries (or advanced economies) (see, e.g., The World Bank (1989), pp. 54–69). It is noted that there are significant differences in the criteria used for the classification of countries on the basis of their economic development even among international organisations, such as the International Monetary Fund ('IMF') and the World Bank; see on this Nielsen (2011), and at: https://blogs.worldbank.org/opendata/new-world-bank-country-classifications-income-level-2022-2023.

regulations are classified as 'microprudential' or 'macroprudential'.[34] In this context, **'reg-tech'** means any technology used by financial firms for (risk management and) regulatory compliance.

'Financial supervision' means the administrative procedures for the monitoring by competent authorities of individual financial firms' compliance with the provisions of the regulatory framework. Such monitoring is carried out proactively and is also widely known as 'microprudential supervision'. **'Sup-tech'** is any technology used for the purpose of conducting supervisory activities.[35]

'Financial enforcement' means the framework for the imposition of sanctions to financial firms not complying with the provisions of the regulatory framework.

Finally, **'financial oversight'** means the monitoring by competent of the sound operation of a market, a part of the financial system or the financial system as a whole.[36]

(2) The following analysis of financial regulation is based on the **'public interest approach'**, whereby this regulation is intended to promote the public good by calling upon individuals and firms to change their preferred behaviour in ways that will benefit others. This is differentiated from the **'public choice theory approach'**, whereby regulation is the outcome of efforts by interest groups, politicians and bureaucrats to use the political process for their own personal gain, and the **'industrial organisation theory approach'**, whereby financial regulation is a response to the demand of financial firms and their customers for certification of soundness and facilitation of the clearing and settlement of transactions.[37]

(3) The policy objectives justifying financial regulation at any given time cannot be exhaustive, since the prevailing economic and social conditions may call for new objectives in future. The dynamics of this variability are

---

[34] On this distinction and the synergies between these two forms, see below, under 1.2.3 and 1.2.5.

[35] See Azzutti (2023).

[36] Taking road traffic as an example: regulation means laying down rules, e.g. on the maximum speed limit; supervision of compliance with these rules is carried out by traffic wardens, who issue speed tickets to the offenders; and enforcement means imposing (and collecting) fines on (and from) those violating a maximum speed limit. Oversight is conducted by traffic police helicopters that look for congestion problems in given roads, in order to smooth the traffic with appropriate instructions.

[37] See Herring and Litan (1995), pp. 79–82, 82–83 and pp. 83–84, respectively. For an overall review of regulatory intervention in the financial system and its limitations, see Herring and Santomero (2000) and Armour *et al.* (2016), pp. 51–98, with extensive further references. On a cost-benefit (quantitative) analysis of financial regulation in terms of effectiveness as a kind of "meta-regulation", see Murphy (2022), pp. 253–276, based on the work of Grabosky (2017); on the "behavioural finance revolution" as a new approach to financial regulation, see Kahn (2018) and Viale *et al.* (2018) (and on behavioural law and economics in general, Zamir and Teichman (2018)). For an analysis of other (than financial meta-regulation) aspects of regulatory theory (in general), see further contributions in Drahos (2017).

clearly demonstrated by the fact that certain policy objectives which stand today did not stand a few years ago. By means of mere indication: *first*, the rationale for combatting terrorist financing through the financial system emerged mostly following the terrorist attacks in the US on 11 September 2001; and *second*, the debate on the need to deal with the adverse impact on public finances of exposure to insolvency of banks and other financial firms, which have grown 'too-big-to-fail' ('**TBTF**') or, more precisely, 'too-big-to-be-left-to-fail') and are labelled as 'systemically important' financial institutions ('**SIFIs**'),[38] emerged after the GFC.

> **Box 1.2 Problems relating to the operation of TBTF financial firms/SIFIs (1)**
> A significant issue arising in this respect is the, often, unequal ex-post treatment, at times of crisis, of TBTF financial firms/SIFIs as the withdrawal of their authorisation may be deemed to be politically untenable.[39] Within this framework, significant distortions (imbalances) arise as smaller firms are at a comparatively disadvantageous position, market discipline is less effective where it is most needed, i.e., in large banks with low capital adequacy, due to exposure to moral hazard, and the cost of government bail-outs for such businesses in times of crisis is extremely substantial. By default, the main concern is to ensure that these entities will not be exposed to insolvency, or if otherwise exposed, their resolution will be feasible without burdening public finances (use of taxpayers' money). This problem, associated with the policy objective of ensuring financial stability, is not new, but has become more acute during the GFC owing to large-scale government bail-outs of financial firms and the ensuing negative impact on public finances.[40]

---

[38] On the definition of SIFIs, see Huertas and Lastra (2011), pp. 255–258 (who use the term 'systemically significant financial institutions' or 'SSFIs'). See also, by means of indication, Claessens, Herring and Schoenmaker (2010) and the various contributions to Lastra (2011, editor). On policy recommendations to overcome the problems arising from the operation of SIFIs and TBTF banks, see Carmassi, Luchetti and Micossi (2010), Claessens, Herring, and Schoenmaker (2010), Goldstein and Veron (2011), Weber *et al.* (2014), pp. 152–171 and Kane (2016).

[39] On the adequate microprudential supervision, micro- and macroprudential regulation of their business activities, as well as the resolution involving them, see, by means of mere indication, Rajan (2010), pp. 169–176, European Central Bank (2010), Hofer (2014), and various Reports of the Financial Stability Board.

[40] Notwithstanding the above remarks, it is worth noting that financial stability concerns may also arise from the potential failure of medium-sized banks, especially if the informatonal channel of contagion among banks (runs and panics) were to be activated; see on that further under 1.1.3 below.

1.1.2.2 The Objective of Preserving Financial Stability

(1) The *first* (and primary for the purpose of this study) policy objective justifying regulatory intervention in the financial system of advanced economies is ensuring its stability, which may be threatened by the occurrence of systemic crises. It is worth noting that there is no single generally accepted definition of the term **'financial stability'**.[41] Some authors define it as the opposite to the concept of 'financial instability' by referring to episodes of **'financial crises'**,[42] while certain others define it on the basis of the various properties of a stable financial system. In that respect, Schinasi (2006) gives the following definition:

> Financial stability is a situation in which the financial system is capable of satisfactorily performing its three functions simultaneously.[43] First, the financial system is efficiently and smoothly facilitating the intertemporal allocation of resources from savers to investors and the allocation of resources generally. Second, forward-looking financial risks are being assessed and priced reasonably accurately and are being relatively well managed. Third, the financial system is in such condition that it can comfortably if not smoothly absorb financial and real economic surprises and shocks.[44]

Finally, others (including this author) formulate an operational definition by introducing a framework which sets out the objectives of intervention and defines the adequate instruments to achieve them.[45] It is noted it this respect that the DeFi's specific features raise specific concerns about its regulation, since, *on the one hand*, these features may result in financial vulnerabilities (e.g., operational fragilities, liquidity and maturity mismatches, leverage and interconnectedness) and, *on the other hand*, traditional financial regulation seems not be effective in pursuing its objectives.[46]

---

[41] Financial stability is a "global public good"; on this term, see Kaul, Grunberg and Stern (1999), pp. 4–6; on this aspect, see also Chapter 3 below, under 3.1.4.

[42] For a generally accepted definition of this term, see Mishkin (2003), pp. 93–105; see also Partnoy (2015), pp. 69–78. For a historic overview of major 'systemically important' financial crises all over the world, see, by means of indication, Caprio and Klingebiel (1996a), 1996b) (discussing the interesting trilemma whether bank insolvencies are due to bad luck, bad policy or bad banking) and (1999), Reinhart and Rogoff (2008), Laeven and Valencia (2008) and (2012), Lowenfeld (2010), pp. 589–595, and Thiele (2014), pp. 563–569.

[43] According to that author (see pp. 80–82), these functions are intermediation, direct financing through markets and operation of financial infrastructures (as also discussed herein above). See also Allen and Gale (2001).

[44] See Schinasi (2006), p. 82.

[45] On the various definitions of the term 'financial stability', see Houben, Kakes and Schinasi (2004), pp. 10–11 and 38–42. On the third approach, see also Schinasi (2005). See also various contributions in von der Krone and Rochet (2014), as well as Pistor (2019), on the regulation of financial markets from the perspective of her "Legal Theory of Finance" ('LTF').

[46] On the notion of DeFi and the related policy considerations, see, by means of mere indication, Zetzsche, Arner and Buckley (2020) and Harvey, Ramachandran and Santoro

(2) Considering the above mentioned, there are five closely linked financial policy objectives[47]:

The *first* is ensuring the stability of the financial system, including the safeguarding of the stability of the banking sector by preventing negative externalities in the form of contagious bank failures (i.e., by preventing a chain reaction of bank failures or 'bank failure spill-over effects').[48] The depletion of a bank's equity and its insolvency do not have a negative impact on its depositors and other creditor categories alone. A key specificity that sets the banking sector apart in the whole economic system lies in the risk of the entire banking system's destabilisation by an individual bank's insolvency. The real sector (of the economy) may be adversely impacted amidst a banking (or in general a financial) crisis owing to the decline in, or lack of, bank financing to households and enterprises and the fall in total demand. The creation of a **'bank safety net'** is the appropriate means to mitigate this, as further discussed in more detail below.[49]

The *second objective* is safeguarding capital markets' stability that may be disrupted by an abrupt and large-scale price fluctuation of financial instruments traded therein[50] or the bankruptcy of a financial

(2021) (the former including a proposal for the development of a new prototype for financial regulation design, that of 'embedded regulation'). This emerging issue will not be further discussed hereinafter.

[47] It is noted in this respect that in some jurisdictions, legislation may have conferred upon the supervisory authority not only primary but also secondary objectives. A notable example is the Prudential Regulation Authority ('PRA') in the United Kingdom ('UK'), which, in accordance with the Financial Services and Markets Act 2000 ('FSMA', at: https://www.legislation.gov.uk/ukpga/2000/8/contents), in addition to its two main objectives has as a secondary competition objective to facilitate "effective competition" in the markets for services provided by PRA-authorised persons in carrying on regulated activities (see at: https://www.bankofengland.co.uk/prudential-regulation/secondary-competition-objective).

On effective competition as a goal and standard, more specifically as a competition law standard, see, by means of mere indication, Steinbaum and Stucke (2020). In the same vein, see also the "canonical" accounts of Adelman (1948) and Smith (1951). On the PRA, see also below, under 1.2.4.

[48] From the extensive literature on this financial policy objective, see Herring and Litan (1995), pp. 50–61. On the synergies between financial stability and effectiveness, see Barth, Caprio and Levine (2006), pp. 307–309. On the specific issue, how increased financial inclusion may support the task of safeguarding financial stability in banking, see Basel Committee on Banking Supervision (2015); on financial inclusion, of relevance is the work of the Global Partnership for Financial Inclusion ('GPFI') (see Chapter 2 below, under 2.3.3).

[49] See below, under 1.1.3.

[50] This risk is associated with market operation and cannot be addressed in principle with regulatory interventions. However, what is needed is to prevent the emergence of inefficient institutional infrastructures that accentuate any problems caused by strong market fluctuations.

intermediary offering investment services.[51] This is pursued through the adoption of rules concerning: authorisation by competent authorities of investment firms and investment funds' management companies; micro- and macroprudential regulation of these firms; microprudential supervision by competent authorities of all financial firms providing investment services in capital markets (including banks); reorganisation, resolution and winding-up of investment firms; macroprudential financial oversight; authorisation, oversight and ongoing supervision of securities exchanges and other markets for trading in financial instruments; and sound operation of markets and infrastructures for trading in financial instruments (including OTC derivatives).

The *third objective* is safeguarding the stability of the insurance sector of the financial system against the risk of bankruptcy of insurance and reinsurance undertakings (closely linked in some jurisdiction with the objective to protect insurance policyholders).[52] This is achieved by adopting rules on the authorisation, microprudential supervision, micro- and macroprudential regulation, reorganisation and winding-up of insurance and reinsurance undertakings, macroprudential financial oversight, and by the establishment of resolution frameworks for failing insurance undertakings.[53]

The *fourth objective* concerns safeguarding the stability of the entire financial system by preventing systemic crises due to excessive risk-taking by financial conglomerates.[54] This is pursued through the adoption of rules concerning the 'supplementary' microprudential regulation and

---

[51] On these policy objectives and the instruments employed to achieve them, see the Objectives and Principles of Securities Regulation, developed by the International Organization of Securities Commissions (IOSCO) and further discussed in Chapter 2 below, under 2.4.4. The later argument has been criticised by those who consider that in this case the risk of spill-over effects is extremely limited (see Haberman (1987) and Herring and Litan (1995), pp. 72–73 and Allen and Herring (2001)). It can thus reasonably be argued that such provisions are adopted mainly to ensure a level playing field between investment firms and banks in terms of regulation to the extent that the former provide similar services with and are exposed to the same kind of risks as the latter.

[52] See Herring and Litan (1995), pp. 73–74.

[53] On the regulation of the insurance sector, see, by means of mere indication, Everson (2015); on the international financial standards with regard to this aspect, see Chapter 2 below, under 2.4.4.

[54] Financial conglomerates are one of the categories of 'financial groups' (the other being 'groups with homogeneous financial activities'). A group is referred to as a financial conglomerate when at least one of its undertakings is an insurance or reinsurance undertaking and at least another one is a bank or investment firm. On the reasons that led to their creation and the risks they are exposed to, see Dierick (2004), pp. 6–16 and Herring and Carmassi (2010), pp. 195–201; on the three corporate structure standards for groups in this class (namely, parent-to-subsidiary corporation; a holding company at the top of the group; and a horizontal group with joint management of all the participating companies), see Dierick (2004), pp. 17–19.

supervision of such conglomerates by competent (administrative) authorities.[55]

Finally, the *fifth objective* consists in ensuring the smooth operation of payment and settlement systems. The risk to such systems consists in the contagion of liquidity and/or solvency problems from one member of the system to another, with all the adverse systemic consequences that this may potentially have on the functioning of the financial system. Exposure to this risk is controlled through proper oversight of payment and settlement systems.[56]

1.1.2.3 Other Objectives[57]

(1) A further key policy objective for financial regulation is the protection of investors who wish to invest, or already have invested, in financial instruments, as well as safeguarding the integrity, efficiency and transparency of capital markets. The 'closeness' of the connection between these two financial policy objectives with regard to capital markets can be explained by the fact that they share, to a large extent, the same financial policy instruments, making their distinction often difficult. Meeting this objective is pursued by adopting a variety of regulations, which are systematically divided into various categories, depending on their recipients, i.e., issuers of transferable securities, banks and investment firms providing investment services, UCITS, AIFs and their managers, secondary markets, credit rating agencies and auditors.[58]

Rules dictated by the need to protect investors—as those persons who invest in a market with specific characteristics and risk profiles—in order to ensure that they trust and invest in markets respond to special requirements under capital markets law, which are independent of those arising from consumer protection law. An investor may, however, be a consumer as well, depending on the transactions conducted with an investment firm (e.g., execution of orders in relation to financial instruments). Investors/consumers are usually subjected to information asymmetry and have limited negotiating capacity *vis-à-vis* providers, i.e., financial firms, which is why, as a result, consumer protection provisions are put into effect. However, investor protection rules

---

[55] The supervision exercised on such conglomerates is supplementary in nature, exercised additionally to the supervision exercised on the participating financial firms on an individual and/or on a consolidated basis within homogeneous activity groups. See Dierick (2004), pp. 20–26 and Herring and Carmassi (2008), pp. 214–226.

[56] See Committee on Payment and Settlement Systems (2005).

[57] Even though, for the purposes of this study, "financial stability" is highlighted as a predominant objective, it is the author's intention to undermine the importance of the other objectives discussed under this heading (in a rather brief way) and play down a "bottom-up" approach, which, in general, would be more suitable.

[58] On these policy objectives and the instruments employed to achieve them, see the above-mentioned IOSCO Objectives and Principles of Securities Regulation; on the role of information and the regulation of markets, see also Donald (2019).

also aim at redressing information asymmetries which, manifestly, go at the expense of investors and differ from those under consumer protection law, since they are a function of the investor's knowledge regarding the issuer/s of the instruments on which the investor will invest his/her savings or regarding the price formation mechanism in the markets where trading takes place. Furthermore, information asymmetry in capital markets may also exist among investors themselves, such as in the case of insider trading.[59]

(2) Another policy objective for financial regulation refers to the compensation of investors trading with an investment services provider (including banks), if competent supervisory or judicial authorities decide to suspend this provider's operation, normally in the event of insolvency, and the provider cannot return funds or financial assets to investors. The appropriate policy instrument in this case is the establishment of explicit investor compensation systems (or schemes, '**ICSs**'), which are set up to offer 'explicit coverage' to investors (usually up to a certain amount).

(3) Safeguarding the efficiency of payment and settlement systems—including securities clearing and settlement systems—is also a policy objective for financial regulation. Proper oversight of payment and settlement systems is the appropriate policy instrument in this case.[60] The significant role played by central banks in this respect should be highlighted. The assignment of this power to central banks is a corollary of the operational synergies that exist between the tasks of conducting monetary policy, safeguarding the stability of the financial system and overseeing payment systems. The scope of the relevant power covers, mainly, large-value payment and settlement systems given the interest in the smooth execution of monetary policy operations. In relation to small-value payment systems, the scope of the relevant power varies across countries and may include low-value payment systems, systemically important small-value payment systems and systems involving *ad hoc* systemic risk.[61]

(4) The final objective for financial regulation is the protection of the economic interests of consumers contracting with financial firms.[62] Policy concerns in this area are primarily based on generally accepted assumptions in the context of financial services provision, which apply across the board in

---

[59] On this aspect, see further details in Armour *et al.* (2016), pp. 205–225.

[60] Regarding the synergies between the stability of payment and settlement systems (discussed above) and their efficiency, see Committee on Payment and Settlement Systems (2005), paragraph 60.

[61] See indicatively European Central Bank (2011).

[62] See, by means of mere indication, Herring and Litan (1995), pp. 61–62.

relation to the protection of consumers' economic interests[63] and are related to three aspects.

The *first* is reducing the information asymmetry between consumers and financial firms about available information on a service to be provided, which can be attributed to the provider's typically greater expertise and knowledge on the financial service's features, function and characteristics, and the consumers' lack of experience and acquaintance with financial transactions due to weak financial literacy.[64]

The *second* aspect is addressing the problem of consumers' limited negotiating capacity *vis-à-vis* financial firms, which is presumed to consist in the contractual relationship between the Contracting Parties, mainly owing to the broad use of general terms of transactions.[65]

Third, as over the last decades households have shown an increased tendency towards over-indebtedness due to several reasons,[66] a related policy objective is to prevent consumer over-indebtedness and avoid the negative consequences with a view to avoiding the potential negative social and economic consequences of consumers' excessive exposure to debt.[67]

---

[63] These policy objectives and instruments refer to the precontractual period and the contractual relationship developing between the provider and the consumer in terms of a service's promotion and provision.

[64] This information asymmetry, accentuated in the case of specialised and complex financial services, in combination with the consumer's typical lack of the resources necessary to fill the information gap, upset the balance between the two parties given that the consumer cannot opt for the financial service of his/her choice based on an accurate assessment of its features. See on this Cartwright (2004), pp. 49–84, Calais-Aulois and Steinmetz (2006), pp. 53–67 and Rasmusen (1989), pp. 133–153.

On financial literacy, see, *inter alia*, the "Core competencies frameworks on financial literacy" developed by the Organisation for Economic Co-operation and Development ('OECD') jointly with the European Commission, the International Organisation of Securities Commissions ('IOSCO') and the OECD International Network on Financial Education (OECD/INFE) (at: https://www.oecd.org/daf/fin/financial-education/core-competencies-frameworks-for-financial-literacy.htm). These are at set of documents on financial literacy for adults, youth, investors, owners and managers of micro, small and medium-sized enterprises ('MSMEs'), as well as potential entrepreneurs.

[65] See Calais-Aulois and Steinmetz (2006), pp. 188–203, and Howells and Weatherill (2005), p. 261 *et seq.*

[66] The term 'over-indebtedness' refers to a consumer's inability to meet his/her financial obligations (default) arising from a loan contract he/she has signed or his/her current household financial obligations (i.e., payment of utility bills). However, there are quite different approaches regarding the notion of such a default (e.g., genuine inability to repay loans or inability considered to be unbearable), the default's timing (after how long is there a default) and the criteria for its calculation (based on the person's total assets or net income).

[67] See Finlay (2009), pp. 73–76. The provision of adequate information to consumers in respect of the nature, characteristics and risks entailed by the service, the content of

1.1.3 Instruments to Achieve the Policy Objective of Ensuring Banking Stability: The 'Bank Safety Net'

1.1.3.1 The Conceptual Framework: Market Failures in Banking and Their Implications

Information Asymmetries in Banking

(1) Business loans which account for a large part of banks' asset portfolios are non-marketable and illiquid due to the following:

> Banks are observing information about each loan which is exclusively shared between the borrower and itself. If the intermediary were to sell the loan and transfer the monitoring and the enforcement to someone else, the new claimant would have to incur the monitoring cost again, duplicating the effort of the first intermediary.[68]

To the extent that there is no secondary market for business and other bank loans (which exists, in practice, only in the case of asset securitisation), these financial assets cannot be marked to market and thus cannot be precisely valued.[69] This makes it difficult for depositors to determine the current value of the bank asset portfolio and evaluate a bank's net worth. The problem of information asymmetry, inherently present in money and capital markets, also emerges in the banking sector since bank managers and depositors do not share equal information about a bank's financial performance.

(2) The asymmetric division of information between depositors and the bank has several implications: *first*, it is the main cause of the reduced market discipline exerted by depositors.[70] *Second*, it creates **moral hazard** problems.[71]

---

concluded contracts, as well as the ensuing rights and obligations is an appropriate instrument employed. Furthermore, unfair commercial practices which might be misleading for consumers in terms of a given service's properties and features or may exert pressure on them to accept a service that they would not have accepted, had they not been misled or pressured, are prohibited. The problem of consumers' limited negotiating capacity is addressed by provisions aiming at controlling and prohibiting abusive terms, safeguarding certain crucial contractual rights (e.g., the right of withdrawal) to ensure their ability to execute them under certain circumstances and providing them with the right to have recourse to judicial proceedings through collective actions or to out-of-court dispute settlement systems. Finally, in relation to consumer over-indebtedness, the adequate policy instrument is the adoption of rules on 'responsible lending' and consumer bankruptcy.

[68] See Diamond (1984), p. 410.

[69] Marking-to-market is an accounting principle requiring the valuation of tradable financial instruments according to market prices, usually on a daily basis.

[70] The 'market discipline test' refers to whether or not the market value of a firm's liabilities responds to individual risk-taking activity.

[71] Moral hazard arises when parties have incentives to accept more risk because the costs are borne, in whole or in part, by others. Rasmusen (1989), at p. 133 *et seq.*, distinguishes between games of moral hazard with hidden action and those with hidden information. In both cases, the principal offers a contract, the agent accepts, and then noise is added to the task to be performed.

Bank insiders with superior information about the expected performance of the loan portfolio are tempted, as would any agent exercising control over information, to assume higher risk exposure, because the level of their effort cannot be observed by the principals (i.e., depositors).[72] *Third*, due to the lack of adequate information in the market, reputation and trust play a proportionally more important role in banking than in most other sectors of the economy. Imprudently, managed banks can free-ride and benefit from the reputation established by others which have managed risks prudently.[73] *Finally*, from the perspective of public policy, the most serious consequence of information asymmetries in banking is that depositors (especially if not covered by deposit guarantee) are tempted to participate in banking panics, inducing thus under conditions negative externalities as well, as discussed just below.

Negative Externalities: Channels of Contagion Among Banks
The informational channel—banking panics: Banks play a crucial role in the transmission of a financial crisis. The first channel for spill-over effects in the banking sector with the potential to lead to systemic crises is the '**informational channel**' and is associated with the emergence of either a run on an individual bank or a run on the entire banking system (literally a 'banking panic'). Panics occur when "*bank debtholders at all, or many, banks in the banking system suddenly demand that banks convert their debt into cash at par to such an extent that banks suspend convertibility of their debt into cash*".[74] Depending on the economic event triggering depositors' sudden demand for convertibility, the models on banking panics are classified based on two theories (as briefly discussed in **Box** 1.3 just below).[75]

Box 1.3 Theories of banking panics

'Non-fundamental theory'	According to this theory, panics are caused by 'random', large withdrawals of funds from the banking system. Under this 'sunspot' hypothesis', they can be triggered by "*anything that causes depositors to anticipate a run such as a bad earnings report, a negative government forecast or even a sunspot*"[76]

(continued)

---

[72] *Ibid.*, p. 140.
[73] This important argument was raised by Goodhart (1988).
[74] This definition of panics is given by Calomiris and Gorton (1990).
[75] These models are reviewed in Carisano (1992), pp. 32–56.
[76] See on this Diamond and Dybvig (1983), p. 410.

(continued)	
'Fundamental theory'	The alternative **'fundamental theory'** considers that panics are caused by any 'economic event' that can induce depositors to change perceptions about bank risk exposure: "*If depositors change, on a rational basis, their perception of asset riskiness they will not be able to discern which bank is underperforming. They will be induced to withdraw from the banking system as a whole, leading the system into panic*".[77] There are three versions of this theory[78]: (a) Under the **'recession hypothesis'**, depositors withdraw funds from the banking system after the dissemination of information about a looming severe recession; when an economic variable predicting recession (e.g., unemployment rate, sales) reaches a critical value, depositors hurry to convert their deposits into cash in the anticipation of several bank failures; (b) According to the **'seasonal hypothesis'**, the origin of panics lies in the existence of stringent money market conditions (e.g., the failure of specific firms, depressed stock prices or high interest rates); (c) Finally, the **'failure hypothesis'** maintains that panics are generated by the unexpected failure of a usually, albeit not necessarily, large bank
Common element	Under both theories, panics are caused by the behaviour of depositors and the existence of information asymmetries, which makes them unable to distinguish between 'good' and 'bad' banks and, under conditions, induces them to massively withdraw their bank deposits

Banking panics are the cause of market failure to the extent that, as they evolve, even solvent banks can face a heavy liquidity strain which in turn may trigger solvency problems.[79] Whereas a bank run need not always lead to a (generalised) panic, the potential failure of one bank can become contagious and trigger a spill-over effect of illiquidity-caused failures of other banks

---

[77] See Carisano (1992), p. 48.

[78] See Gorton (1988a), pp. 224–225.

[79] See Guttentag and Herring (1988), p. 3 and Carisano (1992), p. 14. A bank becomes insolvent when either its liquidity is so low that it cannot repay its outstanding debt, or the market value of its non-equity liabilities exceeds that of its assets. Any bank can be exposed to insolvency, which is a positive function of two factors: the intensity of potential risks and the extent of its vulnerability to risks: while 'risk intensity' depends on the insolvency's frequency and predictability, as well as the extent of losses that could be caused if it were to occur, 'risk vulnerability' depends on both the current exposure of a bank to each individual risk and its capacity to absorb losses, if risks occur (see Guttentag and Herring (1988), p. 27).

for two reasons: either because depositors assume that their bank is or may become exposed to the same risks as an insolvent one ('**pure information contagion**') or because they place it in the same class of riskiness as others exposed to a troubled bank regardless of whether or not a failure has occurred ('**signal information contagion**').[80] Hence, during a generalised withdrawal of funds from the banking sector, even solvent banks can fail due to their **structural vulnerability to liquidity risk**.[81] Under such circumstances, business firms are forced to interrupt their productive investments, leading the economy into a sudden recession. The impact on depositors' transaction balances (the '**macro-domino' effect**), on the functioning of payment systems and on the conduct of monetary policy is grave as well.[82]

The real channel—systemic risk: The *second* channel of contagion in the banking sector is the '**real channel**' and refers to the transmission of problems from one market segment to another following the emergence of systemic risk as a result of the interconnectedness of banks with other banks (and financial firms, in general), e.g., through the interbank market,[83] the markets for OTC derivatives (swaps, forwards, options) or the holding of assets (equity and debt).[84] '**Systemic risk**' is defined as the risk of disruption to the provision of (and/or inability to provide) key financial services that is caused by all or part of the entire financial system, with the likelihood of serious negative impacts ("**knock-on effects**") on the real sector of the economy.[85] It has two dimensions: the '**time dimension**', i.e., the development of systemic risk in the course of time, and the '**cross-sectional dimension**', i.e., how risk is distributed in the financial system at a given point in time.[86]

---

[80] See Saunders (1987), p. 205. Uninformed depositors, and especially those uninsured (or all depositors in the absence of a reliable deposit guarantee scheme, 'DGS'), do not have the time, the competence or even the incentive to monitor and control their bank. Conversion may be required even from creditors who would have preferred to leave their savings with the bank but decide to monitor it by withdrawing deposits, as they cannot adequately assess its net worth (see Diamond and Dybvig (1983), p. 402). This process is facilitated by the fact that the claim of bank depositors has a fixed nominal value, which does not vary with changes in the market value of the bank portfolio in assets (see Freedman (1987), p. 189). Uncertain and unable to coordinate with others, each depositor (reasonably) wants to collect its claim before reimbursement is suspended.

[81] See below, under 1.2.1.

[82] See Guttentag and Herring (1987a), pp. 158–159.

[83] See Saunders (1987), as early as in the 1980s.

[84] For an overview of all transmission channels (mechanisms), see Lastra (2015a), pp. 183–193.

[85] See Committee on the Global Financial System (2010a), Section 2.1, Schwarcz (2008), Chapter II, and Brunnermeier *et al.* (2009), Chapter 2.

[86] These two dimensions are further discussed below, under 1.2.5. On the theory on banking crises and their transmission channels, see Guttentag and Herring (1986a), Saunders (1987), Calomiris and Gorton (1990), Herring and Litan (1995), pp. 50–61, and Caprio and Klingebiel (1996a), (1996b).

1.1.3.2 The Components of the 'Bank Safety Net'

(1) As noted above, the need for regulatory intervention in the banking system is aimed at ensuring its stability against the risk of simultaneous or successive bank authorisation withdrawals. Ensuring the stability of the banking system, by preventing the above-mentioned spill-over effects among banks, renders necessary the adoption of various prudential measures, as well as protection (or 'crisis management') policies. In order, thus, to prevent negative externalities, they command a broad range of instruments, which comprise the **'bank safety net'**. Even though the various components of this prudential, crisis prevention and crisis management system are somewhat complementary, each of them has a specific contribution to the safeguarding of the banking system's stability. According to Guttentag and Herring (1988), the components of the bank safety net can be viewed as "*a series of circuit breakers designed to prevent a shock to one part of the financial system from surging through the financial network to damage the rest of the system*".[87] They include:

first, prudential measures, namely, the authorisation of banks by supervisory authorities, micro- and macroprudential regulation, the monitoring of their compliance with the above regulations (microprudential supervision) and the macroprudential oversight of the financial system;
second, crisis prevention measures, such as recovery plans set up by banks, assessment of banks' resolvability and development of resolution plans by resolution authorities, as well as early intervention measures;
third, last-resort lending by the central bank to solvent banks exposed to temporary illiquidity, which is typically excessive in periods of crisis; and
finally, solvency crisis management measures, including resolution action and winding-up proceedings in respect of banks assessed as "failing or likely to fail" ('**FOLF**'), as well as the operation of deposit guarantee systems ('**DGSs**').[88]

If insolvency problems arise and banks cannot meet capital shortfalls by resort to private sector recapitalisation solutions, competent authorities are faced with a **'trilemma'** whether to[89]: *first*, bail-out undercapitalised (usually systemically significant) banks by using taxpayers' money, judging that a withdrawal

---

[87] See Guttentag and Herring (1988), p. 9. For an overview of the components of the 'bank safety net', aimed at contributing to the stability of the banking system, see Guttentag and Herring (1986a), and Demirgüç-Kunt and Huizinga (1999). See also premise of Kane (2000) that optimal regulation is not a one-size-fits-all proposition.

[88] On differences in the terminology used, namely 'deposit guarantee' *vs.* 'deposit insurance' *vs.* 'deposit protection' and 'deposit guarantee / insurance systems' *vs.* 'deposit guarantee / insurance schemes', see Box 3.5 in Chapter 3 below.

[89] This trilemma is different from (and total unrelated to) Schoenmaker's (2011) 'financial trilemma', stating that in an open market economy the objectives of financial stability, financial integration and national financial policies are incompatible; any two can be combined but not all three.

of their authorisation would have significant systemic consequences[90]; *second*, resolve insolvent banks through the competent resolution authorities[91]; or *third*, withdraw their authorisation and subsequently activate the DGS.[92] It is noted in this respect that resort to the bail-out option, which constitutes a state-aid and is, thus, subject to approval by competition authorities, tends to be (especially in the wake of the **GFC**) the exception and is usually granted under very strict conditions.

(2) Apart from these components to be analysed below, the bank safety net also includes measures by monetary authorities to eliminate any tendencies on the part of depositors for excessive cash withdrawals in periods of crisis. This measure is inextricably linked with the conduct of monetary policy and is a manifestation of the close relationship between the operation of the banking and the monetary system. Of more general character are the **'structural regulations'**, i.e., those determining the range of financial services that banks are allowed to provide in the financial system. The issue whether banks should be allowed to *directly* provide investment services (and to what extent) and be direct members of the markets for the trading of securities and derivatives has been and is a source of major debate. In fact, in some jurisdictions, there are, in principle, no restrictions according to the **'universal banking model'**, while in other jurisdictions limitations are put in place.[93]

(3) The demand for a strengthened regulatory framework and tougher supervision in the banking sector comes back stronger, and rightly so, every time a major crisis arises in the financial system of one or more countries. It can be a **banking crisis**, a **foreign exchange crisis** or a **'twin' crisis**.[94] In this

---

[90] On this, see Padoa-Schioppa (2000), pp. 24–26.

[91] For more on this form of regulatory intervention, see indicatively Avgouleas, Goodhart and Schoenmaker (2009), Claessens, Herring and Schoenmaker (2010), and the Financial Stability Board's Key Attributes of Effective Resolution Regimes for Financial Institutions, further discussed in Chapter 2 below, under 2.4.3.

[92] See below, under 1.3.4.

[93] On this model, see Macey (1993), Benston (1994), Saunders and Walter (1994), pp. 3–9 and 84–126, Goodhart (2000) and Rheinholdson and Olsson (2012). On structural regulation in general (including the universal banking model), see Armour *et al.* (2016), pp. 505–529 and Alexander (2019), pp. 207–222 and 229–230, with further references. *In extremis*, under US federal financial law, banks were not allowed either to provide investment services directly or to have subsidiaries offering investment services pursuant to the 1933 "Glass-Steagall Act" (see Möschel (1978) and Lichtenstein (2010), pp. 219–224). This law was partly repealed in 1999 with the "Financial Services Modernisation Act" (known as 'Gramm-Leach-Bliley Act', Public Law 106-102, 113 Stat. 1338; see O' Neal (2000) and Yeager, Yeager and Harshman (2004)). On whether the adoption of the 1999 Act, which also eliminated legal barriers to affiliations between banks and insurance undertakings, contributed to the eruption of the GFC in the US, see my means of mere indication Grant (2010) (supporting this view), and Wallison (2009) and Norberg (2009), pp. 86–87 (arguing against it).

[94] On this distinction, see Brakman *et al.* (2006), pp. 217–263 (in particular pp. 256–258).

respect, it is useful to highlight four key gaps and sources of inefficiency relating to regulatory and supervisory mechanisms: the potential for regulatory and supervisory failure; the unequal treatment at times of crisis of **SIFIs** (as already discussed); regulatory arbitrage; as well as regulatory and supervisory 'overshooting', also at times following a crisis (Table 1.1).

Table 1.1 Financial policy objective: instruments for safeguarding the stability of the banking system—the 'bank safety net'

Policy instruments	Competent institution
1. Prudential measures	
Authorisation requirements for banks	Supervisory authority—central bank or other administrative authority
Microprudential banking regulations	Legislator (including the Parliament) and/or supervisory authority (under a delegated regulatory capacity)
Microprudential banking supervision	Supervisory authority—central bank or other administrative authority
Macroprudential policies (regulation and oversight)	Central bank or monetary authority/agency (in most cases)
2. Crisis prevention measures	
Preparation for resolution (recovery and resolution planning, intra-group financial support agreements)	Supervisory or judicial authority Resolution authority Deposit guarantee scheme (DGS)
Reorganisation and/or early intervention measures	Supervisory authority
Asset management companies for NPLs -State guarantees	Government agencies
3. Crisis management measures	
3.1 Management of liquidity crises	
Lending of last resort	Central bank or monetary authority/agency
3.2 Management of solvency crises	
Recapitalisation of banks by public funds	Ministry of Finance or delegated government agency
Resolution of banks	Resolution authority (and resolution fund)
Winding-up of banks	Administrative or judicial authority
Deposit guarantee (paybox function)	Deposit guarantee scheme

1.2 Prudential Measures in Banking

1.2.1 Risks to Which Banks May Be Exposed as the Key Driver for Adopting Prudential Measures

1.2.1.1 General Overview

Banks are exposed to several financial and non-financial risks, which are classified in six categories[95]:

(a) The risks in the first three categories (further discussed in detail below) include the following: *first*, those arising from the transformation function of banks, such as credit, liquidity and (interest rate) income risk[96]; *second*, market risks to the extent that banks also operate in capital, foreign exchange and commodities markets (position risk, foreign exchange risk and risk from open positions in commodities); and *third*, environmental risks.[97]

(b) The three other categories comprise settlement risk in payment, clearing and settlement systems[98]; operational risk, which refers to the probability of loss attributed either to inappropriate or incorrect internal processes/systems or human error, or to external causes[99]; and, finally, political and reputational risks.[100]

---

[95] On all these risks, apart from the extensive literature, reference should also be made to the relevant work of two international financial fora, namely the Basel Committee on Banking Supervision ('BCBS') and the Committee on Payments and Market Infrastructures ('CPMI') (on these international financial fora, see details in Chapter 3 below, under 3.1 and 3.3.4, respectively).

[96] In order to control their exposure to these risks, banks transfer part of their loans to special purpose vehicles ('SPVs') through 'asset securitisation' in the context of the 'originate and distribute' model. On the significant extent to which banks used this practice as a major cause of the financial crisis in 2007–2009, see Borio (2008), pp. 1–13 and European Central Bank (2008).

[97] The risks in the first two categories are financial risks; environmental risks translate into financial risks, as well as operational risks (as further discussed below).

[98] Settlement risk, which is another type of financial risk, refers to the probability of loss attributed to a counterparty's failure to settle its end of the deal, thereby preventing other counterparties to settle its commitments. It usually arises when payments are not exchanged simultaneously and its nature differs, depending on whether a participant defaults before any transfer of securities or funds (pre-settlement risk) or once final transfer of securities or funds has begun but not been completed (*stricto sensu* settlement risk).

[99] Operational risk, which does not specifically affect banks' transformation function, also covers cyber risk and legal risk but not strategic or reputational risks (see Basel Committee on Banking Supervision (2011a)). For a detailed definition of legal risk, see McCormick (2006).

[100] Political risk refers to the probability of loss attributed to political instability in a country that may result in cancellation of a license or otherwise affect the bank's ability to provide financial services. In principle, this risk is insurable and overlaps with the political component of *force majeure* (see Siegwart et al. (1989)). On the other hand, reputational risk refers to the probability of loss attributed to the actions of the bank itself (direct

1.2.1.2 Risks Arising from the Transformation Function of Banks
Credit Risk

(1) Credit risk is, in principle, the probability of a bank's risk of loss following a borrower's default or, in the case of undertakings, a credit rating downgrade, which puts borrower debt-servicing ability at risk. Banks' exposure to credit risk arises from their main function, i.e., transformation related to the allocation of liquidity risk according to the above. When managing this risk, banks (and in particular the larger ones) calculate four specific parameters for each exposure: *first*, a borrower's probability of default ('**PD**'); *second*, loss given default ('**LGD**'), which refers to the calculation of a bank's (average) expected loss per claim (a function of accepted collateral) in the event of a borrower's inability to meet liabilities (a concept which incorporates capital losses, loss of interest income and operating expenses); *third*, exposure at default ('**EAD**'), which is the total exposure upon default of a borrower; and *finally*, the asset's maturity.[101] Banks' exposure to credit risk does not only arise from loan and credit supply, but also from the total sum of claims, both on- and off-balance sheet (e.g., bonds or positions in OTC derivatives). Of importance within this framework is the credit risk to which banks are exposed due to positions in tradable debt securities, equities and derivative instruments held in their trading book.

(2) A special dimension is '**counterparty credit risk**' ('**CCR**'), defined as the risk that a counterparty to a transaction could default before the final settlement of the transaction's cash flows. Furthermore, the credit valuation adjustment ('**CVA**') risk is also of relevance. CVA is an adjustment to the fair value (or price) of derivative instruments to account for counterparty credit risk; it is thus commonly viewed as the price of the latter risk. This price depends on counterparty credit spreads and the market risk factors that drive derivatives' values and hence exposure. The probability of loss due to future changes in CVA is defined as CVA risk. Another specific dimension of credit risk is '**country risk**', which refers to the probability of adverse, and normally unforeseen, economic, political or social circumstances in a given state, which do not allow borrowers to repay their foreign currency denominated debt when due, in accordance with applicable contractual terms.[102] The most frequent manifestation thereof is '**transfer risk**', namely the probability of a borrower's reduced ability or limited willingness to secure foreign currency to repay foreign currency denominated debt.

---

approach), an employee or employees (indirect approach) or tangentially third parties (i.e., suppliers).

[101] These parameters are also of importance for the calculation of banks' capital requirements in accordance with the 'internal ratings-based approach'.

[102] See Siegwart *et al*. (1989).

Liquidity Risk

Liquidity is the ability to fund assets and to settle obligations when due.[103] Liquidity risk refers to the likelihood of a bank's liquidity position drying up following an unforeseen increase in liquidity needs. This risk arises from maturity transformation and has two aspects: the *first* is **'funding (or liability) liquidity risk'**, which refers to the probability of loss due to a bank's inability to borrow funds at an acceptable cost to refinance its debt. Typical examples are a rapid, mass withdrawal of deposits, a crisis in the interbank market not allowing fund-raising through it[104] and the inability to issue or refinance debt instruments in money and capital markets.[105] The *second* aspect is **'asset (or market) liquidity risk'**, i.e., the risk of loss resulting from the inability to liquidate assets at prices that do not deviate significantly from their nominal value to meet obligations when due. The decline in asset value due to haircuts and, in the most adverse case, the complete inability to liquidate, as shown during the GFC, are indicative examples. Banks are structurally vulnerable to liquidity risk; this structural vulnerability is caused by the inherent process of transforming liquid liabilities into illiquid assets, which concurrently constitutes the *raison d'être* of banking intermediation.[106]

Income Risk

This refers to the likelihood of a decline in bank interest rate income following an unexpected rise/fall of nominal rates. Banks are vulnerable to this risk due to the structure of their portfolio, given that on-balance sheet assets typically have longer maturities than liabilities and as a result are less vulnerable to interest rate fluctuations. The greater the short-term repricing gap—defined as the ratio of assets to liabilities, repriced within one year to own funds—and the stronger the fluctuation of interest rates, the more vulnerable banks are to this risk (and thus the greater the decline/increase in its prospective interest income due to interest rate volatility).

---

[103] Liquidity risk and the alternative measures for its assessment, management and supervision are discussed in detail in Basel Committee on Banking Supervision (2008).

[104] An indicative example is the 2008 crisis in the interbank market as a result of the GFC.

[105] For example, Greek banks were exposed to this risk in the period 2010–2017 due to the considerable downgrading in the credit rating of Greece's government bonds, which brought about the downgrades of their own credit ratings as well.

[106] To the extent that bank and its assets are marketable, a bank can overcome a sudden exposure to liquidity risk by selling such assets in the secondary market. However, since corporate and consumer loans are illiquid, it is unable to satisfy its depositors if they all choose to exercise their withdrawal option. In principle then, a bank with a substantial portfolio of illiquid and non-marketable assets is vulnerable to losses incurred due to the need to liquidate assets (namely financial instruments) at emergency prices, or to be funded in the money or interbank market at a high premium, which may lead to exposure to illiquidity-caused insolvency.

Market Risks

Position risk: This risk is defined as the probability of loss associated with open positions in debt instruments, equities and derivative instruments (or foreign currency) due to changes in various market parameters, to the extent that these positions are held for the purpose of resale or speculation. According to the prevalent **'building-blocks approach'**, position risk arising from open positions in debt securities and equities contains two components:

> *First*, **specific position risk** is defined as the probability of loss due to a negative change in a debt security's price, mainly due to parameters associated with its issuer. The notion of this component of position risk encompasses **'non-systematic risk'**, defined as a debt security's volatility (of returns) relative to the market rate of return; **'event risk'**, i.e., the risk of a negative change in the price of debt securities under exceptional events, including issuer default (default risk); the risk of inability to liquidate an open position in the market; and **'execution risk'** in arbitrage transactions.
>
> *Second*, **general position risk** means the probability of loss arising from open positions in tradable debt securities and equities following an abrupt change in their market value due to either (unfavourable) changes in nominal rates (in the case of debt instruments); or a strong price fluctuation in the markets where equities are traded, which is not attributed to specific issuers' characteristics. General position risk arising from open positions in debt instruments, also known as **'investment risk'**, is the first of two components of interest rate risk. The second component is (the above-mentioned) **'income risk'**.

The 'building-blocks approach' is also used for derivative instruments included in banks' trading books. In this case, *specific position risk* is the result of an abrupt change in the derivative instrument's market value for reasons associated with the underlying security's issuer. On the other hand, *general position risk* arises from open positions in derivative instruments or portfolios, which can be divided into two categories (the so-called **'Greek alphabet' risks**): the *first* encompasses those forms of market risk that arise from open positions in all derivative instruments, be they based on forward or option contracts, such as 'delta risk'/'absolute price risk', 'rho risk'/'discount rate risk', 'basis risk' and 'spread risk'; the *second* category includes forms of market risk arising exclusively from open positions in option derivatives, such as 'gamma risk'/'convexity risk', 'vega risk'/'volatility risk' and 'theta risk'.[107]

Foreign exchange risk and the risk arising from open positions in commodities: This risk relates to a bank's possible loss due to unpredictable, unfavourable revaluation of the currencies in which on- and off-balance sheet

---

[107] See on this Gortsos (2012), p. 82.

items are denominated *vis-à-vis* the currency of the bank's financial statements.[108] In the context of a system of variable exchange rates, in effect internationally since 1971,[109] the risk arising from foreign exchange open positions is a result of the fluctuation of nominal exchange rates. In fact, due to the frequency and intensity of foreign exchange fluctuations, supervisory authorities are not only interested in the eventuality of loss, but also in the extent to which banks' open position portfolios could be affected in such an eventuality, as a function of three factors: exchange rate volatility[110]; potential correlation between currency pairs[111]; and the duration of foreign exchange open positions. The (related) risk arising from open positions in commodities is associated with the probability of loss from open positions in commodities held in a bank's trading book as a result of changes in commodity prices.

Environmental Risks[112]
(1) Environmental risks in the financial system are closely linked to the discussion on sustainable finance.[113] They do not constitute a separate category of

---

[108] This definition refers to the first aspect of foreign exchange risk, i.e., transaction risk, and delineates it *vis-à-vis* its other two aspects, i.e., translation risk and economic risk.

[109] See Chapter 2 below, under 2.2.2.

[110] Experience of how international foreign exchange markets work so far suggests that certain foreign exchange positions are more risky than others, as certain currency pairs present relatively stronger volatility.

[111] Market experience and institutional restrictions (e.g., the Exchange Rate Mechanism of the European Monetary System) also show that exchange rates for certain currencies have a high degree of correlation.

[112] This sub-section is based on the following sources: (a) a publication by the Task Force on Climate-related Financial Disclosures ('TCFD', further discussed in Chapter 2 below, under 2.4.1), a private-sector taskforce established by the Financial Stability Board ('FSB', further discussed in Chapter 2 below, under 2.3.4) following a request made in April 2015 by the G20 Finance Ministers and Central Bank Governors, which provides recommendations for consistent, comparable, reliable, clear and efficient climate-related financial disclosures by companies (see Task Force on Climate-related Financial Disclosures (2017)); (b) the 2020 publication by the Network for Greening the Financial System ('NGFS'), whose members are central banks and supervisory authorities (see Network for Greening the Financial System (2020); on this network, which was set up in 2017, see at: https://www.ngfs.net/en); and (c) the documents referred to as European Central Bank (2020), Basel Committee on Banking Supervision (2021) and EBA Discussion Paper (2022).

[113] The G20 Sustainable Finance Study Group (2018) Report defines 'sustainable finance' as the aggregate of financing and related institutional and market arrangements that contribute to the achievement of strong, sustainable, balanced and inclusive growth, through supporting directly and indirectly the framework of the Sustainable Development Goals ('SDGs') as laid down in the 2015 United Nations ('UN') global sustainable development framework ("The 2030 Agenda for Sustainable Development"), which covers sustainability's three dimensions: economic, social and environmental ('ESG') (at: https://sustainabledevelopment.un.org/content/documents/21252030%20Agenda%20for%20Sustainable%20Development%20web.pdf). An effective way for achieving this is to make available financial products which pursue environmentally sustainable objectives; see on this Bose, Dong and Simpson (2019).

financial risks but are **risk drivers**—physical and transition risks (discussed just below), which translate into financial (e.g., credit, liquidity and market) risks, as well as operational risks (as discussed above) through various **transmission channels**, such as lower profitability, real estate value, household wealth or asset performance or increased compliance and/or legal cost.[114] They can be defined as the risks of any negative financial impact on a financial firm arising from the current or prospective impacts of environmental factors on its counterparties or invested assets.[115] Reflecting their potential double materiality, they can materialise in two ways: *first*, on the **"financial materiality side"**, the financial performance of a counterparty (or the invested assets) can be affected by environmental factors; *second*, on the **"environmental materiality side"**, the activities of a counterparty (or the invested assets) may have a negative impact on the environment, which may then become financially material for this counterparty through triggering or reinforcing a negative outside-in impact. Environmental risks include, but are not confined to, climate-related financial risks, namely the financial risks posed by the exposure of financial firms to counterparties that may potentially contribute to or be affected by climate change. These are closely interlinked with other environmental risk types since climate change contributes to the degradation of the environment and *vice versa*.

(2) Environmental factors can give rise to negative financial impacts through a variety of risk drivers, which are categorised—as already noted—into physical and transition risks, which closely interact with each other:

> *First*, **physical risks** are those arising from the physical effects of climate change and environmental degradation; they are classified either as acute—when arising from climate and weather-related events and an acute destruction of the environment, or as chronic—when arising from progressive shifts in climate and weather patterns or a gradual loss of ecosystem services.

---

[114] See on this EBA Discussion Paper (2022), pp. 17–19.

[115] These risks are also included in the (rather heterogeneous) category of environmental, social and governance ('ESG') risks, which are defined as the risks of any negative financial impact on the institution stemming from the current or prospective impacts of ESG factors on its counterparties or invested assets. 'ESG factors' are defined as ESG matters that may have a positive or negative impact on the financial performance or solvency of an entity, sovereign or individual; in this respect, 'environmental factors' are related to the quality and functioning of the natural environment and of natural systems, such as climate change and other forms of environmental degradation (e.g., air pollution, water pollution, scarcity of fresh water, land contamination, biodiversity loss and deforestation).

Second, **transition risk** typically refers to the uncertainty related to the timing and speed of the process of adjustment to an environmentally sustainable economy that may be affected by three drivers[116]: *first*, climate-related policy action or potentially disordered mitigation strategies may have an impact on asset prices in carbon-intensive sectors; *second*, technological changes may make existing technologies obsolete or uncompetitive, changing their affordability and affecting the relative pricing of alternative products, leading to assets' repricing; and *third*, changes in consumers' and investors' preferences and behaviour could also affect financial firms, through increasing litigation against counterparties on environmental issues, culminating in increased costs and reputational risks and avoidance of investing in non-sustainable assets, impacting their investment product offerings.

1.2.2 Authorisation Requirements

The first component of the bank safety net consists in laying down certain conditions, whose fulfilment is a *sine qua non* for the taking up of banking activity. Authorisation requirements serve a screening function, aimed at preventing market entry by natural or legal persons whose management could lead to heavy losses in a bank and impair the reputation of the entire banking system.[117] They also ensure that the bank has sufficient financial resources to finance its initial investments and absorb any losses. Standard requirements imposed by supervisory authorities in the context of the licensing procedure are the following: a minimum initial capital requirement; requirements on the organisational structure of the bank; specific fit-and-proper criteria for major shareholders; and similar criteria for bank management.

1.2.3 Microprudential Banking Regulation

1.2.3.1 Content of Microprudential Regulations

Microprudential banking regulation seeks to enforce the safety and soundness of banks by limiting their exposure either to insolvency or to liquidity risks (which, under circumstances, can lead to insolvency[118]) and curbing their risk vulnerability by *on the one hand*, limiting their exposure to various categories of financial risks, and all other risks associated with the conduct of thethreaten financial stabilityir business to which they might be exposed,

---

[116] The TCFD identifies similar risk drivers but classifies them into four categories on the basis of risks (policy and legal; technology; market; and reputational).

[117] Guttentag and Herring (1988), pp. 12–13.

[118] The same authors (at pp. 34–45) (correctly) argue that supervisors should focus more on banks' *potential exposure* to insolvency, because it is such insolvency-exposed banks that seriously.

and *on the other hand*, increasing their capacity to absorb losses incurred in the event of such risks.[119] Hence, it serves a failure-preventing function, by preventing the failure of individual banks, the risk of contagion and subsequent negative externalities in terms of confidence in the entire financial system.[120]

1.2.3.2 Policy Instruments
(1) Microprudential banking regulation is mainly performed by laying down rules on the following aspects: capital adequacy ratios against exposure to risks associated with the conduct of their business; liquidity ratios, a leverage ratio; corporate governance rules, including the organisation and operation of in-house risk management units[121]; the limitation of banks' holdings in other companies, mainly outside the financial system; provisioning for future exposure to risks; portfolio diversification (namely rules on 'large exposures'); and public disclosure of information on those matters.[122]

(2) In particular, **'capital adequacy ratio'** means (in principle) the minimum amount of regulatory capital as a percentage of total assets and off-balance sheet exposures weighted by specific risk factors ('risk-weighted assets', **'RWAs'**).[123] In designing this ratio: with regard to its *numerator*, decisions must be taken in relation to the elements that should be included in regulatory capital and under which qualitative and quantitative conditions; as regards the *denominator*, key aspects to be decided upon include the determination

---

[119] The measures taken by banks themselves in managing their risk exposure are aimed at the same objective. Indeed, supervisory authorities issue guidelines to banks regarding their risk exposure management.

[120] Microprudential banking regulation and its policy instruments (as well as its correlation with microprudential supervision) are discussed in greater detail in Barth, Caprio and Levine (2006), pp. 110–132 (a study published before the outbreak of the GFC).

[121] On related international standards, see the (revised) Guidelines of the BCBS of 15 July 2015 on "Corporate governance principles for banks" (at: https://www.bis.org/bcbs/publ/d328.pdf), as well as the 2015 "G20/OECD Principles of Corporate Governance" (at: https://www.oecd.org/corporate/principles-corporate-governance.htm), which are briefly discussed in Chapter 3 below, under 3.4.3. The BCBS Guidelines address sector-specific prudential regulation concerns, while the G20/OECD Principles are addressed (mainly) to listed companies, including banks (they are, hence, included in capital markets (soft) law).
On this important aspect, which is not core to this study (but some aspects are nonetheless be further discussed mainly in Volume II), see, by means of mere indication, Ferrarini and Giudici (2006), Filatotchev and Nakajima (2010), Hopt (2011) and (2012), McCahery *et al.* (2013), Armour *et al.* (2016), pp. 370–390, Gilson (2016), Goergen (2018), Gordon and Ringe (2018, editors), Alexander (2019), pp. 127–161, Anheier and Baums (2020, editors) and Afsharipour and Gelter (2021, editors).

[122] On these regulatory measures, see Aikman *et al.* (2019), pp. 162–175.

[123] On the different meanings of the 'capital' concept, including regulatory capital, see Norton (1995), pp. 3–8 and Alexander (2015). On the concept and necessity of introducing capital adequacy ratios, see also, by means of mere indication, Kim and Santomero (1988), Furlong and Keeley (1989), Rochet (1992), Berger, Herring and Szego (1995), Kahane (1977) and Armour *et al.* (2016), pp. 290–315.

of the risks to be taken into account and the risk weights to be applied to assets and off-balance sheet exposures. Finally, the level of the ratio must also be determined.[124] Capital adequacy requirements (and ratios) are designed for banks whose operations are continued on a going-concern basis. There is also a 'contingent capital' mechanism, designed for banks reaching the point of non-viability (capital requirements on a gone-concern basis).[125]

Furthermore, the **'leverage ratio'** is calculated as the minimum amount of regulatory capital (usually core own funds) as a percentage of total assets and off-balance sheet exposures *without weighting*.[126] Finally, there are also two (main) liquidity ratios[127]: the **'liquidity coverage ratio'** (**'LCR'**), meaning the ratio of the stock of high-quality liquid assets to total net cash flows over a short period of time (e.g., the next 30 calendar days); and the **'net stable funding ratio'** (**'NSFR'**), meaning the ratio of the *available* amount of stable funding to a *required* amount of stable funding.

1.2.3.3 Specific Issues

Regulatory failures: While market failures are the policy objective for regulatory intervention in modern economies, failures can also occur on the part of regulatory authorities (**'regulatory failures'**). In this context, Norberg (2009) correctly remarks the following:

> It is pointless to compare the real-life market economy, in all its imperfection, with an ideal image of how hypothetical, perfect authorities would govern the economy. It goes without saying that we must compare it with the real, imperfect authorities that we actually have.[128]

As a matter of fact, regulations do not always serve in the best way the purpose of their implementation, *inter alia*, due to the lack of an appropriate risk-benefit analysis.[129] For example, capital adequacy requirements,

---

[124] See Armour et al. (2016), p. 296. The same authors correctly point out (at p. 297) that, in the aftermath of the GFC, further aspects that have been addressed are the means to avoid the 'proportionality issue' (i.e., whether the capital adequacy ratio should be the same for all banks irrespective of their systemic importance) and whether the ratio should vary depending on factors that increase banks' risk of failure. For a detailed overview of the vast literature on capital adequacy regulation, see Allen and Gale (2002), pp. 1–12.

[125] On this aspect, see Coffee (2010), Pazarbasioglu et al. (2011) and Joosen (2015), pp. 210–221.

[126] On the concept and necessity leverage ratios, see Hildebrand (2008) and Murphy (2022), pp. 101–102.

[127] On the concept and necessity of liquidity ratios, see indicatively Armour et al. (2016), pp. 316–339.

[128] See Norberg (2009), p. 134. Intervention failure is one of five aspects of regulatory failure, the others being analytical failure, coordination failure, political failure and design failure.

[129] On regulatory failures, see the contribution of Kroszner in Kroszner and Schiller (2011).

which seek to strengthen banks' resilience, i.e., their capacity to absorb losses arising from unexpected (credit, interest rate, foreign exchange, and operational) risks undertaken as part of their business, amplify **'procyclicality'**, namely by encouraging banks to grant more loans (and ease credit standards) during economic upturns, but reduce credit supply (and stiffen credit standards) during the downward phase of the cycle.[130] It is also important to consider, beyond the predominant 'public interest approach', the circumstances under which rules are being adopted. The 'public choice theory approach' shows that regulatory intervention is the outcome of the actions of politicians, bureaucrats and lobby groups involved in the policy-making process for their own self-interest,[131] raising, *inter alia*, the issue of the influence of companies affected by regulatory intervention rules on those who adopt them (**'regulatory capture'**). In any case, the most relevant factor is not the quantity of regulations but rather their quality and targeting.[132]

The risk of over-regulation: At times of crisis, there is always an unwarranted risk of over-regulation—regulatory intervention and the concomitant supervision in every segment of economic and social activity usually overshoots its purpose. This is a reasonable reaction on the part of the intervening body to—at least—pander to public opinion, and common practice in areas such as air transport, in case of accidents, health care, in case of epidemics, or in the financial system, in case of financial firm insolvencies. In due course, 'excessive' intervention measures tend to become lax, inert or surpassed by the market itself. In this context and in realistic terms, expectations regarding current policy initiatives should be to minimise the eventuality of future crises of the magnitude and extent that we are experiencing today, and not to eliminate financial crises completely.

Regulatory arbitrage: Financial regulations must be designed to ensure a level playing field across all categories of financial firms operating in a given area, offering similar services and exposed to similar risks. In this context, it is of paramount significance to identify the necessary financial policy objectives (goals) and the appropriate financial policy instruments to achieve them.[133] The adoption of rules on regulatory intervention provides firms, irrespective of time or sector, with an incentive to minimise the ensuing cost, by transferring their activity over either to less regulated/unregulated services or to countries with a less stringent regulatory framework. Regulatory arbitrage on the part of private firms is a lesson drawn from economic (including financial)

---

[130] See on this Committee on the Global Financial System (2010a), Section 2.1. This is the main element of the systemic risk's 'time dimension', which necessitates the adoption of macroprudential policies (see below, under 1.2.5).

[131] On these approaches, see above, under 1.1.2.

[132] See on this Herring and Santomero (2000).

[133] By application of the rule established by the seminal work of Tinbergen (1952), the achievement of a specific set of policy objectives requires an equal number of instruments.

history. It is the basis of the **'dialectic relationship'** constantly forged between supervisory authorities and supervised parties (establishment of rules–transgression of rules–establishment of stricter rules, usually with a time lag),[134] and is even more facilitated by technological advances and in our days by the development of financial technology (**'FinTech'**). Even more so, given that supervised entities have been shown, in several cases, to outpace regulators and supervisory authorities, a case in point of such regulatory arbitrage has been the development of the shadow banking system.[135] *In addition*, regulatory arbitrage between countries (coupled with their tendency to adopt lax rules to attract more businesses to their territory, known as 'competitive deregulation' or **'competition in laxity'**) is the premise for the need to lay down harmonised rules at international or regional level.[136]

1.2.4   *Microprudential Banking Supervision*

1.2.4.1   General Remarks and Institutional Aspects

(1) In order to be effective, microprudential banking regulation should be coupled with microprudential supervision by competent supervisory authorities, with a view to assessing the quality of banks' portfolios and ascertaining compliance with the applicable regulatory framework in order to prevent their exposure to unmanageable risk levels. This supervision is conducted, *inter alia*, by means of microprudential **'supervisory stress tests'**,[137] regular and *ad hoc* examinations performed by supervisory authorities, as well as the audit of annual accounts and other financial and organisational aspects by external auditors on behalf of supervisory authorities.

---

[134] On this 'regulatory dialectic', see Kane (1987), pp. 114–116.

[135] See also the analysis of Norberg (2009) in pp. 52–53.

[136] This aspect is thoroughly analysed in Kapstein (1989) and (1992).

[137] A supervisory stress test is a forward-looking supervisory tool (used as a complement to probabilistic techniques), which assesses the resilience of banks (and, in particular, the adequacy of their capital and liquidity) under specific (even extreme) circumstances, taking into account low-probability (frequency) but high-impact risks to which they may be exposed; such risks tend to expose banks to 'disaster myopia' (see on this Guttentag and Herring (1986b)). Key to the supervisory purpose is the ability of the bank "to pass or not to pass the test", as well as the subsequent supervisory measures that may be needed to build up cushions if the bank fails to pass it. Stress tests differ from 'scenario analyses', which focus on the probability of future risks occurring, their consequences and the appropriate measures to be taken in order to mitigate them.

For a relatively recent stocktaking of range of practices in relation to supervisory (and bank) stress testing at a global level, see Basel Committee on Banking Supervision (2017). See also Feldberg and Metrick (2021), who support the view that supervisory authorities should tailor stress tests to focus on their comparative advantages by taking a macroprudential focus, emphasise risk-management practices and be wary of forcing rapid changes in capital levels for individual banks, while linking stress-test results with the imposition of countercyclical capital buffers.

(2) There are several alternative approaches to the institutional structure of microprudential banking (and, more generally, financial) supervision[138] (as discussed in **Box 1.4** below). Irrespective of the approach opted for, supervisory authorities also have the power to impose sanctions, but also to regulate to a certain extent (on a delegated basis)[139]; hence, they are also regulatory authorities. Furthermore, crucial elements are also the safeguarding of the institutional, personal, financial and functional independence of supervisory authorities (following the model of central banks as bodies which design and implement monetary policy[140]), while concurrently safeguarding proper accountability; their appropriate staffing to ensure the quality of the microprudential supervision exercised; the efficient and smooth exercise of their sanctioning powers; and the establishment of an appropriate framework on their responsibility *vis-à-vis* depositors, as well as supervised banks and their shareholders.[141]

Box 1.4 Approaches to the institutional structure of microprudential supervision

(1) In accordance with the **"sectoral approach"**, a different supervisory authority is entrusted with the authorisation and microprudential supervision of financial firms for each of the three main sectors of the financial system.[142] The task of checking compliance with rules on ensuring capital market efficiency is assigned to the supervisory authority responsible for the authorisation and microprudential supervision of investment firms. Under this approach, an issue arises regarding the competence for the microprudential supervision of banks providing investment services in terms of their compliance with rules on ensuring capital market efficiency and investor protection, given that such supervision can be carried

---

[138] For an overview of these approaches, see Lastra (2006), pp. 324–328, Group of Thirty (2008), Central Bank Governance Group (2011) and Armour *et al.* (2016), pp. 577–586. As regards the different governance practices of the financial regulatory and supervisory agencies in 103 Member States of the International Monetary Fund ('IMF') before the onset of the GFC, see Seelig and Novoa (2009).

[139] As a rule, regulatory powers are assigned to supervisory authorities by law, on the basis of either a general procurement or an ad hoc basis.

[140] In most advanced economies, central banks are independent authorities (in personal, institutional, financial and operational terms); on central bank independence, see, by means of mere indication, Amtenbrink (1999), Eijffinger and Hoeberichts (2000), Central Bank Governance Group (2009), Chapters 5–6 and Buiter (2014).

[141] On this distinction, see Rini (2008), pp. 61–68.

[142] One is also responsible for conducting supplementary supervision over financial conglomerates. Typically, this competence is assigned to the supervisory authority responsible for the supervision of a group's parent company or, in the case of horizontal groups, the supervisory authority responsible for the microprudential supervision of the group's largest company.

out either by the supervisory authority responsible for the microprudential supervision of banks or by the capital market supervisory authority. As regards banks, the supervisory authority may be either the central bank, namely the monetary authority or an administrative authority. Under the **"modified sectoral approach"**, there may be only two supervisory authorities: the first for the two main sectors of the financial system (usually banking and capital markets) and the second for the third sector.

(2) If the **"full integration approach"** is adopted, a single supervisory authority is exclusively competent for the microprudential supervision of financial firms operating in the three main sectors of the financial system. Usually, this supervisory authority is an administrative authority, even though in certain countries (such as Ireland) the task is assigned to the central bank.

(3) Under the **"functional"** or **"twin peaks approach"**, responsibilities are allocated between two authorities, as follows: the first is competent for the authorisation and microprudential supervision of financial firms operating in the main sectors of the financial system, as well as for ancillary supervision of financial conglomerates; and the second for monitoring their compliance with **"conduct regulation"**.[143] The former may be the central bank or another administrative authority; the latter is predominantly an administrative authority and not the central bank.[144]

1.2.4.2 Separation of Monetary Policy from Banking Supervisory Tasks

Even though safeguarding financial stability has historically been a major objective of central banks[145] and prudential supervision over banks a main task of several thereof, an ever-increasing number of countries around the

---

[143] On the principles of conduct of business ('COB') regulation for financial firms in general, see Tuch (2015). According to that author, COB regulation governs financial intermediaries' conduct towards their clients, meaning towards the actors (whether individuals or institutions) with whom financial intermediaries transact in providing financial products and services.

[144] See Wymeersch (2006) and Schoenmaker and Veron (2021) (specifically for Europe), Michael, Goo and Wojcik (2020) (for Hong Kong), and various (other) contributions in Godwin and Schmulow (2021) (theory and comparative aspects, with extensive further references). According to Carmichael (2021), at p. 35, in Australia, a "quadruple peaks approach" has been adopted: one authority is responsible for prudential supervision; a second for conduct regulation; a third for competition regulation; and the central bank for systemic stability regulation. It is noted, however, that it is common in all jurisdictions that have (even) adopted the twin peaks approach that competition regulation and financial stability oversight are the responsibility of the competition authority and the central bank, respectively.

[145] For an overview, see Gortsos (2020), pp. 14–19.

world have assigned such supervision since the 1980s to independent authorities other than the central bank.[146] The rationale has been that the exercise of supervisory powers by the central bank may give rise to conflicts of interest that would undermine the efficient achievement of its monetary policy objectives (including, price stability).[147] However, this trend has been (partially) reversed in the aftermath of the GFC due to failures attributed to independent supervisory authorities in many jurisdictions.[148] Along with the Bank of England ('**BoE**') since 1 April 2013,[149] the European Central Bank ('**ECB**') has become another notable example of this trend reversal as discussed in detail in **Part II below**.

1.2.4.3 Supervisory Failures
Apart from regulatory failures, failures by supervisory authorities ('**supervisory failures**') may occur as well. As rightfully argued, the case may be that supervisory authorities are (chronically) unable to restructure banks before their net worth has been depleted. Guttentag and Herring (1987b) identify three reasons for this slow response[150]: the '**recognition lag**' is a lag between the time the bank has become unviable and when authorities recognise this; the '**reaction lag**' extends from the time the authorities recognise the non-viability of the bank until they decide to terminate it; and the '**implementation lag**' is the period between the time the authorities initiate the procedure on closing down an unviable bank and the moment when the bank actually terminates its operations.

In this respect, it is noted that, in several countries, the financial system was not exposed (at least primarily) or was less exposed to the GFC, not only

---

[146] See on this indicatively Herring and Carmassi (2008) and Central Bank Governance Group (2011). On the trend towards integrating sectoral financial supervisory authorities (for banking, capital markets and insurance) into a single body, see Hadjiemmanuil (2004), Wymeersch (2006) (specifically in Europe), Filipova (2007), Group of Thirty (2008) and Seelig and Novoa (2009).

[147] For an overview of the debate on whether it is appropriate for a central bank, as a monetary authority, to also perform prudential banking supervision tasks, see the seminal paper by Goodhart and Schoenmaker (1993), as well as Haubrich (1996), Di Noia and Di Giorgio (1999), Goodhart (2000), Gianviti (2010), pp. 480–482, Eijffinger and Nijskens (2012) and Beck and Gros (2013).

[148] See Davies and Green (2010), pp. 187–213.

[149] Under the UK Financial Services Act 2012 (at: https://www.legislation.gov.uk/ukpga/2012/21/contents/enacted), which (*inter alia*) amended the Financial Services and Markets Act 2000, the (above-mentioned) PRA was established as a subsidiary of the BoE, responsible for the microprudential supervision of banks, building societies and credit unions, insurers and major investment firms. This Act also established the Financial Conduct Authority ('FCA') as a conduct-of-business regulator. Finally, an independent Financial Policy Committee ('FPC') has also been set up, entrusted with the objective of identifying, monitoring and taking action to remove or mitigate risks to financial stability with a view to protecting and enhancing the resilience of the UK financial system.

[150] See Guttentag and Herring (1987b), pp. 48–50.

because these were equipped with a strong institutional and regulatory framework, but also because microprudential supervision of their banking system was, admittedly, suitable. To illustrate this, it is worth quoting the wording of paragraph 151 of the 2009 Report drawn up by the *de Larosière* High-Level Group,[151] tasked with identifying the causes of the crisis:

> The supervisory objective of maintaining financial stability must take into account an important constraint which is to allow the financial industry to perform its allocative economic function with the greatest possible efficiency, and thereby contribute to sustainable economic growth. Supervision should aim to encourage the smooth functioning of markets and the development of a competitive industry. **Poor supervisory organisation or unduly intrusive supervisory rules and practices** will translate into costs for the financial sector and, in turn, for customers, taxpayers and the wider economy. **Therefore, supervision should be carried out as effectively as possible and at the lowest possible cost.**

1.2.5 Macroprudential Policies

1.2.5.1 Content

The term **'macroprudential policies'** comprises the set of policies implemented to limit the risk of system-wide financial distress (**'systemic risk'**) arising from factors not associated with the risk profile of individual financial firms or individual markets and structures of the financial system.[152] Macroprudential policies seek to address the two dimensions of systemic risk (see **Box 1.5** just below).

---

[151] This Report is presented in detail in Chapter 4 below, under 4.3.1.

[152] See Financial Stability Board, International Monetary Fund and Bank for International Settlements (2011), Section 2; on the relation between financial stability risks, monetary policy and macroprudential policies, see Constâncio (2015), Lastra (2015b), Goodhart (2018), and Liang (2019); on the relation between micro- and macroprudential policies, see Green (2012), Faia and Schnabel (2015), Mülbert (2015) and Gortsos (2020), pp. 23–25; on the relation between the twin peaks approach and macroprudential policies, see Godwin, Kourabas and Ramsay (2021); see also Armour *et al.* (2016), pp. 409–432.

Box 1.5 The two dimensions of systemic risk[153]

(1) The *first* is the **'time dimension'**, namely systemic risk's evolution over time (**'cyclical systemic risk'**). In this context, macroprudential policies seek to strengthen the resilience of the financial system, i.e., its capacity to absorb losses during the downward phases of the financial cycle by reducing procyclicality, which is inherent in the financial system and has the potential to accentuate systemic risk because of the interactions developed either within the financial system, or between the financial system and the real sector of the economy.[154] The objective in this case is to **'lean against the financial cycle'**,[155] bearing in mind that it has been proven historically that failures as a result of credit expansion are generated during upswings but become apparent during the downward phases of the financial cycle, especially during downturns.[156]

(2) The *second* dimension is the **'cross-sectional dimension'**, namely how risk is distributed in the financial system at a given point in time. In this case, macroprudential policies are aimed at limiting systemic risk concentration (**'structural systemic risk'**), which could result either from the concurrent exposure of financial firms to risks arising from the same or similar exposures or from their potential interconnectedness, especially if they are SIFIs.

---

[153] See Committee on the Global Financial System (2010a), Annex 1, Section 2, and Financial Stability Board, International Monetary Fund and Bank for International Settlements (2011), Section 2. On the concept of systemic risk, see European Central Bank (2009); on the origin—and so-called new definition—of systemic risk, see Montagna, Torri and Covi (2020).

[154] For an overview of contagion channels between the financial system and the real sector of the economy, see Basel Committee on Banking Supervision (2011a) and Galati and Moessner (2011), Section 5.2.

[155] See Committee on the Global Financial System (2010a), Section 2.1.

[156] More specifically, in the upward phases of the financial cycle, there is typically a credit boom (strong and rapid credit growth), surges in (and potential overvaluation of) real estate, collateral and other asset prices, significant leveraging of banks and money and capital markets, as well as maturity mismatches of assets and liabilities in the balance sheet of banks. In the absence of sufficient protection of the financial system, when the financial cycle is in a downward phase, problems may emerge for financial firms and can be aggravated by a need for de-risking and deleveraging. Usually, under such circumstances, the capacity to extend loans and credits is limited, impacting negatively on the real sector of the economy. On this issue, which came to the forefront particularly in the wake of the GFC, see Borio (2010), Committee on the Global Financial System (2010a), Financial Stability Board, International Monetary Fund and Bank for International Settlements (2011), Galati and Moessner (2011), Section 5.1, and Gluch, Skovranová and Stenström (2013).

1.2.5.2 Policy Instruments
Introductory Remarks

A mix of macroprudential policy instruments, collectively known as the **'macroprudential toolkit'**, is introduced to address cyclical and structural systemic risks. Specifically:

> *First*, it is necessary to set up institutions and procedures for ensuring the **'macroprudential oversight of the financial system'**, enabling thus the identification, measurement and assessment of systemic risk.[157] The objective of macroprudential oversight (typically assigned to central banks, alternatively to multi-agency financial stability committees/ councils[158] and in exceptional cases to financial supervisory authorities), which has now become a key element for achieving financial stability, is to limit any potential distress to the financial system as a whole in order to protect the overall economy against significant losses in real output. In this respect it is noted that, while risks to the financial system may, in principle, stem from the failure of an individual financial firm (if it is large enough in relation to the country concerned and/or if it has multiple branches/subsidiaries in other jurisdictions), systemic risk may arise from the concurrent (direct) exposure of several financial firms to the same or similar risk factors or their potential interconnectedness. Hence, macroprudential analysis should focus on common or correlated shocks and shocks to the financial system that trigger spill-over effects. Macroprudential oversight cannot be meaningful unless it can somehow impact on supervision at the micro-level, whilst microprudential regulation and supervision cannot effectively safeguard financial stability without adequately taking account of macro-level aspects.
>
> *Second*, it is necessary to adopt **'macroprudential policy measures'**, often in the form of regulations addressed to banks and/or other financial firms, as well as money and capital markets, and are differentiated depending on the systemic risk dimension they are called upon to address.[159] The task assigned to supervisory authorities to check financial firms' compliance with these regulations is that of **'macroprudential supervision'**.

---

[157] See Financial Stability Board, International Monetary Fund and Bank for International Settlements (2011), Section 3. On its content, see, by means of mere indication, Borio (2003) and Clement (2010).

[158] On the governance mechanisms of financial stability committees in the wake of the GFC, see indicatively Edge and Liang (2020).

[159] See Committee on the Global Financial System (2010a), Section 3 and Galati and Moessner (2011), Section 4. For an overall review of how these measures were adopted, see Financial Stability Board, International Monetary Fund and Bank for International Settlements (2011), pp. 5–9.

Measures to Address Cyclical Systemic Risk (Time Dimension)
The policy instruments used to achieve the objective of addressing the systemic risk's time dimension (cyclical systemic risk), and notably financial system procyclicality, mainly include the following:

> *First*, it is necessary to adopt rules imposing an obligation on banks to set a 'capital conservation buffer' and a 'countercyclical capital buffer' (see **Box 1.6** below), as well as take 'forward-looking' measures.[160]
>
> *Second*, the macroprudential toolkit also includes other measures which affect *either* the prices of services provided by banks (**'price-based prudential tools'**) such as introducing stricter risk weights on the upside of the financial cycle when calculating the capital adequacy ratio on specific exposures (mainly exposures secured by immovable property, but also, for instance, loans denominated in foreign exchange or loans for the purchase of securities and positions in derivatives); *or* the quantity of their services (**'quantity-based prudential tools'**), such as time variation tools, deployed depending on the financial cycle's phase, and borrower-based measures, such as limits on loan-to-value ratios for mortgage loans secured by immovable property, limits on debt-to-income, or debt-service-to-income ratios in mortgage and consumer loans.
>
> *Finally*, the systemic risk's time dimension (and notably procyclicality as a result of leveraging capital markets) can be addressed by stricter rules imposing margins and haircuts on positions in securities and derivatives during economic upturns.[161]

Measures to Address Structural Systemic Risk (Cross-Sectional Dimension)
The macroprudential toolkit is complemented by policy instruments used to address the systemic risk's cross-sectional dimension, which mainly include the following capital-based measures: *first*, measures in the form of higher loss absorbency requirements for global and domestic systemically important banks to reduce the likelihood and severity of failure of such banks and mitigate its potential impact on taxpayers and the domestic economy, respectively. Macroprudential capital surcharges imposed (usually on SIFIs) are calculated as a percentage of these institutions' total RWAs. Also composed of CET1 capital, their amount is commensurate with the degree of their systemic importance.

---

[160] See Brunnenmeier *et al.* (2009), Chapter 4.
[161] See Committee on the Global Financial System (2010b).

Second, EU banking law provides for additional CET1 capital requirements, known as '**systemic risk buffers**' (see **Box 1.6** just below).[162]

> **Box 1.6 Definition of Various Buffers**
>
> **(1) 'Capital conservation buffers'** are mandatory capital requirements, composed of Common Equity Tier 1 ('**CET1**') capital,[163] that must be fulfilled at all times and may be used to absorb losses in times of stress. The use of these buffers, calculated as a percentage of banks' total RWAs (according to the provisions on the capital adequacy ratio[164]), may necessitate recourse to other regulatory capital elements for absorbing losses, but is subject to restrictions, e.g., on dividend payments or bonus pay-outs.
>
> **(2) 'Countercyclical capital buffers'** ('**CCyBs**') are to be activated and built up in times of economic growth and credit expansion to ensure that the macrofinancial environment in which banks operate is taken into account.[165] They are also composed of **CET1** capital and calculated as a percentage of banks' total RWAs, creating an additional layer of capital to be drawn down in periods of stress. According to relevant BCBS guidance, such a requirement is subject to the discretionary judgement of each jurisdiction, i.e., to be activated when national macroprudential

---

[162] Authorities other than those in charge of macroprudential policy may also adopt regulations targeted at safeguarding financial stability by addressing the systemic risk's cross-sectional dimension, such as: *first*, rules on the resolution of SIFIs exposed to insolvency enabling (in part or in whole) the suspension of their operations without jeopardising the stability of the banking (and, more generally, the financial) system or making state intervention necessary for their bail-out, invoking the argument that they are TBTF; *second*, appropriate specific microprudential regulations (e.g., rules to cover banks' exposure to credit risk from specific assets items); *third*, measures to strengthen infrastructures in relation to OTC derivatives (i.e., the obligation for clearing OTC transactions through central counterparties; see the 2010 Financial Stability Board Report "Implementing OTC Derivatives Market Reforms", October (at: https://www.financialstabilityboard.org/public ations/r_101025.pdf); *fourth*, restrictions on the range of services provided by SIFIs which can also address the cross-sectional dimension (see Financial Stability Board, International Monetary Fund and Bank for International Settlements (2011), p. 9, paragraph 5(iv)); and *finally*, oversight of payment and settlement systems, which can address the cross-sectional dimension as well.

[163] This is the highest quality of regulatory capital, as it immediately absorbs losses as they occur.

[164] See above, under 1.2.3.

[165] The term "macrofinancial environment" refers to the linkages and the (two-way) interactions between the real economy and the financial sector; see on this Claessens and Kose (2018). The macrofinancial implications of a shock may increase uncertainties about the evolution of the economy and expose financial markets and the banking sector to elevated risks. Vice versa, a banking crisis may spill over to the real sector of the economy.

authorities consider that excess aggregate credit growth is deemed to be associated with a build-up of systemic risk. To this end, authorities are called upon to monitor credit growth and additional cyclical indicators that may signal changes in the intensity of systemic risk, assess whether (and to what extent) credit growth is excessive and is leading to the build-up of systemic risk, and set an appropriate level of CCyBs.

(3) In addition, under EU law,[166] **'systemic risk buffers'** may be imposed by Member State authorities to prevent and mitigate a wide range of structural systemic risks that are not covered by any of the above-mentioned macroprudential policy measures, namely the *"risk of disruption to the financial system with the potential for serious negative consequences for the financial system and the real economy in a specific Member State"*. They may be applied across all exposures/institutions or (on a sectoral basis) to subsets thereof in cases where banks exhibit similar risk profiles in their business activities, e.g., real estate exposures.

1.3 Crisis Prevention and Management Measures in Banking

1.3.1 Crisis Prevention Measures

1.3.1.1 General Overview

(1) In the light of the above analysis, a key difference between the banking sector and the other sectors of the financial system (as well as other sectors of the economy) that renders necessary the adoption of measures on micro- and macroprudential regulation is that an individual bank's insolvency, which may be associated, *inter alia*, with depositor behaviour, the macroeconomic conjuncture, its financial structure and/or its business model, can lead to the default of other banks (through various contagion channels) and destabilise the banking sector with a serious negative impact on the functioning of the real economy. This makes the case for the introduction as well of a variety of 'crisis prevention' policies and measures,[167] which include the following: *first*, **'recovery planning'** and **'resolution planning'**[168] (also called

---

[166] This buffer scheme has not been developed at all in the "Basel III regulatory framework" developed by the BCBS; see on this in Chapter 2 below, under 2.4.1.

[167] On these measures, see the seminal work of Calomiris, Klingebiel, Laeven (2004), Claessens, Herring and Schoenmaker (2010), as well as the individual contributions to Lastra (2011, editor), all with extensive further references.

[168] According to a famous *dictum* by Benjamin Franklin, *"if you fail to plan, you are planning to fail"*.

'living wills'[169]); *second*, measures relating to the assessment of banks' resolvability, including the exercise of powers to remove impediments thereto; *third*, **'early intervention measures'** in the operation of banks (discussed in more detail just below); *fourth*, other reorganisation measures for banks exposed to insolvency (e.g., increasing their own funds on a mandatory basis, subject to limitations set by company law with regard to the rights of existing shareholders); *fifth*, the setting up of asset management companies (**'AMCs'**) with the objective of restructuring distressed but viable banks and serving as a vehicle for removing non-performing loans (**'NPLs'**) from their balance sheet[170]; *sixth*, the implementation of earmarked bank debt, account and blanket (state) guarantee programmes; and *finally*, the write-down in the nominal value and/or conversion of a bank's capital instruments into ordinary shares (prior to its potential resolution).[171]

(2) As further discussed below,[172] the historically first and primary function of **DGSs** (linked to banking panics) is to serve as a 'paybox' for depositors. However, DGSs may also be required to use their funds in support of measures (*e.g.*, liquidity provisions, guarantees) to prevent the failure of a bank and reduce the likelihood of future claims against them (the **'failure management function'**). Hence, DGSs may not only operate for the management of a banking crisis but also for its prevention.

1.3.1.2 In Particular: Early Intervention

(1) Early intervention serves to prevent an identified weakness or deficiency of a bank from developing into a threat to financial stability. According to literature, the nature and size of problems in the banking system should be recognised early, and intervention should follow quickly. The purpose of such an early recognition and intervention by supervisory authorities is to avoid a hidden deterioration in banks' financial conditions, before they become insolvent, which could magnify the costs of eventual crisis management operations.

---

[169] Recovery plans, prepared by the banks and approved by competent authorities, should set out credible options for restoring financial or operational soundness in a range of idiosyncratic and market-wide stress scenarios. On resolution planning, see Avgouleas, Goodhart and Schoenmaker (2009), Carmassi and Hering (2013) and Amorello and Huber (2014).

[170] AMCs, which are also referred to as 'bad banks', also serve two other functions: the resolution of insolvent banks by application of the asset separation tool (see under 1.3.3 below) and the privatisation of government-owned banks. On AMCs, see details in Gortsos (2021a), pp. 14–22, with extensive further references to literature.

[171] On an intertemporal, comparative study of key design decisions relating to bank crisis prevention (and crisis management), see the *New Bagehot Project* of the "Yale Program on Financial Stability"; this online platform is available at: https://newbagehot.yale.edu.

[172] See below, under 1.3.4.

(2) A necessary condition for effective early intervention is the existence of supportive institutions and appropriate instruments. In particular, it is facilitated by a resolution regime for banks, which empowers supervisory authorities to intervene promptly before a failure occurs, triggering a costly and lengthy liquidation process:

> In the absence of such a regime, early intervention will require swift policy decisions, typically backed by legislative action, which would avoid the temptation to resort to regulatory forbearance as a temporary expedient until the necessary policies and supporting legislation can be passed. Forbearance can produce serious long-term collateral damage in terms of incentives and the credibility of the framework.[173]

(3) According to Section I of the 2012 **"Core Principles for Effective Banking Supervision"** of the Basel Committee on Banking Supervision (**BCBS**),[174] a greater focus should be placed on effective risk-based supervision and the need for early intervention and timely supervisory actions. By setting out the powers that supervisory authorities should have to address safety and soundness concerns, the Core Principles provide that supervisory authorities should use these powers once weaknesses or deficiencies are identified. Adopting a forward-looking approach to supervision through early intervention can prevent an identified weakness from developing into a threat to safety and soundness. This applies, in particular, to highly complex and bank specific issues (such as liquidity risk) where effective supervisory actions must be tailored to a bank's individual circumstances.[175]

(4) Early intervention is, *inter alia*, also of interest to deposit guarantee. Pursuant to the "IADI Core Principles for Effective Deposit Insurance Systems",[176] if implementation of corrective measures is deficient, early intervention and an effective resolution regime can help lower the costs associated with bank failures, while the effectiveness of the resolution regime strengthens the financial system's architecture and *directly* contributes to financial stability.[177] According to the Chair of the Financial Stability Institute ('**FSI**') at the Bank for International Settlements ('**BIS**'), for supervisory

---

[173] See on this Borio *et al.* (2010), pp. 3–4. On the theory of early intervention, see Krimminger and Lastra (2011), pp. 58–61 and Svoronos (2018); on related international policy proposals, see Basel Committee on Banking Supervision (2018), addressing the challenges of early intervention (pp. 8–11), the appropriate frameworks and processes (pp. 11–20), as well as supervisory capacity, ability development and willingness to act (pp. 21–26).

[174] On this Report, see Chapter 2 below, under 2.4.3.

[175] Core Principles for Effective Banking Supervision (2012), paras 12–13.

[176] These Core Principles and the International Association of Deposit Insurers ('IADI'), which adopted them on 1 November 2014, are further discussed below in Chapter 2, under 2.4.3 and in Chapter 3, under 3.2.

[177] See IADI Core Principles, pp. 12–14 (under 2 and 3).

authorities, early intervention might be about the ability to change management behaviour, through moral suasion or more formal supervisory actions, while a bank's financial condition remains sound, which is broadly consistent with the goals of "risk-based supervision". On the other hand, for deposit insurers and resolution authorities, the focus might be narrower on taking intervention measures to try and avert a bank failure when a bank shows signs of distress, or in their absence, closing a bank when capital is still positive in the hope of minimising losses to the deposit insurer or the taxpayers.[178]

1.3.2 Lending of Last Resort (LLR) by the Central Bank

1.3.2.1 Definition, Functions and Delimitation

(1) In accordance with the (predominant) traditional approach,[179] lending of last resort ('**LLR**')[180] means the provision of liquidity by a monetary authority, i.e., a central bank, to individual solvent banks in exceptional circumstances and on a temporary basis.[181] This power is typically associated with the business of central banks given the synergies existing between the provision of liquidity to banks, safeguarding the stability of payments systems and ensuring financial system stability[182]; the close relationship between monetary and financial systems is hence highlighted. Thus, last-resort lending is part of the bank safety net.[183]

Two remarks deserve attention in this context: *first*, the term 'lending of last resort' is also used for the provision of financial support to countries exposed to public debt refinancing problems; this role is assumed on an international

---

[178] On this aspect, see Restoy (2017), pp. 1–2.

[179] This approach is based on the seminal work by Bagehot, written already in 1873 (which Tucker calls the "classic" Bagehot view; see Tucker (2014), p. 16). For more details on the other three alternative approaches (the "free banking school", the "Richmond Fed view" and the "New York view"), see *ibid.*, pp. 16–19.

[180] Frequent is also the use of the acronym 'LoLR'.

[181] On whether LLR should also be provided to financial firms other than banks, see Tucker (2014), pp. 27–28. This question was particularly relevant in the case of the US investment bank *Lehman Brothers* in September 2008, when the Federal Reserve declined to act as an LLR given the lack of statutory authority to do so. See indicatively Posner (2010), pp. 63–67. With regard to the Fed's general interventions amidst the GFC, see Baxter and Gross (2010), Oganesyan (2013), Gorton and Metrick (2013), pp. 58–60 and Nelson (2014).

[182] See European Central Bank (2007), pp. 80–81.

[183] For an overview of the functions of last-resort lending, see Guttentag and Herring (1983), (1986a) and (1987a), the various contributions in Goodhart (2000) and in Bank for International Settlements (2014), as well as Manna (2009), Nijskens and Eijffinger (2010), and Tucker (2014) and (2018). For a historical analysis of the role of central banks as last-resort lenders, see Gorton and Metrick (2013) and Bordo (2014); for a more detailed account of divergences in the efficiency of last-resort lending depending on the structure of the financial system, see the extremely interesting (and quite technical) paper by Fecht and Tyrell (2004).

level, by the IMF.[184] *Second*, at times of liquidity crises, alternatively to the **'central bank money solution'**, i.e., central banks acting as LLR, there are three other options: financing of a troubled bank through coordinated actions of the private banking sector (the **'private money solution'**); intervention of public authorities as market-makers of last resort[185]; and/or emergency, unconventional monetary policy measures taken by a central bank (in this case, for the entire banking system).[186]

(2) A central bank's intervention as LLR is driven by the need to meet one or more solvent banks' emergency liquidity needs, should they arise. Thus, last-resort lending performs two functions: the *first* consists in enabling solvent banks to address their exposure to exceptional liquidity risk and prevent illiquidity-caused solvency problems; the *second* function is activated when circumstances emerge that would lead banks with exceptional liquidity problems to become insolvent; in this case, LLR is provided to prevent a generalised banking crisis as a result of the simultaneous or successive exposure of several banks to insolvency and avoid negative effects on the economy's real sector.

(3) LLR as an instrument of liquidity crisis management should be conceptually distinguished from measures undertaken at the level of solvency crisis management.[187] Even though central banks may also play an active role in the resolution and withdrawal of the authorisation of insolvent banks (in the *former case*, if they are the competent resolution authorities and in the *latter case*, if they are the competent supervisory authorities), such powers should not be confused with their power to act as an LLR. Last-resort lending should also be distinguished from monetary policy measures implemented by central banks. In both cases, the central bank provides liquidity to the banking system, but in the case of monetary policy actions *first*, the objective is not to ensure the stability of the financial system, but (primarily or secondarily) to maintain price stability; *second*, the liquidity granted is not of an emergency nature, but rather permanent; and *third*, the liquidity is provided to the banking system as a whole (without exception), rather than to individual banks.[188] It is finally noted that deposits are by no means guaranteed by central banks, despite the fact that national law usually may provide for their participation in the

---

[184] See Chapter 2 below, under 2.3.5. On the equivalent arrangement at EU level, the European Stability Mechanism (ESM), see Chapter 5 below, under 5.1.5.

[185] On this aspect, see Tucker (2014), pp. 28–32.

[186] On this, see Borio and Disyatat (2009), and Lenza, Pill and Reichlin (2010), Domanski, Moessner and Nelson (2014) use the term 'emergency liquidity assistance' as equivalent to the term 'last-resort lending', actually to describe central bank intervention at times of liquidity crisis. The term 'ELA' is also the standard term used for last-resort lending in the euro area (see below the *Excursus* at the end of Chapter 6).

[187] For the relation between these two types of measures, see Freixas and Parigi (2008).

[188] On the differences between these two key objectives of central banks, see Central Bank Governance Group (2009), pp. 21–28.

management of **DGSs**, which are primarily (if not exclusively) funded by their member banks.[189]

1.3.2.2 Principles Governing the Implementation of Last-Resort Lending

(1) According to theory, a bank's solvency is a prerequisite for its ability to have recourse to lending of last resort.[190] Relevant information must be provided to the central bank by the competent supervisory authority, which may be an independent administrative authority or the central bank itself. However, there are past examples of last-resort lending to insolvent banks as well, depending on a central bank's evaluation of the probability of risk for a generalised banking crisis.[191]

(2) According to theory as well, last-resort lending should be provided against adequate collateral[192] and at a rate higher than that of monetary policy operations.[193] In this respect, two remarks are useful:

> *First*, as a rule, the collateral that can be provided by counterparty banks includes assets (securities), which are not eligible, given their low credit rating, in the context of open market operations (as part of a central bank's conduct of monetary policy). This is particularly the case if a bank has lost the ability to raise liquidity on money and capital markets, does not have assets on its balance sheet that are eligible in the context of central bank monetary policy operations, is hence excluded from access to open market operations as a counterparty, and is finally forced to have recourse to last-resort lending in order to raise liquidity.
>
> *Second*, the reasoning behind charging significantly higher rates than those applied to monetary policy operations[194] (thus causing a proportionate burden on the financial accounts of counterparty banks) is based on the premise that this rate should be of a punitive nature and, thus, act in a way to discourage banks. Nevertheless, it is also related to

---

[189] DGSs are discussed below, under 1.3.4. On the relationship between microprudential banking supervision, last-resort lending and deposit guarantee, see Kahn and Santos (2001).

[190] See on this Guttentag and Herring (1987a), pp. 163–165, and Tucker (2014), pp. 19–23 and (2020), who considers solvency as a 'fundamental constraint' in the provision of LLR.

[191] Guttentag and Herring (1987a, p. 164) cite many relevant examples.

[192] See on this Tucker (2014), pp. 26–27.

[193] *Ibid.*, pp. 23–24, directly citing Bagehot (1873).

[194] On central bank collateral frameworks and practices as part of the implementation of monetary policy, see Markets Committee (2013).

the preceding remark about the (lower) quality of the collateral provided, not eligible for any other use (not only in *a priori* assessments).

(3) The terms for exercising the power of central banks to act as lenders of last resort are not usually set out explicitly in legislative or regulatory provisions.[195] This is attributed to the fact that, according to the principle of **'constructive ambiguity'**[196] relating to the conditions that must be met in order for the central bank to intervene in the capacity of lender of last resort, the central bank must have discretion in order to be in a position to appropriately weigh the risks and act accordingly to each case. More specifically, it is argued that the existence of an explicit legislative or regulatory provision would put the stability of the financial system at a higher risk as a result of a greater exposure of banks to moral hazard and hence ultimately to insolvency,[197] and, as a result, necessitate stricter microprudential regulations than generally required, in view of preventing banks' exposure to risks undertaken when conducting business.

1.3.3   Banking Resolution

1.3.3.1   General Overview—Objectives

(1) In order to address the TBTF issue and ward off the moral hazard in case of **SIFIs**, the winding up of which would endanger banking (and, more generally, financial) stability (in addition to prevent resort to a government bail-out) 'crisis management measures' in the form of resolution actions may be put in place; as a matter of fact, in the aftermath of the **GFS**, several (albeit not all) national legal frameworks have introduced a banking resolution regime. Resolution is carried out by administrative resolution authorities, which should have clear statutory objectives; the resolution regime should give them the necessary powers and tools to intervene when a bank is (or is likely to be) no longer viable (FLOF), with no reasonable prospect of return to viability, i.e., before it is "balance sheet insolvent" and decide on the dichotomy between either resolving it or initiating liquidation proceedings.[198]

---

[195] A different issue is that certain central banks have a clear statutory task to act as lenders of last resort.

[196] According to Herring and Littan (1995), pp. 126–131, the 'constructive ambiguity' policy has significant negative side-effects, as it leads in reality to unequal treatment of big (usually systemically important) and small banks. For a detailed overview of this topic, and notably whether constructive ambiguity is necessary or not ('explicit last-resort lending function'), see Guttentag and Herring (1987a), pp. 167–172.

[197] Last-resort lending at a rate higher than monetary policy operations rates, as argued above, is deemed to partly resolve the issue of moral hazard (see Tucker (2014), p. 23).

[198] By the application of the 'gone-concern' resolution tools (discussed just below), the bank under resolution would also be liquidated; however, in this case, some of its assets and liabilities would have been transferred to another bank; *on the other hand*, by application of the 'bail-in tool' (also discussed below), the bank under resolution would

(2) The main objectives of resolution, which is referred to (correctly in the author's opinion) as a specialised regime for bank failures,[199] are the following: *first*, ensure the continuity of **'critical functions'** of the bank under resolution, i.e., activities, services or operations which are systemically important and the discontinuance of which is likely to lead to the disruption of services that are essential to the real economy or to disrupt financial stability due to the size, market share, external and internal interconnectedness, complexity or cross-border activities of an institution or group, with particular regard to the substitutability of those activities, services or operations. *Second*, avoid significant adverse effects on financial stability, in particular by preventing contagion effects, including market infrastructures (i.e., payment and settlement systems). *Third*, protect public funds by *minimising reliance* on public financial support (public ownership or bail-out)[200]; consequently, the provision of such support must be restrictive both in terms of having recourse to it and in terms of the amounts provided. *Fourth*, protect depositors and investors covered by DGSs and investor guarantee schemes, respectively, as well as client funds and client assets (which are off-balance sheet items). Hence, the resolution regime encompasses all the measures taken to resolve problems arising from the exposure to insolvency of (mainly, but not exclusively, systemically important) banks and avoid an initiation of liquidation proceedings (thus preventing spill-over effects of a bank's failure on the economy) or resort to bail-out measures through public financial assistance facilities.[201]

1.3.3.2 *Resolution Planning and Resolvability Assessment*

Resolution plans are developed by resolution authorities using information provided by banks. They set out the resolution strategy and the tools to be applied if the conditions for resolution are met, as well as a detailed operational plan for the implementation of that strategy and are of particular importance for large banks whose resolvability entails several complexities. An inherent

---

continue to operate. This aspect, which is of significant importance under EU banking law, will be further discussed in detail in Volume II. It is also noted that in several jurisdictions failed banks are liquidated by resort to corporate insolvency proceedings, while in others a bank-specific liquidation framework is in place, requiring the appointment of a special bank liquidator.

[199] See on this Psaroudakis (2014), pp. 62–71 and Binder (2017), pp. 69–70, who use the term "Sonderinsolvenzrecht der Banken". Hadjiemmanuil (2014) makes use of the term 'special resolution regime (SRR) for banking institutions', with reference to the work of Sjöberg (2014). See also Cihák and Nier (2009) and Muñoz (2017).

[200] It is worth noting that this is contrast to insolvency law where the main (albeit usually not the only) objective is the maximisation of creditor value. See on this Haentjens (2017), p. 220.

[201] On the concept(s) and the evolution of this crisis management measure, see Huertas and Lastra (2011), pp. 258–267, White and Yorulmazer (2014), Armour (2015), Armour et al. (2016), pp. 340–358 and Binder (2016), Section 2.2; on the cross-border resolution of global banks, see Hüpkes and Devos (2010), Davies (2014), and Faia and Mauro (2015).

part of resolution planning is the power conferred upon resolution authorities to carry out **"resolvability assessments"** in order to ensure that (at least systemically important) banks could be resolvable. Their aim being to assess the feasibility and credibility of the resolution strategy, they are coupled with the power of resolution authorities to require banks to adopt measures to address impediments to their resolvability.

1.3.3.3 Resolution Tools and Powers
(1) For the purpose of resolution, four 'resolution tools' are available to resolution authorities if the conditions for resolution are met: the sale of business tool, the bridge institution tool, the asset separation tool and the bail-in tool:

> **'Sale of business tool'** means the mechanism for effecting a transfer by a resolution authority of instruments of ownership issued by a bank under resolution, or of its assets, rights or liabilities, to another bank that is not a bridge institution; **'bridge institution tool'** means the mechanism for transferring, instruments of ownership issued by a bank under resolution, or of its assets, rights or liabilities, to a bridge institution[202]; and **'asset separation tool'** means the mechanism for effecting a transfer of assets, rights or liabilities of a bank under resolution to an 'asset management vehicle'. In all cases, the transfer of instruments of ownership or of assets, rights or liabilities is effected without the consent of shareholders or creditors.[203]
> **'Bail-in tool'** means the mechanism for effecting the exercise of the write-down and conversion powers in relation to liabilities (including deposits up to the level of their coverage in accordance with the rules governing the **DGS**) of a bank under resolution.[204]

In addition, to ensure continuity of banks' critical functions, resolution authorities should, *inter alia*, have the power to impose a temporary stay on early termination rights under financial contracts.

(2) On the basis of the resolution plan and the decision taken after the assessment has been made that the bank is FOLF (which may deviate from

---

[202] In both of these cases, the authorisation of the bank under resolution is withdrawn and the bank is placed under liquidation (hence, they are called 'gone-concern' resolution tools). Nevertheless, its deposits up to the level of their coverage under the DGS are previously transferred either to another bank or to the bridge institution; hence, the DGS does not need to be activated.

[203] In principle, this resolution tool would not be applied on a stand-alone basis but in combination with another one (typically the bail-in tool).

[204] On this 'going-concern' resolution tool, see, out of a vast existing literature, Coffee (2010), Huertas (2012), Goodhart and Avgouleas (2014), Hadjiemmanuil (2014) and (2015), Avgouleas and Goodhart (2015), Krahnen and Moretti (2015) and Armour *et al.* (2016), pp. 358–365.

the provisions of the resolution plan) in relation to the dichotomy between either resolving the bank or putting it under liquidation, resolution authorities should have the power to liquidate all or part of the bank, with timely payout or transfer of insured deposits and with prompt access to client funds and assets.

1.3.3.4 Legal Safeguards: The 'No Creditor Worse Off Principle' (NCWO) Principle

Since resolution actions may interfere, even disproportionately, with contractual, statutory or constitutional rights, legal safeguards are necessary. In this respect and *inter alia*, of specific importance in the application of resolution tools is the **'no creditor worse off ('NCWO') principle (safeguard)'**. According to this, no creditor and shareholder of a bank in resolution should incur greater losses than would have been incurred if this would have been liquidated at the time that the resolution decision is taken, in accordance with specific safeguards. Hence, the resolution framework should provide that creditors and shareholders receiving less due the resolution action than they would have received in liquidation should have a right to compensation and contain rules specifying its exercise. This requirement aims at establishing (to a reasonable level of satisfaction) that this right is substantive, by specifying the authority responsible for administering the process of compensation and for paying it; application procedures for compensation; a transparent process by which the amount of compensation payable and point in time for purposes of valuation are determined; as well as procedures for review and challenge of that determination.

In public international financial law, this principle is specified in Section 5 (titled: Safeguards) of the **2014** "Key Attributes of Effective Resolution Regimes for Financial Institutions" of the Financial Stability Board (**FSB**) providing the following:

> Creditors should have a right to compensation where they do not receive at a minimum what they would have received in a liquidation of the firm under the applicable insolvency regime ("no creditor worse off than in liquidation" safeguard).[205]

1.3.3.5 Resolution Financing

(1) It is common in (almost) all jurisdictions that the funding necessary to effect resolution actions is provided by a resolution fund, which is financed, in principle, by the banking system; privately funded **DGSs** may also be used in resolution financing.[206] Resolution funds are as critical an element of the

---

[205] FSB Key Attributes (2014), Section 5, par. 5.3. On these international standards, see Chapter 2 below, under 2.4.3.

[206] On resolution financing and resolution funds, see Goodhart (2012), Nieto and Garcia (2012), Grünewald (2014), Armour (2015), pp. 479–482, Burke (2015) and

resolution framework as is the bail-in resolution tool in terms of protection of public funds. However, while the latter is designed to shift the financial burden of bailing out credit institutions which have been assessed as FLOF from taxpayers to their shareholders and creditors, the former are designed to shift this financial burden from taxpayers to the banking system.[207] If public funds are used in resolution, there should be mechanisms to recover them from the bank in resolution, its creditors or the financial system in general.

(2) Resolution funding should be clearly distinguished from LLR by central banks. As already discussed,[208] the latter is a tool for the management of banking liquidity crises, while resolution (including its financing) is a tool for the management of banking solvency crises, which may, in certain cases, be caused by liquidity problems, implying that LLR may have already been provided. A related, albeit distinct, issue is that pertaining to the provision of liquidity after the decision has been taken by the resolution authorities to resolve a bank; hence, arrangements should also be in place to ensure access to temporary liquidity for banks in (or more precisely after) resolution. However, in relation to this issue, which is an essential part of an effective resolution framework, the role of central banks as liquidity providers may be essential as well.[209]

In public international financial law, the following standards govern the financing of resolution and its relationship to the **NCWO** principle[210]: *first*, to avoid the bail out or public ownership of banks and (hence) to protect public funds, jurisdictions should have in place either a privately financed resolution or deposit insurance fund, or a funding mechanism with *ex-post* recovery from industry of the costs of providing temporary financing to facilitate their resolution. Resolution funding should be raised from banks, their creditors and, if necessary, other financial industry participants while the resolution fund or mechanism can be administered either privately or publicly; *second*, funding arrangements should provide for adequate resources in a resolution, allowing resolution authorities to effectively use their powers to achieve their statutory resolution objectives, including, *inter alia*, the resources and legal powers to provide funds to support a deposit transfer, to capitalise or fund a bridge institution and to provide temporary guarantees to facilitate the implementation of the resolution and maintain the provision of essential services; and *third*, if temporary sources of funding to maintain essential functions are needed

---

Croitoru, Dobler and Molin (2018). On the role of DGSs in resolution, see Beck and Laeven (2006).

[207] See on this Wiggins, Wedow and Metrick (2019), p. 143.

[208] See above, under 1.3.2.

[209] On these aspects, see, by means of mere indication and with extensive further references, Gortsos (2020), pp. 385–388 and 445–446, respectively. See also Chapter 2 below, under 2.4.3.

[210] FSB Key Attributes (2014), Section 6.

to accomplish orderly resolution, the resolution authority or the authority extending the temporary funding should make provision to recover any losses incurred from shareholders and unsecured creditors subject to the NCWO safeguard or, if necessary, from the financial system widely.

1.3.4 Deposit Guarantee

1.3.4.1 Policy Objectives of Deposit Guarantee Systems

(1) The **principal policy objectives** of DGSs are two: the protection of (small) depositors and acting as buffer mechanisms in the event of a banking crisis and contributing to ensuring banking (and in general financial) stability by preventing bank runs and banking panics, being part of the **'bank safety net'**. The establishment of a **DGS** is first required for the protection of depositors, who should have access to a safe financial instrument for saving purposes and for conducting payments. This category of positive savers usually holds a significant share of their total savings in bank accounts and, on average, cannot be expected to exercise market discipline. Taking into account that banks are exposed to insolvency risk, it is only through regulatory intervention, i.e., the establishment of **DGS**s, that bank deposits become relatively safer. This argument applies *a fortiori* to 'unsophisticated' depositors, namely those who, given their limited knowledge and expertise, are insufficiently informed to be able to assess the solvency of banks to which they entrust their savings and differentiate between safe and unsafe banks.

(2) **DGSs** also act as buffer mechanisms in the event of a banking crisis, contributing to ensuring the stability of the banking system from massive withdrawals by panic-stricken depositors.[211] Since depositor panic results in mass deposit withdrawals, even the most solvent bank is not in a position to meet its obligations, unless it can borrow funds in money and capital markets, which under prevailing conditions may prove difficult, or it liquidates assets at unfavourably low prices, which may turn a liquidity crisis to a solvency one. The failure of coordination among depositors under adverse market conditions, leading to runs and panics, as already discussed, can be addressed *either* by suspending the convertibility of deposits into cash (including by means of capital controls) *or* by the establishment of **DGS**s, which seek to curb incentives for depositor involvement in runs and panics by guaranteeing the transformation of illiquid bank assets into cash.[212]

DGSs assure that depositors will be compensated (up to a certain level) if their bank is unable to convert deposits into cash.[213] Their effectiveness is, however, contingent upon their credibility to meet their obligations and

---

[211] On banking panics, see above, under 1.1.3.

[212] LLR from central banks can also contribute to financial stability under these circumstances.

[213] See Carisano (1992), p. 17.

is lower under conditions of a generalised economic crisis, leading to a situation of several banks (including large ones) being simultaneously exposed to insolvency. In that sense, **DGSs** are not designed to perform the abovementioned function in case of a systemic crisis (as they are also not designed to compensate depositors of large banks in general).[214]

1.3.4.2 Functions (Mandates) of Deposit Guarantee Systems and the Mandatory Membership Rule

(1) As already noted,[215] the historically first (linked to banking panics) and primary function of **DGSs** is to serve as a 'paybox' for depositors, guaranteeing the default-free character of deposits in the event of a bank failure (the **'payout** (or **paybox**) **function'**). Gradually, however, their mandate has been broadened, since they may also be called upon to serve one or more of the following **'non-payout functions'**: *first*, their funds may be used (as discussed[216]) to contribute to the financing of the resolution of banks, if the conditions for resolution are met (the **'contribution to resolution financing function'**); *second*, their funds can be used to finance measures that aim to preserve the access of depositors to covered deposits in the context of insolvency proceedings, other than a direct payout (e.g., a transfer to an acquiring bank); and *third*, they may also be required (as also noted) to serve a **'failure management function'**.[217]

Accordingly, DGSs' mandates can range from narrow "paybox" systems to those with extensive responsibilities, such as preventive action and loss or risk management, with a variety of combinations in between. These can be broadly classified into four categories: *first*, a **"paybox" mandate**, where the **DGS** is only responsible for the reimbursement of covered (insured) depositors (these two terms are used in this study as synonymous); *second*, a **"paybox plus" mandate**, where it also performs the 'contribution to resolution financing function'; *third*, a **"loss minimiser" mandate**, where it is actively engaged in a selection from a range of least-cost resolution strategies; and *fourth*, a **"risk minimiser" mandate**, where it has comprehensive risk minimisation functions that include risk assessment/management, a full suite of early intervention and resolution powers, and in some cases prudential oversight responsibilities.

(2) Membership of banks in the officially recognised **DGS** operating in the jurisdiction where they have been granted authorisation by competent authorities should be mandatory and constitute a *sine qua non* condition for their

---

[214] For further details on these two objectives, see, by means of mere indication, Kleftouri (2015), pp. 3–13 and Alexander (2019), pp. 165–168.

[215] See above, under 1.3.1.

[216] See above, under 1.3.3.

[217] On this function, see details in Baudino *et al.* (2019).

right to accept deposits from the public.[218] This **"mandatory membership rule"** should also apply to credit union and state-owned banks with or without explicit guarantees. *Exceptionally*, banks which are not subject to the prudential supervision of competent authorities may be exempted. When membership in a DGS is terminated, competent authority should have the powers to immediately withdraw the bank's deposit-taking license.[219]

1.3.4.3 Institutional Design of DGSs as to the 'Payout (or Paybox) Function'

Key Elements

(1) Funding for DGSs should be provided based on clearly legally defined funding arrangements establishing an *ex-ante* deposit guarantee fund. Responsibility for paying the cost of deposit guarantee should, in principle, be borne by banks, which might also be called upon to pay *ex-post* contributions, as prescribed by law as well. Initial "start-up" or "seed" funding from government is usually permitted to help establish a DGS. In addition, emergency funding arrangements for DGSs, including pre-arranged and assured sources of liquidity funding, such as a funding agreement with the government, the central bank, market borrowing or borrowing from other DGSs, should explicitly be set out in law and ensure effective and timely access when required, while market borrowing should not be the sole source of funding.

(2) A **"target fund size"** (measured as a proportion of the assessment base (e.g., total or covered deposits)) should also be *ex-ante* determined. This should be sufficient to meet DGSs' expected future obligations and cover their operational and other costs. If a DGS uses "risk-based premiums" (differential premium systems), the system for calculating these premiums (based on criteria such as individual bank risk profiles) should be transparent to all participating banks, the scoring/premium categories be significantly differentiated, and the ratings and rankings resulting from the system for individual banks be kept confidential.

(3) Operational independence, accountability, good governance, transparency and legal protection are core elements which should be embedded in the legal framework governing DGSs. They should 'stress test' their systems as to their performance under extreme conditions and their ability to repay depositors,

---

[218] Due to rapidly evolving availability of digital stored-value products ('DSPs', which from the consumer's perspective have similar characteristics to deposits) as a mechanism to foster financial inclusion, an issue arising is whether such products should be treated as deposits, especially when offered by non-bank financial firms, such as deposit-taking microfinance institutions. A related issue refers to 'fintech' financial services offered by non-bank financial firms (see World Bank Group (2019), pp. 27–28 and Ehrentraud *et al.* (2020)).

[219] On several of these issues, which are based on the IADI Core Principles, see further Gortsos (2021b).

contribute to orderly resolution proceedings with a view to ensuring continuous access to depositors' funds and support the prevention of a bank's failure (if applicable). Stress tests should also verify the appropriateness of DGSs' operational and funding capability to ensure deposit protection in times of increased pressure, under alternative scenarios.

(4) An essential element is the provision of information to the public on an ongoing basis about the benefits and limitations of the DGS covering their deposits. The responsibility for promoting public awareness should lie with DGSs using communication tools that form part of a comprehensive public awareness (communication) programme. This programme should convey information, *inter alia*, about the list of banks which are members of the DGS, as well as the scope and level of coverage. In the event of bank failure, the relevant DGS should notify covered depositors, by any appropriate means of the details relating to the following aspects (at least): place, means and time of payment of compensation; information to be provided to obtain payment; and the availability of advance or interim payments.

Scope and Level of Coverage—Determination of the Repayable Amount

(1) Covered deposits should be clearly and publicly defined in law, including the level and scope of coverage, and reflect the stated policy objectives. Certain types of deposits which are not eligible[220] for deposit protection should be clearly specified, easily determined and not affect the speed of reimbursements.[221] The level and scope of coverage should be limited, designed to be credible for the sake of minimising the risk of bank runs (which can—in our days—can also be digital ones) and ensuring market discipline, apply equally to all member banks of the DGS and not incorporate co-insurance. They should be set so that most depositors across banks are fully protected, while leaving a substantial proportion of the value of deposits unprotected. If coverage is excessively high, **moral hazard** should be mitigated by strong regulation and supervision, as well as by the other design features of DGSs.

(2) In principle, the coverage level should apply to the aggregate deposits of each depositor under the principle of '**coverage** *per depositor per bank*', irrespective of the number of accounts, the currency of the account(s) or the

---

[220] These include, *inter alia*, interbank deposits, deposits arising out of transactions in connection with a criminal conviction for money laundering and deposits of individuals who are regarded as responsible for the deterioration of a bank, including those belonging to its directors, managers, large shareholders and auditors.

[221] By way of derogation, national legislation may provide that, for social policy reasons, certain categories of non-eligible deposits (e.g., those held by personal pension schemes, occupational pension schemes of small or medium-sized enterprises and local authorities) are eligible up to the coverage level, and/or that the protection of deposits resulting from certain transactions may temporarily be higher than the coverage level, considering the significance of the protection for depositors and living conditions.

bank's branches keeping the account is established. The set-off of covered deposits against past due claims (e.g., debt service) or matured loans is usually not considered when determining the repayable amount. When it is taken, it should be timely and not delay prompt reimbursement of covered depositors' claims or undermine financial stability; depositors should also be informed accordingly by the bank prior to the conclusion of the contract.

Repayment (Reimbursement) of Covered Deposits: The Repayment ('Payout') Procedure

(1) DGSs should reimburse depositors' covered deposits promptly based on a clear and unequivocal **trigger for covered depositor reimbursement**. *In principle*, most covered depositors should be reimbursed within seven working days (the **'seven-day payout target'**), unless this is operationally difficult (e.g., in the case of trust accounts with multiple beneficiaries). DGSs should ensure that the repayable amount 'is available' within that period, having fulfilled all the conditions dependent on them for repayment of the amount, including availability of funds, usually through a designated 'paying bank'. *Exceptionally*, taking into account that in many cases the necessary procedures for this short repayment period may not be able to meet, there should be a credible alternative plan upon specific pre-determined criteria. *In addition*, in cases where DGSs have difficulty in determining the amount of repayment and depositors' rights, the deposits of 'absolutely entitled persons' may be subject to a longer repayment period. *Finally*, if a depositor or any person entitled to or interested in sums held in an account has been charged with an offence arising out of or in relation to money laundering, DGSs should suspend any payment relating to the depositor concerned, pending the court's judgement.

(2) In order to provide depositors with prompt access to their funds, DGSs should have continuous access to their records, the authority to undertake advance or preparatory examinations on the reliability of depositor records, and a range of reimbursement options (e.g., cash/cheque payments and electronic transfers). *In addition*, in order to be able to promptly carry out the reimbursement process, they should have adequate resources and personnel, systems to process depositor information in a systematic and accurate manner, as well as scenario planning and simulations, including simulations on bank closings with supervisory and resolution authorities.

(3) After having made payments to covered depositors, a DGS should have a 'right of subrogation' to their rights in liquidation proceedings for an amount equal to the payments made to them. Hence, given its role in the recovery process as a creditor of the failed bank by subrogation, it should also have the right to recover its claims in accordance with the statutory creditor hierarchy (in practice always based on the ranking of depositors) and the right of access to information from the liquidator to monitor the liquidation process. If the repayment procedure has been triggered, covered depositors should have a

right to compensation, which should be the subject of a legal action against the DGS.

Attributes of DGSs in Relation to the Payout Function
(1) As to their payout (paybox) function, **explicit DGSs** are characterised by six main attributes: *in principle*, they are activated only if a bank's authorisation has been withdrawn (without resolution); that is, its deposits have become unavailable to the public; *second*, they assume an *explicit obligation*; upon the withdrawal of a bank's authorisation (without resolution), they are required to compensate, within a pre-specified (short) period, its depositors to the extent that their deposits are covered; *third*, the guarantee provided is *non-discretionary*; once a bank's authorisation has been withdrawn (without resolution), depositors have in principle a direct claim for compensation against DGSs (unless the claim is on the bank's liquidator), irrespective of the conditions underlying the bank failure; *fourth*, deposit guarantee is an *ex-ante 'safe device'* for depositors; it makes them certain of compensation, thus curbing the incentives for bank runs and panics; *fifth*, the *coverage level* offered by a DGS is usually *limited*; the amount of compensation has a ceiling mainly for the mitigation of moral hazard problems[222] (even though there is evidence of a differential treatment in favour of banks deemed to be **TBTF**, see **Box 1.7** just below); and *finally*, the cost of bank failures is incurred by the banking sector ('no taxpayers' money solution').
(2) DGSs are typically funded exclusively by contributions of the participating banks (with limited only contributions by the government and/or the central bank, which may be participating in their administration[223]). These include annual *ex-ante* contributions, as well as various *ex-post* financing arrangements. Borrowing between DGSs may also be provided for.

Box 1.7 Problems relating to the operation of TBTF financial firms/SIFIs (2)

(1) The *ex-post* treatment of small and large banks participating in a DGS can be unequal under given circumstances. In particular, in the absence of a credible and adequately designed bank resolution framework, governments may feel urged to bail-out large failing banks, especially those considered as TBTF, due to the extent of the losses they

---

[222] The coverage level is also of importance if, in a resolution procedure, the bail-in instrument is applied, since in most jurisdictions, deposits covered by the DGS may not be bailed-in; see on that further just below.

[223] The body responsible for the management of a DGS *may* also have supervisory competencies on its member banks; this is the case of the Federal Deposit Insurance Corporation ('FDIC') in the US.

would cause to their creditors and the economy as a whole. The possibility cannot also be excluded that the decision would be taken to wind up such banks and activate the payout mechanism of the DGS with depositors covered *ex-post* more comprehensively.[224] On the contrary, smaller banks are, as a rule, not bailed out and if the decision is taken to wind up such a bank, depositors would be compensated only up to the 'coverage level', since the risk of spill-over effects would be considered not to be significant.

(2) Furthermore (in particular), SIFIs may be tempted to resort to regulatory arbitrage under two diametrically different circumstances. *In normal times*, they may wish to become a member of a DGS with comparatively low contributions, since the cost of membership would be considered as a 'subsidy' to other participating banks for which the activation of the repayment procedure of the DGS might be more probable, while the benefits neutral. *In periods of crisis*, on the other hand, affiliation to an 'affluent' DGS, offering a comparatively high coverage level, might be of value in view of depositors' increased sensitivity to safety. This became evident during the GFC between DGS in neighbouring EU Member States (notably between the UK and Ireland when the latter increased the coverage level of its DGS from 20,000 to 100,000 euro).

1.3.4.4 *Contribution of DGSs to Resolution Financing*

Depending on their mandate, DGSs may be called upon to contribute to the financing of resolution actions.[225] In a resolution scenario, DGSs should have the option to authorise the use of their funds for the resolution of member institutions (other than liquidation) under specific conditions.[226] Furthermore, where a DGS makes payments in the context of resolution proceedings, including the application of resolution tools or the exercise of resolution powers, it should have a claim against the bank in resolution for an amount equal to its payments. That claim should rank *pari passu* as covered deposits under national law governing normal insolvency proceedings. By application of the **NCWO** principle, covered deposits are also protected in the case of a bank's resolution, since, when applying the resolution tools and exercising their resolution powers, resolution authorities should take all appropriate measures to ensure that the resolution action is taken in accordance

---

[224] This was the case of depositors with two large, failed US banking institutions, Continental Illinois Bank (defunct in 1984) and the Bank of New England (closed in 1991), who received compensation for the entirety of their deposits.

[225] See above, under 1.3.3.

[226] On these six conditions, see the IADI Core Principle 9 (point (8)).

with the 'general principles governing resolution', including the principle that *'covered deposits are fully protected'*.

1.3.5 Institutional Relationship Among 'Bank Safety Net' Institutions—Relation with Macroeconomic Policies

(1) A well-structured and effective bank safety net should allow the effective interaction among its components in order to establish a credible interinstitutional relationship and solid foundations for financial stability. In this respect, the following three pillars are noteworthy: *first*, of primary importance is the existence of an explicit, formal and comprehensive framework for the close coordination of activities and information sharing, on an ongoing basis, between the DGS (and, if there are multiple DGSs in a national jurisdiction, among them) and other safety net elements. Information should be exchanged in particular, with due respect to confidentiality, when material supervisory actions are being taken in respect of member banks. *Second*, in order, *inter alia*, to ensure effective market discipline and mitigate moral hazard,[227] DGSs should be part of an effective framework within the safety net providing for enhanced prudential supervision, strong frameworks for, and enforcement of, prudential regulation and supervision and timely intervention in banks in financial difficulty before they become non-viable, including clearly defined qualitative and quantitative criteria used to trigger timely intervention or corrective action. These criteria should include safety and soundness indicators such as the institution's capital, asset quality, management, earnings, liquidity and sensitivity to market risk; and be reviewed periodically. *Third*, DGSs should develop, jointly with all safety net institutions, and regularly test own effective contingency planning and crisis management policies and procedures to ensure the ability to effectively respond to the risk of, and actual, bank failures and other events. They should also participate in regular contingency planning and simulation exercises related to system-wide crisis preparedness and management, as well as in the development of pre- and post-crisis management communication plans to ensure comprehensive and

---

[227] Inadequate market discipline on behalf of depositors can be explained by the fact that they do not have an incentive to monitor the development of their bank's financial condition and, hence, do not request (as would normally happen in a market without DGS) higher interest rates from a bank with relatively lower solvency. On the other hand, banks' exposure to moral hazard is a result of the fact that *first*, participation in a DGS provides then with an incentive to take greater risks than they would have taken if their depositors were uninsured and *second*, in the presence of deposit guarantee, they may be tempted to keep their capital adequacy ratio at the minimum required by the regulatory framework. In this case, a spill-over mechanism may be set in motion; the smaller a bank's capital base, the greater its tendency to take excessive risks, as the profits from higher returns would stay with shareholders while losses would be rolled over (*inter alia*) to the DGS. Key DGS design features aimed at mitigating moral hazard include, as discussed above, limited coverage levels and scope, differential premiums and timely intervention and resolution by the DGS and resolution authorities.

consistent public awareness and communications (with the involvement of all safety net institutions).

(2) It is also noted that, when comparing DGSs to lending of last resort (LLR), the following differences manifest themselves[228]: *first*, in principle, LLR is addressing liquidity crises, while DGSs are (mainly) activated when a bank has been declared insolvent; *second*, since the liquidity provided by the central bank to a bank experiencing liquidity strains is not contingent upon legal constraints, this function is discretionary and depends, in principle at least, on the central bank's assessment of that bank's solvency; and *third*, the liquidity provided by the central bank in its function as lender of last resort has no constraints; *in extremis*, it can be limitless.

(3) Last but not least, sound monetary and fiscal policies also play a significant role in the preservation of banking (and, in general, financial) stability. This applies to both monetary and fiscal policies.[229] In particular, the fiscal crisis in the euro area[230] has demonstrated in a manifest way how poor fiscal policies may lead to the destabilisation of the financial system. In fact, fiscal crises may turn into financial crises through several channels of transmission. A study of the Committee on the Global Financial System ('**CGFS**')[231] identifies four such channels: the impact of negative sovereign ratings on (individual) bank ratings; losses incurred by banks from their sovereign debt holdings; the 'collateral/liquidity channel'; and (explicit and implicit) losses arising from state guarantees granted to banks. On top of these comes the negative impact on the performance of bank loans in the event of a downturn.[232]

Secondary Sources

A

Adelman, M.A. (1948): Effective Competition and the Antitrust Laws, *Harvard Law Review*, Volume 61, Issue 8, pp. 1289–1350

Adrian, T. and A. Ashcraft (2012): *Shadow Banking Regulation*, Federal Reserve Bank of New York, Staff Report No. 559

---

[228] See Carisano (1992), pp. 22–29.

[229] On the interaction between monetary policy and financial stability, see, by means of mere indication, Bank for International Settlements (2003), Lastra and Goodhart (2015), Viñals *et al.* (2015) (also discussing the interaction between monetary and macroprudential policies), Brunnenmeier (2019) and Martin *et al.* (2021) (specifically on the interaction between monetary and macroprudential policies).

[230] See Chapter 4 below, under 4.4.1.

[231] See Committee on the Global Financial System (2011); on this international financial forum, see Chapter 3 below, under 3.4.4.

[232] For more details, see also, by means of mere of indication, Shambaugh (2012) pp. 157–162 and 187–190.

Afsharipour, A. and M. Gelter (2021, editors): *Comparative Corporate Governance*, Research Handbooks in Comparative Law Series, Edward Elgar Publishing, Cheltenham, UK – Northampton, MA, USA

Aggarwal, R. (2002): Demutualization and Corporate Governance of Stock Exchanges, *Journal of Applied Corporate Finance*, Spring

Aikman, D., Haldane, A.G., Hinterschweiger, M. and S. Kapadia (2019): Rethinking Financial Stability, in Blanchard, Ol. and L.H. Summers (2019, editors): *Evolution or Revolution? – Rethinking Macroeconomic Policy After the Great Recession*, Peterson Institute for International Economics (PIIE), The MIT Press, Cambridge, Massachusetts – London, England, Chapter 11, pp. 143–193

Alexander, K. (2019): *Principles of Banking Regulation*, Cambridge University Press, Cambridge, United Kingdom

Alexander, K. (2015): The Role of Capital in Supporting Banking Stability, in Moloney, N., Ferran, E. and J. Payne (2015, editors): *The Oxford Handbook of Financial Regulation*, Oxford University Press, United Kingdom, Chapter 12, pp. 334–363

Allen, F. (2001): *Do Financial Institutions Matter?*, Financial Institutions Center, Wharton, Working Paper Series, 01-04

Allen, F. and D. Gale (2002): *Capital Adequacy Regulation: In Search of a Rationale*, Financial Institutions Center, Wharton, September, Working Paper Series, 03-07

Allen, F. and D. Gale (2001): *Comparative Financial Systems: A Survey*, Financial Institutions Center, Wharton, April, Working Paper Series, 01-15

Allen, F. and R.J. Herring (2001): *Banking Regulation Versus Securities Market Regulation*, Financial Institutions Center, Wharton, Working Paper Series, 01-29

Allen, F. and A.M. Santomero (1999): *What Do Financial Intermediaries Do?*, Financial Institutions Center, Wharton, Working Paper Series, 99-30-B

Amorello, L. and S. Huber (2014): Recovery Planning: A New Valuable Corporate Governance Framework for Credit Institutions, *Law and Economics Yearly Review*, Volume 3, Part 2, pp. 296–317

Amtenbrink, F. (1999): *The Democratic Accountability of Central Banks – A Comparative Study of the European Central Bank*, Hart Publishing, Oxford

Anheier, H. and T. Baums (2020, editors): *Advances in Corporate Governance: Comparative Perspectives*, Oxford University Press, Oxford

Armour, J. (2015): Making Bank Resolution Credible, in Moloney, N., Ferran, E. and J. Payne (2015, editors): *The Oxford Handbook of Financial Regulation*, Oxford University Press, United Kingdom, Chapter 16, pp. 453–486

Armour, J. Awrey, D., Davies, P., Enriques, L., Gordon, J., Mayer, C. and J. Payne (2016): *Principles of Financial Regulation*, Oxford University Press, Oxford

Athanassiou (2012, editor): *Research Handbook on Hedge Funds, Private Equity and Alternative Investments*, Research Handbooks in Financial Law, Edward Elgar, Cheltenham, UK – Northampton, MA, USA

Avgouleas, E. and Ch. Goodhart (2015): Critical Reflections on Bank Bail-ins, *Journal of Financial Regulation*, 1, available at: https://jfr.oxfordjournals.org/content/early/2015/02/03/jfr.fju009

Avgouleas, E., Goodhart, C.A.E. and D. Schoenmaker (2009): *Living Wills as a Catalyst for Action*, DSF Policy Papers No. 4, Duisenberg School of Finance, Amsterdam

Ayadi, R., Arbak, E. and W. De Groen (2012): *Regulation of European Banks and Business Models: Towards a New Paradigm?*, Centre for European Policy Studies, Brussels

Azzutti, Al. (2023): The Algorithmic Future of EU Market Conduct Supervision: A Preliminary Check, in Böffel, L. and J. Schürger (2023, editors): *Digitalisation, Sustainability, and the Banking and Capital Markets Union*, EBI Studies in Banking and Capital Markets Law, Palgrave Macmillan, Cham – Switzerland, Chapter 2, pp. 53–98

B

Bagehot, W. (1873): *Lombard Street*, new edition of 1901, Kegan Paul, Trench, Trumber & Co., London

Bank for International Settlements (2014): *Re-thinking the Lender of Last Resort*, BIS Papers No 79, September, available at: https://www.bis.org/publ/bppdf/bispap79.htm

Bank for International Settlements (2003): *Monetary Policy, Financial Stability and the Business Cycle: Five Views*, BIS Papers No 18, September, Monetary and Economic Department, Bank of International Settlements, available at: https://www.bis.org/publ/bppdf/bispap18.pdf

Barth, J.R., Caprio, G. and R. Levine (2006): *Rethinking Bank Regulation – Till Angels Govern*, Cambridge University Press, Cambridge, New York, Melbourne, Madrid, Cape Town, Singapore, São Paolo

Basel Committee on Banking Supervision (2021): *Climate-Related Risk Drivers and Their Transmission Channels*, Bank for International Settlements, April, available at: https://www.bis.org/bcbs/publ/d517

Basel Committee on Banking Supervision (2018): *Frameworks for Early Supervisory Intervention*, March, Bank for International Settlements, available at: https://www.bis.org/bcbs/publ/d439.pdf

Basel Committee on Banking Supervision (2017): *Supervisory and Bank Stress Testing: Range of Practices*, December, Bank for International Settlements, available at: https://www.bis.org/bcbs/publ/d427.pdf

Basel Committee on Banking Supervision (2015): *Range of Practice in the Regulation and Supervision of Institutions Relevant to Financial Inclusion*, January, available at: https://www.bis.org/bcbs/publ/d310.pdf

Basel Committee on Banking Supervision (2011a): *Principles for the Sound Management of Operational Risk*, June, available at: https://www.bis.org/publ/bcbs144.htm

Basel Committee on Banking Supervision (2011b): *The Transmission Channels Between the Financial and Real Sectors: A Critical Survey of the Literature*, Working Paper No. 18, February

Basel Committee on Banking Supervision (2008): *Principles for Sound Liquidity Risk Management and Supervision*, September, available at: https://www.bis.org/publ/bcbs144.htm

Baudino, P., Defina, R., Real, J.M.F., Hajra, K. and R. Walters (2019): Bank Failure Management – The Role of Deposit Insurance, *FSI Insights on Policy Implementation*, No 17, Financial Stability Institute, Bank for International Settlements, August, available at: https://www.bis.org/fsi/publ/insights17.htm

Baumann, S. (2014): *Crowdinvesting im Finanzmarktrecht*, Schweizer Schriften zum Finanzmarktrecht, Band 117, Schulthess Verlag, Zürich

Baxter, T.C. Jr. and D. Gross (2010): The Federal Reserve's Response to the Crisis: Doing Whatever it Takes Within its Legal Authority, in Giovanoli, M. and D. Devos (2010, editors): *International Monetary and Financial Law: The Global Crisis*, Oxford University Press, Oxford-New York, Chapter 14, pp. 293–304

Beck, T. and D. Gros (2013): *Monetary Policy and Banking Supervision: Coordination Instead of Separation*, CEPS Policy Brief No. 286, available at: https://ssrn.com/abstract=2189364

Beck, T. and L. Laeven (2006): *Resolution of Failed Banks by Deposit Insurers: Cross-Country Evidence*, World Bank Policy Research Working Paper No. 3920, World Bank Publications

Benjamin, J. (2007): *Financial Law*, Oxford University Press, Oxford – New York

Benston, G. (1994): Universal Banking, *Journal of Economic Perspectives*, Volume 8, Number 3, Summer, pp. 121–143

Berger, A., Herring, R. and G. Szego (1995): The Role of Capital in Financial Institutions, *Journal of Banking and Finance*, Volume 19, pp. 393–430

Binder, J.-H. (2017): Systemkrisenbewältigung durch Bankenabwicklung? Aktuelle Bemerkungen zu unrealistischen Erwartungen, *Zeitschrift für Bankrecht und Bankwirtschaft*, Aufsätze, 29. Jahrgang, Heft 2, 15. April, pp. 57–71

Binder, J.-H. (2016): The Position of Creditors Under the BRRD, in *Commemorative Volume for Leonidas Georgakopoulos*, Bank of Greece, Centre for Culture, Research and Documentation, Athens, Volume I, pp. 37–62

Binning, T. and S. Willey (2008): The MiFID Regime for Trading Venues; Regulated Markets, Multilateral Trading Facilities and Systematic Internalisers, in E. Avgouleas (general editor): *The Regulation of Investment Services in Europe Under MiFID: Implementation and Practice*, Tottel Publishing, West Sussex, pp. 73–100

Bordo, M. (2014): *Rules for a lender of last resort: An historical perspective*, Journal of Economic Dynamics and Control, Volume 49, December, pp. 126–134 (also available at: https://doi.org/10.1016/j.jedc.2014.09.023)

Borio, C. (2010): *Implementing a Macroprudential Framework: Blending Boldness and Realism*, keynote address for the BIS-HKMA research conference on Financial Stability: Towards a Macroprudential approach, Honk Kong SAR, July, available at: https://www.bis.org/repofficepubl/hkimr201007.12c.pdf

Borio, C. (2008): *The Financial Turmoil of 2007-?: A Preliminary Assessment and Some Policy Considerations*, BIS working Papers No 251, Bank for International Settlements, March, pp. 1–13

Borio, C. (2003): *Towards a Macro-Prudential Framework for Financial Supervision and Regulation?*, Bank for International Settlements, Working Papers, No 128, Basel, February

Borio, Cl., Vale, B. and G. von Peter (2010): *Resolving the Financial Crisis: Are We Heeding the Lessons from the Nordics?*, BIS Working Papers No 311, Monetary and Economic Department, Bank for International Settlements, June, available at: https://www.bis.org/publ/work311.pdf and at: https://ssrn.com/abstract=1631794

Borio, C. and P. Disyatat (2009): *Unconventional Monetary Policies: An Appraisal*, BIS Working Papers No. 292, Monetary and Economic Department, Bank for International Settlements, November

Bose, S., Dong, G. and A. Simpson (2019): *The Financial Ecosystem: The Role of Finance in Achieving Sustainability*, Palgrave Studies in Impact Finance, Palgrave Macmillan, Cham – Switzerland

Brakman, S., Garretsen, H., van Marrenwijk, Ch. and Ar. Van Witteloostuijn (2006): *Nations and Firms in the Global Economy – An Introduction to International Economics and Business*, Cambridge University Press, Cambridge, United Kingdom

Brunnenmeier, M.K. (2019): The Role of Monetary Policy in Guaranteeing Financial Stability, in Blanchard, Ol. And L.H. Summers (2019, editors): *Evolution or Revolution? – Rethinking Macroeconomic Policy After the Great Recession*, Peterson Institute for International Economics (PIIE), The MIT Press, Cambridge, Massachusetts – London, England, Chapter 12, pp. 195–202

Brunnenmeier, M.K., Crockett, A., Goodhart, Ch., Persaud, A.D. and H. Shin (2009): *The Fundamental Principles of Financial Regulation*, Geneva Reports on the World Economy, No. 11, International Center for Monetary and Banking Studies (ICMB) – Centre for Economic Policy Research (CEPR)

Buiter, W.H. (2014): *Central Banks: Powerful, Political and Unaccountable?*, CEPR Discussion Paper No. DP10223, available at: https://ssrn.com/abstract=2526351

Burke, J.V. (2015): *Building a Bank Resolution Fund over Time: When Should Each Individual Bank Contribute?*, available at: https://ssrn.com/abstract=2535722

C

Calais-Aulay, J. and F. Steinmetz (2006): *Droit de la Consummation*, 7éme édition, Dalloz, Paris

Calomiris, Ch.W., Klingebiel, D. and L.A. Laeven (2004): *A Taxonomy of Financial Crisis Resolution Mechanisms: Cross-Country Experience*, World Bank Policy Research Working Paper No. 3379, August, available at: https://ssrn.com/abstract=625256

Calomiris, Ch.W. and B.G. Gorton (1990): *The Origin of Banking Panic Models: Facts and Banking Regulation*, The Wharton School, University of Pennsylvania, No. 11

Caprio, J. and D. Klingebiel (1999): *Episodes of Systemic and Borderline Financial Crises*, World Bank database

Caprio, J. and D. Klingebiel (1996a): *Bank Insolvencies: Cross-Country Experience*, World Bank Policy Research Working Paper No 1620, World Bank, Washington, DC

Caprio, J. and D. Klingebiel (1996b): *Bank Insolvency: Bad luck, Bad Policy, or Bad Banking?*, Annual World Bank Conference on Development Economics, available at: https://www.academia.edu/31434791/Bank_insolvency_bad_luck_bad_policy_or_bad_banking?email_work_card=title

Carisano, R. (1992): *Deposit Insurance: Theory, Policy and Evidence*, Luiss, Dartmouth

Carmassi, J. and R. Herring (2013): Living Wills and Cross-Border Resolution of Systemically Important Banks, *Journal of Financial Economic Policy*, Volume 5, pp. 361–387

Carmassi, J., Luchetti, El. and S. Micossi (2010): *Overcoming Too-Big-to-Fail: A Regulatory Framework to Limit Moral Hazard and Free Riding in the Financial Sector*, Report of the CEPS-Assonime Task Force on Bank Crisis Resolution, Centre for European Policy Studies, Brussels

Carmichael, J. (2021): Reflections on Twenty Years of Regulation Under Twin Peaks, in Godwin, A. and A. Schmulow (2021, editors): *The Cambridge Handbook of Twin*

Peaks Financial Regulation, Cambridge Law Handbooks, Cambridge University Press, Cambridge, United Kingdom, Chapter 2, pp. 32–50

Cartwright, P. (2004): *Banks, Consumers and Regulation*, Hart Publishing, Oxford

Central Bank Governance Group (2011): *Central Bank Governance and Financial Stability: A Report by a Study Group*, Bank for International Settlements, May, available at: https://www.bis.org/publ/othp14.pdf

Central Bank Governance Group (2009): *Issues in the Governance of Central Banks*, Report, Bank for International Settlements, May, available at: https://www.bis.org/publ/othp04.pdf

Chan, N., Getmansky, M., Haas, S.M. and A.W. LO (2006): Do Hedge Funds Increase Systemic Risk?, *Economic Review*, fourth quarter, Federal Reserve Bank of Atlanta, pp. 49–80

Cihák, M. and E. Nier (2009): *The Need for Special Resolution Regimes for Financial Institutions – The Case of the European Union*, IMF Working Papers, WP/09/200, available at: https://www.imf.org/en/Publications/WP/Issues/2016/12/31/The-Need-for-Special-Resolution-Regimes-for-Financial-Institutions-The-Case-of-the-European-23286

Claessens, S., Herring, R.J. and D. Schoenmaker (2010): *A Safer World Financial System: Improving the Resolution of Systemic Institutions*, Geneva Reports on the World Economy, No 12, International Center for Monetary and Banking Studies, Centre for Economic Policy Research, London, UK

Claessens, S. and M.A. Kose (2018): *Frontiers of Macrofinancial Linkages*, BIS Papers No 95, Bank for International Settlements, Monetary and Economic Department, January, available at: https://www.bis.org/publ/bppdf/bispap95.pdf

Claessens, S., Pozsar, Z., Ratnovski, L. and M. Singh (2012): *Shadow Banking: Economics and Policy*, IMF Staff Discussion Note, SDN/12/12, December

Clement, P. (2010): The Term "Macroprudential": Origins and Evolution, *BIS Quarterly Review*, March, pp. 59–67

Coffee, J.C. (2010): *Bail-ins Versus Bail-outs: Using Contingent Capital to Mitigate Systemic Risk*, The Center for Law and Economic Studies, Columbia University School of Law, Working Paper No. 380, available at: https://www.law.columbia.edu/lawec

Committee on the Global Financial System (2011): *The Impact of Sovereign Credit Risk on Bank Funding Conditions*, CGFS Papers, No. 43, Bank for International Settlements, July

Committee on the Global Financial System (2010a): *Macroprudential Instruments and Frameworks: A Stocktaking of Issues and Experiences*, CGFS Papers, No. 38, May

Committee on the Global Financial System (2010b): *The Role of Margin Requirements and Haircuts in Procyclicality*, CGFS Papers, No. 36, March

Committee on Payment and Settlement Systems (2005): *Central Bank Oversight of Payment and Settlement Systems*, Bank for International Settlements, May, available at: https://www.bis.org/publ/cpss68.htm

Constâncio, V. (2015): *Financial Stability Risks, Monetary Policy and the Need for Macro-Prudential Policy*, European Central Bank, Frankfurt am Main, 13 February

Cox, J.C. and M. Rubinstein (1985): *Options Markets*, Prentice-Hall, New Jersey

Croitoru, O.M., Dobler, M.C. and J. Molin (2018): *Resolution Funding: Who Pays When Financial Institutions Fail?*, IMF, Monetary and Capital Markets Department, Technical Notes and Manuals, July, available at: https://www.imf.org/en/Publications/TNM/Issues/2018/08/16/Resolution-Funding-Who-Pays-When-Financial-Institutions-Fail-46124

Crocket, A. (2007): The Evolution and Regulation of Hedge Funds, *Banque de France, Financial Stability Review, Special Issue Hedge Funds*, No. 10, April, pp. 19–28

D

Davies, P. (2014): Resolution of Cross-Border Banking Groups, in Haentjens, M. and B. Wessels (2014, editors): *Research Handbook on Crisis Management in the Banking Sector*, Edward Elgar Publishing Ltd, Cheltenham, UK (also available as Oxford Legal Studies Research Paper No. 89/2014, at: https://ssrn.com/abstract=2534156)

Davies, H. and D. Green (2010): *Global Financial Regulation. The Essential Guide*, Polity Press, Cambridge, UK - Malden, USA

De Haan, J. and Al. Bruinshhofd (2014, editors): *The Value of Banks and their Business Models to Society*, SUERF – The European Money and Finance Forum (a joint publication with De Nederlandsche Bank and Rabobank), SUERF Study 2014/2, Vienna, available at: https://www.suerf.org/docx/s_5463b514e21fbd3fec3772fba142a46e_4065_suerf.pdf

De Haan, J., Oosterloo, S., and D. Schoenmaker (2009): *European Financial Markets and Institutions*, Cambridge University Press, Cambridge, New York, Melbourne, Madrid, Cape Town, Singapore, São Paolo

Demirgüç-Kunt, A. and H. Huizinga (1999): *Market Discipline and Financial Safety Net Design*, World Bank Policy Research Working Paper No. 2183

Di Noia, C. and G. Di Giorgio (1999): *Should Banking Supervision and Monetary Policy Tasks Be Given to Different Agencies?*, Universitat Pompeu Fabra, Economic Working Paper No. 411, available at: https://ssrn.com/abstract=193730

Diamond, D. (1984): Financial Intermediation and Delegated Monitoring, *Review of Economic Studies*, 51, August, pp. 393–414

Diamond, D. and P. Dybvig (1983): Bank Runs, Deposit Insurance and Liquidity, *Journal of Political Economy*, 91, July, pp. 401–419

Dierick, F. (2004): *The Supervision of Mixed Financial Services Groups in Europe*, European Central Bank, Occasional Paper Series, No. 20, August, European Central Bank

Dionne, G. (2013, editor): *Handbook of Insurance*, Second Edition, Springer

Domanski, D., Moessner, R. and W. Nelson (2014): Central Banks as Lenders of Last Resort: Experiences During the 2007–2010 Crisis and Lessons for the Future, in Bank for International Settlements (2014): *Re-thinking the Lender of Last Resort*, BIS Papers No 79, September, pp. 43–75

Donald, D.C. (2019): Information, and the Regulation of Inefficient Markets, in Avgouleas, E. and D.C. Donald (2015, editors): *The Political Economy of Financial Regulation*, International Corporate Law and Financial Market Regulation, Cambridge University Press, Cambridge, United Kingdom, Chapter 2, pp. 38–62

Drahos, P. (2017, editor): *Regulatory Theory – Foundations and Applications*, Australian National University Press

E

EBA Discussion Paper (2022): *Discussion Paper on the Role of Environmental Risks in the Prudential Framework*, 2 May, available at: https://www.eba.europa.eu/eba-launches-discussion-role-environmental-risks-prudential-framework

Edge, R.M. and N. Liang (2020): *Financial Stability Committees and the Countercyclical Capital Buffer*, Deutsche Bundesbank Discussion Paper No. 04/2020, available at: https://ssrn.com/abstract=3556505

Ehrentraud, J., Ocampo, D.G, Garzoni, L. and M Piccolo (2020): Policy Responses to Fintech: A Cross-Country Overview, *FSI Insights on Policy Implementation*, No 23, Financial Stability Institute, Bank for International Settlements, January, available at: https://www.bis.org/fsi/publ/insights23.htm

Eijffinger, S. and R. Nijskens (2012): *Monetary Policy and Banking Supervision*, European Parliament, Directorate General for Internal Policies, available at: https://www.europarl.europa.eu/studies

Eijffinger, S. and M. Hoeberichts (2000): *Central Bank Accountability and Transparency: Theory and Some Evidence*, Discussion Paper 6/00, Economic Research Centre of the Deutsche Bundesbank, November, available at: https://www.bundesbank.de/Redaktion/EN/Downloads/Publications/Discussion_Paper_1/2000/2000_12_21_dkp_06.pdf?_blob=publicationFile

European Central Bank (2020): *Guide on Climate-Related and Environmental Risks: Supervisory Expectations Relating to Risk Management and Disclosure*, 27 November, available at: https://www.bankingsupervision.europa.eu/ecb/pub/pdf/ssm.202011finalguideonclimate-relatedandenvironmentalrisks~58213f6564.en.pdf

European Central Bank (2011): *Eurosystem Oversight Policy Framework*, July, European Central Bank

European Central Bank (2010): Recent Regulatory Initiatives to Address the Role of Systemically Important Financial Institutions, in: *Financial Stability Review*, IV. Special Features, Section C, June

European Central Bank (2009): The Concept of Systemic Risk, *ECB Financial Stability Review*, December, pp. 134–142 (also available at: https://www.ecb.europa.eu/press/pr/date/2009/html/pr091218.en.html)

European Central Bank (2008): *The Incentive Structure of the 'Originate and Distribute' Model*, European Central Bank, December, available at: https://www.ecb.europa.eu/incentivestructureoriginatedistributemodel200812en.pdf

European Central Bank (2007): The EU Arrangements for Financial Crisis Management, *Monthly Bulletin*, February, pp. 73–84

European Commission (2012): *Non-bank Financial Institutions: Assessment of Their Impact on the Stability of the Financial System*, European Economy – Economic Papers No. 472, December

Everson, M. (2015): Regulating the Insurance Sector, in Moloney, N., Ferran, E. and J. Payne (2015, editors): *The Oxford Handbook of Financial Regulation*, Oxford University Press, United Kingdom, Chapter 14, pp. 409–452

F

Faia, E. and B. Weder di Mauro (2015): *Cross-Border Resolution of Global Banks*, House of Finance SAFE (Sustainable Architecture for Finance in Europe), Working Paper No 88, March

Faia, E. and I. Schnabel (2015): The Road from Micro-prudential to Macro-prudential Regulation, in Faia, E., Hackethal, Haliassos, M. and K. Langenbucher (2015, editors): *Financial Regulation – A Transatlantic Perspective*, Cambridge University Press, Cambridge, United Kingdom, Chapter 1, pp. 3–22

Fecht, F. and M. Tyrell (2004): *Optimal Lender of Last Resort Policy in Different Financial Systems*, Discussion Paper Series 1: Studies of the Economic Research Centre No 39, Deutsche Bundesbank, Frankfurt am Main

Feldberg, G. and A. Metrick (2021): Stress Tests and Policy, *Journal of Financial Crises*, Volume 3, Issue 1, pp. 1–19, available at: https://elischolar.library.yale.edu/journal-of-financial-crises/vol3/iss1/1

Ferguson, R.W., Jr, Hartmann, Ph., Panetta, F. and R. Portes (2007): *International Financial Stability*, Geneva Reports on the World Economy 9, International Center for Monetary and Banking Studies (ICMB), Geneva, Switzerland

Ferrarini, G. and P. Giudici (2006): *Financial Scandals and the Role of Private Enforcement: The Parmalat Case*, ECGI – Law Working Paper N° 40/2005

Filatotchev, I. and Ch. Nakajima (2010): Internal and External Corporate Governance: An Interface Between an Organization and its Environment, *British Journal of Management*, p. 591 et seq.

Filipova, T. (2007): *The Concept of Integrated Financial Supervision and Regulation of Financial Conglomerates in Germany and the United Kingdom*, Verlag C.H. Beck, München – Nomos Verlagsgesellschaft, Baden-Baden

Financial Stability Board (2011): *Shadow Banking: Scoping the Issues*, available at: https://www.financialstabilityboard.org/list/fsb_publications/tid_150/index.htm

Financial Stability Board (2010): *Implementing OTC Derivatives Market Reforms*, October, available at: https://www.financialstabilityboard.org/publications/r_101025.pdf

Financial Stability Board, International Monetary Fund and Bank for International Settlements (2011): *Macroprudential Policy Tools and Frameworks*, February 14, available at: https://www.financialstabilityboard.org/publications/r_1103.pdf

Finlay, St. (2009): *Consumer Credit Fundamentals*, second edition, Palgrave Macmillan, Hampshire, New York

Freedman, C. (1987): Discussion on Guttentag and Herring (1987): Emergency Liquidity Assistance for International Banks), in Portes, R. and A.K. Swoboda (1987, editors): *Threats to International Financial Stability*, Cambridge University Press, Cambridge, United Kingdom, pp. 189–194

Freixas, X. and B. Parigi (2008): *Lender of Last Resort and Bank Closure Policy*, Center for Economic Studies Ifo, CESifo Working Paper No. 2286, February, Munich

Furlong, F. and M. Keeley (1989): Capital Regulation and Bank Risk Taking: A Note, *Journal of Banking and Finance*, Volume 13, pp. 883–891

G

G20 Sustainable Finance Study Group (2018): *Synthesis Report*, July, available at: https://www.g20.utoronto.ca/2018/g20_sustainable_finance_synthesis_report.pdf

Galati, G. and R. Moessner (2011): *Macroprudential Policy – A Literature Review*, BIS Working Papers No. 337, Monetary and Economic Department, Bank for International Settlements, February

Garbaravicius, T. and F. Dierick (2005): *Hedge Funds and Their Implications for Financial Stability*, European Central Bank, Occasional Paper Series, No. 34, European Central Bank, August

Gerding, E. (2011): *The Shadow Banking System and Its Legal Origins*, available at: https://ssrn.com/abstract=1990816

Gianviti, F. (2010): The Objectives of Central Banks, in Giovanoli, M. and D. Devos (2010, editors): *International Monetary and Financial Law: The Global Crisis*, Oxford University Press, Oxford – New York, Chapter 22, pp. 449–483

Gilson, R. (2016): *From Corporate Law to Corporate Governance*, Oxford Handbook of Corporate Law and Governance, Oxford University Press, Oxford also available at: https://ssrn.com/abstract=2819128

Głuch, D., Skovranová, L. and M. Stenström (2013): *Central Bank Involvement in Macro-prudential Oversight*, European Central Bank, Legal Working Paper Series, No 14, 11 January, available at: https://www.ecb.europa.eu/pub/pdf/scplps/ecblwp14.pdf

Godwin, A. and A. Schmulow (2021, editors): *The Cambridge Handbook of Twin Peaks Financial Regulation*, Cambridge Law Handbooks, Cambridge University Press, Cambridge, United Kingdom

Godwin, A., Kourabas, St. and I. Ramsay (2021): Twin Peaks, Macroprudential Regulation and Systemic Financial Stability, in Godwin, A. and A. Schmulow (2021, editors): *The Cambridge Handbook of Twin Peaks Financial Regulation*, Cambridge Law Handbooks, Cambridge University Press, Cambridge, United Kingdom, Chapter 20, pp. 347–363

Goergen, M. (2018): *Corporate Governance: A Global Perspective*, 1st Edition, Cengage Learning EMEA

Goldstein, M. and N. Veron (2011): *Too Big to Fail: The Transatlantic Debate*, Peterson Institute for International Economics Working Paper No. 11–2, 24 January, available at: https://ssrn.com/abstract=1746982

Goodhart, Ch. (2018): The Role of Macro-prudential Policy, in Conti-Brown, P. and R.M. Lastra (2018, editors): *Research Handbook on Central Banking*, Research Handbooks in Financial Law, Edward Elgar Publishing Limited, UK – Edward Elgar Publishing, Inc., USA, Chapter 24, pp. 508–517

Goodhart, Ch. (2012): Funding Arrangements and Burden Sharing in Banking Resolution, in Beck, T. (2012, editor): *Banking Union for Europe – Risks and Challenges*, Centre for Economic Policy Research (CEPR), London, UK, pp. 105–113

Goodhart, C.A.E. (2000): *The Organizational Structure of Banking Supervision*, Financial Stability Institute, Occasional Paper No 1, October, available at: https://www.bis.org/fsi/fsipapers.htm

Goodhart, C.A.E. (1988): *The Evolution of Central Banks*, The MIT Press, Cambridge, Massachusetts

Goodhart, Ch. and E. Avgouleas (2014): A Critical Evaluation of Bail-in as a Bank Recapitalisation Mechanism, in Allen, F., Carletti, E. and J. Gray (2014, editors): *Bearing the Losses from Bank and Sovereign Default in the Eurozone*, FIC Press, Wharton Financial Institutions Center, Philadelphia, USA, Chapter 7, pp. 65–97, available at: https://hdl.handle.net/1814/34437

Goodhart, C.A.E. and D. Schoenmaker (1993): Institutional Separation Between Supervisory and Monetary Agencies, in Goodhart, C.A.E. (1993, editor): *The Central Bank and the Financial System*, Macmillan Press, London

Gordon, J. and W.-G. Ringe (2018, editors): *The Oxford Handbook of Corporate Law and Governance*, Oxford Handbooks, Oxford University Press, Oxford

Gorton, G.B. (1988a): Banking Panics and Business Cycles, *Oxford Economic Papers*, 40, pp. 751–781

Gorton, G.B. (1988b): Why Are Banks Regulated? Comments, *Paper Presented for the Conference on the Perspectives of Banking Regulation*, Cleveland Federal Reserve Bank

Gorton, G.B. and A. Metrick (2013): The Federal Reserve and Panic Prevention: The Roles of Financial Regulation and Lender of Last Resort, *Journal of Economic Perspectives*, Volume 27, No. 4, Fall, pp. 45–64

Gorton, G.B. and A. Metrick (2010): Regulating the Shadow Banking System, *Brookings Papers on Economic Activity*, Volume 2, Fall, pp. 261–312, available at: https://ssrn.com/abstract=1676947

Gorton, G.B. and A. Winton (2002): *Financial Intermediation*, Financial Institutions Center, Wharton, Working Paper Series, 02-28

Gortsos, Ch.V. (2021a): *Non-performing Loans – New Risks and Policies? What Factors Drive the Performance of National Asset Management Companies?*, Briefing Paper for the Committee on Economic and Monetary Affairs (ECON) of the European Parliament, March, available at: https://www.europarl.europa.eu/RegData/etudes/IDAN/2021/659647/IPOL_IDA(2021)659647_EN.pdf

Gortsos, Ch.V. (2021b): *The Evolution of European (EU) Banking Law Under the Influence of (Public) International Banking Law: A Comprehensive Overview*, e-book, Third fully updated edition, available at: https://ssrn.com/abstract=3334493

Gortsos, Ch.V. (2020): *European Central Banking Law – The Role of the European Central Bank and National Central Banks under European Law*, Palgrave Macmillan Studies in Banking and Financial Institutions, Palgrave Macmillan, Cham – Switzerland

Gortsos, Ch.V. (2012): *Fundamentals of Public International Financial Law: International Banking Law within the System of Public International Financial Law*, Schriften des Europa-Instituts der Universität des Saarlandes – Rechtswissenschaft, Nomos Verlag, Baden-Baden

Grabosky, P. (2017): Meta-regulation, in Drahos, P. (2017, editor): *Regulatory Theory – Foundations and Applications*, Australian National University Press, Chapter 9, pp. 149–162

Grant, J.K. (2010): *What the Financial Services Industry Puts Together Let No Person Put Asunder: How the Gramm-Leach Bliley Act Contributed to the 2008–2009 American Capital Markets Crisis*, available at: https://ssrn.com/abstract=1525670

Green, D. (2012): The Relationship Between Micro-Macro-Prudential Supervision and Central Banking, in Wymeersch, Ed., Hopt, K.J. and G. Ferrarini (2012, editors): *Financial Regulation and Supervision - A Post-Crisis Analysis*, Oxford University Press, Oxford, Chapter 3, pp. 57–68

Group of Thirty (2008): *The Structure of Financial Supervision – Approaches and Challenges in a Global Marketplace*, Group of Thirty, Washington, DC, available at: https://group30.org/images/uploads/publications/G30_StructureFinancialSupervision2008.pdf

Grünewald, S.N. (2014): *The Resolution of Cross-Border Banking Crises in the European Union – A Legal Study from the Perspective of Burden Sharing*, International Banking and Finance Law Series, Volume 23, Wolters Kluwer Law & Business, Kluwer Law International, The Netherlands

Guttentag, J. and R.J Herring (1988): *Prudential Supervision to Manage Systemic Vulnerability*, Proceedings of a Conference on Bank Structure and Competition Federal Reserve Bank of Chicago, pp. 502–633

Guttentag, J. and R. Herring (1987a): Emergency Liquidity Assistance for International Banks, in Portes, R. and A.K. Swoboda (1987a, editors): *Threats to International Financial Stability*, Cambridge University Press, Cambridge, United Kingdom, pp. 150–186

Guttentag, J. and R.J. Herring (1987b): *Restructuring Depository Institutions*, International Banking Center, the Wharton School, University of Pennsylvania, *mimeo*

Guttentag, J. and R. Herring (1986a): *Innovations and the Financial Safety Net*, The Wharton Program in International Banking and Finance, University of Pennsylvania, Philadelphia, *mimeo*

Guttentag, J. and R.J. Herring (1986b): *Disaster Myopia in International Banking*, Essays in International Finance, No.163, Princeton, N.J., Princeton University, International Finance Section

Guttentag, J. and R. Herring (1983): The Lender-of-Last-Resort Function in an International Context, *Essays in International Finance*, No. 151, Princeton, N.J., Princeton University, International Finance Section

H

Haberman, G. (1987): Capital Requirements of Commercial and Investment Banks: Contrasts in Regulation, *Federal Reserve Bank of New York Quarterly Review*, Autumn, pp. 1–10

Hadjiemmanuil, Ch. (2015): *Bank Resolution Financing in the Banking Union*, LSE Law, Society and Economy Working Papers 6/2015, available at: https://ssrn.com/abstract=2575372

Hadjiemmanuil, Ch. (2014): Special Resolution Regimes for Banking Institutions: Objectives and Limitations, in Ringe, W.G. and P.M. Huber (2014, editors): *Legal Challenges in the Global Financial Crisis – Bail-outs, the Euro and Regulation*, Chapter 13, Hart Publishing – Oxford and Portland, Oregon

Hadjiemmanuil, Ch. (2004): Institutional Structure of Financial Regulation, A Trend Towards "Megaregulators"?, in *Yearbook of International Financial and Economic Law*, pp. 127–190

Haentjens, M. (2017): Selected Commentary on the Bank Recovery and Resolution Directive, in Moss, G., Wessels, B. and M. Haentjens (2017, editors): *EU Banking and Insurance Insolvency*, Chapter IV, Second edition, Oxford University Press, Oxford, pp. 177–318

Harvey, C.R., Ramachandran, Ash. and J. Santoro (2021): *DeFi and the Future of Finance*, 5 April, available at: https://ssrn.com/abstract=3711777

Haubrich, J. (1996): *Combining Bank Supervision and Monetary Policy*, Economic Commentary, No. 11

Herring, R.J. and J. Carmassi (2010): The Corporate Structure of International Financial Conglomerates: Complexity and Its Implications for Safety and Soundness, in Berger, A.N., Molyneux, P. and J. Wilson (2010, editors): *Oxford Handbook of Banking*, Chapter 8, Oxford University Press, Oxford – New York, pp. 195–229

Herring, R.J. and J. Carmassi (2008): The Structure of Cross-Sector Financial Supervision, *Financial Markets, Institutions & Instruments*, Volume 17, No. 1, February

Herring, R.J. and A.M. Santomero (2000): *What Is Optimal Financial Regulation?*, Financial Institutions Center, Wharton, Working Paper Series, 00-34

Herring, R.J. and R.E. Litan (1995): *Financial Regulation in the Global Economy*, The Brookings Institution, Washington, DC, at: https://www.brookings.edu/comm/conferencereport/cr14.htm

Hildebrand, Ph.M. (2008): *Is Basel II Enough? The Benefits of a Leverage Ratio*, Financial Markets Group Lecture, London School of Economics, London, December

Hofer, U. (2014): *Too Big to Fail and Structural Reforms: A Comparative Look at Structural Banking Reforms in Switzerland and the UK and the Underlying Legal and Economic Background*, Schulthess Juristische Medien AG, Zürich

Hopt, K. (2012): Corporate Governance of Banks after the Financial Crisis, in Wymeersch, Ed., Hopt, K.J. and G. Ferrarini (2012, editors): *Financial Regulation and Supervision – A Post-Crisis Analysis*, Oxford University Press, Oxford, Chapter 11, pp. 337–367 (also available at: https://ssrn.com/abstract=1918851)

Hopt, K. (2011): Comparative Corporate Governance: The State of the Art and International Regulation, *American Journal of Comparative Law*, Volume 59, pp. 1–83, January (also available as ECGI – Law Working Paper No. 170/2011, at: https://ssrn.com/abstract=1713750)

Houben, A., Kakes, J. and G. Schinasi (2004): *Toward a Framework for Safeguarding Financial Stability*, IMF Working Papers, WP/04/101, available at: https://www.imf.org/external/pubs/ft/wp/2004/wp04101.pdf

Howells, G. and S. Weatherill (2005): *Consumer Protection Law*, second edition, Ashgate, England, USA

Huertas, T. (2012): *The case for bail-ins*, Wharton Financial Institutions Center, Working Paper No 17

Huertas, T.F. and R.M. Lastra (2011): The perimeter issue: to what extent should *lex specialis* be extended to systemically significant financial institutions? An exit strategy from too big to fail, in Lastra, R.M. (2011, editor): *Cross-Border Bank Insolvency*, Oxford University Press, Oxford – New York, pp. 250–280

Hull, J.C. (1997): *Options, Futures, and other Derivatives*, International Edition, Prentice Hall International, London

Hüpkes, E. and D. Devos (2010): Cross-border Bank Resolution, in Giovanoli, M. and D. Devos (2010, editors): *International Monetary and Financial Law: The global crisis*, Oxford University Press, Oxford – New York, Chapter 17, pp. 359–377

I-J-K

Ippolito, R.A. (2005): *Economics for Lawyers*, Princeton University Press, Princeton and Oxford

Joosen, B. (2015): Regulatory Capital Requirements and Bail in Mechanisms, in Haentjens, M. and B. Wessels (2015, editors): *Research Handbook on Crisis Management in the Banking Sector*, Edward Elgar Publishing Ltd, Cheltenham, UK, Chapter 9, pp. 175–235

Kahane, Y. (1977): Capital Adequacy and the Regulation of Financial Intermediaries, *Journal of Banking and Finance*, Volume 1, pp. 207–218

Kahn (2018): *A Behavioral Approach to Financial Supervision, Regulation, and Central Banking*, IMF Working Papers, WP/2018/178, available at: https://ww.imf.org/en/Publications/WP/Issues/2018/08/02/A-Behavioral-Approach-to-Financial-Supervision-Regulation-and-Central-Banking-46146

Kahn, Ch.M. and J.A.C. Santos (2001): *Allocating Bank Regulatory Powers: Lender of Last Resort, Deposit Insurance and Supervision*, BIS Working Papers No 79, Bank for International Settlements, August, pp. 93–96

Kane, Ed.J. (2016): Stretching the Financial Safety Net to Its Breaking Point, July, available at: https://ssrn.com/abstract=2820355

Kane, Ed.J. (2014): *Shadowy Banking: Theft by the Safety Net*, available at: https://ssrn.com/abstract=2255065

Kane, Ed.J. (2000): *Designing Financial Safety Nets to Fit Country Circumstances*, September, available at: https://ssrn.com/abstaract=632523

Kane, Ed.J. (1987): Competitive Financial Regulation: An International Perspective, in Portes, R. and A.K. Swoboda (1987, editors): *Threats to International Financial Stability*, Cambridge University Press, Cambridge, United Kingdom, pp. 112–129

Kapstein, E.B. (1989): Resolving the Regulator's Dilemma: International Coordination of Banking Regulations, *International Organisation*, Volume 43, no. 2, pp. 323–345

Kapstein, E.B. (1992): Between Power and Purpose: Central Bankers and the Politics of Regulatory Convergence, *International Organisation*, Volume 46, no. 1

Kaul, I., Grunberg, I. and M.A. Stern (1999): Defining Global Public Goods, in Kaul, I., Grunberg, I. and M.A. Stern (1999, editors): *Global Public Goods: International Cooperation in the 21st Century*, The United Nations Development Programme (UNDP), Oxford University Press, New York – Oxford, pp. 2–19

Kim, D. and A. Santomero (1988): Risk in Banking and Capital Regulation, *Journal of Finance*, Volume 43, Issue 5, pp. 1219–1233

Kleftouri, N. (2015): *Deposit Protection and Bank Resolution*, Oxford University Press, Oxford

Kokkola, T. (2010): *The Payment System: Payments, Securities and Derivatives, and the Role of the Eurosystem*, European Central Bank

Krahnen, J.P. and L. Moretti (2015): Bail-in Clauses, in Faia, E., Hackethal, Haliassos, M. and K. Langenbucher (2015, editors): *Financial Regulation – A Transatlantic Perspective*, Cambridge University Press, Cambridge, United Kingdom, Chapter 6, pp. 125–149

Krimminger, P. and R.M. Lastra (2011): Early Intervention, in Lastra, R.M. (2011, editor): *Cross-Border Bank Insolvency*, Oxford University Press, Oxford – New York, Chapter 3, pp. 57–71

Kroszner, R.S. and R.J. Shiller (2011): *Reforming the U.S. Financial Markets: Reflections Before and Beyond Dodd-Frank*, edited by B.M. Friedman, The MIT Press, Cambridge, MA, January

L

Laeven, L. and F. Valencia (2012): *Systemic Banking Crises Database: An Update*, IMF Working Papers, WP/12/163, available at: https://www.imf.org/external/pubs/ft/wp/2012/wp12163.pdf

Laeven, L. and F. Valencia (2008): *Systemic Banking Crises: A New Database*, IMF Working Papers, WP/08/224, available at: https://www.imf.org/external/pubs/ft/wp/2008/wp08224.pdf

Lastra, R.M. (2015a): *International Financial and Monetary Law*, second edition, Oxford University Press, United Kingdom

Lastra, R.M. (2015b): Systemic Risk and Macro-prudential Supervision, in Moloney, N., Ferran, E. and J. Payne (2015, editors): *The Oxford Handbook of Financial Regulation*, Oxford University Press, United Kingdom, Chapter 11, pp. 309–333

Lastra, R.M. (2011, editor): *Cross-Border Bank Insolvency*, Oxford University Press, Oxford – New York

Lastra, R.M. (2006): *Legal Foundations of International Monetary Stability*, Oxford University Press, Oxford – New York

Lastra, R.M. and Ch. Goodhart (2015): *Interaction Between Monetary and Bank Regulation*, Monetary Dialogue Papers, European Parliament, September, pp. 37–54, at: https://op.europa.eu/en/publication-detail/-/publication/3d05d3ec-fcb9-11e6-8a35-01aa75ed71a1/language-en

Lenza, M., Pill, H. and L. Reichlin (2010): *Monetary Policy in Exceptional Times*, Working Paper Series, no. 1253, European Central Bank – Eurosystem, October

Liang, N. (2019): Financial Stability and Macroeconomic Policies, in Blanchard, Ol. And L.H. Summers (2019, editors): *Evolution or Revolution? – Rethinking Macroeconomic Policy After the Great Recession*, Peterson Institute for International Economics (PIIE), The MIT Press, Cambridge, Massachusetts – London, England, Chapter 14, pp. 213–220

Lichtenstein, C. (2010): Lessons for 21st-Century Central Bankers: Differences Between Investment and Depositary Banking, in Giovanoli, M. and D. Devos (2010, editors): *International Monetary and Financial Law: The Global Crisis*, Oxford University Press, Oxford – New York, Chapter 10, pp. 217–233

Lowenfeld, A.F. (2010): The International Monetary System: A Look Back Over Seven Decades, *Journal of International Economic Law*, Volume 13, No. 3, September, pp. 575–595

M

Macey, J. (1993): *The Inevitability of Universal Banking*, Yale University, Faculty Scholarship Series, Paper 1654

McCahery, J., Vermeulen, E. and H. Masato (2013): *The Present and Future of Corporate Governance: Re-Examining the Role of the Board of Directors and Investor Relations in Listed Companies*, ECGI – Law Working Paper No. 211, available at: https://ssrn.com/abstract=2254520

Manna, M. (2009): Emergency Liquidity Assistance at Work: Both Words and Deeds Matter, *Montepaschi di Siena Studi e Note di Economia*, Anno XIV, n. 2, pp. 155–186

Markets Committee (2013): *Central Bank Collateral Frameworks and Practices*, Bank for International Settlements, March

Martin, Al., Mendicino, C. and Al. Van der Ghote (2021): *On the Interaction Between Monetary and Macroprudential Policies*, ECB Working Paper Series No 2527, February, available at: https://www.ecb.europa.eu/pub/pdf/scpwps/ecb.wp2527~b90657e08c.en.pdf?2888f6ea3013733854dfb02e99bfb9d1

McCormick, R. (2006): *Legal Risk in the Financial Markets*, Oxford University Press, Oxford – New York

McKnight, A. (2008): *The Law of International Finance*, Oxford University Press, Oxford – New York

Mercuro, N. and S.G. Medema (2006): *Economics and the Law, from Posner to Post-Modernism and Beyond*, second edition, Princeton University Press, Princeton and Oxford

Michael, B., Goo, S.H. and D. Wojcik (2020): Does Objectives-Based Financial Regulation Imply a Rethink of Legislatively Mandated Economic Regulation? The Case of Hong Kong and Twin Peaks Financial Regulation, *Capital Markets Law Journal* 15(1) (for the first half) and *Notre Dame Journal of Legislation 46(4)* (for second half) (also available at: https://ssrn.com/abstract=2523346)

Mishkin, F.S. (2003): Financial Policies and the Prevention of Financial Crises in Emerging Market Economies, in Feldstein, M. (2003, editor): *Economic and Financial Crises in Emerging Market Economies*, A National Bureau of Economic Research (NBER) Conference Report, The University of Chicago Press, Chicago and London, pp. 93–130

Montagna, M., Torri G. and G. Covi (2020): *On the Origin of Systemic Risk*, ECB Working Papers No. 2502, December (also available at: https://ssrn.com/abstract=3778199)

Möschel, W. (1978): Das Trennsystem in der U.S.-amerikanischen Bankwirtschaft: Eine normative und faktische Analyse, Studien zum Bank- und Börsenrecht, Band 3, Nomos Verlagsgesellschaft, Baden-Baden

Moritz, A. and J.H. Block (2014): Crowdfunding und Crowdinvesting: State-of-the-Art der wissenschaftlichen Literatur (Crowdfunding and Crowdinvesting: A Review of the Literature), *Zeitschrift für KMU und Entrepreneurship*, Volume 62, No. 1, pp. 57–89 (also available at: https://ssrn.com/abstract=2274141)

Mülbert. P.O (2015): Managing Risk in the Financial System, in Moloney, N., Ferran, E. and J. Payne (2015, editors): *The Oxford Handbook of Financial Regulation*, Oxford University Press, United Kingdom, Chapter 13, pp. 364–408

Muñoz, D.R. (2017): Bank Resolution and Insolvency Ranking and Priorities, in *ECB Legal Conference 2017 – Shaping a New Legal Order for Europe: A Tale of Crises and Opportunities*, European Central Bank, December, pp. 256–286 (also available at: https://www.ecb.europa.eu/pub/pdf/other/ecblegalconferenceproceedings201712.en.pdf)

Murphy, D. (2022): *Derivatives Regulation – Rules and Reasoning from Lehman to Covid*, Oxford University Press, Oxford

N

Nelson, W. (2014): Lessons from Last Resort Operations During the Financial Crisis: The Federal Reserve Experience, in Bank for International Settlements (2014): *Rethinking the Lender of Last Resort*, BIS Papers No 79, September, pp. 76–80

Network for Greening the Financial System (2020): "Guide for Supervisors – Integrating Climate-Related and Environmental Risks into Prudential Supervision", May, available at: https://www.ngfs.net/sites/default/files/medias/documents/ngfs_guide_for_supervisors.pdf

Nielsen L. (2011): *Classification of Countries Based on Their Level of Development. How It Is Done and How It Could Be Done*, IMF Working Papers, WP/11/31, available at: https://www.imf.org/external/pubs/ft/wp/2011/wp1131.pdf

Nieto, M. and G. Garcia (2012): *The Insufficiency of Traditional Safety Nets: What Bank Resolution Fund for Europe?*, LSE Financial Markets Group Paper Series, Special Paper 209, London, UK

Nijskens, R. and S. Eijffinger (2010): *The Lender of Last Resort: Liquidity Provisions Versus the Possibility of Bail-Out*, European Banking Center Discussion Paper No. 2010-2, available at https://ssrn.com/abstract=1562709

Nijskens, R. and W. Wagner (2011): Credit Risk Transfer and Systemic Risk: How Banks Became Less Risky Individually but Posed Greater Risks to the Financial System at the Same Time, *Journal of Banking and Finance*, 35, pp. 1391–1398

Norberg, J. (2009): *Financial Fiasco: How America's Infatuation with Homeownership and Easy Money Created the Economic Crisis*, Cato Institute, Washington, DC

Norton, J.J. (1995): *Devising International Bank Supervisory Standards*, Graham & Trotman, Martinus Nijhoff, London – Dordrecht – Boston

O-P

O' Neal, M.K. (2000): Summary and Analysis of the Gramm-Leach Bliley Act, *Securities Regulation Law Journal*, 28

Oganesyan, G. (2013): *The Changed Role of the Lender of Last Resort: Crisis Responses of the Federal Reserve*, European Central Bank and Bank of England, Working Paper, No. 19/2013, Institute for International Political Economy, Berlin

Pacces, Alessio M. and H. Nabilou (2017): The Law and Economics of Shadow Banking, European Corporate Governance Institute (ECGI) – Law Working Paper No. 339/2017, available at: https://ssrn.com/abstract=2884374

Padoa-Schioppa, T. (2000): EMU and Banking Supervision, in Goodhard, C.A.E. (2000, editor): *Which Lender of Last Resort for Europe?*, Chapter 1, Central Banking Publications, London, pp. 15–29

Partnoy, F. (2015): Financial Systems, Crises, and Regulation, in Moloney, N., Ferran, E. and J. Payne (2015, editors): *The Oxford Handbook of Financial Regulation*, Oxford University Press, United Kingdom, Chapter 3, pp. 68–93

Pazarbasioglu, C., Zhou, J., Le Leslé, V. and M. Moore (2011): *Contingent Capital: Economic Rationale and Design Features*, Monetary and Capital Markets Department, International Monetary Fund, January 25, available at: https://www.imf.org/external/pubs/ft/sdn/2011/sdn1101.pdf

Pistor, K. (2019): Regulating Financial Markets – An LTF Perspective, in Avgouleas, E. and D.C. Donald (2015, editors): *The Political Economy of Financial Regulation*, International Corporate Law and Financial Market Regulation, Cambridge University Press, Cambridge, United Kingdom, Chapter 1, pp. 19-37

Posner, R.A. (2010): *The Crisis of Capitalist Democracy*, Harvard University Press, Cambridge, Massachusetts – London, England

Pozsar, Z., Adrian, T., Ashcraft, A. and H. Boesky (2010): *Shadow Banking*, Federal Reserve Bank of New York, Staff Report No. 458

Psaroudakis, G. (2014): Das Recht der Bankenrestrukturierung in Zeiten der Wirtschaftskrise, in Hopt, K.J. und D. Tzouganatos (Herausgeber): *Das Europäische Wirtschaftsrecht vor neuen Herausforderungen: Beiträge aus Deutschland und Griechenland*, Mohr Siebeck, Tübingen, pp. 41–76

R

Rajan, R.G. (2010): *Fault Lines: How Hidden Fractures Still Threaten the World Economy*, Princeton University Press, Princeton

Rasmusen, Er. (1989): *Games and Information*, Basil Blackwell, Oxford

Reinhart, C.M. and K.S. Rogoff (2008): *This Time Is Different: A Panoramic View of Eight Centuries of Financial Crises*, NBER Working Paper Series, Working Paper 13882, National Bureau of Economic Research (NBER), available at: https://www.nber.org/papers/w13882

Restoy, F. (2017): *Early Intervention Regimes: The Balance Between Rules vs Discretion*, FSI-IADI Meeting on early supervisory intervention, resolution and deposit insurance, Basel, Switzerland, 12 September, available at: https://www.bis.org/speeches/sp170912.pdf

Rheinholdson, F. and H. Olsson (2012): *The Separation of Commercial and Investment Banking: A Literature Review*, University of Gothenburg

Rini, R. (2008): *La responsabilité des autorités de surveillance bancaire en Europe - Étude comparée du droit suisse et des droits allemand, anglais et français dans le contexte de l' Union européenne*, Schweizer Schriften zum Finanzmarktrecht, Band 88, Schulthess Verlag, Zürich

Rochet, J. (1992): Capital Requirements and the Behaviour of Commercial Banks, *European Economic Review*, Volume 36, pp. 1137–1178

S

Saunders, A. (1987): The Interbank Market, Contagion Effects and International Financial Crises, in R. Portes and A.K. Swoboda (1987, editors): *Threats to International Financial Stability*, Cambridge University Press, Cambridge, United Kingdom, pp. 196–232

Saunders, A. and I. Walter (1994): *Universal Banking in the United States, What Could We Gain? What Could We Lose?*, Oxford University Press, New York – Oxford

Schinasi, G.J. (2006): *Safeguarding Financial Stability – Theory and Practice*, International Monetary Fund, Washington, DC

Schinasi, G.J. (2005): *Preserving Financial Stability*, Economic Issues 36, International Monetary Fund, Washington, DC

Schoenmaker, D. (2011): The Financial Trilemma, *Economics Letters*, Volume 111, pp. 57–59 (also available as Duisenberg School of Finance – Tinbergen Institute Discussion Papers No. TI 11–019/DSF 7, at: https://ssrn.com/abstract=1340395)

Schoenmaker, D. and N. Veron (2021): A "Twin Peaks" Vision for Europe, in Godwin, A. and A. Schmulow (2021, editors): *The Cambridge Handbook of Twin Peaks Financial Regulation*, Cambridge Law Handbooks, Cambridge University Press, Cambridge, United Kingdom, Chapter 16, pp. 282–291

Schwarcz, S.L. (2015): The Governance Structure of Shadow Banking: Rethinking Assumptions About Limited Liability, *The Journal of Financial Perspectives*, EY Global Financial Services Institute, March, Volume 3, Issue 1, pp. 65–81

Schwarcz, S.L. (2008): *Systemic Risk*, Duke Law School Legal Studies, Research Paper Series, No. 163, March, available at: https://ssrn.com/abstract=1008326

Seelig, S. and Al. Novoa (2009): *Governance Practices at Financial Regulatory and Supervisory Agencies*, IMF Working Papers, WP/09/135, available at: https://www.imf.org/external/pubs/ft/wp/2009/wp09135.pdf

Shambaugh, J.C. (2012): The Euro's Three Crises, *Brookings Papers on Economic Activity*, Spring, The Brookings Institution, pp. 157–231, available at: https://www.brookings.edu/~/media/Projects/BPEA/Spring%202012/2012a_Shambaugh.pdf

Siegwart, H., Caytas, I.G. and J.I. Mahari (1989): *Global Political Risk*, Helbing and Lichtenhahn, Basle and Frankfurt am Main

Sjöberg, G. (2014): Banking Special Resolution Regimes as a Governance Tool, in Ringe, W.G. and P.M. Huber (2014, editors): *Legal Challenges in the Global Financial Crisis – Bail-outs, the Euro and Regulation*, Chapter 12, Hart Publishing, Oxford and Portland, Oregon

Smith, B. (1951): Effective Competition: Hypothesis for Modernizing the Antitrust Law, *New York University Law Review*, Volume 26, p. 405 et seq.

Steil, B. (2002): *Changes in the Ownership and Governance of Securities Exchanges: Causes and Consequences*, February

Steinbaum, M. and M.E. Stucke (2020): The Effective Competition Standard: A New Standard for Antitrust, *The University of Chicago Law Review*, Volume 87, Issue 2, pp. 595–623

Stiglitz, J.E. and C.E. Walsh (2006): *Principles of Microeconomics*, W.W. Norton & Company, fourth edition, New York – London

Stillhart, G. (2002): *Theorie der Finanzintermediation und Regulierung von Banken*, Bank- und finanzwirtschaftliche Forschungen, Verlag Paul Haupt, Bern – Stuttgart – Wien

Svoronos, J.-Ph. (2018): *Early Intervention Regimes for Weak Banks*, FSI Insights on Policy Implementation, No 6, Financial Stability Institute, April, available at: https://www.bis.org/fsi/publ/insights6.ht

T

Task Force on Climate-related Financial Disclosures (2017): *"Recommendations of the Task Force on Climate-Related Financial Disclosures"*, 29 June, available at: https://www.fsb.org/2017/06/recommendations-of-the-task-force-on-climate-related-financial-disclosures-2

The World Bank (1989): *World Development Report: Financial Systems and Development*, Oxford University Press, Oxford – New York, pp. 49–61

Thiele, Al. (2014): *Finanzaufsicht*, Jus Publicum 229, Mohr Siebeck, Tübingen

Tinbergen, J. (1952): *On the Theory of Economic Policy*, North Holland, Amsterdam

Tuch, A.F. (2015): Conduct of Business Regulation, in Moloney, N., Ferran, E. and J. Payne (2015, editors): *The Oxford Handbook of Financial Regulation*, Oxford University Press, United Kingdom, Chapter 18, pp. 537–567

Tucker, P. (2020): Solvency as a Fundamental Constraint on LOLR Policy for Independent Central Banks: Principles, History, Law, *Journal of Financial Crises*, Volume 2, Issues 2, pp. 1–33, available at: https://elischolar.library.yale.edu/journal-of-financial-crises/vol2/iss2/1

Tucker, P. (2018): The Lender of Last Resort: Regimes for Stability and Legitimacy, in Conti-Brown, P. and R.M. Lastra (2018, editors): *Research Handbook on Central Banking*, Research Handbooks in Financial Law, Edward Elgar Publishing Limited, UK – Edward Elgar Publishing, Inc., USA, Chapter 26, pp. 535–552

Tucker, P. (2014): The Lender of Last Resort and Modern Central Banking: Principles and Reconstruction, in Bank for International Settlements (2014): *Re-thinking the Lender of Last Resort*, BIS Papers No 79, September, pp. 10–42

V-W-Y-Z

Viale, R., Mousavi, Sh., Alemanni, B. and U. Filotto (2018): *The Behavioral Finance Revolution – A New Approach to Financial Policies and Regulations*, Edward Elgar Publishing Limited, Cheltenham, UK – Edward Elgar Publishing, Inc., Northampton, USA

Viñals, J., Blanchard, O., and S. Tiwari (2015): *Monetary Policy and Financial Stability*, IMF Policy Paper, International Monetary Fund, September, available at: https://www.imf.org/external/np/pp/eng/2015/082815a.pdf

Von der Crone, H.C. and J.-Ch. Rochet (2014, Herausgeber): *Finanzstabilität: Status und Perspektiven*, Schweizer Schriften zum Finanzmarktrecht, Band 112, Schulthess Verlag, Zürich

Wallison, P.G. (2009): *Did the 'Repeal' of Glass-Steagall Have any Role on the Financial Crisis? Not Guilty; Not Even Close*, available at: https://ssrn.com/abstract=1507803

Weber, R.H, Arner, D.W., Gibson, E.C. and S. Baumann (2014): Addressing Systemic Risk: Financial Regulatory Design, *Texas International Law Journal*, The University of Texas School of Law, Volume 49, Number 2, Spring, pp. 149–200

Wehinger, G. (2013): Banking in a Challenging Environment: Business Models, Ethics and Approaches Towards Risks, *OECD Journal: Financial Market Trends*, Issue 2, OECD

White, P. and T. Yorulmazer (2014): *Bank Resolution Concepts, Tradeoffs, and Changes in Practices*, Federal Reserve Bank of New York, Economic Policy Review, Volume 20, No. 2, March

Wiggins, R., Wedow, M. and A. Metrick (2019): European Banking Union B: The Single Resolution Mechanism, *Journal of Financial Crises*, Volume 1, Issue 3, pp. 130–149, available at: https://elischolar.library.yale.edu/journal-of-financial-crises/vol1/iss3/8

World Bank Group (2019): *Prudential Regulatory and Supervisory Practices for Fintech: Payments, Credit and Deposits*, Finance, Competitiveness and Innovation Insight, available at: https://documents1.worldbank.org/curated/en/954851578602363164/pdf/Prudential-Regulatory-and-Supervisory-Practices-for-Fintech-Payments-Credit-and-Deposits.pdf

Wymeersch, Ed. (2006): *The Structure of Financial Supervision in Europe: About Single, Twin Peaks and Multiple Financial Supervisors*, Working Paper, available at: https://ssrn.com/abstract=946695

Yeager, T.J., Yeager, F.C. and E.F. Harshman (2004): *The Financial Modernisation Act: Evolution or Revolution?*, available at: https://ssrn.com/abstract=636261

Zamir, E. and D. Teichman (2018): *Behavioral Law and Economics*, Oxford University Press, New York, United States of America

Zetzsche, D.A., Arner, D.W. and R.P. Buckley (2020): Decentralized Finance (DeFi), *Journal of Financial Regulation* 6, pp. 172–203, available at: https://ssrn.com/abstract=3539194

CHAPTER 2

Key Aspects of Public International Financial Law: International Financial Standards

2.1 Definition, Branches and Delimitation

2.1.1 Definition

(1) Certain intergovernmental fora, along with several international financial fora, predominantly composed of financial system national authorities, and a limited number of international organisations (including the Bank for International Settlements [**BIS**] and the International Monetary Fund [**IMF**]) constitute, since the early 1970s the 'new international financial architecture' ('**NIFA**')[1] or the current international institutional framework governing the financial system. They are the main actors in the process of making and enforcing the rules of public international financial law.[2]

(2) Public international financial law (also referred to as 'international financial law'[3]), together with public international monetary law, constitutes one of

---

[1] This term was used for the first time by Crocket (2002), p. 7. See on this Norton (2001), pp. 45–46, who challenges the accuracy of this term regarding all its components; see also Bryant (1999) and Bergsten (2000).

[2] Even though reference to 'international financial law' is more common, the author prefers to add 'public' international in order to clearly distinguish the (soft law) rules discussed in this chapter from the various categories of private international financial law (see under 2.1.3, under "other delimitations").

[3] Norton (2001), pp. 11–13, talks about 'global public financial law'. The rules adopted are also characterised as 'global administrative law' (see Cassese [2005] and Cassese and D' Alterio [2016], pp. 4–7).

the three branches of international economic law, the other two being international trade law and international law of foreign investments.[4] It is defined as the sum of rules of international economic law aimed at the liberalisation of international trade in financial services,[5] and the achievement, by resort to international cooperation, of specific policy objectives justifying regulatory intervention in the financial system. In this respect, attention should be drawn to the following initial remarks on public international financial law: *first*, as '**law**', it refers to institutions and to rules, which, no matter whether legally binding or not, have an impact on the legal order of individual states; *second*, as '**international law**', it is adopted at multilateral level and does not include the rules of administrative financial law adopted on a bilateral basis, or the rules of financial law adopted on a regional basis, such the rules of the European financial law; *third*, as '**public international law**', it does not contain any rules of private law[6]; and *finally*, as '**financial law**', it uses as a point of reference the two functions of the financial system, its infrastructures and the services provided in it, as well as the objectives of regulatory intervention in the financial system.

(3) The formation of public international financial law requires resort to specific principles of international law, of which some pertain only to the liberalisation of international trade in financial services, others pertain only to regulatory intervention in the financial system and some pertain to both. The liberalisation of international trade in financial services is a subset of the liberalisation of international trade in services concerning the abolition of measures adopted unilaterally by states and restrictively affecting trade in services. Hence, it is reasonable to argue that the relevant provisions are part of international trade law.

2.1.2 *Branches*

2.1.2.1 *Introduction*

Taking into account the considerations developed above with regard to the policy objectives justifying regulatory intervention in the financial system, the author views public international financial law as containing four (separate but closely linked) individual branches: public international banking law; public international capital markets law (including public international payment and

---

[4] For the definition and content of international economic law, see Carreau et Juillard (2005), pp. 1–6, Herdegen (2008), pp. 1–6 and Lowenfeld (2009), pp. 1–8.

[5] The liberalisation of international trade in financial services is an integral part but still a distinct subset of the liberalisation of international trade in services, which refers to the abolition of measures adopted unilaterally by states, in the form of laws, regulations, procedures, decisions or administrative actions, and restrictively affecting trade in services. Hence, it is also reasonable to argue that the relevant provisions are part of international trade law. This is a marginal case.

[6] On the delimitation, see below, under 2.1.3.

settlement systems law); public international insurance law; and public international financial conglomerates law. The approach adopted for the definition of the individual branches of public international financial law is the (sectoral) **"functional approach"**[7] for two reasons:

> *First*, in the author's view, this approach is not only suitable, but also necessary given that, if the definition were to be based on an **"institutional approach"** (focusing on the categories of financial firms falling within the personal field of application of relevant provisions), there would be extensive overlapping between individual branches. Indicatively, it can be mentioned that the provisions of a significant subset of the rules contained in the legal acts constituting the sources of all branches of international financial law, as defined above, are applied to banks. If the institutional approach were to be adopted, these provisions would need to be concurrently included in public international banking law, alternatively defined in this case as the 'law of banks', and in public international capital markets law, if they also apply to investment firms.
> *Second*, considering that banks (and all other categories of financial firms) are also subject to the provisions of other branches of international economic law not included in public international financial law (e.g., international competition law), these provisions should also be included, for reasons of consistency, in international banking law, if the functional approach is not adopted, which would lead, in the author's view, to inappropriate results.

2.1.2.2 Public International Banking Law

Public international banking law is defined as the set of rules of international financial law, which apply exclusively to banks, whereby the following two objectives are sought: the *first* is to ensure the liberalisation of trade in banking services,[8] and the second to ensure the stability of the banking system, which could be disrupted due to contagious bank failures. For the achievement of the latter objective, public international banking law contains rules on the authorisation, the micro- and macroprudential regulation and the microprudential supervision of banks; the macroprudential oversight of the banking (and, more generally, the financial) system; the reorganisation, resolution and winding-up of banks; and deposit guarantee.[9] *On the contrary*, in principle, there are no

---

[7] This "functional approach" is different from the post-sectoral functional approach used in relation to the regulation of "shadow banks".

[8] To the extent that payment services are provided by banks (which is the case in several states), it is legitimate to include the rules on the liberalisation of these services in international banking law as well.

[9] For an overview of these components of the 'bank safety net', see Chapter 1, under 1.1.3.

rules on the functioning of central banks as lenders of last resort, since this function is exercised in an environment of 'constructive ambiguity'.[10]

2.1.2.3 Public International Capital Markets Law

Public international capital markets law is the branch of international financial law containing provisions aimed at ensuring the liberalisation of trade in investment services; the stability of capital markets; investor protection as well as capital markets' integrity, efficiency and transparency; and the compensation of investors in case of suspension of operations of a firm providing investment services (bank or investment firm) if such a firm is not in a position to return funds or financial instruments belonging to investors. Even though it could also be considered as a separate branch, public international payment and settlement systems law is also included herein; it contains provisions seeking to meet two policy objectives: safeguarding the stability of payment and settlement systems and ensuring their efficiency.

2.1.2.4 Public International Insurance Law

Public international insurance law contains provisions seeking to ensure the liberalisation of trade in insurance and reinsurance services and safeguard the stability of the insurance sector of the financial system. Notwithstanding very few exceptions, the provisions of public international insurance law usually do not apply to banks. This is due to the fact that in the majority of states the provision of insurance and reinsurance services is only permitted for undertakings specifically authorised for this purpose (namely insurance and reinsurance undertakings), and in any event, not banks.

2.1.2.5 Public International Financial Conglomerates Law

Public international financial conglomerates law contains provisions regarding the supplementary supervision of financial conglomerates in order to safeguard the stability of the financial system as a whole as regards their activity. The provisions of this branch apply to banks only to the extent of their participation in financial conglomerates, and over and above the provisions of public international banking law on the supervision of banks, on an individual and consolidated basis.

2.1.3 Delimitations

2.1.3.1 Delimitation vis-à-vis Public International Monetary Law

Public international financial law must be distinguished from public international monetary law. The latter is defined as the set of rules of international

---

[10] On this aspect, see Chapter 1, under 1.3.2.

law governing the monetary and foreign exchange relations between independent states, hence the operation of the international monetary system.[11] Public international monetary law also contains rules with regard to the following: the adequacy of reserve assets, acceptable to the international community, to financially support international economic transactions (the 'question of liquidity'); the make-up of the portfolio of assets that may be requested and supplied as international (foreign) reserves (the 'question of credibility'); the suitability of the procedures by means of which states can neutralise the imbalances in international payments by having recourse to the use of international reserves (the 'question of adjustment'); the transparency in the conduct of monetary policy (as well as public finance policy, which directly and indirectly affects the operation of the monetary and financial system), and ensuring the correctness and accuracy of the economic data published by states in connection with such policies; the safeguarding of conditions of normality in the international movement of capital; and the adequacy of procedures for the analysis of the sensitivity of economies to crises and the planning of national economic policies.[12]

2.1.3.2 *Delimitation* vis-à-vis *Public International Law on Combatting the Use of the Financial System for the Commitment of Economic Crimes*

The public international law on combatting the use of the financial system for the commitment of economic crimes is the branch of international financial law that contains provisions seeking to prevent the use of the financial system for the conduct of economic crimes (such as 'money laundering', terrorist financing and payment instruments fraud), and to contain such crimes. The relevant provisions apply fully to banks, and it can be reasonably argued that the main reason for their adoption was to combat economic crime committed through the banking sector of the financial system. However, it is not only banks that may come under the scope of these provisions but also the vast majority of the other categories of financial firms. Moreover, several provisions of this branch of international financial law (especially the ones relating to 'money laundering') apply not only to financial firms, but also to undertakings and professionals outside the financial system (such as casinos, notaries and lawyers), with a view to addressing regulatory arbitrage. In this sense, it can be argued, *in extremis*, that a new branch of international economic law has emerged outside of international financial law, but fully applicable to financial firms, referred to as the "international law on combatting the use of the economic system for the commitment of economic crimes".

---

[11] See Gortsos (2012), pp. 110–112. From the extensive literature on this issue, see Lastra (2006), pp. 345–370 (on the historical evolution of international monetary law), Lowenfeld (2009), pp. 628–666 and Bordo and James (2010) (on role and the law governing the IMF), and Hagan (2010a) and (2010b).

[12] See Genberg and Swoboda (1991).

2.1.3.3 Other Delimitations

Public international financial law, as defined above, is also to be clearly distinguished from the following branches of law:

> The *first* is the international law of international (or cross-border) financial transactions,[13] a sub-category of the international law of business transactions, which contains rules adopted at international level on the contractual content of such transactions. Such rules are adopted by inter-governmental organisations, such as the United Nations Commission on International Trade Law ('**UNCITRAL**'),[14] the International Institute for the Unification of Private Law ('**UNIDROIT**'),[15] and trade associations, such as the International Chamber of Commerce ('**ICC**')[16] and the International Swaps and Derivatives Association ('**ISDA**').[17]
>
> The *second* branch is private international financial law, which governs international financial transactions as regards: the determination of the law applicable to each individual international financial transaction, which depends on the choice of the parties or the most significant connection to a particular state ('conflicts of law'); the public policy (or overriding mandatory) rules; as well as on uniform rules of civil or commercial law, which directly govern cross-border financial transactions.[18] The relevant provisions may be adopted either at national level or by means of international treaties. In practice, many of the rules governing international financial transactions are provided through standard contract terms and conditions. Where they incorporate rules drafted by international trade associations, they fall into one with the law of international financial transactions.
>
> Finally, the *third* branch is the law pertaining to inter-state financial transactions, which is usually covered by bilateral agreements.

---

[13] For a definition and the sub-categories of these transactions, see Bizzozero and Robinson (2010), pp. 25–35.

[14] See https://www.uncitral.org, as well as Gross (2007), Berger (2010) and UNCITRAL (2007).

[15] See https://www.unidroit.org, as well as Oser (2008) and Berger (2010).

[16] For more information, see https://www.iccwbo.org.

[17] See https://www.isda.org, as well as McKnight (2008), pp. 611–615 and Zerey (2010, Hrsg.), pp. 143–180.

[18] On this, see McKnight (2008), pp. 167–257.

2.2 Evolution

2.2.1 *Introductory Remarks*

2.2.1.1 *The Environment Until 1971*

(1) Until 1971, there was no single international institution to discuss issues of international financial law. This was due to the fact that the banking systems, the capital markets, the insurance markets, as well as the payment and settlement systems in (several even) advanced economies and (predominantly) in EMEs and less developed countries operated under conditions of protectionism and marked restrictive regulatory intervention, since they served as levers for the conduct of national economic policy (with few exceptions). Consequently, given that the international interconnectedness of systems and markets was limited and the international movement of capital (and therefore most cross-border financial transactions) was very limited throughout this period, the need did not arise either for the setting up of an international organisation or an international forum to deal with matters relating to the operation of financial markets and payment and settlement systems as well as to the regulation and supervision of financial firms providing services within them, or for the adoption of harmonised rules with regard to these aspects. Despite being set up in during this period, the OECD was not yet given competences on matters relating to the financial system (as currently held); the same is true for the General Agreement on Trade and Tariffs ('**GATT**'), which did not deal with the issue of liberalisation of trade in services, including financial services.[19]

(2) On the contrary, during the period 1945–1971, the international architecture of the monetary system was structured, governed by the operation of a mechanism of fixed (but adjustable) foreign exchange rates, known as the IMF-governed Bretton Woods system of fixed exchange rates (hereinafter the "**Bretton Woods system**"). The management and supervision of this system was entrusted to the **IMF**, which at the same time had (and still has) the statutory task of providing financing to its member states when faced with balance of payments problems.[20] In the same field, another international economic organisation, the **BIS** was also operating during this period. Founded in 1930, it had as a principal statutory aim to promote cooperation between its central bank members and facilitate the decision-making process on their part in light of the international impact of their operations.[21]

---

[19] See below, under 2.3.3.
[20] See below, under 2.3.5.
[21] See below, under 2.3.3.

2.2.1.2 The Three Periods for the Formation of Public International Financial Law

The two main characteristics of the evolution of public international financial law are that it was gradual, occurring in relatively modest steps since 1971, and the international community's response to the onset of crises, in particular those with international dimensions which occurred after the abolition of the Bretton Woods system. By means of indication, the Basel Committee on Banking Supervision (**BCBS**) was set up (in 1974) as a reaction of the G10 Central Bank Governors to the bankruptcy of the German "Herstatt Bank",[22] while the **Financial Stability Forum** and the **G20** were set up (in 1999) as a G7 reaction to the 'Asian crisis'.[23] *Furthermore*, the aim of the principles and standards contained in many of the reports, which are adopted by international financial organisations and (mainly) fora and constitute the sources of public international financial law, was to deal with the problems that ensued from specific crises; hence, institutions and rules in the banking (and, more generally, financial) system are often the **'children of crises'**.[24]

Accordingly, public international financial law was shaped, in terms of both institutions and rules (in the form of financial standards[25]), during the last four decades. Its formation can be divided into three main historical periods (see below, under 2.2.2–2.2.4, respectively): the *first period* from the abolition of Bretton Woods system until the 'Asian crisis' (1997–1998); the *second period* from the 'Asian crisis' until the (2007–2009) Global Financial Crisis; and the current *third period* after the global financial crisis, which is also characterised by the implications of the (still ongoing) pandemic crisis.[26]

2.2.2 The Period from the Abolition of the Bretton Woods System Until the 'Asian Crisis' (1997–1998)

2.2.2.1 The New Environment
The Change in the Terms of Operation of the Post-War System
(1) The conditions of operation of national monetary and financial systems began to change significantly in advanced economies from the beginning of the 1970s onwards. Three main catalysts triggered the amendments[27]: the *first* was the development of 'Euromarkets', which made it clear for the first time to national authorities responsible for managing national monetary and

---

[22] See Chapter 3 below, under .

[23] See below, under 2.3.4.

[24] For a critical view of the assertion that key financial regulations (in the example of the US) only follows from crises (the "crisis-legislation hypothesis"), see Conti-Brown and Ohlrogge (2022).

[25] See below, under 2.4.2.

[26] It is noted that the current global inflation crisis has not per se prompted the adoption of new international financial rules (standards).

[27] See Steil (1994), pp. 2–5, and Herring and Litan (1995), pp. 13–48.

financial systems that financial firms could be engaged in financial transactions which went beyond the scope of their regulatory range[28]; the *second* catalyst was an institutional change which consisted in the abolition of the Bretton Woods system of internationally fixed exchange rates and the transition, in 1971, to a free-floating regime[29]; and *finally*, a decisive contribution was made by the rapid progress achieved in the fields of information technology and telecommunications, as this enabled the conduct of large-value cross-border financial transactions in a very short time.

(2) As a result of the concurrence of these factors, significant developments ensued. In particular, a constantly increasing number of states proceeded with the abolition of both the restrictions imposed on cross-border movement of capital and direct administrative interventions, which they had imposed on the operation of national financial systems. This process is known in academic literature as the 'deregulation process'. In view of the above, three important amendments were introduced to the operational conditions of financial systems: an increase in the variety of products offered by financial intermediaries and other financial firms both to enterprises and to private consumers; an increase in the volume of the international movement of capital for the conduct of cross-border commercial and financial transactions; and the integration of advanced economies states into the internationalised financial system.[30] These developments did not occur simultaneously in all economies, nor were they equally intensive. It is, however, a fact that forty years after the abolition of the Bretton Woods system in most of the world's economies, the financial system is governed (to a greater or lesser extent) by the above conditions and no comparison can be made with those prevailing in the early 1970s.

---

[28] These were national markets for the trading of securities and the acceptance of deposits denominated in a currency different from the official currency of the state where trading took place (e.g., acceptance of deposits in US dollars in banks established in the UK). This restricted the capacity of national monetary authorities to impose controls on assets denominated in their currency but held by institutions in other states. On Euromarkets (and Eurocurrencies), see Robinson (1972), pp. 155–275, Kim (1993), pp. 179–200 and Proctor (2012), pp. 58–63.

[29] Despite the abolition of the international system of fixed exchange rates, there were (and still are) many states which chose either to peg the foreign exchange rate of their national currency to a 'strong' international currency (e.g., the US dollar and, most recently, the euro), retained as an international reserve (a policy known as 'pegging', see Proctor (2012), pp. 868–871) or to accede to regional regimes of controlled floating foreign exchange rates (e.g., the Member States of the (then) European Economic Community as early as in 1971).

[30] See Brakman *et al.* (2006), pp. 196–202.

The Increased Importance of Risk Exposure in the Financial System and the Emergence of 'Systemic Crises' with International Dimensions

(1) The increase in the volume of international capital movements, the liberalisation of national financial systems from the restrictive regulatory framework in which they had operated, and the internationalisation of financial activity (as discussed above) have undoubtedly made a particularly positive contribution to the growth rates achieved in recent decades in the world economy. At the same time however, these developments led to the appearance of risks which either did not exist or were not of the same significance in the post-war system up to 1972. More specifically, the following remarks deserve attention:

> *First*, due to the transition to an international system of floating exchange rates, there was increased exposure of economic agents conducting international (commercial and financial) transactions to exchange rate risk—a risk which is intensified in periods of significant fluctuation of exchange rates. At the same time, the development of capital markets has also increased the exposure of investors (private and institutional) to other market risks arising from price volatility in equities, bonds and derivative financial instruments.
>
> *Second*, the increased bank lending activity (due to the higher volume of domestic business credit and international trade financing and the rapid development of housing and consumer credit) has resulted in greater potential exposure to credit and country risk. In this context, it is noted that during the last decades, the rapid development of financial markets has also enabled financial intermediaries and other financial undertakings to make use of various techniques for hedging the risks to which they are exposed by the use of derivative financial instruments, and develop internal risk management systems which, in some cases, have proven more effective in forestalling risk exposure than the rules of prudential supervision which the supervisory authorities impose.[31]
>
> *Third*, the increase in the volume of commercial and financial transactions (domestic and cross-border) has highlighted the importance of the settlement risk inherent in payment and settlement systems for financial instruments and foreign exchange transactions.

(2) In addition to the above-mentioned financial risks to which financial firms and systems may be exposed, it became evident that in an internationalised environment, given certain spill-over effects, a national banking (or more generally, financial) crisis may have negative implications also abroad. As a matter of fact, the period after 1973 was characterised by several banking crises

---

[31] This is the reason why the Basel Committee on Banking Supervision included banks' internal risk management systems in the elaboration of the capital adequacy rules adopted in 2004.

with international ramifications, namely the crises prompted by the failure of *Herstatt Bank* (1974),[32] *Banco Ambrosiano Holding S.A.* (1980),[33] *Continental Illinois* (1984)[34]; *BCCI* (Bank of Commerce and Credit International) (1993)[35] and *Barings Bank* (1996).[36] During this period remarkable was also the debt crisis in Latin America, which had severe adverse effects on the US banking system due to the heavy exposure of US banks to credit risk from positions in sovereign debt and loans in states of this region.[37]

National Initiatives to Redesign Financial Systems
The amendments in the operation of the financial system, in conjunction with the crises described above, have made it clear that in a liberalised financial system there is increased risk exposure and interconnectedness of economic agents, including financial firms, and that as regards banks in particular, exposure to these risks may activate negative chain reactions with an immediate impact on the stability of the financial system and the economy at large. In view of the above, several (but unfortunately not the majority) of the states which proceeded to the liberalisation of their financial systems have also undertaken initiatives aimed at safeguarding the stability of their monetary and financial systems, while identifying the deficiencies existing in national institutional infrastructures. This was achieved in principle with the adoption of rules on microprudential regulation with a view to reducing financial firms' exposure to financial and other risks. Concurrently, measures were taken to reinforce the efficiency of capital markets and the protection of investors, strengthen market infrastructures and combat the use of the financial system for the conduct of economic crimes.

2.2.2.2   *Institutional Developments in the Field of Public International Financial Law*
(1) The new conditions for the internationalised financial system's operation rendered necessary the establishment of new international institutions. While financial internationalisation began to take on significant dimensions, international cooperation on addressing the problems which arose as a result did not immediately follow the same course. As correctly argued:

> The regulation of financial activities and the institutions that conduct them continues to be carried out mostly by national (...) governments.[38]

---

[32] As already noted, this crisis is discussed in Chapter 3, under 3.1.1.

[33] See below, under 2.4.1.

[34] On this crisis, see Dewatripont and Tirole (1994), pp. 16, 21 and 70.

[35] On this crisis, see Kapstein (1994), pp. 155–166.

[36] On this crisis, see Dale (1996), pp. 189–195, and Walker (2001), pp. 275–282.

[37] On this crisis, which was the main trigger for the adoption by the Basel Committee on Banking Supervision of the 1988 'Basel Capital Accord', see Kapstein (1994), pp. 81–102.

[38] Herring and Litan (1995), p. 1; see also Giovanoli (2000), p. 6.

Amidst these conditions, several international fora were gradually established with a view to enhancing cooperation among national authorities (mainly central banks and financial supervisory authorities) and adopting rules, in the form of international standards contained in reports which constitute the sources of public international financial law. These fora, established within the framework of the **NIFA** and still operating, in certain cases considerably modified regarding their composition and tasks, are the by-product of the historical period under review (with one exception, namely the International Association of Deposit Insurers [**IADI**]).[39]

(2) It is also worth noting that in 1976 the G7 was created, the second intergovernmental international forum that played a significant role in the shaping of institutions of public international financial law.[40] Finally, by the end of the period under review the World Trade Organization ('**WTO**') was also established, the second pillar of which—the General Agreement on Trade in Services—laid down the basis for the liberalisation of trade in financial services.

2.2.3 The Period from the 'Asian Crisis' Until the Global Financial Crisis (2007–2009)

2.2.3.1 General Overview

The speed at which international capital movements began to take place (following their liberalisation) highlighted the systemic risk that might result from the sudden liquidation of financial investments, mainly due to amendments in national macroeconomic policies (or altered expectations—well-founded or speculative—for such a change), resulting, in its turn, in increased exposure of financial firms and markets to potential market and liquidity risks. The occurrence of such risks was the principal underlying factor (but not the cause) of the sovereign and generalised financial crises which erupted in Mexico (1994–1995), in several states of south-eastern Asia (1997–1998), in the Russian Federation (1998–1999), in Brazil (1998) and in Argentina (2000).[41]

Consequently, partly as a result of imperfect understanding of such risks (owing to a lack of experience) and hence an inability to effectively manage risks which are inherent in liberalised and strongly internationalised financial

---

[39] For an overview of all these fora, including the IADI, see under 2.3.3 below and in more detail in Chapter 3.

[40] See below, under 2.3.2.

[41] For a detailed analysis of the crises in question, which were crucial for the evolution of international regulatory interventions in contemporary financial systems, see, *inter alia*, Caprio and Klingebiel (1996) and (1999), Radelet and Sachs (1998) and Kane (2000) (both on the Asian crisis), Goldstein, Kaminsky and Reinhart (2000), Eichengreen and Bordo (2002), Yokoi-Arai (2002), pp. 5–52, Lowenfeld (2009), pp. 694–748 and Park and Wyplosz (2010), pp. 3–34. See also Gortsos (2012), pp. 125–126, for a representative example of how a generalised financial crisis may unfold in economically developing countries.

systems, and also partly due to a lack of adequate institutional and regulatory mechanisms for protecting financial firms and systems against exposure to such risks, the positive effects of the internationalisation of the financial system on economic growth were offset (in some cases to a great extent) by the occurrence of repeated crises, including the (2007–2009) global financial crisis (see just below).

2.2.3.2 Institutional Developments in the Field of Public International Financial Law

The above-mentioned crises and in particular that in south-eastern Asia (hereinafter the '**Asian crisis**') worked as a catalyst for two institutional developments of major importance in the field of public international financial law: the *first* was the creation in September 1999, upon a G7 initiative, of a third intergovernmental international forum, the G20. This forum was set up with the intention to bolster cooperation between advanced economies and economically 'dynamic' developing countries on economic and financial issues, and therewith take initiatives for the preservation of international financial stability to the benefit of sustainable global economic growth.[42] The *second*, equally important, institutional development was the creation of the Financial Stability Forum ('**FSF**'). Its objective was the coordination of the actions of its members, including most of the above-mentioned international fora, with a view to safeguarding the international financial system's stability, improving the conditions for market operation, and limiting the exposure of the financial system to systemic risks.[43]

2.2.4 The Period Since the Global Financial Crisis (GFC)

2.2.4.1 On the Causes and the Consequences of the (2007–2009) Global Financial Crisis

(1) Despite the existence of an extensive international financial framework, which was established gradually since the 1970s, the GFC erupted in 2007. This was triggered by events in the financial system of the US, spilled over to the world economy seriously affecting the stability of the financial system in several other states around the globe, had a serious negative impact on the real economy worldwide, and negatively affected confidence in the financial system at a large scale. The analysis of the causes of this crisis is beyond the

---

[42] It is worth noting that (unlike the definition of 'monetary stability', as synonymous to price stability) there is no widely accepted definition of 'financial stability'; on the various definitions of this term, see Houben, Kakes and Schinasi (2004), Schinasi (2006) and Pistor (2019) pp. 19–37, on the regulation of financial markets from the perspective of her (also above-mentioned) legal theory of finance (LTF).

[43] See further below, under 2.3.4.

scope of the present study. Very briefly, it can be pointed out that the crisis mainly relates to the following aspects[44]:

first, the implementation of inadequate monetary and fiscal policies in several states[45];

second, failures by financial firms, in particular[46] with regard to excesses in the asset securitisation processes according to the 'originate and distribute' banking model,[47] and excessive complexity of transactions; poor lending practices (especially in the US with regard to the household sector); excessive leverage and inefficient management of liquidity risk by banks; and imprudent remuneration policies adopted by several institutions;

third, inefficiencies and failures in the regulatory framework of the financial system, such as: lack of macroprudential policies (both in terms of regulation and oversight), of a regulatory framework for the operation of the shadow banking system (especially in the US), credit rating agencies and alternative investment funds (such as hedge funds); other failures in the microprudential regulation of financial firms; lack of transparency in trading of certain categories of financial instruments (namely bonds and financial derivatives); inadequacy of certain valuation methods for financial instruments in accordance with international accounting standards; and inadequacy of corporate governance rules for listed companies;

fourth, the extensive scope for regulatory arbitrage among financial products, markets and jurisdictions; and

finally, failures in the conduct of microprudential supervision of financial firms in several states.[48]

---

[44] On the causes of this crisis see, by means of indication (out of a vast existing literature), European Central Bank (2008), Kiff and Mills (2007), Borio (2008), Calomiris (2008), Eichengreen (2008), Laeven and Valencia (2008), Swoboda (2008), Gorton (2009), Goodhart (2009), pp. 2–29, Norberg (2009), Wehinger (2009), Gorton (2010), Posner (2010), pp. 13–245, Rajan (2010), Lastra and Wood (2010), pp. 537–545, Tirole (2010), pp. 11–47, Scott (2014) and Murphy (2022), pp. 47–81 (with specific emphasis on the role of OTC derivatives). For a comparison of the GFC with the international financial crisis of 1931 (both in terms of causes and in terms of regulatory reaction), see Moessner and Allen (2010). On the range of legal authorities and procedural issues presented by key facilities, which were implemented during that crisis in the US, see Alvarez, Baxter and Hoyt (2020).

[45] The primacy of this aspect is illustrated in the studies of Norberg (2009) and Rajan (2010).

[46] Lastra and Woods (2010) correctly point out also the 'usual suspects', i.e., greed and euphoria in periods of rapid growth and extensive credit provision.

[47] On this model, see also above in Chapter 1, under 1.2.1.

[48] See on this, especially with regard to the EU financial system, the de Larosire Report (2009), Chapter I, paragraphs 6–37 (pp. 7–12), and Smits (2010).

This crisis is eventually a manifest example supporting the view that the causes of a major financial crisis are not (and cannot be) one-dimensional but are a function of a combination of market, supervisory, regulatory and macroeconomic failures.[49] In the words of Honohan (1997, under 1.1):

> Systemic failures in the financial system are typically complex and they differ one from the other. In order to understand the processes involved it is necessary to schematize and simplify, but extreme reductionism is misleading.

(2) The consequence of this crisis, especially after the failure of the US investment bank *Lehman Brothers Inc.*,[50] was that several banks and other financial firms around the world (small or big, even SIFIs) were not able to absorb the losses from their risk exposure.[51] This development resulted, *inter alia*, in negative effects on the real economy, and obliged several governments (especially in the US and the EU) to adopt rescue packages and recovery plans in order to support or even bail out individual banks (and, in some cases, the entire banking system)[52]. Such governmental interventions weighed on state budgets and, in some cases, created serious fiscal imbalances, some of which evolved to fiscal crises,[53] which, in turn, spread to become new financial crises.[54]

2.2.4.2 Institutional Developments in the Field of Public International Financial Law

Expectedly, this crisis has become a catalyst for 're-adjusting' the rules of public international financial law that applied before the crisis broke out, as is the case with every crisis, no matter if it is a banking crisis, a foreign exchange

---

[49] On the related above-mentioned "financial instability hypothesis" of Minsky of 1992, which has been at the centre of academic discussions after the eruption of that crisis, see Krugman (2012), pp. 41–53.

[50] See on this, by means of mere indication, Claessens, Herring and Schoenmaker (2010), pp. 42–46.

[51] On the case of the Swiss bank *UBS*, see, by means of mere indication, Thévenoz (2010) and Alexander (2019), pp. 105–106. On the cases of the US-based insurance undertaking *American International Group Inc. (AIG)*, the Belgium-based *Fortis Bank* and *Dexia Bank* (whose holding company was also seated in Belgium), see Claessens, Herring and Schoenmaker (2010), pp. 46–51.

[52] The most striking example is that of Iceland. See Claessens, Herring and Schoenmaker (2010), pp. 51–53.

[53] The most striking examples are those of Ireland and Cyprus. In the former case, with a sole exception, all Irish credit institutions were exposed to insolvency after the financial crisis and needed to be recapitalised; on the Irish crisis, see Eichengreen (2015), Zeissler, Ikeda and Metrick (2014) and Hadjiemmanuil (2020), pp. 1198–1305. On the Cypriot crisis, see, by means of mere indication, Orphanides (2014), Hadjiemmanuil (2020), pp. 1343–1345, Piantelli (2021), pp. 72–76 and Gortsos (2022a), with extensive further references.

[54] See also the 2011 study of the CGFS discussed in Chapter 1 above, under 1.1.3.

crisis or a **'twin' crisis**.⁵⁵ On the contrary, institutional developments were quite restricted and less spectacular. In particular, since November 2008, the G20 started holding summits at the level of Heads of State or Government. *Furthermore*, at the G20 London Summit, held in April 2009, the decision was taken to re-establish the Financial Stability Forum as 'Financial Stability Board', to expand its membership and enhance its tasks. At the same Summit, the decision was taken to expand the membership of several international fora participated in by all G20 Member States in order to enhance their representativeness.

2.2.4.3   The Impact of the COVID-19 Pandemic Crisis
(1) The COVID-19 pandemic crisis (hereinafter **'pandemic crisis'**), an extraordinary challenge **in living memory** with severe human and social consequences around the globe, was triggered by a low-probability non-financial risk. Its onset also presented a significant shock to the global economy; as eloquently pointed out by the General Manager of the BIS, Agustin Carstens:

> The Covid-19 pandemic and the induced global lockdown are a truly historic event. Never before has the global economy been deliberately put into an induced coma. This is no normal recession, but one that results from explicit policy choices to avoid a large-scale public health disaster. The unique character of this recession poses unfamiliar challenges.⁵⁶

(2) Even worse economic outcomes were prevented by extraordinary policy support. All countries affected by the pandemic immediately took bold measures aiming at four (equally important) objectives: dealing with health emergency needs; supporting economic activity and employment; preserving monetary and financial stability; and preparing the ground for recovery. These contained a mix of extensive government fiscal *stimuli*, emergency liquidity measures⁵⁷ and monetary policy measures by central banks, as well as

---

⁵⁵ See Chapter 1 above, under 1.1.3, as well.

⁵⁶ See Carstens (2020), pp. 1–2. According to the IMF's World Economic Outlook Update for April 2020 (at: https://www.imf.org/en/Publications/WEO/Issues/2020/04/14/weo-april-2020), the global economy was projected to contract sharply by 3% in 2020, much worse than during the 2007–2009 financial crisis; nevertheless, the risks for even more severe outcomes were substantial and as a matter of fact the contraction reached the level of 3.3% (4.7% for advanced economies).

⁵⁷ In this respect, central banks (including predominantly the U.S. Federal Reserve) acted as lenders of last resort by entering into international currency swaps in order to alleviate funding problems among foreign banks. They also acted as (temporary) market makers of last resort ('MMLR') in order to improve the liquidity of markets whose illiquidity pose a threat to financial stability or to the transmission mechanism of monetary policy. See on this also Committee on the Global Financial System (2020).

measures relating to the application of financial micro- and macroprudential regulations.[58]

With regard to the focus of the measures taken, four pillars can be identified: expectedly, the *first* was the provision of funding to address (mainly or concurrently) spending on public health care; *second*, direct support of financing for companies in the real sector of the economy, especially for (but not confined to) small and medium enterprises, has also been addressed in a thorough way; this was also the goal (*via* indirect channels) of the monetary policy measures adopted by central banks, the flexibility proposed by supervisory authorities in the application of microprudential banking regulations, and the release of capital and liquidity buffers[59]; the *third* pillar of the measures taken, closely related to the second, was employment support; and finally, the *fourth* pillar was the support of economies' recovery in the medium to long term. Their life cycle varied as well: while some were earmarked for the entire (albeit not clear yet) duration of the crisis and would thereafter be discontinued, others were designed as **temporary**, i.e., to have a medium- to long-term horizon.

(3) Two elements clearly set the current pandemic crisis apart from the GFC: *first*, its **root cause**: the crisis originated outside the financial system, and it is a rather **'black swan' event**, which originated in a health disaster; and *second*, the **first-round focus** was on the rescue of companies in the economy's real sector. Global financial reforms implemented following the GFC significantly helped banks, which were at the centre of that crisis, absorb the shock caused by the pandemic and, hence, they were, on a global scale, much better capitalised and with stronger liquidity (the **"Basel III impact"**).[60] As noted in the Press release of the BSCB at the initial phase of the pandemic, namely on **20 March 2020**[61]:

> The Basel III standards have strengthened the resilience of the banking system over the past decade (and the) the global banking system has significantly higher levels of capital and liquidity and is therefore in a stronger position to absorb shocks and mitigate interruptions to banking services.

---

[58] For a summary of the measures taken on a global basis, see the IMF Policy Tracker "Policy Responses to COVID-19" (at: https://www.imf.org/en/Topics/imf-and-covid19/Policy-Responses-to-COVID-19) and the Yale Program on Financial Stability's "COVID-19 Financial Response Tracker" (at: https://docs.google.com/spreadsheets/d/1s6EgMa4KGDfFzcsZJKqwiH7yqkhnCQtW7gI7eHpZuqg/edit#gid=0).

[59] Noteworthy was the guidance on micro- and macroprudential banking regulations aimed at inducing banks to finance the real sector of the economy without allowing (at least in the short term) for the built-up of conditions of financial instability (which is, indeed, a very delicate exercise).

[60] On the "Basel III regulatory framework", see further below, under 2.4.1.

[61] "Basel Committee coordinates policy and supervisory response to Covid-19", at: https://www.bis.org/press/p200320.htm.

(4) Nevertheless, the pandemic was the first major test of the global financial system since the **G20 global financial reforms** were put in place following the GFC. Even though the nature of measures taken in almost all jurisdictions was quite similar in the field of financial regulation, the interventions of the G20, at the level of heads of state and government, were comparatively vague, at least during the initial phase of the pandemic and the strategy at international level was not as coordinated and comprehensive as at the onset and in the aftermath of the **GFC**.[62] *On the other hand*, the role of international financial fora (standard setting bodies, **SSBs**), such as the **FSB**, the Basel Committee and the **IOSCO**, and to a lesser extent the **IADI** and the **IAIS**, in contributing to the preservation of 'global financial stability' amidst the pandemic was quite significant. Remarkable were also the widespread interventions of the **OECD** whose work, nevertheless, is not centred to financial stability issues. Pursuant to the (then) FSB Chair, Randal Quarles,[63] the work of the FSB during the pandemic focused on five aspects[64]: *first*, assessment of vulnerabilities during the pandemic; *second*, reinforcement of resilient non-bank financial intermediation ('**NBFI**'); *third*, identification and assessment of policy responses (mainly via the identification of indicators to help assess the efficiency of policy actions and the coordination of national supervisory and regulatory actions, taking account of cross-border spill-over effects); *fourth*, monitoring consistency with international financial standards taking into account its commitment to agreed-upon financial reforms); and *finally*, using flexibility in standards and buffer use[65] (for a summary, see Table 2.1).

---

[62] Initially, there were only two official "G20 Statements on COVID-19", of 12 and 26 March (at: https://g20.org/en/media/Documents/G20%20Sherpas%27%20Statement%20on%20COVID-19%20-%20March%2012%2c%202020_v9%20%28clean%29.pdf and https://www.gov.uk/government/news/g20-leaders-summit-statement-on-covid-19-26-march-2020). On this "global dysfunction" problem, see Patrick (2020).

[63] At: https://www.fsb.org/2020/07/fsb-chairs-letter-to-g20-finance-ministers-and-central-bank-governors-july-2020. Randal Quarles is Governor and Vice Chair of the US Federal Reserve.

[64] The letter also emphasised the FSB's commitment to continue working towards supporting a smooth transition away from the London Interbank Offer Rate ('LIBOR') and developing a roadmap to improve cross-border payments.

[65] A stocktaking of the BCBS's actions is laid down in its Report of 6 July 2021, titled "Early lessons from the Covid-19 pandemic on the Basel reforms" (at: https://www.bis.org/bcbs/bcbs_work.htm) which addresses three key aspects: *first*, throughout the pandemic, banks continued to provide critical services, including lending; *second*, the banking system would have faced greater stress had the Basel III framework not been adopted and in the absence of extraordinary support measures taken by public authorities to mitigate the impact of the pandemic; and *third*, the financial reforms after the GFC have achieved their broad objective of strengthening the resilience of the banking system, since the increased quality and higher levels of capital and liquidity in the global banking system helped banks to absorb the significant economic impact of the pandemic. This Report makes part of the BCBS's "Work program and strategic priorities for 2021/2022", published on 16 April 2021 (at: https://www.bis.org/bcbs/publ/d521.htm), which highlighted several areas to be further monitored, such as pandemic resilience and recovery, horizon scanning, analysis of structural trends and mitigation of risks, as well as the

Table 2.1 The work of the Financial Stability Board (FSB) and the Basel Committee (BCBS) amidst the first phases of the pandemic crisis

(1) The work of the Financial Stability Board (FSB)

2020	
20 March	Press release on active global cooperation to maintain global financial stability (especially during the pandemic-induced March 2020 market turmoil), keep markets open and functioning and preserve the financial system's capacity to finance growth
2 April	Press release on action taken by FSB members to ensure continuity of critical functions of financial services throughout the pandemic
15 April	Report on "International cooperation to address the financial stability implications of COVID-19"
1 July	Statement "on the impact of COVID-19 on global benchmark reform"
15 July	First Report after the onset of the pandemic to the G20 Finance Ministers and Governors on "COVID-19 Pandemic: Financial Stability Implications and Policy Measures Taken"
17 November	FSB Chair's first letter to G20 Leaders after the pandemic's onset ahead of their 2020 Summit
	Report on "COVID-19 Pandemic: Financial Stability Impact and Policy Responses"
	Report on "Holistic Review of the March Market Turmoil"
18 November	"2020 Resolution Report: Be prepared"
16 December	"Global Monitoring Report on Non-Bank Financial Intermediation 2020"
2021	
31 March	Resolution-related Final Report on the "Evaluation of the effects of too-big-to-fail reforms"
6 April	Report on "COVID-19 support measures: Extending, amending and ending"
7 July	FSB Chair letter to the G20 Finance Ministers and Central Bank Governors
13 July	Interim Report on "Lessons learnt from the COVID-19 pandemic from a financial stability perspective"
20 March	Press release on the banking supervisory implications of the pandemic, actively coordinating its responses with the FSB and other standard setting bodies

(continued)

Table 2.1 (continued)

(1) The work of the Financial Stability Board (FSB)	
27 March	Postponement of the implementation of the revised market risk framework, the Complement to Basel III and the revised Pillar 3 disclosure requirements to 1 January 2023; and the transitional arrangements for the output floor accompanying the Complement to 1 January 2028
2020	
3 April	Set of additional measures to alleviate the financial and economic impact of the pandemic on the global banking system relating to expected credit loss ('ECL') accounting frameworks; margin requirements for non-centrally cleared derivative; as well as the annual assessment of G-SIBs and the revised G-SIB framework
2021	
31 March	"Principles for operational resilience"
16 April	"Work program and strategic priorities for 2021/2022"
6 July	Report on "Early lessons from the Covid-19 pandemic on the Basel reforms"

2.3 The Four Levels of Making and Enforcement of Law and Policy

2.3.1 Introduction

In examining, in the previous Section, the gradual evolution of public international financial law over the last decades we identified the existence of several international fora, which along with certain intergovernmental fora and a limited number of international organisations are the main actors in the process of making and enforcing the rules of public international financial law. In the present chapter, we undertake a more in-depth analysis of this process. The starting point is that the making and enforcement of the rules of public international financial law takes place at four levels: the level of political decision-making; the level of the adoption of the rules of international financial law; the coordination level; *and* that of the indirect enforcement of the rules of international financial law.[66]

2.3.2 The Level of Political Decision-Making

2.3.2.1 Introductory Remarks

The dominant political role within the framework of the international architecture of the financial system has been entrusted to three intergovernmental fora (presented in chronological order of establishment): the Group of Ten (or G10), the Group of Seven (or G7) and the Group of Twenty (or G20), which currently play the most important role. Distinct from these fora is the G30, which was set up in 1978 as a not-for-profit international body of private law, with the participation not only of the public, but also of the private sector, as well as the academic community. Its work consists in deepening the understanding of international economic and financial issues, investigating the effects of the decisions made by the public and private sector, and examining feasible alternative solutions. It periodically issues reports, with recommendations on monetary and financial issues.[67]

2.3.2.2 The G10

The G10 was set up in 1962 with the participation of Belgium, Canada, France, Germany, Italy, Japan, The Netherlands, the UK, the US and Sweden. Switzerland also participates in this forum since 1984 (hence, the members

---

strengthening of supervisory coordination and practices. For a comprehensive discussion about the role of international financial fora in preserving global financial stability amidst the first cycle of the pandemic crisis, see Gortsos (2023).

[66] See just below, under 2.3.2–2.3.5, respectively. The following analysis is based—albeit differentiated regarding certain aspects—on Giovanoli (2000) and was further developed in Gortsos (2012), pp. 131–159.

[67] For more information on the work of this Group, see: https://www.group30.org.

of the G10 are eleven).⁶⁸ The justification for setting up the G10 was the creation of a financing mechanism, the so-called General Arrangements to Borrow ('**GAB**').⁶⁹ This was established for the provision of funds to the **IMF** when its existing funds proved to be insufficient for the fulfilment of one of its main statutory tasks, which consists in the financial assistance of its members when facing problems in their balance of payments.⁷⁰ The meetings of the G10 take place either at the level of Finance Ministers and Central Bank Governors (twice a year), or only at the level of Central Bank Governors (six times a year).⁷¹ Without prejudice to the initiatives of the G7, for more than thirty years, the G10 has been the main intergovernmental forum responsible for matters relating to the governance of the international monetary and financial system. Since 1999 though, these issues are mainly discussed at the G20.

2.3.2.3 The G7

(1) The G7 was set up in 1976, a few years after the abolition of the international system of fixed exchange rates of the IMF, and the first oil crisis, with a view to dealing at a political level with the problems that had arisen accordingly. Its original and current members are the seven economically most developed countries in the world (at the time of its creation), notably: the US, Germany, France, Canada, Japan, the UK and Italy (i.e., the members of the G10, with the exception of Belgium, The Netherlands, Sweden and Switzerland),⁷² as well as the EU, which is represented by the European Commission, the ECB and the President of the Eurogroup.⁷³ The meetings of this forum take place at the level of Finance Ministers and Central Bank Governors, where issues concerning the international economic and financial system are discussed. The findings of the discussions in question are published in the form of 'final communiqués'. It is noted, however, that the annual 'G7 summits' are attended by the Heads of State or Government of the above-mentioned states, as well as by the EU, represented jointly by the Presidents of the European Commission and the European Council.⁷⁴

---

⁶⁸ The IMF, the BIS, the OECD and the European Commission have observer status.

⁶⁹ The central bank of Switzerland also takes part in the GAB since April 1984, while an equivalent agreement has been signed with the government of Saudi Arabia as well. On this mechanism, as well as the mechanism of the New Arrangements to Borrow ('NAB'), see Lowenfeld (2009), pp. 658–662.

⁷⁰ On the role of the IMF, see below, under 2.3.5.

⁷¹ This Forum's work figures on the website of the BIS at: https://www.bis.org/publ/g10.htm.

⁷² This Forum does not have an internet address either. G7 is to be distinguished from G8, with the participation of the members of G7 plus the Russian Federation. The G8 holds meetings on an annual basis at the level of Heads of State or Government to discuss broader political and economic issues of international interest.

⁷³ COM/2015/602 final, Section 2.

⁷⁴ *Ibid.*

(2) Indicative G7 initiatives on the international architecture of the financial system include the creation of other international intergovernmental fora, such as the G22 and the G20, international fora adopting international standards pertaining to the achievement of specific policy objectives relating to regulatory intervention in the financial system, such as the Financial Action Task Force (FATF) and the Financial Stability Forum (FSF).[75]

2.3.2.4 The G20

As already noted,[76] the G20 was set up in 1999 on the initiative of the G7, as a successor to G22 which had been set up a year earlier.[77] The purpose of its creation, in the aftermath of the above-mentioned international financial crises of the 1990s, was the need for a forum to enhance the cooperation between advanced economies and economically 'dynamic' developing countries (mainly EMEs). Its main task consists in seeking compromise solutions between the (sometimes contradictory) positions of these two groups of states on international monetary and financial matters to ensure the achievement of all the related policy objectives.[78]

Members of the G20 are the following: the Member States of the G7, represented at the level of Finance Ministers and Central Bank Governors; twelve economically developing states/EMEs (Argentina, Australia, Brazil, China, India, Indonesia, Mexico, Russian Federation, South Africa, Saudi Arabia, the Republic of Korea (South Korea) and Turkey), also represented at the level of Finance Ministers and Central Bank Governors, considered as 'systemically important', in the sense that the occurrence of a crisis in their financial system might have an international impact; the EU, represented by the Presidents of the Commission, the Council and the **ECB**[79]; and *ex officio*, the Managing Director of the **IMF**, the President of the World Bank, and the

---

[75] See below, under 2.3.3 and 2.3.4, respectively.

[76] See above, under 2.2.3.

[77] The G20 is also defined as a group of economically developing countries (currently 23), which was set up in 2003 in the framework of the World Trade Organization (WTO), and whose main task consists in the further liberalisation of international trade in goods (at: https://en.wikipedia.org/wiki/G20_developing_nations).

[78] On the G20 see indicatively Giovanoli (2010), pp. 15–17, Thiele (2014), pp. 534–545, Alexander, Lorez, Jackson and Moloney (2014) and Nobel (2019), pp. 274–288 (see also at: https://www.g20.org). Bremmer and Roubini (2011) have heavily criticised the efficiency of the G20's work (talking about a 'G-zero world'). A more general criticism of the efficiency of the G20 to deal with issues pertaining to the financial system is based on three (legitimate) arguments: its Member States are usually not at the same point of the economic cycle; the exposure to fragility of its Member States' financial systems is usually significantly different; and several of its Member States (obviously the economically less developed and developing) do not have deep financial markets and SIFIs.

[79] COM/2015/602 final, Sect. 2.

Table 2.2 G20 members

States represented by their Ministers of Finance and Central Bank Governors		Ex officio
G7 member states	Other states	
Canada France Germany Italy Japan United Kingdom United States	Argentina Australia Brazil China India Indonesia Mexico Republic of Korea Russian Federation Saudi Arabia South Africa Turkey	• Managing Director of the IMF • President of the World Bank • President of the International Monetary and Financial Committee of the IMF and • President of the Development Committee of the IMF and the World Bank

The EU is represented by the Presidents of the European Commission, the Council and the ECB

heads of the International Monetary and Financial Committee and the Development Committee—the two committees which function, respectively, under the auspices of the two international organisations in question.[80] In order to ensure a regional balance over time, the G20 Presidency rotates on an annual basis. Due to the severity of the **GFC**, since November 2008, '**G20 Summits**' have been held at the level of Heads of State or Government. In these Summits, the Presidency formally invites also representatives from other countries to participate under observer status (Table 2.2).

2.3.3 The Level of Adoption of the Rules of Public International Financial Law

2.3.3.1 International Fora: Importance, Legal Characteristics and Criteria for Classification

(1) The vast majority of the rules of public international financial law, in the form of international financial standards, which are aimed at the achievement, with resort to international cooperation, of the policy objectives relating to

---

[80] It is noted that Switzerland is not a member of the G20, even though Basel is the seat for the BIS and for most of the international fora, including the Financial Stability Board, adopting international financial standards, which are included in the reports constituting the sources of public international financial law.

regulatory intervention in the financial system, are being adopted by international fora which do not have the capacity of an international organisation. These fora have not been established by virtue of an international treaty, but are usually set up, as already mentioned, *ad hoc* and in several cases as a response of the international community to major financial crises with international dimensions. In several cases, they do not have a charter or articles of association and are not administered by formal organs and are referred to as 'standard-setting bodies', or 'standard-setters'. Their main objective (except for the Committee on the Global Financial System (CGFS)) consists in the adoption of international financial standards.[81] They are considered as members of the "**international financial regulatory community**". Boyle and Chinkin (2007) characterise them as 'transnational networks', making a distinction between 'sub-state networks with the participation of administrative agencies' and 'professional networks'.[82]

(2) The international fora under review can be classified into different categories according to several criteria. Based *on their composition*, these international fora can be systematically classified in the following five categories (presented in more detail in Chapter **3**):

> The *first* category consists of four international fora with the participation of representatives from national supervisory and regulatory authorities from the three main sectors of the financial system (public administrative authorities and, in certain cases, central banks, mainly for the banking sector). These fora are also usually referred to as 'sector-specific groupings of supervisors and regulators' and include: the **Basel Committee on Banking Supervision**, acting in the subject-area of micro- and macroprudential banking regulation; the **International Organisation of Securities Commissions (IOSCO)**, acting in the subject-areas of micro- and macroprudential regulation and microprudential supervision of investment firms; the **International Association of Insurance Supervisors ('IAIS')**, acting in the subject-area of micro- and macroprudential regulation and microprudential supervision of insurance and reinsurance undertakings; and the **Joint Forum**, acting in the subject-area of microprudential regulation and supervision of financial conglomerates.
>
> The *second* category consists of two international fora with the participation of representatives (experts) from national central banks (also called 'committees of central bank experts'): the **Committee on Payments and Markets Infrastructures ('CPMI'**, formerly known as 'Committee on Payment and Settlement Systems, **'CPSS'**), acting in the issue-area of payment and settlement systems' oversight; and the **Committee on the Global Financial System (CGFS)**, which is the only international

---

[81] On this term, see Giovanoli (2000), p. 8, and Norton (2001), p. 14.

[82] See Boyle and Chinkin (2007), pp. 50–52, with reference to Slaughter (2000) and to Baldwin (1907), respectively.

forum which is not a standard-setter, but still very important in terms of research.

The *third* category consists of the **International Association of Deposit Insurers ('IADI')** with the participation of representatives from national deposit insurance organisations.

The *fourth* category comprises two private professional associations, and more specifically the **International Accounting Standards Board ('IASB')**, which adopts international accounting standards, and the **International Federation of Accountants ('IFAC')**, which adopts international auditing standards.

The *fifth* category comprises the **Financial Action Task Force on Money Laundering ('FATF')**, with a (mainly) intergovernmental composition, which is active in the subject-area of combatting money laundering and terrorist financing.[83]

It is also noted that at the Toronto G20 Summit in June 2010, the G20 leaders reiterated their commitment to improve access to financial services for the poor by endorsing a set of "Principles for Innovative Financial Inclusion", aimed at forming the basis of a concrete and pragmatic action plan for improving access to financial services among the poor. The G20 approved the Financial Inclusion Action Plan and set up a new international forum, the **Global Partnership for Financial Inclusion (GPFI)**, to provide a systematic coordination and implementation structure for this action plan, which is also participated in by the World Bank and the OECD.[84]

Other criteria for the classification of these international fora are the period during the evolution of international law in which they were established; their 'global representativeness[85]; and their headquarters, especially taking into account that the majority is based in Basel at the seat of the BIS as part of the so-called **'Basel Process'** (as further discussed in this Section below) (Table 2.3).

2.3.3.2 *International Organisations*
Introductory Remarks

The only international economic organisations involved in the making of public international financial law are the **WTO** with regard to the liberalisation of international trade in financial services, and the **OECD** with regard to the

---

[83] These fora are further presented in Chapter 3 below; see also Giovanoli (2000), pp. 20–29, Chiti and Wessel (2011), Thiele (2014), pp. 552–554, Wandel (2014), pp. 30–44, Lastra (2015), pp. 501–507 and Armour *et al.* (2016), pp. 619–625.

[84] See on this Global Partnership for Financial Inclusion (2014).

[85] This aspect is addressed in Giovanoli (2000), pp. 30–32.

Table 2.3 International fora (in chronological order of establishment)

Forum	Year of establishment	Seat	Regular membership	Objective
Committee on the Global Financial System (CGFS)	1971	Basel	Central banks	Study of financial systems
International Accounting Standards Board (IASB)	1973	London	Accountancy	International accounting standards
Basel Committee on Banking Supervision (BCBS)	1974	Basel	Banking supervisory authorities	Banking regulation and supervision
International Federation of Accountants (IFAC)	1977	New York	Professional accounting associations	International auditing standards
International Organisation of Securities Commissions (IOSCO)	1983	Madrid	Capital markets' supervisory authorities	Capital markets' regulation and supervision
Financial Action Task Force on Money Laundering (FATF)	1989	Paris	G7 States, European Commission and Gulf Cooperation Council	Combatting money laundering and terrorist financing
Committee on Payments and Market Infrastructures (CPMI)	1990	Basel	Central banks	Oversight of payments and market infrastructures
International Association of Insurance Supervisors (IAIS)	1994	Basel	Supervisory authorities for the insurance sector	Insurance sector regulation and supervision
Joint Forum	1996	Basel	BCBS, IOSCO, IAIS and national supervisory authorities	Regulation and supervision of financial conglomerates
International Association of Deposit Insurers (IADI)	2002	Basel	Deposit guarantee organisations	Operation of deposit guarantee systems
Global Partnership for Financial Inclusion (GPFI)	2010		Various	Financial inclusion

adoption of international financial standards on corporate governance.[86] In this context, specific reference must first be made to the BIS, even though this international organisation neither participates *per se* in the adoption of international financial standards nor adopts any rules related to public international financial law.

The Bank for International Settlements

(a) General aspects: The Bank for International Settlements (**BIS**) is an international organisation established in 1930 by the Hague Convention and signed among six states and Switzerland.[87] As of **December 2022**, shareholders of the BIS, a private limited liability company by shares[88] under Swiss law,[89] whose seat is located in Basel, were sixty-two national central banks and monetary authorities, as well as the ECB, which have voting rights and right of representation at its General Meetings.[90] The statutory tasks of the BIS consist of the following: promotion of cooperation between its member central banks, provision of additional facilities to central banks for international financial transactions (in this sense, it is also a bank, since it has the power to accept deposits from central banks and international organisations and provide short-term credit to other central banks), and acting as a trustee or agent with regard to international financial settlements entrusted to it under agreements with the parties concerned.[91]

(b) In particular, the 'Basel Process': In fulfilling its first task as above, the BIS plays an important role in the context of the international financial architecture. This is due to the close links existing between the monetary and the financial system and the fact that in several states the central bank is the supervisory and regulatory authority of one or more main sectors of the financial system. In this framework, the BIS is host to ten committees, groups and associations, which are part of the **'Basel Process'**. This term the role of the BIS

---

[86] International standards are also adopted by the IMF on issues of macroeconomic policy and relevant data transparency, and by the World Bank on issues concerning, on a horizontal level, the insolvency of businesses.

[87] The text of this Convention is available at: https://www.bis.org/about/convention-en.pdf. The initial Statutes of the BIS are available at: https://www.bis.org/about/charter-en.pdf.

[88] Statutes (2005), Article 1. The BIS Statutes of 20 January 1930, as in force after the last amendment of 7 November 2016 (and effective from 1 January 2010) are available at: https://www.bis.org/about/statutes-en.pdf.

[89] The operation of the BIS in Switzerland is governed by the provisions of the "Headquarters Agreement" of 1987 (as currently in force). This agreement is available at: https://www.bis.org/about/headquart-en.pdf.

[90] The ECB became a shareholder of the BIS in 2000, by amendment of Article 15 of the BIS's Statutes to the effect its members are central banks in general, and not only national central banks (as initially provided for).

[91] Statutes (2005), Article 3, as further specified in Articles 19–25. For an analytical study on the work of the BIS during the period 1930–1973, see Toniolo (2005). On its more recent tasks, see Nobel (2019), pp. 300–305.

in hosting and supporting the work of the international secretariats engaged in standard-setting in the pursuit of financial stability. It is based on three key features: *first*, synergies of co-location; *second*, flexibility and openness in the exchange of information; and *third*, support from BIS expertise in the fields of economics, banking and regulation.[92]

The BIS provides secretarial support to six of the above-mentioned international fora (namely, the Basel Committee (and through this also to the Joint Forum), the IAIS, the CPMI, the CGFS and the IADI), and to the Financial Stability Board (FSB).[93] For all these fora, the BIS secretariat prepares meetings, draws up background papers and reports and publishes their work. The following international fora are also operating under the auspices of the BIS: the **Markets Committee** (formerly known as the 'Committee on Gold and Foreign Exchange'), dealing with structural developments that can have an impact on short-term market dynamics. Members of this committee are senior officials responsible for market operations in the G10 central banks and the ECB[94]; the **Irving Fisher Committee on Central Bank Statistics**, whose members are senior officials responsible for statistics in the G10 central banks and the ECB[95]; and the **Central Bank Governance Forum**, which serves as a venue for the exchange of views on matters of interest relating to the design and operation of central banks; its Members are central bankers *in personam*[96] and it consists of the **'Central Bank Governance Network'**, connecting individuals with central banks, and the **'Central Bank Governance Group'**, which provides a discussion forum for central bank governors and acts as a steering committee for the Forum.

In terms of governance, three BIS bodies are involved, while the FSB, the IAIS and the IADI each have their own governance arrangements:

> *First*, the Basel Committee's oversight body is the **Group of Governors and Heads of Supervision ('GHOS')**, which is further discussed in Chapter 3.[97]
>
> *Second*, the **Global Economy Meeting ('GEM')**, which comprises the Governors from thirty-one BIS member central banks in major advanced economies and in **EMEs** that account for about 4/5 of the global gross domestic product (**'GDP'**),[98] provides guidance to three central

---

[92] See also at: https://www.bis.org/about/basel_process.htm.

[93] See just below, under 2.3.4.

[94] On the work of this Committee, see: https://www.bis.org/about/factmktc.htm.

[95] On the work of this Committee, see: https://www.bis.org/ifc/index.htm.

[96] On the work of this Forum, see: https://www.bis.org/hub/cbgf.htm.

[97] See Chapter 3, under 3.1.5.

[98] Members of the GEM are the central bank Governors of Argentina, Australia, Belgium, Brazil, Canada, China, France, Germany, Hong Kong SAR, India, Indonesia, Italy, Japan, Korea, Malaysia, Mexico, The Netherlands, Poland, Russian Federation, Saudi Arabia, Singapore, South Africa, Spain, Sweden, Switzerland, Thailand, Turkey, the UK

Table 2.4 Governance of the 'Basel process'

Oversight body	Fora oversighted
Group of Governors and Heads of Supervision (GHOS)	Basel Committee on Banking Supervision
Global Economy Meeting (GEM)	CGFS—CPMI—Markets Committee
All Governors' Meeting	Central Bank Governance Forum
	Irving Fisher Committee on Central Bank Statistics
No oversight body	FSB—IAIS—IADI

bank committees/fora, namely the CGFS, the CPMI and the Markets Committee. The GEM oversees their organisation and appoints their chairs, receives reports from the committees, decides on their publication and provides guidance on work priorities. A smaller group of central bank Governors in the Economic Consultative Committee ('**ECC**') supports the GEM by preparing proposals for discussion and decision.[99] The GEM's second main task is the monitoring and assessment of developments, risks and opportunities in the world economy and the global financial system.

Finally, the **All Governors' Meeting**, whose membership is broader than that of the GEM since it comprises the Governors of all BIS member central banks, oversees the work of two other fora, namely the Central Bank Governance Forum and the Irving Fisher Committee (Table 2.4).

The World Trade Organization (WTO)

(1) The WTO was set up in 1994, within the framework of the 'Uruguay Round' of international trade negotiations. The Uruguay Round was the first round of multilateral negotiations, where the issue of the liberalisation of international trade in services was discussed. Part of the Final Act with which the Uruguay Round was completed was the General Agreement on Trade in Services ('**GATS**').[100] This was the first multilateral framework of rules and principles by which the Member States of the WTO, headquartered in Geneva, undertook general obligations and specific commitments with regard to the

---

and the US, as well as the Presidents of the ECB and of the Federal Reserve Bank of New York. The Governors of another 19 central banks attend the GEM as observers.

[99] The ECC includes all BIS Board member Governors, the central bank Governors from India and Brazil and the BIS General Manager and assembles proposals for consideration by the GEM. Its Chair (the Chairperson of the GEM) also initiates recommendations to the GEM on the appointment of chairs of the main central bank committees and on the composition and organisation of those committees.

[100] The Treaty establishing the WTO was signed in Marrakech (Morocco) on 15 April 1994 and its provisions came into force on 1 January 1995.

liberalisation of international trade in services, in a way which corresponded to the regime governing international trade in goods.[101] However, negotiations on financial services were not completed when the Uruguay Round came to a close, even though the specific provisions which govern trade in financial services were finalised at that time with the signing of the "First Annex on Financial Services", and the "Understanding on Commitments in Financial Services".[102]

(2) Since the range of specific commitments which most Member States had undertaken with regard to financial services was not broad, while many Member States made extensive use of the exemptions from the obligations of Article II (including the US), the prolongation of the negotiations until 30 June 1995 was decided upon, in accordance with the "Second Annex on Financial Services".[103] However, the completion of the negotiations in 1995 did not prove possible either, since the progress which was made by the members as to the undertaking of specific commitments and the abolition of exemptions from the obligations of Article II continued to be unsatisfactory.

(3) The "Second Protocol to the General Agreement on Trade in Services" contains the product of a so-called "Interim Agreement" of 24 July 1995,[104] by which some of its members undertook additional specific commitments in the field of financial services entering into force on 1 September 1996, and the next deadline for the completion of the negotiations was set on 12 December 1997. This new deadline was abided by. The outcome of the negotiations is included in the "Fifth Protocol to the General Agreement on Trade in Services",[105] which had to be approved by all WTO members that submitted a Table of specific commitments by 29 January 1999 and came into force on 1 March of that year. Annexed to this Protocol were sixteen lists of exemptions from the obligations of Article II and fifty-six Tables of specific commitments (which involved 70 members, since the Member States of the EU were represented by the European Commission and submitted a single Table).[106]

---

[101] See Lowenfeld (2009), pp. 117–128 and Van den Bossche (2008).

[102] See, by means of mere indication, Von Bogdandy and Windsor (2008), pp. 618–639 and 647–666, respectively. Para 2 of the Annex on Financial Services lays down a "prudential carve out", according to which "*members are not prevented from taking measures for prudential reasons, including for the protection of investors, depositors [and (insurance)] policy holders (...)*". Accordingly, any such measure shall not be subject to the specific commitments made to GATS; see *Ibid.*, pp. 634–636 and in detail Yokoi-Arai (2008).

[103] Von Bogdandy and Windsor (2008), p. 640.

[104] *Ibid.*, pp. 641–642.

[105] *Ibid.*, pp. 643–646.

[106] On a Guide to the Uruguay Round Agreements, see World Trade Organization (1999).

The Organisation for Economic Co-operation and Development (OECD)

(1) The OECD was set up in 1961 by the Paris Convention.[107] Based in Paris, it is participated in by thirty-eight (mainly) advanced economies and EMEs from across the world.[108] Its statutory tasks consist in the following: *first*, achieving the highest sustainable economic growth and development and a rising standard of living among its members, while maintaining financial stability, to contribute to the development of the world economy; *second*, contributing to sound economic expansion in its member states, as well as in its non-member states in the process of economic development; and *third*, contributing to the expansion of world trade on a multilateral, non-discriminatory basis pursuant to international obligations.[109]

(2) The inclusion of the OECD in the group of international economic organisations taking part in the governance of the international financial architecture can be attributed to three factors: *first*, it is they only one that elaborates international financial standards with regard to the corporate governance of companies which are listed in regulated markets[110]; *furthermore*, the above-mentioned Financial Action Task Force operates under its auspices and *finally*, it is under its aegis that international cooperation in the fields of consumer protection and financial literacy takes place.

2.3.4 The Level of Coordination: The Financial Stability Board (FSB)

2.3.4.1 The Financial Stability Forum (FSF) as a 'Forerunner': Establishment Membership and Tasks

(1) The significant number of international fora set up in the context of the international architecture of the financial system with regard to the adoption of international financial standards, according to the above analysis, and subsequently the fragmented nature of the system, is a direct corollary of the fact that the achievement of policy objectives relating to regulatory intervention in the financial system, as well as instruments for their achievement are up to various national authorities and systems. Accordingly, the representation of all these authorities and systems in one single international forum would render its operation ineffective. In view of this institutional fragmentation, the coordination of the work of all these fora is deemed of primary importance. This role was entrusted, in 1999, to the Financial Stability Forum ('**FSF**'). Its creation was the result of proposals included in the so-called '**Tietmeyer Report**' (titled "International Cooperation and Coordination in the Area of Financial Market Supervision and Surveillance"), which had been submitted

---

[107] The text of this Convention is available at: https://www.oecd.org.

[108] The list of OECD members is available at: https://www.oecd.org/document/25.

[109] Paris Convention (1960), Article 1. On the role of the OECD, see Nobel (2019), pp. 376–382.

[110] See below, under 2.4.4.

to the G7 Bonn meeting of Finance Ministers and Central Bank Governors, in 1999.[111]

(2) The FSF numbered forty-three members. Except for its President who participated *in personam*, members were states and international bodies responsible, directly or indirectly, for the supervision, regulation and oversight of financial firms and the financial system. More specifically, the following were represented in the FSF: the G7 Member States, all represented by three members from the Ministry of Finance, the central bank and the relevant supervisory authority (in total, 21 members); five states considered as international financial centres (Australia, Hong Kong SAR, The Netherlands, Singapore and Switzerland, represented by one member (in total, 5 members)[112]; the international economic organisations participating in the governance of the international financial system, i.e., the IMF and the World Bank, both represented by two members, as well as the BIS and the OECD, both represented by one member (in total, 6 members); three international fora with the participation of national supervisory authorities in the three main sectors of the financial system, i.e., the BCBS, the IOSCO and the IAIS, each represented by two members (in total, 6 members); the IASB, represented by one member; the (above-mentioned) international fora with the participation of central banks, i.e., the CPSS and the CGFS, each one represented by one member (in total, 2 members); and the ECB, represented by one member.

(3) The objective of the FSF, which was located in Basel and received secretarial support from the BIS, was to coordinate the actions of its members with a view to safeguarding the international financial system's stability, improving the conditions for market operation and limiting the exposure of the financial system to systemic risks. As mentioned in the Tietmeyer Report:

> Although there are various international fora which monitor developments in the international financial system and have taken important initiatives to ensure its stability, the need to set up the Forum stems from the fact that these fora have their attention focused on the three sectors of the financial system (...) and consequently are not in a position to study and deal effectively with the problems which arise in financial conglomerates and complex structures.

(4) There are three fields of activity in which initiatives were required immediately, which constituted the tasks of the FSF: identification and assessment

---

[111] This Report was the result of the mandate, given in October 2008, to the then Governor of the Central Bank of Germany (Deutsche Bundesbank), Hans Tietmeyer, by the G7 Finance Ministers and Central Bank Governors for the submission of proposals on setting up new institutions necessary to bolster cooperation between supervisory authorities and international organisations and fora for enhancing financial stability.

[112] Out of these states, only Australia belongs to the sub-group of the twelve economically developing countries of the G20, which initially became a member of the FSF.

Table 2.5 Members of the Financial Stability Board (FSB)

Member jurisdictions	G20 member states & the EU (represented by the ECB and the European Commission)
	Other states (5): Hong Kong SAR, The Netherlands, Singapore, Spain, Switzerland
International financial institutions	BIS—IMF—OECD—World Bank
International financial fora	Basel Committee—IOSCO—IAIS—IASB—CPMI—CGFS
In personam	President

of the causes of systemic risks in the financial system and the submission of proposals for dealing with these risks in a timely manner; adoption and implementation of standards of good practice to be implemented in a uniform manner by all categories of financial firms; and strengthening of cross-border cooperation and information exchange among all sectoral financial supervisory and regulatory authorities. Among other initiatives, in April 2001, the FSF published a Compendium titled "International Standards and Codes to Strengthen Financial Systems". This **'Compendium of Standards and Codes'** has been gradually expanded by the FSB to include numerous reports issued by international organisations and several of the above-mentioned international financial fora dealing with the governance of both the international monetary and the international financial system.[113]

2.3.4.2 *The Financial Stability Board (FSB)*
Seat, Charter, Organisational Structure and Membership
(1) At the G20 London Summit in April 2009, the decision was taken to re-establish the Financial Stability Forum by renaming it 'Financial Stability Board' (**'FSB'**).[114] In this way, the G20 signalled the enhancement of this body's institutional role regarding safeguarding the stability of the international financial system. In September 2009, the FSB, which is located in Basel at the BIS, became the first international financial forum to adopt a formal Charter (**'FSB Charter'**),[115] which constituted a major institutional development. This contains provisions on the objectives, the mandate and the tasks,

---

[113] The Compendium is further discussed under 2.4.1 below.

[114] See G20 (2009): "Declaration on Strengthening the Financial System" (at: https://www.g20.org/Documents/Fin_Deps_Fin_Reg_Annex_020409-1615_final.pdf) and "The Global Plan for Recovery and Reform", paragraph 15, second sentence, first point. See also Financial Stability Forum (2009a): "Press release: Financial Stability Forum re-established as the Financial Stability Board", 2 April (at: https://www.fsforum.org/press/pr_090402b.pdf), paragraph 1. For more details on the work of this international financial forum, see Giovanoli (2010), pp. 19–25, Gortsos (2012), pp. 145–150, Thiele (2014), pp. 541–545 and Nobel (2019), pp. 288–299.

[115] The FSB Charter, as last amended in June 2012, is available at: https://www.fsb.org/wp-content/uploads/FSB-Charter-with-revised-Annex-FINAL.pdf.

the resort to consultations, as well as the accountability and transparency of the FSB **(Articles 1–4)**; the criteria for admission as member and members' commitments **(Articles 5–6)**; and the FSB's internal organisation **(Articles 7–22)**. The latter consists of the Plenary, which is the decision-making body; the Steering Committee, which implements operational work in between the Plenary's meetings; the Standing Committees (see Box 2.1); Working Groups; the Regional Consultative Groups (as listed in **Annex B**[116]); the Chair[117]; and the Secretariat. Finally, pursuant to **Article 23** the Charter *"is not intended to create any legal rights or obligations"*.

---

[116] The FSB has six Regional Consultative Groups covering the Americas, Asia, the Commonwealth of Independent States, Europe, the Middle East and North Africa, and Sub-Saharan Africa and bringing together financial authorities from FSB member and non-member countries to exchange views on vulnerabilities affecting financial systems and on initiatives to promote financial stability.

[117] In December 2022, Chair of the FSB was Klaas Knot, President of the Dutch central bank (De Nederlandsche Bank).

Box 2.1 The SRB's Standing Committees[118]

Committee	Mandate
Standing Committee on Assessment of Vulnerabilities ('**SCAV**')	Main mechanism for identifying and assessing risks in the financial system
Standing Committee on Supervisory and Regulatory Cooperation ('**SCSRC**')	Undertaking of further supervisory analysis or framing of regulatory or supervisory policy responses to a material vulnerability identified by the SCAV
Standing Committee on Standards Implementation ('**SCSI**')	Monitoring the implementation of agreed FSB policy initiatives and international standards
Standing Committee on Budget and Resources ('**SCBR**')	Oversight of the resources and the budget of the FSB and presentation of recommendations to the Plenary, as necessary

(**2**) Members of the FSB include authorities from jurisdictions responsible for maintaining financial stability (e.g., ministries of finance, central banks, as well as supervisory and resolution authorities), international financial institutions (organisations), as well as international standard-setting bodies. The eligibility of members is being reviewed periodically by the FSB Plenary considering the FSB's objectives. The current members of the FSB are listed in **Annex A** of the Charter.[119] The EU and its Member States are represented in the FSB by three member jurisdictions (France, Germany and Italy) which are members of the G20, the ECB and the European Commission (Table 2.5).[120]

---

[118] FSB Charter (2012), Articles 14–17.

[119] FSB Charter (2012), Article 5. Annex A was amended for the last time on 26 June 2018; see also Table 2.5.

[120] See on this Donelly (2019).

Objectives and Tasks—Accountability and Transparency

(1) The statutory objective of the FSB consists in coordinating, at international level, the work of national financial authorities and international standard-setting bodies to develop and promote the implementation of effective regulatory, supervisory and other financial sector policies. In association with international financial institutions, the FSB also addresses vulnerabilities affecting financial systems in the interest of international financial stability.[121] In order to meet these objectives, the tasks of the FSB have been defined as follows:

> The *main tasks* of the FSB consist of the following[122]: advising on and monitoring best practices in meeting regulatory standards; assessing vulnerabilities affecting the international financial system and identifying and reviewing on a timely and ongoing basis the regulatory, supervisory and related actions needed to address them, as well as their outcomes[123]; promoting coordination and information exchange among national authorities responsible for financial stability; monitoring and advising on market developments and their implications for regulatory policy; undertaking joint strategic reviews of the policy development work of the international standard-setting bodies to ensure their work is timely, coordinated, focused on priorities and addressing gaps; setting guidelines for and supporting the establishment of 'supervisory colleges'[124]; supporting contingency planning for cross-border crisis management, particularly with respect to systemically important firms; collaborating with the IMF to conduct "Early Warning Exercises"; promoting member jurisdictions' implementation of standards, and policy recommendations through monitoring of implementation, peer review and disclosure; and undertaking any other tasks agreed by its members in the course of its activities and within the framework of its Charter.
>
> Its *additional tasks* include promoting the coordination of aligning the activities of standard-setting bodies to address any overlaps or gaps and clarifying demarcations in view of amendments in national and regional regulatory structures relating to prudential and systemic risk, market

---

[121] FSB Charter (2012), Article 1. Members thus commit to pursue the maintenance of financial stability, maintain the financial system's openness and transparency, implement international financial standards and agree to undergo periodic per reviews.

[122] *Ibid.*, Article 2(1).

[123] In this respect, the SRB adopts international financial standards itself; see below, under 2.4.3.

[124] A 'supervisory college' is a group of national supervisors from different states in which an international bank is established and has foreign presence through subsidiaries and branches. Hence, each international bank has a different college of supervisory authorities ('variable geometry').

integrity, investor and consumer protection, infrastructures, as well as accounting and auditing.[125]

(2) In order to discharge its accountability beyond its members, the SRB is required by its Charter[126] to publish Reports and, in particular, periodical Progress Reports of its work to the G20 Finance Ministers and Central Bank Governors, as well as to G20 Heads of State and Governments.

2.3.5 The Level of Indirect Enforcement of the Rules of Public International Financial Law

2.3.5.1 Introductory Remarks

The fourth level consists in the (indirect) enforcement of the rules of international financial law (typically in the form of standards), which can be achieved through peer group pressure exerted within the international financial fora (including the FSB); '**Assessment Programs**' conducted by these fora[127]; '**thematic**' and '**country peer reviews**' conducted by the FSB[128]; and/or the IMF's Financial Sector Assessment Program ('**FSAP**') as part of its regulatory authority (presented below).

2.3.5.2 Tasks and Powers of the IMF

(1) The power for the indirect enforcement of the rules of public international financial law, in the form of international financial standards adopted by the above-mentioned international fora, which as soft law have no legally binding nature, is a competence of the **IMF**. It is an international economic organisation of one hundred and ninety member countries, belongs to the group of UN specialised organisations,[129] and was set up by virtue of an international treaty concluded at the UN Monetary and Financial Conference in Bretton Woods (New Hampshire, US, widely known as the "**Bretton Woods Agreement**"), which was signed in 1944 and entered into force on 27 December 1945.

(2) According to its Articles of Articles of Agreement of 1945,[130] the initial principal tasks consisted of monitoring the international system of fixed (but

---

[125] FSB Charter (2012), Article 2(2).

[126] *Ibid.*, Article 4.

[127] On the Basel Committee's Regulatory Consistency Assessment Programme (RCAP) in particular, see below in Chapter 3, under 3.1.7.

[128] For a stocktaking of these reviews, see at: https://www.fsb.org/policy_area/peer-reviews.

[129] This category includes fifteen international organisations which are linked to the UN by special agreements and whose activity covers a wide range of issues (monetary relations, economic development, agricultural policy, education, health, telecommunications, meteorology).

[130] The Articles of Agreement have been amended seven times, with the latest amendment adopted on 15 December 2010 (effective as of 26 January 2016).

adjustable) exchange rates[131] (already mentioned above as the Bretton Woods system) and providing financial assistance to its Member States when faced with problems in their balance of payments,[132] upon conditionality.[133] Hence, the IMF was established as both an international monetary organisation and as a lender of last resort for sovereign states.[134] The Bretton Woods system was *de facto* abolished in December 1971 following the signing of the 'Smithsonian Agreement' by the Group of Ten (G10). *De jure*, the system was abolished in 1978 by the second amendment of the Articles of Agreement of the IMF, which entered into force on 1 April 1978.[135] Based on this amendment, the IMF was assigned the task to:

> oversee the international monetary system in order to ensure its effective operation and (…) the compliance of each member with its obligations under Chapter 1 of this Article.[136]

In order to fulfil this function, the IMF has the right "to exercise firm surveillance over the exchange rate policies of (its) members, and (…) adopt specific principles for the guidance of all members with respect to those policies".[137] This is also the basis of the IMF's mandate to monitor global financial stability. Within this framework, the Member States must provide the IMF with any information deemed necessary for the effective exercise of its supervisory competence. They must also take part in consultation with executives of the IMF (widely referred to as **'Article IV consultation'**[138] or **'Article IV surveillance'**) to render possible an assessment of the compatibility of national economic policy measures with the general obligations they have undertaken

---

[131] Articles of Agreement (1945), Article IV.

[132] The "balance of payments" is an accounting statement of a country showing the economic transactions that its residents carry out with foreign residents during a certain period of time (usually one year). This balance sheet is broken down into three sub-accounts: the trade balance, which tracks imports and exports of goods and services; the undeclared balance sheet, which shows undeclared resources and undeclared payments; and the capital account, which keeps track of financial assets and liabilities of the private and public sectors. The accounting sum of the trade balance and the undeclared balance constitutes the "current account".

[133] Articles of Agreement (2016), Article V ("Operations and Transactions of the Fund"). On these tasks see Lowenfeld (2009), pp. 613–617 and 622–624, and Lastra (2015), pp. 415–422.

[134] On the role of the IMF as a lender of last resort, its alternatives and proposals for its improvement, see Sachs (1999), Fisher (1999) (with extensive further references), as well as the seminal work of Mishkin and Hall (2000) and Jeanne and Wyplosz (2001).

[135] For a review of this system and the conditions for its abolishment, see Hooke (1981), Eichengreen (1994), pp. 50–54, Kapstein (1994), Lowenfeld (2009), pp. 622–633, and Lastra (2015), pp. 412–426.

[136] Articles of Agreement (2016), Article IV ("Obligations Regarding Exchange Arrangements"), Chapter 3, paragraph (a).

[137] *Ibid.*, Article IV, Chapter 3, paragraph (b), first sentence.

[138] See Lowenfeld (2009), pp. 634–644, and Lastra (2015), pp. 456–460.

towards the IMF.[139] In the context of this consultation/surveillance, risks to financial stability are also analysed at the country level[140] (and, then, less frequently though, in the Financial Sector Assessment Program (FSAP) discussed just below). Conditionality at the provision of financial assistance has been maintained under the amended Articles of Agreement.[141]

2.3.5.3 The Financial Sector Assessment Program (FSAP)
Introductory Remarks

(1) In order to fulfil its supervisory task under **Article IV of its Articles of Agreement**, the IMF formulates specific guidelines addressed to its Member States determining the framework within which their foreign exchange policy must be exercised. In 1995, the Executive Council laid down the main principles pertaining to the strategy of the IMF in connection with its supervisory task.[142] Two points of this strategy are of particular importance: the *first* is imposing the obligation on its Member States to provide to the IMF promptly reliable and immediately available statistics of economic and financial nature, in accordance with the general data dissemination and specific data dissemination standards. The *second* is the IMF's interest in the stability of the financial system of its Member States, in view of the frequency and the critical nature of systemic problems that have manifested themselves in recent years affecting the stability of the international financial system.

(2) Within this context, the IMF, in cooperation with the World Bank, adopted the Financial Sector Assessment Program[143] (hereinafter '**FSAP**' or '**Programme**') in May 1999, after the Asian crisis, which is open to any country irrespective of whether or not it is borrowing from the IMF or the

---

[139] Articles of Agreement (2016), Article IV, Chapter 3, paragraph (b), second sentence.

[140] At the multilateral level, these risks are analysed in the series "Global Financial Stability Report" (for a stocktaking, see at: https://www.imf.org/en/publications/gfsr). The most recent Report, of 11 October 2022, is available at: https://www.imf.org/en/Publications/GFSR/Issues/2022/10/11/global-financial-stability-report-october-2022.

[141] See Lowenfeld (2009), pp. 644–651, and Lastra (2015), pp. 468–483.

[142] It is often claimed that in that respect the IMF endorsed the ten recommended policy reforms of the 1989 "Washington Consensus" (a term first used in Williamson (1990) in response to the macroeconomic turbulence and the debt crisis of the early to mid-1980s. On the Washington Consensus, the new agenda at the late 1990s (the "Augmented Washington Consensus" according to Rodrik (2002)) and its gradual abolition by the Fund, see, by means of mere indication, Montaverdi (2017), with extensive further references (also on the impact of the Washington Consensus on EU policies).

[143] Interestingly, the FSAP refers to the "financial sector" and not to the "financial system", apparently in distinction to the real sector of the economy. In the rest of this Sub-section, reference is made to financial systems.

World Bank.[144] The aim of this initiative was to provide in-depth examinations of countries' financial systems in order to facilitate the (independent) assessment of financial systems' resilience and countries' compliance with the international standards and codes in the FSB Compendium, to identify weaknesses and sources of instability in the international financial system and to ensure that countries undertake efforts to correct macroeconomic policies and strengthen their financial system and their economy.[145] Related are also the 'Reports on the Observance of Standards and Codes' ('**ROSCs**'); these are an optional for the country component of the FSAP and can also be conducted outside an FSAP, on a stand-alone basis.

(**3**) The reports prepared under the FSAP address several aspects: economic and monetary transparency, banking supervision, securities regulation, insurance supervision, oversight of payment systems and, more rarely, corporate governance or accounting and auditing standards.[146] Banking supervision as well as economic and monetary transparency aspects are examined in every case, while some of the above aspects may be examined individually, under the Technical Assistance Programs, rather than within the framework of the FSAP. The wide range of subjects usually covered by the FSAP has also made it necessary to mobilise experts outside the IMF and the World Bank (such as from central banks and international organisations and fora).

Methodological Tools

In order to be able to play a decisive role in strengthening the financial system of interested states, it was considered that the FSAP should provide high-quality assessments, taking into account the particularities of the economies examined. To this end, expert groups working on the Program used (almost)

---

[144] The IMF Executive Board has established prioritisation criteria for all country requests (except for those for which stability assessments under the FSAP are a mandatory part of surveillance, which take priority), such as the systemic importance of the country; macroeconomic or financial vulnerabilities; major reform programmes that might benefit from a comprehensive financial sector assessment; and features of the exchange rate and monetary policy regime that make the financial system more vulnerable.

[145] The FSAP was first launched as a one-year pilot project, including twelve member states representing the entire range of economic development levels. One year later, upon review of the progress made, the IMF and the World Bank decided to continue the programme in the following year and included another twenty-four states, with the prospect of including all Member States of the IMF within five years. On the FSAP, see Conthe and Ingves (2001), Reddy (2001) and Lastra (2015), pp. 461–463.

It is noted that the IMF also has the power to indirectly impose on member states resorting to it for financial assistance the implementation of the international financial standards contained in the FSB's Compendium (and mainly its "Key Standards for Sound Financial Systems") based on the 'conditionality principle' (Articles of Agreement (2016), Article IV, Chapter 3, paragraph (a)); on the Compendium, see below, under 2.4.

[146] In the pilot project, each of the twelve FSAPs that were conducted examined on average 3.8 sectors.

since its launch methodology tools specifically designed for its purposes, such as macroprudential analysis, study and implementation of potential negative scenarios for the economy, as well as assessment of the adoption and implementation of international financial standards (as further discussed in Box 2.2).

Box 2.2 The three key methodological tools in the FSAP

Macroprudential analysis	The macroprudential analysis is aimed at showing the two-way relationship that exists between the economy's macroeconomic robustness and the positive financial system performance. For the purposes of this analysis, **Macro-Prudential Indicators ('MPIs')** are used to make an in-depth examination of both the robustness and solvency of commercial banks and of the broader framework of national economic policy choices. Experience has shown that when analysis reveals weaknesses in both these aspects, the likelihood of a future economic crisis is increased

(continued)

(continued)	
Study and implementation of potential negative scenarios for the economy	The study and implementation of various scenarios (**stress tests**, sensitivity and contagion analysis) aim at examining the impact of a potential serious financial crisis would have on market operation and the solvency of banks. These are applied to large commercial banks as well as to banking systems. To properly conduct stress tests, it is imperative that the IMF and the World Bank have all the information deemed necessary[147]
Assessment of the adoption and implementation of international financial standards	Assessment of the progress achieved by a member state in adopting and implementing international financial standards, aims at revealing the positive aspects of the economy in question regarding its adaptability to new situations, on the one hand, and at identifying any institutional gaps and the weaknesses of its financial system, on the other. The interest here is mainly focused on the fields of banking supervision, economic and monetary transparency, payment systems, capital markets and insurance

Adjustment of the Program After the GFC
(1) The GFC highlighted many of the FSAP's strengths, but also revealed its weaknesses (including its voluntary nature).[148] In this respect and on the basis

---

[147] The problem in this case is that some competent national authorities are hesitant to reveal such information, even though this is subject to a confidentiality clause. Another problem relates to the different level of economic development between the states that set up scenarios (in advanced economies) and the ones applying them (mostly developing countries and EMEs). It is usually claimed that such scenarios presume the existence of a well-organised banking system, a robust capital markets and many well-informed actors. Such prerequisites are rarely encountered in many developing countries participating in the Program.

[148] On various proposals in relation to the enhancement of the IMF following that crisis, see, by means of mere indication, Bordo and James (2010), as well as Hagan (2010a) and (2010b).

of the 2009 FSAP Review, in **September 2009**, the IMF and the World Bank 'revamped' the FSAP[149] to include four new features:

> *First*, a **'Risk Assessment Matrix'** was introduced, designed to render the analysis of stability assessments in the context of the FSAP more systematic, candid and transparent; FSAPs should anymore be structured into core three pillars: risk analysis (which puts specific emphasis on **"macroprudential stress testing"** by incorporating various feedback and spill-over effects[150]) and vulnerability analysis, oversight and financial safety nets and risk analysis.
>
> *Second*, new assessment methodologies were developed to better identify linkages between the broader economy and the financial system and cover a greater variety of risk sources (such as those from the rise of non-bank financial institutions (including digital market infrastructures), as well as emerging risks from fintech, cyber risks and risks related to climate change), while more emphasis has been put on cross-country links, spill-over effects and coordination arrangements. Risk-based assessments of the standards that apply to the regulation and supervision of banks, securities markets and insurance were introduced to better target the assessments of these standards.
>
> *Third*, in order to allow the FSAP to be better integrated with the IMF surveillance and (also) allow more continuous monitoring of developments and quicker responses, as of September 2010, countries with SIFS would be required to undergo financial stability assessments every five years. This would allow the IMF to monitor more closely those members that would have the most impact on systemic stability in the event of a crisis because of the size or the interconnectedness of their financial systems.
>
> *Finally*, a clearer delineation of institutional responsibilities for stability and development, with greater institutional accountability, was introduced regarding the conduct by the IMF or the World Bank, respectively, of financial stability or development assessments in separate modules

---

[149] "Statement of Surveillance Priorities-Revisions of Economic Priorities and Progress on Operational Priorities", Policy Paper No. 2009/4367, September 2, 2009 (at: https://www.imf.org/en/Publications/Policy-Papers/Issues/2016/12/31/Statement-of-Surveillance-Priorities-Revisions-of-Economic-Priorities-and-Progress-on-PP4367).

[150] IMF macroprudential stress tests are a methodology to assess financial vulnerabilities that can trigger systemic risk and the need of systemwide mitigating measures. On this stress test and its differences with the microprudential 'supervisory stress tests' (see Chapter 1 above, under 1.2.4), see Adrian, Morsink and Schumacher (2020). It is also noted that, on the occasion of the pandemic crisis, it was considered important to develop a "global bank stress testing approach", which would undertake consistent risk analysis of the impact on countries of common global shocks and incorporate cross-country spill-over effects. On the Global Bank Stress Test ('GST'), which was launched in October 2020, see Ding *et al.* (2022).

(instead of 'one-size-fits-all' assessments). The **2009 FSAP Review** introduced two modules of FSAPs: the **"financial stability module"** (led by the IMF) and **"financial developmental module"** (led by the World Bank); all FSAPs to advanced economies are financial stability modules.

Accordingly, the FSAP still remains a joint IMF-World Bank programme (except for the countries where FSAPs are the sole responsibility of the IMF), and country participation is still voluntary for countries with non-systemic financial systems (notably developing countries and EMEs), where FSAPs are done jointly by World Bank and IMF staff. The two components may be assessed at the same time during a joint IMF-World Bank mission or at different times in separate financial stability and financial development modules conducted by the IMF and the World Bank, respectively.

(2) On the basis of the above, in **April 2010**, the IMF's Executive Board decided to make stability assessments under the FSAP a mandatory part of its surveillance policy. This decision resulted in a more risk-based approach to financial system surveillance and better integration of FSAPs into Article IV consultation in these jurisdictions. In **September 2010**, this agreement was concretised, when the IMF made it mandatory for twenty-five jurisdictions with financial systems/sectors that have the greatest impact on global financial stability ("systemically important financial sectors", '**SIFS**') to undergo financial stability assessments under the FSAP every *five years*.

Furthermore, on the basis of the updated legal framework governing mandatory financial stability assessments to reflect the "Integrated Surveillance Decision" of July 2012, on **6 December 2013**, the Executive Board reviewed experience with the implementation of its 2010 decision, revisited the original approach for determining jurisdictions with SIFS and adopted a new methodology for such determinations. This places greater emphasis on interconnectedness, expands the range of covered exposures and takes into consideration the potential for price contagion across financial systems, while adhering to the principles of relevance and transparency established by the 2010 Executive Board decision.[151] On that basis, four jurisdictions were added to the list of those that have a SIFS.

Finally, on **12 May 2021**, the IMF's Executive Board, upon conclusion of the quintennial FSAP Review,[152] reexamined the methodology to identify SIFS and the list of members with SIFS and endorsed the 2013 methodology (as remaining adequate) with a couple of minor adjustments. The Review aimed to make mandatory financial stability assessments even more risk-based,

---

[151] A country's broader economic or political importance and financial system vulnerabilities are not considered in that respect.

[152] "2021 Financial Sector Assessment Programs Review—Towards A More Stable And Sustainable Financial System", Policy Paper No. 2021/040 (at: https://www.imf.org/en/Publications/Policy-Papers/Issues/2021/05/28/2021-Financial-Sector-Assessment-Program-Review-Towards-A-More-Stable-And-Sustainable-460517).

following the directions set out in the concurrent **Comprehensive Surveillance Review**[153] to make surveillance more risk-based. The list of jurisdictions with SIFS was further expanded to forty-seven: thirty-three jurisdictions with relatively more SIFS should participate in FSAP every once in five years, while the other fifteen (mainly EMEs) should participate every once in ten years.[154]

The Financial Stability and the Financial Development Assessment: A Closer Look
(1) As already, noted, initially, the assessment procedure was always launched upon request of the interested state. In the wake of the GFC and the decision taken to revamp the FSAP, the following applies:

> *First*, the *financial stability assessment* is the main responsibility of the IMF and covers an evaluation of three components: the source, probability and near-term potential impact of the main risks to macro-financial stability; the country's financial stability policy framework; and the authorities' capacity to manage and resolve a financial crisis should the risks materialise. The key findings of the stability assessment are summarised in the 'Financial Sector Stability Assessment' ('**FSSA**'), which is prepared by the IMF team for the IMF Executive Board and is a key input to IMF surveillance. The above apply both in countries where FSAPs are jointly conducted with the World Bank and in the case that the financial stability assessment is conducted on a stand-alone basis as a financial stability module.
> *Second*, the *financial development assessment* is the main responsibility of the World Bank, which participates in FSAPs conducted in developing countries and in EMEs, focuses on medium- to long-term needs for the deepening and strengthening of the financial system and addresses major weaknesses affecting the system's efficiency, soundness and contribution to long-term growth and social development. These may include assessments of financial system infrastructure development needs; financial system oversight; related public policies; the impact of an underdeveloped financial system on financial stability; and long-term financial system reforms. In this respect, the World Bank prepares a Financial Sector Assessment ('**FSA**') for its Executive Board. The above apply both in countries where FSAPs are jointly conducted with the World Bank and

---

[153] This review comprises ten policy papers, which are available at: https://www.imf.org/en/Topics/Comprehensive-Surveillance-Review).

[154] Since systemic importance is a dynamic concept, both the list of jurisdictions and the methodology for assessing systemic importance is under periodic review (see at: https://www.imf.org/external/np/exr/facts/fsap.htm). Related IMF's FSAP Policy Papers are available at: https://www.imf.org/en/Publications/SPROLLs/Financial-Sector-Assessment-Program-FSAP-Policy-Papers#sort=%40imfdate%20descending.

in the case that the assessment is conducted on a stand-alone basis as a financial development module.[155]

(2) In both cases, an Aide-Mémoire is prepared by the FSAP team for the country authorities; this summarises the main findings and recommendations of the mission, remains confidential and cannot be published or shared with third parties.[156] These are coupled by Technical Notes on selected topics and Detailed Assessments Reports ('**DARs**') of compliance with international standards and codes, whose publication is voluntary. Publication of the FSSAs and the FSAs is also voluntary but presumed. Even though, as already mentioned, the FSAP is an independent assessment of the financial system by the staff of the IMF and the World Bank (if relevant), input and feedback are sought from the authorities, which can review and provide comments on the Aide Memoire, the Technical Notes and DARs on the financial standards assessed. Like the Article IV Staff Report, the FSSA is not provided to the authorities for comments before it is circulated to the IMF's Executive Board (Tables 2.6 and 2.7).[157]

2.4   Key Sources

2.4.1   *Introductory Remarks*

2.4.1.1   *General Overview*

(1) The international fora mentioned above have issued hundreds of Reports since their establishment, which contain international financial standards and constitute the sources of public international financial law, in its various branches. Another (partial) source of public international financial law is the General Agreement on Trade in Services (GATS), and in particular with regard to international trade in financial services, the "Second Annex of GATS on Financial Services", the "Second Protocol to GATS", which replaced the

---

[155] The FDA findings are used in various World Bank programmes, such as the Country Assistance Strategies ('CASs'), the Social and Structural Reviews ('SSRs') and the Poverty Reduction Strategy Papers.

[156] Since the handling of confidential and market-sensitive data is of primary importance, upon request, the authorities can be provided with a formal letter of undertaking to maintain confidentiality or sign a confidentiality protocol.

[157] The FSAP team would also usually meet with financial firms and other market participants to gain a better understanding of market developments, as well as structure, outlook, risk management practices (under strict conditions of confidentiality). More information on the FSAP can be found at: https://www.imf.org/en/Publications/fssa, and at: https://www.worldbank.org/finance/html/fsap.html.

Table 2.6 Institutions of public international financial law

G7, G10, G20: Political decisions

G20 members (including the EU)—five other states (significant financial centres: Hong Kong SAR, Singapore, Spain, Switzerland, The Netherlands)

International fora (subject-area of objective)

BCBS (banking regulation)	Financial Stability Board (FSB)	*IMF*
IOSCO (capital markets regulation)	no financial supervisory authority	no financial supervisory authority
IAIS (insurance regulation)	standard-setting body on specific areas (e.g., financial resolution)	standard-setting body (on macroeconomic issues)
CPMI (payment systems oversight)	forum for international coordination of financial standards	monitoring body for implementation of financial standards (FSAP—conditionality)
CGFS (market functioning)	early warning system monitoring body (in cooperation with IMF)	early warning system monitoring body (in cooperation with FSB)
IASB (accounting standards)		

International organisations

BIS (international monetary cooperation)	*World Bank* (economic development, standard-setter)	*OECD* (corporate governance)

Joint Forum (supervision of financial conglomerates)
IFAC (auditing standards)
FATF (money laundering and terrorist financing)
IADI (deposit guarantee)

Italics indicate states, international organisations and fora represented in the FSB

Table 2.7 States' participation in the institutional structure of the international architecture of the financial system following the G20 Summit in London

G7 member states	• Canada, France, Germany, Italy, Japan, United Kingdom, United States
G10 member states (11)	G7 member states Belgium, The Netherlands, Sweden, Switzerland
G20 member states (19) (the EU is also a member of the G20)	G7 member states Argentina, Australia, Brazil, China, India, Indonesia, Mexico, Russian Federation, Saudi Arabia, South Africa, Republic of Korea, Turkey (12)
States represented in the FSB (24)	G20 member states (19) Hong Kong SAR, The Netherlands, Singapore, Spain, Switzerland
States represented in the BCBS (27)	G20 member states (19) G10 member states not represented in the G20: Belgium, The Netherlands, Sweden, Switzerland Hong Kong SAR, Luxembourg, Singapore, Spain

schedules of specific commitments and lists of exemptions relating to financial services set out in Article II of the GATS, and the "Understanding on Commitments in Financial Services".[158]

(2) With regard to public international banking law, a *first* group contains three Reports included in the FSB's **"Key Standards for Sound Financial Systems"**, which constitutes the main component of the FSB's 'Compendium of Standards and Codes',[159] namely: the Basel Committee's "Core Principles for Effective Banking Supervision"; the "IADI Core Principles for Effective Deposit Insurance Systems"; and the FSB's "Key Attributes of Effective Resolution Regimes for Financial Institutions". Of significant importance are also the Basel Committee's (first) Reports on the prudential supervision of international banks and the cross-border cooperation between supervisory authorities (the original (1975) "Basel Concordat", in the aftermath of the *Herstatt Bank* crisis,[160] and the revised (1983) "Basel Concordat" following the bankruptcy of the Luxembourg-based holding company *Banco Ambrosiano Holding S.A*, a subsidiary of the Italian credit institution *Banco Ambrosiano*[161]), as well as the **"Basel III regulatory framework"**.

(3) The BCBS's Reports on the micro- and macroprudential regulation of (predominantly international) banks, known as the **"Basel III regulatory framework"**, are (eventually) the globally most influential sources of public international banking law—even though due to their quite technical character they are not included in the FSB's Key Standard for Sound Financial Systems.[162] This framework improved banks' ability to absorb financial

---

[158] See Von Bogdandy and Windsor (2008) and Lowenfeld (2009), pp. 129–132. On the reason(s) why there are only a few international treaties as sources of public international financial law, see Tietje and Lehmann (2010).

[159] On this Compendium and these Key Standards, see just below.

[160] See Chapter 3 below, under 3.1.1. Indicative of the purely informal character of the Basel Committee's operation until 1983 was the fact that the Basel Concordat was not disclosed until 1981 when it was published as an appendix to a book.

[161] For a detailed analysis of this case, see Dale (1984), pp. 156–167, and Kapstein (1994), pp. 53–57. The revised "Basel Concordat" was further revised in 1990, 1992, 1996 and 1983; see details in Walker (2001), pp. 84–131 and Gortsos (2012), pp. 238–248.

[162] This international regulatory framework was initially introduced in 1988, when the Basel Committee adopted its Report "International convergence of capital measurement and capital standards", known as 'Basel Capital Accord' or 'Basel I framework' (July 1988, at: https://www.bis.org/publ/bcbs111.htm). During the period 1991-1995, 'Basel I' was amended on five occasions in terms of individual technical points. On the 'Basel I' framework, see Bardos (1988), Hausmann (1995), pp. 141–152 and 229–247, Norton (1995), pp. 171–241, and Gortsos (2012), pp. 250–252.

The 'Basel I' framework was then fully revised in 2004 by the Committee's Report "Basel II: International Convergence of Capital Measurement and Capital Standards, A Revised Framework", known as 'Basel II framework' (June 2004, at: https://www.bis.org/publ/bcbs107.htm). On this framework, see Saidenberg and Schuermann (2003), Ayadi and Resti (2004), Herring (2005), the various contributions in Wiegand (2006) (and in particular Sigrist [2006]), Macht (2007) and Gleeson (2010). On the evolution of the Basel Committee's capital adequacy and (since 2010) regulatory frameworks and their

shocks through significantly higher levels of capital and liquidity, enhanced the supervision of the global banking system and resulted in a number of structural changes to strengthen banks' financial resilience. It consists of three Reports[163]:

Basel III: A global regulatory framework for more resilient banks and banking systems[164];

Basel III: The Liquidity Coverage Ratio [**LCR**] and liquidity risk monitoring tools[165]; and

Basel III: The Net Stable Funding Ratio [**NSFR**].[166]

(4) This regulatory framework is under adjustment on an ongoing basis (see Table 2.8). In this respect, a major amendment was undertaken in December 2017, when the BCBS's oversight body (GHOS), endorsed the Report "Basel III: Finalising post-crisis reforms"[167] (also referred to as the **"Basel IV regulatory framework"**, even though the BCBS tends to view it as a "complement to Basel III"). Furthermore, a revised **market risk framework** was also introduced in 2017, which was finalised in 2019,[168] and an updated set of **revised Pillar 3 disclosure requirements** was tabled on 11 December 2018.[169] Amidst the pandemic crisis, on **27 March 2020**, the BCBS decided (through the GHOS again) to postpone the implementation of the revised market risk framework, the Complement to Basel III and the **revised Pillar 3 disclosure requirements** to 1 January 2023, with a view to increasing the operational capacity of banks under the circumstances. The transitional arrangements for

---

implementation into EU law, see Gortsos (2022b); on the evolution, see also Alexander (2019), pp. 92–116.

[163] On the 'Basel III' framework, in its original version of 2010, see details in Gortsos (2012), pp. 254–281.

[164] June 2011, at: https://www.bis.org/publ/bcbs189.htm.

[165] January 2013, at: https://www.bis.org/publ/bcbs238.htm.

[166] October 2014, at: https://www.bis.org/publ/bcbs295.htm. It is noted that the capital and liquidity buffers introduced by the Basel III regulatory framework, including the capital conservation buffer and, by extension, the countercyclical capital buffer, buffers for systemically important banks and banks' stock of high-quality liquid assets ('HQLA'), are designed to be used in periods of stress, like the pandemic one.

[167] This Report is available at: https://www.bis.org/bcbs/publ/d424.htm. For a compilation of the Basel Committee's documents forming this regulatory framework, including the current review proposals, see at: https://www.bis.org/bcbs/basel3/compilation.htm (constantly updated).

[168] "Minimum capital requirements for market risk", February 2019—revised text (at: https://www.bis.org/bcbs/publ/d457.pdf).

[169] At: https://www.bis.org/bcbs/publ/d455.htm. For a detailed presentation of the Basel III framework, including its amendments, see Gortsos (2022b), Sects. 1.4.–1.5. The first holistic evaluation by the BCBS of the impact and efficacy of the implemented Basel III reforms was published on 14 December 2022 (at: https://www.bis.org/bcbs/publ/d544.htm).

the output floor accompanying the Complement have also been extended by one year to 1 January 2028.[170]

The full set of BCBS documents and standards in this field are nowadays included in the "consolidated **Basel Framework**".[171]

Table 2.8 The evolution of the BCBS' capital adequacy and (since 2010) regulatory frameworks

---

The Basel I capital adequacy framework
(1988): "International convergence of capital measurement and capital standards", July
(1991): "Amendment of the Basel capital accord in respect of the inclusion of general provisions/general loan—loss reserves in capital", November
(1994a): "Amendment to the Basel Capital Accord of July 1988", July
(1994b): "Basel Capital Accord: the treatment of the credit risk associated with certain off-balance-sheet items", July
(1994c): "Basel Committee Amendment to the 1988 Capital Accord: Recognition of Collateral", December
(1995): "Basel Capital Accord: treatment of potential exposure for off-balance-sheet items", April
(1996): "Amendment to the Capital Accord to incorporate market risks"
The Basel II capital adequacy framework
(2004): "Basel II: International Convergence of Capital Measurement and Capital Standards, A Revised Framework", June
(2006): "International Convergence of Capital Measurement and Capital Standards, A Revised Framework—Comprehensive Version", June—codification of Basel I and Basle II
(2009): "Revisions to the Basel II market risk framework", July
The Basel III regulatory framework
(2010a): "Basel III: A global regulatory framework for more resilient banks and banking systems", December
(2010b): "Basel III: International framework for liquidity risk measurement, standards and monitoring", December
(2010c): "Guidance for national authorities operating the countercyclical capital buffer", December
(2011): "Basel III: A global regulatory framework for more resilient banks and banking systems", June—revised text
(2012): "Regulatory treatment of valuation adjustments to derivative liabilities", July
(2013): "Basel III: The Liquidity Coverage Ratio and liquidity risk monitoring tools", January
(2014): "Basel III: The net stable funding ratio", October
(2016): "Minimum capital requirements for market risk", January
(2017): "Basel III: Finalising post-crisis reforms", December
(2018): "Pillar 3 disclosure requirements—updated framework, December
(2019a): "Minimum capital requirements for market risk", February—revised text
(2019b): "Leverage ratio treatment of client cleared derivatives", June

---

[170] "Governors and Heads of Supervision announce deferral of Basel III implementation to increase operational capacity of banks and supervisors to respond to Covid-19", Press release (at: https://www.bis.org/press/p200327.htm).

[171] At: https://www.bis.org/basel_framework.

(5) Of significant importance are also, *inter alia*, the BCBS "Principles for operational resilience" of **31 March 2021**,[172] which seek to promote a principles-based approach to improving operational resilience. The underlying rationale for this initiative was the consideration that (even prior to the pandemic) there was a need to strengthen banks' ability to absorb operational risk-related events, such as pandemics, cyber risks, technology failures and natural disasters, which could cause significant operational failures or wide-scale disruptions in financial markets. Nevertheless, after the onset of the pandemic, banks rapidly adapted their operational posture in response to new hazards or changes in existing ones and the BCBS considered that a pragmatic, flexible approach to operational resilience can enhance the ability of banks to withstand, adapt to and recover from potential hazards and thereby mitigate potentially severe adverse impacts.[173]

(6) It is finally noted that, taking into account that during the last few years sustainable finance has become an issue of high priority in the agenda of international organisations and fora, including the FSB, which, following a request made in April 2015[174] by the G20 Finance Ministers and Central Bank Governors, established the (above-mentioned) TCFD.[175] On **7 July 2021**, the urgency for stronger global cooperation in the field of sustainable finance was manifested by the publication by the FSB of its "Roadmap for Addressing Climate-Related Financial Risks",[176] a Report on "The availability of data with which to monitor climate-related financial stability risks"[177] and a Report on "Promoting climate-related disclosures".[178] This Roadmap, prepared in consultation with (other) international standard-setting bodies

---

[172] At: https://www.bis.org/bcbs/publ/d516.pdf.

[173] The approach adopted builds on updates to its "Principles for the Sound Management of Operational Risk" of March 2021 (at: https://ww.bis.org/bcbs/publ/d515.htm) and draws from previously issued principles on corporate governance for banks, outsourcing-related, business continuity-related and relevant risk management-related guidance and the work undertaken by several jurisdictions and standard-setting bodies.

[174] Of importance in this context is also the Paris Agreement that was adopted by 196 Parties at the UN Climate Change Conference in Paris on 12 December and entered into force on 4 November 2016 (its text is available at: https://unfccc.int/files/essential_background/convention/application/pdf/english_paris_agreement.pdf); in the EU it was approved by Council Decision (EU) 2016/1841 of 5 October 2016 (OJ L 282, 19.10.2016, pp. 1–3). Pursuant to Article 2(1), point (c), this international treaty aims to strengthen the global response to the threat of climate change in the context of sustainable development and efforts to eradicate poverty, *inter alia*, "*by making finance flows consistent with a pathway towards low greenhouse gas emissions and climate-resilient development*".

[175] On its latest Status Report (October 2022), see at: https://assets.bbhub.io/company/sites/60/2022/10/2022-TCFD-Status-Report.pdf.

[176] At: https://www.fsb.org/2021/07/fsb-roadmap-for-addressing-climate-related-financial-risks.

[177] At: https://www.fsb.org/2021/07/the-availability-of-data-with-which-to-monitor-and-assess-climate-related-risks-to-financial-stability.

[178] At: https://www.fsb.org/2021/07/report-on-promoting-climate-related-disclosures.

and international organisations, was delivered to the G20 Finance Ministers and Central Bank Governors meeting in July 2021[179] but does not (as yet) contain specific financial standards. Its objective is to support international coordination in the field by setting out a comprehensive and coordinated plan for addressing climate-related financial risks and paving the way for implementation and focuses on assessing and addressing such risks through four interrelated areas: firm-level disclosures, data, vulnerability analysis, as well as regulatory and supervisory tools.[180]

2.4.1.2 In Particular: The 'Compendium' of the Financial Stability Board

(1) As already noted, in April 2001, the FSF published a 'Compendium of Standards and Codes' titled "International Standards and Codes to Strengthen Financial Systems" (hereinafter the **'Compendium'**), which is being updated on a continuous basis by the FSB.[181] According to the latter:

> The standards under the broad policy areas (…) have been designated by the FSB as key for sound financial systems and deserving of priority implementation depending on country circumstances. These standards are broadly accepted as representing minimum requirements for good practice that countries are encouraged to meet or exceed.

(2) In terms of **scope**, the FSB classifies the standards as either *sectoral*, covering the various economic and institutional sectors (e.g., government, central bank, the four sectors of the financial system (banking, securities, insurance and payments) and corporate sector), or *functional*, covering, within each sector, specific areas (such as governance, accounting, disclosure and transparency, regulation and supervision, information-sharing, risk management, payment and settlement, as well as business ethics). From an implementation perspective and in terms of **"specificity"**, standards are classified by the FSB into three categories: **principles** are fundamental tenets pertaining to a broad policy area, usually set out in a general way and offering a degree of flexibility in implementation to suit country circumstances; **practices** are more specific and spell out the practical application of principles (drawing on country experiences) within a more narrowly defined context; and **guidelines** provide detailed guidance on steps to be taken or requirements to be met in a particular area.

(3) The **"Key Standards for Sound Financial Systems"** are the main component of the FSB's Compendium; they are designated by the FSB as

---

[179] At: https://www.fsb.org/2021/07/fsb-chairs-letter-to-g20-finance-ministers-and-central-bank-governors-july-2021.

[180] On this, see Quarles (2021).

[181] At: https://www.fsb.org/work-of-the-fsb/about-the-compendium-of-standards.

deserving of priority implementation depending on country circumstances.[182] As of **December 2022**, they included sixteen of the numerous reports issued by the above-mentioned international organisations and fora, which are divided into three categories (all shortly presented, in turn, below—for an overview, see also Table 2.9): four reports pertaining to national macroeconomic and financial policies and the transparency of the data supplied by competent authorities; eight reports pertaining to institutional and market infrastructure; and four reports pertaining to financial regulation and supervision.[183]

2.4.2 The Legal Nature of International Financial Standards

(1) With the sole exception of the provisions of the General Agreement on Trade in Services ('**GATS**') on financial services,[184] the rules of public international financial law are not included in the traditional sources of international law under **Article 38(1) of the Statute** of the **International Court of Justice**[185] according to which:

> The traditional statement of the sources of international law, the Statute of the International Court of Justice (…) assumes states to be the primary actors in international law-making and gives no indication of the ways in which non-state actors impact upon its function.[186]

Sources of international financial law include the reports issued by the above-mentioned international fora, i.e., by non-state actors, as well as by international organisations (such as the IMF, the World Bank and the OECD).

(2) The rules contained in these reports take up the form of 'standards' and this is the reason why these fora are designated as 'standard-setting bodies'.[187]

---

[182] At: https://www.fsb.org/work-of-the-fsb/about-the-compendium-of-standards/key_standards.

[183] There are five criteria for determining the list of key standards for sound financial systems: *relevance* and *criticality* for a stable, robust and well-functioning financial system, in order to impart a sense of prioritisation in implementation; *universality* in applicability, by covering areas that are important in most jurisdictions; *flexibility* in implementation, by being general enough to take into account different national particularities; *broad endorsement*, namely, adoption by an internationally recognised body in the relevant area in extensive consultation with relevant stakeholders (this criterion would be satisfied when the standard-setting body has wide representation, or when the standard has been endorsed by international financial institutions, such as the IMF and the World Bank); and *accessibility* by national authorities or by such institutions.

[184] For a detailed presentation of these provisions, see Von Bogdandy and Windsor (2008).

[185] See Stein and von Buttlar (2009), pp. 9–76.

[186] See Boyle and Chinkin (2007), p. 41.

[187] See Kane (2001). It is noteworthy that many international organisations and international fora do not name the standards they issue as such, but they use terms such as:

Table 2.9 The Compendium of Standards of the Financial Stability Board (FSB): *Key Standards for Sound Financial Systems*

Area	Report	Issuing body
A. Macroeconomic Policy and Data Transparency		
Monetary and financial policy transparency	Code of Good Practices on Transparency in Monetary and Financial Policies (2000)	IMF
Fiscal policy transparency	Code of Good Practices on Fiscal Transparency (2017)	IMF
Data dissemination	Enhanced General Data Dissemination System (2015) & Special Data Dissemination Standard (1996)	IMF
B. Institutional and Market Infrastructure		
Insolvency	Insolvency and Creditor Rights Standard (ICR Standard) (2011)	World Bank
Corporate governance	G20/OECD Principles of Corporate Governance (2015)	OECD
Accounting	International Financial Reporting Standards (IFRSs) (2021)	IASB
Auditing	International Standards on Auditing (ISA) (2015)	IFAC
Payment and settlement	Principles for Financial Market Infrastructures (2012)	CPMI/IOSCO
Market integrity	FATF Recommendations on Combatting Money Laundering and the Financing of Terrorism & Proliferation (2012)	FATF
Deposit guarantee	IADI Core Principles for Effective Deposit Insurance Systems (2014)	IADI
Resolution	Key Attributes of Effective Resolution Regimes for Financial Institutions (2014)	FSB

In its simplest form, a standard is a 'model rule' which often needs to be further specified due to its inherent vagueness. The specification of their content is made *ad hoc* when there is resort to them. Due to their widespread acceptance, standards are a common point of reference among their recipients, which means that a minimum level of international harmonisation is achieved on the regulation of a given issue.[188] It is broadly accepted that these standards constitute international 'soft law',[189] namely rules whose key feature is that they lack any legally binding character.

recommendations, core principles, best practices, guidelines, codes of conduct or codes of best practice. Schreiber (2005) (at pp. 10, with further references, and 230) correctly points out that all these concepts should be considered as synonym to the concept of standards. In this sense, the clear definition of terms in the Basel Committee's Charter (see Chapter 3 below) is an exception and can be used as a solid point of reference.

[188] For details, see Schreiber (2005), pp. 44–52.

[189] On the concept of international soft law, see Alexander (2000), Giovanoli (2000), pp. 33–44, Schreiber (2005), pp. 189–229, Boyle and Chinkin (2007), pp. 211–229, Stein and von Buttlar (2009), p. 150, Brummer (2010), Giovanoli (2010), pp. 34–37, Wandel (2014), pp. 25–27, and Lastra (2015), pp. 501–503, 510–513, and 521–524 (arguing that

However, even though they are not 'legally binding', they are **'legally significant'**. This significance is demonstrated by the following: *First*, they constitute a benchmark which all central banks and supervisory authorities that constitute the membership of international fora are expected to comply with and lead *de facto* to the harmonisation of public international financial law.[190] *Second*, they affect the national law of the states that implement them: on a voluntary basis; by means of peer pressure; or in the context of the IMF's supervisory competences, based on its statutory task to oversee the economic policies of its Member States—currently also including issues related to the safeguarding of the financial system's stability. *Third*, these rules have definitively been exerting an influence on the shaping of European financial law and most importantly of the rules of European banking law governing the micro- and macroprudential regulation of EU credit institutions.[191] *Finally*, some standards are not only adopted by the members of international fora, but also by third states since they are considered as global regulatory benchmarks.

2.4.3 Key Sources of Public International Banking Law Included in the Compendium

2.4.3.1 Core Principles for Effective Banking Supervision
Introductory Remarks

The Basel Committee's **"Core Principles for Effective Banking Supervision"** are the result of its cooperation with non-participating banking supervisory authorities. They were issued in 1997[192] and then revised in October 2006 and again in September 2012.[193] In their current form, they contain a list of twenty-nine principles that serve as a main point of reference for banking supervisory authorities and govern the microprudential supervision (and regulation) of banks in every state to ensure its effectiveness. In order to facilitate implementation and evaluation of these principles, the BCBS issued a methodology report in 1999 titled **"Core Principles Methodology"** (revised in 2006). In the 2012 Report, the Core Principles and the assessment methodology were merged into a single (comprehensive) document. The 2012 Core Principles were heavily influenced by the GFC. As noted in the Foreword:

---

we should expect a degree of formalisation of an 'emerging *lex financiera*', points 14.88–14.94). On the issue of legitimacy and accountability of international standard setting, see, by means of mere indication, Wandel (2014), pp. 139–176.

[190] See on this Norton (2001), pp. 20–21, Schreiber (2005), pp. 189–229, and Brummer (2010). On the specific aspect relating to the relevance of international financial standards in the law of the WTO, see Bismuth (2010).

[191] See, by means of mere indication, Sousi-Roubi (1995), pp. 198–206, Hadjiemmanuil (2006), pp. 786–829, Lastra (2006), pp. 297–303, and Fernandez–Bollo et Tabourin (2007), pp. 114–128.

[192] On that version, see Alford (2005).

[193] At: https://www.financialstabilityboard.org/2012/09/cos_061030a.

Important enhancements have been introduced into the individual Core Principles, particularly in those areas that are necessary to strengthen supervisory practices and risk management. As a result, certain "additional criteria" have been upgraded to "essential criteria", while new assessment criteria were warranted in other instances. Close attention was given to addressing many of the significant risk management weaknesses and other vulnerabilities highlighted in the financial crisis. In addition, the review has taken account of several key trends and developments that emerged during the last few years of market turmoil: the need for greater supervisory intensity and adequate resources to deal effectively with systemically important banks; the importance of applying a system-wide, macro perspective to the **micro-prudential supervision** of banks to assist in identifying, analysing and taking pre-emptive action to address systemic risk; and the increasing focus on effective crisis management, recovery and resolution measures in reducing both the probability and impact of a bank failure.

Structure of the Report
(1) The 2012 Report is structured into five sections. While **Section I** contains the "Foreword to the review",[194] the 29 principles are listed in **Section II**[195] (see below in **Table 14**). For the most part, they are derived from Recommendations and Guidelines contained in other Basel Committee reports and can be grouped into the following nine subject-areas: *first*, the institutional requirements that must be fulfilled so that the supervisory authorities can exercise effective prudential banking supervision (responsibilities, objectives and powers, independence and, its necessary counterpart, accountability,[196] resourcing and legal protection, as well as cooperation and collaboration, Principles 1–3); *second*, the conditions for the provision of operating licences to banks, their permissible activities, as well as the approval of amendments in shareholders' structure (Principles 4–7); *third*, supervisory approach, supervisory techniques and tools, supervisory reporting, as well as corrective and sanctioning powers of supervisors (Principles 8–11); *fourth*, consolidated supervision and home-host relationships (Principles 12–13); *fifth*, corporate governance and risk management processes (Principles 14–15); *sixth*, the regulatory framework for exercising prudential banking supervision (i.e., capital adequacy, exposure to credit risk, problem assets, provisions and reserves, exposure to concentration risk and large exposure limits, transactions with related parties, as well as exposure to country and transfer risks, market risk, interest rate risk in the banking book, liquidity risk and operational risk,

---

[194] Basel Committee Core Principles (2012), pp. 4–9.
[195] *Ibid*., pp. 9–14.
[196] Banking supervisors' independence is analysed in Quintyn and Taylor (2002), Doherty and Lenihan (2005), Quintyn, Ramirez and Taylor (2007), Pellegrina *et al.* (2010) and Lastra (2015), pp. 94–96; on their accountability, see Hüpkes, Quintyn and Taylor (2005), Quintyn, Ramirez and Taylor (2007), Lastra and Amtenbrink (2008) and Lastra (2015, *Ibid*).

Principles 16–25); *seventh*, supervisory methods, in cooperation with internal and external auditors, for the control of supervised banks (Principles 26–27); *eighth*, the range of information to be submitted by banks to their supervisory authorities and disclosed to the public (disclosure and transparency, Principle 28); and *finally*, abuse of financial services (Principle 29).

(2) **Section III** of the Report[197] refers to the six preconditions for effective banking supervision. These include sound and sustainable macroeconomic policies; a well-established framework for financial stability policy formulation; a well-developed public infrastructure; a clear framework for crisis management, recovery and resolution; an appropriate level of systemic protection (or public safety net); and effective market discipline. **Section IV**[198] contains the assessment methodology, with specific reference to its use, the assessment of compliance and the practical considerations in conducting assessments; **Section V**[199] sets out analytically the criteria for assessing compliance with the Core Principles, including the powers, responsibilities and functions of supervisory authorities.

(3) The report contains two Annexes: **Annex 1** on the comparison between the revised and 2006 versions of the Core Principles,[200] and **Annex 2** on the structure and guidance for assessment reports prepared by the IMF and the World Bank.[201]

2.4.3.2 The Key Attributes of Effective Resolution Regimes
for Financial Institutions (and Some Related FSB Documents)
(1) The twelve "Key Attributes of Effective Resolution Regimes for Financial Institutions" were adopted in **October 2011** by the FSB.[202] The international financial standards contained therein were adopted in the wake of the GFC with a view to addressing the TBTF issue and contributing to the preservation of financial stability. They lay down the essential features that resolution regimes should incorporate to enable administrative (resolution) authorities to resolve failing financial firms that could be systemic in failure in an orderly manner that limits the overall impact on economic activity, by ensuring, thus, the continuity of critical financial functions and protecting financial stability and without exposing public funds to loss, and in particular measures representing a **"two-pronged strategy"** to reduce both the probability of failure

---

[197] Basel Committee Core Principles (2012), pp. 14–16.
[198] *Ibid.*, pp. 16–20.
[199] *Ibid.*, pp. 21–67.
[200] *Ibid.*, pp. 68–69.
[201] *Ibid.*, pp. 70–79.
[202] At: https://www.financialstabilityboard.org/publications/r_111104cc.htm. For an overview, see Grünewald (2014), pp. 79–80 and Kleftouri (2015), pp. 160–165.

of SIFIs[203] and the impact thereof. According to the Preamble of the Key Attributes:

> The objective of an effective resolution regime is to make feasible the resolution of financial institutions without severe systemic disruption and without exposing taxpayers to loss, while protecting vital economic functions through mechanisms which make it possible for shareholders and unsecured and uninsured creditors to absorb losses in a manner that respects the hierarchy of claims in liquidation.[204]

The standards set out in the Key Attributes refer to the following: the scope of application; the obligation of national lawmakers to designate an (operationally) independent administrative authority responsible for exercising resolution powers over financial institutions and to clearly define their resolution powers; set-off, netting, collateralisation and segregation of client assets; safeguards, including the (above-mentioned) **'no creditor worse off principle'** (**'NCWO'** principle)[205]; funding of firms in resolution; legal framework conditions for cross-border cooperation; cross-border Crisis Management Groups (**'CMGs'**) (the related two standards apply only in relation to **G-SIFIs**); institution-specific cross-border cooperation agreements; recovery and resolution planning and resolvability assessments; as well as access to information and information-sharing.

(2) On **15 October 2014**, the FSB adopted additional guidance documents, which elaborate on specific Key Attributes relating to information-sharing for resolution purposes and sector-specific guidance setting out how they should be applied for insurers, financial market infrastructures (**'FMIs'**)[206] and the protection of client assets in resolution. These documents were incorporated as Annexes into the 2014 version of the Key Attributes but did not modify the 2011 text (**'FSB Key Attributes (2014)'**[207]). *Furthermore*, in **October 2016**, the FSB adopted the "Key Attributes Assessment Methodology for the Banking Sector", which lay down essential criteria

---

[203] Measures to reduce the probability of failure include requirements for additional loss absorption capacity for global SIFIs ('G-SIFIs') and more intensive and effective supervision of financial institutions.

[204] On resolution objectives, see also Chapter 1 above, under 1.3.3.

[205] *Ibid*.

[206] An FMI is a multilateral system among participating financial institutions, including the operator of the system, used for the purposes of, clearing, settling or recording payments, securities, derivatives or other financial transactions. It includes payment systems, central securities depositories, securities settlement systems, central counterparties and trade repositories.

[207] At: https://www.Financialstabilityboard.org/2014/10/r_141015.

guiding the assessment of compliance with the key attributes ('**FSB Assessment Methodology (2016)**').[208]

(3) The work of the FSB on resolution is not confined to the Key Attributes. In this respect, *inter alia*, reference should also be made to two related documents for global systemically important banks ('**G-SIBs**')[209]:

> *First*, taking into account that bail-in powers should be supported by the requirements for G-SIBs to hold bail-in-able liabilities, on **9 November 2015**, it issued its Report "Principles on Loss-absorbing and Recapitalisation Capacity of G-SIBs in Resolution—Total Loss-absorbing Capacity (TLAC) Term Sheet".[210] This document: (a) set out thirteen Principles on a new international standard for international banks identified by the FSB as G-SIBs[211]; (b) laid down the minimum external 'total loss absorbing capacity' standard (the 'minimum TLAC standard') for G-SIBs deemed as TBTF[212]; and (c) introduced an 'internal TLAC standard', governing the loss-absorbing capacity that resolution entities should commit to 'material sub-groups' to facilitate cooperation between home and host authorities *and* the implementation of effective cross-border resolution strategies for the appropriate distribution of loss-absorbing and recapitalisation capacity within groups outside the resolution entity's home jurisdiction.[213]
>
> *Second*, in relation to the issue of liquidity in (or after) resolution, in 2016 FSB adopted its **Guiding Principles** "on the temporary funding needed to support the orderly resolution of a global systemically important bank".[214] According to these Principles, a credit institution's ability to use private sources of funding in resolution depends, *inter alia*, on the following: *first*, the timing of resolution action; *second*, the amount and quality of available collateral to the extent of asset encumbrance

---

[208] This document lays down essential criteria guiding the assessment of national bank resolution frameworks' compliance with the key attributes (at: https://www.fsb.org/2016/10/key-attributes-assessment-methodology-for-the-banking-sector).

[209] On the corporate complexity of G-SIBs, see Carmassi and Herring (2016); for an analysis suggesting that requiring G-SIBs to hold additional capital is likely to reduce volatility spill-over effects to other large banks, see McNelis and Yetman (2020).

[210] At: https://www.fsb.org/2015/11/total-loss-absorbing-capacity-tlac-principles-and-term-sheet.

[211] At: https://www.fsb.org/wp-content/uploads/2015-update-of-list-of-global-systemically-important-banks-G-SIBs.pdf.

[212] On the TLAC, see Borsuk (2015), Huertas (2015), Kupiec (2015), Speyer (2015), Szczepańska (2015) and Mauchle (2017).

[213] FSB TLAC Report (2015), Term Sheet, paras 16–17. On 6 July 2017, the FSB also adopted its "Guidance on Continuity of Access to [FMIs] for a Firm in Resolution" (at: https://www.fsb.org/2017/07/guidance-on-continuity-of-access-to-financial-market-infrastructures-fmis-for-a-firm-in-resolution-2).

[214] At: https://www.fsb.org/2016/08/guiding-principles-on-the-temporary-funding-needed-to-support-the-orderly-resolution-of-a-global-systemically-important-bank-g-sib.

prior to resolution; *third*, the prevailing macroeconomic environment, including market liquidity; *fourth*, market confidence towards the recapitalised credit institutions; and *finally*, the existence of an effective public sector backstop funding mechanism. In relation to the latter aspect, it is provided that this mechanism must be able to cover the liquidity needs of several credit institutions in case of a systemic crisis and operationally capable to grant liquidity in time to address liquidity gaps of the institutions concerned. Furthermore, the backstop funding mechanisms must provide temporary funding under strict conditions in order to mitigate ensuing moral hazard risks.[215]

2.4.3.3 Core Principles for Effective Deposit Insurance Systems

(1) On 18 June 2009, the Basel Committee and IADI jointly issued a Report on "Core Principles for Effective Deposit Insurance Systems"[216]; this was followed by the "IADI Core Principles for Effective Deposit Insurance Systems" of 1 November 2014.[217] The updated IADI Core Principles, which reflect the need for effective deposit insurance in preserving financial stability, were heavily influenced by the GFC. As mentioned in the Introduction:

> In the aftermath of the crisis, many deposit insurers saw their mandates enhanced and, in some cases, expanded to include resolution tools in addition to depositor reimbursement. As a result of the crisis, a greater emphasis has also been placed on ensuring that the deposit insurer has the necessary operational independence to fulfil its mandate. The crisis has shown that deposit insurers need to have additional tools and an ability to be better integrated into the financial safety-net.

(2) The 2014 IADI Report is structured into five sections (including the introductory **Section I**[218]). **Section II** gives the definitions of key terms,[219] **Section III** deals with moral hazard, operating environment and other considerations,[220] **Section IV** deals with some special issues in applying the Core Principles[221] while the sixteen Core Principles (including the compliance assessment) are listed in **Section V**.[222] The Core Principles refer to the following aspects: the policy objectives of deposit insurance systems; their

---

[215] FSB Guiding Principles, pp. 9–14.

[216] This Report is available at: https://www.iadi.org/en/core-principles-and-guidance/core-principles.

[217] On this Report, see at: https://www.financialstabilityboard.org/2014/11/cos_090618.

[218] IADI Core Principles (2014), pp. 5–8.

[219] *Ibid.*, pp. 8–10.

[220] *Ibid.*, pp. 11–15.

[221] *Ibid.*, pp. 16–17.

[222] *Ibid.*, pp. 18–41.

mandate and powers; their governance; the relationship with other components of the 'bank safety net'; the international dimension ('cross-border issues', *new*); the deposit insurers' role in contingency planning and crisis management *(new)*; the obligation for all banks to participate in principle in a deposit insurance system; the coverage provided to depositors by these systems; their funding mechanisms ('sources and uses of funds'); the information provided to depositors ('public awareness'); specific legal issues ('legal protection'); the dealing with parties at fault in a bank failure; early detection and timely intervention *(new)*; failure resolution; the pay-out to depositors; and recoveries by deposit insurance systems *(new)*.

The Report is supplemented by two Annexes: **Annex I** which presents guidance and a format for compliance assessment, as well as the structure of the assessment reports[223]; and **Annex II** which lists the members of the IADI Steering Committee and the Joint Working Group which contributed to the elaboration of the revised Core Principles.[224] A list of references to relevant primary and secondary sources completes the Report.[225]

2.4.4 The Other FSB "Key Standards for Sound Financial Systems"

2.4.4.1 Codes Pertaining to National Macroeconomic Policies and the Transparency of Data Supplied by Competent Authorities

Code of Good Practices on Transparency in Monetary and Financial Policies: Issued by the IMF in 1999 and revised in 2000, this Code identifies transparency practices for central banks in their conduct of monetary policy, and for central banks and other supervisory authorities in the individual financial system sectors in the performance of their supervisory and regulatory responsibilities. These practices are desirable, according to the IMF, for two main reasons: *first*, the effectiveness of monetary and financial policies can be enhanced if the objectives and the means of achieving them are known to the public; and *second*, accountability of supervisory authorities (including central banks) may strengthen their governance and ensure policy consistency, especially when these authorities have a high degree of independence.

Fiscal Transparency Code: This Code, issued as well by the IMF in 2014 (and in force as amended on 7 November 2017), constitutes the global standard for disclosure of information about public finances. It replaced the 2007 Code and the related "Fiscal Module of the Reports on the Observance of Standards and Codes" as an adjustment to the lessons from the GFC. It identifies the desirable transparency requirements regarding the clarity of the role and the responsibilities between government and commercial activities; 'open' budget processes; public availability of information with respect to the

---

[223] *Ibid.*, pp. 42–48.
[224] *Ibid.*, pp. 49–53.
[225] *Ibid.*, pp. 54–56.

(past, current and projected) fiscal activity and major fiscal risks; and assurances relating to the integrity of fiscal data and practices. The Code's principles are built around four pillars: fiscal reporting, fiscal forecasting and budgeting, fiscal risk analysis and management, and resource revenue management. For each transparency principle, the Code differentiates between basic, good and advanced practices to provide countries with clear milestones towards full compliance with the Code and ensure its applicability to the broad range of IMF member countries.

Special Data Dissemination Standard and enhanced General Data Dissemination System: This framework of standards, also elaborated by the IMF, was issued in 1996 and 1997 and contains two parts: the *first part* ('**SDDS**') is addressed to states that have, or that might seek, access to international capital markets with respect to dissemination of economic and financial data to the public; the *second part* ('**e-GDDS**'), as in force since 1 May 2015, is addressed to states which do not have or intend to obtain access to international capital markets, taking into account the particularities of each state's economy, as well as the data dissemination systems developed. States adopting the SDDS or the e-GDDS commit to abide by good statistical practices regarding coverage, periodicity and timeliness of disseminated data, access by the public, as well as correctness and quality of data. Data dissemination practices under these two codes cover twenty categories of data, referring to the real, fiscal, financial and external sectors of the economy.

2.4.4.2 Codes Pertaining to Institutional and Market Infrastructure[226]

Principles for Effective Insolvency and Creditor Rights Systems: The World Bank and the UNCITRAL, in consultation with the IMF, have adopted the Insolvency and Creditor Rights' Standard (the '**ICR Standard**'). This contains international best practices concerning. That report, issued in 2001 and lastly amended in 2011, contains principles concerning effective: systems for formal reorganisation and liquidation/insolvency proceedings; organisation and functioning of commercial courts and insolvency professionals; out-of-court restructuring practices and procedure; credit access and protection mechanisms; as well as commercial enforcement and credit risk management frameworks.

Principles of corporate governance: In 1999, the OECD issued a report with specific principles aimed at improving the legal, institutional and regulatory framework on corporate governance in its member states and in non-OECD states; they are in force as lastly amended in November 2015.[227]

---

[226] By exception, the International Financial Reporting Standards, the International Standards on Auditing and the FATF Recommendations are presented in Chapter 3 below, under 3.3.2, 3.3.3 and 3.4.3, respectively. This was deemed necessary in order to link them with the operation of the international fora adopting them.

[227] OECD (2015), G20/OECD Principles of Corporate Governance, OECD Publishing, Paris (at: https://dx.doi.org/10.1787/9789264236882-en). A draft of the Principles was discussed by the G20/OECD Corporate Governance Forum in April 2015.

Even though their main focus is listed companies, their application to companies whose shares are not listed in markets is not excluded. They refer to the rights and equal treatment of shareholders; the role of stakeholders in corporate governance; disclosure and transparency obligations to ensure timely and accurate disclosure on all material matters regarding the operation of companies; the responsibilities of board members to ensure their strategic guidance (pursuing objectives in the interest of the company and its shareholders); and the effective monitoring of management.

Principles for financial market infrastructures (FMIs): These twenty-four principles, adopted on 18 April 2012 by the CPMI and the IOSCO's Technical Committee, replaced and codified three previous reports (issued in the period 2001-2004) on the principles which should govern sound FMIs, duly taking into account existing experience, lessons from the GFC and policy work by the CPSS and IOSCO.[228] The principles apply to systemically important payment systems, central securities depositories ('**CSDs**'), securities settlements systems, central counterparties ('**CCPs**')[229] and trade repositories and concern the following subject areas: credit and liquidity risk management, including risk-based collateral and margin; settlement finality and money settlement; governance of CSPs and securities settlement systems; participants' default rules and procedures; general business and operational risk management; access and participation requirements to FMIs; their efficiency, effectiveness and transparency; as well as responsibilities of authorities to provide for their effective regulation, supervision and oversight.

2.4.4.3 Codes on financial microprudential regulation and supervision

Objectives and Principles of Securities Regulation: This IOSCO Report was issued in 1998 and revised repeatedly, most recently on 31 May 2017.[230] It sets out thirty-eight principles, accompanied by examples of specific existing practices, as regards microprudential supervision and regulation in capital markets with a view to safeguard the protection of investors, ensure capital markets' integrity, efficiency and transparency, as well as safeguard their

---

The OECD Council adopted the Principles on 8 July 2015. The Principles were then submitted to the G20 Leaders' Summit on 15–16 November 2015 in Antalya, where they were endorsed as the G20/OECD Principles of Corporate Governance. These principles are currently being reviewed; see at: https://www.oecd.org/corporate/review-oecd-g20-principles-corporate-governance.htm. It is expected that the review will be completed in 2023.

[228] CPMI/IOSCO "Principles for financial market infrastructures" (at: https://www.bis.org/cpmi/publ/d101a.pdf). In addition to these standards, the CPMI and the IOSCO have published a number of related documents and further guidance on the implementation of these standards.

[229] On CCPs and the case for their regulation, see details, by means of mere indication, in Murphy (2022), pp. 177–226.

[230] At: https://www.iosco.org/library/pubdocs/pdf/IOSCOPD561.pdf.

stability (by reducing systemic risk).[231] The IOSCO principles are grouped into ten categories depending on their recipient and subject matter, as follows: eight principles relating to the supervisory authorities (mentioned as 'the regulator'), one principle for self-regulation, three principles for the enforcement of securities regulation, three principles for cooperation in supervision (mentioned as 'regulation'), three principles for issuers of securities, five principles for auditors, credit rating agencies and other information service providers, five principles for collective investment schemes, four principles for market intermediaries, five principles for secondary and other markets, and one principle on clearing and settlement of securities. The accompanying document "Methodology for Assessing Implementation of the IOSCO Objectives and Principles of Securities Regulation" of 2011 (revised in May 2017) provides interpretation of the principles and gives guidance on the conduct of a self-assessment or third-party assessment of the level of their implementation.[232]

Insurance Core Principles, Standards, Guidance and Assessment Methodology: The twenty-six principles of the IAIS were included in a 1997 Report, which was repeatedly amended (in 2000 and 2003, substantially in 2011, and then again in 2013, in 2017 and most recently on 9 November 2019, when a multi-year review and revision process was completed). They refer to the conditions that need to be met for a national (private) insurance supervisory and regulatory system to be effective. The document sets out the framework for insurance microprudential supervision and identifies areas of major importance that need to be addressed through microprudential regulations in this financial sector, and relevant powers of the competent supervisory authorities. It is accompanied by an "Assessment Methodology".

Core Principles for Islamic Financial Regulation (Banking Segment): These Core Principles of 1 April 2015, along with their associated assessment methodology, were adopted by the Islamic Financial Services Board ('**IFSB**').[233] They refer to the regulation and supervision of the Islamic financial services industry taking into consideration the specificities of institutions offering such services in the banking sector. They complement existing international standards, principally the Basel Committee's Core Principles for Effective Banking Supervision.[234]

---

[231] It is clarified therein that the term 'investor' includes customers or other consumers of financial services.

[232] At: https://www.iosco.org/library/pubdocs/pdf/IOSCOPD562.pdf.

[233] On this Board, see at: https://www.ifsb.org.

[234] On Islamic banking, see, by means of mere indication, Antoniazzi (2022), with extensive further references.

Secondary Sources

A

Adrian, T., Morsink, J. and L.B. Schumacher (2020): *Stress Testing at the IMF*, Monetary and Capital Markets Department, International Monetary Fund, No. 20/4, 5 February, available at: https://www.imf.org/en/Publications/Departmental-Papers-Policy-Papers/Issues/2020/01/31/Stress-Testing-at-the-IMF-48825

Alexander, K. (2019): *Principles of Banking Regulation*, Cambridge University Press, Cambridge, United Kingdom

Alexander, K. (2000): *The Role of Soft Law in the Legalization of International Banking Supervision: A Conceptual Approach*, ESRC Centre for Business Research, Department of Applied Economics, University of Cambridge, Cambridge, England

Alexander, K., Lorez, K., Jackson, H.E. and N. Moloney (2014): *The Legitimacy of the G20—A Critique under International Law*, available at: https://ssrn.com/abstract=2431164

Alford, D.E. (2005): Core Principles for Effective Banking Supervision: An Enforceable International Financial Standard?, *Boston College International and Comparative Law Review*, Volume 28, issue 2, pp. 237–297, available at: https://lawdigitalcommons.bc.edu/iclr/vol28/iss2/2

Alvarez, S.G., Baxter, T.C. Jr. and R.F. Hoyt (2020): The Legal Authorities Framing the Government's Response to the Global Financial Crisis, *Journal of Financial Crises*: Volume 2, Issue 1, pp. 3–32, available at: https://elischolar.library.yale.edu/journal-of-financial-crises/vol2/iss1/2

Antoniazzi, S. (2022): *Islamic Banks and the European Banking System: Critical Profiles and Law*, European Banking Institute Working Paper Series, No. 125, available at: https://ssrn.com/abstract_id=4155340

Armour, J. Awrey, D., Davies, P., Enriques, L., Gordon, J., Mayer, C. and J. Payne (2016): *Principles of Financial Regulation*, Oxford University Press, Oxford

Ayadi, R. and A. Resti (2004): *The New Basel Capital Accord and the Future of the European Financial System*, CEPS Task Force Report No. 51, April, Centre for European Policy Studies

B

Baldwin, S.E. (1907): The International Congresses And Conferences Of The Last Century As Forces Working Toward The Solidarity Of The World, *American Journal of International Law*, p. 565 et seq. (reprinted as paperback, 13 March 2012, Nabu Press, Germany)

Bardos, J. (1988): The Risk-based Capital Agreement: A Further Step towards Policy Convergence, *Federal Reserve Bank of New York Quarterly Review*, winter, pp. 26–34

Berger, K.P. (2010): *The Creeping Codification of the New Lex Mercatoria*, 2nd edtion, Alphen aan den Rijn, Kluwer, The Netherlands

Bergsten, F. (2000): *Reforming the International Financial Architecture*, Testimony before the Committee on Banking and Financial Services, United States House of Representatives, Peterson Institute for International Economics, Washington, DC, available at: https://www.piie.com/commentary/testimonies/reforming-international-financial-architecture

Bismuth, R. (2010): Financial Sector Regulation and Financial Services Liberalization at the Crossroads: The Relevance of International Financial Standards in WTO Law, Journal of World Trade, Volume 44, no. 2, pp. 489–514

Bizzozero, A. and Ch. Robinson (2010): *Activités financières cross-border vers et depuis la Suisse*, Bizzozero & Robinson—Brlegal, Bulle, Switzerland

Bordo, M. and H. James (2010): The past and future of IMF reform: a proposal, in Wyplosz, Ch. (2010, editor): *The New International Monetary System - Essays in honor of Alexander Swoboda*, Routledge International Studies in Money and Banking, Rutledge, USA—Canada, pp. 9–28

Borio, C. (2008): *The Financial Turmoil of 2007-?: A Preliminary Assessment and Some Policy Considerations*, BIS working Papers No 251, Bank for International Settlements, March, pp. 1–13

Borsuk, M. (2015): *Adequate loss-absorbing capacity in the resolution process*, Safe Bank, Bank Guarantee Fund, no 3(60), pp. 54–77

Boyle, A. and Ch. Chinkin (2007): *The Making of International Law*, Oxford University Press, Oxford—New York

Brakman, S., Garretsen, H., van Marrenwijk, Ch. and Ar. Van Witteloostuijn (2006): *Nations and Firms in the Global Economy—An Introduction to International Economics and Business*, Cambridge University Press, Cambridge, pp. 217–263

Bremmer, I. and N. Roubini (2011): A G-Zero World, *Foreign Affairs*, Volume 91, Number 2 (March/April), pp. 2–7

Brummer, C. (2010): Why soft law dominates international finance—and not trade, *Journal of International Economic Law*, Volume 13, No. 3, September, Oxford University Press, Oxford, September, pp. 623–644

Bryant, R.C. (1999): *Reforming the International Financial Architecture*, Brookings Discussion Papers in International Economics, No. 146, July, available at: https://www.brookings.edu/wp-content/uploads/2016/06/146.pdf

C

Calomiris, Ch.W. (2008): The subprime turmoil: What's old, what's new, and what's next, Jackson Hole Symposium: *Maintaining Stability in a Changing Financial System*, Federal Reserve Bank of Kansas City, August

Caprio, J. and D. Klingebiel (1999): *Episodes of Systemic and Borderline Financial Crises*, World Bank database

Caprio, J. and D. Klingebiel (1996): *Bank Insolvencies: Cross-Country Experience*, World Bank Policy Research Working Paper, No. 1620, World Bank, Washington, DC

Carmassi, J. and R. Herring (2016): The corporate complexity of global systemically important banks, *Journal of Financial Services Research*, Volume 49, issue 2, pp. 175–201

Carreau, D. et P. Juillard (2005): *Droit International Economique*, Dalloz, Paris

Carstens, A. G. (2020): *Countering Covid-19: The nature of central banks' policy response*, Opening remarks at the UBS High-level Discussion on the Economic and Monetary Policy Outlook, Zurich, 27 May, available at: https://www.bis.org/speeches/sp200527.htm

Cassese, S. (2016): *Research Handbook on Global Administrative Law*, Research Handbooks on Globalisation and the Law series, Edward Elgar Publishing, Cheltenham, UK—Northampton, MA, USA

Cassese, S. (2005): Global Administrative Law: An Introduction, *Journal of International Law and Politics*, Volume 37, Issue 4, pp. 663–694

Cassese and E. D' Alterio (2016): Introduction: the development of Global Administrative Law, in Cassese, S. , 2016. Cassese, S. and E. D' Alterio (2016): Introduction: the development of Global Administrative Law, in Cassese, S. (2016): *Research Handbook on Global Administrative Law*, Research Handbooks on Globalisation and the Law series, Edward Elgar Publishing, Cheltenham, UK—Northampton, MA, USA

Chiti, Ed. and R.A. Wessel (2011): The emergence of international agencies in the global administrative space: Autonomous actors or state servants?, in Collins, R. and N.G. White (2011, editors): *International Organizations and the Idea of Autonomy: Institutional Independence in the International Legal Order*, pp. 142–159

Claessens, S., Herring, R.J. and D. Schoenmaker (2010): *A Safer World Financial System: Improving the Resolution of Systemic Institutions*, Geneva Reports on the World Economy, no 12, International Center for Monetary and Banking Studies, Centre for Economic Policy Research, London, UK

Committee on the Global Financial System (2020): *US dollar funding: an international perspective*, CGFS Papers, No 65, 18 June, available at: https://www.bis.org/publ/cgfs65.pdf

Conthe, M. and S. Ingves (2001): *Financial Sector Assessment Program*, available at: https://www.imf.org/external/np/fsap/fsap.asp

Conti-Brown, P. and M. Ohlrogge (2022): Financial Crises and Legislation, *Journal of Financial Crises*, Volume 4, Issue 3, pp. 1–59 (also available as NYU Law and Economics Research Paper No. 22-02, at: https://ssrn.com/abstract=2360698

Crocket, A. (2002): Thoughts on the New Financial Architecture, in Dickinson, D.G. and W.A. Allen (2002, editors): *Monetary Policy, Capital Flows and Exchange Rates*, 1st Edition, Routledge, London–New York, pp. 78–91

D

Dale, R. (1996): *Risk and Regulation in Global Securities Markets*, Wiley Publishers, Chichester-New York-Brisbane-Toronto-Singapore

Dale, R. (1984): *The Regulation of International Banking*, Wood-head-Faulkneur, Cambridge and Prentice-Hall, Inc., Englewood Cliffs, N.J.

Dewatripont, M., and J. Tirole (1994): *The Prudential Regulation of Banks*, The Walras-Pareto Lectures, No. 1, The MIT Press, Cambridge-London

Ding, X., Gross, M., Krznar, I., Laliotis, D., Lipinsky, F., Lukyantsau, P. and Th. Tressel (2022): *The Global Bank Stress Test*, Monetary and Capital Markets Department, International Monetary Fund, Departmental Paper Series, DP/2022/009 available at: https://www.imf.org/en/Publications/Departmental-Papers-Policy-Papers/Issues/2022/04/04/The-Global-Bank-Stress-Test-513818

Doherty, J. and N. Lenihan (2005): Central bank independence and responsibility for financial supervision within the ESCB: the case of Ireland, in European Central Bank (2005): *Legal Aspects of the European System of Central Banks: Liber Amicorum Paolo Zamboni Garavelli*, European Central Bank, pp. 215–232

Donelly, Sh. (2019): Financial Stability Board (FSB), Bank for International Settlements (BIS) and Financial Market Regulation Bodies: ECB and Commission participation alongside the Member States, in Wessel, R. and J. Odermatt (2019, editors), *Research Handbook on the European Union and International Organizations*, Edward Elgar Publishing, Cheltenham, UK—Northampton, MA, USA (also available at: https://www.academia.edu/40185329)

E-F

Eichengreen, B. (2015): *The Irish Crisis and the EU from a Distance*, January, available at: https://www.imf.org/external/np/seminars/eng/2014/ireland/pdf/Eichengreen_IrishCrisisEU.pdf

Eichengreen, B. (2008): *Thirteen Questions about the Subprime Crisis*, Conference of the Tobin Project: Toward a new Theory of Financial Regulation, While Oak Conference and Residency Center, February

Eichengreen, B. (1994): *International Monetary Arrangements for the 21st Century*, Integrating National Economies, The Brookings Institution, Washington, DC

Eichengreen, B. and M. Bordo (2002): *Crises Now and Then: What Lessons from the Last Era of Financial Globalization?* NBER Working Paper No. 8716

European Central Bank (2008): *The incentive structure of the 'originate and distribute' model*, European Central Bank, December, available at: https://www.ecb.europa.eu/incentivestructureoriginatedistributemodel200812en.pdf

Fernandez-Bollo, E. et G. Tabourin (2007): Les établissements de credit, in Commentaire J. Megret: *Integration des marchés financiers*, Direction Dominique Servais, Institut d' Etudes Européennes, Editions de l' Université de Bruxelles, Bruxelles, pp. 91–148

Fisher, St. (1999): *On the Need for an International Lender of Last Resort*, Speech at the International Monetary Fund, January 3, available at: https://www.imf.org/en/News/Articles/2015/09/28/04/53/sp010399

G

Genberg H. and A.K. Swoboda (1991): *The Provision of Liquidity in the Bretton-Woods System*, Discussion Papers in International Economics, The Graduate Institute of International Studiers, Geneva

Giovanoli, M. (2010): The International Financial Architecture and its Reform after the Global Crisis, in Giovanoli, M. and D. Devos (2010, editors): *International Monetary and Financial Law: The global crisis*, Oxford University Press, Oxford–New York, pp. 3–39

Giovanoli, M. (2000a, editor): *International Monetary Law—Issues for the New Millennium*, Oxford University Press, Oxford

Giovanoli, M. (2000b): A New Architecture for the Global Financial Market: Legal Aspects of International Financial Standard Setting, in Giovanoli, M. (2000, editor): *International Monetary Law—Issues for the New Millennium*, Oxford University Press, Oxford—New York, pp. 3–59

Giovanoli, M. and D. Devos (2010, editors): *International Monetary and Financial Law: The global crisis*, Oxford University Press, Oxford–New York

Gleeson, S. (2010): *International Regulation of Banking—Basel II: Capital and Risk Requirements*, Oxford University Press, Oxford—New York

Global Partnership for Financial Inclusion (2014): *2014 Financial Inclusion Action Plan*, September, available at: https://www.g20.utoronto.ca/2014/2014_g20_financial_inclusion_action_plan.pdf

Goldstein, M., Kaminsky, G. and C. Reinhart (2000): Assessing Financial Vulnerability in Emerging Economies: A Summary of Empirical Results, *East Asian Economic Review*, Volume 4, No. 2, pp. 101–147 (also available at: https://ssrn.com/abstract=3080019)

Goodhart, C.A.E. (2009): *The Regulatory Response to the Financial Crisis*, Edward Elgar, Cheltenham, UK–Northampton, MA, USA

Gorton, G. (2010): *Questions and Answers about the Financial Crisis, Prepared for the U.S Financial Crisis Inquiry Commission*, available at: https://ssrn.com/abstract=1557279

Gorton, G. (2009): *Slapped in the face by the Invisible Hand: Bank and Panic of 2007*, Prepared for the Federal Reserve Bank of Atlanta's 2009 Financial Markets Conference: Financial Innovation and Crisis, May 11–13, 2009, available at: https://ssrn.com/abstract=1401882

Gortsos, Ch.V. (2023): The role of international financial fora in preserving global financial stability amidst the pandemic crisis: the first 18 months, in Blair, W., Zilioli, Ch. and Ch.V. Gortsos (2023, editors), *International Monetary and Banking Law in the post COVID-19 World*, Chapter 1, Oxford University Press, Oxford

Gortsos, Ch.V. (2022a): On the Cypriot 2012–2013 Banking Crisis and the 2013 Banking Resolution, *Festschrift in Honour of Benjamin Geva, Banking & Finance Law Review*, Volume 38, Section III: The legal nature of money and banking law, pp. 271–284

Gortsos, Ch.V. (2022b): Historical Evolution of Bank Capital Requirements in the European Union, in Joosen, B., Lamandini, M. and T. Tröger (2022, editors): *Capital and Liquidity Requirements for European Banks: CRRII and CRDV*, Oxford EU Financial Regulation Series (main editors D. Busch and G. Ferrarini), Oxford University Press, Oxford, Part I, Chapter 1, pp. 3–42

Gortsos, Ch.V. (2012): *Fundamentals of Public International Financial Law: International Banking Law within the System of Public International Financial Law*, Schriften des Europa-Instituts der Universität des Saarlandes—Rechtswissenschaft, Nomos Verlag, Baden-Baden

Gross, D. (2007): UNCITRAL at 40: An overview of current achievements and challenges, *Uniform Law Review 12*, p. 178 *et seq.*

Grünewald, S.N. (2014): *The Resolution of Cross-Border Banking Crises in the European Union – A Legal Study from the Perspective of Burden Sharing*, International Banking and Finance Law Series, Volume 23, Wolters Kluwer Law & Business, Kluwer Law International, The Netherlands

H

Hadjiemmanuil, Ch. (2020): The Euro Area in Crisis: 2008–2018, in Amtenbrink, F. and Ch. Herrmann (2019, editors): *Oxford Handbook on the EU Law of Economic and Monetary Union*, Oxford University Press, Oxford, Chapter 40, pp. 1253–1362 (also published in LSE Law, Society and Economy Working Papers 12/2019, available at: https://ssrn.com/abstract=3413000)

Hadjiemmanuil, Ch. (2006): Financial Services, in Chalmers, D., Hadjiemmanuil, Ch., Monti, G. and A. Tomkins (2006, editors): *European Union Law*, Cambridge University Press, Cambridge, New York, Melbourne, Madrid, Cape Town, Singapore, São Paolo, Chapter 18, pp. 781–829

Hagan, S. (2010a): Enhancing the IMF's regulatory authority, *Journal of International Economic Law*, Volume 13, Number 3, September, Oxford University Press, Oxford, pp. 955–968

Hagan, S. (2010b): Reforming the IMF, in Giovanoli, M. and D. Devos (2010b, editors): *International Monetary and Financial Law: The Global Crisis*, Oxford University Press, Oxford, pp. 40–68

Hausmann, Y. (1995): *Die Eigenmittelvorschriften des schweizerischen Bankengesetzes im Vergleich zu den Bestimmungen der Europäischen Union und des Basler Ausschusses für Bankenbestimmungen und -überwachung*, Schweizer Schriften zum Bankrecht, Band 31, Schulthess Polygraphischer Verlag, Zürich

Herdegen, M. (2008): *Internationales Wirtschaftsrecht*, 7, Auflage, Verlag C.H.Beck, München

Herring, R. (2005): Implementing Basel II: Is the Game Worth the Candle?, *Financial markets, Institutions & Instruments*, Volume 14, No. 5, pp. 267–287, December (also available at: https://ssrn.com/abstract=869287)

Herring, R.J. and R.E. Litan (1995): *Financial Regulation in the Global Economy*, The Brookings Institution, Washington, DC, available at: https://www.brookings.edu/comm/conferencereport/cr14.htm

Honohan, P. (1997): *Banking system failures in developing and transition countries: diagnosis and prediction*, BIS Working Papers No. 39, Bank for International Settlements, Monetary and Economic Department, January

Hooke, A.W. (1981): *The International Monetary Fund, its Evolution, Organisation and Activities*, Pamphlet Series No. 37, International Monetary Fund, Washington, DC

Houben, A., Kakes, J. and G. Schinasi (2004): *Toward a Framework for Safeguarding Financial Stability*, IMF Working Papers, WP/04/101, available at: https://www.imf.org/external/pubs/ft/wp/2004/wp04101.pdf

Huertas, T. (2015): *Six structures in search of stability*, LSE Financial Markets Group Paper Series, Special Paper no 236, July, available at: https://ssrn.com/abstract=2662251

Hüpkes, E., Quintyn, M. and M. Taylor (2005): *The Accountability of Financial Sector Supervisors: Principles and Practice*, IMF Working Papers, WP/05/51, available at: https://www.imf.org/external/pubs/ft/wp/2005/wp0551.pdf

J-K

Jeanne, Ol. and Ch. Wyplosz (2001): *The International Lender of Last Resort: How Large is Large Enough?*, National Bureau of Economic Research (NBER), Working Paper 8381, July, available at: https://www.nber.org/system/files/working_papers/w8381/w8381.pdf

Kane, E.J. (2001): Relevance and Need for International Regulatory Standards, in Litan, R.E. and R.J. Herring (2001, editors): *Brookings-Wharton Papers on Financial Services*, Brookings Institution Press, July pp. 87–115

Kane, E.J. (2000): *Capital Movements Banking Insolvency, and Silent Runs in the Asian Financial Crisis*, NBER Working Paper Series, Working Paper, January, available at: https://www.nber.org/papers/w7514

Kapstein, E.B. (1994): *Governing the Global Economy: International Finance and the State*, Harvard University Press, Cambridge, Massachusetts–London, England

Kiff, J. and P. Mills (2007): *Money for Nothing and Checks for Free: Recent Developments in U.S. Subprime Mortgage Markets*, IMF Working Papers, WP/07/188, available at: https://www.imf.org/external/pubs/ft/wp/2007/wp07188.pdf

Kim, T. (1993): *International Money & Banking*, Routledge, New York

Kleftouri, N. (2015): *Deposit Protection and Bank Resolution*, Oxford University Press, Oxford

Krugman, P. (2012): *End this depression now!* W.W. Norton & Company, New York–London

Kupiec, P. (2015): *Will TLAC Regulations Fix the G-SIB Too-Big-To-Fail Problem?*, AEI Economic Policy Working Paper 2015–08, 25 November, available at: https://ssrn.com/abstract=2631617

L

Lastra, R.M. (2015): *International Financial and Monetary Law*, second edition, Oxford University Press, United Kingdom

Lastra, R.M. (2006): *Legal foundations of international monetary stability*, Oxford University Press, Oxford–New York

Lastra, R.M. and G. Wood (2010): The crisis of 2007–2009: nature, causes and reactions, *Journal of International Economic Law*, Volume 13, no. 3, September, Oxford University Press, Oxford, September, pp. 531–550

Lastra, R.M. and R. Amtenbrink (2008): Securing Democratic Accountability of Financial Regulatory Agencies—A Theoretical framework, in de Mulder Rotterdam: Erasmus School of Law & Research School for Safety and Security (OMV) (2008, editor): *Mitigating Risk in the Context of Safety and Security. How Relevant is a Rational Approach?*, pp. 115–132

Laeven, L. and F. Valencia (2008): *Systemic Banking Crises: A New Database*, IMF Working Papers, WP/08/224, available at: https://www.imf.org/external/pubs/ft/wp/2008/wp08224.pdf

Lowenfeld, A. F. (2009): *International Economic Law*, Second edition, International Economic Law Series, Oxford University Press, Oxford–New York

M-N

Macht, C. (2007): *Der Baseler Ausschuss für Bankenaufsicht und Basel II—Bankenregulierung auf einem internationalen level paying field*, Studien zum Bank- und Börsenrecht, Band 64, Nomos Verlagsgesellschaft, Baden-Baden

Mauchle, Y. (2017): *Bail-In and Total Loss-Absorbing Capacity (TLAC)—Legal and Economic Perspectives on Bank Resolution with Functional Comparisons of Swiss and EU Law*, International Banking and Finance Law Series Volume 32, Kluwer Law International BV, The Netherlands

McKnight, A. (2008): *The Law of International Finance*, Oxford University Press, Oxford

McNelis, P.D. and J. Yetman (2020): *Volatility spillovers and capital buffers among the G-SIBs*, BIS Working Papers No 856, April, available at: https://www.bis.org/publ/work856.pdf

Mishkin, F.C. and U. Hall (2000): *The International Lender of Last Resort: What are the Issues?* available at: https://www0.gsb.columbia.edu/faculty/fmishkin/PDFpapers/00KIEL.pdf

Moessner, R. and W. Allen (2010): *Banking Crises and the International Monetary System in the Great Depression and now*, BIS Working Papers No. 333, Monetary and Economic Department, Bank for International Settlements, December

Monteverdi, A. (2017): From Washington Consensus to Brussels Consensus, in: Sciso E. (2017, editor): *Accountability, Transparency and Democracy in the Functioning of Bretton Woods Institutions*, Springer, Cham—Switzerland, pp. 73–90 (also available at: https://www.academia.edu/34156956/From_Washington_Consensus_to_Brussels_Consensus?email_work_card=abstract-read-more)

Murphy, D. (2022): *Derivatives Regulation—Rules and Reasoning from Lehman to Covid*, Oxford University Press, Oxford

Nobel, P. (2019): *Schweizerisches Finanzmarktrecht*, 4., vollständig überarbeitete Auflage, Stämpfli Verlag AG Bern

Norberg, J. (2009): *Financial Fiasco: How America's infatuation with homeownership and easy money created the economic crisis*, Cato Institute, Washington, DC

Norton, J.J. (2001): Pondering the Parameters of the 'New International Financial Architecture': A legal Perspective, in Lastra R.M. (2001, editor): *The Reform of the International Financial Architecture*, International Banking, Finance and Economic Law Series, Kluwer Law International, The Hague–London–New York, pp. 3–46

Norton, J.J. (1995): *Devising International Bank Supervisory Standards*, Graham & Trotman, Martinus Nijhoff, London–Dordrecht–Boston

O-P-Q

Orphanides, A. (2014): *What Happened in Cyprus? The Economic Consequences of the Last Communist Government in Europe*, MIT Sloan School Working Paper No. 5089, May, Cambridge, MA

Oser, D. (2008): *The UNIDROIT Principles of International Commercial Contracts: A Governing Law?*, Brill Academic Publishers, Leiden

Park, Y.Ch. and Ch. Wyplosz (2010): The future of the IMF and of regional cooperation in East Asia, in Wyplosz, Ch. (2010, editor): *The New International Monetary System—Essays in honor of Alexander Swoboda*, Routledge International Studies in Money and Banking, Rutledge, USA–Canada, pp. 29–43

Patrick, St. (2020): COVID-19 and the Costs of Global Dysfunction, *Foreign Affairs*, July/August, pp. 40–50

Pellegrina, L.D., Masciandaro, D. and R.V. Pansini (2010): *Government, Central Bank and Banking Supervision Reforms: Does Independence Matter?*, "Paolo Baffi" Centre Research Paper Series No.2010-74, available at: https://ssrn.com/abstract=1641091

Piantelli, A.M. (2021): *Managing Banking Crises in Europe after the Great Crisis*, Radboud Business Law Institute, Series Law of Business and Finance, Volume 20, Wolters Kluwer Nederland B.V.

Pistor, K. (2019): Regulating Financial Markets—An LTF Perspective, in Avgouleas, E. and D.C. Donald (2019, editors): *The Political Economy of Financial Regulation*, International Corporate Law and Financial Market Regulation, Cambridge University Press, Cambridge, United Kingdom, Chapter 1, pp. 19–37

Posner, R.A. (2010): *The Crisis of Capitalist Democracy*, Harvard University Press, Cambridge-Massachussets-London, England

Proctor (2012): *Mann on the Legal Aspect of Money*, seventh edition, Oxford University Press, Oxford–New York

Quarles, R.K. (2021): *Disclosures and Data: Building Strong Foundations for Addressing Climate-Related Financial Risks* (Venice International Conference on Climate Change, 11 July 2021, available at: https://www.fsb.org/2021/07/disclosures-and-data-building-strong-foundations-for-addressing-climate-related-financial-risks

Quintyn, M., Ramirez, S. and M.W. Taylor (2007): *The Fear of Freedom: Politicians and the Independence and Accountability of Financial Sector Supervisors*, IMF Working Papers, WP/07/25, available at: https://www.imf.org/external/pubs/ft/wp/2007/wp0725.pdf

Quintyn, M. and M. Taylor (2002): *Regulatory and Supervisory Independence and Financial Stability*, IMF Working Papers, WP/02/46, available at: https://www.imf.org/external/pubs/ft/wp/2002/wp0246.pdf

R-S

Radelet, St. and J. Sachs (1998): *The Onset of the East Asian Financial Crisis*, NBER, Working Paper 6680, August, available at: https://www.nber.org/papers/w6680

Rajan, R.G. (2010): *Fault Lines: How Hidden Fractures Still Threaten the World Economy*, Princeton University Press, Princeton

Reddy, Y. (2001): Issues in implementing international financial standards and codes, BIS Review 62/2001, p. 21 et seq.

Robinson, St.W. (1972): *Multinational Banking: A Study of Certain Legal and Financial Aspects of the Postwar Operating of the United States Branch banks in Western Europe*, Sijthoff, Leyden

Rodrik, D. (2002): *After Neoliberalism, What?*, Remarks at a conference on Alternatives to Neoliberalism, June, available at: https://drodrik.scholar.harvard.edu/files/dani-rodrik/files/after-neoliberalism-what.pdf

Sachs, J. (1999): *International lender of last resort? What the alternatives?* Conference Series Proceedings, 1 February, available at: https://www.researchgate.net/publication/5027120_International_lender_of_last_resort_what_are_the_alternatives

Saidenberg, M. and T. Schuermann (2003): *The New Basel Capital Accord and Questions for Research*, Financial Institutions Center, Wharton Working Paper Series No. 03-14

Schinasi, G.J. (2006): *Safeguarding Financial Stability—Theory and Practice*, International Monetary Fund, Washington, DC

Schreiber, V. (2005): *International Standards: Neues Recht für die Weltmärkte*, St. Galler Studien zum Privat-, Handels- und Wirtschaftsrecht, Haupt Verlag, Bern-Stuttgart-Wien

Scott, H.L. (2014): *Interconnectedness and Contagion—Financial Panics and the Crisis of 2008*, available at: https://ssrn.com/abstract=2178475

Sigrist, D. (2006): Basel II—kurz erklärt, in Wiegand, W. (2006, Herausgeber): *Basel II: die rechtlichen Konsequenzen*, Institut für Bankrecht an der Universität Bern, Berner Bankrechtstag, Band 12, Stämpfli Verlag, Bern, pp. 1–11

Slaughter, A.-M. (2000): Governing the Global Economy through Government Networks, in Byers, M. (editor): *The Role of Law in International Politics: Essays in International Relations and International Law*, Oxford University Press, Oxford, Chapter 9, pp. 177–206

Smits, R. (2010): European Supervisors in the Credit Crisis: Issues of Competence and Competition, in Giovanoli, M. and D. Devos (2010, editors): *International*

Monetary and Financial Law: The Global Crisis, Oxford University Press, Oxford–New York, Chapter 15, pp. 305–328
Sousi-Roubi, B. (1995): *Droit bancaire européen*, Dalloz, Paris
Speyer, B. (2015): *TLAC: Systemic risk issues and the impact on strategies of cross-border banks*, Safe Bank, Bank Guarantee Fund, no 3(60), pp. 23–36
Steil, B. (1994): *International Financial Markets Regulation*, Wiley Publishers, Chichester-New York-Brisbane-Toronto-Singapore
Stein, T. and Ch. von Buttlar (2009): *Völkerrecht*, 12. Auflage, Academia Iuris, Carl Heymanns Verlag, Köln-München
Swoboda, A. (2008): Restoring International Financial Stability: Five Guidelines for Regulatory Reform, paper prepared for the conference *"Building an International Monetary and Financial System for the 21st Century: Agenda for Reform"*, The Reinventing Bretton Woods Committee, New York, November
Szczepańska, O. (2015): *MREL and TLAC i.e., How to increase the loss absorption capacity of banks*, Safe Bank, Bank Guarantee Fund, no 3(60), pp. 37–53

T

Thévenoz, L. (2010): The Rescue of the UBS, in: Giovanoli, M. and D. Devos (2010, editors): *International Monetary and Financial Law: The Global Crisis*, Oxford University Press, Oxford–New York, pp. 378–391
Thiele, Al. (2014): *Finanzaufsicht*, Jus Publicum 229, Mohr Siebeck, Tübingen
Tietje, Ch. and M. Lehmann (2010): The Role and Prospects of International Law in Financial Regulation and Supervision, *Journal of International Economic Law*, Volume 13, Issue 3, pp. 663–682 (also available at: https://doi.org/10.1093/jiel/jgq030)
Tirole, J. (2010): Lessons from the Crisis, in: Dewatripont, M., Rochet, J-Ch. and J. Tirole (2012): *Balancing the Banks: Global Lessons from the Financial Crisis*, Princeton University Press, Princeton and Oxford, Chapter 2, pp. 10–77
Toniolo, G. (2005): *Central Bank Cooperation at the Bank for International Settlements, 1930–1973*, Cambridge University Press, Cambridge, United Kingdom

U-V-W & Y-Z

UNCITRAL (2007): *Modern Law for Global Commerce*, Proceeding of the Congress of the United Nations Commission on International Trade Law Held on the Occasion of the Fortieth Session of the Commission, available at: https://www.uncitral.org/pdf/english/congress/09-83930Ebook.pdf
Van den Bossche, P. (2008): *The Law and Policy of the World Trade Organisation: Text, Cases and Materials*, 2nd edition, Cambridge University Press, Cambridge, United Kingdom
Von Bogdandy, A. and J. Windsor (2008): Annex on Financial Services, Second Annex on Financial Services, Second Protocol to the GATS, Fifth Protocol to the GATS, Understanding on Commitment in Financial Services, in Wolfrum, R., Stoll, P.T. and C. Feinäugle (2018, editors): *WTO—Trade in Services*, Max Planck Commentaries on World Trade Law, Martinus Nijhoff Publishers, Leiden-Boston, pp. 618–666
Walker, G.A. (2001): *International Banking Regulation: Law, Policy and Practice*, International Banking, Finance and Economic Law Series, Kluwer Law International, The Hague–London–New York

Wandel, S.A. (2014): *International Regulatory Cooperation: An Analysis of Standard Setting in Financial Law*, Schweizer Schriften zum Finanzmarktrecht, Band 119, Schulthess Verlag, Zürich

Wehinger, G. (2009): Lessons from the financial market turmoil: Challenges ahead for the financial industry and policy makers, *OECD Journal: Financial Market Trends*, Issue 2 (also available at: https://doi.org/10.1787/fmt-v2008-art11-en)

Wiegand, W. (2006, Herausgeber): *Basel II: die rechtlichen Konsequenzen*, Institut für Bankrecht an der Universität Bern, Berner Bankrechtstag, Band 12, Stämpfli Verlag, Bern

Williamson, J. (1990): What Washington Means by Policy Reform, in Williamson, J. (1990): *Latin American Adjustment: How Much Has Happened*, Chapter 2, available at: https://www.piie.com/commentary/speeches-papers/what-washington-means-policy-reform

World Trade Organization (1999): *Guide to the Uruguay Round Agreements*, Kluwer, The Hague

Yokoi-Arai, M. (2008): GATS' Prudential Carve Out in Financial Services and its Relation with Prudential Regulation, *International & Comparative Law Quarterly*, Volume 57, Issue 3, July, pp. 613–646

Yokoi-Arai, M. (2002): *Financial Stability Issues: The case of East-Asia*, International Banking, Finance and Economic Law Series, Kluwer Law International, The Hague–London–New York

Zerey, J.C. (2010, Hrsg.): *Finananzderivate—Rechtshandbuch*, 2. Auflage, Nomos Verlag, Baden-Baden—facultas.wuv Verlag, Wien—Helbing & Lichtenhahn Verlag, Basel

Zeissler, A.G., Ikeda, D. and A. Metrick (2014): *Ireland and Iceland in Crisis D: Similarities and Differences*, Yale Program on Financial Stability, Case Study 2014–4D-V1, available at: https://ssrn.com/abstract=2579081

CHAPTER 3

Key Institutional Aspects of the International Financial Architecture and an Interim Assessment

3.1 The Basel Committee on Banking Supervision (BCBS)

3.1.1 Establishment, Seat and Charter

(1) The Basel Committee on Banking Supervision (hereinafter '**Basel Committee**' or 'BCBS'[1]) is probably the most widely known among the international financial fora founded after 1971, the year when the Bretton Woods system of fixed exchange rates was de facto abolished.[2] The aim was to contribute to safeguarding the stability of the international financial system

---

[1] The literature on the Basel Committee is vast. My means of indication, see Kapstein (1994), pp. 44–57 and 103–128, Herring and Litan (1995), pp. 95–113, Norton (1995), pp. 171–243, Walker (2001), pp. 17–162, Giovanoli (2010), pp. 25–26, Goodhart (2011) (on the history of its first 25 years), Wandel (2014), pp. 78–79, Lastra (2015), pp. 505–507, Alexander (2019), pp. 69–72 (on the accountability and legitimacy of decision-making), Nobel (2019), pp. 305–328, as well as Ortino (2019) and the other contributions in the related special issue of the Journal of International Economic Law. For a brief historical outline of the Committee, see also the Committee's paper "History of the Basel Committee and its Membership", August 2009 (at: https://www.bis.org/bcbs/history.htm).

[2] See above in Chapter 2, under 2.2.2.

This Chapter discusses the international fora except for the FSB, which was presented in Chapter 2 above, under 2.3.4. Due to their predominant importance for the purposes of this study, the Basel Committee and the IADI are discussed in more detail.

and, in particular, the international banking system.[3] It was set up on 8 October 1974 by an informal decision of the Governors of G10 members' central banks and the Governor of the Swiss National Bank as a reaction of the international community to the systemic impact caused, at the international level, by the withdrawal of **Herstatt Bank's** operating licence (for details on this bank's crisis, see Box 3.1 below). Indicative of the very informal character of the BCBS, at the time is the fact that the original mandate assigned to the Committee by the Governors was included in a press release issued by the BIS on 12 February 1975.[4] From the beginning of its operations until 1988, it was named 'Standing Committee on Banking Regulations and Supervisory Practices'. In its early years, it was also known as the 'Blunden Committee' and then 'Cooke Committee', after the names of its first two Chairpersons.[5]

(2) Since its establishment, the BCBS has its seat at the BIS in Basel.[6] Its Charter was adopted in January 2013, almost 40 years after its establishment, upon approval by the GHOS.[7] It contains seventeen Sections included in eight Chapters and is in force as last updated on 5 June 2018.[8]

Box 3.1 The Herstatt Bank crisis

In 1974, a grave banking crisis of worldwide magnitude occurred, set off by the excessive exposure of the German bank *Bankhaus I.D. Herstatt* ('**Herstatt Bank**') to exchange-rate risk due to major open positions in forward foreign-exchange transactions. Due to this event, the risk involving the possibility of loss from transactions in foreign currency due to failure of settlement has since been recorded as '**Herstatt risk**'.[9] Its fallout was not only the withdrawal on 26 June of the

---

[3] See Giovanoli (2000), pp. 11–12 and 20–27 and Norton (2001), pp. 20–21.

[4] See Norton (1995), p. 177.

[5] See Walker (2001), p. 41. For a list of all former Basel Committee Chairpersons, see the above-mentioned 2009 paper on the "History of the Basel Committee and its Membership", p. 1.

[6] This is now also provided in Sect. 11.4 of the Committee's Charter. Even though several other international fora receive secretarial support by the BIS, as already mentioned, one cannot overlook the fact that this international financial forum is the only one seated in Basel to be named after this city, despite it was the second to be established there (the first having been the CGFS in 1971).

[7] See further below, under 3.1.5.

[8] The Charter, as in force after its updating on 5 June 2018, is available at: https://www.bis.org/bcbs/charter.htm.

[9] See the 1996 Report of the CPSS: "Settlement risk in foreign transactions" (known as the "Allsopp Report", available at: https://www.bis.org/cpsspubl).

bank's operating licence by its supervisory authority (Bundesaufsichtsamt für das Kreditwesen), but also an unprecedented upheaval in the international interbank market, given that:

in August 1974, the German supervisory authority also revoked the operating license of three other (smaller) German banks (*Bass & Herz Bankhaus, Bankhaus Wolff KG, and Frankfurter Handelsbank AG*); while

several banks in other states (such as the British *Hill Samuel Group Ltd*, as well as *Morgan Guarantee Trust Company and Seattle First National Bank* in the US) were severely exposed to foreign-exchange risk due to open positions in forward contracts with Herstatt Bank, which could not be settled.[10]

Concurrently with the initiatives of the banking supervisory authorities in several states aimed at dealing with the causes and effects of this occurrence, the bankruptcy of Herstatt Bank and the crisis which ensued from the bankruptcy of American Franklin National Bank of New York in the two-year period between 1973 and 1974,[11] demonstrated the need to strengthen international cooperation in the field of banking supervision. The concern of the G10 central bank governors (including Switzerland) about the solvency of banks operating in their territory in an environment of increased volatility of key macroeconomic indicators, coupled with the expansion of banking activities because of their internationalisation:

first, made a priority the establishment of international cooperation between the monetary and (for the first time in history) banking supervisory authorities with a view to preventing systemic crises and safeguarding the stability of the international banking system,[12] and *second*, led to the establishment of the Basel Committee.

---

[10] For an in-depth analysis of this banking crisis and its impact, see Walker (2001), pp. 28–30, Herring and Litan (1995), pp. 95–96, and Kapstein (1994), pp. 39–45.

[11] For more details, see Walker (2001), pp. 26–28.

[12] It is worth noting that, whereas the bankruptcy of Bankhaus Herstatt brought about problems mainly as regards the operation of payment and settlement systems, these problems were nevertheless dealt with at a global level much later. See the CPSS paper titled "Report of the Committee on Interbank Netting Schemes of the central banks of the Group of Ten countries" (the "Lamfalussy Report (1990)", available at: https://www.bis.org/cpsspubl).

3.1.2 Mandate and Legal Status

According to its Charter, the Basel Committee is the primary global standard-setter for the prudential regulation of banks and provides a forum for cooperation on banking supervisory matters; its mandate is *"to strengthen the regulation, supervision and practices of banks worldwide with the purpose of enhancing financial stability"*.[13] As already noted, the BCBS is an international financial forum and not an international organisation; it does not have legal personality[14] nor does it possess any formal supranational authority.[15] Even though it is involved in issues pertaining to microprudential banking supervision (as well as micro- and macroprudential banking regulation), it is not a supervisory authority. Indeed, it does not have the formal authority and powers to directly supervise banks which are incorporated in the states whose central banks and banking (or, more generally, financial) supervisory authorities are represented in it. With one sole exception (namely the case of the euro area[16]), microprudential banking supervision continues to be carried out by (the competent) national supervisory authorities, either central banks or independent administrative authorities as laid down in national law.

3.1.3 Activities

3.1.3.1 A Historical Overview of the Perimeter of Activities

As already mentioned, the start of operations of the BCBS dates to 1971, when the international monetary system of fixed exchange rates was abolished, leading to a remarkable increase in the volatility of nominal foreign exchange and interest rates in developed economies. This resulted, *inter alia*, in making banks particularly vulnerable to the risks arising from this volatility. Cooperation within the Basel Committee since 1974 has revolved around six key pillars (as discussed in Box 3.2 just below).

---

[13] BCBS Charter, Sect. 1.

[14] The lack of legal personality implies that the Basel Committee is politically responsible for its decisions, but no direct claims can be raised against it since it does not have any legal liability.

[15] BCBS Charter, Sect. 3, first sentence.

[16] This is discussed in Parts II and II below.

Box 3.2 The six key pillars of the Basel Committee's initial perimeter of activities

Pillars	Content
First pillar	The *first pillar* concerned the exchange of views among its members to better understand the new environment of the international banking system after the abolition of the Bretton Woods system and the ascertainment of various financial risks to which banks are exposed as part of their operations. Indeed, the BCBS started to serve as an informal forum for the exchange of views between its members regarding the stability of the international banking system, given the significant amendments in its operating conditions[17]
Second pillar	The *second pillar* concerned the strengthening of multilateral cooperation between banking supervisory authorities, the elaboration of rules on the incorporation of international banks operating in more than one state through branches and/or subsidiaries within the jurisdiction of supervisory authorities (by allocating responsibilities among home and host supervisors), and the creation of effective communication channels for the exchange of essential information (and the provision of mutual assistance) between home and host state supervisory authorities, in order to ensure effective oversight of international banks. Some of the Committee's Reports also contained rules on the conditions for the authorisation their foreign subsidiaries and branches
Third pillar	The *third pillar* was more ambitious: it referred to the elaboration of international financial standards on banking micro- and macroprudential regulation, which, even though not legally binding, were expected to be adopted by its members, and be appropriate to contribute to the reduction of banks' exposure to insolvency and, in this way, the safeguarding of the stability of the international banking system. In the early years of the Basel Committee's operation, its Reports dealt exclusively with banks having significant international activity and a statutory registered office (of the parent undertaking) in one of its members
Fourth pillar	Gradually, however, and in the aftermath of the severe financial crises of the mid-1990s in various EMEs, it became evident that, because of the globalisation of financial activities, appropriate supervision of only a sub-total of the international economy's banks was not sufficient for achieving the policy objective of ensuring the stability of the international banking system.[18] It was therefore deemed necessary to undertake initiatives to enhance the banking supervisory and regulatory framework in developing states as well. This objective has become the *fourth pillar* of cooperation within the BCBS

(continued)

---

[17] See Walker (2001), pp. 47 and 51–54 and Kapstein (1994), pp. 45–46.

[18] See Norton (2001), pp. 6–13, Walker (2001), pp. 282–302, and Giovanoli (2000), pp. 6–8.

(continued)	
Pillars	Content
Fifth pillar	Recourse to international cooperation within the BCBS was also deemed necessary to achieve conditions of competitive equality between international banks incorporated in states represented in it (the *fifth pillar*). The achievement of this objective was also pursued through the standards set by the Committee's Reports[19]
Sixth pillar	*Finally*, the last activity of the BCBS was the adoption of equivalent rules pertaining to the prudential regulation of international banks and international investment firms, in terms of their exposure to the same risks from similar financial (and, more particularly, investment) services. The objective is met by means of the Committee's Reports issued in collaboration with the IOSCO

3.1.3.2 Activities Outside the Reach of the Basel Committee
(1) According to its explicit statements, made since 1983, the Basel Committee's work does not touch upon the role of the central banks as lenders of last resort in crisis periods providing financial support to solvent banks which have been temporarily exposed to liquidity risk. This position results from a statement of the Governors of its member central banks, according to which they are not willing to extend their relevant competence to the foreign subsidiaries of banks incorporated within their jurisdiction.[20] The Charter is silent on this aspect, reinforcing the established practice.

(2) The issue of the reorganisation and winding-up of international banks exposed to insolvency has preoccupied the Committee only to a limited extent until very recently. Its work was confined to a Report in December 1992

---

[19] In the early 1980s, economically developed countries concluded that existing prudential banking regulations did not suffice to cover the stability needs of the international banking system in view of newly internationalised conditions. None, however, was willing to take a unilateral initiative for the adoption of the necessary measures that would strengthen prudential supervision exercised over banks in their territory. Such an initiative would bring national banks in an unfavourable position in the face of ever-increasing global competition. In light of this and given the problems which ensued in the mid-1980s from the crisis of the less developed, heavily indebted states, it became imperative to enhance cooperation in the context of the BCBS, aimed at the international coordination of microprudential regulations, and mainly capital adequacy rules, while ensuring not only the international banking system's stability but also competition equality (as far as the regulatory framework is concerned) among international banks incorporated in states represented in it.

[20] See the Committee's 1983 Report on "Principles for the Supervision of Banks' Foreign Establishments" (May), Chapter 1, second sub-paragraph.

titled "The insolvency liquidation of an international bank".[21] It is also worth noting that the BCBS is not dealing directly with the framework pertaining to the resolution of banks, which is laid down in the FSB's 2011 Report "Key Attributes of Effective Resolution Regimes for Financial Institutions".[22]

(3) Finally, the international coordination of the rules governing deposit guarantee systems and the coverage of deposits with foreign branches[23] of international banks had also not been touched upon initially by the BCBS. On this topic, its work was confined to a comparative study in May 1998 ("Deposit protection schemes in the member countries of the Basel Committee") in connection with the main features of deposit guarantee systems operating in its members. In the decade of 2000, however, it started addressing this issue as well, in close cooperation with the IADI.

3.1.3.3 The Provisions of the Charter

The chapter formalised the above courses of action and provides that the BCBS shall seek to achieve its (above-mentioned) mandate through the following activities[24]: *first*, exchanging information on developments in the banking sector and financial markets to help identify current or emerging risks for the global financial system; *second*, sharing supervisory issues, approaches and techniques to promote common understanding and to improve cross-border cooperation; *third*, establishing and promoting global standards for the regulation and supervision of banks as well as guidelines and sound practices[25]; *fourth*, addressing regulatory and supervisory gaps posing risk to financial stability; *fifth*, monitoring the implementation of its standards in member jurisdictions and beyond with the purpose of ensuring their timely, consistent and effective implementation and contributing to a 'level playing field' among international banks; *sixth*, consulting with central banks and banking supervisory authorities which are not its members to benefit from their input into the process of policy formulation and promote

---

[21] This listed the problems faced by supervisory authorities as regards the reorganisation of banks operating in more than one state through branches and/or subsidiaries without touching upon issues concerning the harmonisation of the rules governing the winding-up, reorganisation and liquidation of insolvent banking undertakings. It also discussed the allocation of competences among home and host competent authorities (supervisory and/or judicial) regarding the winding-up and reorganisation of international banks with foreign establishments. Relevant in this context was also the Basel Committee's 2002 Report "Supervisory guidance on dealing with weak banks", which was updated in July 2015 by the "Guidelines for identifying and dealing with weak banks". The latter is available at: https://www.bis.org/bcbs/publ/d330.htm.

[22] See Chapter 2 above, under 2.4.3.

[23] The prevalent term under international economic law for such establishments is 'commercial presence' (GATS, Article XXVIII(d)).

[24] BCBS Charter, Sect. 2.

[25] On this aspect, see details below, under 3.1.7. It is noted, however, that the vast majority of its standards refer to banking regulation and not to banking supervision.

the implementation of its standards, guidelines and sound practices beyond its member countries; and finally, coordinating and cooperating with other financial sector standard-setters and international bodies, in particular those involved in promoting financial stability.[26]

3.1.4 Membership

3.1.4.1 Historical Development

(1) The initial members of the BCBS, from its establishment in 1974 until June 2009, were on the one hand, the central banks of the G10 members, Switzerland and Spain (since 2001),[27] and on the other hand, banking (or, more generally, financial) supervisory (and regulatory) authorities in these states, to the extent that their central bank was not exclusively responsible for the conduct of prudential banking supervision, as well as the financial authority of Luxembourg.[28] The inclusion of both monetary and (other) supervisory authorities in its composition was decided on the consideration that central banks are competent for safeguarding the stability of the banking system (which is the main policy objective of the Committee), even in states which have adopted the **'principle of separation'** of the monetary and supervisory functions of central banks.

(2) In its meeting of 10–11 March 2009, the BCBS decided to broaden its membership[29] upon an invitation by the G20 to all international fora to review their composition. The expansion was completed three months later (in June).[30] New members became the central banks and (as appropriate) the banking (or, more generally, financial) supervisory authorities from the twelve G20 members that were not represented in it, as well as the ECB representing the EU.[31] The BCBS further expanded its membership in 2014.

---

[26] On the last two activities, see details below, under 3.1.8 and 3.1.9. The work programme and strategic priorities for 2023/24 were adopted on 16 December 2022 (at: https://www.bis.org/bcbs/bcbs_work.pdf).

[27] These central banks are also the most important shareholders of the BIS.

[28] Luxembourg, albeit not a G10 member, was included mainly due to its great importance as an international financial centre and partly because of its monetary agreement with Belgium (on this argument, see Walker [2001, pp. 42–43]). Until 1998, it participated only through its 'Monetary Institute', which was not a central bank; even today the Central Bank of Luxembourg—whose establishment in 1998 was deemed necessary following Luxembourg's accession in the EU monetary union—is not a member of the Basel Committee.

[29] Basel Committee on Banking Supervision (2009): "Expansion of membership announced by the Basel Committee", Press release, 13 March (at: https://www.bis.org/press/p090313.htm).

[30] Basel Committee on Banking Supervision (2009): "Basel Committee broadens its membership", Press release, 10 June (at: https://www.bis.org/press/p090610.htm).

[31] Since 1999 and until then the ECB had observer status.

3.1.4.2 The Provisions of the Charter

Pursuant to the Charter,[32] Basel Committee members include organisations with direct banking supervisory authority and central banks. After consulting the Committee,[33] the Chair may invite other organisations to become observers. The list of members and observers is set on its website, while Membership and observer status must be reviewed periodically. In accepting new members, due regard must be given to the importance of their national banking sectors to international financial stability and Recommendations must be made to the BCBS oversight body (GHOS).[34] Members are committed to the following responsibilities: *first*, closely work for the achievement of the Committee's mandate and, in particular, promote financial stability and continuously enhance the quality of prudential banking regulation and supervision; *second*, actively contribute to the development of standards, guidelines and sound practices, implement and apply these in their domestic jurisdictions within pre-defined timeframes, as well as undergo and participate in BCBS reviews to assess the consistency and effectiveness of domestic rules and supervisory practices in relation to those; and *third*, promote not solely national interests but also those of 'global financial stability',[35] while participating in the work and decision-making of the BCBS.

3.1.4.3 Current Membership Structure—Observers

(1) As of **December 2022**, the BCBS comprised forty-five members from twenty-eight jurisdictions, consisting of central banks and monetary authorities, as well as other banking (or generally financial) supervisory authorities of all members of the G20, the four G10 members which are not G20 members (Belgium, Sweden, Switzerland and The Netherlands), as well as Hong Kong SAR, Luxembourg, Singapore and Spain. The EU is represented by the ECB and the Single Supervisory Mechanism (**SSM**)[36] (for a summary, see Table 3.1).

(2) As already mentioned, the Basel Committee members include both national central banks and national (administrative) authorities responsible for microprudential banking supervision. In that respect, it is worth making the following remarks:

> The *first category* comprises the national central banks of all members represented (with the mere exception, as already mentioned, of Luxembourg). According to the relevant national law in force, fourteen of these central banks

---

[32] BCBS Charter, Sect. 4.

[33] On the Committee, which is the Basel Committee's ultimate decision-making body, see below, under 3.1.6.

[34] BCBS Charter, Sect. 5.

[35] See on this also Chapter 1 above, under 1.1.2.

[36] On the SSM, see details in Chapter 8 below.

Table 3.1 Members of the Basel Committee

States	National central banks	National administrative authorities
Argentina	Central Bank of Argentina	
Australia	Reserve Bank of Australia	Australian Prudential Regulation Authority
Belgium	National Bank of Belgium	
Brasil	Central Bank of Brasil	
Canada	Bank of Canada	Office of the Superintendent of Financial Institutions
China	People's Bank of China	China Banking Regulatory Commission
European Union	European Central Bank	Single Supervisory Mechanism (SSM)
France	Banque de France	Autorité de contrôle prudentiel et de résolution (ACPR) (Prudential Supervision and Resolution Authority)
Germany	Deutsche Bundesbank	Bundesanstalt für Finanzdienstleistungsaufsicht (BaFin) (Federal Financial Supervisory Authority)
Hong Kong SAR	Hong Kong Monetary Authority	
India	Reserve Bank of India	
Indonesia	Bank of Indonesia	Indonesia Financial Services Authority
Italy	Bank of Italy	
Japan	Bank of Japan	Financial Services Agency
Korea	Bank of Korea	Financial Supervisory Service
Luxembourg		Surveillance Commission for the Financial Sector
Mexico	Bank of Mexico	National Banking and Securities Commission
The Netherlands	Netherlands Bank	
Russian Federation	Central Bank of the Russian Federation	
Saudi Arabia	Saudi Monetary Agency	
Singapore	Monetary Authority of Singapore	
South Africa	South African Reserve Bank	
Spain	Bank of Spain	
Sweden	Sveriges Riksbank	Finansinspektionen (Swedish Financial Supervisory Authority)
Switzerland	Swiss National Bank	Swiss Financial Market Supervisory Authority (FINMA)
Turkey	Central Bank of the Republic of Türkiye	Banking Regulation and Supervision Agency
United Kingdom	Bank of England (BoE)	Prudential Regulation Authority (PRA)

(continued)

Table 3.1 (continued)

States	National central banks	National administrative authorities
United States	Board of Governors of the Federal Reserve System Federal Reserve Bank of New York	Office of the Comptroller of the Currency Federal Deposit Insurance Corporation (FDIC)

(exactly the half) are formally competent for conducting direct microprudential banking supervision.[37] In twelve cases, these are solely responsible for the direct supervision of banks, according to the 'sectoral approach' to financial supervision; in Belgium and The Netherlands applicable is the 'functional approach'.

The *second category* comprises the national administrative (supervisory and regulatory) authorities of some of its members who have been empowered, pursuant to applicable national administrative law, to conduct microprudential banking supervision according to the 'principle of separation' of the monetary and supervisory functions of central banks. These fourteen supervisory authorities can be classified in four groups depending on the range of their supervisory powers over the financial system (see Table 3.2): The *first* group comprises three supervisory authorities (those in China, Turkey and the US[38]), which are solely responsible for banking prudential supervision in accordance with the 'sectoral approach'. The *second* group comprises the supervisory authorities of Luxembourg and Mexico, which are responsible for prudential supervision both in banking and capital markets in accordance with the 'modified sectoral approach'.[39] In France, the Autorité de contrôle prudentiel et de résolution ('**ACPR**') (Prudential Supervision and Resolution Authority), is in charge of supervision in both the banking and the insurance sector, while being also responsible for the resolution of credit institutions and insurance undertakings.[40] The *fourth* (and larger) group contains the remaining eight supervisory authorities which are responsible for the prudential supervision of the entire

---

[37] As already noted in Chapter 1 (under 1.2.4), in the UK the PRA is a subsidiary of the BoE; in the euro are the ECB has specific tasks with regard to the prudential supervision as the credit institutions designated as significant with the Single Supervisory Mechanism (SSM), as further discussed in Chapter 8 below.

[38] The US is the only state participating in the Basel Committee with three federal banking supervisory authorities, in addition to its dual participation in the field of central banking.

[39] In Luxembourg, this supervisory authority is also responsible for the supervision of pension funds, which in most other states usually falls under the competence of insurance supervisors (or the single financial supervisor, where the full integration approach applies).

[40] Even though the ACPR is operationally attached to the Banque de France, it is an independent administrative authority both in financial terms and in the performance of its tasks.

Table 3.2 Classification of members of the Basel Committee according to their competences in microprudential banking (financial) supervision

		Members of Basel Committee (reference to the relevant state)	
		National central banks (14)	National administrative authorities (14)
Approaches to microprudential financial supervision	Sectoral approach	Argentina Brasil Euro area: SSM Hong Kong SAR India Italy Russian Federation Saudi Arabia Singapore South Africa Spain United Kingdom (the PRA being a BoE subsidiary)	Only for banking: China Turkey United States Both for banking and capital markets: Luxembourg Mexico
	Functional approach	Belgium The Netherlands	France
	Full integration approach	–	Australia Canada Germany Indonesia Japan Korea Sweden Switzerland

range of financial firms. Accordingly, these are single financial supervisory authorities in accordance with the 'full integration approach'.[41]

(3) The BCBS has also eight observers. As of **December 2022**, 'country observers' were the Central Banks of Malaysia and of the United Arab Emirates, as well as the Chilean Banking and Financial Institutions Supervisory Agency; other observers were the BIS, the IMF, the European Commission, the European Banking Authority (EBA) and the Basel Consultative Group.[42]

---

[41] On all these approaches, see Chapter 1 above, under 1.2.4.

[42] On the EBA, see details in Chapter 7 below; on the Basel Consultative Group, see under 3.1.6 below.

3.1.5 Oversight—The Group of Governors and Heads of Supervision (GHOS)

As already repeatedly mentioned, the GHOS is the oversight (and hence governing) body of the BCBS, which reports to the GHOS and seeks its endorsement for major decisions. The GHOS consists of the central bank Governors and non-central bank heads of supervision of its member jurisdictions. In addition, it approves the Basel Committee's Charter and any amendments thereto, provides general direction for its work programme and appoints its Chairperson from among its members.[43]

3.1.6 Organisation

The internal organisational structure of the BCBS comprises the Committee, Groups, Working Groups, Virtual Networks and Task Forces, the Chair and the Secretariat.[44] The Committee is the ultimate decision-making body with responsibility for ensuring that the mandate of the BCBS is achieved. In principle, it meets three times per year; however, the Chair may convene additional or fewer meetings as necessary. All BCBS members and observers are entitled to appoint one representative to attend these meetings, which are presided by the Chair.[45] Decisions are taken by *consensus* among the members; those of public interest are communicated through the BCBS website, while the Committee may issue, if appropriate, press statements to communicate its decisions.[46] The Committee is responsible for developing, guiding and monitoring the BCBS work programme within the general direction provided by GHOS; establishing and promoting standards, guidelines and sound practices; establishing and disbanding Groups, Working Groups, Virtual Networks and Task Forces, approving and modifying their mandates and monitoring their progress; recommending to the GHOS amendments to the Charter; and deciding on the organisational regulations governing its activities.[47]

---

[43] If the Chair ceases to be a GHOS member before the end of his/her term, the GHOS must appoint a new one. Until a new Chair has been appointed, the Secretary General assumes the Chair's functions (BCBS Charter, Sect. 6). On the GHOS's composition and work, see at: https://www.bis.org/about/orggov.htm?m=1%7C2%7C603. In December 2022, its Chair was Tiff Macklem, Governor of the Bank of Canada.

[44] BCBS Charter, Sect. 7.

[45] The representatives are senior officials of their organisations (e.g., at the level of head of banking supervision, head banking policy/regulation, deputy governor or head of financial stability department) and have the authority to commit their institutions.

[46] BCBS Charter, Sects. 8.2–8.5.

[47] Ibid., Sect. 8.1.

3.1.6.1 *Groups, Working Groups, Virtual Networks and Task Forces*

The BCBS's work is largely organised around Groups, Working Groups and Task Forces[48]:

'BCBS Groups' are composed of senior staff from BCBS members that guide or undertake themselves major areas of the Committee's work. They report directly to the Committee, form part of its permanent internal structure and operate without a specific deliverable or end date. As of **December 2022**, they included the Risks and Vulnerabilities Assessment Group, the Supervisory Cooperation Group, the Policy and Standards Group and the Basel Consultative Group (see Box 3.3 just below).

'BCBS Working groups' consist of experts from BCBS members supporting the technical work of its Groups.

'Virtual Networks' serve as an expert group; they are called upon as needed by the parent group or the Committee and their primary function is to monitor existing policies.

'BCBS Task Forces' are created to provide specific and expert assistance and are generally composed of technical experts from BCBS members. Since they are temporary in nature, they do not form part of the permanent structure of the BCBS. As of **December 2022**, these included the Task Force on Climate-related Financial Risks ('**TFCR**'), charged with undertaking the work of the BCBS on these financial risks[49]; and the Task Force on Evaluations ('**TFE**'), which is charged with examining the impact of **"Basel III post (GFC) crisis reforms"**, including their functioning considering the pandemic crisis[50] and, under a more 'holistic' evaluation, their impact on bank resilience and behaviour.

---

[48] Ibid., Sect. 9.1–9.4, respectively.

[49] Its workplan and future deliverables include, *first*, a set of analytical reports on climate-related financial risks and reports on their transmission channels to the banking system and on measurement methodologies; and *second*, the development of effective supervisory practices to mitigate such risks. See also the recent (8 December 2022) BCBS document: "Frequently asked questions on climate-related financial risks", available at: https://www.bis.org/bcbs/publ/d543.htm.

[50] See Chapter 2 above, under 2.2.4.

Box 3.3 The current structure and mandates of BCBS Groups

Group	Mandate
Risks and Vulnerabilities Assessment Group ('RVG')	This Group leads the BCBS's work on the monitoring and assessment of risks and vulnerabilities that could impact the resilience of the global banking system. Such vulnerabilities are associated, *inter alia*, with the financial stability implications of the pandemic crisis, as well as with leveraged loans and collateralised loan obligations ('CLOs')[51]
Supervisory Cooperation Group ('SCG')	The initial mandate of this Group (formerly known as Standards Implementation Group and then Supervision and Implementation Group (both '*SIG*') was to share information and promote consistency in the implementation of the '*Basel II capital adequacy framework*'. Gradually, its mandate has been modified and currently relates to strengthening banking supervision worldwide and promoting strong and effective supervisory cooperation on cross-border banking issues
Policy and Standards Group ('PSG')	The mandate of this Group, formerly known as Policy Development Group ('PDG'), is to support the BCBS on the development and implementation of common prudential supervisory standards, *inter alia*, on capital, credit, market an operational risk, ratings and securitisation, the leverage ratio, liquidity, large exposures and expected loss provisioning. AEG working groups/task forces
Basel Consultative Group ('BCG')	This is a forum for deepening the BCBS' cooperation with non-member banking supervisors from across the world on a broad range of issues, by facilitating broad supervisory dialogue on new initiatives early in the process.[52] Members of the BCG, which (as already mentioned[53]) has observer status in the BCBS, are central banks and supervisory authorities from all 28 BCBS members, supervisory groups, international agencies, and other bodies

3.1.6.2 Chair

The Chair directs the work of the BCBS in accordance with its mandate. He/she is appointed by the GHOS for a term of three years that is renewable once. His/her main responsibilities are to convene and chair Committee meetings, monitor the progress of the Committee's work programme, provide operational guidance between meetings to carry forward its decisions and directions,

---

[51] CLOs are securities backed by a pool of loans, i.e., repackaged loans sold to investors; see at: https://corporatefinanceinstitute.com/resources/fixed-income/collateralized-loan-obligations-clo.

[52] BCBS Charter, Sect. 15.1. It is also noted that these supervisors also participate as observers in BCBS Groups, Working Groups, Virtual Networks and Task Forces, contributing thus to its policy development work (ibid., Sect. 15.3).

[53] See above, under 3.1.4.

report to the GHOS, represent the Committee externally and be its principal spokesperson.[54]

3.1.6.3 The Secretariat

The Basel Committee's Secretariat is provided by the BIS and mainly consists of professional staff, mostly on temporary secondment from Committee's members. Its main responsibilities are to provide support and assistance to the other components of the internal organisational structure, ensure the timely and effective information flow to all BCBS members, facilitate coordination across Groups, Working Groups, Virtual Networks and Task Forces and a close contact between members and non-member authorities, as well to support the cooperation between the BCBS and other institutions.[55]

The Secretary General is selected by the Chair on recommendation of a selection panel comprising BCBS and/or GHOS members, as well as a senior BIS representative. The term of appointment is typically three years and extendable. The Secretary General reports to the Chair, directs the Secretariat's work, manages the financial, material and human resources allocated to the Secretariat and assists the Chair in representing the Committee externally.[56] Deputy Secretaries General, selected by the Secretary General in conjunction with the Chair, report to and assist the former in discharging his/her duties and substitute for him/her in case of absence and incapacity or upon request.[57]

3.1.7 Standards, Guidelines and Sound Practices

3.1.7.1 The Provisions of the Charter

(1) The BCBS sets '**standards**' (mainly for the micro- and macroprudential regulation of banks) and expects their full implementation by its members and their internationally active banks; they constitute minimum requirements, which its members may exceed. The Committee expects standards to be incorporated into national legal frameworks through the rulemaking process in each jurisdiction (and in the EU through the 'regional **rulemaking** process'[58]) within the pre-defined timeframe set. If literal transposition into national legal frameworks is not possible, members should seek the greatest possible equivalence of standards and their outcome.[59] *On the other hand*, '**Guidelines**' elaborate the standards in areas where they are considered desirable

---

[54] BCBS Charter, Sect. 10; since March 2019, Chair is Pablo Hernández De Cos, Governor of the Bank of Spain.

[55] Ibid., Sect. 11.1.

[56] Ibid., Sect. 11.2. Since February 2022, Secretary General is Neil Esho.

[57] Ibid., Sect. 11.3.

[58] See below in Chapter 7, under 7.5.

[59] BCBS Charter, Sect. 12.

for the prudential regulation and supervision of banks, in particular international ones. They generally supplement standards by providing additional guidance for the purpose of their implementation.[60] Finally, **'sound practices'** describe actual observed practices, with the goal of promoting common understanding and improving supervisory or banking practices. BCBS members should compare these practices with those applied by themselves and by their supervised institutions to identify potential areas for improvement.[61]

(2) The standards set (and the guidelines elaborated) by the BCBS are not legally binding and enforceable and the BCBS works on the conviction that its members endeavour for their implementation, by any appropriate means, in their national law. According to the Charter:

> "[The BCBS] decisions do not have legal force. Rather, the BCBS relies on its members' commitments, as described in Section 5,[62] to achieve its mandate".[63]

Nevertheless, their legal significance is important both within and outside the ranks of its members.

3.1.7.2 Categories of Standards, Guidelines and Sound Practices

From a systematic point of view,[64] the standards, guidelines and sound practices set by the BCBS through its various Reports can be classified into nine categories: the cross-border cooperation of banking supervisory authorities and the allocation of responsibilities between home and host authorities; international harmonisation of methods for exercising micro- and (since 2009) macroprudential banking regulation; the supervisory aspects of the management of risks to which banks are exposed; the provision of information by banks to supervisory authorities and the dissemination of information by banks to the public; core principles of banking supervision and regulation; the resolution of international banks following the outbreak of the GFC (in cooperation with the FSB); the operation of deposit guarantee systems (in cooperation with the IADI); bank accounting issues and, in particular, accounting for loans extended and the provisions needed for potential losses of banks from 'bad loans' (in cooperation with the IASB); and combatting the use of the financial system for the commitment of economic crimes (in cooperation with the

---

[60] *Ibid.*, Sect. 13.
[61] *Ibid.*, Sect. 14.
[62] See above, under 3.1.4.
[63] BCBS Charter, Sect. 3, second and third sentences.
[64] However, many of the Basel Committee's Reports address in parallel several issues rather than exclusively one, since the degree of affinity of these issues is particularly high, in certain cases at least.

FATF).[65] As already mentioned,[66] among the hundreds of Reports adopted by the BCBS, it is only the 2012 "Core Principles for Effective Banking Supervision", which have been included in the FSB's Key Standards for Sound Financial Systems.

3.1.7.3 Public Consultation Process

The BCBS seeks input from all relevant stakeholders on policy proposals. The consultation process includes issuing a public invitation to interested parties to provide comments in writing to the Secretariat on policy proposals within a specified timeframe (typically 90 calendar days). As a rule, responses to public invitations for comments are published on the BCBS website, unless confidential treatment is requested by respondents. This process is compulsory for its standards.[67]

3.1.7.4 In Particular: The Regulatory Consistency Assessment Programme (RCAP)

Based on its expectation that its member jurisdictions and their internationally active banks will fully implement its standards, including the "**Basel III regulatory framework**", the BCBS monitors 'locally' their timely, consistent and effective implementation. To facilitate this process, it established in 2012 a "Regulatory Consistency Assessment Programme" ('**RCAP**'). This Programme, which also supports the FSB in monitoring the implementation of the '**global financial reforms**' agreed by the G20,[68] consists of two closely interlinked modules (see Box 3.4 just below).[69]

---

[65] A chronological list of all Basel Committee's standards, guidelines and sound practices is available at: https://www.bis.org/bcbs/about/work_publication_types.pdf.

[66] See above in Chapter 2, under 2.4.3.

[67] BCBS Charter, Sect. 17.

[68] These were laid down in the Statement of 2 April 2009 by the G20 Leaders in London "Global Plan for Recovery and Reform" (hence, are also referred to as 'G20 financial reforms'), paras 1–5 and 13–21 (at: https://www.g20.utoronto.ca/2009/2009communique0402.pdf).

[69] Noteworthy is also the "Basel III implementation dashboard", which uses a combination of numerical grades and colour codes to signal the different stages of adoption of the standards to ensure compliance with the agreed timeline. On the most recent (September 2020) summary, see at: https://www.bis.org/bcbs/implementation/rcap_reports.htm.

Box 3.4 The modules of the Regulatory Consistency Assessment Program (RCAP)

Module	Mandate
Module 1: Basel III Monitoring Reports	The monitoring of implementation of the Basel III regulatory framework (and its standards) on the basis of information provided by each member jurisdiction is conducted by means of semi-annual Progress Reports ("**Basel III Monitoring Reports**").[70] Until the end of 2016, the focus of this monitoring exercise (the "**Level 1 Assessment**") was confined to the adoption of the 'Basel III' capital standards. Since 2017, it also covers the 'Basel III' standards relating to leverage, liquidity, and loss absorbency requirements for *global* and *domestic* systemically important banks (**G-SIBs** and '**D-SIBs**'),[71] including the December 2017 finalisation of the Basel III reforms and the January 2019 finalisation of the market risk framework
Module 2: Consistency assessments	(1) '**Member jurisdiction assessments**' (the "**Level 2 Assessments**") review the extent to which domestic regulations are aligned with the minimum Basel requirements and help identify material gaps in these regulations. Until the end of 2016, the focus of these assessments has been on three aspects: the risk-based capital standards, the liquidity coverage ratio (**LCR**) and the framework governing G-SIBs and D-SIBs. Since 2017, they also cover the Basel III standards on the net stable funding ratio (**NSFR**) and the leverage ratio.[72] The procedures and the process for conducting such assessments are included in a '**Handbook for Jurisdictional Assessments**' of March 2016, which describes the complete assessment program and introduces the RCAP questionnaires, which member jurisdictions complete ahead of the assessment and update it regularly[73] (2) '**Thematic assessments**' (the "**Level 3 Assessments**") examine implementation of the requirements laid down in the Basel III regulatory framework and seek to ensure that prudential ratios are calculated consistently by banks across jurisdictions to improve comparability across outcomes. The assessments are extending the findings of the BCBS's implementation monitoring and member jurisdiction assessments to implementation at the bank level[74]

---

[70] The most recent Report, of 21 February 2022 (based on data as of 30 June 2021), is available at: https://www.bis.org/bcbs/publ/d531.htm.

[71] A list of G-SIBs, based on an assessment methodology designed by the BCBS, is published by the FSB; the most recent list, of 21 November 2022, in which the thirty banks remain the same as the 2021 list, is available at: https://www.fsb.org/2022/11/fsb-publishes-2022-g-sib-list.

[72] The published member jurisdiction assessments, together with *post* RCAP follow-up actions (based on self-reporting), are available at: https://www.bis.org/bcbs/implementation/l2.htm.

[73] At: https://www.bis.org/bcbs/publ/d361.pdf.

[74] These RCAP Reports are available at: https://www.bis.org/bcbs/implementation/l3.htm.

3.1.8 Consultation with Non-member Authorities

3.1.8.1 The History of International Consultation

Since the mid-1980s, the BCBS has pursued ongoing cooperation with the banking supervisory authorities of third states, which are not included in its membership by fostering bilateral relations. Furthermore, it provides technical assistance to such supervisory authorities to support their banking and, more generally, financial system through the Financial Stability Institute ('**FSI**'). This is a joint initiative of the BCBS and the BIS, created in 1999 to assist supervisors around the world in improving and strengthening their financial systems. Its objectives are the promotion of sound prudential supervisory standards and practices and the support of their full implementation globally; the provision of a venue for policy discussion and sharing of market developments, practices and techniques, as well as supervisory practices and experiences; and the promotion of cross-sectoral supervisory contacts and cooperation.[75] The BCBS was also in close cooperation with regional associations of banking supervisors worldwide, many of which were assisted by the Committee at their initial phase.[76]

3.1.8.2 The Provisions of the Charter

In consistency with its activities under Sect. 2 of its Charter,[77] the BCBS is committed to consulting widely on its activities with non-member authorities through several structures and mechanisms, in addition to the above-mentioned Basel Consultative Group.[78] In particular, the biennial International Conferences of Banking Supervisors ('**ICBS**') provide a venue for supervisors around the world to discuss issues of common interest, while non-member authorities can contribute to the BCBS's policy development work by participating as observers in its bodies.[79] *In addition*, support is given to FSI activities, including the '**BCBS-FSI High Level Meetings**'. These are targeted at senior policy-makers within central banks and supervisory authorities and provide a series of regional fora for distributing information on the BCBS's standards, keeping participants updated on its work, sharing supervisory practices and concerns, as well as establishing and maintaining strong contacts. *Finally*, the BCBS supports the work and activities of regional groups

---

[75] An overview of the FSI's activities is available at: https://www.bis.org/fsi/index.htm; on its activity as of end-2021, see also the document "FSI—2021 in Review" (at: https://www.bis.org/fsi/fsi2021review.pdf). Its publications (some which are referred to in this book) are available at: https://www.bis.org/fsi/publications.htm?m=1%7C17%7C161.

[76] For more detail on these associations, see Walker (2001, pp. 60–67).

[77] See above, under 3.1.3.

[78] BCBS Charter, Sect. 15.2; on the Basel Consultative Group, see above, under 3.1.6.

[79] On the most recent Conference, held on 29 November–1 December 2022, see at: https://www.bis.org/bcbs/events/icbs22/overview.htm.

of banking supervisors worldwide by participating, through its secretariat staff, in their meetings to exchange ideas and seek feedback on its work.[80]

3.1.9 International Cooperation

The BCBS cooperates with other international financial standard-setters and public sector bodies with a view to achieving an enhanced coordination of policy development and implementation. In carrying out their responsibilities to support this cooperation, the Chair and the Secretariat must pay particular attention to the need to comply with the BCBS's due process and governance arrangements. Together with the IOSCO and the IAIS, it sponsors and provides secretarial support to the Joint Forum, where issues of common concern to the standard-setters can be addressed and recommendations for coordinated action can be developed. It is also a member of the FSB and participates in its work with a view to developing, coordinating and promoting the implementation of effective regulatory, supervisory and other financial sector policies.[81]

3.2 THE INTERNATIONAL ASSOCIATION OF DEPOSIT INSURERS (IADI)

3.2.1 Establishment, Seat, Membership, Legal Personality and Governance

(1) The IADI was set up in May 2002, upon an initiative of the FSF,[82] pursuant to Article 60 of the Swiss Civil Code as a non-profit organisation with an unlimited duration and domiciled in Basel.[83] In accordance with the categorisation set out in its Statutes,[84] as of **December 2022**, the IADI had 92 Members representing national deposit insurance[85] organisations responsible for the management of their deposit guarantee systems[86]; 10 Associates representing other 'bank safety-net organisations' (i.e., central banks, supervisors

---

[80] BCBS Charter, Sect. 15.4–15.5.

[81] Ibid., Sect. 16.

[82] The FSF set up a 'Study Group on Deposit Insurance' in 1999 and, drawing from its findings, constituted a 'Working Group on Deposit Insurance' in 2000, which led to the creation of the IADI two years later.

[83] IADI Statutes, Article 1. The Statutes and By-laws of the IADI are available at: https://www.iadi.org/aboutIADI.aspx?id=71.

[84] Ibid., Articles 6–7 and 10.

[85] The IADI makes consistent use of the term 'deposit insurance' (also in its name) rather than the term 'deposit guarantee', which prevails in European banking law; see on this. Without undermining the significance of the underlying differences, in the author's view the two terms can be used alternatively.

[86] Unlike other international fora, membership of the IADI is open in the sense that any deposit guarantee organisation may become a member.

and regulators) from states having established or considering the establishment of a deposit insurance system; and 17 Partners, i.e., entities that entered in a cooperative arrangement with IADI in the pursuit and furtherance of its objects, including the IMF, the World Bank, the European Bank for Reconstruction and Development ('**EBRD**'[87]), the Inter-American Development Bank and the European Forum of Deposit Insurers ('**EFDI**'). Not-for-profit entities which do not fulfil the criteria to be an Associate but have a direct interest in the effectiveness of deposit insurance systems (e.g., international organisations) have an Observers status.[88]

Box 3.5 Differences in terminology

Attention should be drawn to differences in the terminology used: *first*, the **IADI** make use of the term '**deposit insurance**'; *second*, in EU legislation use is made of the term '**deposit guarantee**' (a "Deposit Guarantee Schemes Directive") but also of the term '**deposit insurance**' (a "European Deposit Insurance Scheme")[89]; *third*, Swiss law refers to '**deposit protection**'.[90]

In the IADI Core Principles a distinction is made between: "deposit insurance", defined as a system established to protect depositors against the loss of their insured deposits in the event that a bank is unable to meet its obligations to the depositors; "deposit insurer", namely the specific legal entity responsible for providing deposit insurance, deposit guarantees or similar deposit protection arrangements; and "deposit insurance system" ('**DIS**'), i.e., the deposit insurer *and* its relationships with the financial safety-net participants that support deposit insurance functions and resolution processes. Hence, the **IADI** makes use of the term 'deposit insurance **systems**', while the term used in EU and Swiss law is 'deposit guarantee/protection **schemes**'.

Without undermining the significance of the underlying differences, in the author's view all these terms can be used alternatively.

---

(2) Unlike other international financial fora, the IADI has a separate legal personality; hence, it has the power to contract, sue and be sued in its own

---

[87] On the EFDI, see further below in Chapter 4, under 4.4.5.

[88] At: https://www.iadi.org/en/about-iadi/iadi-members-and-participants.

[89] On the EU legislation, see Chapter 4 below.

[90] The provider of the deposit protection scheme in Switzerland is "esisuisse", an association established pursuant to Articles 60–79 of the Swiss Civil Code (Articles of Association, Article 1); see Nobel (2019), pp. 1034–1036.

name, acquire and dispose of property and take any other action as necessary or useful for its purposes and activities.[91] Its governing bodies are the General Meeting of Members and the Executive Council composed of individuals elected by the Members; a Secretary General appointed by the Executive Council assists these bodies.[92] The Chairperson of the Executive Council also acts in the capacity of President of the IADI.[93] The Executive Council is assisted in its work by six **Council Committees** (on Audit and Risk, Core Principles and Research, Member Relations and Training and Technical Assistance) participated in by members of the Executive Council. In view of reflecting regional interests and common issues through the sharing and exchange of information, eight **Regional Committees** have also been created for Africa, Asia–Pacific, the Caribbean, Eurasia, Europe, Latin America, the Middle East and North Africa, and North America.[94] The accounts and the annual financial statements of the IADI for each financial year are audited by an external Auditor appointed by the General Meeting.[95]

3.2.2 Objectives

The IADI has two objectives: *first*, contribute to the stability of financial systems by promoting international cooperation in the field of deposit insurance and providing guidance for establishing new, and enhancing existing (national[96]) DISs; and *second*, encourage wide international contact among deposit insurers and other interested parties. This is being pursued by the following means: *first*, development of principles, standards and guidance to enhance the effectiveness of DISs, which, *inter alia*, lead in 2009 to the joint adoption with the BCBS of the "Core Principles for Effective Deposit Insurance Systems" that are included in FSB's "Key Standards for Sound Financial Systems",[97] encouragement of their consideration and *voluntary* application, as well as development of methodologies for the assessment of compliance with those and facilitation of related assessment processes; *second*, enhancing

---

[91] IADI Statutes, Article 4.

[92] Ibid., Articles 11 and 19.

[93] Ibid., Article 16, second sub-paragraph. In December 2022, President and Chair of the Executive Council was Alejandro López from the Argentinian deposit insurance scheme (Seguro de Depósitos Sociedad Anónima).

[94] On this Committees, see at: https://www.iadi.org/en/about-iadi/organisation/committees.

[95] IADI Statutes, Article 20, first sub-paragraph.

[96] On the proposal to establish an international deposit insurance scheme (which has never been taken over), see Grubel (1979).

[97] See Chapter 2 above, under 2.4.3. It is noted that in July 2011 the IADI also adopted, jointly with the (above-mentioned) Islamic Financial Services Board (IFSB), the Core Principles for Effective Islamic Deposit Insurance Systems (at: https://www.iadi.org/en/assets/File/Core%20Principles/IADI-IFSB%20CPIDIS_IFSB%20Approved_05%20July%202021%20Clean.pdf).

the understanding of common interests and issues related to deposit insurance; *third*, facilitating the sharing and exchange of expertise and information on deposit insurance issues through training, development and educational programmes, as well as provision of advice on the establishment or enhancement of effective DISs through its Training and Capacity Building Unit ('**TCBU**')[98]; *fourth*, undertaking of research on issues relating to deposit insurance[99]; and *finally*, cooperation with other international organisations, and creation of awareness among financial supervisors and regulators on the key role of DISs in maintaining financial stability.[100]

3.3 INTERNATIONAL FORA IN THE FIELD OF CAPITAL MARKETS LAW[101]

3.3.1 *The International Organisation of Securities Commissions (IOSCO)*

3.3.1.1 *Establishment, Seat, Membership and Governance*

(1) The IOSCO was set up in 1983 as an international association of securities regulators and has its seat (as of its creation) in Madrid.[102] As of **December 2022**, it numbered 131 **Ordinary Members**, which are national securities commissions in their respective jurisdiction (typically, public administrative authorities). There were also thirty-three **Associate Members**, such as agencies or branches of government (other than the principal national securities regulator in their respective jurisdictions) that have some regulatory competence over securities markets, intergovernmental international organisations (such as the IMF and the World Bank) and other international standard-setting bodies with a mission related to either the development or the regulation of securities markets. The third category of members are the seventy **Affiliate Members**, which are self-regulatory organisations, stock exchanges, FMIs,

---

[98] On this activity, see at: https://www.iadi.org/en/training-and-capacity-building.

[99] The "IADI Research Papers" and the "Regional Research Papers" are available at: https://www.iadi.org/en/research/research-papers.

[100] IADI Statutes, Article 3; for current developments, see also at: https://www.iadi.org.

[101] Since this study is mainly on banking regulation, the presentation of the international fora in this and the following Sections is more descriptive and not based on the rules of their Statutes or By-laws (where such statutory documents exist at all).

[102] On the establishment, membership, legal nature, and (initial) objectives of the IOSCO, see Gortsos (2012), pp. 162–164, Wandel (2014), pp. 79–81 and Lastra (2015), pp. 508–509. Its By-laws are available at: https://www.iosco.org/library/by_laws/pdf/IOSCO-By-Laws-Section-1-English.pdf.

investor protection and compensation funds, as well as other bodies with an appropriate interest in securities regulation.[103]

(2) The IOSCO has two governing bodies. The **"Presidents' Committee"**, which meets once a year during its Annual Conference, is composed of the Presidents of its Ordinary and Associate Members and pursues the achievement of the purpose of IOSCO, while the **"IOSCO Board"**, which is composed of thirty-five securities regulators, reviews the regulatory issues facing global securities markets and coordinates practical responses to any concerns arising.[104] The IOSCO's policy work is conducted by eight policy committees, in the following policy areas: Issuer Accounting, Audit and Disclosure; Regulation of Secondary Markets; Regulation of Market Intermediaries; Enforcement and the Exchange of Information and the IOSCO Multilateral Memorandum of Understanding ('**MMoU**') Concerning Consultation and Cooperation and the Exchange of Information Screening Group[105]; Investment Management; Credit Rating Agencies; Derivatives; and Retail Investors. The largest among them is the Growth and Emerging Markets Committee ('**GEMC**'), which seeks to promote the development and greater efficiency of emerging securities and future markets.[106]

The IOSCO also has four Regional Standing Committees dealing with specific regional problems of its members: the Africa/Middle-East Regional Committee, the Asia–Pacific Regional Committee, the European Regional Committee and the Inter-American Regional Committee.

3.3.1.2 Objectives

(1) The objectives of IOSCO, which closely works with the G20 and the FSB (of which it is a member) and cooperates with other standard-setting bodies (such as the BCBS[107] and the Payments and Market Infrastructures (CPMI)[108]), are the following: *first*, the promotion of cooperation between its members' supervisory and regulatory authorities and the provision of mutual assistance among them for the enhancement of market integrity; *second*, the

---

[103] It is apparent that, if compared to other international fora, the IOSCO has a much broader global representativeness in terms of membership.

[104] In December 2022, Chair of the Board was Jean-Paul Servais, Chair of Belgium's Financial Services and Markets Authority.

[105] On the impact of this MMoU, see at: https://www.iosco.org/news/pdf/IOSCON EWS666.pdf.

[106] As noted in its most recent Fact Sheet document (at: https://www.iosco.org/about/pdf/IOSCO-Fact-Sheet.pdf), the IOSCO is one of the few international standard-setters that have a committee solely responsible for emerging market issues.

[107] For example, Recommendations relating to the disclosure of information by banks and investment firms are jointly adopted with the BCBS through the "BCBS Transparency Group and IOSCO TC Working Party on the Regulation of Financial Intermediaries".

[108] See, e.g., the recent joint Report on "Client clearing: access and portability" of 8 September 2022 (at: https://www.bis.org/cpmi/publ/d210.pdf); see also at: https://www.iosco.org/about/?subsection=cpmi_iosco.

elaboration and adoption of international financial standards relating to the stability of capital markets, the protection of investors, and capital markets' integrity, efficiency and transparency[109]; and *third*, the provision of high-quality technical assistance, education, training and research to its members and other regulators for the enhancement of sound global capital markets and a robust global regulatory framework.

(2) At its Annual Conference in June 2015, IOSCO approved its "**Strategic Direction 2015–2020**", which envisaged the reinforcement of its position as the key global reference point for securities regulation[110]; the strategy and the related goals should be implemented through an extensive set of (forty-three) initiatives laid down in Action Plans, which covered six priority areas. This was followed, in February 2021, by the "**2021–2022 Work Program**", which called on IOSCO to work on the eight priorities during that period, amidst the pandemic crisis.[111]

3.3.2 *The International Accounting Standards Board (IASB)*

3.3.2.1 *Establishment, Seat, Membership, Governance and Objective*

The IASB was set up in 1973 and has its seat in London. It is one of the two independent standard-setting bodies of the 'International Financial Reporting Standards ['**IFRS**'] Foundation', a not-for-profit private organisation.[112] Since 1 December 2016, the Board has fourteen members, which combine a geographically diversified mix of recent practical experience in accounting standard-setting, in preparing, auditing or using financial reports, as well as in accounting education. They are appointed and overseen by the IFRS Foundation Trustees, which in turn are accountable to a monitoring board of public authorities (IFRS Foundation Monitoring Board).[113] The IASB's objective consists in the elaboration and adoption and promotion of

---

[109] As in the case of the BCBS, it is only the IOSCO Report on "Objectives and Principles of Securities Regulation" which is included in the FSB's "Key Standards for Sound Financial Systems"; for a list of the most recent (numerous) Reports, see pp. 8–10 of the Fact Sheet document.

[110] The relevant document is available at: https://www.iosco.org/library/pubdocs/pdf/IOSCOPD496.pdf.

[111] At: https://www.iosco.org/news/pdf/IOSCONEWS596.pdf. On the work of the IOSCO amidst the pandemic, see Gortsos (2023). As of 31 December 2022, a new Working Programme was not publicly available. There is only a "Crypto-Asset Roadmap for 2022-2023" of 7 July 2022 (available at: https://www.iosco.org/news/pdf/IOSCONEWS649.pdf).

[112] On the second independent body, the International Sustainability Standards Board, see just below. The 2021 IFRS Foundation Constitution sets out the foundation's purpose and objectives, as well as its governance structure and the composition requirements for the different groups within that structure (at: https://www.ifrs.org/content/dam/ifrs/about-us/legal-and-governance/constitution-docs/ifrs-foundation-constitution-2021.pdf).

[113] As of December 2022, Chair of the IASB was Dr. Andreas Barckow from Germany.

the International Financial Reporting Standards (**IFRSs**), including the *IFRS for SMEs* Accounting Standard.[114]

3.3.2.2 The IFRSs

The IFRSs, previously known as 'International Accounting Standards', were adopted on 1 October 2002, are constantly updated (last update in October 2022) and are accompanied by Interpretations (in total twenty-eight), which are developed by the fourteen-members of the IFRS Interpretations Committee and then approved by the Board. IFRSs are a set of accounting standards, developed and maintained by the IASB with the intention of those standards being capable of being applied on a globally consistent basis. They are used for drawing up the financial statements of companies, particularly those listed in regulated markets, and with a view to establishing transparency, accountability and efficiency to financial markets.[115]

According to the IASB, transparency is established by enhancing the international comparability and quality of financial information, enabling investors and other market participants to make informed economic decisions; accountability is established by reducing the information gap between companies and investors; and economic efficiency is established by helping investors to identify opportunities and risks across the world, thus improving capital allocation. The IFRSs are aimed for implementation mainly, but not exclusively, by enterprises listed in regulated markets (always on a consolidated basis, namely at 'group level'). In order for enterprises to be considered as compliant, they must meet all of the individual IFRSs and IFRS Interpretations issued by the IASB.

The second independent body of the IFRS Foundation, the **International Sustainability Standards Board** ('**ISSB**') was created in November 2021. Its objective is the development of a global baseline of sustainability-related disclosure standards to provide investors and other capital market participants with information about companies' sustainability-related risks and opportunities to help them make informed decisions.[116]

---

[114] As already mentioned in Chapter 2 above (under 2.4.4), these standards are included in the FSB's "Key Standards for Sound Financial Systems".

[115] From 1973 to 2000, these standards were issued by the International Accounting Standards Committee, founded by agreement of the professional accounting agencies in ten advanced economies. Its present composition is a result of amendments adopted in 1999 and approved in 2000. For more details on the history and the work of the IASB, see at: https://www.ifrs.org/groups/international-accounting-standards-board.

[116] In 2007, the US Securities and Exchange Commission ('SEC') allowed foreign registrants to file IFRS-based financial statements without reconciling to the US Generally Accepted Accounting Principles ('GAAP'). That was a major step towards truly globally useable accounting standards. The usage is meanwhile allowed or required in more than 150 countries worldwide.

3.3.3 The International Federation of Accountants (IFAC)

3.3.3.1 Establishment, Seat, Membership, Governance and Objective

The IFAC was set up in 1977 as the international forum for the accountancy profession and has its seat in New York. As of **November 2022**, its members (regular and associate) included 180 professional accountancy organisations ('**PAOs**') across 130 jurisdictions (representing more than three million professional accountants globally). Its work is monitored by a Board of Directors consisting of twenty-three members and is assisted by earmarked advisory groups[117]; its objective consists in enhancing the relevance, reputation and value of the global accountancy profession.

3.3.3.2 The International Standards on Auditing (ISAs)

In this respect, *inter alia*, through a technical committee, the International Auditing and Assurance Standards Board,[118] the IFAC issues international financial standards on the convergence of national rules and standards pertaining to the external audit of the financial statements of enterprises and other data provided to shareholders (and for companies listed in regulated markets, to the public). The International Standards on Auditing ('**ISA**'), as in force since 4 December 2015, concern, *inter alia*: aspects of financial statements that generally have a higher risk of material misstatement (e.g., estimates, fair values and related parties); the quality of audit evidence; and auditors' communications and reporting.[119]

3.3.4 The Committee on Payments and Market Infrastructures (CPMI)[120]

3.3.4.1 Establishment, Seat, Membership and Governance

The CPMI is, as of 1 September 2014, the successor of the Committee on Payment and Settlement Systems ('CPSS'), which was set up in 1990 by the G10 Central Bank Governors. As of **December 2022**, members of the CPMI, which has its seat in Basel, were senior officials from central banks or monetary authorities and agencies of the G20 Member States (the US being represented both through the Board of Governors of the Federal Reserve System and the

---

[117] See at: https://www.ifac.org/who-we-are/membership and https://www.ifac.org/who-we-are/advisory-groups, respectively. Since November 2022, President of the Board is Asmâa Resmouki from Morocco.

[118] At: https://www.ifac.org/search?keys=International%20Auditing%20and%20Assurance%20Standards%20Board.

[119] As mentioned in Chapter 2 above (under 2.4.4), these standards are also included in the FSB's "Key Standards for Sound Financial Systems".

[120] This forum is included under that heading in consistency with the above-mentioned in Chapter 2 (under 2.1.2) that public international payment and settlement systems law is part of public international capital markets law (even though it could be considered, as mentioned, as a separate branch, cutting across sectors).

Federal Reserve Bank of New York and the EU by the ECB); the three G10 Member States that are not members of the G20 (Belgium, Switzerland and Sweden), as well as Hong Kong SAR, The Netherlands, Singapore and Spain. The CPMI's Charter, adopted in September 2014,[121] provides that its regular meetings are held on the occasion of four of the bimonthly meetings of the Governors of the BIS member central banks. As of January 2010, the Chair of the CPMI[122] reports on its monitoring discussions and other initiatives to the GEM.[123]

3.3.4.2 Objective

The objective of the CPMI consists in supporting financial stability and the wider economy by promoting, monitoring and making Recommendations about the safety and efficiency of payment, clearing, settlement and related systems and arrangements. In this respect, it adopts (and monitors the implementation of) international financial standards contained in Reports on large-value payment systems; retail payment instruments (including electronic money) and systems; securities clearing and settlement systems, as well as clearing and settlement arrangements for derivatives transactions; settlement risk in foreign-exchange transactions; as well as interdependencies of payment and settlement systems and central bank oversight therein. *Furthermore*, it identifies risks for the safety and efficiency of payment, clearing and settlement systems, serves as a forum for central bank cooperation in related oversight, policy and operational matters, supports cooperative oversight and cross-border information-sharing (including crisis communication and contingency planning for cross-border crisis management) and maintains relationships with non-CPMI central banks to share experiences and promote the implementation of CPMI standards and recommendations beyond member jurisdictions. *Finally*, it is a member of the FSB and cooperates with other standard-setting bodies (in particular the Basel Committee and the IOSCO), the CGFS, international financial institutions and public sector bodies on matters falling within its mandate to enhance coordination of policy development and implementation.[124]

---

[121] This Charter is available at: https://www.bis.org/cpmi/info.htm?m=3%7C16%7C29.

[122] In December 2022, Chair of the CPMI was Sir Jon Cunliffe, Deputy Governor of the BoE.

[123] On the Global Economy Meeting (GEM), see Chapter 2 above, under 2.3.3 (when discussing the Basel Process).

[124] On the work of this forum, see at: https://www.bis.org/cpmi/about/overview.htm. Some reports are jointly issued with IOSCO through the "Task Force on Securities Settlement Systems". The above-mentioned joint CPMI/IOSCO 2012 Report on "Principles for Financial Market Infrastructures" is included in the FSB's "Key Standards for Sound Financial Systems".

3.4 OTHER INTERNATIONAL FINANCIAL FORA

3.4.1 The International Association of Insurance Supervisors (IAIS) in the Field of Public International Insurance Law

(1) The **IAIS** was set up in 1994 and has its seat in Basel at the BIS. It is an international non-profit, voluntary membership organisation of insurance supervisors. As of December 2022, its members totalled 210 (constituting 97% of the world's insurance premiums); there were also more than one hundred observers representing industry associations, professional associations, insurance and reinsurance undertakings, consultants and international financial institutions. The main governing body of the IAIS is the Executive Committee, whose thirty-eight members represent different geographical regions, and which is responsible for the provision of strategic direction and for the management of the forum's activities in accordance with its by-laws.[125] Its operation is supported by a Secretariat, under the direction of a Secretary General, and by five committees: the Audit and Risk Committee, the Budget Committee, the Implementation and Assessment Committee, the Macroprudential Committee and the Policy Development Committee.[126] The IAIS is a member of the FSB and a Parent Committee of the Joint Forum.[127]

(2) The main objectives of the IAIS consist the following: *first*, elaboration of principles, standards and guidance relating to the microprudential supervision, as well as the micro- and macroprudential regulation of insurance and reinsurance undertakings,[128] and provision of assistance to its members for their implementation; *second*, promotion of cooperation and experience-sharing among its members, as well as provision of training services and support on issues related to insurance regulation and supervision; and *third*, performance of a forward-looking role in identifying key trends and developments that could reshape the insurance business of insurance, supporting its members in addressing emerging risks and challenges (such as digital innovation, cyber risks, climate risk, financial inclusion, as well as sustainable economic development and diversity, equity and inclusion).

---

[125] In December 2022, Chair of the Executive Committee was Vicky Saporta, Executive Director of Prudential Policy Directorate at the BoE. The IAIS By-laws, as in force, are available at: https://www.iaisweb.org/uploads/2022/01/181207-2018-By-Law-Amendments-8-November-2018.pdf.

[126] On the organisational structure, see at: https://www.iaisweb.org/about-the-iais/organisational-structure.

[127] See just below, under 3.4.2.

[128] Its main report ("Insurance Core Principles") is also included in the FSB's "Key Standards".

3.4.2 The Joint Forum in the Field of Public International Financial Conglomerates Law

(1) The Joint Forum, initially known as 'Joint Forum on Financial Conglomerates', was set up in 1996 as a successor to the 'Tripartite Group' under the auspices of the Basel Committee, the IOSCO and the IAIS (the "**Parent Committees**").[129] As of **December 2022**, members of this international financial forum, which also has its seat in Basel at the BIS, were senior representatives of the Parent Committees and of national supervisory (and regulatory) authorities of the three main sectors of the financial system from twelve G20 Member States, Belgium, The Netherlands and Spain. The IMF, the European Commission and the FSI have observer status.[130] The Joint Forum does not have a founding charter or by-laws. Its Chairmanship, for a two-year term, rotates between the Parent Committees,[131] usually meets three times a year.

(2) The Joint Forum's objective is the provision of support to banking, insurance and securities supervisors in meeting their regulatory and supervisory objectives and, more broadly, the contribution to the international regulatory agenda in particular in relation to inter-sectoral risks and gaps. This is pursued by *first*, addressing and promoting the understanding of issues common to the three sectors of the financial system, including the supervision of financial conglomerates; *second*, analysing cross-sectoral market and regulatory developments, as well as examining cross-sectoral gaps and conflicts in regulation and supervision; *third*, developing guidance and principles and identifying best practices on cross-sectoral technical, regulatory and/or policy issues to encourage cross-sectoral consistency and alignment, and reduce opportunities for regulatory arbitrage; and *finally*, facilitating cooperation, coordination and information-sharing among banking, insurance and securities supervisors (or representatives of the Parent Committees) and further supports the Parent Committees by identifying synergies or duplication in their work efforts.[132] Its work is supported by two Sub-Groups, on Risk Assessment and Capital, and on Conglomerate Supervision.

---

[129] The Tripartite Group was set up in 1993, at the initiative of the Basel Committee, to address issues relating to the prudential supervision and regulation of financial conglomerates. The Forum's name was shortened to 'Joint Forum' in 1999 since its mandate was extended beyond issues relating to financial conglomerates to cover issues of common interest to all three sectors of the financial system, i.e., the banking, capital markets and insurance sectors. Nevertheless, its main objective remains the same, which is why, in the author's view, the Joint Forum should be considered mainly as a standard-setter with regard to international financial conglomerates law.

[130] On the FSI, see under 3.1.8 above.

[131] In December 2022, the Joint Forum was chaired by Thomas Schmitz-Lippert, Executive Director at the German single financial supervisory authority (BaFin).

[132] See at: https://www.bis.org/bcbs/jfmandate.htm.

3.4.3 The Financial Action Task Force (FATF) in the Field of Combatting the Use of the Financial System for the Commitment of Economic Crimes

(1) The FATF was founded in 1989, on the initiative of the G7 during its annual summit in Paris, as an intergovernmental body. As of **December 2022**, the FATF, which has its seat in Paris and receives secretarial support from the OECD, numbered thirty-nine members (thirty-seven member jurisdictions and two regional organisations, namely the European Commission and the Gulf Cooperation Council ('**GCC**')), including the founding-members of the G7. In addition, the FATF relies on a strong global network of FATF-Style Regional Bodies ('**FSRBs**'), which have the status of Associate Members.[133] The FATF does not have a strictly defined constitution or an unlimited life span[134]; its decision-making body is the FATF Plenary which meets three times per year.

(2) The FATF's objective consists in the adoption of international financial standards to counter (i.e., prevent and contain) the use of the financial system by criminals, and in particular the legitimisation of proceeds from illegal activities (a practice and criminal activity known as 'money laundering') and terrorist financing. In this respect, it issued a Report in 1990 (updated in 1996 and 2003) laying down forty Recommendations, which set out the framework for combatting money laundering. In 2001, just a few months after the terrorist attacks of 11 September, it also issued eight special Recommendations on combatting terrorist financing (complemented by a ninth Recommendation of 2004). Comprehensive, revised Recommendations were re-issued on 1 February 2012, which, as in force, provide the framework to detect, prevent and contain such crimes, and cover, *inter alia*: risk identification and criminalisation of money laundering and terrorist financing; preventive measures to be adopted by financial institutions and designated non-financial professions; institutional measures, such as the creation of a Financial Intelligence Unit ('**FIU**'); transparency measures; and international cooperation.[135]

---

[133] These include, *inter alia*, the Asia/Pacific Group on Money Laundering (APG), the Caribbean Financial Action Task Force (CFATF), the Eurasian Group (EAG), the Eastern and Southern Africa Anti-Money Laundering Group (ESAAMLG), the Council of Europe Committee of Experts on the Evaluation of Anti-Money Laundering Measures and the Financing of Terrorism (MONEYVAL), the Financial Action Task Force on Money Laundering in South America (GAFISUD), the Inter-Governmental Action Group against Money Laundering in West Africa (GIABA) and the Middle East and North Africa Financial Action Task Force (MENAFATF). Indonesia, the United Nations Office on Drugs and Crime (UNODC), the IMF, the World Bank, the OECD, the ECB, Interpol, Europol and the World Customs Organisation have observer status.

[134] Since 1 July 2022, the FATF is chaired, for a two-year term, by T. Raja Kumar from Singapore.

[135] These Recommendations are also included in the FSB's "Key Standards for Sound Financial Systems" (see Chapter 2 above (under 2.4.4)).

(3) The FATF monitors members' progress in implementing the above standards; prepares reports on money laundering and terrorist financing techniques; and promotes the adoption and implementation of appropriate measures globally. Its objective is achieved by means of the compilation and assessment of annual reports on the results of international cooperation initiatives on combatting money laundering and terrorist financing, as well as the examination and adoption of further measures to enhance international cooperation.[136]

3.4.4 *The Committee on the Global Financial System (CGFS)*

3.4.4.1 Establishment, Seat, Membership and Governance
(1) The CGFS was set up in 1971 by the G10 Central Bank Governors as the 'Euro-Currency Standing Committee' (hence it was the first international financial forum established). At that time, its mandate was to monitor international banking markets and the monetary implications of the rapid growth of offshore deposit and lending markets ('Euromarkets'). It was given its current name in 1999 to reflect that the focus of its work gradually shifted to issues of financial stability and broader issues related to structural amendments in the financial system.

(2) The initial members of the CGFS, which also has its seat in Basel at the BIS, were Deputy-Governors and high-level officials from the G10 central banks (the US being represented in this forum, as in the Joint Forum, by the Board of Governors of the Federal Reserve System and the Federal Reserve Bank of New York) and Luxembourg. The Economic Adviser of the BIS is also a member. Gradually, membership increased with the participation of representatives from the central banks of Spain, Hong Kong SAR and Singapore, as well as the ECB. In 2009, membership was extended to another six central banks of G20 Member States (Australia, Brazil, China, India, Korea and Mexico). As of **December 2022**, its member institutions totalled twenty-eight.

(3) The CGFS does not have a founding Charter or by-laws, and its regular meetings are held on the occasion of four of the bimonthly meetings of the Governors of the BIS member central banks. In addition, since January 2010, the Chair of the CGFS[137] reports to the 'Global Economy Meeting' (GEM) on its monitoring discussions and other initiatives.

---

[136] For a more detailed overview of the work of this forum, see https://fatf-gafi.org. Its main Report ("Forty Recommendations on Money Laundering/Nine Special Recommendations on Terrorist Financing") is included in the FSB's "Key Standards for Sound Financial Systems".

[137] In December 2022, Chair of the CGFS was Philip Lowe, Governor of the Reserve Bank of Australia.

3.4.4.2 Objectives

Unlike all other international fora mentioned above, the CGFS is not a standard-setting body. Its current objectives were set out in a statement of the G10 Central Bank Governors of 8 February 1999[138] and consist in the following. The *first* is to seek to identify and assess potential sources of stress in the international financial environment. The means to achieve this objective is the regular and systematic monitoring of developments in financial markets and systems, including through evaluation of macroeconomic developments.[139] The *second* objective is to further the understanding of the functioning and underpinnings of financial markets and systems. With a view to achieving it, the CGFS is monitoring the evolution of financial markets and systems, and conducting in-depth analyses, with particular reference to the implications for central bank operations and broader responsibilities for monetary and financial stability. In this respect, the CGFS has issued several reports, which during and in the aftermath of the GFC constituted valuable sources for the analysis of its causes, its impact and the necessary regulatory intervention (see Box 3.6 below).[140] Finally, the *third* objective is to promote the development of well-functioning and stable financial markets and systems; the targets set to achieve this objective are examining alternative policy responses and drawing up corresponding policy recommendations. The CGFS also oversees the collection of international banking and financial statistics compiled by the BIS.

Box 3.6 Key CGFS publications since 2007

2007–2010

Financial stability and local currency bond markets (June 2007).

Research on global financial stability: the use of BIS international financial statistics (December 2007).

Private equity and leveraged finance markets (July 2008).

Central bank operations in response to the financial turmoil (July 2008).

Ratings in structured finance: what went wrong and what can be done to address shortcomings? (July 2008).

Capital flows and emerging market economies (January 2009).

The role of valuation and leverage in procyclicality (April 2009).

Credit risk transfer statistics (September 2009).

---

[138] See also https://www.bis.org/cgfs/mandate.htm.

[139] According to its mandate, this forum was responsible for the macroprudential oversight of the international (or global) financial system, a task it has obviously not fully discharged.

[140] These reports are available at: https://www.bis.org/list/cgfs/index.htm.

The role of margin requirements and haircuts (March 2010).
The functioning and resilience of cross-border funding markets (March 2010).
Macro-prudential instruments and frameworks: a stocktaking of issues and experiences (May 2010).
Funding patterns and liquidity management of internationally active banks (May 2010).
Research on global financial stability: the use of BIS international financial statistics (June 2010).
Long-term issues in international banking (June 2010).

2011–2015
Interactions of sovereign debt management with monetary conditions and Financial stability (May 2011).
The impact of sovereign credit risk on bank funding conditions (July 2011).
Fixed income strategies of insurance companies and pension funds (July 2011).
Global liquidity—concept, measurement and policy implications (November 2011).
The macrofinancial implications of alternative configurations for access to central counterparties in OTC derivatives markets (November 2011).
Global liquidity—concept, measurement and policy implications (November 2011).
Operationalising the selection and application of macroprudential instruments (December 2012).
Asset encumbrance, financial reform and the demand for collateral assets (May 2013).
Regulatory change and monetary policy (May 2015).

2016–2022
Experiences with the ex-ante appraisal of macroprudential instruments (July 2016).
Objective-setting and communication of macroprudential policies (November 2016).
Designing frameworks for central bank liquidity assistance: addressing new challenges (April 2017).
Fin Tech credit: Market structure, business models and financial stability implications (May 2017).
Structural changes in banking after the crisis (January 2018).
Financial stability implications of a prolonged period of low interest rates (July 2018).
Establishing viable capital markets (January 2019).

> Unconventional monetary policy tools: a cross-country analysis (October 2019).
> US dollar funding: an international perspective (June 2020).
> Changing patterns of capital flows (May 2021).
> Private sector debt and financial stability (May 2022).

3.5 An Interim Assessment and the Link to Parts II and III of This Study

It can be strongly argued that the new international financial architecture has taken on historically unprecedented dimensions, even before the GFC. The main constituents of this architecture, which, as mentioned above, were shaped gradually and have been marked by ongoing readjustments to new conditions, can be summarised as follows: *First*, in contrast with the initial post-war period, until 1970, there is symmetry between the international monetary and the international financial architectures, with the second having become equally important (and evidently more detailed). *Second*, the governance of the international architecture is carried out on a decentralised basis, since there is no international organisation or forum entrusted with the management even of a single aspect of the internationally intertwined national monetary and financial systems. National authorities remain competent for the conduct of monetary policy (with the exception of the cases of regional monetary unions, like the one in the euro area) and various aspects of financial policy. *Third*, the governance of the international financial architecture is also characterised by institutional fragmentation, given that several intergovernmental fora, international organisations, international financial fora with the participation of national authorities or other and (in two cases) private professional associations are active, and these differ significantly both in their make-up and in the way international cooperation is carried out. However, cooperation between them has been significantly bolstered since 1999 within the framework of the FSB, which plays a significant role at the level of coordination. Furthermore, international organisations and fora, over and above the remainder of their activities, play an important role as fora for cooperation and information exchange between their members.[141] *Finally*, an important aspect with regard

---

[141] Despite the geopolitical tensions caused by the Russian Federation's invasion of Ukraine in 2022 and, in terms of trade in goods and services the shift towards relative "deglobalisation" (the discussion of which is beyond the scope of this study), the level of cooperation within the international financial fora does not seem to have been (as yet at least) negatively affected. However, during the current period, the resilience of the global financial system will be tested through various amplification channels, including, *inter alia*, financial firms' exposures to Russian and Ukrainian assets.

to the making and enforcement of international financial law is that it takes place at four levels. It is to this latter aspect that the author will now turn his attention, in the following Parts of this study.

Secondary Sources

A & G–H

Alexander, K. (2019): Principles of Banking Regulation, Cambridge University Press, Cambridge, United Kingdom

Giovanoli, M. (2010): The International Financial Architecture and its Reform after the Global Crisis, in Giovanoli, M. and D. Devos (2010, editors): *International Monetary and Financial Law: The global crisis*, Oxford University Press, Oxford–New York, Chapter 1, pp. 3–39

Giovanoli, M. (2000, editor): International Monetary Law—Issues for the New Millennium, Oxford University Press, Oxford

Giovanoli, M. (2000): A New Architecture for the Global Financial Market: Legal Aspects of International Financial Standard Setting, in Giovanoli, M. (2000, editor): International Monetary Law – Issues for the New Millennium, Oxford University Press, Oxford–New York, pp. 3–59

Goodhart, C. (2011): The Basel Committee on Banking Supervision: A History of the Early Years 1974–1997, Cambridge University Press, Cambridge, United Kingdom

Gortsos, Ch.V. (2023): The Role of International Financial Fora in Preserving Global Financial Stability Amidst the Pandemic Crisis: The First 18 Months, in Blair, W., Zilioli, Ch. and Ch.V. Gortsos (2023, editors), International Monetary and Banking Law in the post COVID-19 World, Chapter 1, Oxford University Press, Oxford

Gortsos, Ch.V. (2012): Fundamentals of Public International Financial Law: International Banking Law within the System of Public International Financial Law, Schriften des Europa-Instituts der Universität des Saarlandes – Rechtswissenschaft, Nomos Verlag, Baden-Baden

Grubel, H. G. (1979): A Proposal for the Establishment of an International Deposit Insurance Corporation, Essays in International Finance, No. 133, Princeton, NJ, Princeton University, International Finance Section

Herring, R.J. and R.E. Litan (1995): Financial Regulation in the Global Economy, The Brookings Institution, Washington, DC, available at: https://www.brookings.edu/comm/conferencereport/cr14.htm

K–L

Kapstein, E.B. (1994): Governing the Global Economy: International Finance and the State, Harvard University Press, Cambridge, MA–London, England

Lastra, R.M. (2015): International Financial and Monetary Law, second edition, Oxford University Press, United Kingdom

N–O

Nobel, P. (2019): Schweizerisches Finanzmarktrecht, 4., vollständig überarbeitete Auflage, Stämpfli Verlag AG Bern

Norton, J.J. (2001): Pondering the Parameters of the 'New International Financial Architecture': A legal Perspective, in Lastra R.M. (2001, editor): The Reform of the International Financial Architecture, International Banking, Finance and Economic Law Series, Kluwer Law International, The Hague–London–New York, pp. 3–46

Norton, J.J. (1995): Devising International Bank Supervisory Standards, Graham & Trotman, Martinus Nijhoff, London–Dordrecht–Boston

Ortino, M. (2019): Thirty Years After the Basel Accord and Ten After the Financial Crisis: the Basel Committee on Banking Supervision and its Place in International Economic Law, Journal of International Economic Law, Special Issue: The Basel Committee on Banking Supervision, Volume 22, Issue 2, June, pp. 159–161 (also available at: https://doi.org/10.1093/jiel/jgz019)

W

Walker, G.A. (2001): International Banking Regulation: Law, Policy and Practice, International Banking, Finance and Economic Law Series, Kluwer Law International, The Hague - London - New York

Wandel, S.A. (2014): International Regulatory Cooperation: An Analysis of Standard Setting in Financial Law, Schweizer Schriften zum Finanzmarktrecht, Band 119, Schulthess Verlag, Zürich

PART II

European Banking Regulation (Law): Definition, Evolution and Sources

CHAPTER 4

Definition and Evolution up to the Creation of the Banking Union

4.1 General Introduction

4.1.1 Financial Integration as the Conceptual Basis of European (EU) Financial Law

4.1.1.1 The Concept of Financial Integration

(1) The process of financial integration has been advancing in the **EU** mainly over the last five decades, in stages, but at a gradually intensifying pace. This process, the starting point of which was the complete fragmentation of its Member States' financial systems, is constantly evolving and aims at shaping a single financial area within its single market.[1] Financial integration between two or more sovereign states is one of the dimensions of these states' microeconomic integration[2] which, along with their macroeconomic integration, compose the whole of economic integration. At the same time, financial integration forms part of the broader process of financial internationalisation,[3] but

---

[1] On the degree of fragmentation between the financial systems of EU Member States, see, by means of mere indication, Avgouleas and Arner (2013) and Schoenmaker and Peek (2014). See also the ECB/Eurosystem most recent (April 2022) Report "Financial Integration and Structure in the Euro Area" (ECB Committee on Financial Integration, at: https://www.ecb.europa.eu/pub/pdf/fie/ecb.fie202204~4c4f5f572f.cs.pdf).

[2] The author defines 'microeconomic integration' as the aggregation of markets (for goods and services) of the sovereign states participating in the integration process, aimed at creating a single economic area. On the other hand, 'macroeconomic integration' is defined as the harmonisation/unification of the instruments used in the conduct of macroeconomic policies of these participating states with a view to implementing a single macroeconomic policy; see also below, under 4.1.4.

[3] See Herring and Litan (1995), pp. 13–48.

usually materialises at regional level and penetrates deeper into the financial system of participating states. According to a 2007 study of the ECB[4]:

> Taking as a starting point the view that national financial systems have historically been segmented, financial integration is part of the currently heavily emerging process of financial internationalisation. Evidently, however, the process of financial integration aims at deeper results in comparison to that of financial internationalisation, because its ultimate purpose is the establishment and functioning of a single financial area within the context of a common economic area ("microeconomic integration"). It may be even deeper if the states concerned strive also at "macroeconomic integration", as it is the case in the European Union, which has already achieved its monetary unification.

(2) To the best of the author's knowledge, there is no commonly accepted definition of financial integration in literature. In view of this, the point of reference used is the ECB's definition:

> The ECB [...] considers the market for a given set of financial instruments or services to be fully integrated when all potential market participants in such market are subject to a single set of rules when they decide to deal with those financial instruments or services, have equal access to this set of financial instruments or services, and are treated equally when they operate in the market. This integration can be achieved through initiatives of the market itself ("market-led process of integration"), through self-regulation, and/or through binding rules arising from intergovernmental or supranational institutions.[5]

For the purposes of this study, financial integration is thus defined as the aggregation of the financial systems of two or more sovereign (member) states within the framework of the operation of a *single* economic area, which is aimed at meeting the three above-mentioned conditions pertaining to the operation of a single financial area *and* pursued through the regulatory framework, *via* self-regulation or by means of market-led initiatives.[6]

4.1.1.2 The Two Dimensions of Financial Integration

Negative financial integration: To the extent that financial integration is pursued through the regulatory framework, two dimensions can be identified: a negative and a positive one. The materialisation of negative financial integration requires, on the one hand, the liberalisation of trade in financial services and, on the other hand, the adoption of rules to ensure free competition in the financial system, a policy objective of primary importance for the entire

---

[4] See European Central Bank (2007).
[5] See European Central Bank (2008), p. 6.
[6] *Ibid.*, pp. 64–65.

common economic area (i.e., not particular to the financial system only).[7] Implementation of this dimension of financial integration should be regarded as the 'necessary' condition for achieving full financial integration.

Positive financial integration: The content of positive financial integration, which constitutes the 'sufficient' condition for achieving full financial integration, is, in the author's view, twofold:

(a) According to a *stricto sensu* approach, the achievement of positive integration initially requires the adoption of rules that, within a single financial area, enable meeting the objectives of regulatory intervention in the financial system, i.e., specific financial policy objectives. These rules must be designed to ensure conditions of competitive equality across all categories of financial service providers operating in the single area, offering similar services and exposed to similar risks. In this context, there are three key issues that need to be addressed[8]:

> The *first* concerns identifying the necessary financial policy objectives and appropriate financial policy instruments to achieve them.
> The *second issue* concerns the level and extent of harmonisation of rules, within a single financial area, which prescribe regulatory intervention to meet the identified financial policy objectives: ***minimum*** or ***maximum*** in terms of extent[9]; ***partial or full*** in terms of scope.[10]
> The *third (related) issue* concerns pinpointing administrative authorities (and, in certain cases, schemes), which should be competent for the implementation of regulatory intervention in the financial system. In this respect, decisions need to be taken on two sub-issues: whether these authorities and schemes should remain national or become supranational; and if national, which states' authorities and schemes should be competent for foreign establishments (i.e., branches and subsidiaries) of financial firms operating in several states within the single financial area.

(b) The second (and undoubtedly more ambitious) aspect of positive financial integration consists in the adoption of a single set of rules with respect to

---

[7] An example of liberalisation would be the role of the free movement of capital in rendering discriminatory national laws inapplicable, while an example of free competition rules would be the—in principle—prohibition of state aid granted by a Member State in support of its financial system.

[8] For more details, see Gortsos (1996), pp. 79–89.

[9] For an analysis of the relevant issues at stake, when deciding between maximum *versus* minimum harmonisation, see, by means of mere indication, Weatherill (2012).

[10] In accordance with the 'economic transplants' analysis of Langenbucher (2017), in a situation of diversity between national legislations, (harmonisation through) economic transplants at EU level provide a "*common language, outside of the idiosyncrasies of individual Member States' laws*" (see at pp. 68–69 and then the following chapters, with a focus on aspects of capital markets law).

the provision of financial services, namely a single 'financial contracts law'. Meeting this parallel target, according to a *lato sensu* approach of positive financial integration, would require the full harmonisation of corresponding aspects of private law of the states participating in the single financial area.[11]

4.1.2 A Definition of European (EU) Financial Law

(1) As just mentioned above, implementation of financial integration is sought either through the regulatory framework established by intergovernmental and/or supranational authorities, through self-regulation, or, finally, through market-led initiatives. In the EU, implementation of financial integration through the regulatory framework is sought (and achieved) by means of the provisions of those legal acts that constitute the sources of EU financial law, a subset of European economic law.[12] Based on the definition of the concept and the two dimensions of financial integration, the author considers that EU financial law can be defined, in principle, as the set of provisions of secondary EU law aimed at the achievement of the EU's negative and positive financial integration, with a view to creating a single financial area in the single market, positive financial integration relating to the achievement at EU level of specific financial policy objectives. Hence, this concept of EU financial law, based on a functional approach, is demarcated by legal acts issued by the competent EU institutions aimed at materialising three of EU law's fundamental freedoms (on capital movement, establishment and provision of services) in relation to various categories of EU financial firms, in the context of negative financial integration, and adopting provisions on the implementation of specific *financial policies*, in the context of positive financial integration.[13]

Under an alternative *lato sensu* definition, EU financial law is defined as the set of provisions of secondary EU law aimed at the achievement of the EU's negative and positive financial integration, with a view to creating a single financial area in the common market, positive financial integration relating in this case both to the achievement at EU level of specific financial policy objectives and the creation of a European 'financial contracts law'.[14] The vast majority of the legal acts constituting the sources of the EU financial law in force (still) contain provisions consistent with the main definition. Hence, the following analysis is confined to this.

---

[11] On the evolution of EU contract law in the Banking and Financial Union, see, by means of mere indication, Grundmann and Sirena (2019).

[12] On the concept and content of EU economic law, see, by means of mere indication, Kellerhals (2006), Schwarze (2007) and Kilian (2008).

[13] On the indirect "export" of rules of EU financial law to third countries through the mechanism of equivalence, see Pennesi (2021) and in more detail (2022), both with extensive further references.

[14] The first definition is consistent with the above-mentioned *stricto sensu* approach to positive financial integration, and the alternative consistent with the *lato sensu* approach to this integration.

(2) The **perimeter of Member States** to which the rules of the various legal acts which constitute the sources of EU financial law apply is variable: *first*, usually, these legal acts are addressed to all Member States[15]; *second*, the provisions of the legal acts which constitute the legal basis of the main pillars of the (European) Banking Union ('**BU**') apply only to the Member States which have adopted the euro as a currency, even though other Member States may also participate therein; in this case, these legal acts apply equally to BU participating states ("eurozone +")[16]; *finally*, the legal acts adopted (mainly) in the form of Directives also apply to Iceland, Liechtenstein and Norway, i.e., the three of the four Member States of the European Free Trade Association ('**EFTA**'), which, together with the EU Member States, form the European Economic Area ('**EEA**').[17] Switzerland, the fourth EFTA Member State, is not a member of the EEA.

4.1.3   The Branches of European (EU) Financial Law

4.1.3.1   General Overview

Considering the above and in full consistency with the categorisation of the branches of public international financial law,[18] the author distinguishes between four separate albeit closely linked branches of EU financial law: EU banking law; EU capital markets law (including EU payment and settlement systems law); EU insurance law; and EU financial conglomerates law. These individual branches of EU financial law, especially as regards the dimension of positive financial integration, are defined on the basis of a functional approach for the reasons already mentioned.[19] As an indication, the regime governing the operation of EU credit institutions (and partly also branches of third-country credit institutions established in the EU) is also affected by the provisions of other branches of EU financial law (except for EU insurance law). If the institutional approach were to be adopted, these provisions would need to be concurrently included in European (EU) banking law (alternatively defined in this case as "European law of credit institutions"), as well as in EU capital markets law, if they also apply to investment firms. Moreover, given that EU credit institutions (and all other categories of EU financial firms) are also subject to the provisions of several other legal acts constituting the sources of other branches of EU economic law not included in EU financial law, if the functional approach would not be adopted, these provisions should also be included, for reasons of consistency, in EU banking law.

---

[15] On the differentiated integration of Member States, see, by mere indication, Enoch (2021), pp. 271–288.

[16] On the BU, see details under 4.4 below.

[17] For more details on the EFTA and the EEA, see at: https://www.efta.int.

[18] See above in Chapter 2, under 2.1.1.

[19] *Ibid*.

4.1.3.2 *European (EU) Banking Law*

(1) EU banking law is defined as the set of provisions of EU financial law, aimed at the following two objectives: to materialise, with regard to EU credit institutions, the two basic freedoms laid down in primary law (i.e., the freedom of establishment by setting up branches and the freedom to provide services), and to ensure the stability of the European banking system. For the achievement of the latter objective, EU banking law contains rules on the authorisation, micro- and macroprudential regulation and the prudential supervision of credit institutions; the macroprudential oversight of the banking (and, more generally the financial) system; the reorganisation, resolution and winding-up of credit institutions; and deposit guarantee. On the contrary, in principle, there are no rules on the functioning of central banks as lenders of last resort since this function is exercised in an environment of 'constructive ambiguity'.[20]

(2) The overwhelming majority of the provisions of EU banking law apply to EU credit institutions. They also apply to credit institutions incorporated in member countries of the EEA. This branch of EU financial law also contains provisions on the establishment and operation of branches of non-EU credit institutions in Member States. Finally, some provisions of EU banking law also apply to EU 'financial institutions', which are subsidiary undertakings of EU credit institutions. This category comprises mainly finance, leasing and factoring companies.

Box 4.1 Definition of the terms credit institution and financial institution

(1) The term **'credit institution'** was (initially) defined to mean any undertaking whose business is to receive deposits or other repayable funds from the public and to grant credits for its own account.[21] It was selected as an overarching concept, covering all types of financial firms which accept deposits and grant loans for their own account, even if they are/were not named 'banks' (e.g., cajas in Spain, casse di risparmio in Italy, Ταχυδρομικό Ταμιευτήριο in Greece) in order to establish a uniform framework regarding their operation.

---

[20] See on this the *Excursus* at the end of Chapter 6.

[21] This definition was introduced for the first time in 1977 by the 'First Banking Directive' (see below, under 4.2.1). It was recurrently adopted *verbatim* in subsequent legal acts constituting the sources of EU banking law and was expanded in 2019, as discussed in Chapter 6 below, under 6.1.2.

> An **'EU credit institution'** means a credit institution incorporated under the laws of an EU/EEA Member State. On the other hand, a **'non-EU credit institution'** means a credit institution incorporated under the laws of a third country, which is not a Member State of the EU or the EEA.
>
> **(2)** Under EU secondary law, **'financial institution'** means, in principle, an undertaking, *other than a credit institution*, the principal activity of which is to acquire holdings *or* to pursue any of the activities listed in points (2)–(12) and (15) of Annex I to one of the sources of EU banking law, the **Capital Requirements Directive No IV**.[22] Accordingly, the use of this term when referring to firms exercising general activity in the financial sector is not appropriate; suitable in that context is the term **'financial firms'**.[23]

4.1.3.3 European (EU) Capital Markets Law
(1) EU capital markets law is the branch of EU financial law containing provisions aimed at complying with five rationales: materialise the freedom of establishment and the freedom to provide services by EU financial firms in capital markets; ensure the compensation of investors in case of suspension of operations of a firm providing investment services (bank or investment firm), if such firm is not in a position to return investors' funds or financial instruments; ensure the stability of capital markets; ensure the protection of investors that wish to invest, or already invest, in primary and derivative financial instruments, that are either going to be listed in a regulated market (the 'primary market'), or are already being traded therein (the 'secondary market'); as well as ensure capital markets' integrity, efficiency and transparency. In consistency with the discussions on public international financial law in Chapter 2 above, this branch of EU financial law also contains provisions seeking to safeguard the stability and efficiency of payment and settlement systems.

(2) Most of the provisions of EU capital markets law apply to credit institutions for three reasons: *first*, as further discussed below,[24] these are entitled since 1996 to provide the entire range of investment services and activities on an individual basis, according to the 'universal banking model'[25]; *second*,

---

[22] See under 4.4.3 below.

[23] It is, however, worth noting that in primary EU law and in particular in Article 127(6) of the Treaty on the Functioning of the European Union ('TFEU', Consolidated version, OJ C 202, 7.6.2016, pp. 47–200), this term is referred to as if credit institutions were also financial institutions. This creates an inconsistency (as further discussed in the following chapters).

[24] See under 4.2.2 below.

[25] On this model, see Chapter 1 above, under 1.1.3.

a significant number of credit institutions are listed in regulated markets and, hence, the provisions on the regulatory obligations imposed on listed companies also apply to them; and *third*, in relation to payment and settlement systems, credit institutions are participating therein as members and/or shareholders.

4.1.3.4 *European (EU) Insurance Law*

EU insurance law is the branch of EU financial law containing provisions seeking to materialise the freedom of establishment and the freedom to provide services regarding EU financial firms providing insurance and reinsurance services, protect insurance policyholders and insurance contract beneficiaries, and (to a lesser extent) safeguard the stability of the insurance sector. Notwithstanding very few exceptions, the provisions of EU insurance law do not apply to credit institutions since in most Member States the provision of insurance and reinsurance services is only permitted for undertakings specifically authorised for this purpose, namely insurance and reinsurance undertakings.

4.1.3.5 *European (EU) Financial Conglomerates Law*

EU financial conglomerates law is the branch of EU financial law that contains provisions regarding the supplementary supervision of financial conglomerates (groups comprising insurance undertakings, as well as credit institutions or investment firms), in order to safeguard the stability of the financial system as regards their activity. The provisions of this branch apply to credit institutions to the extent of their participation in financial conglomerates, over and above the provisions of EU banking law on their prudential supervision (on an individual and a consolidated basis).

4.1.3.6 *Final Remark: The Sector-Specific Nature of EU Financial Law*

As further discussed in the following sections of this chapter, the three key branches of EU financial law, namely banking, capital markets and insurance law, contain rules which were and remain mainly sector specific. This was dictated by the need to pursue, through harmonisation at EU level, and meet specific policy objectives relating to each of the three main sectors of the financial system (payment systems being the fourth), albeit at the expense of a coherent cross-sectoral approach, where this would be deemed necessary.[26]

---

[26] To a certain extent, it was (and still is) also the by-product of an inherent element of the 'international financial architecture', as gradually shaped since the 1970s, which is based on the sectoral approach, as discussed in Chapters 2 and 3 above. On the limitations and inefficiencies of sectoral legislation, see, by means of indication, Colaert, Busch and Incalza (2019, editors) (the by-product of a research project); see also Annunziata (2022), discussing the creation of a comprehensive "EU Charter" for the protection of end users in financial markets.

4.1.4 Delimitation vis-à-vis *European Monetary Law*

4.1.4.1 Introductory Remarks

EU financial law must be distinguished from **'European (or EU) monetary law'**, which is defined as the set of primary and secondary EU law provisions which govern the 'M' of the Economic and Monetary Union (**'EMU'**). The EMU was established by the "Treaty establishing the European Community" (**'TEC'**),[27] which incorporated the **Treaty of Maastricht** of **7 February 1992**.[28] In this respect, the following is noted:

(1) The establishment of the European monetary union was based on **Article 4(2) TEC**, whereby:

> (…) These activities (of the Member States and the Community) shall include the irrevocable fixing of exchange rates, leading to the introduction of a single currency, the ECU, and the definition and conduct of a single monetary policy and exchange rate policy (…).[29]

Currently, the legal anchor for the monetary union, the first and main element of the EMU, is the **TFEU**.[30] Participation in the EMU is confined to the Member States meeting specific economic and legal 'convergence criteria'[31]; those not meeting these criteria are referred to as 'Member States with a derogation'.[32] The group of Member States with a derogation also includes Denmark, the only Member State with an opt-out clause from the monetary union under the conditions laid down in **Protocol (No 16)** annexed to the

---

[27] Consolidated version, OJ C 321, 29.12.2006, pp. 47–200.

[28] OJ C 191, 29.7.1992, pp. 1–112.

[29] For a detailed presentation of the road towards the EMU, see Bini-Smaghi *et al.* (1994) and Issing (2008).

[30] Monetary integration is part of macroeconomic and not of microeconomic integration in the EU. Hence, and based on the functional approach adopted for the definition of EU financial law, its delimitation from EU monetary law is justified by the mere fact that their provisions aim at different policy objectives. It is noted, furthermore, that in a monetary union, it is possible to establish a common currency, which, following the irrevocable fixing of exchange rates, may circulate in parallel with national currencies of participating states. However, the *full achievement* of monetary integration further requires the introduction of a single currency in the form of both scriptural and physical money (coins and banknotes), and the withdrawal from circulation of banknotes and coins in the national currencies of the Member States participating therein.

[31] TEC, Articles 108–109 and 121(1) (currently, Articles 130–131 and 140(1) TFEU) and Protocol (No 13) attached to the Treaties (Consolidated version, OJ C 202, 7.6.2016, pp. 281–282).

[32] Member States with a derogation were subject to Articles 121–124 TEC (currently, Articles 139–144 TFEU).

Treaty on European Union ('**TEU**')[33] and the TFEU (jointly hereinafter the '**Treaties**').[34]

(2) The operation of a monetary union presupposes the concurrence of institutional and functional conditions, so that the conduct of a single monetary policy is enabled. Obviously, it is not possible for subsidiarity, i.e., a partially national monetary policy, to exist in a single monetary area.[35] In the context of the operation of the European monetary union, which is undoubtedly the core of the EMU, the establishment of a supranational entity, competent for defining and implementing a single monetary policy, was thus deemed necessary. With the **Treaty of Maastricht**, the Member States made the political decision to proceed to the establishment of such entity, the ECB within a "*quasi* federal system of central banks", the European System of Central Banks ('**ESCB**'). This comprises the ECB, which (since 1 December 2009) is a Treaty-based EU institution,[36] and the national central banks ('**NCBs**') of all EU Member States, while the term '**Eurosystem**' is defined to comprise the ECB and the NCBs of the Member States whose currency is the euro (i.e., those of the euro area).[37]

(3) The operation of the ECB, the ESCB and the Eurosystem is governed by the TFEU and the Statute of the ESCB and the ECB (hereinafter the '**ESCB/ECB Statute**').[38] The relationship between the ECB and the NCBs of the Member States whose currency is the euro is governed by **Article 14.3.**

---

[33] Consolidated version, OJ C 202, 7.6.2016, pp. 13–45.

[34] Consolidated version, OJ C 202, 7.6.2016, p. 287. This Protocol "on certain provisions relating to Denmark" established Denmark's right to opt-out from participation in the third stage of EMU, and provides that in case of exercising this right, its regime equals the one of the other Member States with a derogation. According to Article 51 TEU (Article 311 TEC), the Protocols annexed to the Treaties form an integral part thereof and, consequently, their provisions constitute primary EU law.

[35] On the economics of the monetary union, see, by means of indication, De Grauwe (2020). On a related matter, according to Article 5(3) TEU, the EU law principle of subsidiarity does not apply in areas of exclusive EU competence.

[36] TEU, Article 13(1), second sub-paragraph, sixth indent. On the institutional aspects of the ECB, see, by means of mere indication, Lastra (2015), pp. 247–273, Zilioli and Athanassiou (2018), pp. 613–624, De Grauwe (2020), pp. 173–177, Gortsos (2020), pp. 245–278 and Ioannidis (2020). On the role of NCBs in the ESCB and the Eurosystem, see Gortsos (2020), pp. 188–194.

[37] Pursuant to Article 8 TEC, from the beginning of the (then called 'third stage' of the) EMU on 1 January 1999, the ESCB and the ECB are expected to "(…) *act within the limits of the powers conferred upon them by this Treaty and by the (Protocol on the) Statute of the [ESCB and of the ECB] annexed thereto*". Both the ESCB and the Eurosystem do not have legal personality.

[38] This Statute was initially included in a Protocol annexed to the TEC and the 1992 TEU. Currently, it is included, broadly unchanged, in Protocol (No 4) annexed to the Treaties (Consolidated version, OJ C 202, 7.6.2016, pp. 230–250). On the ECB, the ESCB and the monetary union, see, by means of mere indication out of a vast existing bibliography, Smits (1997), Zilioli and Selmayr (2000), Issing *et al.* (2001), the various

In the performance of their Eurosystem tasks, these NCBs must comply with the **Eurosystem Ethics Framework**.[39]

4.1.4.2 Objectives and Tasks of the Eurosystem and of the ECB
(1) The primary objective of the Eurosystem is to maintain price stability.[40] This is its primary, albeit not exclusive objective. The TFEU clearly sets out[41] that, without prejudice to this objective, the Eurosystem shall (also) support the "general economic policies in the EU" to contribute to the achievement of its objectives as laid down in **Article 3 TEU**, acting in accordance with the principle of an open market economy with free competition, favouring an efficient allocation of resources (a 'generic' statement of respect for market economics) and in compliance with the principles set out in **Article 119(3) TFEU**. The rationale behind this hierarchy of objectives lies within the prevailing view that the Eurosystem can only pursue its secondary objectives if it has ensured the primary one. It must thus perform its tasks aimed at combatting inflation (or disinflation) and only if this is achieved at influencing growth and employment conditions (hence, it does not have a dual primary objective, as is the case, exceptionally, with other central banks, such as the US Federal Reserve System).

(2) The basic tasks of the ECB within the Eurosystem are laid down in **Article 127(2) TFEU** (Article 3.1 ESCB/ECB Statute).[42] They include the definition and implementation of the single monetary policy[43]; the conduct of foreign exchange operations consistent with **Article 219 TFEU** (single foreign exchange policy),[44] the holding and management of Member States' official foreign reserves; and the promotion of the smooth operation of

---

contributions in European Central Bank (2005), Smits (2005a) and (2005b), Hadjiemmanuil (2006a), Scheller (2006), Louis (2009), Lastra and Louis (2013), Gortsos (2020), Enoch (2021), pp. 73–102 and Thiele (2021).

[39] ECB Guideline 2021/2253 of 2 November 2021 "laying down the principles of the Eurosystem Ethics Framework (ECB/2021/49) (recast)", OJ L 454, 17.12.2021, pp. 7–16.

[40] TFEU, Article 127(1), first sentence; see also Articles 3(3) TEU and Articles 119(2)–(3), 219(1)–(2) and 282(2) TFEU.

[41] *Ibid.*, Article 127(1), second sentence.

[42] On these tasks, see details in Gortsos (2020), pp. 281–320, with extensive further references.

[43] Responsible for the formulation of this policy is the ECB Governing Council ('GC'), which must adopt Guidelines for the implementation of intermediate monetary objectives, key interest rates and the supply of reserves in the Eurosystem (ESCB/ECB Statute, Article 12.1, first sub-paragraph, second sentence).

[44] If the euro is freely floating in exchange rate markets (as it was the case at the time when the EMU started and is still today), this task is carried out by the Eurosystem in cooperation with the Council (as composed by the Ministers of the Member States whose currency is the euro, the 'Eurogroup') (TFEU, Article 219(2)).

payment systems.[45] The ECB also has been endowed with other tasks, such as the exclusive right to authorise the issue of euro[46] banknotes in the EU, the issuance (along with the NCBs of the euro area Member States) of such notes (which have the status of legal tender within the EU) and the approval for the issuance by Member States of euro coins in accordance with **Article 128 TFEU** (Article 16 ESCB/ECB Statute),[47] the contribution, within the Eurosystem, to the smooth conduct of policies pursued by the national authorities relating to the prudential supervision of credit institutions and the financial system's stability,[48] as well as the collection of statistical information.[49] However, even though the ECB is a monetary authority, it does not act as a lender of last resort to credit institutions established in the euro area. Such lending to solvent credit institutions exposed to severe liquidity problems is provided by the NCBs of the euro area Member State in which they are incorporated under the conditions governing the Emergency Liquidity Assistance ('**ELA**') Mechanism.[50]

(3) Furthermore (and of primary importance for this study), by virtue of **127(6) TFEU** on the specific tasks to be conferred upon the ECB in relation to the prudential supervision of (*inter alia*) credit institutions, the ECB has been assigned specific tasks within the '**European System of Financial Supervision**' ('**ESFS**') in the field of financial macroprudential oversight to address systemic vulnerabilities,[51] taking into account the close links between monetary and macroprudential policies.[52] Then, since **4 November 2014**, the links between EU monetary and banking law have become stronger, since the ECB, apart from being a single monetary authority within the Eurosystem, has also become a banking supervisory authority within the '**Single Supervisory Mechanism**' ('**SSM**'), which is the first main pillar of the European

---

[45] TFEU, Article 127(2). On these tasks, see Gortsos (2020), pp. 281–320, with extensive further references.

[46] According to Article 3(4) TEU, the euro is the currency of the EMU; see on this Becker (2019), pp. 58–59. Since the euro is a single and not a common currency, it is substituted for the (former national) currencies of the Member States participating in the euro area at an irrevocably fixed rate (TFEU, Article 140(3)). Concurrently, the euro is the national currency of those Member States by virtue of national law.

[47] On this aspect, see details in Gortsos (2020), pp. 320–326, with further references.

[48] TFEU, Article 127(5) (further discussed under 4.4.1 below).

[49] ESCB/ECB Statute, Article 16.

[50] On this mechanism, see the *Excursus* at the end of Chapter 6.

[51] On this aspect, see further below, under 4.3.1.

[52] The interaction between monetary policy and financial stability is well established; in this respect, in the aftermath of the GFC, the aim of monetary policy remained price stability and macroprudential policies were tasked with the preservation of financial stability; see Lastra and Goodhart (2015) and Viñals *et al.* (2015).

'**Banking Union' (BU)**, established by a Council Regulation whose legal basis is (indeed) **Article 127(6) TFEU**.[53]

(4) Accordingly, the TFEU distinguishes between three sets of tasks of the ECB: *first*, its monetary and other *basic* tasks within the Eurosystem by virtue of Article 127(2) TFEU; *second*, the *specific* tasks conferred upon it within the ESFS and the SSM by virtue of Article 127(6) TFEU; and *third*, its *other* tasks, including its financial stability task within the Eurosystem under Article 127(5) TFEU.

(5) The EMU is asymmetric by design[54]: whereas in the context of the monetary union the EU has exclusive competence on monetary policy for the Member States whose currency is the euro, the same does not hold for economic (namely fiscal) policy in the framework of the economic union, which remains national, the EU having in this case a coordinating competence, as well as specific powers relating to fiscal discipline and economic solidarity.[55]

4.1.4.3 European (EU) Central Banking Law as a Synthesis

Taking into primary consideration the functions that central banks perform in the monetary, the financial, as well as the payment and settlement systems, a distinct branch of European economic law can be identified, that of '**European (EU) central banking law'**. The author defines it as the set of EU rules governing the operation of the ECB and Member State NCBs. Its primary focus is EU rules, either under primary or under secondary law, and shaping the objectives, tasks and competences of such central banks, as well as their inclusion in the EU institutional framework. It also deals with the rules adopted by the ECB and NCBs under EU law. *On the other hand*, EU central banking law does not touch upon the objectives, tasks and competences of NCBs under their respective national legislation, unless this has an impact on EU law.[56]

---

[53] On the SSM and Article 127(6) TFEU, see further below, under 4.4.3 and Chapter 6, under 6.3.1.

[54] TFEU, Articles 3(1), point (c) and 5(1), respectively.

[55] *Ibid.*, Articles 121 (on economic policy coordination), 123–126 (fiscal discipline) and 122 (economic solidarity). The rules laid down in Articles 122 and 126 are further specified in Council Regulations (EC) No 1466/97 and (EC) No 1467/97 (both of 7 July 1997 (OJ L 209, 2.8.1997, pp. 1–5 and 6–11, respectively) and as in force), which constitute the two pillars of the Stability and Growth Pact ('SGP'); see indicatively Keppenne (2020). A single economic policy, which would become an exclusive EU competence, as the monetary policy, when and if achieved, would mean that Member States would no longer have discretion to conduct macro-economic policy in general. Therefore, the decision for full economic unification in such a form would have to be considered along with EU political integration.

[56] See Gortsos (2019c) and (2020), pp. 43–45.

4.1.5 *Delimitation* vis-à-vis *Other Branches of European Economic Law*

(1) EU consumer law contains provisions seeking to ensure the protection of the economic interests of consumers dealing with financial firms, with a view to mitigating the information asymmetry usually existing between consumers and financial firms, addressing the problem of consumers' reduced negotiating capacity *vis-à-vis* financial service providers, and combatting consumer over-indebtedness. Apart from these 'specific' provisions of EU financial services consumer law, certain provisions of horizontal nature regarding all or certain categories of products or service suppliers may also apply. Therefore, from a systematic viewpoint, the provisions of 'general' EU consumer law that apply to the field of financial services come under three categories: *first*, provisions applicable exclusively to credit institutions and other categories of financial firms entitled to pursue the business of granting credit in the context of their commercial, business or professional activity; *second*, provisions applicable to all categories of financial firms, including credit institutions, but not to other categories of services providers; and *third*, 'horizontal' provisions applicable to all service providers, including financial firms (and credit institutions).[57]

(2) EU law on combatting the use of the financial system for the commitment of economic crimes is the branch of EU financial law that contains provisions seeking to prevent the use of the financial system for the conduct of economic crimes (such as 'money laundering', terrorist financing and payment instruments' fraud), and to contain such crimes. The relevant provisions apply fully to credit institutions, and it can be reasonably argued that the main reason for their adoption was to combat the use of the banking sector for criminal (or terrorist) purposes. However, it is not only credit institutions that may come under the scope of these provisions but also most of the other categories of financial firms. Moreover, the provisions of this branch of EU law do not only apply to financial firms but also to undertakings and professionals outside the financial system (such as casinos, notaries and lawyers), with a view to addressing regulatory arbitrage.

4.1.6 *Evolution of European (EU) Banking Law Within the System of European (EU) Financial Law*

(1) EU financial law is being shaped gradually, always within the limits set by the institutional framework based on the initiatives taken by EU (previously Community) institutions (i.e., the (European) Commission, the European Parliament and the (Ecofin) Council) and, since 1999, under the opinion-giving influence of the ECB, within the context of political conditions prevailing in each given period, as well as developments in public international

---

[57] See, by means of mere indication, Chapters 12–16 in Colaert, Busch and Incalza (2019, editors). For a detailed analysis on EU consumer protection law and consumers as banking clients, see also Ramsay (2016).

financial law, as discussed in Part II above. Despite the self-standing development of the EU financial integration process, much of the content of the legal acts constituting the sources of EU banking law is being shaped under the influence of international banking law, taking into consideration the rules of the BCBS. The same applies, albeit to a lesser extent, with regard to the impact of the work of the IOSCO on the shaping of EU capital markets law.[58]

(2) In the context of a short overview of the evolution of EU financial law, the following four periods can be identified: the period from the beginning of the functioning of the European Economic Community ('**EEC**') until 1988; the period of the establishment of the single financial area (1989–1998); the period of consolidation of the single financial area (1999–2007), extending from the start of the functioning of the EMU until the outbreak of the (2007–2009) GFC; and the current period since 2008.[59] In the author's opinion, the latter period contains two phases, linked to two major crises which erupted since 2007 (namely the GFC and the euro area fiscal crisis) and affected, *inter alia*, the stability of the EU financial system and public confidence therein:

> The *first phase*, apart from the legislative acts adopted, was marked by the publication, immediately after the GFC, of the Report of the "*de Larosière Group*". This laid down the basis for reshaping and further deepening the institutionalisation of arrangements at EU level pertaining to financial prudential supervision and establishing for the first time an EU framework for the financial system's macroprudential oversight.
>
> The *second phase* discusses the legislative acts adopted as a reaction to the fiscal crisis in the euro area, which became manifest in 2010; the main by-product of this response, as regards EU banking law,[60] was the creation of the BU. It also covers legislative actions as a response to the pandemic crisis.[61]

---

[58] On the BCBS and the IOSCO, Chapter 3 above, under 3.1 and 3.2.1, respectively.

[59] For an overview of the evolution of EU financial law, see Dermine (2003), pp. 33–50 (only with respect to EU banking law), Blair *et al.* (2009, editors), pp. 98–102, Hadjiemmanuil (2006b), pp. 786–804 and Jung-Bishof (2015). On the various phases in the evolution of EU banking law before the creation of the BU, see Schnyder (2005), Walker (2007), Tridimas (2011) and Chiu and Wilson (2019), pp. 281–313.

[60] Several institutional developments related to improving the 'E' of the EMU, i.e., the Economic Union. By means of mere indication, see the (2012) Van Rompuy Report, Stephanou (2013) and Drossos (2020).

[61] The latter aspect is discussed in Chapter 5 below, under 5.3. As in the case of public international financial law (see above in Chapter 2, under 2.2.1), the current inflation crisis has not per se prompted the adoption of new financial rules at EU level; on the impact of monetary policy decisions taken by the ECB (within the Eurosystem) as a response to that crisis on financial stability, see Gortsos (2023), pp. 88–92, with extensive further references.

Even though the focus of this study is on EU banking law, the evolution of the other branches of EU financial law is also studied, albeit in significantly less detail.

4.2 THE FIRST THREE PERIODS

4.2.1 *The First Period*

The first period extends from the beginning of the functioning of the (then) EEC, established by the **1958 Treaty of Rome**, until the implementation of the Commission's **1985 White Paper** "on Completing the Internal Market".[62] During this period, developments in EU financial law were slow and piecemeal, the initial legal acts adopted being in the field of EU insurance law.[63] In the field of EU banking law, three Council Directives were adopted:

The *first* was in 1973 "on the abolition of restrictions on freedom of establishment and freedom to provide services in respect of self-employed activities of banks and other financial institutions".[64]

This was followed, in 1977, by the **'First Banking Directive'**,[65] which laid down the conditions, on the basis of the minimum harmonisation principle, for the granting and withdrawal of credit institutions' licences by the Member States' competent (supervisory) authorities and for the granting of licences to branches of credit institutions incorporated either in other Member States, on the basis of the national treatment principle, or in third countries (on the basis of the principle of reciprocity), and established procedures for the cooperation between Member States'

---

[62] COM/85/310 final. On the institutional dimension of the internal market programme, see the contemporary analysis of Dehousse (1989), pp. 133–136.

[63] These included Council Directive 64/225/EEC of 25 February 1964 "on the abolition of restrictions on freedom of establishment and freedom to provide services in respect of reinsurance and retrocession" (OJ L 878, 4.4.1964, pp. 131–132) followed, 8 years later, by Council Directive 72/166/EEC of 24 April 1972 "on the approximation of the laws of Member States relating to insurance against civil liability in respect of the use of motor vehicles, and to the enforcement of the obligation to insure against such liability" (OJ L 103, 2.5.1972, pp. 1–4) and then by the (First Council) Directive 73/239/EEC of 24 July 1973 "on the coordination of laws, regulations and administrative provisions relating to the taking-up and pursuit of the business of direct insurance other than life assurance" (OJ L 103, 16.8.1973, pp. 3–19). In the field of EU capital markets law, the Council adopted its first Council Directive (79/279/EEC) on 5 March 1979 on "coordinating the conditions for the admission of securities to official stock exchange listing" (OJ L 66, 16.3.79, pp. 21–32).

[64] Council Directive 73/183/EEC of 28 June 1973, OJ L 194, 16.7.1973, pp. 1–10.

[65] Council Directive 77/780/EEC of 12 December 1977 "on the coordination of the laws, regulations and administrative provisions relating to the taking up and pursuit of the business of credit institutions", OJ L 322, 17.12.1977, pp. 30–37.

competent authorities, as well as the exchange of information among them and with supervisory authorities of third countries.[66]

Finally, the *third* source of EU banking law of that period was the 1983 **'Consolidated Supervision Directive'**,[67] which was the first legal act adopted under the influence of public international banking law, and namely the 1983 BCBS revised "Basel Concordat".[68]

4.2.2 The Second Period

4.2.2.1 Introductory Remarks

In 1986 took place the first major amendment of the 1958 Treaty of Rome by the 1986 **'Single European Act'**[69] (**'SEA'**). Its main objective was to facilitate the establishment of a single market by 31 December 1992. In that respect, it introduced the **"principle of qualified majority voting"** in the Council (rather than unanimity as a rule of decision) for almost all relevant legal acts, thus paving the way for a higher degree of harmonisation of national legislative and administrative measures, including those in the financial system. Hence, after this amendment, the process of financial integration in the banking sector (and in general in financial system) through legislation gained momentum with a view to establishing a single banking area. The legal acts of EU banking (and in general financial) law of this period were Directives governed by 3 guiding principles: decentralised management (national authorities and schemes), mutual recognition, as well as minimum and partial harmonisation.

---

[66] First Banking Directive, Articles 3, 8, 4, 9, 7 and 12, respectively. On the principle of national treatment, see the seminal work of Sousi-Roubi (1995), p. 66; on the principle of reciprocity, see Vigneron and Smith (1990). See also Chiu and Wilson (2019), pp. 282–283.

[67] Council Directive 83/350/EEC of 13 June 1983 "on the supervision of credit institutions on a consolidated basis", OJ L 193, 18.7.1983, pp. 18–20.

[68] See Chapter 2 above, under 2.4.1. It is also noted that, on 20 December 1985, the first legal act in the field of UCITS was adopted, namely Council Directive 85/611/EEC "on the coordination of laws, regulations and administrative provisions relating to undertakings for collective investment in transferable securities (UCITS)" OJ L 375, 31.12.1985, pp. 3–18 (the so-called UCITS I Directive), which introduced the home-country rule in the field of capital markets. Another significant source of capital markets law of that period was the 'Public Offering Directive' (Council Directive 89/298/EEC of 17 April 1989 "coordinating the requirements for the drawing-up, scrutiny and distribution of the prospectus to be published when transferable securities are offered to the public", OJ L 124, 5.5.1989, pp. 8–15).

[69] OJ L 169, 29.6.1987, pp. 1–28; this Act, adopted on 28 February 1986, entered into force on 1 July 1987. For a contemporary assessment of the SEA, see Weiler (1991); on its importance for the further development of the EU, see Barnard and Peers (2020), Chapter 2, Section 4.2.

The Treaty of Rome was further amended, as already noted, by the **1992 Treaty of Maastricht**,[70] which, *inter alia* and apart from having established (along with the EC) the European Union (EU), introduced the co-decision procedure between the European Parliament and the Council (hereinafter 'the **co-legislators**') for the adoption of (then so-called) basic legal acts in the form of Regulations and Directives.[71] EU financial law provisions were also included in legally non-binding Recommendations of the Commission, issued pursuant to **Article 211 TEC**.

4.2.2.2 The Directives Adopted
(1) In 1989, the Council adopted the **'Second Banking Directive'**,[72] which substantially amended the First Banking Directive. This legal act laid down the groundwork for the exercise by EU credit institutions of the freedoms to provide services and establish branches in other Member States, by virtue of the principle of mutual recognition of the 'single license' (passport) granted to them by their home Member State's national competent authorities ('**NCAs**'),[73] further specified the conditions for granting and withdrawing bank licences by these NCAs, laid down the conditions for credit institutions to carry out their activities under the single licence and established a procedure for the licensing of EU credit institutions being subsidiaries of non-EU parent companies.[74] *Concurrently*, the Council adopted the **'Own Funds Directive'** and the **'Solvency Ratio Directive'**,[75] which transposed into EU banking law the 1988 Basel I framework.[76] These legal acts laid down rules about the

---

[70] See above, under 4.1.4.

[71] As a matter of fact, until November 1993, such acts were adopted solely by the Council and it was only thereafter that they are adopted (in principle, but not exclusively) jointly by the co-legislators pursuant to the 'co-decision procedure' under Article 251 TEC.

[72] Second Council Directive 89/646/EEC of 15 December 1989 "on the coordination of laws, regulations and administrative provisions relating to the taking up and pursuit of the business of credit institutions and amending Directive 77/780/EEC", (hereinafter the 'Second Banking Directive', OJ L 386, 30.12.1989, pp. 1–13). Of importance in this respect was the 1997 Commission interpretative Communication "Freedom to provide services and the interest of the general good in the Second Banking Directive" (OJ C 209, 10.7.1997, pp. 6–22).

[73] On the definition of this term under the EU banking law as in force, see Chapter 6 below, under 6.1.2.

[74] Second Banking Directive, Articles 18, 4–5 and 17, 10–12 and 7, respectively. On this Directive, see Chapters 3–8 in Van Empel and Smits (2001, editors); see also Chiu and Wilson (2019), pp. 283–286.

[75] Council Directive 89/299/EEC of 17 April 1989 "on the own funds of credit institutions" (OJ L 124, 5.5.1989, pp. 16–20) and Council Directive 89/647/EEC of 18 December 1989 "on a solvency ratio for credit institutions" (OJ L 386, 30.12.1989, pp. 14–22). See van den Bergh (2001).

[76] See Chapter 2 above, under 2.4.1.

calculation of credit institutions' minimum capital ratio of 8% as to their exposure to credit (and country) risk, and the elements eligible for use as regulatory 'own funds' to meet this requirement.[77]

(2) Furthermore, the 1983 **'Consolidated Supervision Directive'** was repealed by the 1992 **'Second Consolidated Supervision Directive'**,[78] while a **'Large Exposures Directive'** was also adopted during the same year.[79] Then, in 1993, the Council adopted two further legal acts, which were key sources of EU capital markets law but also of relevance to EU banking law:

> The *first* was **'Capital Adequacy Directive'**[80] (**'CAD'**), which also applied to investment firms and enhanced the regulatory framework governing credit institutions' capital adequacy by laying down rules regarding their exposure to market risks (namely, position risk, foreign exchange risk, settlement risk, counterparty risk and risks arising from large exposures in the trading book).[81]
> *In parallel*, the Council adopted the **'Investment Services Directive'**[82] (**'ISD'**), which introduced for investment firms the same principles governing the operation of credit institutions under the Second Banking Directive. Of specific importance for credit institutions (and hence for EU banking law) was **Article 15(3) ISD**, pursuant to which Member States were prohibited, since 1996, to impose on them limitations regarding the

---

[77] This 8% capital adequacy ratio applies, as a minimum, also under the current framework (this aspect is further discussed in detail in Volume II below). The amendments—during the period 1991–1995—of the Basel I framework prompted tantamount amendments of these EU Directives; see Gortsos (2022), pp. 16–17.

[78] Council Directive 92/30/EEC of 6 April 1992 "on the supervision of credit institutions on a consolidated basis", OJ L 110, 28.4.1992, pp. 52–58. Its objectives were to enhance the intensity of consolidated supervision and submit to its field of application also financial holding companies; see Pearson (2001a).

[79] Council Directive 92/121/EEC of 21 December 1992 "on the monitoring and control of large exposures of credit institutions", OJ L 29, 5.2.1993, pp. 1–8; see Pearson (2001b). It is noted that in March 2000, all the above Directives, including their subsequent amendments, were codified into one single act (Directive 2000/12/EC of the co-legislators "relating to the taking up and pursuit of the business of credit institutions", OJ L 126, 26.5.2000, pp. 1–59).

[80] Council Directive 93/6/EEC of 15 March 1993 "on the capital adequacy of investment firms and credit institutions", OJ L 141, 11.6.1993, pp. 1–26. See Vossen (2001).

[81] This Directive was based on the relevant proposals of the BCBS, which were then finalised in January 1996 upon adoption of its Report titled "Amendment to the Capital Accord to incorporate market risks" (see Table 2.8 above).

[82] Council Directive 93/22/EEC of 10 May 1993 "on investment services in the securities field", OJ L 141, 11.6.1993, pp. 27–46.

direct provision of investment services.[83] Thus, the **'universal banking model'** became the rule under EU financial law.[84]

(3) The 1994 **'Deposit Guarantee Schemes Directive'**[85] was the first source of EU financial law adopted under the co-decision procedure among the **co-legislators**. It introduced the principle of mutual recognition for such (national) schemes[86] and harmonised, at the minimum level, some aspects of their functioning, such as the level and the extent of deposit coverage, the procedure for the compensation of depositors once a participating credit institution's deposits have become 'unavailable', and depositors' information requirements.[87] Applicable to credit institutions (albeit not sources of EU banking law) were also the 1991 first **'Anti-Money Laundering ('AML') Directive**,[88] as well as another source of EU capital markets law, namely the 1997 'Investor Compensation Schemes Directive' (**'ICSD'**),[89] which is the only legal act of that period in EU financial law that is still in force.

4.2.3 The Third Period

4.2.3.1 Institutional Developments
Introductory Remarks
(1) The third period starts with the introduction of the euro as the single euro area currency on 1 January 1999, which, *inter alia*, was a trigger for deepening EU financial integration. Until then, the Council had made limited use of its right to confer on the Commission implementing powers by virtue of a **Decision** pursuant to **Article 202** (third indent) **TEC** (governing—at

---

[83] See Mauerhofer (1998), p. 92.

[84] On the content of all these legal acts of that period, see also Sousi-Roubi (1995), pp. 97–211 and 269–325.

[85] Directive 94/19/EC of 30 May 1994 "on deposit guarantee schemes", OJ L 135, 31.5.1994, pp. 5–14.

[86] Accordingly, deposits taken by an EU credit institution through its branches established in other Member States were (and are still) covered by the DGS of its home Member State.

[87] For details, see Sousi-Roubi (1995), pp. 212–234, Smits (2001) and Kleftouri (2015), pp. 64–75.

[88] Council Directive 91/308/EEC of 10 June 1991, OJ L 166, 28.6.1991, pp. 77–82.

[89] Directive 97/9/EC of the co-legislators of 3 March 1997 "on investor-compensation schemes", OJ L 84, 26.3.1997, pp. 22–31; see on this Sousi-Roubi (1995), pp. 326-332. Another important source of EU capital markets law (on its infrastructures) was Directive 98/26/EC of the co-legislators of 19 May 1998 "on settlement finality in payment and securities settlement systems" (OJ L 166, 11.6.1998, pp. 45–50), which is still in force as amended by Directive 2009/44/EC (OJ L 146, 10.6.2009, pp. 37–43); see Staehelin (2012), pp. 30–32.

that time—the **'comitology'**).[90] However, there was an increased need to manage a constantly growing volume of detailed legislative measures to enable the deepening of financial integration and the increasingly technical nature of regulations.

(2) Under these circumstances, the adoption of measures to speed up procedures towards a single EU capital market, where numerous gaps had been identified, as well as important delays in the law-making process, became a priority after the launch of the euro.[91] Hence, in its session of 17 July 2000, the Council decided to set up a 7-member committee made up of prominent personalities of the financial sector. On **15 February 2001**, this Committee, known as the Committee of Wise Men or the "Lamfalussy Committee" (named after its Chairperson, Baron Alexandre Lamfalussy),[92] submitted its Final Report "On the Regulation of European Securities Markets" ('**Lamfalussy Report 2001**').[93] Chapter I [94] covered an analysis of the reasons necessitating the amendment of the (then applicable) procedure on issuing legal acts on EU capital markets law. The Committee's proposals, presented in Chapter II of the Report,[95] included the establishment of a special procedure comprising four levels for the issuance by EU institutions of basic legal acts on EU capital markets law and their implementation by Member States (since then known as the **'Lamfalussy process'**), as well as the setting up of an Inter-Institutional Monitoring Group and the review of process in 2004.

Application of the Lamfalussy Report
(1) At a political level, the Lamfalussy Report was immediately, fully and unreservedly adopted both by the Council, at its Stockholm meeting on 23

---

[90] Council Decision 1999/468/EC, OJ L 184, 17.07.1999, pp. 23–26; for more details, see the *Excursus* at the end of Chapter 7 below.

[91] The rationale was that, in a single currency environment, conditions had greatly improved for further consolidation of national capital markets, with the elimination of currency risk for investments, as well as enhanced price transparency which enabled investors to compare the performance of listed companies based on one single currency unit denominator, and, as a result, markets would become more liquid. On the impact of the introduction of the euro on EU capital markets, see Galati and Tsatsaronis (2003) and Freixas *et al.* (2004).

[92] Among his other capacities in the financial system, Lamfalussy had served as Chairperson of the European Monetary Institute (i.e., the predecessor of the ECB) throughout its operation (1994–1998).

[93] Both the initial report of 9 November 2000 and the final report are included in a single document, available at: https://ec.europa.eu/internal_market/securities/lamfalussy/index_en.htm.

[94] Lamfalussy Report (2001), pp. 9–18.

[95] *Ibid.*, pp. 19–42.

March 2001,[96] and by the Stockholm European Council on 23–24 March 2001,[97] which also issued a relevant Resolution "on more effective securities market regulation in the [EU]".[98] Under these conditions, on 6 June 2001, the Commission adopted two **Decisions** establishing the two committees proposed in the Report, namely the "European Securities Committee" ('**ESC**') and the "Committee of European Securities Regulators" ('**CESR**'), both of which became operative on **7 June 2001**.[99]

(2) Considering that the contribution of the Lamfalussy process to shaping EU capital markets law was positive, the Council decided its extension also to banking and insurance law, as well as to the law governing **UCITS**. Accordingly, on 5 November 2003, the Commission submitted a package of measures into six new Decisions extending this process as follows: *first*, two new committees were created for the banking sector: the "European Banking Committee" ('**EBC**'), which entered into operation on 13 April 2005, and the "Committee of European Banking Supervisors" ('**CEBS**'), which became operative on 1 January 2004[100]; *second*, two new committees for the insurance, reinsurance and occupational pensions sectors were the "European Insurance and Occupational Pensions Committee" ('**EIOPC**'), which also entered into operation on 13 April 2005, and the "Committee of European Insurance and Occupational Pensions Supervisors" ('**CEIOPS**'); this became operative on 24 November 2003[101]; and *third*, the duties of the ESC and the CESR were extended to UCITS.[102]

---

[96] At: https://europa.eu.int/comm/internal_market/en/finances/mobil/01-memo105.htm.

[97] At: https://europa.eu.int/european_council/conclusions/index_en.htm.

[98] At: https://ue.eu.int/ueDocs?cms_Data/docs/pressData/en/ec/00100-r1.%20annr1.en1.html.

[99] Commission Decisions 2001/528/EC and 2001/527/EC (OJ L 191, 13.7.2001, pp. 45–46 and 43–44, respectively). These Decisions were not based on any specific TEC article but on the Treaty in general. It is also noted that cooperation between national supervisory/regulatory authorities in this field was informally established in 1985 within the "High Level Securities Supervisors Committee" ('HLSSC') and was further strengthened, in 1997, within the "Forum of European Securities Commissions" ('FESCO') (see European Commission [2000], pp. 33–35 and 41–43).

[100] Commission Decisions 2004/10/EC and 2004/5/EC (OJ L 3, 7.1.2004, pp. 36–37 and 28–29, respectively). Cooperation between national banking supervisory authorities was informally established in 1972 within the "Groupe de Contact" and was further strengthened in 1998 within the Banking Supervision Committee ('BSC') of the ESCB (see European Commission [2000], pp. 11–16).

[101] Commission Decisions 2004/9/EC and 2004/6/EC (OJ L 3, 7.1.2004, pp. 34–35 and 30–31, respectively). Cooperation among Member States' insurance supervisory authorities was informally established in 1957 within the "Conference of Insurance Supervisors of the Member States of the European Communities" (see European Commission [2000], pp. 27–29).

[102] Commission Decisions 2004/7/EC and 2004/8/EC (OJ L 3, 7.1.2004, pp. 32, and 33, respectively), amending, respectively, Decisions 2001/527/EC and 2001/528/

(3) The Lamfalussy process was a novelty in the law-making process for the three main branches of EU financial law to the extent that it involved therein, in an advisory capacity, the CEBS, the CESR and the CEIOPS; it can be considered that this was taken over from the international financial architecture, these three Committees reflecting, *mutatis mutandis*, the composition and tasks of the BCBS, the IOSCO and the IAIS. *Furthermore*, the role of the EBC, the ESC and the EIOPC was to support the Commission in relation to its implementing powers (under the comitology procedure). Cooperation among national financial supervisory authorities was also institutionalised, even though—contrary to what applies to monetary policy—the institutional structure of the European financial system's supervision continued to be governed by fragmentation.[103]

4.2.3.2 Regulatory Developments
The 1999 "Financial Services Action Plan" ('FSAP')
(1) In 1999, the Commission adopted the **"Financial Services Action Plan" ('FSAP')**.[104] This laid down a list of legislative measures in the fields of EU financial, company and taxation law, which the Commission deemed necessary for the acceleration of the financial integration process after the introduction of the euro. In relation to financial integration, it contained three key pillars (as further discussed in **Box 4.2 just below**): enhancement of capital markets' integration; shaping of open and safe markets for retail transactions; and shaping of an efficient framework on the prudential supervision and regulation of financial firms. All legal acts proposed were based on the existing set of principles pertaining to financial regulation and supervision (decentralised management, mutual recognition, minimum and partial harmonisation). The FSAP also paved the way for the harmonisation of taxation in the financial sector[105] and proposed the repeal of the first **AML Directive** by a new one ('second **AML Directive**').[106]

EC. The decisions establishing the CESR, the CEBS and the CEIOPS were repealed and replaced in 2009 (Commission Decisions 2009/77/EC, 2009/78/EC and 2009/79/EC, OJ L 25, 29.1.2009, pp. 18–32).

[103] For an assessment, see Ferran (2004), pp. 61–74 and 99–107, Lastra (2006), pp. 334–341, Hadjiemmanuil (2006b), pp. 815–818, Sousi-Roubi (2007), pp. 24–29 and Lastra and Garri (2009).

[104] COM/1999/232 final.

[105] This led to the adoption of Directive 2003/48/EC of the co-legislators of 3 June 2003 "on taxation of savings income in the form of interest payments" (OJ L 157, 26.6.2003, pp. 38–48), which is no longer in force.

[106] Directive 2005/60/EC of the co-legislators of 26 October 2005 "on the prevention of the use of the financial system for the purpose of money laundering and terrorist financing", OJ L 309, 25.11.2005, pp. 15–36.

Box 4.2 The three key pillars of the 1999 Financial Services Action Plan (FSAP)

Pillars	Legislative acts adopted
First pillar	In relation to this pillar, the co-legislators adopted a wide range of legislative acts, which totally reshaped EU capital markets law, including (in chronological order) two Directives which substantially amended the (above-mentioned) 1985 UCITS I Directive,[107] the 'Listing Particulars Directive',[108] the 'Financial Collateral Arrangements Directive',[109] the Markets Abuse Directive ('MAD I'),[110] the 'Prospectus Directive',[111] the 'Takeover Bids Directive',[112] the 'Markets in Financial Instruments Directive' ('MiFID I'),[113] repealing the ISD, and the 'Transparency Directive'[114]
Second pillar	The objectives of this pillar were to ensure a high level of consumer information and transparency of cross-border transactions and the uniform implementation by Member States of consumer protection legislation, as well as the development of an appropriate framework pertaining to electronic commerce in financial services, and the creation of a single small-value payments area, following the precursor to the 'TARGET' system for large-value payments, which was

(continued)

---

[107] Directives 2001/107/EC and 2001/108/EC of 21 January 2002, OJ L 41, 13.2.2002, pp. 20–34 and 35–42.

[108] Directive 2001/34/EC of 28 May 2001, OJ L 184, 6.7.2001, pp. 1–66.

[109] Directive 2002/47/EC of 6 June 2002, OJ L 168, 27.6.2002, pp. 43–50. See Staehelin (2012), pp. 30–32.

[110] Directive 2003/6/EC of 28 January 2003 "on insider dealing and market manipulation", OJ L 96, 12.4.2003, pp. 16–25.

[111] Directive 2003/71/EC of 4 November 2003 "on the prospectus to be published when securities are offered to the public or admitted to trading", OJ L 345, 31.12.2003, pp. 64–89, which repealed the above-mentioned Council Directive 89/298/EEC.

[112] Directive 2004/25/EC of 21 April 2004 "on takeover bids", OJ L 142, 30.4.2004, pp. 12–23. On this legislative act, as in force, see Veil (2022b).

[113] Directive 2004/39/EC of 21 April 2004, OJ L 145, 30.4.2004, pp. 1–44. On this legislative act, which also applied to credit institutions providing investment services, see, by means of mere indication Moloney (2005), the various contributions in Ferrarini and Wymeersch (2006, editors), Moloney (2008), pp. 337–535, and the various contributions in Avgouleas (2008, general editor).

[114] Directive 2004/109/EC of 15 December 2004 "on the harmonisation of transparency requirements in relation to information about issuers whose securities are admitted to trading on a regulated market", OJ L 390, 31.12.2004, pp. 38–57. For a comprehensive overview of EU capital markets law of that period, see Moloney (2008).

Pillars	Legislative acts adopted
(continued)	established in 1999 to support the single monetary policy.[115] The key legislative acts adopted in this respect (by the co-legislators) were the first '**E-money Institutions Directive**',[116] the '**Cross-border Payments in Euro Regulation**',[117] the '**Distance Marketing of Consumer Financial Services Directive**',[118] the 'Insurance Mediation Directive'[119] ('**IMD**') and the 'Payment Services Directive'[120] ('**PSD I**')
Third pillar	The third pillar was the shaping of an efficient framework on the microprudential regulation and supervision of financial firms. In this respect (and in chronological order) the co-legislators adopted several legal acts as well. In particular: *First*, on 4 April 2001, the '**Reorganisation and winding-up (of credit institutions) Directive**'[121] was adopted. This Directive (the only source of EU banking law still in force) was the first legal act of EU financial law which introduced the principle of mutual recognition without providing for a minimum harmonisation of national reorganisation measures and winding-up proceedings[122]

(continued)

[115] On this system, see Gortsos (2020), pp. 309–320. On the current status of this system and its continuous development, see at: https://www.ecb.europa.eu/paym/target/html/index.en.html.

[116] Directive 2000/46/EC of 18 September 2000 "on the taking up, pursuit of and prudential supervision of electronic money institutions", OJ L 275, 27.10.2000, pp. 39–43.

[117] Regulation (EC) No 2560/2001 of 19 December 2001 "on cross-border payments in euro", OJ L 344, 28.12.2001, pp. 13–16.

[118] Directive 2002/65/EC of 23 September 2002 "concerning the distance marketing of consumer financial services (…)", OJ L 271, 9.10.2002, pp. 16–24.

[119] Directive 2002/92/EC of 9 December 2002 "on insurance mediation", OJ L 9, 15.1.2003, pp. 3–10.

[120] Directive 2007/64/EC of 13 November 2007 "on payment services in the internal market (…)", OJ L 319, 5.12.2007, pp. 1–36.

[121] Directive 2001/24/EC of the co-legislators of 4 April 2001 "on the reorganisation and winding-up of credit institutions", OJ L 125, 5.5.2001, pp. 15–23. The adoption of this act was pending since 1987.

[122] This legislative act is further discussed in Chapter 6 below, under 6.7.

(continued)

Second, the regulatory framework pertaining to insurance undertakings was substantially enhanced with the adoption of three legislative acts of the co-legislators[123]; related was also '**Institutions for Occupational Retirement Provision Directive No I**'[124] ('**IORPD I**')

Third, another by-product was the 2002 **Financial Conglomerates Directive** ('**FICOD I**'),[125] which was adopted based on the international financial standards adopted by the Joint Forum on this field[126] and still constitutes (as in force[127]) the source of the fourth branch of EU financial law

Finally, of significant importance for EU banking law was the transposition, in June 2006, into EU law of the Basel II framework by two legal acts, jointly known as '**Capital Requirements Directive No I**' ('**CRD I**').[128] These introduced the Basel II framework's 'three pillar-system', an alternative approach for the calculation of credit risk capital requirements, amended capital requirements for market risk and new capital requirements for operational risk[129]

---

[123] Directive 2001/17/EC of 19 March 2001 "on the reorganisation and winding-up of insurance undertakings", OJ L 110, 20.4.2001, pp. 28–39; Directive 2002/13/EC of 5 March 2002 "amending Council Directive 73/239/EEC as regards the solvency margin requirements for non-life insurance undertakings" (OJ L 77, 20.3.2002, pp. 17–22); and Directive 2002/83/EC of 5 November 2002 "concerning life assurance" (OJ L 345, 19.12.2002, pp. 1–51).

[124] Directive 2003/41/EC of 3 June 2003 "on the activities and supervision of institutions for occupational retirement provision", OJ L 235, 23.9.2003, pp. 10–21.

[125] Directive 2002/87/EC of 16 December 2002 "on the supplementary supervision of financial conglomerates", OJ L 35, 11.2.2003, pp. 1–27.

[126] See Chapter 3 above, under 3.4.2.

[127] This legal act is in force as amended (mainly) by Directive 2011/89/EU of 16 November 2011 (OJ L 326, 8.12.2011, pp. 113–141, 'FICOD II'). The current consolidated version is available at: https://eur-lex.europa.eu/legal-content/EN/TXT/?uri=CELEX%3A02002L0087-20210626. On this legislative act, see Gruson (2004) and Gortsos (2019a).

[128] Directives 2006/48/EC "relating to the taking up and pursuit of the business of credit institutions" and 2006/49/EC "on the capital adequacy of investment firms and credit institutions" (both of the co-legislators and of 14 June 2006, OJ L 177, 30.6.2006, pp. 1–200 and 201–255, respectively). In 2007, certain Articles of Directive 2006/48/EC, mainly on the evaluation criteria for the prudential assessment of acquisitions and increase of holdings in the financial sector, were amended by Directive 2007/44/EC ('Qualifying Holdings Directive', OJ L 247, 21.9.2007, pp. 1–16). See on this Kerjean (2008), pp. 47–79.

[129] See on this Ayadi and Resti (2004) and Dierick et al. (2005).

The 2005 White Paper "Financial Services Policy 2005–2010" ('Post FSAP')

A second benchmark initiative of this period was the Commission's **2005 White Paper** "Financial Services Policy 2005-2010" (**'Post FSAP'**). This document outlined the Commission's financial services policy for the said period with a view to the further regulation-driven deepening of EU financial integration.[130] It was published well before the evaluation of the efficiency of the measures adopted under the FSAP was completed (and despite a widespread consensus on the need for a 'regulatory pause', necessary in order to digest the regulatory storm of the previous years) and was based on 4 pillars: the dynamic integration of the single financial area; the preservation of sound regulatory and supervisory procedures; the taking up of a limited amount of new legislative initiatives; and the upgrading of the EU role in the shaping of international financial law.

Despite its proposals for improvements in a wide range of issues, the Post-FSAP (just like the FSAP) continued to rely on the existing set of principles pertaining to financial regulation and supervision (decentralised management, mutual recognition, as well as minimum and partial harmonisation) and did not contain any proposals on modifying the architecture of EU financial law. In any case, the progress towards its implementation was interrupted abruptly in 2007, when the GFC broke out, and rendered necessary, *inter alia*, a more comprehensive readjustment of EU financial law.

4.3 THE (CURRENT) FOURTH PERIOD, UNTIL THE CREATION OF THE BANKING UNION

4.3.1 Institutional Development: Creation of the European System of Financial Supervision (ESFS)

4.3.1.1 Introductory Remarks

(1) The academic debate on the creation of supranational supervisory authorities for the European financial system can be basically traced back to the mid-2000s.[131] At the political level, the prospect of establishing pan-European financial supervisory authorities was first put forward in 2009 in the wake of the GFC. The scale and intensity of this crisis have shown, as one should reasonably expect, the need to review the then existing EU financial regulatory and supervisory framework. The Commission assigned the task of investigating the appropriate means to attain the objective of re-adjusting the provisions of the applicable EU financial law pertaining to the supervision of EU financial firms to a special, high-level, group of experts, chaired by the France's former

---

[130] COM/2005/629 final. For the EU Commission's own assessment of the 2005 White Paper, see the speech of the (then) European Commissioner for Internal Market and Services Charlie McCreevy (SPEECH/05/448).

[131] See, by means of mere indication, Lastra (2006), pp. 324–328.

central banker Jacques *de Larosière*[132] (the *High-Level Group on Financial Supervision in the EU*).

(2) The Group submitted its Report (hereinafter the '*de Larosière* **Report**') on 25 February 2009.[133] Apart from (briefly but thoroughly) analysing the causes of the GFC, it included recommendations on improving the existing regulatory framework in order to strengthen existing rules and to fill the regulatory gaps identified due to that crisis.[134] In addition, it addressed the readjustment of the supervisory framework in the European financial system,[135] coming to the conclusion that it was neither necessary nor feasible, in the near future, to set up supranational supervisory authorities at European level,[136] and in any case, the prudential supervision of financial firms, including credit institutions, should not be assigned to the ECB.[137] However, it included a proposal on the eventuality of moving, in the long term, towards a system that would rely on two authorities, following a **functional approach** to the institutional architecture of the financial system's prudential supervision (in use in several Member States).[138]

(3) For the short-term horizon, the Report proposed the creation of a 'European System of Financial Supervision'[139] ('**ESFS**'), which was indeed created and became fully operational on 1 January 2011. The ESFS applies to all EU Member States and consists of the European Systemic Risk Board ('**ESRB**'), the three 'European Supervisory Authorities' ('**ESAs**'), their Joint Committee, as well as the NCAs in the three main sectors of the EU financial system

---

[132] Jacques *de Larosière* served as Managing Director of the International Monetary Fund (1978–1987), Governor of the Central Bank of France (Banque de France, 1987–1993), and President of the European Bank for Reconstruction and Development (EBRD, 1993–1998).

[133] For an overview, see Ferrarini and Chiodini (2009), Gortsos (2010) and Chiu and Wilson (2019), pp. 289–291.

[134] *De Larosière* Report (2009), Chapter I, paras 6–37 and Chapter II, paras 38–143, respectively.

[135] *Ibid.*, Chapter III, paras 144–218. The examination of this issue was the main rationale behind the assignment of the Report to the *de Larosière Group*, which is not coincidentally called, as already mentioned, "Group on Financial Supervision in the EU". As noted in the Report, the financial system of several states was not exposed (at least primarily) or was less significantly exposed, to the GFC not only because they were equipped with a strong institutional and regulatory framework, but also because prudential supervision of their banking sector (system) was, admittedly, suitable; and that was not the case throughout the EU.

[136] *Ibid.*, par. 184, second and third sentences.

[137] *Ibid.*, paras 171 and 172, first sentence.

[138] *Ibid.*, Chapter III, Section V ("Reviewing and possibly strengthening the European System of Financial Supervision (ESFS)"). On the functional approach, see Chapter 1 above, under 1.2.4.

[139] *Ibid.*, paras 194–214.

and the ECB with regard to its specific supervisory tasks within the Single Supervisory Mechanism (**SSM**).[140]

4.3.1.2 The Three 'European Supervisory Authorities' (ESAs) as Successors of the Lamfalussy Committees

(1) The ESAs were established by three Regulations of the co-legislators of 24 November 2010 whose legal basis is the harmonisation clause of **Article 114 TFEU** (on the approximation of laws[141]): the European Banking Authority ('**EBA**') under the 'EBA Regulation' ('**EBAR**'); the European Insurance and Occupational Pensions Authority ('**EIOPA**') under the 'EIOPA Regulation' ('**EIOPAR**'); and the European Securities and Markets Authority ('**ESMA**') under the 'ESMA Regulation' ('**ESMAR**').[142] The EBAR was amended in 2013 in the prospect of conferring specific tasks to the ECB within the SSM[143]; furthermore, all Regulations were amended in 2019[144] to clarify and strengthen existing powers and to attribute new powers to the ESAs in targeted areas.

(2) The ESAs succeeded the Lamfalussy Committees, namely the CEBS, the CEIOPS and the CESR, which (as mentioned) were set up following the recommendations in the 2001 Lamfalussy Report; hence, the 'sectoral approach' regarding EU institutional arrangements concerning the financial system's prudential supervision was maintained.[145] Given that they are mainly regulatory authorities with some specifically designated supervisory powers, in principle, financial prudential supervision remained national, although financial regulation was for the most part gradually Europeanised. Padoa-Schioppa (2004, at p. 121) referred to this situation as "*European regulation with national supervision*". In the same vein, Lastra (2006, at p. 298) characteristically notes:

---

[140] All these components are discussed below as appropriate.

[141] On this TFEU Article, see Herrnfeld (2019) and Craig and de Búrca (2020), pp. 123–124 and 649–654. For further analysis, see also Wyatt (2009), Craig (2011), as well as Weatherill (2011) and (2016), pp. 356–361.

[142] Regulations (EU) No 1093/2010, (EU) No 1094/2010 and (EU) No 1095/2010, OJ L 331, 15.12.2010, pp. 12–47, 48–84 and 84–119, respectively. It is noteworthy that, unlike their predecessors, the ESAs were not established by Commission Decisions but by co-legislators' Regulations.

[143] Regulation (EU) No 1022/2013 of the co-legislators of 22 October 2013 "amending Regulation (EU) No 1093/2010 establishing the European Supervisory Authority (…) as regards the conferral of specific tasks on the [ECB] pursuant to Council Regulation (EU) No 1024/2013" (OJ L 287, 29.10.2013, pp. 5–14).

[144] Regulation (EU) 2019/2175 of the co-legislators of 18 December 2019, OJ L 334, 27.12.2019, pp. 1–145.

[145] According to Busch and Gortsos (2022), at p. 10: "*Not only European legislation is still predominantly sectoral in nature, but European financial supervisors are also largely organized along sectoral lines*".

Table 4.1 Cooperation of national banking supervisory authorities at European level: from informal *fora* to 'European (*quasi-*)Supervisory Authorities'

	Banking	Capital markets	Insurance, reinsurance and pension funds
Before the adoption of the Lamfalussy process: informal (except BSC)	GdC (Groupe de Contact, 1972), and BSC (Banking Supervision Committee, since 1998)[a]	HLSSC (High-Level Securities Supervisors Committee, 1985) and FESCO (Forum of European Securities Commissions, 1997)	CIS (Conference of Insurance Supervisors, 1957)
After the adoption of the Lamfalussy process: institutionalised	CEBS (Committee of European Banking Supervisors, 2004), and BSC[a]	CESR (Committee of European Securities Regulators, 2001)	CEIOPS (Committee of European Insurance and Occupational Pensions Supervisors, 2004)
After the creation of the ESFS: further institutionalised	EBA (European Banking Authority, 2011), and BSC[a]	ESMA (European Securities and Markets Authority, 2011)	EIOPA (European Insurance and Occupational Pensions Authority, 2011)

[a] Within the context of the ESCB, with the representation of NCBs from all Member States

There is an inevitable tension in the current EU structure: a **national mandate** in prudential supervision, combined with a single European currency and a **European mandate** in the completion of the single market in financial services.

Accordingly, the creation of the ESFS did not, literally speaking, lead to the creation of supranational financial supervisory authorities at EU level (Table 4.1).[146]

4.3.1.3 The European Systemic Risk Board (ESRB) and the Specific Tasks Conferred upon the ECB Therein

The ESRB

(1) The ESRB was established by **Regulation (EU) No 1092/2010**,[147] whose legal basis is (also) **Article 114 TFEU**, and which entered into force

---

[146] The EBA is further discussed in detail in Chapter 7 below.

[147] Regulation (EU) No 1092/2010 of the co-legislators of 24 November 2010 "on European Union macroprudential oversight of the financial system and establishing a European Systemic Risk Board", OJ L 331, 15.12.2010, pp. 1–11 ('ESRBR'). This Regulation is in force as amended by Regulation (EU) 2019/2176 of 18 December 2019 (OJ L 334, 27.12.2019, pp. 146–154). The current consolidated version is available at: https://eur-lex.europa.eu/legal-content/EN/TXT/?uri=CELEX%3A02010R1092-20191230.

on 1 January 2011. It became operational (along with the ESAs) on 1 January 2011 and has its seat in Frankfurt; unlike the ESAs, it is not a 'Union body' nor does it have legal personality.[148] Hence, as far as non-contractual liability is concerned, it cannot be directly held liable, and any damages claims should be instituted against the EU by virtue of **Article 340, second sub-paragraph TFEU**.[149] Each Member State should also designate an authority entrusted with the conduct of macroprudential policy at national level.[150]

(2) No supervisory powers have been conferred upon the ESRB. Its objective consists in the macroprudential oversight of the EU financial system at large in order to contribute to the prevention or mitigation of systemic risks to financial stability in the EU arising from developments within the financial system, taking into account macroeconomic developments, to avoid periods of widespread financial distress. It must also contribute to the smooth functioning of the internal market and thereby ensure a sustainable contribution of the financial system to economic growth.[151] Hence, the macroprudential oversight of the European financial system became the first (and single until 2014) component of the "Europeanised bank safety net" and, unlike the ESAs, is not based on the sectoral approach. In order to fulfil its objective, the ESRB carries out, *inter alia*, the following tasks[152]:

> *first*, determination and/or collection and analysis of all relevant and necessary information; *secondly*, identification and prioritisation of systemic risks;
> *second*, issuance of Warnings, where systemic risks are deemed to be significant,[153] and of Recommendations for remedial action in response to the risks identified and monitoring their follow-up; this task relates to remedial action in response to identified significant risks, which can be of a general or of a specific nature and are addressed to the EU, to the

---

[148] ESRBR, Article 1(1)-(2); see also recital (15), last sentence. Its Rules of Procedure are laid down in its Decision of 20 March 2020, which amended Decision ESRB/2011/1 (ESRB/2020/3) (OJ C 140, 29.4.2020, pp. 5–10).

[149] See Busch and Gortsos (2022), pp. 28 (at 2.64) and 39 (at 2.99–2.100). For an analysis of this TFEU Article, see Berg (2019).

[150] ESRB Recommendation of 22 December 2011 "on the macroprudential mandate of national authorities" (ESRB/2011/3), OJ C 41, 14.2.2012, pp. 1–4. All Member States have complied with.

[151] ESRBR, Article 3(1).

[152] *Ibid.*, Article 3(2).

[153] See, e.g., the recent (22 September 2022) Warning "on vulnerabilities in the Union financial system" (OJ C 423, 7.11.2022, pp. 1–6), which identified a few severe and elevated systemic risks to financial stability caused by the Russian Federation's invasion of Ukraine and the current inflation crisis.

Commission in respect of the relevant EU legislation, as well as to one or more EU Member States, ESAs or NCAs[154];

third, close cooperation with the ESAs for the development of a common set of quantitative and qualitative indicators for the identification and measurement of systemic risk, as well as coordination of its actions with international financial organisations and fora, such as the IMF and the FSB, and relevant bodies in third countries on matters related to macroprudential oversight.

The Specific Tasks of the ECB

(1) Even though the *de Larosière* Report advised against the ECB's exercising prudential supervision over the European financial system, it pointed out that specific tasks concerning the macroprudential oversight of the financial system should be conferred on it.[155] To this end, in connection to the operation of the ESRB specific tasks have been conferred on the ECB by **Council Regulation (EU) No 1096/2010** of 17 November 2010.[156] Its legal basis is the enabling clause of **Article 127(6) TFEU** (carried over in **Article 25.2 ESCB/ECB Statute**), activated for the first time in this case.[157]

(2) In this respect, the ECB is represented in the ESRB's General Board and in Steering Committee. Its President and Vice-President are members of the General Board and, respectively, Chair and first Vice-Chair, while 5 other members of the General Board who are also members of the ECB General Council are members of the Steering Committee. *Furthermore*, the ECB has been assigned the specific task to provide to the ESRB analytical, statistical, logistical and administrative support by ensuring its Secretariat. According to **recital (9)**:

---

[154] The addressees of an ESRB Recommendation must communicate to it and to the Council the actions undertaken and provide adequate justification for any inaction ('act or explain'). If the addressees do not follow the Recommendation or fail to provide adequate justification for their inaction, the ESRB must, subject to strict rules of confidentiality, inform them, along with the Council and, if relevant, the ESA concerned. The ESRB decides whether a Warning or a Recommendation should be made public on a case-by-case basis and after having consulted the Council (ESRBR, Articles 16(1)–(2), 17(1)–(2) and 18(1)–(3)).

[155] *De Larosière* Report (2009), par. 172, second sentence and paras 173–182.

[156] OJ L 331, 15.12.2010, pp. 162–164. On both these Regulations and the functioning of the ESRB, see Ferran and Alexander (2011), Papathanassiou and Zagouras (2012), McPhilemy and Roche (2013), Chiu and Wilson (2019), pp. 306–310, Gortsos (2020), pp. 224–228 and in detail Enoch (2021), pp. 175–232 (with extensive further references).

[157] The second time this TFEU Article was activated was in 2013, when used as a legal basis for adopting the 'SSM Regulation', i.e., the main legal source of the first pillar of the BU (as further discussed below).

As it is the task of the ESRB to cover all aspects and areas of financial stability, the ECB should involve [NCBs] and supervisors to provide their specific expertise. The option to confer specific tasks concerning policies relating to prudential supervision upon the ECB provided for by the [TFEU] should therefore be exercised, by conferring on the ECB the task of ensuring the Secretariat to the ESRB.[158]

In fulfilling this task, it must provide sufficient human and financial resources and appoint the Secretariat's head, in consultation with the ESRB's General Board.[159] The Secretariat's mission consists in preparing ESRB meetings, collecting and processing statistical and other information[160] on behalf of the ESRB and for the fulfilment its tasks, and preparing analyses necessary for the ESRB to carry out its tasks, drawing on technical advice from NCBs and supervisors. *In addition*, it supports the ESRB in its international cooperation at administrative level with other relevant bodies on macroprudential issues, as well as the work of its General Board and Committees. The Secretariat's head attends the meetings of the ESRB's bodies and takes directions, on behalf of the ESRB, by its Chair and its Steering Committee.[161]

4.3.2 Regulatory Developments

4.3.2.1 The Impact of Public International Financial Law
A General Overview
For the most part, regulatory measures adopted as a regulatory response to the GFC were taken over from the international financial reform agenda, mainly

---

[158] It is noted that recitals are not in themselves legally binding and cannot overrule a substantive provision of a legislative act; however, they can be important in the interpretation of ambiguous provisions by the CJEU. See on this Den Heijer, Van den Abeelen and Maslyka (2019), with extensive references to case law.

[159] Regulation (EU) No 1096/2010, Articles 2, first sentence and 3.

[160] In fulfilling its mission in relation to the collection of information on behalf of the ESRB, the Secretariat must, on a regular and ad hoc basis, collect all the necessary information, which has been determined by the ESRB as necessary for the purposes of the performance of its tasks and make available to the ESAs the information on risks necessary for the performance of their tasks.

[161] Regulation (EU) No 1096/2010, Articles 2, second sentence, 4 and 5 (with reference to Article 15 ESRBR). It is noted that, on the basis of Articles 8(2) and (4) and 15 ESRBR and Articles 5–6 of this Regulation, the ESRB has signed an Agreement with the ESAs on "The establishment at the ESRB Secretariat of specific confidentiality procedures in order to safeguard information regarding individual financial institutions can be identified" (at: https://www.eba.europa.eu/sites/default/documents/files/documents/10180/62404/958a3bda-f9a7-436d-b238-142d57580075/Agreement-ESAs-ESRB-on-confidentiality-procedures2.pdf?retry=1).

the work orchestrated by the FSB and the financial standards adopted by the FSB, the BCBS, the IOSCO and the FATF. In this respect:

> *First*, the impact of the work of the FSB was considerable, since its **2011 Report** on "Key Attributes of Effective Resolution Regimes for Financial Institutions" influenced the initiatives for creating an EU legal framework for the resolution of credit institutions and investment firms. This led to the adoption, in 2014, by the co-legislators of the Bank Recovery and Resolution Directive **(BRRD)** establishing a framework for the recovery and resolution of credit institutions and investment firms.[162] In addition, the FSB's initiatives regarding to the regulation of the shadow banking system triggered EU regulatory developments as well.
>
> *Second*, the initiatives of the BCBS for the review of the international framework on micro- and macroprudential banking regulation were the basis for the adoption, in 2013, by the co-legislators of the **Capital Requirements Regulation** and the **Capital Requirements Directive (No IV)**.[163]
>
> *Third*, the work of the IOSCO substantially influenced the revised EU capital markets law.
>
> *Fourth*, the third **AML Directive**,[164] which repealed the second (2005/60/EC) with effect from **26 June 2017**, was adopted taking account of the revised FATF Recommendations.[165]

'Structural Reform'

(1) The issue concerning whether banks should be allowed to *directly* provide investment services, and to what extent,[166] re-emerged in the wake of the GFC. The US enacted legislation restricting the power of banks to provide investment services, according to the provisions of the 'Volcker Rule', which is implemented by Title VI of the 2010 "Dodd-Frank Wall Street Reform and

---

[162] This Directive, an integral element by now of the BU, is presented under 4.4.4 below.

[163] These two legislative acts, which are also an integral element of the BU (hence a by-product of the fiscal crisis in the euro area), are also presented below, under 4.4.3.

[164] Directive (EU) 2015/849 of the co-legislators of 20 May 2015 "on the prevention of the use of the financial system for the purposes of money laundering or terrorist financing (...)", OJ L 141, 5.6.2015, pp. 73–117, as in force. Upon the Commission's proposal of 20 July 2021 (COM/2021/423 final), this legislative act will be repealed.

[165] See Chapter 3 above, under 3.4.3.

[166] The rule of the ISD (see above, under 4.2.2), according to which Member States were prohibited, since 1996, to impose on EU credit institutions limitations with regard to the provision of investment services, still applies under the EU capital markets law as in force.

Consumer Protection Act".[167] The same applied in the UK on the basis of the **'Vickers Report'**,[168] as well as in Belgium, France and Germany.

(2) In the EU, in **November 2011**, a High-level Expert Group was set up ("High-level Expert Group on structural aspects of the EU banking sector") in order to assess the need for structural reform of the EU banking sector, chaired by Erkki Liikanen, Governor of the Bank of Finland (**"Liikanen Group"**). Its mandate consisted in determining whether structural reforms of EU credit institutions, alongside other regulatory reforms, would strengthen financial stability and improve efficiency and consumer protection.[169] On the basis of the Report submitted by the "Liikanen Group"[170] on 29 January 2014, the Commission adopted a **Proposal for a Regulation** of the co-legislators "on structural measures improving the resilience of EU credit institutions" to prevent the largest banking groups from engaging in proprietary trading, and give supervisory authorities the power to require those banking groups to separate risky trading activities from their deposit-taking business.[171] This legislative act has not (yet) been put forward.

Shadow Banking

The GFC highlighted the need for improved transparency and monitoring not only in the traditional banking sector, but also in areas where non-bank credit activities take place, in direct competition to the traditional and regulated banking activities.[172] Following consultation on a **Green Paper of 19 March 2012**,[173] on 4 September 2013, the Commission adopted a **Communication** (i.e., an instrument of EU soft law) on "Shadow Banking – Addressing

---

[167] Public Law 111-203, 124 Stat. 1376-2223; on this Act, see Acharya *et al.* (2011), Whitehead (2011), Thakor (2012) and Dumler (2013).

[168] At: https://bankingcommission.independent.gov.uk.

[169] For its mandate and list of members, see at: https://ec.europa.eu/internal_market/bank/docs/high-level_expert_group/mandate_en.pdf.

[170] High-Level Expert Group on Reforming the Structure of the EU Banking Sector, Final Report (2012) (at: https://ec.europa.eu/internal_market/bank/docs/high-level_expert_group/report_en.pdf). See Krahnen (2013).

[171] COM/2014/40 final—COD/2014/17. On the provisions of the Regulation's proposal, see Binder (2014), pp. 23–27. For an overview of all the above-mentioned structural reforms, see Gambacorta and van Rixtel (2013), Vinals *et al.* (2013), Binder (2016), pp. 16–22 and 27–32 and Alexander (2019), pp. 222–228. See also Montalbano (2021), pp. 277–309 (with extensive further references).

[172] According to the 2011 FSB Recommendations (Sect. 3.2), the regulatory measures to be examined by authorities refer to the following main aspects: the indirect regulation of banks' interaction with shadow banking entities; the regulatory reform of money market funds ('MMFs'); the regulation of other shadow banking entities, such as hedge funds; the regulation of securitisation; and the regulation of securities financing transactions ('SFTs'), such as securities lending and repurchase agreements. For an overview of shadow banking in the euro area, see Bakk-Simon *et al.* (2012) and Muñoz (2016).

[173] COM/2012/102 final.

New Sources of Risk in the Financial Sector", setting out a roadmap to limit the emergence of risks in the unregulated or less regulated financial system, particularly those of systemic nature through the shadow banking system's interconnectedness with the banking sector through contagion risk.[174] Most of the related aspects were dealt with by the adoption of new legislative acts, which constitute sources of EU capital markets law (as discussed just below).

4.3.2.2 'Pure' EU Regulatory Interventions

Even though such interventions were fewer, in the wake of (and as a regulatory response to) the GFC, substantial amendments were introduced in 2019 to the (above-mentioned) 1994 Directive on DGSs as regards the coverage level and the payout delay[175]: deposit protection was firstly increased to 50,000 euro and then (by end-2010) to 100,000 euro. Furthermore, in 2014 that Directive was repealed by the new **DGS Directive** (another element of the BU, discussed below). Other legislative acts of the co-legislators included the new **'E-money Institutions Directive'**,[176] which repealed with effect from 30 April 2011 the pre-existing legislative act in this field,[177] as well as several acts in the field of consumer protection in financial services, such as: **Directive 2014/17/EU** "on credit agreements for consumers relating to residential immovable property (...)", **Regulation (EU) 2015/751** "on interchange fees for card-based payment transactions",[178] the 'Payment Accounts Directive' (**'PAD'**),[179] the 'Payments Services Directive' No II (**'PSD II'**),[180] and the 'Single Euro Payments Area (**'SEPA'**) Regulation'.[181]

---

[174] COM/2013/614 final.

[175] Directive 2009/14/EC of the co-legislators of 11 March 2009, OJ L 68, 13.3.2009, pp. 3–7.

[176] Directive 2009/110/EC of 16 September 2009 "on the taking up, pursuit and prudential supervision of the business of electronic money institutions (...)" (OJ L 267, 10.10.2009, pp. 7–17), as in force.

[177] See above, under 4.2.3.

[178] OJ L 60, 28.2.2014, pp. 34–85 and OJ L 123, 19.5.2015, pp. 1–15, respectively.

[179] Directive 2014/92/EU of 23 July 2014 "on the comparability of fees related to payment accounts, payment account switching and access to payment accounts with basic features", OJ L 257, 28.8.2014, pp. 214–246. On this legislative act, see Jans (2022), pp. 74–95.

[180] Directive (EU) 2015/2366 of 25 November 2015 "on payment services in the internal market (...)", OJ L 337, 23.12.2015, pp. 35–127; this repealed Directive 2007/64/EC (OJ L 319, 5.12.2007, pp. 1–36, 'PSD'). On this legislative act, see Jans (2022), pp. 95–107. Both the PAD and the PSD II are of interest for the purposes of this study since they fall in the scope of action of the EBA in accordance with Article 1(2) EBAR (see Chapter 7 below, under 7.3.1).

[181] Regulation (EU) No 260/2012 of 14 March 2012 "establishing technical and business requirements for credit transfers and direct debits in euro (...)" OJ L 94, 30.3.2012, pp. 22–37. On this legislative act, see Jans (2022), pp. 107–112.

4.3.2.3 Developments in EU Capital Markets Law
General Overview

Regulatory developments in EU capital markets law were aimed at three primary goals: enhancing market stability, ensuring the protection of investors and safeguarding the integrity, efficiency and transparency of capital markets.[182] To this end, the co-legislators adopted several legislative acts, which were either directly or indirectly linked to the GFC and can be divided into two groups: acts amending or even repealing existing legal acts on the same field[183]; and new acts, the content of the majority of which was heavily influenced by the work of the IOSCO (discussed in turn below). It is also remarked that during that period that EU institutions heavily resorted to the adoption of Regulations (along with a few Directives) with a view to achieving the highest possible degree of harmonised application of the relevant rules.[184]

Legislative Acts Amending/Repealing Existing Ones—Legislative Acts on New Fields

(1) In relation to the *first group* of significant importance are the 'Markets in Financial Instruments Directive' No II ('**MiFID II**') and the 'Markets in Financial Instruments Regulation' ('**MiFIR**'), both of 15 May 2014.[185] Even though these acts are sources of EU capital markets law, most of their provisions also apply to credit institutions[186] if their licence covers the provision of investment services and/or the performance of investment activities. *In addition*, in the field of market abuse, the **MAD I** was repealed, with effect from **3 July 2016**, by a Regulation ('**MAR**') and a Directive ('**MAD II**')[187]; the

---

[182] See Commission Communication of 2 June 2010 "Regulating financial services for sustainable growth" (COM/2010/301 final).

[183] In some cases, political decisions to introduce these amendments were taken prior to the crisis, but as the latter broke out new aspects came to the fore, which were subsequently incorporated in the final texts of the adopted legislative acts and are *indirectly linked* to the crisis.

[184] For a comprehensive overview of EU capital markets law of that period, see Moloney (2014a) and Veil (2017, editor). For an overview, see also Appendix V in Gortsos (2018a), pp. 206–209.

[185] Directive 2014/65/EU and Regulation (EU) No 600/2014 of the co-legislators of 15 May 2014 "on markets in financial instruments (…)", OJ L 173, 12.6.2014, pp. 349–496 and 84–148, respectively. The former repealed Directive 2004/39/EU on the same subject (OJ L 145, 30.4.2004, pp. 1–44, 'MiFID I'). On these twin acts, see, by means of mere indication, Moloney (2014a) in various Chapters (on a thematic basis), Sethe (2014) (in relation to its impact on Swiss law), the contributions in Busch and Ferrarini (2017, editors), Gortsos (2017) (on public enforcement) and (2018a) (on investor protection, Articles 24–30) and various contributions (on a thematic basis) in Veil (2022a, editor). On the regime governing third-country firms thereunder, see Armour, Bengtzen and Enriques (2017), pp. 59–60 and Busch and Louisse (2017).

[186] MiFID II, Article 1(3), point (b).

[187] Regulation (EU) No 596/2014 (OJ L 173, 12.6.2014, pp. 1–61) and Directive 2014/57/EU (OJ L 173, 12.6.2014, pp. 179–189) of the co-legislators of 16 April

latter introduced, for the first time, harmonised provisions on the criminal sanctions regarding market abuse. *Furthermore*, the prospectus and the transparency regimes were also enhanced,[188] while the 1985 UCITS I Directive (in force as repeatedly amended) was repealed in 2009 with effect from 1 July 2011 by the '**UCITS IV Directive**'[189] (further amended in 2014[190]).

(2) The *second group* of legislative acts contains mainly Regulations (and a few Directives only) of the co-legislators which are *directly linked* to the crisis and are new. These refer to several aspects and the content of the rules of their majority was heavily influenced by the work of the IOSCO. By means of indication:

First, as early as on 16 September 2009, the '**Credit Rating Agencies Regulation**' was adopted,[191] which is in force as subsequently amended.[192] By virtue of the first amendment, credit rating agencies established in Member States are directly supervised by the ESMA, which, hence and as an exception, is a genuinely supervisory body among the ESAs (as already mentioned).

Second, in relation to investment funds, several new legislative acts were adopted (apart from the amendment of the UCITS Directive), in the field of alternative investment funds and (mainly) their managers: the 'Alternative Investment Fund Managers Directive'[193] ('**AIFMD**'), which lays down harmonised rules on the authorisation, ongoing operation and transparency of the managers of AIFs ('**AIFMs**'), managing

---

2014. The latter contains for the first-time provisions on criminal sanctions. On the evolution and the content of the MAR, see Di Noia (2012), Fleischer and Schmolke (2012), Tountopoulos (2014), Willemaers (2014), Hellstén (2015) and, in detail, Ventoruzzo and Mock (2017, editors) and Veil (2022b). On the MAD II, see Faure and Leger (2014) and Willemaers (2014).

[188] Directive 2010/73/EU of the co-legislators of 24 November 2010 (OJ L 327, 11.12.2010, pp. 1–12) and Directive 2013/50/EU of 22 October 2013 (OJ L 294, 6.11.2013, pp. 13–27), which modified the (then) existing framework.

[189] Directive 2009/65/EC of the co-legislators of 13 July 2009 "on the coordination of laws, regulations and administrative provisions relating to [UCITS]", OJ L 302, 17.11.2009, pp. 32–96.

[190] Directive 2014/91/EU of the co-legislators of 23 July 2014, OJ L 257, 28.8.2014, pp. 186–213 ('UCITS V'), which applies from 18 March 2016. On the UCITS IV, see Moloney (2014a), pp. 200–269 and Zetzsche (2017).

[191] Regulation (EC) No 1060/2009, OJ L 302, 17.11.2009, pp. 1–31.

[192] Regulations (EU) No 513/2011 of 11 May 2001 (OJ L 145, 31.5.2011, pp. 30–56) and 462/2013 of 21 May 2003 (OJ L 146, 31.5.2013, pp. 1–33). For a detailed review of this legislative act, as in force, see Staikouras (2012), Moloney (2014a), pp. 637–682, Miglionico (2019), García Alcubilla and Ruiz del Pozo (2012) and Veil (2022c).

[193] Directive 2011/61/EU of 8 June 2011, OJ L 174, 1.7.2011, pp. 1–73.

and/or marketing **AIFs** in the EU[194]; the 'European Venture Capital Funds Regulation' ('**EuVeCaR**'); the 'European Social Entrepreneurship Funds Regulation' ('**EuSEFR**')[195]; the 'European Long-Term Investment Funds Regulation' ('**ELTIFR**')[196]; and the 'Money Market Funds Regulation[197] ('**MMFR**').

Third, the legal framework on market infrastructures was further enhanced by adoption of two Regulations: the '**European Markets Infrastructure Regulation**'[198] ('**EMIR**') to increase the transparency of the OTC derivatives markets, which was heavily highlighted during the GFC and particular due to the almost collapse of *Bear Sterns*, the bankruptcy of *Lehman Brothers* and the rescue through public support of the insurance undertaking *AIG*[199]; and the '**Central Securities Depositories Regulation**'[200] ('**CSDR**') to harmonise rules on cross-border securities settlement.

Finally, other new sources of EU capital markets law are the '**Short Selling Regulation**',[201] governing short selling and certain aspects of

---

[194] On the AIFMD, see Busch and van Setten (2014), Zetzsche and Preiner (2015), various other contributions in Zetzsche (2015, editor) and Gortsos (2018b).

[195] Regulations (EU) No 345/2013 and (EU) No 346/2013 of 17 April 2013 (OJ L 115, 25.4.2013, pp. 1–17 and 18–38, respectively). Both these funds are AIFs managed by 'small AIFMs' (exempted from the field of application of the AIFMD pursuant to Article 3(2)) with a specific investment strategy: the first in SMEs and the second in companies with a socially beneficial approach and strategy.

[196] Regulation (EU) 2015/760 of 29 April 2015, OJ L 123, 19.5.2015, pp. 98–121. ELTIFs are also a specifically regulated type of EU AIFs or compartments thereof, which are marketed to *professional and certain retail investors* in the EU and are raising and channelling capital towards European long-term investments in the real economy, in line with the EU objective of smart, sustainable and inclusive growth.

[197] Regulation (EU) 2017/1131 of 14 June 2017, OJ L 169, 30.6.2017, pp. 8–45.

[198] Regulation (EU) No 648/2012 of 4 July 2012 "on OTC derivatives, central counterparties and trade repositories", OJ L 201, 27.7.2012, pp. 1–59. On this legal act, see Aditya (2013), Ferrarini and Saguato (2013) and (2014) and Provino (2015). See also the Commentary by Sethe *et al.* (2017, Hrsg.) on the equivalent Swiss law (Finanzmarktinfrastrukturgesetz, FinfraG), at the beginning of the analysis of several Articles of which there is a short description of the relevant EMIR provisions.

[199] These episodes emphasised the gaps in the *modus operandi* of the OTC derivatives market and created concerns in relation with the role of credit default swaps during the crisis. See indicatively Norberg (2009), pp. 84–94, Posner (2010), pp. 56–65, and Rajan (2010), pp. 134–153.

[200] Regulation (EU) No 909/2014 of 23 July 2014 "on improving securities settlement in the [EU] and on central securities depositories (…)", OJ L 257, 28.08.2014, pp. 1–72. The term 'central securities depository' (CSD) is defined to mean a legal person operating a securities settlement system as referred to in point (3) of Section A of the Annex and providing at least one other core service listed in Section A thereof (*ibid.*, Article 2(1), point (1)).

[201] Regulation (EU) No 236/2012 of 14 March 2012, OJ L 86, 24.3.2012, pp. 1–24. On the highly contested validity of some aspects of this Regulation, as confirmed by the

credit default swaps[202]; the **'PRIIPS Regulation'**, [203] which, *inter alia*, introduced the key information document (**'KID'**) for packaged retail and insurance-based investment products; the 'Securities Financing Transactions Regulation'[204] (**'SFTR'**); and the **'Benchmarks Regulation'**,[205] which governs indices used as benchmarks in financial instruments and financial contracts or to measure the performance of investment funds.[206]

4.3.2.4 Developments in EU Insurance Law

This branch of EU financial law has also been in the focus due to the systemic importance of certain large insurance and reinsurance undertakings and the need to enhance investor protection in that field. The by-product has been the adoption by the co-legislators of three legislative acts: *first*, the **'Solvency II' Directive**,[207] which repealed all previous legislative acts on the

---

CJEU, see Case C-270/12, *United Kingdom v Parliament and Council*, further discussed in Box 7.1 below.

[202] 'Short sale' in relation to a share or debt instrument means any sale of the share or debt instrument which the seller does not own at the time of entering into the agreement to sell including such a sale where at the time of entering into the agreement to sell the seller has borrowed or agreed to borrow the share or debt instrument for delivery at settlement. 'Credit default swap' means a derivative contract in which one party pays a fee to another party in return for a payment or other benefit in the case of a credit event relating to a reference entity and of any other default, relating to that derivative contract, which has a similar economic effect (*ibid.*, Article 2(1), points (b) and (c), respectively). On this Regulation, see Walla (2022).

[203] Regulation (EU) No 1286/2014 of 26 November 2014 on key information documents for packaged retail and insurance-based investment products (PRIIPs)", OJ L 352, 9.12.2014, pp. 1–23. On this Regulation, see Willemaers (2014), Sections 4.2 and 3.8, Möllers (2015), Colaert (2017), Lupoi (2017) and Weber and Baisch (2017), pp. 261–264 and 269–271. See also Veil (2017), at p. 99, linking this legal act with behavioural finance: "(...) *The PRIIPs Regulation align[s] the disclosure obligation relating to financial products with the findings from Behavioural Finance (smart disclosure)*". On the interplay between the PRIIPs' KIDs and the MiFID II conduct of business rules, see Colaert (2017), Section III.

[204] Regulation (EU) 2015/2365 of 25 November 2015, OJ L 337, 23.12.2015, pp. 1–34.

[205] Regulation (EU) 2016/1011 of 8 July 2016, OJ L 171, 29.6.2016, pp. 1-65. See on this see Moloney (2014a), pp. 744–750 and Wundenberg (2022).

[206] 'Benchmark' means any index by reference to which the amount payable under a financial instrument or contract, or the value of a financial instrument, is determined, or an index used to measure the performance of an investment fund with the purpose of tracking the return of such index or of defining the asset allocation of a portfolio or of computing the performance fees (Benchmarks Regulation, Article 3(1), point (3)).

[207] Directive 2009/138/EC of 25 November 2009 "on the taking-up and pursuit of the business of Insurance and Reinsurance)", OJ L 335, 17.12.2009, pp. 1–155. Noteworthy in this respect is also the (quite lengthy) Commission Delegated Regulation (EU) 2015/35 of 10 October 2014 supplementing the Solvency II Directive (OJ L 12, 17.1.2015, pp. 1–797). On this legislative act, see the contributions in Marano and Siri (2017).

authorisation, operation, as well as prudential regulation and supervision of insurance and reinsurance undertakings[208]; *second*, the **'Insurance Distribution Directive'**[209] (**'IDD'**), which repealed, with effect from **23 February 2018**, the IMD; and *third*, the **'Institutions for Occupational Retirement Provision Directive No II'**[210] (**'IORPD II'**), which repealed with effect from **13 January 2019** the IORPD I.

4.4 CREATION OF THE BANKING UNION (BU)

4.4.1 The BU in a Historical Perspective

4.4.1.1 Introductory Remarks

The BU initiative is broader than an initiative aimed at the mere establishment of a pan-European banking (or even financial) supervisory authority, which did not exist either. It is recalled that the launch of the EMU on 1 January 1999 did not bring about any changes to the regime on the authorisation and prudential supervision of credit institutions incorporated in Member States. Contrary to the definition and implementation of the single monetary and foreign exchange policy, for which competences became supranational, the ECB had not been assigned any supervisory powers for the EU financial system. Rather, the relevant competence remained with the Member States.[211] In this respect two remarks are noteworthy:

> *First*, competent for the authorisation and microprudential supervision of EU credit institutions were exclusively (until 4 November 2014) the authorities designated as such by Member States. This was also implicitly provided in **Article 105(5) TEC** (carried over *verbatim* in **Article 3.3 ESCB/ECB Statute**) stipulating that the ESCB *"shall contribute to the smooth conduct of policies pursued by the competent authorities relating to the prudential supervision of credit institutions and the stability*

---

[208] 'Insurance undertaking' means a direct life or non-life insurance undertaking which has received authorisation in accordance with Article 14 of the Solvency II Directive; 'reinsurance undertaking' means an undertaking which has received authorisation in accordance with the same Article to pursue reinsurance activities (*ibid.*, Article 13, points (1) and (4), respectively).

[209] Directive (EU) 2016/97 of 20 January 2016 "on insurance distribution (…)", OJ L 26, 2.2.2016, pp. 19–59.

[210] Directive (EU) 2016/2341 of 14 December 2016 "on the activities and supervision of institutions for occupational retirement provision (IORPs)", OJ L 354, 23.12.2016, pp. 37–85.

[211] For a summary of the various proposals regarding the creation of supranational financial supervisory authorities in the EU, see Lastra (2006), pp. 324–328, and Hadjiemmanuil (2006b), pp. 818–828.

of the financial system".²¹² The relevant competence of the ECB was mainly to submit opinions pursuant to **Article 105(4) TEC** (carried over *verbatim* in **Article 4 ESCB/ECB Statute**), within the limits and under the conditions set out in a **Council Decision**.²¹³ However, **Article 105(6) TEC** (carried over almost *verbatim* in **Article 25.2 ESCB/ECB Statute**) contained an enabling clause, according to which the Council could assign to the ECB 'specific powers' with regard to the prudential supervision of credit institutions, which had not been activated.²¹⁴ The **Treaty of Lisbon**²¹⁵ did not amend these provisions. They are contained (subject to minor modifications relating to the legislative procedure), respectively, in **Article 127(5)** and in **Articles 127(4) and 282(5) TFEU**.²¹⁶

It is noted in this respect, that **Article 127 TFEU** does not provide a solid legal basis for a primary financial stability mandate of the ECB. Nevertheless, it has been argued (correctly in the author's view) that financial stability, as a secondary mandate, is implied in the monetary authority of the ECB, given the functional relation between price and financial stability, albeit confined by **Article 127(5) TFEU**.²¹⁷ In the author's opinion, this is reinforced by **Article 127(1), second sentence TFEU**, according to which the Eurosystem must support the general EU economic policies with a view to contributing to the achievement of the EU objectives as laid down in Article 3 TEU, without prejudice to the objective of price stability.²¹⁸

Second, the ECB never assumed the role of the lender of last resort for any solvent credit institution incorporated in a euro area Member State and exposed to illiquidity. Its role was (and remains) confined to the approval

---

[212] These provisions were in force since the launch of Stage III of the EMU (Article 116(3), second indent TEC, with a reference to Article 105(5)). For a historical background, see Smits (1997), pp. 334–350, Andenas and Hadjiemmanuil (1997), pp. 386–394, Lastra (2006), pp. 216–222, Louis (2009), pp. 162–166 (with specific reference to the powers of the ESCB during the GFC) and Lastra and Louis (2013), pp. 82–94.

[213] Council Decision 98/415/EC of 29 June 1998 "on the consultation of the [ECB] by national authorities regarding draft legislative provisions" (OJ L 189, 3.7.1998, pp. 42–43). On the duty to consult the ECB under Article 127(4) TFEU and the Opinions submitted by the ECB, see Lambrinoc (2009).

[214] On Article 105(5)–(6) TEC, see Smits (1997), pp. 319–362.

[215] OJ C 306, 17.12.2007, pp. 1–271.

[216] Article 127(5) TFEU does not apply to Member States with a derogation (Article 139(2), point 3 TFEU and Article 42.1 ESCB/ECB Statute), including at that time to the UK [Protocol (No 15) (Consolidated version, OJ C 202, 7.6.2016, pp. 284–286), paras 4 and 7]. On its content, see Smits (1997), pp. 338–355, Lastra and Louis (2013), p. 95, Psaroudakis (2018), pp. 134–137, as well as Smolenska and Beukers (2022). On the role of the ESCB in banking supervision, see Smits (2005a) and (2015).

[217] See on this, by means of mere indication, Psaroudakis (2018), pp. 155–156.

[218] See above, under 4.1.4.

of relevant decisions taken by the NCBs-members of the Eurosystem in accordance with **Article 14.4 ESCB/ECB Statute**.[219]

4.4.1.2 Developments Since 2012

(1) The creation of the BU was tabled at the Euro Area Summit of **29 June 2012**, amidst the fiscal crisis in the euro area, which became manifest in 2010 and was triggered by the exceptionally severe fiscal imbalances in Greece, which were then transmitted to other EU Member States of the euro area 'periphery'.[220] The main rationale behind this initiative is summarised in one sentence:

> We affirm that it is imperative to break the vicious circle between banks and sovereigns.[221]

The European Summit which was held concurrently on 28–29 June decided to invite the President of the European Council to develop, in close collaboration with the Presidents of the Commission, the Eurogroup and the ECB, a specific and time-bound roadmap for the achievement of a genuine EMU, in accordance with the **"Van Rompuy Report"**,[222] submitted a few days earlier (on 26 June) by the President of the European Council. One of its 4 elements was the creation of the BU.[223]

---

[219] This aspect is discussed in detail in the *Excursus* at the end of Chapter 6 below.

[220] The author uses the term 'fiscal crisis' instead of the more commonly used terms 'debt crisis' or 'sovereign crisis' as more consistent with the fact that the Member States which, for different reasons each, were severely affected by this crisis (Greece, Portugal, Ireland, and Cyprus), were excluded from international interbank and capital markets and resorted to the (sovereign) lending of last resort facilities of the IMF and the (then) newly created EU facilities, violated the 'hard limit' (3%) deficit/GDP ratio laid down in EU law (TFEU, Article 126(2) and Article 1 of Protocol (No 12) "on the excessive deficit procedure" (Consolidated version, OJ C 202, 7.6.2016, pp. 279–280). For an analysis of this crisis and the policy responses thereto, see Belke (2010), Eichengreen *et al.* (2011), pp. 47–64, Athanassiou (2011), Aizenman (2012), Caminal (2012), Shambaugh (2012), Stephanou (2013), De Grauwe (2013), D' Arvisenet (2015), Zimmermann (2015), Hadjiemmanuil (2020) and Piantelli (2021), pp. 1–84 (all with extensive further references). On supervisory failure as a cause of this crisis, see Masciandaro *et al.* (2012).

[221] Euro Area Summit Statement, 29 June 2012, first para., first sentence (at: https://consilium.europa.eu/uedocs/cms_data/docs/pressdata/en/ec/131359.pdf. On the 'vicious circles' (also called 'vicious cycles', diabolic loops' or 'doom loops') between the banking sector and sovereign bond markets from a historical perspective, see Mitchener (2014), with extensive further references.

[222] "Towards a Genuine Economic and Monetary Union", Report of the President of the European Council in close collaboration with Jose Manuel Barroso, President of the Commission, Jean-Claude Juncker, President of the Eurogroup, and Mario Draghi, President of the ECB, 5 December.

[223] *Ibid.*, Section II.1. The other 3 elements were the establishment of an integrated budgetary framework ('European Fiscal Union'), an integrated economic policy framework

(2) Against this political background, the **Commission Announcement of 12 September 2012** contained "A Roadmap for a Banking Union", a proposal for a Council Regulation "conferring specific tasks on the [ECB] concerning policies relating to the prudential supervision of credit institutions", and a proposal for a Regulation of the co-legislators "amending [the EBA] Regulation (…) as regards its interaction with Council Regulation (EU) No…/ … conferring specific tasks on the [ECB] concerning policies relating to the prudential supervision of credit institutions".[224] In its Announcement the Commission called on the co-legislators to undertake the following[225]:

> *First*, to reach agreement by end-2012 on the two above-mentioned Regulation proposals, as a first step in the creation of the BU.
> *Second*, to approve, also by end-2012, the proposals for the Regulations and Directives (of the co-legislators) on amending the applicable regulatory framework on microprudential banking regulation and setting up a new regulatory framework on macroprudential banking regulation, establishing EU rules on the recovery and resolution of unviable credit institutions (and investment firms), and amending the existing regulatory framework on DGSs.[226]
> *Third*, to examine, in the medium term, how to shape the conditions for the establishment of a supranational entity for the resolution of credit institutions, a supranational resolution fund for covering funding gaps, provided that a decision is made in favour of the resolution of credit institutions, and a supranational DGS, allowing the completion of the BU.

Under this agenda, the creation of the BU should lead to a "Europeanised bank safety net" consisting of three pillars: a Single Supervisory Mechanism for the banking sector (i.e., not for the other two sectors of the financial system) for the prudential supervision of credit institutions (mainly) incorporated in euro area Member States (the **'first pillar'**); a Single Resolution Mechanism for unviable credit institutions (also mainly incorporated in euro area Member States) and a Single Resolution Fund to cover any resulting funding gaps, provided that a decision is made on their resolution (the **'second pillar'**); and a single DGS, which coupled with the Single Resolution Board (a part of the

---

('European Economic Union') and a democratic legitimacy and accountability framework ('European Political Union').

[224] COM/2012/510 final, COM/2012/511 final and COM/2012/512 final, respectively.

[225] COM/2012/510 final, Section 4.

[226] COM/2010/369 final and COM/2012/280 final.

SRM) could form a 'European Deposit Insurance and Resolution Authority' ('**EDIRA**') (the '**third pillar**').[227]

(3) These main pillars of the BU, which were designed to mainly (but not exclusively) apply to euro area Member States, should be coupled by a 'single rulebook'[228] containing substantive rules on all the previous aspects, as part of the single market for financial services,[229] adopted either in the form of legislative acts under **Article 289 TFEU**, or by the Commission (or the Council) with the direct contribution of the EBA (delegated and implementing acts under **Articles 290–291 TFEU**). It is noted that the 'single rulebook', adopted by the co-legislators and further detailed by the Commission and the EBA, is *applicable across all EU Member States*. It is mainly a child of the **GFC**, shaped, to a higher or lesser degree, under the influence of developments in public international banking law in its wake and is based on a 'total harmonisation approach', under consideration of the 'proportionality principle'.[230]

4.4.2 The New Institutional and Regulatory Framework of 2013–2014

The BU is a "highly integrated system" like the ESCB.[231] The key institutional and regulatory developments towards its establishing took place during the period 2013–2014, as presented below. Considering the normal response time of European institutions, these legislative measures were taken, based on proposals by the Commission, in an exceptionally short timeframe. Except

---

[227] For arguments for or against establishing the BU, see (out of a vast existing literature) Acharya (2012), Louis (2012), the various contributions in Beck (2012, editor), Bofinger et al. (2012), House of Lords (2012), Pisani-Ferry et al. 2012), Schoenmaker (2012), Sibert (2012), Wyplosz (2012), Herring (2013) and Huertas (2013). On various aspects of its functioning, see (also) the contributions in Allen, Carletti and Gray (2013), (2014) and (2015) (in all editors).

[228] This term is used to refer to the total harmonisation of rules pertaining to the prudential regulation and supervision of financial firms and was first introduced in June 2009, when the European Council called for the establishment of a "*European single rulebook applicable to all financial institutions in the Single Market*" (11225/2/09 REV 2, at: https://www.consilium.europa.eu/uedocs/cms_data/docs/pressdata/en/ec/108622.pdf), par. 20. For a detailed analysis on the single rulebook, see Lefterov (2015) and Babis (2019).

[229] On the link between the BU and the single market, see Lastra (2013), Alexander (2016), pp. 258–260, Binder (2016), pp. 13–15, and see Ohler (2022), pp. 3–4.

[230] There are three aspects of the proportionality test: suitability/appropriateness, necessity and proportionality *stricto sensu*); see Joosen and Lehmann (2019), pp. 73–74 (with reference to Alexy [2014]). These, of course, are only examined once it is confirmed that the measure pursues a legitimate aim.

[231] See Lehmann (2021), pp. 77–78, with reference to the judgement of the Court (Grand Chamber) of 26 February 2019 in joined Cases C-202/18, *Ilmārs Rimšēvičs v Republic of Latvia* and C-238/18, *European Central Bank v Republic of Latvia* (ECLI:EU:C:2019:139), pp. 69–70.

for the European Deposit Insurance Scheme ('**EDIS**') (as the EDIRA has finally been conceived), the other components, namely the Single Supervisory Mechanism ('**SSM**') and the Single Resolution Mechanism ('**SRM**'), are in place.[232]

4.4.3   Authorisation, Prudential Supervision and Prudential Regulation of Credit Institutions

4.4.3.1   The Single Supervisory Mechanism (SSM)

(1) With regard to the creation of a European banking supervisory authority, within 14 months from the submission of the Commission's proposal, the Council adopted the Single Supervisory Mechanism Regulation[233] ('**SSMR**'). Since the political decision was to make use of the existing EU Treaties, its legal basis is **Article 127(6) TFEU**. This Regulation established the SSM for credit institutions and some other categories of supervised entities established in the '**participating Member States**',[234] which became operative on **4 November 2014**.

Box 4.3 Two significant SSMR recitals

Recital (11)	*"(...) In view of the close links and interactions between Member States whose currency is the euro, the banking union should apply at least to all euro area Member States. With a view to maintaining and deepening the internal market and to the extent that this is institutionally possible, the banking union should also be open to the participation of other Member States"*

(continued)

---

[232] For a general overview and assessment of the legal framework on the BU, see, by means of mere indication, Moloney (2014b), the various contributions in Hinojosa and Beneyto (2015, editors), Lastra (2015), pp. 355–382, Chiu and Wilson (2019), pp. 313–319, Montalbano (2021), Binder and Gortsos (2016), the various contributions in Castaneda et al. (2015, editors), Chiti and Santoro (2019, editors), Chiu and Wilson (2019), pp. 313–327, Busch and Ferrarini (2020, editors), Alexander (2022), and Binder, Gortsos, Lackhoff and Ohler (2022, editors). On additional literature, see Chapters 8–9 below. On the specific aspect of how the BU framework also impacts on private law relationships (duties), see Grundmann (2015) and Badenhoop (2020); on private law in BU litigation, se Haentjens (2021).

[233] Council Regulation (EU) No 1024/2013 of 15 October 2013 "conferring specific tasks on the [ECB] concerning policies relating to the prudential supervision of credit institutions", OJ L 287, 29.10.2013, pp. 63–89.

[234] Article 2 SSMR defines a participating Member State as a Member State whose currency is the euro or a Member State whose currency is not the euro which has established a close cooperation under Article 7 thereof.

Recital (12)	*"As a first step towards a banking union, a single supervisory mechanism should ensure that the Union's policy relating to the prudential supervision of credit institutions is implemented in a coherent and effective manner, that the single rulebook for financial services is applied in the same manner to credit institutions in all Member States concerned, and that those credit institutions are subject to supervision of the highest quality, unfettered by other, non-prudential considerations. In particular, the [SSM] should be consistent with the functioning of the internal market for financial services and with the free movement of capital. A single supervisory mechanism is the basis for the next steps towards the banking union. This reflects the principle that the ESM will, following a regular decision, have the possibility to recapitalise banks directly when an effective single supervisory mechanism is established (...)"*[235]

(2) The institutional framework governing the SSM is further specified in several ECB legal acts, containing provisions on the operational arrangements for the implementation of its supervisory tasks; the most important is the **SSM Framework Regulation ('SSM-FR')**.[236] Furthermore, in 2013 the ECB signed an **Interinstitutional Agreement** with the European Parliament and a **Memorandum of Understanding ('MoU')** with the Council.[237]

4.4.3.2 The Single Rulebook
(1) On **27 June 2013**, the following two legislative acts of the co-legislators of 26 June 2013 were published in the *OJ*: the 'Capital Requirements Regulation' (**'CRR'**) and the 'Capital Requirements Directive No IV'[238] (**'CRD IV'**[239]). They are in force since **1 January 2014** and repealed the CRD I.[240] An integral part of this single rulebook is also the delegated and implementing acts adopted by the Commission (and in some limited cases by the Council) based on the power conferred upon it (them) by virtue of specific CRR and

---

[235] On this direct recapitalisation instrument, see Chapter 5 below, under 5.1.5.

[236] Regulation (EU) No 468/2014 of the ECB of 16 April 2014 "establishing the framework for cooperation within the SSM between the [ECB] and [NCAs] and with national designated authorities (ECB/2014/17)", OJ L 141, 14.5.2014, pp. 1–50.

[237] On the SSMR, see further in Chapter 6 below, under 6.3.

[238] Regulation (EU) No 575/2013 "on prudential requirements for credit institutions and investment firms (...)" and Directive 2013/36/EU "on access to the activity of credit institutions and the prudential supervision of credit institutions and investment firms (...)", OJ L 176, 27.6.2013, pp. 1–337 and 338–436, respectively.

[239] This acronym is a misnomer for the Directive, which addresses several other prudential aspects rather than merely capital requirements.

[240] On these two legislative acts, see further Chapter 6 below, under 6.1 and 6.2.

CRD IV Articles, as well as EBA Guidelines, adopted either on the basis of the CRR and the CRD IV or on its own initiative pursuant to **Article 16 EBAR**.

4.4.4 Resolution of Credit Institutions

4.4.4.1 The Single Resolution Mechanism and the Single Resolution Fund

(1) In 2014, a Single Resolution Mechanism (**SRM**) and a Single Resolution Fund ('**SRF**') were also established by virtue of the Single Resolution Mechanism Regulation[241] ('**SRMR**'). The establishment of the SRM was a necessary complement to the SSM, as it would be a paradox if credit institutions were directly supervised (by the ECB) at EU level, but, in the event of a need for resolution (upon a proposal of the ECB), the relevant decision was to be made at national level. In this regard, the International Monetary Fund, in its Article IV consultation for the euro area in 2013, has starkly stated that:

> (...) without a strong SRM complementing the SSM, the credibility and effectiveness of the banking union would be jeopardized.[242]

The uniform rules and a uniform procedure for the resolution of the categories of entities referred to in **Article 2 SRMR** and established in the '**participating Member States**' are applied by the Single Resolution Board ('**SRB**'), together with the Council, the Commission and the national resolution authorities ('**NRAs**') within the SRM framework.[243] The SRF, which was established by the SRMR,[244] is also governed by the intergovernmental '**SRF Agreement**'[245]; this is an instrument of public international law (international treaty). Contributions are collected by each NRA to the relevant national resolution fund, which are then transferred to the SRF, which is administered by the SRF. After the exit of the UK from the EU, Sweden is the only Member State that is not Contracting Party to the SRF Agreement, which complements and supports the SRMR that established the SRF.[246]

---

[241] Regulation (EU) No 806/2014 of the co-legislators of 15 July "establishing uniform rules and a uniform procedure for the resolution of credit institutions and certain investment firms in the framework of a Single Resolution Mechanism and a Single Resolution Fund (...)", OJ L 225, 30.7.2014, pp. 1–90.

[242] See International Monetary Fund (2013), p. 17.

[243] SRMR, Article 1.

[244] *Ibid.*, Article 67(1), first sentence.

[245] Intergovernmental Agreement (No 8457/14) "on the transfer and mutualisation of contributions to the SRF" (at: https://register.consilium.europa.eu/content/out?lang=EN&typ=ENTRY&i=SMPL&DOC_ID=ST%208457%202014%20COR%201).

[246] On the SRMR, see further Chapter 6 below, under 6.5.

4.4.4.2 The Single Rulebook

(1) On **15 May 2014**, the co-legislators adopted the Bank Recovery and Resolution Directive[247] ('**BRRD**'). It was the first time that harmonised rules were adopted at the EU level in this field, as opposed to other areas for which a regulatory framework had been in place since the late 1980s and mid-1990s, such as those of authorisation, microprudential regulation and supervision of credit institutions (while macroprudential regulation under the CRR and the CRD IV is another innovative element), and that of DGSs.

Box 4.4 Two significant BRRD recitals

Recital (4) — "*There is currently no harmonisation of the procedures for resolving institutions at Union level. Some Member States apply to institutions the same procedures that they apply to other insolvent enterprises, which in certain cases have been adapted for institutions. There are considerable substantial and procedural differences between the laws, regulations and administrative provisions which govern the insolvency of institutions in the Member States. In addition, the financial crisis has exposed the fact that general corporate insolvency procedures may not always be appropriate for institutions as they may not always ensure sufficient speed of intervention, the continuation of the critical functions of institutions and the preservation of financial stability*"

Recital (5) — "*A regime is therefore needed to provide authorities with a credible set of tools to intervene sufficiently early and quickly in an unsound or failing institution so as to ensure the continuity of the institution's critical financial and economic functions, while minimising the impact of an institution's failure on the economy and financial system (…)*"

On the basis of the BRRD, the Commission (and in some limited cases by the Council) have adopted delegated and implementing acts and the EBA Guidelines (part of the single rulebook as well). It is also noted that the BRRD (still) applies to both credit institutions and investment firms (commonly referred to therein as 'institutions').

(2) As in the case of the CRR and the CRD IV, the impact of public international law on the BRRD was also considerable. Its content was

---

[247] Directive 2014/59/EU of the co-legislators "establishing a framework for the recovery and resolution of credit institutions and investment firms (…)", OJ L 173, 12.6.2014, pp. 190–348.

heavily influenced by the **2011 FSB Report** on "Key Attributes of Effective Resolution Regimes for Financial Institutions" (as in force).[248]

4.4.5 *Deposit Guarantee Schemes*

4.4.5.1 *A Single Deposit Guarantee Scheme*
Introductory Remarks
At an initial stage, the prospect of establishing a European deposit guarantee scheme (EDIS), as the third main component of the BU, had only been discussed in terms of principles and 'high-level' politics. Thus, no specific regulatory proposals had been tabled by the Commission on this field; deposit guarantee schemes (DGSs) had thus far remained national, albeit subject to minimum harmonisation under Directive 2014/49/EU.[249] The prospective of creating an EDIS was laid down in the **'Five Presidents Report'** of **22 June 2015** "Completing Europe's Economic and Monetary Union", which was included in the system of proposals for creating an (EU) **'Financial Union'**.[250] According to this Report, the EDIS would increase resilience against future crises and is also more likely to be fiscally neutral over time than national DGSs, since risks are spread more widely, and private contributions are raised over a much larger pool of financial institutions.

The November 2015 Commission's Proposal for a Regulation
(1) On **24 November 2015**, the Commission submitted a proposal for a Regulation of the co-legislators "amending [the SRMR] in order to establish a European Deposit Insurance Scheme".[251] The EDIS should be introduced gradually, in three phases. The proposal included a series of strict safeguards, according to which the EDIS should be built on the existing system, composed of national DGSs; be overall cost-neutral for the banking sector (since credit institutions' contributions to the EDIS would be deducted from those to the national DGSs); be risk-weighted (with 'riskier' credit institutions having to pay relatively higher contributions); and be accompanied by strict safeguards against moral hazard and inappropriate use (giving incentives to national DGSs to manage their potential risks in a prudent way) and by a Communication setting out measures to reduce risks. A European Deposit Insurance Fund (**'EDIF'**) would also have been set up from the outset, directly

---

[248] As already noted in Chapter 2 above (under 2.4.3), these lay down the core elements for an effective regime governing the resolution of financial firms that could be systemic in failure. On the BRRD, see further Chapter 6 below, under 6.4.

[249] See just below.

[250] At: https://ec.europa.eu/priorities/economic-monetary-union/docs/5-presidents-report_en.pdf.

[251] At: https://ec.europa.eu/finance/general-policy/docs/banking-union/european-deposit-insurance-scheme/151124-proposal_en.pdf.

financed through risk-adjusted contributions made by credit institutions. Its management would be entrusted to the SRB.[252]

> **Box 4.5 The three phases in the evolution of the EDIS in accordance with the 2015 Commission's legislative proposal**
>
> | Phases | Development |
> | --- | --- |
> | Phase 1: reinsurance | Applicable during the first three-year phase (**2007–2009**) would have been 'reinsurance', whereby a national DGS would have access to EDIS funds only when all its own resources would have been exhausted and fully comply with the (new) **DGS Directive** (see just below). EDIS funds would have provided additional funds to a national DGS only up to a certain level and the latter would have had access to the EDIS only when justified. Use of EDIS funds would have been closely monitored, and any such funds found to have been inappropriately received by a national DGS should be fully reimbursed[253] |
> | Phase 2: co-insurance | In 2020, the EDIS would have become a progressively mutualised system (the 'co-insurance' phase), still subject to appropriate limits and safeguards against abuse. During this phase, a national DGS would not have been required to exhaust its own funds before accessing EDIS funds and the EDIS would have been available to contribute a share of the costs from the moment when the DGS would have been activated to reimburse depositors, leading to a higher degree of *"risk-sharing between national DGSs through the EDIS"*. The share to have been contributed by the EDIS would have started at a level of 20% and would have gradually increased to 80% over a four-year period[254] |
> | Phase 3: full insurance | The EDIS would have fully insured national DGSs as of **2024**, when the SRF and the requirements of the DGS Directive would have been *fully* phased in.[255] The mechanism would be equal to that in the co-insurance phase, with the EDIS covering, albeit in this case, a share of 100% |

---

[252] Regulation Proposal, Article 2(34), inserting new Articles 74a–74g, Article 2(35), Article 2(36), replacing Article 75 SRMR, Article 2(37), inserting a new Article 77a to the SRMR and Article 2(38)–(41). On this scheme, see, by means of indication, Gros (2015), Carmassi *et al.* (2018), Schnabel and Véron (2018), Brescia Morra (2019), Gortsos (2019b) (in detail) and Montalbano (2021), pp. 197–228 (with extensive further references).

[253] Regulation Proposal, Article 2(10) inserting new Articles 41a–41c.

[254] *Ibid.*, Article 2(10), inserting new Articles 41d–41g.

[255] *Ibid.*, Article 2(10), inserting new Article 41h.

4.4.5.2 The Single Rulebook

The operation of national DGSs is governed by the **'Deposit Guarantee Schemes Directive'** of the co-legislators of 16 April 2014[256] (**'DGSD'**), which repealed Directive 94/19/EC as of **3 July 2015**.[257] By laying down rules and procedures on the establishment and functioning of national DGSs in Member States, the DGSD substantially modified certain aspects of the 1994 Directive, while concurrently containing several innovative elements.[258] The impact of public international financial law on the content of the DGSD is less important than in the case of the CRR, the CRD IV and the BRRD, since most of the principles contained in the 2014 "IADI Core Principles for Effective Deposit Insurance Systems"[259] were already incorporated into EU law (Fig. 4.2).

---

[256] Directive 2014/49/EU "on deposit guarantee schemes", OJ L 173, 12.6.2014, pp. 149–178.

[257] On Directive 94/19/EC, see above, under 4.2.2.

[258] On the DGSD, see further Chapter 6 below, under 6.6. It is also noted that, at the broader European level, national DGSs cooperate within the European Forum of Deposit Insurers ('EFDI'), which was set up in 2002 (like the IADI). In December 2022, the EFDI, which has its seat in Brussels and formally became an international non-profit association in June 2007, was participated in by 68 member institutions (DGSs and ICSs) from 49 countries located in Europe or in a Member State of the Council of Europe (including all EU Member States). Its objective consists mainly in investigating, analysing and exploring cross-border issues, burden-sharing and the efficiency of its members. It also plays an important role, upon explicit request of the Commission, in the ongoing review and amendment of EU legislation on DGSs. It also works closely, *inter alia*, with the ECB, the World Bank, the IMF and the IADI. For more information on its composition and work, see at: https://www.efdi.eu/efdi.

[259] See Chapter 2 above, under 2.4.3.

Table 4.2 The key legal sources of the three main pillars of the Banking Union (BU) for credit institutions

	Prudential supervision and regulation (SSM)	Resolution (SRM)	Deposit guarantee schemes (EDIS)
EU 'Single Mechanisms'	Council Regulation (EU) No 1024/2013 (**SSM Regulation**) ECB Regulation (EU) No 468/2014 (**SSM-FR**) and other ECB legal acts	Regulation (EU) No 806/2014 of the co-legislators (**SRM Regulation**) and Commission delegated and implementing acts Intergovernmental Agreement (2014) (**SRF**)	Proposal for a Regulation of the co-legislators "amending Regulation EU No 806/2014 in order to establish an **EDIS**"
Harmonisation of substantive rules ('single rulebook')	Regulation (EU) No 575/2013 (**CRR**) and Directive 2013/36/EU (**CRD IV**) of the co-legislators, and Commission delegated and implementing acts	Directive 2014/59/EU of the co-legislators (**BRRD**) and Commission delegated and implementing acts	Directive 2014/49/EU of the co-legislators and a Commission delegated act (**DGSD**)

Secondary Sources

A

Acharya, V.V. (2012): Banking Union in Europe and Other Reforms, in Beck, T. (2012, editor): *Banking Union for Europe – Risks and Challenges,* Centre for Economic Policy Research (CEPR), London, UK, pp. 45–49

Acharya, V.V., Cooley, T., Richardson, M. and I. Walter (2011): *Regulating Wall Street - the Dodd-Frank Act and the New Architecture of Global Finance,* Wiley, New York

Aditya, P. D. (2013): *European Markets Infrastructure Regulation (EMIR) and Dodd-Frank Wall Street Reform and Consumer Protection Act (DFA): A New Revolution of OTC Derivatives towards Transparency,* available at: https://ssrn.com/abstract=2314998

Aizenman, J. (2012): US Banking over Two Centuries: Lessons for the Eurozone Crisis, in Beck, T. (2012, editor): *Banking Union for Europe – Risks and Challenges,* Centre for Economic Policy Research (CEPR), London, UK, pp. 129–135

Alexander, K. (2022): The ECB's role in the European Banking Union, in Beukers, T., Fromage, D. and G. Monti (2022, editors): *The New European Central Bank: Taking Stock and Looking Ahead,* Oxford University Press, Oxford, Chapter 7

Alexander, K. (2019): *Principles of Banking Regulation,* Cambridge University Press, Cambridge, United Kingdom

Alexander, K. (2016): The ECB and Banking Supervision: Does Single Supervisory Mechanism Provide an Effective Regulatory Framework?, in Andenas, M.

and G. Deipenbrock (2016, editors): *Regulating and Supervising European Financial Markets – More Risks Than Achievements*, Springer International Publishing, Switzerland, pp. 253–276

Alexy, R. (2014): Constitutional Rights and Proportionality, *Revus – Journal for Constitutional Theory and Philosophy of Law*, Issue 22, pp. 51–65 (also available at: https://journals.openedition.org/revus/2781)

Allen, F., Carletti, E. and J. Gray (2013, editors): *Political, Fiscal and Banking Union in the Eurozone?*, FIC Press, Wharton Financial Institutions Center, Philadelphia, USA, available at: https://hdl.handle.net/1814/28478

Allen, F., Carletti, E. and J. Gray (2014, editors): *Bearing the Losses from Bank and Sovereign Default in the Eurozone*, FIC Press, Wharton Financial Institutions Center, Philadelphia, USA available at: https://hdl.handle.net/1814/34437

Allen, F., Carletti, E. and J. Gray (2015, editors): *The New Financial Architecture in the Eurozone*, European University Institute (EUI)

Andenas, M., Gormley, L., Hadjiemmanuil, Ch. and I. Harden (1997, editors): *European Economic and Monetary Union – The Institutional Framework*, International Banking, Finance and Economic Law Series, Kluwer Law International, United Kingdom

Andenas, M. and Ch. Hadjiemmanuil (1997): Banking Supervision, the Internal Market and European Monetary Union, in Andenas, M., Gormley, L., Hadjiemmanuil, Ch. and I. Harden (1997, editors): *European Economic and Monetary Union – The Institutional Framework*, International Banking, Finance and Economic Law Series, Kluwer Law International, United Kingdom, Chapter 18, pp. 375–417

Annunziata, F. (2022): *Towards an EU Charter for the Protection of End Users in Financial Markets*, Bocconi Legal Studies Research Paper No. 4200502 (also in European Banking Institute Working Paper Series, No. 128, available at: https://ssrn.com/abstract_id=4200502)

Armour, J., Bengtzen, M. and L. Enriques (2017): *Investor Choice in Global Securities Markets*, Law Working Paper No 371/2017, October, available at: https://ssrn.com/abstract=3047734

Athanassiou, Ph. (2011): Of Past Measures and Future Plans for Europe's Exit from the Sovereign Debt Crisis: What is Legally Possible and What Not, *European Law Review*, Volume 36, issue 4, pp. 558–575

Avgouleas, E. (2008): International Financial Regulation, Access to Finance, Systemic Stability, and Development, *LAWASIA Journal*, pp. 62–76

Avgouleas, E. and D.W. Arner (2013): *The Eurozone Debt Crisis and the European Banking Union: A Cautionary Tale of Failure and Reform*, University of Hong Kong Faculty of Law Research Paper No. 2013/037, available at: https://ssrn.com/abstract=2347937

Ayadi, R. and A. Resti (2004): *The New Basel Capital Accord and the Future of the European Financial System*, CEPS Task Force Report No. 51, CEPS

B

Babis, V. (2019): The Single Rulebook and the European Banking Authority, in Fabbrini, F. and M. Ventoruzzo (2019, editors): *Research Handbook on EU Economic Law*, Edward Elgar Publishing, Cheltenham, UK – Northampton, MA, USA, Chapter 10, pp. 262–386

Badenhoop, N. (2020): Europäische Bankenregulierung und private Haftung - Die Durchsetzung von System- und Individualschutz mit Mitteln des Privatrechts, Schriften zum Unternehmens- und Kapitalmarktrecht 81, Mohr Siebeck, Tübingen

Bakk-Simon, K. et al. (2012): Shadow Banking in the Euro Area: An Overview, *ECB Occasional Paper Series No. 2012133*, April, available at: https://ssrn.com/abstract=4022867

Barnard, C. and S. Peers (2020): *European Union Law*, 3rd edition, Oxford University Press, Oxford

Beck, T. (2012, editor): *Banking Union for Europe – Risks and Challenges*, Centre for Economic Policy Research (CEPR), London, UK

Becker, U. (2019): Kommentar zum Artikel 3 EUV, in Schwarze, J., Becker, U., Hatje, A. und J. Schoo (2019, Hrsg.): *EU-Kommentar*, 4. Auflage, Nomos Verlagsgesellschaft, Baden-Baden, pp. 53–59

Belke, A. (2010): *The Euro Area Crisis Management Framework: Consequences and Institutional Follow-ups*, Ruhr Economic Papers No. 207, Ruhr-Universität Bochum, Germany, September, available at: https://econpapers.repec.org/paper/rwirepape/0207.htm

Berg and (2019): Kommentar zum Artikel 340 AEUV, in Becker, U., Hatje, A. Schoo, J. und J. Schwarze, , 2019.Berg, W. (2019): Kommentar zum Artikel 340 AEUV, in Becker, U., Hatje, A. Schoo, J. und J. Schwarze (2019, Herausgeber): *EU-Kommentar*, 4. Auflage, Nomos Verlagsgesellschaft, Baden-Baden, pp. 3244–3283

Binder, J.-H. (2016): The European Banking Union – Rationale and Key Policy Issues, in Binder, J.-H. and Ch.V. Gortsos (2016): *Banking Union: A Compendium*, Verlag C.H. Beck, München – Hart, Oxford – Nomos Verlagsgesellschaft, Baden-Baden

Binder, J.-H. (2014): *To Ring-Fence or Not, and How? Strategic Questions for Post-Crisis Banking Reform in Europe*, available at: https://ssrn.com/abstract=2543860

Binder, J.-H. and Ch.V. Gortsos (2016): *Banking Union: A Compendium*, Verlag C.H. Beck, München – Hart, Oxford – Nomos Verlagsgesellschaft, Baden-Baden

Binder, J.-H., Gortsos, Ch.V., Lackhoff, K. and Ch. Ohler (2022, editors): *Brussels Commentary on the Banking Union*, Verlag C.H. Beck, München – Hart Publishing, Oxford – Nomos Verlagsgesellschaft, Baden-Baden

Bini-Smaghi, L., Padoa-Schioppa, T. and F. Papadia (1994): *The Transition to EMU in the Maastricht Treaty*, Essays in International Finance, No 194, Princeton University, Princeton, N.J.

Blair, M., Walker, G. and R. Purves (2009, editors): *Financial Services Law*, second edition, Oxford University Press, Oxford – New York

Bofinger, P., Bush, Cl.M., Feld, L.P., Franz, W. and C.M. Schmidt (2012): *From the Internal Market to a Banking Union: A proposal by the German Council of Economic Experts*, VOX, 12 November

Brescia Morra, C. (2019): The Third Pillar of the Banking Union and its Troubled Implementation, in Chiti, M.P. and V. Santoro (2019, editors): *The Palgrave Handbook of European Banking Union Law*, Chapter 17, pp. 393–407, Palgrave Macmillan, Cham – Switzerland

Busch, D. and Ch.V. Gortsos (2022): Liability of the European Central Bank, the Single Resolution Board and the ESAs (ESMA, EBA and EIOPA), in Busch, D., Gortsos, Ch.V. and G. McMeel (2022, editors): *Liability of Financial Supervisors and Resolution Authorities*, Chapter 2, pp. 9–54

Busch, D. and G. Ferrarini (2020, editors): *European Banking Union*, Oxford EU Financial Regulation Series, second edition, Oxford University Press, Oxford

Busch, D. and G. Ferrarini (2017, editors): *Regulation of EU Financial Markets: MiFID II*, Oxford University Press, United Kingdom

Busch, D. and M. Louisse (2017): MiFID II/MiFIR's Regime for Third-Country Firms, in Busch, D. and G. Ferrarini (2017, editors): *Regulation of the EU Financial Markets: MiFID II and MiFIR*, Oxford University Press, Oxford, Chapter 10

Busch, D. and L. van Setten (2014): The Alternative Investment Fund Managers Directive, in Busch, D. and L. van Setten (2014, editors): *Alternative Investment Funds in Europe*, Chapter 1, Oxford University Press, Oxford, pp. 1–122

C

Caminal, R.O. (2012): *The EU Architecture to Avert a Sovereign Debt Crisis*, in Organisation for Economic Cooperation and Development (2012): *OECD Journal: Financial Market Trends*, Issue 2, Paris, 23 March, pp. 1–32

Carmassi, J., Dobkowitz, S., Evrard, J., Parisi, L., Silva, A. and M. Wedow (2018): Completing the Banking Union with a European Deposit Insurance Scheme: Who Is Afraid of Cross-Subsidisation?, *ECB Occasional Paper Series No. 208*, April, available at: https://ssrn.com/abstract_id=3161390

Castaneda, J., Karamichailidou, G., Mayes, D. and G. Wood (2015, editors): *European Banking Union. Prospects and Challenges*, Routledge, available at: https://ssrn.com/abstract=2540038

Chiti, M.P. and V. Santoro (2019, editors): *The Palgrave Handbook of European Banking Union Law*, Palgrave Macmillan, Cham – Switzerland

Chiu, I.H-Y. and J. Wilson (2019): *Banking Law and Regulation*, Oxford University Press, Oxford

Colaert, V. (2017): MiFID II in Relation to Other Investor Protection Regulation: Picking Up the Crumbs of a Piecemeal Approach, in Busch, D. and G. Ferrarini (2017, editors): *Regulation of the EU Financial Markets: MiFID II and MiFIR*, Oxford University Press, Oxford, Chapter 21 (also at: https://ssrn.com/abstract=2942688)

Colaert, V., Busch, D. and T. Incalza (2019, editors): *European Financial Regulation: Levelling the Cross-Sectoral Playing Field*, Hart Publishing, Oxford

Craig, P. (2011): The ECJ and *Ultra Vires* Action: a Conceptual Analysis, *Common Market Law Review*, Volume 48, Issue 2, pp. 395–437

Craig, P. and G. de Búrca (2020): *EU Law: Texts, Cases, and Materials*, Seventh edition, Oxford University Press, Oxford – New York

D

D' Arvisenet, Ph. (2015): The Genesis of the Eurozone Sovereign Debt Crisis, in Christodoulakis, G. (2015, editor): *Managing Risks in the European Periphery Debt Crisis: Lessons from the Trade-off Between Economics, Politics and the Financial Markets*, Palgrave Macmillan, Hampshire and New York, pp. 3–37

De Grauwe, P. (2020): *Economics of Monetary Union*, 13th Edition, Oxford University Press, Oxford – New York

De Grauwe, P. (2013): *Design Failures in the Eurozone: Can They Be Fixed?*, London School of Economics, "Europe in Question" Discussion Paper Series, February

Dehousse, R. (1989): 1992 and Beyond: The Institutional Dimension of the Internal Market Programme, *Legal Issues of European Integration*, Volume 1, No. 1, pp. 109–136

Den Heijer, M., Van den Abeelen, T. and A. Maslyka (2019): *On the Use and Misuse of Recitals in European Union Law*, Amsterdam Law School Research Paper No. 2019-31, Amsterdam Center for International Law No. 2019-15, 30 August, available at: https://ssrn.com/abstract=3445372

Dermine, J. (2003): Banking in Europe: Past, Present and Future, in Gaspar, V., Hartmann, Ph. And O. Sleijpen (2003, editors): *The Transformation of the European Financial System*, Second ECB Central Banking Conference, European Central Bank, May, p. 31–95

Di Noia, C. (2012): *Reviewing the EU's Market Abuse Rules*, European Capital Markets Institute (ECMI) Policy Brief No. 19, 27 February

Dierick, F., Pires, F. Scheicher, M. and K.G. Spitzer (2005): *The New Basel Capital Framework and Its Implementation in the European Union*, Occasional Paper Series No. 42, European Central Bank, December (also available at: https://ssrn.com/abstract=807416)

Drossos, Y. (2020): *The Flight of Icarus: European Legal Responses Resulting from the Financial Crisis*, Hart Publishing, Oxford

Dumler, M.T. (2013): *The Volcker Rule: Has Anything Changed?*, Moral Cents Volume 2, Issue 1, Winter/Spring, Seven Pillars Institute

E

Eichengreen, B., Feldmann, R., Liebman, J., von Jürgen, H. and Ch. Wyplosz (2011): *Public Debts: Nuts, Bolts and Worries*, Geneva Report on the World Economy 13, International Center for Monetary and Banking Studies (ICMB), Geneva, Switzerland

Enoch, Ch. (2021): *Europe Beyond the Euro: Building Protection for Europe's Economies in the Times of Risks*, St Antony's Series (Series Editors Healey D. and L. Payne), Palgrave Macmillan, Cham – Switzerland

European Central Bank (2005): *Legal Aspects of the European System of Central Banks – Liber amicorum Paolo Zamboni Garavelli*, European Central Bank, Frankfurt, available at: https://www.ecb.europa.eu/pub/pdf/other/legalaspectsescben.pdf

European Central Bank (2008): *Financial Integration in Europe*, European Central Bank, April

European Central Bank (2007): *Financial Integration in Europe*, European Central Bank, March

European Commission (2000): *Institutional Arrangements for the Regulation and Supervision of the Financial Sector*, Internal Market Directorate General, January

F

Faure, M. and C. Leger (2014): *Towards a Harmonization of Insider Trading Criminal Law at EU Level?*, Rotterdam Institute of Law and Economics (RILE) Working Paper Series No.13

Ferran, E. (2004): *Building an EU Securities Market*, Cambridge University Press, Cambridge, New York, Melbourne, Madrid, Cape Town, Singapore, São Paolo

Ferran, E. and K. Alexander (2011): *Can Soft Law Bodies be Effective? Soft Systemic Risk Oversight Bodies and the Special Case of the European Systemic Risk Board*, University of Cambridge Faculty of Law Research Papers, No. 36, available at: https://ssrn.com/abstract=1676140

Ferrarini, G. and F. Chiodini (2009): Regulating Cross-Border Banks in Europe: A Comment on the de Larosière Report and a Modest Proposal, *Capital Markets Law Journal*, Volume 4, pp. 123–140

Ferrarini, G. and P. Saguato (2014): *Regulating Financial Market Infrastructures*, European Corporate Governance Institute (ECGI) Law Working Paper No 259/2014, June

Ferrarini, G. and P. Saguato (2013): Reforming Securities and Derivatives Trading in the EU: from EMIR to MiFIR, *Journal of Corporate Law Studies*, Volume 13, Issue 2, pp. 319–359

Ferrarini, G. and Ed. Wymeersch (2006, editors): *Investor Protection in Europe, Corporate Law Making, the MiFID and beyond*, Oxford University Press, Oxford – New York

Fleischer, H. and K. Schmolke (2012): *Financial Incentives for Whistleblowers in European Capital Markets Law? Legal Policy Considerations on the Reform of the Market Abuse Regime*, ECGI Law Working Paper No. 189, available at: https://ssrn.com/abstract=2124678

Freixas, X., Hartmann, P. and C. Mayer (2004): The Assessment: European Financial Integration, *Oxford Review of Economic Policy*, Volume 20, no. 4

G

Galati, G. and K. Tsatsaronis (2003): The Impact of the Euro on Europe's Financial Markets, *Financial Markets, Institutions and Instruments*, Volume 12, Issue 2, New York University Salomon Center

Gambacorta, L. and A. van Rixtel (2013): *Structural Bank Regulation Initiatives: Approaches and Implications*, BIS Working Papers No. 412, Monetary and Economic Department, Bank for International Settlements, April

García Alcubilla, R. and J. Ruiz del Pozo (2012): *Credit Rating Agencies on the Watch List: Analysis of European Regulation*, Oxford University Press, Oxford

Gortsos, Ch.V. (2023): *Legal Aspects of the Single Monetary Policy in the Euro Area: From the Establishment of the Eurosystem to the Pandemic Crisis and the Current Inflation Crisis*, Fifth fully updated edition, available at: https://ssrn.com/abstract=3819726

Gortsos, Ch.V. (2022): Historical Evolution of Bank Capital Requirements in the European Union, in Joosen, B., Lamandini, M. and T. Tröger (2022, editors): *Capital and Liquidity Requirements for European Banks: CRRII and CRDV*, Oxford EU Financial Regulation Series (main editors D. Busch and G. Ferrarini), Oxford University Press, Oxford, Part I, Chapter 1, pp. 3–42

Gortsos, Ch.V. (2020): *European Central Banking Law – The Role of the European Central Bank and National Central Banks Under European Law*, Palgrave Macmillan Studies in Banking and Financial Institutions, Palgrave Macmillan, Cham – Switzerland

Gortsos, Ch.V. (2019a): Identifying Groups as 'Financial Conglomerates' Under European Financial Law (Directive 2002/87/EC): A Not so Straightforward Exercise, in *Liber Amicorum of Emeritus Professor Thanassis Papachristou*, Nomiki Bibliothiki – Athens (also available at: https://ssrn.com/abstract=3066037)

Gortsos, Ch.V. (2019b): The European Deposit Insurance Scheme (EDIS), in Fabbrini, F. and M. Ventoruzzo (2019, editors): *Research Handbook on EU Economic Law*, Edward Elgar Publishing, Cheltenham, UK – Northampton, MA, USA, Chapter 13, pp. 366–395

Gortsos, Ch.V. (2019c): European Banking Union Within the System of European Banking and Monetary Law, in Chiti, M.P. and V. Santoro (2019, editors): *The Palgrave Handbook of European Banking Union Law*, Palgrave – Macmillan, USA, Chapter 2, pp. 19–40

Gortsos, Ch.V. (2018a): *Stricto Sensu Investor Protection Under the 'MiFID II': A Systematic Overview of Articles 24-30*, Cambridge Scholars Publishing, Cambridge

Gortsos, Ch.V. (2018b): The Scope of the EU Alternative Investment Fund Managers Directive (2011/61/EU) and Its Significance for EU Investment Funds Law (2018), in *Dignatio Rerum Professor Elias Krispis*, Sakkoulas Publications, Athens – Thessaloniki, pp. 207–232 (also available at: https://ssrn.com/abstract=3000356)

Gortsos, Ch.V. (2017): Public Enforcement of MiFID II, in Busch, D. and G. Ferrarini (2017, editors): *Regulation of the EU Financial Markets: MiFID II and MiFIR*, Chapter 19, Oxford University Press, Oxford

Gortsos, Ch.V. (2010): The Proposals of the Larosière Group on the Future of Financial Supervision in the European Union, in Giovanoli, M. and D. Devos (2010, editors): *International Monetary and Financial Law: The Global Crisis*, Oxford University Press, Oxford – New York, Chapter 6, pp. 127–145

Gortsos, Ch.V. (1996): *Supranational and International Regimes for the Prudential Regulation of International Banks*, Graduate Institute of International Studies, University of Geneva, Geneva

Gros, D. (2015): *Completing the Banking Union: Deposit Insurance*, CEPS Policy Brief No. 335, December, Centre for European Policy Studies, available at: https://ssrn.com/abstract=2721668

Grundmann, S. (2015): The Banking Union Translated into (Private Law) Duties: Infrastructure and Duties, in Grundmann, S. and J.-H. Binder (2015, editors): The Banking Union and the Creation of Duties, *European Business Organisation Law Review*, Volume 16, issue 3, Springer – Asser Press, pp. 357–382

Grundmann, S. and P. Sirena (2019): *European Contract Law in the Banking and Financial Union*, European Contract Law and Theory (EUCOLATH) Series, Volume 4, Intersentia, Cambridge, UK

Gruson, M. (2004): *Supervision of Financial Conglomerates in the European Union*, Paper presented at the Seminar on Current Developments in Monetary and Financial Law (May 24-June 4, 2004), IMF

H

Hadjiemmanuil, Ch. (2020): The Euro Area in Crisis: 2008–2018, in Amtenbrink, F. and Ch. Herrmann (2020, editors): *Oxford Handbook on the EU Law of Economic and Monetary Union*, Oxford University Press, Oxford, Chapter 40, pp. 1253–1362 (also published in LSE Law, Society and Economy Working Papers 12/2019, available at: https://ssrn.com/abstract=3413000)

Hadjiemmanuil, Ch. (2006a): Economic and Monetary Union, in Chalmers, D., Hadjiemmanuil, Ch., Monti, G. and A. Tomkins (2006, editors): *European Union Law*, Cambridge University Press, Cambridge, New York, Melbourne, Madrid, Cape Town, Singapore, São Paolo, Chapter 12, pp. 506–560

Hadjiemmanuil, Ch. (2006b): Financial Services, in Chalmers, D., Hadjiemmanuil, Ch., Monti, G. and A. Tomkins (2006, editors): *European Union Law*, Cambridge University Press, Cambridge, New York, Melbourne, Madrid, Cape Town, Singapore, São Paolo, Chapter 18, pp. 781–829

Haentjens, M. (2021): Private law in Banking Union litigation, in Zilioli, Ch. and K.-Ph. Wojcik (2021, editors): *Judicial review in the European Banking Union*, Edward Elgar Publisher, Cheltenham, UK – Northampton, MA, USA, Chapter 5, pp. 59–76

Hellstén, L. (2015): *Disclosure and Delayed Disclosure of Inside Information in the Light of the EU Market Abuse Regulation*, University of Helsinki

Herring, R.J. (2013): The Danger of Building a Banking Union on a One-Legged Stool, in Allen, F., Carletti, E. and J. Gray (2013, editors): *Political, Fiscal and Banking Union in the Eurozone?*, FIC Press, Wharton Financial Institutions Center, Philadelphia, USA, Chapter 2, pp. 9–28

Herring, R.J. and R.E. Litan (1995): *Financial Regulation in the Global Economy*, The Brookings Institution, Washington, DC, available at: www.brookings.edu/comm/conferencereport/cr14.htm

Herrnfeld, H.-H. (2019): Kommentar zum Artikel 114 AEUV, in Becker, U., Hatje, A. Schoo, J. und J. Schwarze (2019, Herausgeber): *EU-Kommentar*, 4. Auflage, Nomos Verlagsgesellschaft, Baden-Baden, pp. 1869–1935

Hinojosa L.M. and J.M. Beneyto (2015, editors): *European Banking Union: The New Regime*, International Banking and Financial Law Series Volume 27, Kluwer Law International

House of Lords (2012): *European Banking Union: Key Issues and Challenges*, European Union Committee, 7th Report of Session 2012-13, HL Paper 88, London, 12 December

Huertas, T. (2013): Safe to fail, *Butterworths Journal of International Banking and Financial Law*, July/August

I–J

International Monetary Fund (2013): *Euro Area Policies*, 2013 Article IV Consultation, IMF Country Report No. 13/231, Washington, D.C.

Ioannidis, M. (2020): The European Central Bank, in Amtenbrink, F. and Ch. Herrmann (2020, editors): *The EU Law of Economic and Monetary Union*, Oxford University Press, Oxford, Chapter 14, pp. 353–388

Issing, O. (2008): *The Birth of the Euro*, Cambridge University Press, Cambridge, United Kingdom

Issing, O., Gaspar, V., Angeloni, I. and O. Tristani (2001): *Monetary Policy in the Euro Area*, Cambridge University Press, Cambridge, United Kingdom

Jans, J.A. (2022): *Towards a Level-Playing Field Between Banks and Non-Banks in the European Market for Electronic Payments*, Vrije Universiteit Amsterdam

Joosen, B. and M. Lehmann (2019): Proportionality in the Single Rule Book, in Chiti, M.P. and V. Santoro (2019, editors): *The Palgrave Handbook of European Banking Union Law*, Chapter 4, pp. 65–90, Palgrave Macmillan, Cham – Switzerland

Jung, P. – E. Bishof (2015): *Europäisches Finanzmarktecht: Die Regulierung von Märkten, Unternehmen und Dienstleistungen durch die Europäische Union*, Nomos Verlagsgesellschaft, Baden-Baden, Dike Verlag, Zürich/St. Gallen

K

Kellerhals, A. (2006): *Wirtschaftrecht and europäische Integration*, Wirtschaftsrecht und Wirtschaftspolitik, Band 200, Nomos Verlagsgesellschaft, Baden-Baden – Schulthess, Zürich

Keppenne, J.-P. (2020): EU Fiscal Governance on the Member States: The Stability and Growth Pact and Beyond, in Amtenbrink, F. and Ch. Herrmann (2020, editors): *Oxford Handbook on the EU Law of Economic and Monetary Union*, Oxford University Press, Oxford, Chapter 28, pp. 813–849

Kerjean, S. (2008): *The Legal Implications of the Prudential Supervisory Assessment of Bank Mergers and Acquisitions Under EU Law*, European Central Bank, Legal Working Paper Series, No 6, 26 June

Kilian, W. (2008): *Europäisches Wirtschaftrecht*, Juristische Kurzlehrbücher, Verlag C.H. Beck, München

Kleftouri, N. (2015): *Deposit Protection and Bank Resolution*, Oxford University Press, Oxford

Krahnen, J.P. (2013): *Rescue by Regulation? Key Points of the Liikanen Report*, White Paper Series No. 9, Center of Excellence SAFE (Sustainable Architecture for Finance in Europe)

L

Lambrinoc, S.E. (2009): *The Legal Duty to Consult the European Central Bank*, European Central Bank, Frankfurt, Legal Working Paper Series, No 9, November

Langenbucher, K. (2017): *Economic Transplants – On Lawmaking for Corporations and Capital Markets*, International Corporate Law and Financial Market Regulation, Cambridge University Press, Cambridge

Lastra, R.M. (2015): *International Financial and Monetary Law*, second edition, Oxford University Press, United Kingdom

Lastra, R.M. (2013): Banking Union and Single Market: Conflict or Companionship?, *Fordham International Law Journal*, Volume 36, pp. 1189-1223

Lastra, R.M. (2006): *Legal Foundations of International Monetary Stability*, Oxford University Press, Oxford-New York

Lastra, R.M. and Ch. Goodhart (2015): *Interaction Between Monetary and Bank Regulation*, Monetary Dialogue Papers, European Parliament, September at: https://op.europa.eu/en/publication-detail/-/publication/3d05d3ec-fcb9-11e6-8a35-01aa75ed71a1/language-en, pp. 37–54

Lastra, R.M. and J.V. Louis (2013): European Economic and Monetary Union: History, Trends, and Prospects, *Yearbook of Economic Law*, pp. 1–150

Lastra, R.M. and G. Garri (2009): Assessing the Lamfalussy Process: Successes and Failures, *Butterworth's Journal of International Banking and Financial Law*, Volume 24, Issue 7, pp. 379-383

Lehmann, M. (2021): Jurisdiction, Locus Standi and the Circulation of Judgments in the Banking Union, in Zilioli, Ch. and K.-Ph. Wojcik (2021, editors): *Judicial*

review in the European Banking Union, Edward Elgar Publisher, Cheltenham, UK – Northampton, MA, USA, Chapter 6, pp. 77–96
Lefterov, A. (2015): *The Single Rulebook: Legal Issues and Relevance in the SSM Context*, European Central Bank, Legal Working Paper Series, No 15, October
Louis J.-V. (2012): Vers une Union bancaire, *Cahiers de droit européen*, 2012, 2, pp. 289–304
Louis, J.-V. (2009): L'Union européenne et sa monnaie, in Commentaire J. Megret : *Integration des marchés financiers*, 3ᵉ édition, Institut d' Etudes Européennes, Editions de l' Université de Bruxelles, Bruxelles
Lupoi, A. (2017): *The Sunset of Literal Information, the Dawn of 'Data' Information (Financial Products, EU Prospective)*, available at: https://ssrn.com/abstract=3049273

M–N

Marano, P. and M. Siri (2017): *Insurance Regulation in the European Union – Solvency II and Beyond*, Palgrave Macmillan, Cham – Switzerland
Masciandaro, D., Quintyn, M. and R. Vega Pansini (2012): The Economic Crisis: A Story of Supervisory Failure and Ideas for the Way Forward, in Balling, M., Lierman, F., Van den Spiegel, F., Ayadi, R. & D.T. Llewellyn (2012, editors): *New Paradigms in Banking, Financial Markets and Regulation?*, SUERF Study 2012/2, SUERF, Vienna
Mauerhofer, G. (1998): *Die Wertpapierdiensleistungsrichtlinie*, Schriften zum gesamten Europarecht, Manzsche Verlags- und Universitätsbuchhandlung, Wien
McPhilemy, S. and J. Roche (2013): *Review of the New European System of Financial Supervision (ESFS) Part 2: The Work of the European Systemic Risk Board – The ESFS'S Macro-Prudential Pillar*, European Parliament, Directorate General for Internal Policies, IP/A/ECON/ST/2012-23, October, available at: https://op.europa.eu/en/publication-detail/-/publication/77093691-8b67-4e10-8ee5-c777b416067b/language-en
Miglionico, A. (2019): *The Governance of Credit Rating Agencies: Regulatory and Liability Issues*, Elgar Financial Law and Practice, Edward Elgar Publishing, Cheltenham, UK – Northampton, MA, USA, pp. 128–139 and 227–240
Mitchener, K.J. (2014): The Diabolic Loop: Precedents and Legacies, in Allen, F., Carletti, E. and J. Gray (2014, editors): *Bearing the Losses from Bank and Sovereign Default in the Eurozone*, FIC Press, Wharton Financial Institutions Center, Philadelphia, USA, Chapter 12, pp. 165–180
Möllers, T. (2015): *The Progress of German Information Disclosure Requirements: A Comparative Law Prospective in Light of Recent Developments in European Capital Markets Law*, available at: https://ssrn.com/abstract=1709897
Moloney, N. (2014a): *EU Securities and Financial Markets Regulation*, Oxford European Union Law Library, Third edition, Oxford University Press, Oxford
Moloney, N. (2014b): European Banking Union: Assessing Its Risks and Resilience, *Common Market Law Review*, Volume 51, Issue 6, pp. 1609–1670, available at: https://eprints.lse.ac.uk/60572
Moloney, N. (2008): *EC Securities Regulation*, Oxford EC Law Library, Second edition, Oxford University Press, Oxford – New York
Moloney, N. (2005): Building a Retail Investment Culture Through Law: The 2004 Markets in Financial Instruments Directive, *European Business Organization*

Law Review, Volume 6, p. 341–422 (also available at: https://ssrn.com/abstact=819964)

Montalbano, G. (2021): *Competing Interest Groups and Lobbying in the Construction of the European Banking Union*, Palgrave Macmillan, Cham – Switzerland

Muñoz, D.R. (2016): Shadow Banking: The Blind Spot in Banking and Capital Markets Reform, *European Company and Financial Law Review*, Volume 13, no. 1, pp. 157-196

Norberg, J. (2009): *Financial Fiasco: How America's Infatuation with Homeownership and Easy Money Created the Economic crisis*, Cato Institute, Washington, DC

O–P–R

Ohler, Ch. (2022): Commentary on Article 1 SSMR, in Binder, J.-H., Gortsos, Ch.V., Lackhoff, K. and Ch. Ohler (2022, editors): *Brussels Commentary on the Banking Union*, Verlag C.H. Beck, München – Hart Publishing, Oxford – Nomos Verlagsgesellschaft, Baden-Baden, pp. 1–13

Papathanassiou, Ch. and G. Zagouras (2012): The European Framework for Macro-Prudential Oversight, in Wymeersch, Ed., Hopt, K.J. and G. Ferrarini (2012, editors): *Financial Regulation and Supervision - A Post-Crisis Analysis*, Oxford University Press, Oxford, Chapter 6, pp. 159–171

Pearson, P. (2001a): Consolidated Supervision Directive, in Van Empel, M. and R. Smits (2001a, editors), *Banking and EC Law: Commentary*, Kluwer, Chapter 12

Pearson, P. (2001b): Large Exposures Directive, in Van Empel, M. and R. Smits (2001b, editors), *Banking and EC Law: Commentary*, Kluwer, Chapter 13

Pennesi, F. (2022): *Equivalence in Financial Services: A Legal and Policy Analysis*, EBI Studies in Banking and Capital Markets Law, Palgrave Macmillan, Cham – Switzerland

Pennesi, F. (2021): Equivalence in the Area of Financial Services: An Effective Instrument to Protect EU Financial Stability in Global Capital Markets?, *Common Market Law Review*, Volume 58, Kluwer Academic Publishers, the Netherlands, pp. 39–70

Piantelli, A.M. (2021): *Managing Banking Crises in Europe After the Great Crisis*, Radboud Business Law Institute, Series Law of Business and Finance, Volume 20, Wolters Kluwer Nederland B.V.

Pisani-Ferry, J., Sapir, A., Véron, N. and G.B. Wolff (2012): *What Kind of European Banking Union*, Bruegel, D121, A-2012, 25 June

Posner, R.A. (2010): *The Crisis of Capitalist Democracy*, Harvard University Press, Cambridge – Massachusetts – London, England

Provino, D. (2015): Central Counterparties and Trade Repositories in Post-trading Infrastructure Under EMIR Regulation on OTC Derivatives, University Luiss Guido Carli, Rome

Psaroudakis, G. (2018): The Scope of Financial Stability Considerations in the Fulfilment of the Mandate of the ECB/Eurosystem, *Journal of Financial Regulation*, Volume 4, pp. 119–156

Ramsay, I. (2016): Changing Policy Paradigms of EU Consumer Credit and Debt Regulation, in Leczykiewicz, D. and Weatherill, S. (2016, editors): *The Images of the Consumer in EU Law: Legislation, Free Movement and Competition Law*, Studies of the Oxford Institute of European and Comparative Law, Hart Publishing, Oxford, pp. 159–182

Rajan, R.G. (2010): *Fault Lines: How Hidden Fractures Still Threaten the World Economy*, Princeton University Press, Princeton

S

Scheller, H.K. (2006): *The European Central Bank – History, Role and Functions*, European Central Bank, Frankfurt, Second revised edition

Schnabel, I. and N. Véron (2018): *Breaking the Stalemate on European Deposit Insurance*, Commentary in the VoxEU Debate "Euro Area Reform", VoxEU.org, 7 April, available at: https://cepr.org/voxeu/columns/breaking-stalemate-european-deposit-insurance

Schnyder, A.K. (2005): *Europäisches Banken- und Versicherungsrecht*, Ius Communitatis, C.F. Müller Verlag, Heidelberg

Schoenmaker, D. (2012): Banking union: Where We're Going Wrong, in Beck, T. (2012, editor): *Banking Union for Europe – Risks and Challenges*, Centre for Economic Policy Research (CEPR), London, UK, pp. 97–103

Schoenmaker, D. and T. Peek (2014): *The State of the Banking Sector in Europe*, Organisation for Economic Co-operation and Development, Economics Department Working Papers, No. 1102

Schwarze, J. (2007): *Europäisches Wirtschaftsrecht*, Nomos Verlagsgesellschaft, Baden-Baden

Sethe, R. (2014): MiFID II – Eine Herausforderung für den Finanzplatz Schweiz, *Schweizerische Juristen-Zeitung/ Revue Suisse de Jurisprudence (SJZ)*, pp. 477–489

Sethe, R., Favre, Ol., Hess, M., Kramer, S. and Schott An. (2017, Hrsg.): *Kommentar zum Finanzmarktstrukturgesetz FinFraG*, Schulthess Verlag, Zürich – Basel – Genf

Shambaugh, J.C. (2012): The Euro's Three Crises, *Brookings Papers on Economic Activity*, Spring, The Brookings Institution, pp. 157–231, available at: https://www.brookings.edu/~/media/Projects/BPEA/Spring%202012/2012a_Shambaugh.pdf

Sibert, A. (2012): *Banking Union and a Single Bank Supervisory Mechanism*, Directorate-General for Internal Policies, Banking Union and a Single Banking Supervisory Mechanism, Monetary Dialogue 2012, European Parliament, available at: https://www.europarl.europa.eu/RegData/etudes/note/join/2012/492449/IPOL-ECON_NT(2012)492449_EN.pdf

Smits, R. (2015): The Role of the ESCB in Banking Supervision, in *Legal Aspects of the European System of Central Banks*, ECB E-Book, pp. 199–212

Smits, R. (2005a): The role of the ESCB in Banking Supervision, in European Central Bank (2005): *Legal Aspects of the European System of Central Banks: Liber Amicorum Paolo Zamboni Garavelli*, European Central Bank, pp. 199–212

Smits, R. (2005b): The European Constitution and EMU: an Appraisal, *Common Market Law Review*, Volume 42, pp. 425–468

Smits, R. (2001): Deposit-Guarantee Directive, in Van Empel, M. and R. Smits (2001, editors): *Banking and EC Law Commentary*, Chapter 15, Kluwer, The Hague

Smits, R. (1997): *The European Central Bank – Institutional Aspects*, Kluwer Law International, The Hague

Smolenska, A. and T. Beukers (2022): The ECB and financial stability, *Agnieszka Smolenska and Thomas Beukers*, in Beukers, T., Fromage, D. and G. Monti (2022, editors): *The New European Central Bank: Taking Stock and Looking Ahead*, Oxford University Press, Oxford, Chapter 5

Sousi-Roubi, B. (2007): La politique legislative, dans Dom. Servais (directeur): *Intégration des marchés financiers*, Commentaire J. Megrét, éditions de l' Université de Bruxelles, pp. 23–38

Sousi-Roubi, B. (1995): *Droit bancaire européen*, Dalloz, Paris

Staehelin, L. (2012): *Bankinsolvenzrechtliche Finalität bei der systemischen Abwicklung von Zahlungen und Effektentransaktionen*, Schweizer Schriften zum Finanzmarktrecht, Band 100, Schulthess Verlag, Zürich

Staikouras, P.K. (2012): *A Theoretical and Empirical Review of the EU Regulation on Credit Rating Agencies: In Search of Truth, Not Scapegoats*, New York University Salomon Center, Financial Markets, Institutions & Instruments, Topics in Financial Intermediation, New York University Salomon Center and Wiley Periodicals

Stephanou, C.A. (2013): Building Firewalls: European Responses to the Sovereign Debt Crisis, in Hieronymi, O. and C.A. Stephanou (2013, editors): *International Debt: Economic, Financial, Monetary, Political and Regulatory Aspects*, Chapter 4, pp. 127–158, Palgrave Macmillan, CPI Antony Rowe, Chippenham and Eastbourne, Great Britain

T

Thakor, A. (2012): *The Economic Consequences of the Volcker Rule*, Center for Capital Markets Competitiveness, U.S. Chamber of Commerce, Washington, DC

Thiele, Al. (2021): *Die Europäische Zentralbank*, 2. Auflage, Mohr Siebeck, Tübingen

Tountopoulos, V. (2014): Market Abuse and Private Enforcement, *European Company and Financial Law Review*, Volume 11, no. 3, pp. 297–332

Tridimas, T. (2011): EU Financial Regulation: Federalization, Crisis Management, and Law Reform, in Craig, P. and G. de Búrca (2011, editors): *The Evolution of EU Law*, 2nd edition, Oxford University Press, Oxford - New York, pp. 783–804

V

Van den Bergh, M. (2001): Solvency Ratio Directive and Own Funds Directive, in Van Empel, M. and R. Smits (2001, editors), *Banking and EC Law: Commentary* Kluwer, Chapter 11

Van Empel, M. and R. Smits (2001, editors), *Banking and EC Law: Commentary*, Kluwer

Van Rompuy Report (2012): "Towards a Genuine Economic and Monetary Union", Report of the President of the European Council in Close Collaboration with Jose Manuel Barroso, President of the Commission, Jean-Claude Juncker, President of the Eurogroup, and Mario Draghi, President of the ECB, 5 December, available at: https://www.consilium.europa.eu/uedocs/cms_data/docs/pressdata/en/ec/134069.pdf.

Veil, R. (2022a, editor): *European Capital Markets Law*, Third edition, Hart Publishing, Oxford, UK – New York, NY

Veil, R. (2022b): Takeover Law, in Veil, R. (2022a, editor): *European Capital Markets Law*, Third edition, Hart Publishing, Oxford, UK – New York, NY, Chapters 37–40, pp. 673–699

Veil, R. (2022c): Market Abuse, in Veil, R. (2022b, editor): *European Capital Markets Law*, Third edition, Hart Publishing, Oxford, UK – New York, NY, Chapter 27, pp. 521–545

Veil, R. (2022c): Rating Agencies, in Veil, R. (2022, editor): *European Capital Markets Law*, Third edition, Hart Publishing, Oxford, UK – New York, NY, Chapters 13–15, pp. 183–256

Veil, R. (2017, editor): *European Capital Markets Law*, Second edition, Hart Publishing, Oxford and Portland, Oregon (USA)

Ventoruzzo, M. and S. Mock (2017, editors): *Market Abuse Regulation: Commentary and Annotated Guide*, Oxford University Press, United States of America

Vigneron, P. and A. Smith (1990): The Concept of Reciprocity in Community Legislation: The Example of the Second Banking Directive, *Journal of International Banking Law*, volume 5, pp. 181-191

Viñals, J., Blanchard, O., and S. Tiwari (2015): *Monetary Policy and Financial Stability*, IMF Policy Paper, IMF, September, available at: https://www.imf.org/external/np/pp/eng/2015/082815a.pdf

Vinals, J., Pazarbasioglu, C., Surti, J., Narain, A., Erbenova, M. and J. Chow (2013): *Creating a Safer Financial System: Will the Volcker, Vickers and Liikanen Structural Measures Help?*, IMF Staff Discussion Note, SDN/13/4, International Monetary Fund, Washington, DC

Vossen, A. (2001): Capital Adequacy Directive, in Van Empel, M. and R. Smits (2001, editors), *Banking and EC Law: Commentary*, Kluwer, Chapter 14

W & Z

Walker, G.A. (2007): *European Banking Law – Policy and Programme Construction*, Sir Joseph Gold Memorial Series, International Financial & Economic Law, Volume 6, The British Institute of International and Comparative Law, London

Walla, F. (2022): Short Sales and Credit Default Swaps, in Veil, R. (2022, editor): *European Capital Markets Law*, Third edition, Hart Publishing, Oxford, UK – New York, NY, Chapter 24, pp. 439–456

Weatherill S. (2016): *Law and Values in the European Union*, Oxford University Press, Oxford

Weatherill, S. (2012): Maximum versus Minimum Harmonization: Choosing between Unity and Diversity in the Search for the Soul of the Internal Market, in Shuibhne, N.N and L.W. Gormley (2012, editors): *From Single Market to Economic Union: Essays in Memory of John A. Usher*, Oxford University Press, Oxford

Weatherill S. (2011): The Limits of Legislative Harmonisation Ten Years after *Tobacco Advertising*: How the Court's Case Law Has Become a "Drafting Guide", *German Law Journal*, Volume 12, p. 832 et seq.

Weber, R.H. and R. Baisch (2017): Finanzdienstleistungsveträge, in Trüten, D. Baumgartner, T. and A. Bruneer (Hrsg.): *Verbaucherverwtragsrecht der Europäischen Union*, Nomos – Verlag Österreich – Schulthess, pp. 251–278

Weiler, J. (1991): The Transformation of Europe, Yale Law Journal, 100, p. 2403 et seq.

Whitehead, C. (2011): The Volcker Rule and Evolving Financial Markets, *Harvard Business Law Review*, issue 1, pp. 39–72

Willemaers, G. (2014): Client Protection on European Financial Markets–From Inform Your Client to Know Your Product and Beyond: An Assessment of the PRIIPs Regulation, MiFID II/MiFIR and IMD 2, *Revue Trimestrielle de Droit Financier*, Autumn 2014 (also available at: https://ssrn.com/abstract=2494842)

Wundenberg, M. (2022): Regulation of Benchmarks, in Veil, R. (2022, editor): *European Capital Markets Law*, Third edition, Hart Publishing, Oxford, UK – New York, NY, Chapters 35–36, pp. 645–670

Wyatt, D. (2009): Community Competence to Regulate the Internal Market, in Dougan, M. and S. Currie (2009, editors): *Fifty Years of the European Treaties: Looking Back and Thinking Forward* Hart Publishing, Oxford

Wyplosz, Ch. (2012): Banking Union as a Crisis-Management tool, in Beck, T. (2012, editor): *Banking Union for Europe – Risks and Challenges*, Centre for Economic Policy Research (CEPR), London, UK, pp. 19–23

Zetzsche, D.A. (2017): *The Anatomy of European Investment Fund Law*, available at: https://ssrn.com/abstract=2951681

Zetzsche, D.A. (2015, editor): *The Alternative Investment Fund Managers Directive*, Second Edition, International Banking and Finance Law Series, Wolters Kluwer Law & Business, The Netherlands

Zetzsche, D.A. and Ch. D. Preiner (2015): Scope of the AIFMD, in Zetzsche, D.A. (2015, editor): *The Alternative Investment Fund Managers Directive*, Second Edition, International Banking and Finance Law Series, Chapter 3, Wolters Kluwer Law & Business, The Netherlands

Zilioli, Ch. and Ph. L. Athanassiou (2018): The European Central Bank, in Schütze, R. and T. Tridimas (2018, editors): *Oxford Principles European Union Law – Volume I: The European Union Legal Order*, Oxford University Press, Oxford, Part III: Institutional Framework, Chapter 19, pp. 610–650

Zilioli, Ch. and M. Selmayr (2000): The ECB – An Independent Specialized Organization of Community Law, *Common Market Law Review*, Volume 37, pp. 591–643

Zimmermann, H. (2015): The Deep Roots of the Government Debt Crisis, *The Journal of Financial Perspectives*, EY Global Financial Services Institute, March, Volume 3, Issue 1, pp. 33–42

CHAPTER 5

Developments After the Establishment of the Banking Union

5.1 The Commission's 2016–2017 Reform Agenda and Its (Partial) Implementation

5.1.1 General Overview

(1) The initial legal framework governing the BU and (mainly) the underlying single rulebook has been amended. The **Commission Communications of 24 November 2015** "Towards the completion of the [BU]"[1] and (then) of **11 October 2017** "on completing the [BU]",[2] broadly based on the conclusions of the **Commission Reflection Paper** "on the deepening of the economic and monetary union" **of 31 May 2017**[3] (hereinafter the '**EMU reflection paper**'), laid down in this respect the following priorities, which can be categorised in two groups: the *first* contained '**risk reduction' measures**, including the adoption of the 2016 "legislative banking package", the creation of sovereign bond-backed securities and the undertaking of actions to address **NPLs** in accordance with the **Council Action Plan** of July 2017; and the *second* group comprised two '**risk sharing' measures** (implementation of which might follow the effective application of the above-mentioned risk reduction measures), and in particular the creation of a 'common backstop' to the SRB for the SRF and the creation of the EDIS.[4]

(2) The prioritisation of these actions was further reinforced in the **Commission Communication of 6 December 2017** "Further steps towards

---

[1] COM/2015/587 final.

[2] COM/2017/592 final.

[3] At: https://ec.europa.eu/commission/publications/reflection-paper-deepening-economic-and-monetary-union_en.

[4] All these aspects are briefly discussed in turn below, under 5.1.2–5.1.6.

completing Europe's [EMU]: A roadmap",[5] which outlines the comprehensive package of 6 proposals to strengthen the EMU—including the BU and the Capital Markets Union ('**CMU**'),[6] i.e., the two pillars of the '**Financial Union**'. These initiatives were without prejudice to other regulatory measures adopted in order to strengthen financial stability,[7] including the IASB's international accounting standard '**IFRS 9**' on the classification and measurement of financial instruments, applicable since 1 January 2018.[8]

5.1.2 Finalisation of the 2016 "Legislative Banking Package"

(1) On 23 November 2016, the Commission tabled a legislative banking package concerning the amendment of several aspects of the BRRD, the SRMR, the CRR and the CRD IV with a view to reducing risks and further strengthening the resilience of EU credit institutions.

Box 5.1 The three pillars of the 2016 "legislative banking package"

Pillars	Content
Pillar 1	A Directive of the co-legislators amending **Article 108 BRRD** as regards the ranking of unsecured debt instruments in insolvency was adopted on 12 December 2017[9]
Pillar 2	A combined legislative proposal referred to the amendment of both the SRMR and the BRRD, reviewing the minimum requirement for own funds and eligible liabilities ('**MREL**') and implementing in the EU legal framework the total loss-absorbing capacity ('**TLAC**') standard set out in the FSB 2015 Report "Principles on Loss-absorbing and Recapitalisation Capacity of G-SIBs in Resolution – Total Loss-absorbing Capacity (TLAC) Term Sheet".[10] Two legislative acts of the co-legislators were ultimately

(continued)

---

[5] COM/2017/821 final, 6.12.1017, pp. 11–12.

[6] On the CMU, see under 5.2 below.

[7] For the role of financial stability in post-crisis Europe, see Losada and Tuori (2021).

[8] On this accounting standard and its financial stability implications, see European Systemic Risk Board (2017). Relevant is also Regulation (EU) 2017/2395 of the co-legislators of 12 December 2017 "amending the [CRR] as regards transitional arrangements for mitigating the impact of the introduction of IFRS 9 on own funds and for the large exposures treatment of certain public sector exposures denominated in the domestic currency of any Member State" (OJ L 345, 27.12.2017, pp. 27–33).

[9] Directive (EU) 2017/2399 of the co-legislators of 12 December 2017 "amending Directive 2014/59/EU as regards the ranking of unsecured debt instruments in insolvency hierarchy", OJ L 345, 27.1.2.2017, pp. 96–101.

[10] At: https://www.fsb.org/2015/11/total-loss-absorbing-capacity-tlac-principles-and-term-sheet.

5 DEVELOPMENTS AFTER THE ESTABLISHMENT ... 271

Pillars	Content
(continued)	
	adopted on 20 May 2019 and published on 7 June 2019: the 'SRMR II' and the 'BRRD II'[11] The former applies from **28 December 2020**, while the latter's provisions have been transposed into national law by all Member States, albeit with delays in some cases, i.e., after the **28 December 2020** deadline. For this reason, according to the latest Commission update, infringement proceedings by the Commission are pending against twenty-one Member States[12]
Pillar 3	The amendments to the CRR included in the 'CRR II'[13] refer to the leverage and the net stable funding ratios; requirements for own funds and eligible liabilities; counterparty credit and market risks; exposures to CCPs and collective investment undertakings; large exposures; and reporting and disclosure requirements. The CRR II rules, including amendments to the calculation of the leverage ratio, apply from **28 June 2021**. *In addition*, the 'CRD V'[14] amends CRD IV rules as regards exempted entities, supervision of financial holding companies and mixed financial holding companies, remuneration, supervisory measures and powers, as well as capital conservation measures
	The vast majority of the proposals on the amendment of the CRR and the CRD IV are broadly based on aspects of the **"Basel III regulatory framework"**, which had not been included in these two EU legal acts at the time of their adoption (in 2013). The CRD V provisions have been transposed into national law by almost all Member States (except Portugal),

[11] Regulation (EU) 2019/877 of the co-legislators of 20 May 2019 "amending Regulation (EU) No 806/2014 as regards the loss-absorbing and recapitalisation capacity of credit institutions and investment firms" (OJ 150, 7.6.2019, pp. 226–252) and Directive (EU) 2019/879 of the co-legislators of 20 May 2019 "amending Directive 2014/59/EU as regards the loss-absorbing and recapitalisation capacity of credit institutions and investment firms (…)" (OJ 150, 7.6.2019, pp. 296–344).

[12] See at: https://finance.ec.europa.eu/regulation-and-supervision/financial-services-legislation/enforcement-and-infringements-banking-and-finance-law/monitoring-banking-and-finance-directives/bank-recovery-and-resolution-directive-2_en#enforcement.

[13] Regulation (EU) 2019/876 of the co-legislators of 20 May 2019 "amending Regulation (EU) 575/2013 as regards the leverage ratio, the net stable funding ratio, requirements for own funds and eligible liabilities, counterparty credit risk, market risk, exposures to central counterparties, exposures to collective investment undertakings, large exposures, reporting and disclosure requirements (…)", OJ 150, 7.6.2019, pp. 1–225.

[14] Directive (EU) 2019/878 of the co-legislators of the same date "amending Directive 2013/36/EU as regards exempted entities, financial holding companies, mixed financial holding companies, remuneration, supervisory measures and powers and capital conservation measures", OJ 150, 7.6.2019, pp. 253–295.

> albeit with delays in some cases, i.e., after the **28 December 2020** deadline. For this reason, according to the latest Commission update, infringement proceedings by the Commission are pending against thirteen Member States[15]

5.1.3 Introduction of Sovereign Bond-Backed Securities

(1) The development of sovereign bond-backed securities ('**SBBSs**', also referred to as sovereign-backed securities) is an aspect primarily dealt with by the ESRB.[16] Its aim is twofold: *first*, to reduce systemic risk by allowing credit institutions, insurance undertakings and other investors to diversify their government bond portfolios at relatively low transaction costs; and *second*, to mitigate financial fragmentation (and ultimately reduce the 'bank-sovereign loop') by allowing *all* participating Member States to contribute to the symmetrical supply of low-risk euro assets.[17]

This initiative can be viewed as a by-product of the need to overcome *smoothly* a major '**regulatory failure**' linked to the provisions of the CRR, which stipulate, in relation to the calculation of capital requirements for credit risk (mainly under the Standardised Approach, still used by several less sophisticated credit institutions[18]), that claims on Member State governments, if denominated in the local currency, have a zero per cent (0%) risk weight.[19] The experience from the 'voluntary' haircut on Greek government bonds under the Private Sector Involvement ('**PSI**'), which resulted in Greek credit institutions suffering extremely severe losses from their participation therein to the extent that their capital basis was depleted, has shown that these provisions are not appropriate. They provide credit institutions with perverse

---

[15] See at: https://finance.ec.europa.eu/regulation-and-supervision/financial-services-legislation/enforcement-and-infringements-banking-and-finance-law/monitoring-banking-and-finance-directives/bank-recovery-and-resolution-directive-2_en#enforcementhttps://finance.ec.europa.eu/regulation-and-supervision/financial-services-legislation/enforcement-and-infringements-banking-and-finance-law/monitoring-banking-and-finance-directives/capital-requirements-directive-5-investment-firms_en.

[16] See European Systemic Risk Board (2016), Brunnermeier *et al.* (2016) and Demary and Matthes (2017).

[17] European Systemic Risk Board (2016), Sect. 3. On the basic characteristics of SBBSs, see Sect. 2 and on their design, see Sect. 4.

[18] This aspect is discussed in detail in Volume II.

[19] CRR, Article 114(4). For an analytical study of this case, see European Systemic Risk Board (2015). On the same aspect from a global point of view, see the discussion paper of the Basel Committee of 7 December 2017 on the "Regulatory treatment of sovereign exposures" (at: https://www.bis.org/bcbs/publ/d425.htm).

incentives when including government bonds in their portfolios (especially in their banking books).[20] However, any (even adequate) increase of risk weights might lead to a distortion of capital markets, given the volumes of higher-risk government bonds involved.

(2) On **24 May 2018**, the Commission submitted a "Proposal for a Regulation (…) on sovereign bond-backed securities", aimed at laying down an EU "general framework" for SBBSs.[21] This legislative act has not yet been finalised.

5.1.4 *The NPL Problem and Measures Taken to Address It*

(1) The problem of credit institutions' NPLs, which form part of a wider set of non-performing exposures ('**NPEs**'), is not new in recent EU economic history. In the wake of the GFC and the subsequent fiscal crisis in the euro area, NPL amounts increased exponentially in all Member States albeit to a different extent (the so-called **legacy NPLs**).[22] During subsequent years, however, the accumulated stock of NPLs started to significantly decrease as a percentage of both their overall assets and their regulatory capital. This was due to a combination of accommodating macroeconomic conditions and the increase of credit institutions' regulatory capital resulting from the application of the micro- and macroprudential components of the 2013 single rulebook (i.e., the CRR and the CRD IV). Furthermore, the creation (and establishment) of the BU and particularly its first pillar, the SSM, seems to have more effectively addressed the supervisory '**home bias**' problem and

---

[20] On the key terms of the PSI following the 26 October 2011 Euro Summit, see Gortsos (2013), pp. 166–169, and more analytically Zettelmeyer, Trebesch and Gulati (2013) and Buchheit (2016). In relation to the PSI programme, of particular interest is the judgement of the General Court (Third Chamber) of 9 February 2022 in Case T-868/16, *QI and Others v European Commission and European Central Bank* (ECLI:EU:T:2022:28). The application, which was brought under Article 268 TFEU and dismissed in its entirety, sought compensation for the damage allegedly suffered by the applicants (holders of Greek government bonds) following the implementation of the PSI due to the conduct and actions of, in particular, the European Council, the Council, the Commission and the ECB. On Article 268 TFEU, which provides that the CJEU has jurisdiction in disputes relating to compensation under Article 340 (second and third paragraphs) concerning the non-contractual liability of the EU and of the ECB, respectively, see (by means of mere indication) Lenaerts, Maselis and Gutman (2014), pp. 480–549 and Craig and de Búrca (2020), pp. 616–640.

[21] COM/2018/839 final. The Commission's Staff Working Document "Impact Assessment" (SWD/2018/252 final, 24.5.2018, is available at: https://ec.europa.eu/info/law/better-regulation/initiatives/ares-2018-400473. This proposal is analysed in Gortsos (2018).

[22] On the development of NPLs after these crises, on the obstacles to NPL resolution in the EU and proposals for a comprehensive EU strategy on NPLs, see Aiyar *et al.* (2015), pp. 6–9, Lamandini *et al.* (2017), pp. 1–4, various contributions in Monokroussos and Gortsos (2017, editors), Montanaro (2019), pp. 215–220 and Gortsos (2021a). On legacy NPLs as a market failure problem, see Lamandini *et al.* (2017), pp. 5–6.

greatly improved the quality of prudential banking supervision within the SSM (pursuant to **Article 6 SSMR**).

(2) Within this context, the ECB "Guidance to banks on [NPLs]" of May 2017 set out best practices which constitute its supervisory expectation within the SSM,[23] followed in July 2017 by the Council "Action Plan to tackle [NPLs] in Europe".[24] The follow-up Commission Progress Reports on this Action Plan are also noteworthy and, in particular, the Commission Staff Working Document of 14 March 2018 "Asset Management Companies Blueprint" accompanying the Communication "Second Progress Report on the Reduction of [NPEs] in Europe".[25] Relevant are also the **EBA "Guidelines** on management of non-performing and forborne exposures" of 31 October 2018 (**EBA/GL/2018/06**)[26] and **Regulation (EU) 2019/630** of the co-legislators of 17 April 2019 "amending the [CRR] as regards minimum loss coverage for [NPEs]".[27]

In accordance with the 2018 EBA Guidelines, NPLs are defined as loans and advances as (further) defined in Annex V to **Commission Implementing Regulation (EU) No 680/2014** of 16 April 2014 "laying down implementing technical standards with regard to supervisory reporting of institutions according to [the CRR]"[28] and classified as non-performing in accordance with that same Annex; and NPEs are defined as exposures classified as non-performing in accordance with Annex V to that same Commission Implementing Regulation. Beyond loans and advances, such exposures include other debt instruments, such as debt securities, advances and demand deposits. Forborne exposures ('**FBEs**') are defined as exposures to which forbearance measures have been applied pursuant to Annex V to the above-mentioned Commission Implementing Regulation.[29]

---

[23] At: https://www.bankingsupervision.europa.eu/ecb/pub/pdf/guidance_on_npl.en.pdf. The ECB Guidance is based on the Guidance of the BCBS of 4 April 2017 on the "Prudential treatment of problem assets – definitions of [NPEs] and forbearance" (at: https://www.bis.org/bcbs/publ/d403.htm).These international financial standards were adopted with a view to promoting global harmonisation in the measurement and application of these two important measures of asset quality (NPEs and forbearance) and complement the existing accounting and regulatory framework for asset categorisation.

[24] The conclusions of this Action Plan are available at: https://www.consilium.europa.eu/en/press/press-releases/2017/07/11/conclusions-non-performing-loans. The Commission's proposals are set out in pp. 17–18 of the Communication. For a detailed overview, see Montanaro (2019).

[25] SWD/2018/072 final and COM/2018/133 final, respectively.

[26] At: https://www.eba.europa.eu/regulation-and-policy/credit-risk/guidelines-on-management-of-non-performing-and-forborne-exposures.

[27] OJ L 111, 25.4.2019, pp. 4–12.

[28] OJ L 191, 28.6.2014, pp. 1–1861.

[29] Credit institutions are also required to report the NPL ratio as a measure of their exposure to credit risk and the quality of outstanding loans. In calculating this ratio, the gross carrying amount of NPLs and advances is divided by the gross carrying amount

5.1.5 The 'Common Backstop' to the Single Resolution Board (SRB) for the Single Resolution Fund (SRF)

5.1.5.1 The Initial Proposals for Establishing a European Monetary Fund (EMF)

(1) One of the main elements of the comprehensive package of measures proposed by the Commission in its (above-mentioned) **Communication of 6 December 2017** was the proposal for a Council Regulation "on the establishment of the European Monetary Fund"[30] ('**EMF Regulation**'). Its legal basis would have been **Article 352 TFEU**.[31] The Commission proposed that the Regulation should be adopted by **mid-2019**. The proposal provided for the establishment of a European Monetary Fund ('**EMF**'), whose Statute (hereinafter the '**EMF Statute**') was set out in the Annex to the Regulation and formed an integral part thereof.[32]

(2) The EMF would succeed and replace the European Stability Mechanism ('**ESM**'),[33] which was established as a permanent sovereign crisis management mechanism in the euro area, by virtue of an intergovernmental Treaty of 2 February 2012,[34] outside the EU framework, and is based in Luxembourg.[35] The ESM fully substituted for the European Financial Stability

---

of total loans and advances pursuant to the NPE definition (EBA Guidelines (EBA/GL/2018/06), pp. 16–17).

[30] COM/2017/827 final, 6.12.2017.

[31] On this TFEU Article, resort to which is rare, see Gundel (2019), Craig and de Búrca (2020), pp. 121–122 and Weatherill (2016), pp. 31–33. It is noted that, under this Article, unanimity is required in the Council. Moreover, certain national courts are very sceptical when it comes to measures adopted on its basis. See in this respect the judgement of the German Federal Constitutional Court ('FCC') of 30 June 2009 in the *Lisbon case*, which assessed the compatibility of the Lisbon Treaty with German law, judging that there are no decisive constitutional objections to the Act approving the Lisbon Treaty (Bundesverfassungsgericht, BVerfG, 2 BvE 2/08), especially at paras 326-328. On this judgement, see Steinbach (2010).

[32] EMF Regulation, Article 1(1) and 1(2); see also recital (18).

[33] This substitution would have included its legal position and the assumption of all its rights and obligations, with its current financial and institutional structures essentially preserved.

[34] The consolidated version of the ESM Treaty, which is currently under revision (as discussed below), is available at: https://www.esm.europa.eu/legal-documents/esm-treaty.

[35] Treaty establishing the ESM, Articles 1(1) and 31(1), respectively. On this mechanism, see, by means of mere indication, Hadjiemmanuil (2020a), pp. 1290–1292 and in more detail Martucci (2020), pp. 301–317. In relation to the amendment to Article 136 TFEU and the validity of the ESM Treaty (in view of, *inter alia*, Articles 2–3 and 13 TEU and Articles 119–123 and 125–127 TFEU) of relevance is also the judgement of the Court (sitting as a full Court) of 27 November 2012 in Case C-370/12, *Thomas Pringle v Government of Ireland and Others* (ECLI:EU:C:2012:756). On this case, see, by means of mere indication, Hadjiemmanuil (2020a), pp. 1293–1294.

Facility ('**EFSF**'),[36] following the **European Council Decision 2011/199/ EU** of 25 March 2011[37] by which the Member States introduced the (only during the fiscal crisis) amendment to the TFEU by inserting a **new paragraph (3) in Article 136 TFEU.**[38]

The objective of the EMF would be the contribution to safeguarding the financial stability of the euro area and of the participating Member States.[39] To achieve its objective, the EMF would have been assigned two tasks.[40] The *first* would be to mobilise funding and provide stability support under strict policy conditions, appropriate to the financial assistance instrument chosen, to the benefit of its members experiencing, or are threatened by, severe financing problems. This would include, *inter alia*, the provision of direct public financial assistance by the ESM to credit institutions through the 'Direct Recapitalisation Instrument' ('**DRI**'),[41] which was created in 2014 but has never been activated (see Box 5.2). The *second* task would consist in providing credit lines or setting guarantees in support of the SRB (the '**common backstop**').

Box 5.2 The Direct Recapitalisation Instrument (DRI)

This instrument was established on **8 December 2014** by a unanimous **Resolution of the ESM Board of Governors**, which on the same date also adopted a detailed **Guideline** on its modalities. Its aim was to safeguard financial stability in the euro area and in its Member States, by catering for those cases in which an ESM Member would be confronted with severe financial disturbances that could not be remedied without significantly jeopardising fiscal sustainability, given the heightened risk

---

[36] *Ibid.*, preamble, point (1). Resort to this facility was made by Greece (2010), Ireland (2010) and Portugal (April 2011). On the Greek support programmes, see Drossos (2020), Chapter 4, Section IV, Hadjiemmanuil (2020a), pp. 1281–1286 and Piantelli (2021), pp. 70–72; for Portugal's support programme, see Drossos (2020), Chapter 4, Section V, Hadjiemmanuil (2020a), pp. 1305–1311 and Piantelli (2021), pp. 67-70. It is noted that the EFSF is no longer involved in support programmes but continues to be active in the international bond markets to manage its debt.

[37] OJ L 91, 6.4.2011, pp. 1–2.

[38] Cyprus was the first Member State to approach the ESM. The financial assistance programme for Cyprus was formally approved by the ESM on 24 April 2013 and subsequently approved by the Cypriot Parliament on 30 April and by the IMF Executive Board on 15 May (IMF, "Request for arrangement under the extended fund facility", May 2013, available at: https://imf.org/external/pubs/ft/scr/2013/cr13125.pdf). On the Cypriot crisis, see the literature in Chapter 2 above, under 2.2.4, part of which also discusses the support programme received by Cyprus.

[39] EMF Statute, Article 3(1).

[40] *Ibid.*, Article 3(2).

[41] *Ibid.*, Article 19(1), second sentence and EMF Regulation, recital (46).

> of contagion from the financial sector to the sovereign. The DRI was mainly available to systemically relevant credit institutions unable to meet the capital requirements established by the ECB in its capacity as supervisor within the SSM, and obtain sufficient capital from private sources, if the application of the 'bail-in' resolution tool could not adequately meet the anticipated capital shortfall.[42] A burden-sharing scheme determined the contributions of the requesting ESM Member and the ESM. Financial assistance under the DRI should be granted under strict conditionality, accompanied by an MoU addressing the sources of difficulties in the financial sector and the overall economic situation of the requesting ESM Member.[43]

Hence, the EMF Regulation and the EMF Statute would have established the EMF as a *comprehensive crisis management EU body* with legal personality,[44] which would serve as a 'lender of last resort' both for the Member States whose currency is the euro, and for the SRF, in the form of the common backstop. The function of last-resort lending to credit institutions operating in the euro area would remain with the NCBs—members of the Eurosystem, under the conditions laid down in **Article 14.4 ESCB/ECB Statute**.[45]

(3) The legal basis for the provision of financial support to the SRF by the EMF would be **Article 22 EMF Statute**, which provides that such support must be jointly provided by the EMF *and* the participating Member States within the meaning of **Article 2 SSMR** whose currency is not the euro, on equivalent terms and conditions, through 'credit lines or ceilings', or both, for guarantees on liabilities of the SRB. Its ultimate legal basis would be **Article 74 SRMR** (titled **'access to financial facility'**). This provides that the (single Resolution) Board can contract for the SRF public financial arrangements regarding the *immediate availability* of **'additional financial means'** to be used (in accordance with **Article 76** on the SRF's mission) if the bank contributions raised or available are not sufficient to meet the SRF's obligations. Such amounts of support would be provided in proportion to a key to be communicated by the Board when requesting the support.

In order to ensure that the EMF would continue to be able to provide financial support to its Members when needed, it was proposed that the combined outstanding commitments available for the purposes of support to

---

[42] This resolution tool (along with the other three) is presented in detail in Volume II.

[43] For further details, see European Stability Mechanism (2014) and Hadjiemmanuil (2015), pp. 29–34. For the DRI's (potential but never materialised) impact on sovereign debt, see Varela (2015).

[44] EMF Statute, Article 1, first sentence.

[45] See the *Excursus* at the end of Chapter 6 below.

the SRB arising from decisions adopted under the above provisions would be subject to an initial ceiling of 60 billion euro.[46] However, to also ensure that the EMF would be able to respond flexibly to unforeseen funding needs arising from resolution operations, the Board of Governors should be empowered to increase the ceiling.[47]

5.1.5.2   Operationalisation of the Common Backstop

(1) Any progress on the adoption of the above-mentioned legislative act is halted. However, during the Euro Summit meeting of **29 June 2018**,[48] agreement was reached that the common backstop should be activated and be provided by a more strengthened ESM.[49] Taking also into consideration the relative urgency of the situation, the Euro Summit noted that the Eurogroup will have to prepare the terms of reference of the common backstop and agree on a term sheet for the further development of the ESM by December 2018.[50] The following Euro Summit meeting, of **14 December 2018**, endorsed *first*, the terms of reference for the operationalisation of the common backstop, as developed by the Eurogroup, on condition (in that case as well, as for the creation of the EDIS) that *"sufficient progress has been made in risk reduction"*[51]; and *second*, the term sheet developed by the Eurogroup on the further development, by reform, of the ESM, asking the Eurogroup to prepare, by June 2019, the necessary amendments to the ESM Treaty, including on the common backstop.[52]

(2) The Euro Summit meeting, of **21 June 2019**, noted the broad agreement reached on the revision of the ESM Treaty, stating its expectation that it will continue its work to allow for a final agreement in December 2019.[53]

---

[46] EMF Statute, Article 22(2).

[47] *Ibid.*, Article 22(4), point (b) and EMF Regulation, recital (61). For a systematic presentation and an assessment of the proposed legal framework on the EMF, see Gortsos (2017). On the case for establishing a common backstop, see, by means of mere indication, Schoenmaker (2014) and (2017) and Schlosser (2017) (all completed before the publication of the Commission's proposal).

[48] Euro Summit meetings are participated in by the heads of state or government of the euro area Member States, the Euro Summit President and the President of the Commission and provide strategic guidelines on euro area economic policy. The rules for the organisation of the proceedings of Euro Summits are set out in a document available at: https://www.consilium.europa.eu/media/20377/qc3013400enc_web.pdf.

[49] See on this Aerts and Bizarro (2020).

[50] Euro Summit meeting (29 June 2018), Statement, point 2.

[51] Euro Summit meeting (14 December 2018), Statement, point 1. The terms of reference are annexed to the Statement of the Eurogroup's report of 4 December 2018 (at: https://www.consilium.europa.eu/media/37268/tor-backstop_041218_final_clean.pdf).

[52] *Ibid.*, Statement, point 2. The term sheet is annexed to the Statement as well (at: https://www.consilium.europa.eu/media/37267/esm-term-sheet-041218_final_clean.pdf).

[53] Euro Summit meeting (21 June 2019), Statement, point 1, first bullet.

However, the statement of the Euro Summit meeting of **13 December 2019** was brief as well, noting that the Eurogroup should continue to work on both the ESM package of reforms, pending national procedures and on all elements of the further strengthening of the BU.[54] It was, finally, during the Euro Summit meeting, of **11 December 2020**, that the backstop was endorsed[55] on the basis of the letter of the Eurogroup's President of **4 December 2020**,[56] which noted the agreement reached in the Eurogroup in inclusive format on the ESM reform. In this context, that Eurogroup was invited to prepare, on a consensual basis, a stepwise and time-bound work plan on all outstanding elements needed to complete the BU.[57]

(3) The ESM reform entails a few new tasks, including the further development of ESM instruments, enhancing the ESM's role and setting up the common backstop.[58] Accordingly, on **27 January and 8 February 2021**, the Contracting Parties signed the Agreements amending the ESM Treaty (the amendments going well beyond the introduction of the backstop facility) and **Articles 5(1) and 7(1) SRF Agreement**.[59] In accordance with (the new) **Article 12(1a) ESM Treaty**, the ESM may provide the backstop facility for the SRF, without prejudice to EU law and the competences of EU institutions and bodies. Loans under this facility shall only be granted as a last resort and to the extent that it is fiscally neutral in the medium term. The rules governing the backstop facility, which will become operational in **January 2022**,[60] are laid down in (the new as well) **Article 18a ESM Treaty**.

---

[54] Euro Summit meeting (13 December 2019), Statement, point 2. The text of this Statement is available at: https://www.consilium.europa.eu/en/press/press-releases/2019/12/13/statement-of-the-euro-summit-13-december-2019.

[55] Euro Summit meeting (11 December), Statement, point 3, first bullet. The text of this Statement is available at: https://www.consilium.europa.eu/media/47298/11-12-20-euro-summit-statement-en.pdf.

[56] At: https://www.consilium.europa.eu/media/47177/20201204-letter-to-president-charles-michel.pdf.

[57] Euro Summit meeting (11 December 2020), Statement, point 3. The text of this Statement is available at: https://www.consilium.europa.eu/media/47298/11-12-20-euro-summit-statement-en.pdf.

[58] At: https://www.esm.europa.eu/about-esm/esm-reform. All relevant draft documents are available at: https://www.esm.europa.eu/about-esm/esm-reform-documents.

[59] Furthermore, in their Joint Declaration attached to the Agreement amending the SRF Agreement, the Contracting Parties committed to strive to complete the process of ratification of this amending Agreement at the same time as that of the Agreement amending the ESM Treaty, *"where possible, and taking into account their national requirements, and, in any event, as soon as necessary for the early introduction of the common backstop as confirmed by the political decision as referred to in the Terms of Reference of the Common Backstop to the [SRF]"* (see at: https://www.consilium.europa.eu/media/48070/joint-declaration-attached-to-the-amending-agreement-on-the-single-resolution-fund_en.pdf).

[60] See at: https://www.esm.europa.eu/content/when-will-common-backstop-be-introduced.

Both Agreements will enter into force on the date when the instruments of ratification, approval or acceptance have been deposited by all Signatories[61] (which was not the case by end-2022).

5.1.6 Creation of the EDIS

(1) No progress was made on adopting the Regulation establishing the EDIS on the basis of the above-mentioned 2015 Commission's proposal.[62] In light of this development, the Commission identified in its (also above-mentioned[63]) **EMU reflection paper** the creation of the EDIS (ideally by 2019, with a view to be in place and fully operational by 2025) as one of the key outstanding components for the completion of the BU.[64] In this respect, in its (also above-mentioned[65]) **Communication of 11 October 2017** concerning the completion of all parts of the BU by 2018, the Commission submitted a compromise solution, proposing a more gradual introduction of the EDIS compared with the original proposal in only two phases as follows: during the more limited **'reinsurance phase'**, the EDIS would only provide liquidity coverage to national DGSs, temporarily providing the means to ensure full payout if a credit institution's deposits were to become unavailable; national DGSs would need to pay back this support, ensuring that losses would continue to be covered at national level; during the following **'co-insurance phase'**, migration to which should be conditional on progress achieved in reducing risks, the EDIS would also progressively cover losses.

(2) In the Statement of the Euro Summit meeting, of **29 June 2018**, it was agreed that work on a roadmap for beginning political negotiations on the EDIS should start immediately after the adoption of risk reduction measures.[66] The Euro Summit meeting, of **14 December 2018**, did not make any explicit reference to the progress of negotiations on the EDIS. Nevertheless, according to the **"Eurogroup Report to Leaders on EMU deepening"** of **4 December 2018**,[67] work had started on a roadmap for beginning political negotiations

---

[61] The text of the Agreement amending the ESM is available at: https://www.esm.europa.eu/about-esm/esm-reform-documents/esm-treaty-amending-agreement. All ESM reform documents are available at: https://www.esm.europa.eu/about-esm/esm-reform-documents. The common backstop will be further discussed in Volume II.

[62] See Chapter 4 above, under 4.4.5.

[63] See above, under 5.1.1.

[64] EMU reflection paper (2017), pp. 19–20.

[65] See above, under 5.1.1.

[66] Euro Summit meeting (29 June 2018), Statement, point 1 (second sentence). The text of this Statement is available at: https://www.consilium.europa.eu/media/35999/29-euro-summit-statement-en.pdf.

[67] The text of this Report's Statement is available at: https://www.consilium.europa.eu/en/press/press-releases/2018/12/04/eurogroup-report-to-leaders-on-emu-deepening/pdf.

on the EDIS in line with the mandate from the June 2018 Euro Summit. In addition, the establishment of a high-level working group was decided to work on the next steps and report to the Euro Summit of June 2019.

(3) The Euro Summit meeting, of **21 June 2019**, on the other hand, was silent on this subject, even though the risk reduction measures had been adopted a month ago, its statement concluding with a general remark: "*We look forward to the continuation of the technical work on the further strengthening of the Banking Union*".[68] The same applied to the Euro Summit meetings, of **13 December 2019**, **11 December 2020** and **16 December 2021**, while in the meeting of **24 June 2022** the Euro Summit, which was mainly preoccupied with the economic and macrofinancial implications of the Russian Federation's invasion of Ukraine, simply welcomed the commitment of the Eurogroup in inclusive format to subsequently identify in a consensual manner possible further measures with regard to the other outstanding elements to strengthen and complete the BU.[69] Under these conditions, the creation of the EDIS and the EDIF is (in realistic terms) not envisaged before 2024.

5.2 Creation of the Capital Markets Union (CMU)

5.2.1 The Initial Phase

(1) The creation of the BU was the driving force behind the discussions pertaining to building a (European) **CMU** as well, a concept first introduced in the Political Guidelines for the next Commission issued by the, then candidate, President of the Commission Jean-Claude Juncker on **15 July 2014**. In the mission letter sent on 1 November of that year to the newly appointed Commissioner for Financial Stability, Financial Services and CMU Lord Jonathan Hill, Juncker incorporated the project of creating a CMU, alongside the BU, as another step towards ending financial fragmentation in lending markets.

On **22 October 2014**, during his speech at the Joint EIB-IMF High-Level Workshop, Yves Mersch, at that time member of the ECB Executive Board, highlighted the desirable infrastructure of an upcoming CMU, defining it as the proper follow-up to the sea change the BU brought to the EU banking and financial markets and as an appropriate action in the struggle to re-ignite growth in the heavily traumatised EU economy, which is described as "*a plane*

---

[68] Euro Summit meeting (21 June 2019), Statement, point 2. The text of this Statement is available at: https://www.consilium.europa.eu/media/39968/20190621-euro-summit-statement.pdf.

[69] Euro Summit meeting (24 June 2022), Statement, point 3(b). The text of this Statement is available at: https://www.consilium.europa.eu/media/57443/20220624-euro-summit-statement-en.pdf. To the best of the author's knowledge, no Euro Summit meeting was held in December 2022.

flying on one engine, the bank financing."[70] However, unlike the BU, the CMU project is not predominantly dealing with financial stability issues and does not provide for the creation of a single, pan-European securities markets authority,[71] even though the enhancement of efficiency in supervising capital markets is a key objective.[72]

(2) On **18 February 2015**, the Commission issued a **Green Paper** on "Building a [CMU]",[73] paving the way for further action. This was followed, in **September 2015**, by a Communication on an "Action Plan on building a [CMU]"[74] (the '**2015 CMU Action Plan**'), which set out a list of actions and related measures to establish the building blocks of an integrated capital market in the EU by 2019.[75] These actions are summarised in six pillars relating to the following aspects (as laid down in Annex 1): provision of financing for innovation, start-ups and non-listed companies; reduction of barriers for companies wishing to raise capital on public markets; provision of facilities for long-term, infrastructure and sustainable investment; fostering retail and institutional investment; leveraging banking capacity to support the wider economy; and facilitating cross-border investing.

(3) The first "Mid-Term Review of the [CMU] Action Plan" was made public in a Commission Communication dated **8 June 2017**. According to this Review, over the preceding 18 months the Commission had delivered, in accordance with the original timetable, more than half of the measures (20 out of 33) announced in the 2015 CMU Action Plan, while another three legislative proposals were also at a final stage.[76] In addition, the Mid-Term Review set **new priority actions** concerning the **7 issue-areas**, which, along with the outstanding CMU workstreams, constitute the basis for a decisive and lasting contribution to laying the foundations for a true CMU by 2019.[77]

(4) The Commission's **Communication of 28 November 2018** on"[CMU]: time for renewed efforts to deliver for investment, growth and a stronger role of the euro",[78] considered that the CMU is essential to increase the resilience

---

[70] See Mersch (2014).

[71] On this prospect, see Lannoo (1999), Avgerinos (2003), pp. 145–224, and Ferran (2004).

[72] See Avgouleas and Ferrarini (2018) and Busch (2018).

[73] COM/2015/63 final.

[74] COM/2015/468 final.

[75] For some critical comments on the lack of ambition of the 2015 CMU Action Plan, see Lannoo (2015).

[76] See on this the Annex to the Review.

[77] The consolidated set of measures is presented in the Communication's Annex. For an assessment of the CMU project, see Dixon (2014), House of Lords (2015) and Véron and Wolff (2015). For a comprehensive analysis of its various elements, see the contributions in Busch, Avgouleas and Ferrarini (2018, editors).

[78] COM/2018/767 final.

of Member States' and the EMU's economy, foster convergence, safeguard financial stability and strengthen the international role of the euro.[79] Assessing the state-of-play with regard to the CMU,[80] the Commission identified that only three of the legislative proposals contained in the 2015 CMU Action Plan and the 2017 Mid-Term Review programme were completed (all in 2017, as briefly discussed in Box 5.3 just below).

> **Box 5.3 The three legislative acts on the Capital Markets Union (CMU) adopted in 2017**
>
> The *first* was the **'Prospectus Regulation'**[81]; this entered into force in July 2019, repealed the Directive of the same name (2003/71/EC[82]) and lays down harmonised requirements for the drawing up, approval and distribution of the prospectus to be published when securities are offered to the public or admitted to trading on a regulated market situated or operating within a Member State.[83]
>
> The *second* was **Regulation (EU) 2017/1991** of 25 October 2017,[84] which amended the existing Regulations on European venture capital funds and European social entrepreneurship funds.[85] The purpose was to further facilitate investments in innovative small and medium-sized enterprises by opening-up the regulation to fund managers of all sizes and expanding the range of companies that can be invested in. In addition to the new rules, the Commission launched in 2018 a Pan-European "Venture Capital Fund-of-Funds" programme in support of innovative investments.[86]

---

[79] Commission Communication, Sect. 5, first paragraph.

[80] *Ibid.*, Sect. 2.

[81] Regulation (EU) 2017/1129 of 14 June 2017 "on the prospectus to be published when securities are offered to the public or admitted to trading on a regulated market (…)", OJ L 168, 30.6.2017, pp. 12–82.

[82] See above in Chapter 2, under 2.4.3.

[83] *Ibid.*, Article 1(1). On this legislative act, see Pietrancosta and Marraud des Grottes (2018), the contributions in Busch, Ferrarini and Franx (2020, editors), as well as Gortsos and Terzi (2020), pp. 2–24.

[84] OJ L 293, 10.11.2017, pp. 1–18.

[85] See Chapter 4 above, under 4.3.2.

[86] Commission factsheet of 10 April 2018; see at: https://europa.eu/rapid/press-release_MEMO-18-2764_en.htm.

> *Finally*, the '**STS Securitisation Regulation**'[87] aims at re-building confidence in the securitisation market and, hence, allow credit institutions to deleverage their balance sheets.[88]

Furthermore, in its **Communication** of **15 March 2019**, titled "[CMU]: progress on building a Single Market for capital for a strong [EMU]",[89] the Commission stated that the CMU is necessary to complement the BU and strengthen the EMU and the international role of the euro, since:

> "*Deeper integration of capital markets, together with more integrated banking systems, can help to maintain cross-border capital flows and sustain investment in Member States suffering large asymmetric macroeconomic shocks.*"

5.2.2 The Full Implementation of the 2015 CMU Action Plan

The 2015 CMU Action Plan and the 2017 Mid-Term Review programme were completed in 2019–2020. In particular, apart from the amendment of the Regulations establishing the ESAs by virtue of (the above-mentioned) **Regulation (EU) 2019/2175**[90] and the sustainable finance trilogy (separately discussed just below[91]) the following (new or amending) acts were adopted by the co-legislators:

(1) In **May 2019**, the **EMIR** was amended by **Regulation (EU) 2019/834**[92] as regards the clearing obligation, the suspension of the clearing obligation, the reporting requirements, the risk-mitigation techniques for OTC derivative contracts not cleared by a central counterparty, the registration and

---

[87] Regulation (EU) 2017/2402 of 12 December 2017 "laying down a general framework for securitisation and creating a specific framework for simple, transparent and standardised ['STS'] securitisation (…)", OJ L 347, 28.12.2017, pp. 35–80. This legislative act amends several Directives (2009/65/EC, 2009/138/EC and 2011/61/EU) and Regulations [(EC) No 1060/2009 and (EU) No 648/2012].

[88] See on this Kastelein (2018) and Joosen and Lieverse (2018), Section V. In addition, the Commission amended its Delegated Regulation (EU) 2015/35 of 10 October 2014 (OJ L 12, 17.1.2015, pp. 1–797 (!!!)), which was adopted by virtue of the 'Solvency II' Directive' (i.e., the main source of EU insurance law) to facilitate investments in STS securitisations and infrastructure by insurance undertakings as well. See on this Joosen and Lieverse (2018), Section VI.

[89] COM/2019/136 final.

[90] See above in Chapter 4, under 4.3.1.

[91] See under 5.3.2. below. According to Colaert (2022), sustainable finance could be considered (anymore) as an autonomous objective of financial regulation in the EU.

[92] Regulation (EU) 2019/834 of the co-legislators of 20 May 2019 "amending Regulation (EU) No 648/2012 as regards the clearing obligation (…)", OJ L 141, 28.5.2019, pp. 42–63. This legislative act applies from 17 June 2019 (*ibid.*, Article 2).

supervision of trade repositories and the requirements for trade repositories ('**EMIR REFIT**').[93]

(2) On **20 June 2019**, the co-legislators adopted several legislative acts and namely a combined package of a Directive and a Regulation in relation to the cross-border distribution of collective investment funds and the *facilitation* of such a distribution, respectively[94]; a Regulation "on a Pan-European Personal Pension Product ('**PEPP**')",[95] which lays down uniform rules on the registration, manufacturing, distribution and supervision of personal pension products that are distributed in the EU under that designation; and the (highly important) Directive on restructuring and insolvency.[96]

(3) Another combined package of a Regulation and a Directive was adopted on **27 November 2019**: the 'Investment Firms Directive' ('**IFD**')[97] lays down rules concerning the initial capital of investment firms; supervisory powers and tools for their prudential supervision of by NCAs in a manner that is consistent with the rules set out in the 'Investment Firms Regulation' ('**IFR**'); and publication requirements for NCAs in the field of prudential regulation and supervision of investment firms[98]; and the IFR[99] lays down uniform prudential requirements which apply to investment firms supervised for compliance with prudential requirements under the IFD in relation to the own funds requirements relating to quantifiable, uniform and standardised elements of risk-to-firm, risk-to-client and risk-to-market; requirements

---

[93] 'REFIT' stands for the Commission's "Regulatory Fitness and Performance Programme", under which legislative acts are periodically reviewed with a view to their improvement.

[94] Directive (EU) 2019/1160 of 20 June 2019, amending the UCITS IV and the AIFMD with regard to cross-border distribution of collective investment undertakings (OJ L 188, 12.7.2019, pp. 106–115), and Regulation (EU) 2019/1156 of 20 June 2019 "on facilitating cross-border distribution of collective investment undertakings (…)" (OJ L 188, 12.7.2019, pp. 55–66). The Regulation and the national rules adopted for the implementation of the Directive apply from August 2021 (Regulation (EU) 2019/1156, Article 19 and Directive (EU) 2019/1160, Article 3(1)). See on this Gargantini *et al.* (2018).

[95] Regulation (EU) 2019/1238 of 20 June 2019, OJ L 198, 25.7.2019, pp. 1–63. On the Commission's proposal regarding this legislative act, see Heemskerk, Maatman and Werker (2018).

[96] Directive (EU) 2019/1023 of 20 June 2019 "on preventive restructuring frameworks, on discharge of debt and disqualifications, and on measures to increase the efficiency of procedures concerning restructuring, insolvency and discharge of debt (…)", OJ L 172, 26.6.2019, pp. 18-55. On this legislative act, which must have been transposed by Member States (in principle) from 21 July 2021 (*ibid.*, Articles 19(1) and 34), see Pulgar Ezquerra and Signes de Mesa (2021).

[97] Directive (EU) 2019/2034 of 27 November 2019 "on the prudential supervision of investment firms and amending (…) [the CRD IV]", OJ L 314, 5.12.2019, pp. 64–114.

[98] IFD, Article 1.

[99] Regulation (EU) 2019/2033 of 27 November 2019 "on the prudential requirements of investment firms", OJ L 314, 5.12.2019, pp. 1–63.

limiting concentration risk; liquidity requirements relating to quantifiable, uniform and standardised elements of liquidity risk; reporting requirements related to the above aspects; and public disclosure requirements.[100]

In addition, on the same date, a third combined package of a Regulation and a Directive was adopted by the co-legislators in relation to covered bonds.[101]

(4) On **7 October 2020**, the co-legislators adopted the "European Crowdfunding Service Providers Regulation"[102] ('**ECSPR**'), which lays down uniform requirements for the provision of crowdfunding services, for the organisation, authorisation and supervision of crowdfunding service providers, for the operation of crowdfunding platforms, as well as for transparency and marketing communications in relation to the provision of crowdfunding services in the EU.[103]

(5) *Finally*, on **16 December 2020**, the co-legislators adopted **Regulation (EU) 2021/23** "on a framework for the recovery and resolution of central counterparties (…)".[104] This legislative act lays down rules and procedures relating to the recovery and resolution of **CCPs** authorised in accordance with the EMIR, as well as rules relating to arrangements with third countries in that field.[105]

---

[100] IFR, Article 1(1). The IFR and the IFR established a new proportional prudential regime for investment firms, by creating a three-class classification for those firms. The IFR and the national rules to be adopted for the implementation of the IFD apply from 26 June 2021 (IFR, Article 66(2) and IFD, Article 67(1)).

[101] Regulation (EU) 2019/2160 of 27 November 2019 amended the CRR as regards exposures in the form of covered bonds (OJ L 328, 18.12.2019, pp. 1–6); Directive (EU) 2019/2162 of the same date governs the issues of covered bonds and covered bond public supervision (OJ L 328, 18.12.2019, pp. 29–57). The Regulation and the national rules to be adopted on the basis of the Directive apply from 8 July 2022 (Regulation (EU) 2019/2160, Article 2 and Directive (EU) 2019/2162, Article 32).

[102] Regulation (EU) 2020/1503 of 7 October 2020 "on European crowdfunding service providers for business (…)", OJ L 347, 20.10.2020, pp. 1–49.

[103] *Ibid.*, Article 1(1). 'Crowdfunding service provider' means a legal person who provides 'crowdfunding services'; these are defined as the matching of business funding interests of investors and project owners through the use of a crowdfunding platform and which consists of either the facilitation of granting of loans; or the placing without a firm commitment basis (as referred to in point (7) of Section A of Annex I to MiFID II) of transferable securities and admitted instruments for crowdfunding purposes issued by project owners or a special purpose vehicle, and the reception and transmission of client orders, as referred to in point (1) of that Section, in relation to those transferable securities and admitted instruments for crowdfunding purposes (*ibid.*, Article 2(1), points (e) and (a), respectively). On this legislative act, see, by means of mere indication, Ferrarini and Macchiavello (2018).

[104] OJ L 22, 22.1.2021, pp. 1–102.

[105] Regulation (EU) 2021/23, Article 1. This legislative act is analysed in Binder (2021a).

5.2.3 In Particular: The Sustainable Finance Agenda

(1) The EU sustainable finance[106] agenda dates back to September 2015, when the Commission issued its (above-mentioned) CMU Action Plan. Following its Communication of 14 September 2016 on "Capital markets union – accelerating reform",[107] it set up a 'High-Level Expert Group ('**HLEG**') on Sustainable Finance'[108] to develop an EU strategy on sustainable finance[109] addressing climate-related and environmental risks.[110] Furthermore, one of the priority actions of its (also above-mentioned) 2017 "Mid-Term Review of the [CMU] Action Plan" concerned a concrete follow-up to the Recommendations of the **HLEG** on Sustainable Finance. In this respect, the Commission submitted proposals aimed at improving disclosure and fully integrating sustainability, as well as environmental, social and governance ('**ESG**') considerations in rating methodologies and supervisory processes and in the investment mandates of institutional investors and asset managers. It also committed to develop an approach for taking sustainability considerations into account in upcoming legislative reviews of financial legislation. Of significant importance was also its '**2018 Sustainable Finance Action Plan**',[111] which laid down the foundations for a comprehensive EU sustainable finance framework.[112]

(2) Within this context, on 27 November 2019, the **co-legislators** adopted two Regulations. The first is the '**Sustainable Finance Disclosure Regulation**'[113] ('**SFDR**'), which lays down harmonised rules for financial market

---

[106] On the definition of sustainable finance, see Chapter 1 above, under 1.2.1.

[107] COM/2016/601 final.

[108] On the work of the HLEG, see Alexander (2019), pp. 366–369.

[109] The establishment of an internal market working for the sustainable development of the EU and based, *inter alia*, on balanced economic growth and a high level of protection and improvement of the quality of the environment, is laid down in Article 3(3) TEU (on this, see indicatively Becker (2019), pp. 57–58).

[110] On these risks, which combine two main risk drivers (i.e., physical and transition risk), see the 2020 ECB "Guide on Climate-Related and Environmental Risks: Supervisory Expectations Relating to Risk Management and Disclosure", 27 November, pp. 10–15 (at: https://www.bankingsupervision.europa.eu/ecb/pub/pdf/ssm.202011finalguideoncli mate-relatedandenvironmentalrisks~58213f6564.en.pdf).

[111] Communication of 8 March 2018: "Action Plan: Financing Sustainable Growth", COM/2018/097. In November 2020, the European Court of Auditors ('ECA') assessed, *inter alia*, the 2018 Action Plan, and concluded (in its Special Report 25/2020) that more consistent EU action was needed to redirect private and public finance towards sustainable investments; see European Court of Auditors (2020).

[112] Action 1 called for the establishment of the EU taxonomy, discussed just below.

[113] Regulation (EU) 2019/2088 of the co-legislators of 27 November 2019 "on sustainability-related disclosures in the financial services sector" (OJ L 317, 9.12.2019, 1-16); see details in Busch (2021). According to Busch (2022), at p. 65: "*The SFDR is an important step forward as harmonized sustainability transparency is a dire necessity, basically because the alternative is not workable*".

participants and financial advisers on transparency regarding the integration of **'sustainability risks'**[114] and the consideration of adverse sustainability impacts in their processes and the provision of sustainability-related information with respect to financial products[115] to increase transparency and comparability of sustainability-related disclosures. The second is the **'Low Carbon Benchmarks Regulation'**,[116] which sets out rules as regards EU climate transition and EU Paris-aligned benchmarks and sustainability-related disclosures for benchmarks.[117] In **June 2020**, these were complemented, by the **'Taxonomy Regulation'**[118] ('**TR**'), which builds on the work of the HLEG, amended the SFDR and sets out a unified classification system, the Taxonomy framework.[119]

Box 5.4 Key elements of the Taxonomy Regulation (TR)

In accordance with its title, the TR establishes *"a framework to facilitate sustainable investment"* by setting the criteria for determining whether *an economic activity* qualifies as environmentally sustainable for the purposes of establishing the degree to which *an investment* is

---

[114] The term 'sustainability risk' is defined to mean an ESG event or condition that, if occurring, could cause an actual or a potential material negative impact on the value of the investment (*ibid.*, Article 2, point (22)).

[115] *Ibid.*, Article 1.

[116] Regulation (EU) 2019/2089 of the co-legislators of 27 November 2019 "amending Regulation (EU) 2016/1011 as regards EU Climate Transition Benchmarks, EU Paris-aligned Benchmarks and sustainability-related disclosures for benchmarks", OJ L 317, 9.12.2019, 17-27.

[117] *Ibid.*, recital (17). The benchmarks are defined in (the new) points (23a) and (23b) of Article 3(1) of Regulation (EU) 2016/1011.

[118] Regulation (EU) 2020/852 of the co-legislators of 18 June 2020 "on the establishment of a framework to facilitate sustainable investment (...)" (OJ L 198, 22.6.2020, 13-43). *Inter alia*, this is based on the Commission Report "Financing a Sustainable European Economy" of 31 January 2018, which called for the creation of a technically robust EU classification system to establish clarity on which activities qualify as 'green' or 'sustainable' (at: https://ec.europa.eu/info/sites/info/files/180131-sustainable-finance-final-report_en.pdf).

[119] On this legislative act, see Pacces (2021) and in more detail Gortsos (2021b). One of its key objectives is to prevent 'greenwashing', meaning the practice of gaining an unfair competitive advantage by inaccurately marketing a financial product as environmentally friendly or 'green', when key environmental standards have not been met. See, by means of mere indication, Helleringer (2021), Mollers (2022) and Zukas and Trafkofski (2023). Overall, the implementation of the sustainable finance agenda brought about significant regulatory changes in the banking and insurance regulatory frameworks.

environmentally sustainable as well.[120] The benchmarks are six environmental objectives,[121] grouped in two categories: the *first* contains the two climate-related ones, namely climate change mitigation (i.e., the process of holding the increase in the global average temperature to well below 2 °C and pursuing efforts to limit it to 1.5 °C above pre-industrial levels pursuant to the Paris Agreement) and climate change adaptation (i.e., the process of adjustment to actual and expected climate change and its impacts); the environmental objectives in the *second category* are sustainable use and protection of water and marine resources; transition to a "circular economy"; pollution prevention and control; as well as protection and restoration of biodiversity and ecosystems (healthy ecosystem).

Inter alia, an economic activity should comply with applicable technical screening criteria ('**TSC**') set out in the Commission delegated acts supplementing the TR. Since the TR does not itself establish a label for sustainable financial products, the determination of whether an economic activity qualifies as sustainable should be made in these delegated acts.[122]

(3) The above-mentioned legislative acts constitute the regulatory 'trilogy' implementing the Commission's 2015 CMU Action Plan in relation to sustainable finance to remove hurdles to the internal market's functioning

---

[120] TR, Article 1(1).

[121] *Ibid.*, Article 9; see also recital (23).

[122] Pursuant to Articles 10(3), 11(3), 12(2), 13(2), 14(2) and 15(2) TR. In this respect, the Commission adopted on 4 June 2021 its "EU Taxonomy Climate Delegated Act" of 4 June 2021 (Commission Delegated Regulation (EU) 2021/2139 "supplementing Regulation (EU) 2020/852 (…) by establishing the [TSC] for determining the conditions under which an economic activity qualifies as contributing substantially to climate change mitigation or climate change adaptation and for determining whether that economic activity causes no significant harm to any of the other environmental objectives" (OJ L 442, 9.12.2021, pp. 1–349). This act, including its two Annexes (respectively), applies from 1 January 2022 (*ibid.*, Articles 10(6) and 11(6)). The Delegated Act on the other environmental objectives should have been adopted by the Commission in 2022 and apply from 1 January 2023 (*ibid.*, Articles 12(5), 13(5), 14(5) and 15(5)). However, this has not been the case.

This delegated act was amended in 2022 by the so-called Complementary Climate Delegated Act, which applies from 1 January 2023 (Commission Delegated Regulation (EU) 2022/1214 of 9 March 2022 "amending Delegated Regulation (EU) 2021/2139 as regards economic activities in certain energy sectors and Delegated Regulation (EU) 2021/2178 as regards specific public disclosures for those economic activities", OJ L 188, 15.7.2022, pp. 1–45). This includes, under strict conditions, specific nuclear and gas energy activities in the list of economic activities covered by the EU taxonomy. The criteria for the specific activities are in line with EU climate and environmental objectives and will help accelerate the shift from solid or liquid fossil fuels, including coal, towards a climate-neutral future.

in terms of obtaining finance for sustainability projects and to avoid future barriers from arising. However, even though the EU is undoubtedly at the forefront of sustainable finance regulation, with more instruments in the pipeline,[123] international convergence has not been effective (despite initiatives undertaken by the FSB) and more major jurisdictions will need to converge on implementing a common set of standards or at least certain key principles.[124]

5.3 THE IMPACT OF THE PANDEMIC CRISIS

5.3.1 Introductory Remarks

(1) As already noted,[125] the root cause of the pandemic crisis was different from the GFC, which was caused by failings (mainly, albeit not exclusively) of the financial sector, and of the subsequent fiscal crisis in the euro area, which is attributed to poor fiscal policies in some Member States and banking instability in others. From an economic point of view and from the outset of the pandemic crisis, the focus has been on the rescue of companies in the real sector of the economy. As noted, *inter alia*, by **Andrea Enria**, Chair of the ECB Supervisory Board:

> "*Unlike in the 2008 financial crisis, banks are not the source of the problem this time. But we need to ensure that they can be part of the solution.*"[126]

(2) Just before the onset of the pandemic, the EU banking sector was quite robust. Credit institutions, several of which were at the centre of the GFC, were much better capitalised and with stronger liquidity, while financial stability was also overall strengthened.[127] This was not only thanks to accommodating macroeconomic conditions and an enhanced supervisory framework, in place since the creation (and establishment) of the SSM, but also (if not primarily) to the **"Basel III impact"**, namely the fact that credit institutions benefited from the introduction of macroprudential capital buffers and liquidity ratios, in line with the international standards of the 2010 **Basel III**

---

[123] See below, under 5.4.3.

[124] According to recital (7) TR, given the systemic nature of global environmental challenges, environmental sustainability should be approached on a systemic and forward-looking basis, addressing growing negative trends. On this aspect, see Gortsos and Kyriazis (2022) and in more detail Gortsos and Blair (2023).

[125] See Chapter 2 above, under 2.2.4.

[126] At: https://www.bankingsupervision.europa.eu/press/interviews/date/2020/html/ssm.in200623~e668f871fa.en.html.

[127] This was manifested, *inter alia*, by the quarterly EBA Risk Dashboard of 14 April 2020, which covered 2019 Q4 data and summarised the main risks and vulnerabilities in the EU banking sector ahead of the crisis (at: https://eba.europa.eu/eu-banks-sail-through-corona-crisis-sound-capital-ratios).

regulatory framework. The buffers at their disposal allowed them to effectively support the short- and longer-term financing of economic activity and recovery in the EU without breaching their own funds requirements, and complemented the higher quality of capital, which had also been a by-product of the Basel III framework, as applied in the EU by means of the CRR and the CRD IV.

(3) Immediately after the outbreak of the pandemic, the EU developed a coherent strategy considering the spill-over effects and interlinkages between EU economies and the need to preserve confidence and stability. The measures adopted to deal with health emergency needs, support economic activity and employment, preserve monetary and financial stability and prepare the ground for recovery, contained a combination of: *first*, government fiscal *stimuli* with extensive resort to the principle of solidarity[128]; *second*, emergency liquidity and monetary policy measures by the ECB within the Eurosystem (designed as temporary), which applied both conventional (interest rate) and unconventional (balance sheet) measures[129]; and *third*, measures relating to financial stability.[130]

(4) Since the EU framework governing credit institutions' micro- and macro-prudential regulation (namely the CRR and the CRD IV) provides certain elements of 'flexibility', and considering that making full use thereof would be essential to overcome the financing pressures faced by firms and households, the ECB, as a banking supervisor within the SSM, adopted specific supervisory measures to ensure that credit institutions retain their capacity to support the real economy by ensuring the smooth provision of credit to households and businesses in a flexible way during (at least the initial phase of) the pandemic, also supported by the EBA.[131] *Furthermore*, the SRB also made targeted interventions in respect to the application of the resolution planning framework in

---

[128] On the early fiscal *stimuli*, see Hadjiemmanuil (2020b). Notable in this context is the "Next Generation EU" fiscal package, including as its key element the Recovery and Resilience Facility ('RRF', established by Regulation (EU) 2021/241 of the co-legislators of 12 February 2021, OJ L 57, 18.2.2021, pp. 17–75), which aims to boost aggregate demand, support the most hard-hit Member States and strengthen EU economic growth. See on this Bosque, Ramos Muñoz and Lamandini (2021) and European Commission (2022).

[129] See on this Bonatti *et al.* (2021), De Cos (2021), European Parliament (2021), Gortsos (2020b), Ohler (2023) and Zilioli and Riso (2023). On the response of central banks on a global basis (in both advanced and emerging economies) to the pandemic, see English *et al.* (2021) and various (other) contributions in Blair, Zilioli and Gortsos (2023, editors). For an overview of the framework governing the ECB's conventional and unconventional monetary policy measures ("general" and "temporary framework" in its own terminology) before the pandemic crisis, see Gortsos (2020a), pp. 286–297 and 297–300, respectively, and Tuori (2020).

[130] For an overview of all measures taken, see also Enoch (2021), pp. 234–250.

[131] Further to the measures discussed under 5.3.2–5.3.4 below, the ECB applied flexibility regarding, *inter alia*, the treatment of NPLs, supported by the EBA. It also

the context of monitoring the situation related to the pandemic crisis in the euro area and its impact on the financial system. *Finally*, very significant was also the ESRB contribution in the field of financial macroprudential oversight (aimed at addressing pandemic-related systemic vulnerabilities), the **Commission 2020 NPL Action Plan** and the measures taken by the ESMA in relation to capital markets regulation.[132]

5.3.2 Macroprudential Measures—Buffers

An essential element of flexibility was the releasability of capital and liquidity buffers included in the macroprudential policy and regulatory framework. In this respect, in its announcement of **12 March 2020**,[133] the ECB provided for the following: *first*, credit institutions were allowed to operate temporarily below the level of capital defined by the Pillar 2 Guidance ('**P2G**'), under the supervisory review and evaluation process ('**SREP**') framework, the capital conservation buffer ('**CCB**') and the liquidity coverage ratio ('**LCR**'). National designated authorities were also allowed to relax or delay the phase-in of certain non-releasable capital buffer requirements.[134] *Second*, they were also allowed to partially use capital instruments that do not qualify as Common Equity Tier 1 ('**CET1**') capital to meet the (additional) Pillar 2 Requirements ('**P2R**'), under the SREP framework as well, bringing forward a measure that was due to take effect in January 2021 pursuant to the amended CRD provisions.[135] These capital relief measures were complemented and enhanced by national macroprudential measures swiftly taken by several euro area

---

recommended the adoption of transitional rules on the international accounting/reporting standard 'IFRS 9' relating to the classification and measurement of financial instruments.

[132] See, respectively, under 5.3.5–5.3.8.

[133] "ECB Banking Supervision provides temporary capital and operational relief in reaction to coronavirus", at: https://www.bankingsupervision.europa.eu/press/pr/date/2020/html/ssm.pr200312~4335lac3ac.en.html.

[134] In the above ECB press release, the term 'national macroprudential authorities' (typically committees comprising several bodies, including the Ministry of Finance, the central bank and the capital markets commission, responsible for identifying, monitoring, assessing, preventing and mitigating systemic risks) is incorrectly used *in lieu* of 'national designated authorities' (see below). Structural non-releasable buffers, i.e., G-SII and O-SII buffers, were not used in response to the pandemic, as opposed to the CCyB and systemic risk buffer; on this, see details in Lagaria (2021). On the definition of 'G-SIIs' and 'O-SIIs', see Box 5.1. For a case study on how EU Member States in Central, Eastern and Southeastern Europe ('CESEE') adjusted their macroprudential policies in response to the COVID-19 crisis, see Eller *et al.* (2021).

[135] On the provisions of the CRD IV and the CRR governing the SREP, the P2G and the P2R, the various buffers and the LCR, see the analysis in Volume II.

designated authorities[136] (i.e., CCyB and systemic risk buffer releases[137]), which freed up more than 20 billion euro of CET1 capital held by euro area credit institutions to facilitate the absorption of credit losses and support lending to the real sector of the economy.[138]

5.3.3 Microprudential Measures

5.3.3.1 Measures by the ECB and the EBA

An additional element of flexibility was the interpretation and application of microprudential supervisory measures under exceptional circumstances. In this respect and pursuant to its above-mentioned[139] announcement of **12 March 2020**, the ECB provided operational flexibility in the implementation of institution-specific supervisory measures, which was then further extended on **20 March**.[140] Furthermore, on **16 April**, by virtue of another announcement, temporary relief was also provided for capital requirements against exposure to market risk.[141]

The EBA's stance was complementary: **on 12 March**, it made a statement on actions to mitigate the impact of COVID-19 on the EU banking sector and also decided to postpone the 2020 EU-wide stress test exercise to 2021.[142] Then, on **25 and 31 March**, it provided clarifications to credit institutions and consumers on the application of the prudential framework in the light of COVID-19 measures.[143] Further guidance on the use of flexibility was provided on **22 April**; in this statement, however, the EBA called

---

[136] Under the CRD IV, it is the national designated authority ('NDA') which is responsible for setting/releasing the rates for the CCyB, the O-SII/G-SII buffer and the systemic risk buffer.

[137] The CCyB and the systemic risk buffer have been designed to be releasable (at the discretion of national authorities and in line with the provisions of Article 5 SSMR).

[138] ECB press release: "ECB supports macroprudential policy actions taken in response to coronavirus outbreak", 15 April 2020 (at: https://www.ecb.europa.eu/press/pr/date/2020/html/ecb.pr200415~96f622e255.en.html). For details on all these measures, see Joosen (2020), pp. 339–360 and Lagaria (2021).

[139] See above, under 5.3.2.

[140] See "ECB Banking Supervision provides further flexibility to banks in reaction to coronavirus" (at: https://www.bankingsupervision.europa.eu/press/pr/date/2020/html/ssm.pr200320~4cdbbcf466.en.html).

[141] At: https://www.bankingsupervision.europa.eu/press/pr/date/2020/html/ssm.pr200416~ecf270bca.en.html.

[142] At: https://eba.europa.eu/eba-statement-actions-mitigate-impact-covid-19-eu-banking-sector and https://eba.europa.eu/sites/default/documents/files/document_library/General%20Pages/Coronavirus/EBA%20Statement%20on%20Coronavirus.pdf. In the same vein, at international level, the BCBS postponed all outstanding jurisdictional assessments planned in 2020 under its RCAP (see Chapter 3 above, under 3.1.7).

[143] At: https://eba.europa.eu/eba-provides-clarity-banks-consumers-application-prudential-framework-light-covid-19-measures and https://eba.europa.eu/eba-provides-additional-clarity-on-measures-mitigate-impact-covid-19-eu-banking-sector.

for heightened attention to ensuing risks.[144] In accordance with **Article 16** of its founding **Regulation,**[145] the EBA also issued on **2 April** its **Guidelines** "on legislative and non-legislative moratoria on loan repayments applied in the light of the COVID-19 crisis" (**EBA/GL/2020/02**)[146];

5.3.3.2   Amendment of the CRR and the CRR II
On **24 June 2020**, the co-legislators adopted a **Regulation** amending the CRR and the CRR II as regards adjustments in response to the pandemic[147] (the '**CRR quick fix**'), whose aim was to maximise the capacity of credit institutions to support households and businesses to recover from the crisis by providing credit. This legislative act applies from **27 June** and contains provisions relating to several aspects, such as: *first*, the amendment to the **minimum capital requirements for NPLs** under the **"prudential backstop"** to extend the preferential treatment of NPLs guaranteed by export credit agencies also to publicly guaranteed loans, subject to EU State aid rules; and *second*, the amendment of several arrangements relating to the **introduction of the IFRS 9**, allowing credit institutions to mitigate the potential negative impact of a likely increase in their provisions for expected credit losses (ECL).[148]

5.3.4   Temporary Ban on the Payment of Dividends by Credit Institutions

Noteworthy is also the ECB Recommendation of **27 March 2020** "on dividend distributions during the COVID-19 pandemic and repealing Recommendation (ECB/2020/1) (**ECB/2020/19**)".[149] Pursuant to this soft law instrument, addressed to significant supervised entities and significant supervised groups, the ECB recommended that, at least **until 1 October 2020**, no dividends (of any form) should be paid out by credit institutions and no irrevocable commitment to pay out dividends should be undertaken for the financial

---

[144] At: https://eba.europa.eu/eba-provides-further-guidance-use-flexibility-relation-covid-19-and-calls-heightened-attention-risks.

[145] OJ L 331, 15.12.2010, pp. 12–47.

[146] At: https://eba.europa.eu/eba-publishes-guidelines-treatment-public-and-private-moratoria-light-covid-19-measures. On 18 June, it made use of the option to extend their application to 30 September (at: https://eba.europa.eu/eba-extends-deadline-application-its-guidelines-payment-moratoria-30-september). In the meantime, on 2 June, it had issued its Guidelines "to address gaps in reporting data and public information in the context of COVID-19" (EBA/GL/2020/07) (at: https://eba.europa.eu/eba-issues-guidelines-address-gaps-reporting-data-and-public-information-context-covid-19).

[147] Regulation (EU) 2020/873, OJ L 204, 26.6.2020, pp. 4–17. Article 1 introduced amendments to the CRR and Article 2 amendments to the CRR II.

[148] *Ibid.*, Article 1, point (1), amending Article 47c (4) and point (7), extensively amending Article 473a CRR. On this legislative act, see Wojcik (2020). On an assessment of the CRR quick fix and on arguments against overshooting prudential relief for credit institutions, see Mack (2020).

[149] OJ C 102I, 30.3.2020, pp. 1–2.

years 2019 and 2020.[150] Furthermore, credit institutions should refrain from share buybacks aimed at remunerating shareholders. Based on the "comply or explain" principle, credit institutions, which are unable to comply with the Recommendation, should immediately explain the underlying reasons to their joint supervisory team ('**JST**').[151] The Recommendation was also addressed to NCAs and NDAs regarding less significant supervised entities and groups, which were expected to apply it to these as deemed appropriate.[152]

5.3.5   *Resolution Planning*

5.3.5.1   Actions by the Single Resolution Board (SRB)
(1) In the context of monitoring the situation related to the onset of the pandemic crisis and its impact on the financial system in the euro area, the Board's Chair, Elke König, made three interventions in respect of the application of the resolution planning framework: on 1 April, a letter was addressed to credit institutions under the Board's remit "on potential operational relief measures related to the COVID-19 outbreak", coupled by a note titled "An extraordinary challenge: SRB actions to support efforts to mitigate the economic impact of the COVID-19 outbreak". One week later, on 8 April, the application of the framework governing the MREL was addressed in another note titled "COVID-19 crisis: the SRB's approach to MREL targets".[153] All interventions were supportive of the measures taken by the ECB to help credit institutions ensure continuity of business and services.

(2) The Board also presented its approach in view of the uncertainty and disruption caused to the economy by the pandemic, setting out its remit on potential operational relief measures, its actions to support efforts to mitigate the economic impact of the crisis and its dealing with MREL targets. This approach was based on two complementary pillars, namely preservation of financial stability and flexibility in the application of the resolution framework.[154] In relation to the *first*, it was stated that the progress made

---

[150] This temporary ban on the payment of dividends was reinforced by the EBA in its (above-mentioned) statement of 31 March, urging "*banks to follow prudent dividend and other distribution policies, including variable remuneration*" as well as relevant ESRB Recommendations (ESRB/2020/7 and ESRB/2020/15). On this aspect, see details in Sciaronne Alibrandi and Frigeni (2020) and Dautovic *et al.* (2021). For a comparative analysis of, *inter alia*, similar temporary bans in other jurisdictions, see Awad *et al.* (2020).

[151] Points I and II of the ECB Recommendation.

[152] *Ibid.*, point III. According to point IV, the ECB should further evaluate the economic situation and consider whether further suspension of dividends was advisable beyond 1 October 2020.

[153] At: https://srb.europa.eu/en/node/965-967, https://srb.europa.eu/en/node/966 and https://srb.europa.eu/en/node/967.

[154] On this aspect, see Gortsos (2020c).

on resolution planning to make credit institutions resolvable and the build-up of MREL was important to maintain a strong banking sector supporting the economic recovery and preserve financial stability amidst the pandemic. As regards the *second pillar*, the Board supported credit institutions with operational relief measures, applying a pragmatic approach and considering, if necessary, to postpone less urgent information or data requests related to the (then) upcoming 2020 resolution planning cycle ('**RPC**'), expecting that they would identify mitigating actions to continue progress towards resolvability. *Furthermore*, considering that the build-up of MREL is key to resolvability, it stated its aim to assess the potential impact on transition periods needed for that build-up and provided clarity on its flexible approach, committing to ensure that short-term MREL constraints would not prevent credit institutions' lending activities. Hence, it expressed the intention to take a 'forward-looking approach' to credit institutions facing difficulties in meeting the (then) existing binding targets, as set out in the 2018 and 2019 RPCs, before new decisions would take effect.[155]

5.3.5.2 *The EBA Statement on Resolution Planning During the Pandemic Crisis*

On **9 July 2020**, the EBA published a statement on "Resolution planning in light of the COVID-19 pandemic"[156] to reiterate the importance of resolution planning even in times of uncertainty in order to ensure that resolution stands as a credible option in case of bank failures. In this respect, the EBA noted that the SRB and NRAs should consider the impact of the pandemic on credit institutions and their business models when taking decisions on resolution plans and the MREL, as well as use and test resolution colleges as key fora to exchange information and share decisions in times of stress.[157] Furthermore, it remarked that, on the one hand, "*resolution authorities should continue to promote institutions' efforts to enhance their capabilities and increase their resolvability*" and, on the other, "*institutions should continue to maintain strong focus on implementing the measures agreed with resolution authorities to overcome these impediments*".[158]

5.3.6 *The Contribution of the ESRB*

In order to address pandemic-related systemic vulnerabilities, the ESRB General Board took, on **6** and **27 May 2020**, respectively, two sets of actions in response to the pandemic crisis, addressing the following major

---

[155] This aspect is discussed in detail in Volume II.

[156] At: https://eba.europa.eu/eba-calls-resolution-authorities-consider-impact-covid-19-resolution-strategies-and-resolvability. Its legal basis is Article 8(1), point (ab) EBAR.

[157] EBA Statement, paras 3–7 and 9. Resolution colleges are also discussed in Volume II.

[158] *Ibid.*, par. 8.

financial stability issues: *first*, financial system implications of fiscal measures taken to protect the real sector of the economy; *second*, market illiquidity and implications for asset managers and insurers; *third*, the impact of large-scale downgrades of corporate bonds on markets and entities across the financial system (as a by-product of increased volatility in capital markets and 'flight to quality' reactions); *fourth*, system-wide restrictions on dividend payments, share buybacks and other payouts; and *fifth*, liquidity risks arising from margin calls.[159] In more detail, the ESRB issued three Recommendations to financial institutions (banks and non-banks): **Recommendation ESRB/2020/6** of 25 May 2020 on liquidity risks arising from margin calls; **Recommendation ESRB/2020/7** of 27 May 2020 on restriction of distributions during the COVID-19 pandemic, which was extended until 30 September 2021 by Recommendation ESRB/2020/15 of 15 December 2020; and **Recommendation ESRB/2020/8** of 27 May 2020 on monitoring the financial stability implications of debt moratoria, and public guarantee schemes and other measures of a fiscal nature taken to protect the real economy in response to the pandemic.[160]

5.3.7 *The Commission's 2020 NPL Action Plan*

(1) Even though the accumulated stock of NPLs before the pandemic crisis were significantly reduced, an additional stability-related issue, of primary importance, was the emerging new wave of NPLs caused by the pandemic crisis. In this respect, on 16 December 2020, amidst the pandemic, the Commission published its Communication "Tackling [NPLs] in the aftermath of the COVID-19 pandemic",[161] which set out its new **2020 NPL Action Plan**, intended to prevent a future build-up of NPLs across the EU due to the pandemic. The strategy proposed contains four pillars: *first*, the further development of secondary markets for distressed assets; *second*, the reform of the EU's corporate insolvency and debt recovery legislation; *third*, the support of the establishment and cooperation of national AMCs and eventually a cross-border network among national AMCs at EU level; and

---

[159] At: https://www.esrb.europa.eu/news/pr/date/2020/html/esrb.pr200514~bb1f96a327.en.html and https://www.esrb.europa.eu/news/pr/date/2020/html/esrb.pr200608~c9d71f035a.en.html, respectively.

[160] Respectively, at: https://www.esrb.europa.eu/pub/pdf/recommendations/esrb.recommendation200608_on_liquidity_risks_arising_from_margin_calls~41c70f16b2.en.pdf; https://www.esrb.europa.eu/pub/pdf/recommendations/esrb.recommendation200608_on_restriction_of_distributions_during_the_COVID-19_pandemic_2~f4cdad4ec1.en.pdf; https://www.esrb.europa.eu/pub/pdf/recommendations/esrb.recommendation201215_on_restriction_of_distributions_during_the_COVID-19_pandemic~2502cd1d1c.en.pdf; and https://www.esrb.europa.eu/pub/pdf/recommendations/esrb.recommendation200608_on_monitoring_financial_implications_of_fiscal_support_measures_in_response_to_the_COVID-19_pandemic_3~c745d54b59.en.pdf?35a81a46f32f9b8d233f3c3d59812675.

[161] COM/2020/822 final.

fourth, the implementation of precautionary public support measures to ensure the continued funding of the real economy under the BRRD and State aid frameworks.[162]

5.3.8 Measures in Relation to Capital Markets Law

Amidst the pandemic crisis, the ESMA has also taken a series of measures in relation to capital markets regulation (and in particular with a view to investor protection), including by prohibiting specific actions and practices (such as postponement of publication dates for periodic reports; measures relating to bans on short selling; maintaining conduct of business obligations under '**MiFID II**'; and highlighting challenges for rating collateralised loan obligations ('**CLOs**')).[163] *Furthermore*, on **24 July 2020**, as part of its overall pandemic-related recovery strategy, the Commission adopted a "**Capital Markets Recovery Package**",[164] which set out targeted amendments to several legislative acts that constitute sources of EU banking and capital markets law, to make it easier for capital markets to support EU businesses recovering from the pandemic crisis. In particular, the proposed measures aimed at encouraging investments in the economy, facilitating the recapitalisation of companies (by having access to new short-term funding) and increasing credit institutions' capacity to finance economic recovery.

In this respect, on **16 February 2021**, the co-legislators adopted two legislative acts: **Regulation (EU) 2021/337** amending the 2017 Prospectus Regulation "as regards the EU Recovery prospectus and targeted adjustments for financial intermediaries" and the Transparency Directive 2004/109/EC (as in force) "as regards the use of the single electronic reporting format for annual financial reports, to support the recovery from the COVID-19 crisis"; and **Directive (EU) 2021/338** amending the MiFID II "as regards information requirements, product governance and position limits" and the CRR "as regards [its] application to investment firms, to help the recovery from the COVID-19 crisis".[165]

---

[162] On the impact of the pandemic on banking stability in the EU, see also Gortsos (2020b) and (2020c), various contributions in Gortsos and Ringe (2020 and 2021, editors), as well as in Lackhoff (2021, editor). On the macroeconomic consequences of the exit from the pandemic, see the study of the same name, available at: https://www.bis.org/publ/work932.htm. On the economic requirements and legal conditions for completing the BU, see Weder di Mauro *et al.* (2022).

[163] See Moloney and Conac (2020), Annunziata and Siri (2021) and Enriques and Pagano (2021). For an update of measures taken by the ESMA, see at: https://www.esma.europa.eu/node/90557 and the (weekly) regulatory tracker of the European Banking Institute ('EBI') (available at: https://ebi-europa.eu/covid-regulatory-tracker). On CLOs, see also Chapter 3 above, under 3.1.6.

[164] European Commission, 'Coronavirus response: Making capital markets work for Europe's recovery', press release IP/20/1382, 24 July 2020.

[165] OJ L 68, 26.2.2021, pp. 1–13 and 14–28, respectively. On the amendments to the Prospectus Regulation (as proposed by the Commission), see Gortsos and Terzi (2020), pp. 24–26.

5.4 CURRENT DEVELOPMENTS

5.4.1 Further Amendment of Key Legislative Acts Relating to the BU

(1) On **26 January 2021**, the Commission published a targeted consultation document on the "Review of the crisis management and deposit insurance framework".[166] Its focus is the amendment of the BRRD, the SRMR and the DGSD. In this respect, it sought to gather both experience with the current crisis management and deposit insurance framework and their views on its revision in the context of completing the BU.[167] This is expected to lead soon to a formal legislative proposal.

(2) Furthermore, on **27 October 2021**, the Commission tabled its **2021 "legislative banking package"**,[168] which contains three legislative proposals amending the single rulebook for banking services in the EU, and namely the CRR and the CRD IV and (to a lesser extent) the BRRD. It forms part of the regular review of that EU banking legislation, which started in 2016 with the 'Risk Reduction Measures Package' that was adopted in 2019; the latest package does not, however, address issues relating to the 'unfinished' agenda for the completion of the BU, such as the creation of the EDIS. The aim of the proposed rules is to reduce risks in the financial system and ensure that EU credit institutions become more resilient to potential future economic shocks, while contributing to the EU's recovery from the pandemic crisis and promoting sustainable financing of the economic activity. The four pillars of this package are presented in Box 5.5 just below.[169]

Box 5.5 The Four Pillars of the 2021 "Legislative Banking Package"

Pillars	Content
Pillar 1	This pillar refers to the incorporation into EU law of recently BCBS international financial standards, duly taking into consideration the specific features of the EU banking system
Pillar 2	The *second pillar* contains proposals for strengthening prudential banking supervision to ensure EU credit institutions' sound management and better protect financial stability

(continued)

---

[166] At: https://ec.europa.eu/info/sites/default/files/business_economy_euro/banking_and_finance/documents/2021-crisis-management-deposit-insurance-review-targeted-consultation-document_en.pdf).

[167] On this consultative document, see Dias *et al.* (2021) (published based on the intended initiative), Binder (2021b) and European Central Bank (2021a).

[168] At: https://ec.europa.eu/info/consultations/finance-2021-esas-review_en.

[169] All these aspects will be further discussed in Volume II, as appropriate.

Pillars	Content
(continued)	
Pillar 3	The objective of the *third pillar*, on sustainability—contributing to the green transition, is to strengthen the resilience of the banking system to **ESG risks** as part of the Commission's 'Sustainable Finance Strategy', as set out in its 2021 **Communication** of a New Sustainable Finance Strategy (discussed below)
Pillar 4	*Finally*, some technical modifications to the banking resolution framework in the CRR and the BRRD were proposed, aimed at clarifying certain aspects regarding the prudential treatment of global systemically important institution ('**G-SII**') groups with a multiple-point-of-entry ('**MPE**') resolution strategy *and* methods for the indirect subscription of instruments eligible for meeting the **MREL** (the so-called **daisy chain** proposal). This is the only element of the package which has been finalised by the adoption by the co-legislators on 19 October 2022 of **Regulation (EU) 2022/2036**[170]

5.4.1.1 The '2020 CMU Action Plan'

(1) On **20 September 2020**, the Commission launched a new Action Plan titled "A [CMU] for people and businesses - new action plan"[171] (the '**2020 CMU Action Plan**').[172] This took into consideration the pandemic crisis, noting that market-based financing is essential to sustain the recovery and the return to long-term growth and to finance the green and digital transitions of the economy. It proposed sixteen legislative and non-legislative actions with three key objectives: *first*, support a green, digital, inclusive and resilient economic recovery by making financing more accessible to European companies; *second*, make the EU an even safer place for individuals to save and invest in the long-term; and *third*, integrate national capital markets into a genuine single market.

(2) A comprehensive package of measures, which included **five legislative proposals** (mainly) delivering on three actions in the 2020 CMU Action Plan, was then adopted on **25 November 2021**.[173] The aim of this

---

[170] OJ L 275, 25.10.2022, pp. 1–10.

[171] COM/2020/590 final.

[172] The measures to support, *inter alia*, a green recovery, are contained in Sect. 1 (7–10, Actions 1–6). On the role of the pandemic as a catalyst to strengthen the CMU and on why the benefit to be gained from some of the measures of the 2020 CMU Action Plan will take longer to emerge than others, see De Guindos et al. (2020).

[173] At: https://ec.europa.eu/info/publications/211125-capital-markets-union-package_en.

legislative package is to further improve EU companies' access to funding, broaden investment opportunities for retail investors and better integrate capital markets.[174] The accompanying Commission Communication, titled "[CMU] – Delivering one year after the Action Plan", explains the interconnectedness between the proposed measures.[175]

5.4.2   Developments in Relation to Sustainable Finance

5.4.2.1   The New Sustainable Finance Strategy

(1) Upon adoption of the above-mentioned regulatory 'trilogy' implementing the Commission's 2015 CMU Action Plan in relation to sustainable finance,[176] the Commission tabled on **21 April 2021**, amidst the pandemic crisis, a new **Communication** on "EU Taxonomy, Corporate Sustainability Reporting, Sustainability Preferences and Fiduciary Duties: Directing finance towards the European Green Deal"[177] marked another major step towards implementing the Green Deal and the Sustainable Finance Action Plan. The Commission relied on this Communication to draft and submit a proposal for a 'Corporate Sustainability Reporting Directive' (**'CSRD'**), which was adopted on 28 November 2022[178] and amended, *inter alia*, the reporting rules laid down in the **2013 'Accounting Directive'** (as in force)[179] as regards reporting on corporate sustainability.[180]

(2) Considering that sustainability is a main pillar of the EU's recovery from the pandemic and that the financial system can heavily contribute to meet the targets of the **"Green Deal"**,[181] the Commission issued then, on **6 July**

---

[174] For an overview, see Gortsos (2021c).

[175] COM/2021/720 final.

[176] See above, under 5.2.3.

[177] COM/2021/188 final. This covers taxonomy and disclosures; labelling (Green Bonds); as well as ratings and benchmarks.

[178] Directive (EU) 2022/2464 of the co-legislators of 14 December 2022 "(…) as regards corporate sustainability reporting", OJ L 322, 16.12.2022, pp. 15–80.

[179] Directive 2013/34/EU of the co-legislators of 26 June 2013 "on the annual financial statements, consolidated financial statements and related reports of certain types of undertakings (…)" (OJ L 182, 29.6.2013, 19-76), which is in force as amended (*inter alia*) by Directive 2014/95/EU of 22 October 2014 "(…) as regards disclosure of non-financial and diversity information by certain large undertakings and groups" (OJ L 330, 15.11.2014, pp. 1–9, known as the 'Non-Financial Reporting Directive', 'NFRD'). The NFRD is broadly governed by the 'comply or explain' principle; see Helleringer (2021).

[180] On the same date, the Commission also adopted six proposals for Delegated Acts on sustainability preferences, fiduciary duties and product governance, to ensure that advisers, asset managers or insurers include sustainability in their procedures and their investment advice to clients (at: https://ec.europa.eu/info/publications/210421-sustainable-finance-communication_en#csrd).

[181] Commission Communication of 11 December 2019 "The European Green Deal", COM/2019/640 final.

2021, a **Communication** on its "New Sustainable Finance Strategy"[182] and submitted a proposal for a Regulation of the co-legislators on an EU Green Bond Standard ('**EUGBS**'),[183] which aims to create a new, EU high-quality 'gold standard' for green bonds that can serve as a benchmark to other market standards.[184] The New Sustainable Finance Strategy identifies four main objectives (pillars) which are necessary for the financial system to fully support the transition of the economy towards sustainability: financing transition; developing a more inclusive sustainable finance framework; improving the financial system's resilience and contribution to sustainability (under a double materiality perspective); and fostering global ambition. Six sets of action are set out therein to obtain these objectives (coupled with proposals)[185]: *first*, development of a more comprehensive framework and facilitation of access to transition finance towards sustainability; *second*, improvement of the inclusiveness of sustainable finance with a view to SMEs and consumers, including supporting the development of 'green' loans and mortgages; *third*, enhancement of the economic and financial systems' resilience as to sustainability risks; *fourth*, increase of the financial system's contribution to sustainability; *fifth*, monitoring the financial system's orderly transition to sustainability and ensuring its integrity; and *sixth*, development of international sustainable finance initiatives and standards, and support of EU partner countries.[186]

5.4.2.2 *Management and Supervision of ESG Risks by Credit Institutions and Investment Firms*

(1) The above-mentioned Taxonomy Regulation (TR) is a legal instrument setting out disclosure requirements only applying to credit institutions either as undertakings subject to the obligation to publish a non-financial statement or a consolidated non-financial statement pursuant to the **2013 Accounting Directive**[187] when issuing environmentally sustainable corporate bonds, or to the extent that their operating licences cover the provision of portfolio management services (acting, hence, as 'market participants').[188] *On the other hand*, it does not *directly* apply to credit institutions' lending activity. However, the compatibility of the latter activity with sustainability criteria

---

[182] Communication on "Strategy for Financing the Transition to a Sustainable Economy", COM/2021/390 final.

[183] COM/2021/391 final.

[184] See on this, by mere indication, Maragopoulos (2021).

[185] Action 1 is linked to the first pillar, Action 2 to the second, Actions 3–5 to the third and Action 6 to the last.

[186] In relation to the last pillar, one day later, on 7 July 2021, the FSB published, *inter alia*, its (above-mentioned) "Roadmap for Addressing Climate-Related Financial Risks" (see Chapter 2 above, under 2.4.1).

[187] Directive 2013/34/EU, Articles 19a and 29a.

[188] TR, Articles 8 and 1(2), respectively.

is envisaged in Guidelines developed by the ECB, proposals of the EBA[189] and the Commission's "New Sustainable Finance Strategy" Communication, which, as noted, aims to improve the financial sector's resilience and its contribution to sustainability.[190]

> **Box 5.6 Two related aspects—not further discussed but quite significant**
>
> The *first* is the impact of climate-related risks on financial stability in general.[191] The *second* refers to the link between climate-related considerations and monetary policy; noteworthy in this respect is the **ECB Action Plan of 8 July 2021** to include climate change considerations in its monetary policy strategy.[192] Furthermore, on **4 July 2022**, the GC announced further steps to include climate change considerations in the Eurosystem's monetary policy framework, adjusting corporate bond holdings in its monetary policy portfolios and its collateral framework, introducing climate-related disclosure requirements and enhancing its risk management practices.[193]

(2) On **26 June 2021**, the EBA published a Report "On management and supervision of ESG risks for credit institutions and investment firms",[194] which discusses how 'ESG factors' and 'ESG risks' should be included in the regulatory and supervisory framework governing these institutions, focusing on their resilience to the potential financial impact of ESG risks across different

---

[189] See the "EBA Action Plan on Sustainable Finance" of 6 December 2019 (at: https://www.eba.europa.eu/eba-pushes-early-action-sustainable-finance) and the EBA "Roadmap on Sustainable Finance" of 13 December 2022 (at: https://www.eba.europa.eu/eba-publishes-its-roadmap-sustainable-finance). It is noted that the CRD V and the CRR II introduced new related mandates for the EBA (see Chapter 7 below, under 7.3.2).

[190] On this aspect see, by means of mere indication, Böffel and Schürger (2023), also with due reference to the impact on insurance regulation.

[191] See on this, by means of mere indication, European Central Bank (2021b) and Grünewald (2021).

[192] At: https://www.ecb.europa.eu/press/pr/date/2021/html/ecb.pr210708_1~f104919225.en.html); see on this Reichlin *et al.* (2021) and Zilioli (2021).

[193] At: https://www.ecb.europa.eu/press/pr/date/2022/html/ecb.pr220704~4f48a72462.en.html. In November 2022, the ECB ranked fourth among the G20 central banks in the "Green Central Banking Scorecard", which scores and ranks the full range of their green policies and initiatives on the basis of several criteria; see at: https://greencentralbanking.com/scorecard. See also Mayer and Schürger (2023).

[194] EBA/REP/2021/18 (at: https://www.eba.europa.eu/eba-publishes-its-report-management-and-supervision-esg-risks-credit-institutions-and-investment). This was adopted pursuant to Article 98(8) CRD IV and Article 35 IFD.

time horizons.[195] In accordance with a phase-in approach and with a view to further enhancing the SREP, the Report proposes the extension of the time horizon of the supervisory assessment of the resilience of institutions' business models, applying at least a 10-year horizon to capture 'physical risks', relevant public policies, or broader transition trends.

(3) In accordance with the *third pillar* of the (above-mentioned) 2021 legislative banking package,[196] supervisory authorities will have to conduct regular climate stress testing and assess ESG risks as part of the **SREP**, while credit institutions will be required to systematically identify, disclose and manage ESG risks as part of their risk management. The content of the new framework is heavily influenced by the EBA Report of 26 June 2021.[197]

5.4.3 The Commission's 2020 Digital Finance Package

Regulatory developments relating to digital finance will also, either directly or indirectly, impact on the operation of the banking system, *mainly* in respect of payment services provided by credit institutions. These developments are linked to the **Communication** "on a Digital Finance Strategy for the EU" of the Commission of **24 September 2020**,[198] which aims at further enabling and supporting the potential of digital finance in terms of innovation and competition, while mitigating the related risks. Part of this "Digital Finance Package" was three proposals for a Regulation of the co-legislators, which constitute a closely related 'trilogy':

> The *first*, "on a Pilot Regime for market infrastructures based on distributed ledger technology (…)" ('**DLTR**'), was adopted by the co-legislators on 30 May 2022[199]; it lays down requirements on multilateral trading facilities and securities settlement systems using distributed ledger technology ('**DLT**') market infrastructures.

---

[195] 'ESG factors' are defined as ESG matters that may have a positive or negative impact on the financial performance or solvency of an entity, sovereign or individual; 'ESG risks' are defined as those of any negative financial impact on an institution arising from the current or prospective impacts of ESG factors on its counterparties or invested assets.

[196] See above, under 5.4.1.

[197] On this pillar, see De Arriba-Sellier (2022). It is noted that on 19 December 2022 the ECB published its "Report on good practices for climate stress testing" (at: https://www.bankingsupervision.europa.eu/ecb/pub/pdf/ssm.202212_ECBreport_on_good_practices_for_CST~539227e0c1.en.pdf?c1b3d7b239907b9530b8cbecb6ebed80).

[198] COM/2020/591 final. This builds on its Communication "FinTech Action Plan: For a More Competitive and Innovative European Financial Sector" (8 March 2018, COM/2018/109 final).

[199] Regulation (EU) 2022/858, OJ L 151, 2.6.2022, pp. 1–33. Most of the provisions of this legislative act shall apply from 23 March 2023 (*ibid.*, Article 19).

The *second* Regulation, "on digital operational resilience for the financial sector (…)"[200] (well-known as Digital Operational Resilience Act, '**DORA**'), was adopted by the co-legislators on 14 December 2022; it lays down uniform requirements concerning the security of network and information systems supporting the business processes of financial entities needed to achieve a high common level of digital operational resilience.[201]

The *third*, and eventually most important legislative initiative, is the proposal for a Regulation "on Markets in Crypto-Assets (…)"[202] ('**MiCAR**'). The aim of this proposed legislation (which had been formally adopted by the co-legislators but not published as of end-2022) is to define the terms 'crypto-assets' and '**DLT**' as widely as possible to capture all types of crypto-assets, which (are highly volatile and) currently fall outside the scope of EU financial law (including asset-referenced and e-money tokens, jointly referred to as '**stablecoins**'[203]).[204] Furthermore, it also aims at contributing to the objective of combatting money laundering and the financing of terrorism; hence, the definition of 'crypto-assets' and 'crypto-asset service providers' shall correspond to the definition of virtual assets and virtual asset service providers ('**VASPs**') as set out in the FAFT Recommendations.[205]

---

[200] Regulation (EU) 2022/2554, OJ L 333, 27.12.2022, pp. 1–79. This legislative act shall apply from 17 January 2025 (*ibid.*, Article 64). *Inter alia*, it is in line with the G7 international standards (G7 Fundamental Elements for Threat-Led Penetration Testing) ('G7FE-TLPT', available at: https://assets.publishing.service.gov.uk/government/uploads/system/uploads/attachment_data/file/1134064/2018-10-24-g7-fundamental-elements-led-penetration-testing-data.pdf).

[201] The term 'digital operational resilience' is defined (DORA, Article 3, point (1)) as a financial entity's ability to build, assure and review its operational integrity and reliability by ensuring, either directly or indirectly through the use of services provided by Information and Communication Technology ('ICT') third-party service providers, the full range of ICT-related capabilities needed to address the security of the network and information systems which a financial entity uses, and which support the continued provision of financial services and their quality, including throughout disruptions.

[202] COM/2020/593 final.

[203] See in this respect the final Report of the FSB of 13 October 2020: "Regulation, Supervision and Oversight of "Global Stablecoin" Arrangements", available at: https://www.fsb.org/2020/10/regulation-supervision-and-oversight-of-global-stablecoin-arrangements/.

[204] For an overview of this proposed legislative act Gortsos (2021d), see also Zetzsche *et al.* (2020) on its relationship with the EU's Digital Finance Strategy.

[205] Financial Action Task Force (2021): "Virtual Assets and Virtual Asset Service Providers: Updated Guidance for a Risk-Based Approach", 28 October 2 (available at: https://www.fatf-gafi.org/media/fatf/documents/recommendations/Updated-Guidance-VA-VASP.pdf).

Crypto-assets should be distinguished from central bank digital currencies ('**CBDCs**'), which are also based on **DLT**, are issued (or are to be issued) by central banks and are excluded from the field of application of the MiCAR. The further discussion of this (quite) recent development, mainly due to changes in payments, finance and technology, is outside the scope of this study.[206]

(3) As already noted, and *inter alia*, these regulatory developments will impact on the operation of the banking sector and payment systems. Most importantly, however, when this 'trilogy' will have been fully adopted and implemented, it will create a level playing field among various providers of means of payments and payment services (including credit institutions) and mitigate the risks relating to the issuance and admission to trading of crypto-assets and the operation of their issuers, the providers of crypto-asset services and the markets of crypto assets, by enhancing transparency and consumer protection and ensuring the integrity of the markets for crypto-assets.[207]

Secondary Sources

A

Aerts, J. and P. Bizarro (2020): The Reform of the European Stability Mechanism, *Capital Markets Law Journal*, Volume 15, Issue 2, April, pp. 159–174

Aiyar, S., Bergthaler, W., Garrido, J., Ilyina, A., Jobst, A., Kang, K., Kovtun, D., Liu, Y., Monaghan, D. and M. Moretti (2015): *A Strategy for Resolving Europe's Problem Loans*, International Monetary Fund, IMF Staff Discussion Note, Volume 15, no. 19, September

Alexander, K. (2019): *Principles of Banking Regulation*, Cambridge University Press, Cambridge, United Kingdom

Annunziata, F. and M. Siri (2021): Fixing the core of EU capital markets legislation during the pandemic: temporary exercises or long-term path?, in Gortsos, Ch.V. and W.G. Ringe (2021, editors): *Financial Stability amidst the Pandemic Crisis: on Top*

---

[206] On this topic, see (on top of an already vast existing literature) the "BIS Innovation Hub work on central bank digital currency (CBDC)" (at: https://www.bis.org/about/bisih/topics/cbdc.htm). See also the most recent (16 December 2022) BCBS Report titled: "Prudential treatment of cryptoasset exposures" (at: https://www.bis.org/bcbs/publ/d545.htm), which the BCBS has agreed to implement by 1 January 2025 and has been included, as a new chapter, in the consolidated "Basel Framework" (see Chapter 2 above, under 2.4.1).

[207] For the sake of completeness, it is also noted that, on 21 April 2021, the Commission submitted a proposal for a Regulation of the co-legislators (based on Articles 16 and 114 TFEU) "laying down harmonised rules on artificial intelligence (Artificial Intelligence Act) (…) (COM/2021/206 final)". The aim of this proposed legislative act, which as of December 2022 had not yet been adopted, is to set out a coordinated EU approach on the human and ethical implications of artificial intelligence ('AI') with a view to promoting the development and across the single market of safe and lawful AI with due respect to fundamental rights.

of the Wave, European Banking Institute (EBI), e-book, Chapter 17, pp. 563–583, available at: https://ssrn.com/abstract=3877946

Avgerinos, Y.V. (2003): *Regulating and Supervising Investment Services in the European Union*, Palgrave Macmillan, Antony Rowe Ltd, Chippenham and Eastbourne, Great Britain

Avgouleas, E. and G. Ferrarini (2018): A Single Listing Authority and Securities Regulator for the CMU and the Future of ESMA: Costs, Benefits and Legal Impediments, in Busch, D., Avgouleas, E. and G. Ferrarini (2018, editors): *Capital Markets Union in Europe*, Oxford EU Financial Regulation Series, Oxford University Press, United Kingdom, Chapter 4, pp. 55–96

Awad, R., Ferreira, C., Jociene, Al. and L. Riedweg (2020): *Restriction of Banks' Capital Distribution during the COVID-19 Pandemic (Dividends, Share Buybacks, and Bonuses)*, IMF Special Series on Covid-19, 7 July, available at: https://www.imf.org/~/media/Files/Publications/covid19-special-notes/en-special-series-on-covid-19-restriction-of-banks-capital-distribution-during-the-covid-19-pandemic.ashx?la=en&utm_medium=email&utm_source=govdelivery

B

Becker, U. (2019): Kommentar zum Artikel 3 EUV, in Schwarze, J., Becker, U., Hatje, A. und J. Schoo (2019, Hrsg.): *EU-Kommentar*, 4. Auflage, Nomos Verlagsgesellschaft, Baden-Baden, pp. 53–59

Binder, J.-H. (2021a): *Central Counterparties' Insolvency and Resolution – The New EU Regulation on CCP Recovery and Resolution*, European Banking Institute Working Paper Series, No. 82, available at: https://ssrn.com/abstract=3778649

Binder, J.-H. (2021b): *The next step: Towards harmonised frameworks for the liquidation of non-systematically relevant credit institutions in the EU? A discussion of policy choices and potential impediments*, European Banking Institute Working Paper Series, No. 86, available at: https://ssrn.com/abstract=3807919

Blair, W., Zilioli, Ch. and Ch.V. Gortsos (2023, editors): *International Monetary and Banking Law in the post COVID-19 World*, Oxford University Press, Oxford

Böffel, L. and J. Schürger (2023): Sustainability: A Current Driver in EU Banking and Insurance Regulation, in Böffel, L. and J. Schürger (2023, editors): *Digitalisation, Sustainability, and the Banking and Capital Markets Union*, EBI Studies in Banking and Capital Markets Law, Palgrave Macmillan, Cham–Switzerland, Chapter 8, pp. 229–271

Bonatti, L. et al. (2021): *Recalibrated Monetary Policy Instruments to Address the Economic Fallout from Covid-19: Compilation of Papers*, Study Requested by ECON Committee, Monetary Dialogue, March, available at: https://mail.google.com/mail/u/0/#label/EBI+-+e-book+2021/FMfcgxwLtQTbWRRvrTnSvsVfSGHTcPTk?projector=1&messagePartId=0.3

Bosque, C., Muñoz, D.R. and M. Lamandini (2021): Next Generation EU: Its meaning, challenges and link to sustainability, in Gortsos, Ch.V. and W.G. Ringe (2021, editors): *Financial Stability amidst the Pandemic Crisis: On Top of the Wave*, European Banking Institute (EBI), e-book, Chapter 10, pp. 325–356, available at: https://ssrn.com/abstract=3877946

Brunnermeier, M.K., Langfield, S., Pagano, M., Reis, R. Van Nieuwerburgh, S. and D. Vayanos (2016): *ESBies: Safety in the tranches*, ESRB Working Paper Series, No

21, September, available at: https://www.esrb.europa.eu/pub/pdf/wp/esrbwp21.en.pdf

Buchheit, L.C. (2016): The Greek debt restructuring of 2012, in European Central Bank (2016): *ECB Legal Conference 2016 – In memory of Ron Luberti, General Counsel of De Nederlandsche Bank and member of the Legal Committee of the ESCB*, available at: https://www.ecb.europa.eu/pub/pdf/other/escblegalconferenc e2016_201702.en.pdf?78c259326d82ec15a0918ffd5a094373, pp. 46–51

Busch, D. (2022): The future of EU financial law, *Capital Markets Law Journal*, Volume 17, Issue 1, pp. 52–94

Busch, D. (2021): Sustainability Disclosure in the financial sector, in Busch, D., Ferrarini, G. and S. Grünewald (2021, editors): *Sustainable Finance in Europe: Corporate Governance, Financial Stability and Financial Markets*, EBI Studies in Banking and Capital Markets Law, Chapter 10, pp. 329–350, Palgrave Macmillan, Cham–Switzerland

Busch, D. (2018): A Stronger Role for the European Supervisory Authorities in the EU?, in Busch, D., Avgouleas, E. and G. Ferrarini (2018, editors): *Capital Markets Union in Europe*, Oxford EU Financial Regulation Series, Oxford University Press, United Kingdom, Chapter 3, pp. 28–54

Busch, D., Avgouleas, E. and G. Ferrarini (2018, editors): *Capital Markets Union in Europe*, Oxford University Press, Oxford

Busch, D., Ferrarini, G. and Franx, J.P. (2020, editors): *Prospectus Regulation and Prospectus Liability*, Oxford EU Financial Regulation Series, Oxford University Press, United Kingdom

C–D

Colaert, V. (2022): The Changing Nature of Financial Regulation: Sustainable Finance as a New EU Policy Objective, *Common Market Law Review*, Volume 59, pp. 1669–1710

Craig, P. and G. de Búrca (2020): *EU Law: Texts, Cases, and Materials*, Seventh edition, Oxford University Press, Oxford – New York

Dautovic, Er. et al. (2021): *Evaluating the benefits of euro area dividend distribution recommendations on lending and provisioning*, ECB Macroprudential Bulletin, available at: https://www.ecb.europa.eu/pub/financial-stability/macroprudential-bulletin/html/ecb.mpbu202106_2~90dc75f42d.en.html

De Arriba-Sellier, N. (2022): Banking on Green: Sustainability in the Commission's Banking Reform, *EU Law Live*, Weekend edition, No 86, January 22, available at: https://eulawlive.com/weekend-edition/weekend-edition-no86

De Cos, P.H. (2021): *The ECB monetary policy response to the pandemic crisis*, 1st Ibero-American Central Bank Conference/Banco de España and Ibero-American General Secretariat, Banco de España, available at: https://www.bis.org/review/r210413a.pdf

De Guindos, L., Panetta, F. and Is. Schnabel (2020): *Europe needs a fully fledged capital markets union—now more than ever*, The ECB Blog, 2 September, available at: https://www.ecb.europa.eu/press/blog/date/2020/html/ecb.blog20090 2~c168038cbc.en.html

Demary, M. and J. Matthes (2017): *An Evaluation of Sovereign-backed Securities (SBSs)—Potentials, Risks and Political Relevance for EMU Reform*, Institut der deutschen Wirtschaft Köln, IW policy paper 12/2017, 23 June, available at: https://www.iwkoeln.de/fileadmin/publikationen/2017/347407/IW-pol icy-paper_2017_12_SBS_evaluation_basis.pdf

Dias, C., Grigaitè, K., Seagall, R. and M. Magnus (2021): *Review of the bank crisis management and deposit insurance frameworks*, European Parliament, Economic Governance Support Unit, Briefing, January, available at: https://www.europarl.eur opa.eu/RegData/etudes/BRIE/2021/659620/IPOL_BRI(2021)659620_EN.pdf

Dixon H. (2014): *Unlocking Europe's capital markets union*, Centre for European Reform, October, available at: https://www.cer.org.uk/sites/default/files/public ations/attachments/pdf/2014/unlocking_europes_capital_markets_union_hugo dixon_15.10.14-9870.pdf

Drossos, Y. (2020): *The Flight of Icarus: European Legal Responses Resulting from the Financial Crisis*, Hart Publishing, Oxford

E–F

Eller M., Martin, R. and L. Vashold (2021): CESEE's macroprudential policy response in the wake of the COVID-19 crisis, *Focus on European Economic Integration*, Oesterreichische Nationalbank (Austrian Central Bank), Issue Q1/21, pp. 55–69, available at: https://www.oenb.at/dam/jcr:a39f859c-7c91-4590-b94c-57cafddae8ef/04_feei_q1-21_cesees-macroprudential-policy-response-in-the-wake-of-the-covid-19-crisis.pdf

English, B., Forbes K. and Á. Ubide (2021): *Monetary policy and central banking in the Covid era: A new eBook*, VoxEU/CEPR, CEPR Press, June, available at: https://voxeu.org/article/monetary-policy-and-central-banking-covid-era-new-ebook

Enoch, Ch. (2021): *Europe Beyond the Euro: Building Protection for Europe's Economies in the Times of Risks*, St Antony's Series (Series Editors Healey D. and L. Payne), Palgrave Macmillan, Cham–Switzerland

Enriques, L. and M. Pagano (2021): Emergency measures for equity trading: the case against short-selling and stock exchange shutdowns, in Gortsos, Ch.V. and W.G. Ringe (2021, editors): *Financial Stability amidst the Pandemic Crisis: on Top of the Wave*, European Banking Institute (EBI), e-book, Chapter 16, pp. 547–561, available at: https://ssrn.com/abstract=3877946

European Central Bank (2021a): *ECB contribution to the European Commission's targeted consultation on the review of the crisis management and deposit insurance framework*, available at: https://www.bankingsupervision.europa.eu/ecb/pub/pdf/ssm.consultation_on_crisis_management_deposit_insurance_202105~0ac1f04e33.en.pdf?f72a2359f0e84b0c5677bd2d673e9480

European Central Bank (2021b): Climate-related risk and financial stability", ECB/ESRB Project Team on climate risk monitoring, July, available at: https://www.ecb.europa.eu/pub/pdf/other/ecb.Climateriskfinancialstabili ty202107~87822fae81.en.pdf?d38340433f58fb658f73574755835661

European Commission (2022): *Synergies between the Sustainable Development Goals and the National Recovery and Resilience Plans—Best Practices from Local and Regional Authorities*, European Committee of the Regions, available at: https://europa.eu/!cyXyN7

European Court of Auditors (2020): *Sustainable finance: More consistent EU action needed to redirect finance towards sustainable investment*, Special Report 25/2022, available at: https://www.eca.europa.eu/Lists/ECADocuments/SR21_22/SR_sustainable-finance_EN.pdf

European Parliament (2021): *The ECB's Monetary Policy Response to the COVID-19 Crisis*, ECON in Focus, 9 February, available at: https://mail.google.com/mail/u/0/#label/EBI+-+e-book+2021/FMfcgxwLtQTbWRRvrTnSvsVfSGHTcPTk?projector=1&messagePartId=0.2

European Stability Mechanism (2014): *FAQ on the ESM direct bank recapitalisation instrument*, Luxembourg, December, available at: https://www.esm.europa.eu/pdf/2014-12-08%20FAQ%20DRI.pdf

European Systemic Risk Board (2017): *Financial stability implications of IFRS 9*, July, available at: https://www.esrb.europa.eu/pub/pdf/reports/20170717_fin_stab_imp_IFRS_9.en.pdf

European Systemic Risk Board (2016): *Survey on sovereign bond-backed securities, Background document*, European Systemic Risk Board High-Level Task Force on Safe Assets, 22 December, available at: https://www.esrb.europa.eu/pub/pdf/surveys/161222_survey_background_document.en.pdf

European Systemic Risk Board (2015): *ESRB report on the regulatory treatment of sovereign exposures*, available at: https://www.esrb.europa.eu/pub/html/index.en.html

Ferran, E. (2004): *Building an EU Securities Market*, Cambridge University Press, Cambridge, New York, Melbourne, Madrid, Cape Town, Singapore, São Paolo

Ferrarini, G. and E. Macchiavello (2018): Fin Tech and Alternative Finance in the CMU: The Regulation of Marketplace Investing, in Busch, D., Avgouleas, E. and G. Ferrarini (2018, editors): *Capital Markets Union in Europe*, Oxford EU Financial Regulation Series, Oxford University Press, United Kingdom, Chapter 10, pp. 208–233

G

Gargantini, M., Di Noia, C. and G. Dimitropoulos (2018): Cross-border Distribution of Collective Investment Products in the EU, in Busch, D., Avgouleas, E. and G. Ferrarini (2018, editors): *Capital Markets Union in Europe*, Oxford EU Financial Regulation Series, Oxford University Press, United Kingdom, Chapter 19, pp. 413–441

Gortsos, Ch.V. (2021a): *Non-performing Loans—New risks and policies? What factors drive the performance of national asset management companies?*, Briefing paper for the Committee on Economic and Monetary Affairs (ECON) of the European Parliament, available at: https://www.europarl.europa.eu/RegData/etudes/IDAN/2021/659647/IPOL_IDA(2021)659647_EN.pdf

Gortsos, Ch.V. (2021b): The EU Taxonomy Regulation: more important than just an element of the Capital Markets Union, in Busch, D., Ferrarini, G. and S. Grünewald (2021 editors): *Sustainable Finance in Europe*, EBI Studies in Banking and Capital Markets Law, Chapter 11, pp. 351–395, Palgrave Macmillan, Cham – Switzerland

Gortsos, Ch.V. (2021c): The 2021 Capital Markets Union Package': A First Comprehensive Set of Legislative Proposals to Implement the 2020 CMU Action Plan, *EU Law Live*, Op-Ed, December, available at: https://eulawlive.com/op-ed-the-2021-capital-markets-union-package-a-first-comprehensive-set-of-legislative-proposals-to-implement-the-2020-cmu-action-plan-by-christos-v-gortsos

Gortsos, Ch.V. (2021d): *The Commission's 2020 Proposal for a Markets in Crypto-Assets Regulation ('MiCAR'): A Brief Introductory Overview*, available at: https://ssrn.com/abstract=3842824

Gortsos, Ch.V. (2020a): *European Central Banking Law —The Role of the European Central Bank and National Central Banks under European Law*, Palgrave Macmillan Studies in Banking and Financial Institutions, Palgrave Macmillan, Cham–Switzerland

Gortsos, Ch.V. (2020b): The response of the European Central Bank to the current pandemic crisis: monetary policy and prudential banking supervision decisions, *European Company and Financial Law Review*, Volume 17, issue 3–4 (also in European Banking Institute Working Paper Series, No. 68, available at: https://ssrn.com/abstract=3650370)

Gortsos, Ch.V. (2020c): The application of the EU banking resolution framework amidst the pandemic crisis, in Gortsos, Ch.V. and G. Ringe (2020, editors): *Pandemic Crisis and Financial Stability*, European Banking Institute (EBI), e-book, Chapter 11, pp. 361–390, available at: https://ssrn.com/abstract=3607930

Gortsos, Ch.V. (2018): *Financial engineering coupled with regulatory incentives: is there a strong market case for sovereign bond-backed securities (SBBSs) in the euro-area? A brief analysis of the European Commission's Proposal for a Regulation on SBBSs*, available at: https://ssrn.com/abstract=3244320

Gortsos, Ch.V. (2017): *The proposed legal framework for establishing a European Monetary Fund (EMF): a systematic presentation and a preliminary assessment*, available at: https://ssrn.com/abstract=3090343

Gortsos, Ch.V. (2013): The Impact of the Current Euro Zone Fiscal Crisis on the Greek Banking Sector and the Measures Adopted to Preserve its Stability, in Hieronymi, O. and C.A. Stephanou (2013, editors): *International Debt: Economic, Financial, Monetary, Political and Regulatory Aspects*, Chapter 6, pp. 164–188, Palgrave Macmillan, CPI Antony Rowe, Chippenham and Eastbourne

Gortsos, Ch.V. and W. Blair (2023): The evolution of the regulatory framework governing climate change and sustainable finance in the EU and UK, in Blair, W., Zilioli, Ch. and Ch.V. Gortsos (2023, editors): *International Monetary and Banking Law in the post COVID-19 World*, Chapter 14, Oxford University Press, Oxford

Gortsos, Ch.V. and D. Kyriazis (2022): *Sustainable Finance: The EU's Legislative Trilogy and the Need for Global Convergence*, available at: https://hub.uoa.gr/sustainable-finance

Gortsos, Ch.V. and G. Ringe (2021, editors): *Financial Stability amidst the Pandemic Crisis: On Top of the Wave*, European Banking Institute (EBI), e-book, available at: https://ssrn.com/abstract=3877946

Gortsos, Ch.V. and G. Ringe (2020, editors): *Pandemic Crisis and Financial Stability*, European Banking Institute (EBI), e-book, available at: https://ssrn.com/abstract=3607930

Gortsos, Ch.V. and M.E. Terzi (2020): *The Prospectus Regulation (Regulation (EU) 2017/1129) and the recent Proposal for an EU Recovery Prospectus: elements of continuity and change with the past and the way forward*, European Banking Institute Working Paper Series, No. 79, available at: https://ssrn.com/abstract=3742863

Grünewald, S. (2021): Climate Change as a Systemic Risk in Finance: Are Macroprudential Authorities Up to the Task?, in Busch, D. Ferrarini, G. and S. Grünewald (2021, editors): *Sustainable Finance in Europe: Corporate Governance, Financial

Stability and Financial Markets, EBI Studies in Banking and Capital Markets Law, Chapter 7, pp. 227–257, Palgrave Macmillan, Cham– witzerland

Gundel, J. (2019): Kommentar zum Artikel 352 AEUV, in Becker, U., Hatje, A. Schoo, J. und J. Schwarze (2019, Herausgeber): *EU-Kommentar*, 4. Auflage, Nomos Verlagsgesellschaft, Baden-Baden, pp. 3334–3346

H

Hadjiemmanuil, Ch. (2020a): The Euro Area in Crisis: 2008–2018, in Amtenbrink, F. and Ch. Herrmann (2020, editors): *Oxford Handbook on the EU Law of Economic and Monetary Union*, Oxford University Press, Oxford, Chapter 40, pp. 1253–1362 (also published in LSE Law, Society and Economy Working Papers 12/2019, available at: https://ssrn.com/abstract=3413000)

Hadjiemmanuil, Ch. (2020b): European economic governance and the pandemic: Fiscal crisis management under a flawed policy process, in Gortsos, Ch.V. and W.G. Ringe (2020, editors): *Pandemic Crisis and Financial Stability*, European Banking Institute (EBI), e-book, Chapter 6, pp. 175–243, available at: https://ssrn.com/abstract=3607930

Hadjiemmanuil, Ch. (2015): *Bank Resolution Financing in the Banking Union*, LSE Law, Society and Economy Working Papers 6/2015, available at: https://ssrn.com/abstract=2575372

Heemskerk, M., Maatman, R. and B. Werker (2018): A Policy Framework for European Personal Pensions, in Busch, D., Avgouleas, E. and G. Ferrarini (2018, editors): *Capital Markets Union in Europe*, Oxford EU Financial Regulation Series, Oxford University Press, United Kingdom, Chapter 17, pp. 372–394

Helleringer, G. (2021): EU vs. Greenwashing: The Birth Pangs of Transparency, Comparability, Cooperation and Leadership, *Oxford Business Law Blog*, 5 July, available at: https://www.law.ox.ac.uk/business-law-blog/blog/2021/07/eu-vs-greenwashing-birth-pangs-transparency-comparability-cooperation

House of Lords (2015): *Capital Markets Union: a welcome start*, European Union Committee, 11th Report of Session 2014–15, HL Paper 136, London, 20 March

J–K–L

Joosen, B. (2020): Balancing macro- and micro-prudential powers in the SSM during the COVID-19 crisis, in Gortsos, Ch.V. and W.G. Ringe (2020, editors): *Pandemic Crisis and Financial Stability*, European Banking Institute (EBI), e-book, Chapter 10, pp. 339–360, available at: https://ssrn.com/abstract=3607930

Joosen, B. and K. Lieverse (2018): Relief from Prudential Requirements to Support the Capital Markets Union, in Busch, D., Avgouleas, E. and G. Ferrarini (2018, editors): *Capital Markets Union in Europe*, Oxford EU Financial Regulation Series, Oxford University Press, United Kingdom, Chapter 20, pp. 446–463

Kastelein, G. (2018): Securitization in the Capital Markets Union: One Step Forward, Two Steps Back, in Busch, D., Avgouleas, E. and G. Ferrarini (2018, editors): *Capital Markets Union in Europe*, Oxford EU Financial Regulation Series, Oxford University Press, United Kingdom, Chapter 21, pp. 464–483

Lackhoff, K. (2021, editor): *Banking Supervision and COVID-19: A Handbook*, Verlag C.H. Beck, München—Hart Publishing, Oxford—Nomos Verlagsgesellschaft, Baden-Baden

Lagaria, K. (2021): Releasable and Non-Releasable Capital Buffers in the European Union: From Puberty to Maturity, *Journal of Accounting & Finance*, Volume 21, Issue 3, available at: https://ssrn.com/abstract_id=3903999

Lamandini, M., Lusignani, G. and D.R. Muñoz (2017): *Does Europe Have What It Takes to Finish the Banking Union: NPLs and Their Hard Choices, Non-Choices and Evolving Choices*, EBI Working Paper Series No 17, available at: https://ssrn.com/abstract=3091944

Lannoo, K. (2015): Detailed CMU Action Plan, but more (ambition) is required, *ECMI Commentary*, No. 39/2, 2 October, available at: https://www.ceps.eu/download/publication/?id=9102&pdf=KL_CMU.pdf

Lannoo, K. (1999): *Does Europe need a SEC?*, European Capital Markets Institute, Madrid

Lenaerts, K., Maselis, Ig. and K. Gutman K (2014): *EU Procedural Law*, Oxford European Union Law Library, Oxford University Press, Oxford

Losada, F. and K. Tuori (2021): Integrating Macroeconomics into the EU Single Legal Order: The Role of Financial Stability in Post-crisis Europe, *European Papers*, Volume 6, Issue 3, pp. 1367–1396

M

Mack, S. (2020): EU banks' vulnerabilities: Capital conservation key to withstanding Corona crisis, Bertelsmann Stiftung Policy Brief, Hertie School, Jacques Delors Centre, 20 May, available at: https://www.bertelsmann-stiftung.de/fileadmin/files/user_upload/20200520_EU_banks__vulnerabilities_Mack.pdf

Maragopoulos, N. (2021): *Towards a European Green Bond: A Commission's proposal to promote sustainable finance*, European Banking Institute Working Paper Series, No. 103, available at: https://ssrn.com/abstract=3933766

Martucci, F. (2020): Non-EU Legal Instruments (EFSF, ESM, and Fiscal Compact), in Amtenbrink, F. and Ch. Herrmann (2020, editors): *Oxford Handbook on the EU Law of Economic and Monetary Union*, Oxford University Press, Oxford, Chapter 12, pp. 293–325

Mayer, M. and J. Schürger, J. (2023): Green Monetary Policy in the EMU and Its Primary Law Limits, in Böffel, L. and J. Schürger (2023, editors): *Digitalisation, Sustainability, and the Banking and Capital Markets Union*, EBI Studies in Banking and Capital Markets Law, Palgrave Macmillan, Cham – Switzerland, Chapter 10, pp. 295–326

Mersch, Y. (2014): *Capital markets union—The "Why" and the "How"*, Speech at the Joint EIB-IMF High Level Workshop, Brussels, 22 October

Mollers, T.M. (2022): European Green Deal: Greenwashing and the Forgotten Good Corporate Citizen as an Investor, *Columbia Journal of European Law*, Volume 28, p. 203 *et seq.*

Moloney, N. and P.-H. Conac (2020): EU Financial Market Governance and the Covid-19 Crisis: ESMA's Nimble, Responsive, and Speedy Response in Coordinating National Authorities through Soft-Law Instruments, *European Company and Financial Law Review*, 2020, Volume 17, Issue 3–4, pp. 363–385

Monokroussos, P. and C. Gortsos (2017, editors): *Non-Performing Loans and Resolving Private Sector Insolvency: Experiences from the EU Periphery and the Case of Greece*, Palgrave Macmillan Studies in Banking and Financial Institutions, Palgrave Macmillan, Cham–Switzerland

Montanaro, E. (2019): Non-Performing Loans and the European Union Legal Framework, in Chiti, M.P. and V. Santoro (2019, editors): *The Palgrave Handbook of European Banking Union Law*, Chapter 10, pp. 213–246, Palgrave Macmillan, Cham–Switzerland

O–P–Q–R

Ohler, Ch.M. (2023): Unconventional monetary policy in the euro area: A comparative analysis with the unconventional monetary policy of the Federal Reserve, in Blair, W., Zilioli, Ch. and Ch.V. Gortsos (2023, editors): *International Monetary and Banking Law in the post COVID-19 World*, Chapter 18, Oxford University Press, Oxford

Pacces, A.M. (2021): *Will the EU Taxonomy Regulation Foster a Sustainable Corporate Governance?*, ECGI, Law Working Paper No 611/2011, October, available at: https://ecgi.global/working-paper/will-eu-taxonomy-regulation-foster-sustainable-corporate-governance

Piantelli, A.M. (2021): *Managing Banking Crises in Europe after the Great Crisis*, Radboud Business Law Institute, Series Law of Business and Finance, Volume 20, Wolters Kluwer Nederland B.V.

Pietrancosta, A. and A. Marraud des Grottes (2018): *Has the Notion of 'Private Offerings' Been Abolished by the Prospectus Regulation of 14 June 2017?*, available at: https://ssrn.com/abstract=3124225

Pulgar Ezquerra, J. and Ig. Signes de Mesa (2021): Non-performing loans in the pandemic crisis and the Directive on preventive corporate restructuring, in Gortsos, Ch.V. and W.G. Ringe (2021, editors): *Financial Stability amidst the Pandemic Crisis: on Top of the Wave*, European Banking Institute (EBI), e-book, Chapter 7, pp. 219–260, available at: https://ssrn.com/abstract=3877946

Reichlin, L., Adam, K., McKibbin, W.J., McMahon, M., Reis, R., Ricco, G. and B. Weder di Mauro (2021): *The ECB strategy: The 2021 review and its future*, VoxEU.org/CEPR, CEPR Press, available at: https://voxeu.org/content/ecb-strategy-2021-review-and-its-future

S–T

Schlosser, P. (2017): Still Looking for the Banking Union's Fiscal Backstop, in Allen, F., Carletti, E., J. Gray and M. Gulati (2017, editors): *The changing geography of finance and regulation in Europe*, European University Institute (EUI), pp. 163–178

Schoenmaker, D. (2017): *A macro approach to international bank resolution*, Bruegel, Policy Contribution, Issue no 20, July, available at: https://bruegel.org/wp-content/uploads/2017/07/PC-20-2017-100717.pdf

Schoenmaker, D. (2014): *On the need for a fiscal backstop to the banking system*, Duisenberg school of finance, DSF Policy Paper, No 44, July, available at: https://www.dsf.nl/wp-content/uploads/2014/10/DSF-Policy-Paper-No-44-On-the-need-for-a-fiscal-backstop-to-the-banking-system.pdf

Sciaronne Alibrandi, A. and G. Frigeni (2020): Restrictions on Shareholder's Distribution in the COVID-19 crisis, in Gortsos, Ch.V. and W.G. Ringe (2020, editors): *Pandemic Crisis and Financial Stability*, European Banking Institute (EBI), e-book, Chapter 14, pp. 429–454, available at: https://ssrn.com/abstract=3607930

Steinbach, A. (2010): The Lisbon Judgment of the German Federal Constitutional Court – New Guidance on the Limits of European Integration?, *German Law Journal*, Volume 11, no. 4, pp. 367–390 (also available at: https://ssrn.com/abstract=2543488)

Tuori, Kl. (2020): Monetary Policy (Objectives and Instruments), in Amtenbrink, F. and Ch. Herrmann (2020, editors): *The EU Law of Economic and Monetary Union*, Oxford University Press, Oxford, Chapter 22, pp. 615–698

V–W & Z

Varela, J.C. (2015): Direct recapitalization of banks and sovereign debt: the ESM direct recapitalization instrument and its impact on sovereign debt, in Hinojosa L.M. and J.M. Beneyto (2015, editors): *European Banking Union: The new regime*, International Banking and Financial Law Series Volume 27, Kluwer Law International, Chapter 9, pp. 121–136

Véron, N. and G. Wolff (2015): *Capital Markets Union: a vision for the long term*, Bruegel Policy Contribution, Issue 2015/05, April

Weatherill, S. (2016): *Cases and Materials on EU Law*, 12th edition, Oxford University Press, Oxford

Weder di Mauro, B. **et al. (2022)**: *Completing the banking union: Economic requirements and legal conditions*, Centre for Economic Policy Research (CEPR) Policy Insights, Policy Insight 119, 27 October, available at: https://cepr.org/publications/policy-insight-119-completing-banking-union-economic-requirements-and-legal-conditions

Wojcik, K.-Ph. (2020): The EU's Response to the COVID-19 Pandemic in the Field of EU Banking Regulation, *EU LAW LIVE*, weekend edition No 24, 4 July, pp. 12–22, available at: https://eulawlive.com/weekend-edition/weekend-edition-no24

Zettelmeyer, J., Trebesch, Ch. and and G.M. Gulati (2013): Managing Holdouts: The Case of the 2012 Greek Exchange, in Lastra, R.M. and L. Buchheit (2013, editors): *Sovereign Debt Management*, Oxford University Press, Oxford, Chapter 3, pp. 25–38

Zetzsche, D.A., Annunziata, F., Arner, D.W. and R.P. Buckley (2021): The Markets in Crypto-Assets regulation (MiCA) and the EU Digital Finance Strategy, *16 Capital Markets Law Journal*, pp. 203–225 (also available in EBI Working Paper Series No 77 (2020), available at: https://ssrn.com/abstract=3725395)

Zilioli, Ch. (2021): The new ECB monetary policy strategy and the ECB's Roadmap of climate change-related actions', *EU Law Live*, Weekend Edition No 67, pp. 2–6

Zilioli, C and A.L. Riso (2023): The response of central banks to the COVID-19 crisis: legal aspects of the ECB's monetary policy measures, in Blair, W., Zilioli, Ch. and Ch.V. Gortsos (2023, editors): *International Monetary and Banking Law in the post COVID-19 World*, Chapter 3, Oxford University Press, Oxford

Zukas, T. and U. Trafkofski (2023): Sustainable Finance: The Regulatory Concept of Greenwashing under EU Law, in Baumgartner, T., Kellerhals, A., W. Uebe (2023, Herausgeber): *EuZ – Zeitschrift für Europarecht – Jahrbuch 2022*, pp. C1–C29

CHAPTER 6

The Legislative Acts Which Constitute the Sources of EU Banking Law

6.1 THE CAPITAL REQUIREMENTS REGULATION (CRR)

6.1.1 General Aspects

(1) The (extremely lengthy) Capital Requirements Regulation [(EU) No 575/2013, **CRR**] was adopted on **26 June 2013** in accordance with **Article 289(1) TFEU** by the ordinary legislative procedure (i.e., by the co-legislators).[1] Its legal basis is **Article 114 TFEU**, it was published in the *OJ* on 27 June and entered into force on the following day.[2] Its content is heavily influenced by and largely reflects the provisions of the **'Basel III regulatory framework'**.

The CRR is binding in its entirety and directly applicable in all Member States (as well as to the **non-EU EEA Member States**, Norway, Liechtenstein and Iceland). It applies from **1 January 2014** with the following exceptions: *first*, the provisions requiring the ESAs to submit to the Commission draft regulatory technical standards (**'RTSs'**) and implementing technical standards (**'ITSs'**) and those empowering the latter to adopt (usually on the basis of these standards) delegated or implementing acts (by virtue of Articles 290–291 TFEU) apply from **31 December 2014**; *second*, **Article 8(3)** on the derogation from the application of liquidity requirements on an individual basis for institutions of a single liquidity sub-group authorised in several Member States, **Article 21** on joint decisions on the level of application of liquidity

---

[1] On this procedure, see Chapter 7 below, under 7.5.1.
[2] CRR, Article 521(1).

requirements and **Article 451(1)** on institutions' obligation to disclose information regarding their leverage ratio and their management of the risk of excessive leverage apply from **1 January 2015**; *finally*, **Article 413(1)** on the 'stable funding liquidity ratio' applies from **1 January 2016**.[3]

(2) As of **December 2022**, the CRR had been repeatedly amended as follows:

> *First*, during the period 2014–2017, it was amended by two Commission Delegated Regulations regarding the leverage ratio and the waiver on own funds requirements for certain covered bonds[4]; and by three Regulations of the co-legislators regarding exemptions for commodity dealers,[5] transitional arrangements (mainly) for mitigating the impact of the introduction of the IFRS 9 on own funds[6] and the treatment of securitisation positions.[7]
>
> *Furthermore*, upon implementation of the Commission's 2016 "legislative banking package" in 2019, it was substantially amended by the **CRR II**. During that year, it was further amended another four times: the first amendment referred to the minimum loss coverage for NPEs[8]; the second was on exposures in the form of covered bonds[9]; the third was by the IFR[10]; and the fourth was on the alternative standardised approach for capital adequacy requirements relating to market risk.[11]
>
> *Third*, amidst the pandemic crisis, the CRR was amended by the (above-mentioned) June 2020 "**CRR quick fix**"[12] and then again in March 2021 concerning adjustments to the securitisation framework, with a view to supporting the economic recovery in response to the crisis, by maximising credit institutions' capacity to lend and absorb crisis-related losses.[13]

---

[3] *Ibid.*, Article 521(2).

[4] Commission Delegated Regulation (EU) 2015/62 of 10 October 2014 (OJ L 11, 17 January 2015, pp. 37–43) and Commission Delegated Regulation (EU) 2017/2188 of 11 August 2017 (OJ L 310, 25 November 2017, pp. 1–2).

[5] Regulation (EU) 2016/1014 of 8 June 2016, OJ L 171, 29 June 2016, pp. 153–154.

[6] Regulation (EU) 2017/2395 of 12 December 2017 (see Chapter 5 above, under 5.1.1).

[7] Regulation (EU) 2017/2401 of 12 December 2017, OJ L 347, 28 December 2017, pp. 1–34.

[8] Regulation (EU) 2019/630 of the co-legislators of 17 April 2019 (see Chapter 5 above, under 5.1.4).

[9] Regulation (EU) 2019/2160 of the co-legislators of 27 November 2019 (see Chapter 5 above, under 5.2.2).

[10] See Chapter 5 above, under 5.2.2 as well.

[11] Commission Delegated Regulation (EU) 2021/424 of 17 December 2019, OJ L 84, 11 March 2021, pp. 1–15.

[12] See Chapter 5 above, under 5.3.3.

[13] Regulation (EU) 2021/558 of the co-legislators of 31 March 2021 (OJ L 116, 6 April 2021, pp. 25–32). An additional (minor) amendment was introduced by Commission Implementing Regulation (EU) 2021/1043 of 24 June 2021 "on the extension of the

Finally, in October 2022 it was amended by **Regulation (EU) 2022/2036**, which (as already noted[14]) is the only element of the 2021 legislative banking package that has been finalised.[15]

As part of this legislative package, the Commission also submitted a legislative proposal on its further amendment, including for incorporating into EU law the BCBS's 2019 revised market risk framework, the **'Complement to Basel III'** and the revised Pillar 3 disclosure requirements,[16] the implementation dates of which have been deferred, as already noted, due to the pandemic.[17]

6.1.2 *Objective and Field of Application*

6.1.2.1 *Objective*

(1) The CRR lays down uniform rules concerning general prudential requirements that institutions, financial holding companies and mixed financial holding companies supervised under the CRD IV must comply with. These requirements relate to the following five items[18]: *first*, own funds requirements relating to entirely quantifiable, uniform and standardised elements of credit risk, market risk, operational risk, settlement risk and leverage; *second*, requirements on the limitation of large exposures; *third*, liquidity requirements relating to entirely quantifiable, uniform and standardised elements of liquidity risk; *fourth*, reporting requirements related to the above points; and *finally*, public disclosure requirements. The CRR also lays down uniform rules concerning the own funds and eligible liabilities requirements that resolution entities that are **G-SIIs** (see **Box** 6.1 below) or part of G-SIIs and material subsidiaries of non-EU G-SIIs must comply with. It does not govern publication requirements for competent authorities in the field of institutions' prudential regulation and supervision set out in **the CRD IV**.[19]

---

transitional provisions related to own funds requirements for exposures to [CCPs] set out in [the CRR]" (OJ L 225, 25 June 2021, pp. 52–53).

[14] See Chapter 5 above, under 5.4.

[15] The current consolidated version (which does not contain Regulation (EU) 2022/2036), is available at: https://eur-lex.europa.eu/legal-content/EN/TXT/?uri=CELEX%3A02013R0575-20220708.

[16] These aspects are discussed in Volume II.

[17] See Chapter 2 above, under 2.4.1.

[18] CRR, Article 1, first sub-paragraph, as amended by the CRR II.

[19] *Ibid.*, Article 1, second and third sub-paragraphs, as amended by the CRR II.

Box 6.1 Definition of G-SIIs (and O-SIIs)

(1) The term **'systemically important institution'** is defined in **Article 3(1), point (30) CRD IV** as meaning an EU parent institution, an EU parent financial holding company, an EU parent mixed financial holding company, or an institution, the failure or malfunction of which could lead to systemic risk.

(2) Global systemically important institutions (**G-SIIs**) are defined in point (133) of Article 4(1) CRR, as those that have been identified in accordance with **Article 131(1) and (2) CRD IV**, as applicable, which provides for the following:

(a) A G-SII is *either* a group headed by a Union (EU) parent institution, a Union (EU) parent financial holding company or a Union (EU) parent mixed financial holding company; *or* an institution that is not a subsidiary of the above institutions/companies.[20]
(b) The methodology for identifying G-SIIs follows the indicator-based measurement approach of the BCBS, setting out specific criteria for assessing systemic significance at the level of the group, i.e., its size; its interconnectedness with the financial system; substitutability of the services or the financial infrastructure that it provides; its complexity; and its cross-border activity, including between Member States and between a Member State and a third country. Each category must receive an equal weighting and consists of quantifiable indicators.[21]
(c) There must be at least five sub-categories of G-SIIs. The lowest boundary and the boundaries between sub-categories must be determined by the scores under the identification methodology. The cut-off scores between adjacent sub-categories must be clearly defined and comply with the principle that there is a constant linear increase of systemic significance, between each sub-category resulting in a linear increase in the requirement of additional CET1 capital, except for the highest sub-category. Systemic significance is the expected impact exerted by the G-SII's distress on the global financial market.[22]
(d) The NCA or the NDA may, in the exercise of sound supervisory judgement, re-allocate a G-SII from a lower sub-category to a higher sub-category or allocate an entity with an overall score that is lower than the cut-off score of the lowest sub-category to that

---

[20] CRD IV, Article 131(1), second sub-paragraph.
[21] *Ibid.*, Article 131(2).
[22] *Ibid.*, Article 131(9), first-fourth sentences.

> sub-category or to a higher sub-category, thereby designating it as a G-SII.[23]
>
> **(3)** G-SIIs are distinguished from other systemically important institutions ('**O-SIIs**'); these may be *either* an institution *or* a group headed by an EU parent institution, an EU parent financial holding company, an EU parent mixed financial holding company, a parent institution in a Member State, a parent financial holding company, a parent financial holding company in a Member State or a parent mixed financial holding in a Member State.[24]

(2) For the purpose of ensuring compliance with this legislative act, **NCAs** have the powers and must follow the procedures set out therein and in the CRD IV; NRAs have the powers and must follow the procedures set out in the BRRD. Institutions are not prevented from holding own funds and their components in excess of or applying measures that are stricter than those required by the CRR.[25] '**National competent authority**' (NCA) means[26] a public authority or body officially recognised by national law, which is empowered by national law to supervise institutions as part of the supervisory system in operation in the Member State concerned.

6.1.2.2 Field of Application
At the time of adoption, the CRR (as well as the CRD IV) equally applied to investment firms (encompassed in the term 'institutions', jointly with credit institutions), and hence constituted source(s) of both EU banking and capital markets. However, some of its articles were amended by the **IFR** to the effect that the CRR (and the CRD IV) ceased to apply to investment firms and was renamed to "*on prudential requirements for credit institutions*". Most importantly, by virtue of the IFR, the definition of the term '**credit institution**' has been expanded, and the term 'institution' has been modified (as discussed in **Box 6.2** just below).

---

[23] *Ibid.*, Article 131(10).

[24] *Ibid.*, Article 131(1), third sub-paragraph. The terms EU parent institution, EU parent financial holding company, EU parent mixed financial holding company, parent institution in a Member State, parent financial holding company, parent financial holding company in a Member State and parent mixed financial holding in a Member State are defined in Article 4(1) CRR. See Table 6.3.

[25] *Ibid.*, Articles 2(1)–(2) and 3.

[26] *Ibid.*, Article 4(1), point (40).

Box 6.2 The new definition of the terms credit institution and institution

(1) Credit institution does (no longer) only mean an undertaking the business of which consists of taking deposits or other repayable funds from the public and granting credits for its own account (under the traditional definition),[27] but also an undertaking the business of which consists in carrying out any of the activities referred to in **points (3) and (6) of Section A of Annex I to MiFID II** (namely dealing on own account and underwriting of financial instruments and/or placing of financial instruments on a firm commitment basis), where any of the following applies (provided, however, that this is not a commodity and emission allowance dealer, a collective investment undertaking or an insurance undertaking):

  (i) the total value of the undertaking's consolidated assets is equal to or exceeds 30 billion euro;
  (ii) the total value of the assets of the undertaking is less than 30 billion euro, and it is part of a group in which the total value of the consolidated assets of all undertakings therein that individually have total assets of less than 30 billion euro and carry out any of the above-mentioned activities of Section A of Annex I to MiFID II is equal to or exceeds 30 billion euro; or
  (iii) the total value of the assets of the undertaking is less than 30 billion euro, and it is part of a group in which the total value of the consolidated assets of all undertakings in the group that carry out any of the above-mentioned activities of Section A of Annex I to MiFID II is equal to or exceeds 30 billion euro, where the consolidating supervisor, in consultation with the supervisory college, so decides in order to address potential risks of circumvention and potential risks for the financial stability of the EU.[28]

(2) For the purposes of the CRR (and the CRD IV) the term '**institution**' is (henceforth) defined to mean a credit institution authorised under Article 8 CRD IV; or an undertaking as referred to in Article 4(1), point (1)(b) CRR (also covered by the new definition of credit institution as just noted), which by 24 December 2019 was carrying out activities as investment firm, authorised under the MiFID II and should

---

[27] *Ibid.*, Article 4(1), point (1)(a).

[28] For the purposes of points (ii)–(iii) above, where the undertaking is part of a third-country group, the total assets of each branch of that group authorised in the EU must be included in the combined total value of the assets of all undertakings therein (*ibid.*, Article 4(1), point (1)(b)).

have applied for authorisation in accordance with Article 8 CRD IV by 27 December 2020 (a rather marginal case).[29]

(3) Due to divergences in the interpretation of elements of the notion of credit institution (under to the traditional definition) across the EU, which depend on national implementations (albeit being contained in the **CRR** and thus directly applicable in all Member States) and in particular regarding the terms 'the business of which', 'deposits', 'other repayable funds' and 'from the public', on **18 September 2020**, the **EBA** issued **an Opinion** "on elements of the definition of credit institution under Article 4(1), point 1, letter (a) [CRR] and on aspects of the scope of the authorisation" (**EBA/OP/2020/15**).[30] In the author's view, it correctly suggested that these terms should be further clarified by the Commission to enhance the single rulebook and ensure that prudential requirements contained in the CRR and the CRD IV are appropriately imposed in relation to entities presenting similar risks to customers and financial stability (based on the 'same activity', 'same risks, same rules' principle of financial regulation).[31]

6.1.3 The System of Rules

In line with the provisions of the 'Basel III regulatory framework' (and even beyond), the CRR and the CRD IV contain rules concerning the **'three pillars'** of this framework (as adjusted, in relation to the earlier Basel II framework). In particular, the CRR contains:

> *first*, a large part of the rules of **'Pillar 1'** on the micro- and macro-prudential regulations imposed on credit institutions, such as those on the elements of own funds (and since 2019 eligible liabilities)[32]; capital requirements against exposure to credit risk (including credit risk mitigation, securitisation and counterparty risk), operational risk, market risks, settlement risk and credit valuation adjustment (CVA) risk in accordance with various methods[33]; rules on large exposures

---

[29] CRR, Article 4(1), point (3), with reference to Article 8a (3) CRD IV, inserted by virtue of the IFD.

[30] At: https://www.eba.europa.eu/eba-publishes-an-opinion-on-the-perimeter-of-credit-institutions.

[31] EBA/OP/2020/15, paras 16–17.

[32] CRR, Articles 25–80 (and 81–88 on minority interest and additional Tier 1 and Tier 2 instruments issued by subsidiaries).

[33] *Ibid.*, Articles 107–311, 312–324, 325–377, 378–380 and 381–386, respectively. On all these risks, see Chapter 1 above, under 1.2.1.

and exposures to transferred credit risk[34]; liquidity requirements[35]; and rules on leverage[36];

second, the rules of **'Pillar 3'** on public disclosure of information by institutions.[37]

6.1.4 Other Aspects

The CRR contains a long list of transitional provisions (the majority of which has expired); it also requires the Commission and the EBA (in some cases after consulting the ESRB) to submit Reports and make Reviews on a wide range of aspects and by various dates.[38] Furthermore, the EBA has been requested to develop an electronic **'compliance tool'** aimed at facilitating institutions' compliance with the CRR (and the CRD IV), as well as with RTSs, ITSs, Guidelines and templates adopted to implement them.[39]

6.2 THE CAPITAL REQUIREMENTS DIRECTIVE No IV (CRD IV)

6.2.1 General Aspects

(1) Like the CRR, the Capital Requirements Directive No IV (2013/36/EU, **CRD IV**) was adopted by the co-legislators on **26 June 2013** by the ordinary legislative procedure, was published in the *OJ* **on 27 June** of the same year and entered into force on the following day.[40] It is addressed to the Member States[41] and is also applicable to the non-EU EEA Member States. Its legal basis is **Article 53(1) TFEU**, which refers to two aspects: the *first* is the right of establishment and, by reference therein also the freedom to provide services as laid down in **Article 62 TFEU**; the *second aspect* is the coordination of national laws, regulations or administrative provisions concerning the taking-up and pursuit of activities as self-employed persons.[42]

---

[34] *Ibid.*, Articles 387–403 and 404–410, respectively.

[35] *Ibid.*, Articles 411–428az.

[36] *Ibid.*, Articles 429–430c.

[37] *Ibid.*, Articles 431–455.

[38] *Ibid.*, Articles 465–501b and 501c–519b, respectively.

[39] This tool is aimed at enabling at least each institution to rapidly identify the provisions that are relevant in terms of its size and business model and monitor the changes made in legislative acts and in the related implementing provisions, Guidelines and templates (*ibid.*, Article 519c, inserted by the CRR II). The substantive aspects of the CRR are presented in detail in Volume II.

[40] CRD IV, Article 164.

[41] *Ibid.*, Article 165.

[42] For an analysis of Article 53 TFEU, see Schlag (2019).

(2) Member States were required to apply the laws, regulations and administrative provisions necessary to comply with the CRD IV, in principle, since **1 January 2014**; with effect from that date, the CRD I (Directives 2006/48/EC and 2006/49/EC[43]) was repealed.[44] *Exceptionally*, provisions on 'capital buffers' in **Articles 128–142** (apart from **Article 133**[45]) apply from **1 January 2016**; **Article 131** on **G-SII buffers** was phased in from that date to apply fully as of 1 January 2019.[46]

(3) The CRD IV has also been repeatedly amended (albeit not as frequently as the CRR):

> *first*, during the period 2014–2015, it was amended by the BRRD and the above-mentioned **Directives 2014/17/EU** on credit agreements for consumers relating to residential immovable property and **(EU) 2015/2366 (PSD II)**;
> *furthermore*, in 2018–2019, it was first (marginally) amended with respect to the prevention of the use of the financial system for the purposes of money laundering or terrorist financing,[47] and then more extensively by the CRD V and the IFD; by virtue of the latter, it was renamed to "on access to the activity of credit institutions and the prudential supervision of credit institutions";
> *finally*, amidst the pandemic crisis, it was amended as regards its application to investment firms to help them address its impact.[48]

The CRD IV will also be further modified by specific rules contained in the **2021** legislative banking package upon its finalisation.

6.2.2 Objective and Field of Application

(1) The CRD IV lays down rules concerning the following aspects[49]: the *first* is access to the activity of credit institutions (granting and withdrawal of authorisation, acquisition and disposal of qualifying holdings), exercise of the right of establishment and the freedom to provide services in the single market

---

[43] See Chapter 4 above, under 4.2.3.

[44] CRD IV, Article 162(1) and 163, respectively.

[45] Article 133 refers to Member States' discretion to introduce and maintain a 'systemic risk buffer' in order to prevent and mitigate macroprudential or systemic risks not covered by the CRR and by Articles 130–131 CRD IV.

[46] *Ibid.*, Article 162(2) and (5).

[47] Directive (EU) 2018/843 of 30 May 2018, OJ L 156, 19 June 2018, pp. 43–74.

[48] The current consolidated version is available at: https://eur-lex.europa.eu/legal-content/EN/TXT/?uri=CELEX%3A02013L0036-20220101.

[49] CRD IV, Article 1.

and relations to third countries[50]; the *second* aspect refers to the supervisory powers and tools for the prudential supervision of institutions by competent authorities, in a manner that is consistent with the rules set out in the CRR, both on a solo and on a consolidated basis, including the SREP[51]; the *third* refers to micro- and macroprudential regulation of credit institutions[52]; these rules reflect to a large extent the **"Basel III regulatory framework"**; and the *final* aspect consists in the publication requirements for competent authorities in the field of prudential regulation and supervision of institutions.

(2) Since January 2021 the CRD IV only applies to institutions[53]; specific provisions also apply to financial holding companies, mixed financial holding companies and mixed-activity holding companies with their head office in the EU.[54] The CRD IV does not apply to central banks, to post office giro institutions, as well to specific institutions in each Member State.[55]

6.2.3 *The System of Rules*

In the context of the **'three pillars'** framework, the rules of the CRD IV on **'Pillar 1'** are included in **Articles 128–142** and pertain to macroprudential capital buffers (namely the capital conservation buffer, the institution-specific CCyB; the G-SII buffer; the O-SII buffer); and a systemic risk buffer[56]) as well as capital conservation measures in the form of restrictions on distributions.[57] The supervisory framework governing credit institutions' compliance with the above rules is laid down in Articles 49–117 CRD IV and covers three aspects: the *first* lays down NCAs' powers to conduct microprudential supervision and impose sanctions[58]; the *second* aspect (**'Pillar 2'**) refers to the 'review processes', which cover five areas[59]: the internal capital adequacy assessment process (**'ICAAP'**)[60]; credit institutions' arrangements, processes and mechanisms, including the technical criteria concerning their organisation and the treatment of risks (including the internal liquidity adequacy assessment

---

[50] *Ibid.*, Articles 8–27, 33–46 and 47–48, respectively.

[51] *Ibid.*, Articles 49–117 (of which Articles 97–101 refer to the SREP).

[52] *Ibid.*, Articles 128–142 (on capital buffers).

[53] *Ibid.*, Article 2(1). As already noted above (see Box 6.2), these are defined in Article 4(1), point (3) CRR.

[54] *Ibid.*, Article 2(4) with reference to Articles 34 and 119–127.

[55] *Ibid.*, Article 2(5). Post office giro institutions and the institutions exempted are treated as financial institutions for the purposes of Article 34 and Title VII, Chapter 3.

[56] These buffers are defined in Article 128, points (1)–(5) and governed by Articles 129–140; they are discussed in detail in Volume II.

[57] *Ibid.*, Articles 141–142.

[58] *Ibid.*, Articles 49–71.

[59] *Ibid.*, Articles 73, 74–96, 97–101, 102–107 and 108–110, respectively.

[60] The ECB "Guide to the (…) ICAAP" of November 2018 is available at: https://www.bankingsupervision.europa.eu/ecb/pub/pdf/ssm.icaap_guide_201811.en.pdf.

process ('**ILAAP**')[61]), as well as their internal governance and remuneration policies; the **SREP**, which has a predominant role in the supervisory framework[62]; supervisory measures and powers; and the field of application of these processes; the *third* aspect covered is microprudential supervision on a consolidated basis.[63]

6.2.4   Other Aspects

The CRD IV contains transitional provisions on the supervision of institutions exercising the freedom of establishment and the freedom to provide services, on financial holding companies and mixed financial holding companies, as well as on capital buffers, all of which have expired.[64] It also requires the Commission and the EBA to submit Reports on several aspects.[65]

6.3   THE SSM REGULATION (SSMR)

6.3.1   General Aspects

6.3.1.1   Introduction

(1) The Single Supervisory Mechanism Regulation [(EU) No 1024/2013, **SSMR**] is the key legal source governing the SSM. It was adopted by the Council in October 2013 within 14 months from the submission of the Commission's proposal, was published in the *OJ* on 29 October 2013 and entered into force on **3 November** of the same year.[66] It respects the principles of subsidiarity and proportionality in accordance with **Article 5 TEU** (and **Protocol (No 2)**) and observes the principles recognised in the **Charter**, in particular the right to the protection of personal data (**Article 8**), the freedom to conduct a business (**Article 16**) and the right to an effective remedy and to a fair trial (**Article 47**).[67] The SSMR, which is in force without any subsequent

---

[61] The ECB "Guide to the (…) ILAAP" of November 2018 as well is available at: https://www.bankingsupervision.europa.eu/ecb/pub/pdf/ssm.ilaap_guide_201811.en.pdf.

[62] On 1 September 2022, the ECB appointed five high-level experts on banking supervision to review the SREP's effectiveness and efficiency and its relation to other supervisory processes (see at: https://www.bankingsupervision.europa.eu/press/pr/date/2022/html/ssm.pr220901~04fea56942.en.html).

[63] CRD IV, Articles 111–127.

[64] *Ibid.*, Articles 151–159, 159a and 160, respectively.

[65] *Ibid.*, Article 161. The substantive aspects of the CRD IV are discussed in detail in Volume II.

[66] SSMR, Article 34.

[67] *Ibid.*, recitals (86)–(87). These Charter's Articles are analysed, respectively, in Knecht (2019), Schwarze and Voet van Vormizeele (2019) and Voet van Vormizeele (2019).

amendment, is binding in its entirety and directly applicable in all Member States.[68]

(2) The ECB was due to assume its tasks under the SSMR on **4 November 2014** and has, indeed, done so.[69] In view of assuming its specific (supervisory) tasks, the ECB was given the power to ask NCAs and the persons referred to in **Article 10(1) SSMR** to provide it, from **3 November 2013**, with all relevant information necessary to carry out a 'Comprehensive Assessment', including a balance-sheet assessment, of the credit institutions and supervised groups to be directly supervised by it.[70] Credit institutions and NCAs should supply the information requested.[71] The results were published on **26 October 2014** in the "Aggregate Report on the Comprehensive Assessment".[72]

in particular:

Article 127(6) TFEU as the legal basis
The legal basis of the SSMR is **Article 127(6) TFEU**.[73] Alternative options were either to confer upon the EBA the specific tasks on prudential supervision of credit institutions or to create a new pan-European banking supervisory authority.[74] In practice, however, the Commission did not have any choice but to opt for this particular solution, since the **Euro Area Summit of 29 June 2012** decided that *"the Commission will present proposals on the basis of Article 127(6) for a single supervisory mechanism shortly"*.[75] Hence, the political decision was to make use of the existing EU Treaties, identifying thus the ECB as the main actor. This decision was also confirmed by the European

---

[68] *Ibid.*, last sentence.

[69] *Ibid.*, Article 33(2), first sub-paragraph. The relevant Press Release of the ECB is available at: https://www.bankingsupervision.europa.eu/press/pr/date/2014/html/sr141104.en.html. Without prejudice to the exercise of the investigatory powers conferred on it by Articles 10–13, the ECB could start carrying out the tasks conferred on it, from 4 November 2013, other than adopting supervisory Decisions, in respect of any credit institution or other supervised entity, following a Decision addressed to those and the NCAs concerned. In addition, if the ESM would unanimously request the ECB to take over direct supervision of such an entity as a precondition for its direct recapitalisation, the ECB could immediately start carrying out its tasks under the SSMR in respect of that supervised entity, following a Decision addressed to it and the NCAs concerned (*ibid.*, Article 33(3)). No use has been made of these options, in the second case because the ESM DRI framework was not in place yet.

[70] These credit institutions were identified in ECB Decision 2014/123/EU of 4 February 2014 (ECB/2014/3) (OJ L 69, 08 March 2014, pp. 107–111).

[71] SSMR, Article 33(4).

[72] See on this European Central Bank (2014a).

[73] As noted in Chapter 4 above (under 4.3.1), Council Regulation (EU) No 1096/2010 conferring specific tasks upon the ECB concerning the functioning of the ESRB was the first one adopted under this TFEU Article.

[74] On the limitations to the implementation of these options, see Wymeersch (2012), pp. 237–240 (an article published before the creation of the BU), with reference to the delegation-related concerns that this would give rise to in light of the *Meroni* doctrine; see on this Box 7.1 below.

[75] Euro Area Summit Statement, 29 June 2012, first paragraph, second sentence.

Council of the same day.[76] On this Article, the use of which as the legal basis for creating the SSM has not escaped criticism,[77] the following is briefly noted (in **Box 6.3** below).[78]

Box 6.3 Some remarks on Article 127(6) TFEU

Adoption by the Council by the special legislative procedure	The SSMR should be adopted by the Council by the special legislative procedure set out in **Article 289(2) TFEU**.[79] However, in this case, the European Parliament was de facto enhanced since it was adopted in parallel with **Regulation (EU) No 1022/2013** on the amendment of the **EBAR**,[80] which should have been adopted by the ordinary legislative procedure. As a result, the European Parliament was able to intervene more intensively during the procedure for the adoption of the SSMR, asking for several substantial amendments, which were, indeed, accepted in the context of the **'Trialogue'** with the Council and the Commission. It was also the political lever for the adoption in October 2013 of the **Interinstitutional Agreement** between the European Parliament and the ECB[81]
Unanimous adoption by the Council	The Regulation must be adopted by the Council unanimously. Since **Article 127(6) TFEU** is applicable to all Member States,[82] the SSMR was adopted by the Ministers of Finance of all Member States[83]; the SSM is open-ended and not confined to the Member States whose currency is the euro[84]

(continued)

---

[76] European Council Conclusions, 28/29 June 2012, paragraph 4(b), *in finem*.

[77] See on this Lastra (2013), p. 1197, with further references, Alexander (2016), pp. 264–267 and Van Rijn (2022), pp. 353–359. On top of those, in the author's view, the embedment of Article 127(6) in Article 127, which, along with Articles 128–133, is included in Chapter 2 of Title VIII in Part Three of the TFEU entitled "Monetary Policy", is conceptually misleading, since it is more than apparent that Article 127(6) (like, *inter alia*, also Article 127(5)) does not relate to monetary policy, but to the specific banking supervisory tasks of the ECB.

[78] For a more detailed analysis of this Article, see also Smits (1997), pp. 355–360, Hadjiemmanuil (2006), pp. 824–825, Louis (2009), pp. 166–168 and Lastra and Louis (2013), pp. 82–94.

[79] See Chapter 7 below, under 7.5.1.

[80] On this legislative act, see further below, under 6.3.5.

[81] On both Regulation amending the EBAR and this Agreement, see below, under 6.3.5.

[82] TFEU, Article 139(2), point 3, and ESCB/ECB Statute, Article 42.1.

[83] Valid scepticism had been expressed as to the feasibility of reaching (in principle) a *unanimous* decision (as required) under this Article (see Wymeersch (2012), p. 240, at 9.22), which, however, has not been the case.

[84] On this aspect, see Chapter 8 below, under 8.2.3 (on the 'Close cooperation' between the ECB and the competent authorities of Member States with a derogation).

(continued)

Conferral to the ECB of specific tasks (only) relating to the prudential supervision of credit institutions and other categories of financial firms	In relation to this, three comments deserve attention: *First*, unlike in the case of Article 127(2) relating to the basic tasks, the specific tasks are not conferred upon the ECB within the Eurosystem but directly on the ECB *Second*, the Regulation may confer specific tasks upon the ECB relating to the prudential supervision not only of credit institutions, but also of other types of financial firms.[85] Hence, the wording of this TFEU Article does not rule out the possibility of conferring upon the ECB specific tasks with regard to the microprudential supervision of investment firms and other financial firms operating in capital markets (an option which, nevertheless, has not been in any political agenda). Explicitly excluded are insurance undertakings *Third*, the Regulation may confer on the ECB 'specific' only supervisory tasks. Accordingly, it should contain a *numerous clausus* of such tasks; those not listed therein remain competences of NCAs
Proposal for amendment	In its "Blueprint for a deep and genuine economic and monetary union – Launching a European debate", of 28 November 2012,[86] the Commission proposed the amendment of **Article 127(6) TFEU** to make the ordinary legislative procedure applicable and eliminate some of the legal constraints it places on the design of the SSM, such as: enshrine a direct and irrevocable opt-in by Member States whose currency is not the euro to the SSM, beyond the model of 'close cooperation'; grant Member States whose currency is not the euro but participating in the SSM fully equal rights in the ECB decision-making, and go even further in the internal separation of decision-making on monetary policy and on supervision[87]

---

[85] It is noted that the wording therein "*credit institutions and other financial institutions*" is not consistent with the definitions in EU banking law, where the definition of the term credit institution is different from that of the term financial institution, and the latter cannot be considered a sub-category of the former. It is also noted that, on the contrary, the field of application of Article 127(5) only covers (in respect of a different ECB task within the Eurosystem) credit institutions.

[86] COM/2012/777 final.

[87] See also recital (85). According to Article 48(6) (second sub-paragraph) TEU, which refers to one of the simplified procedures for amending the Treaties, the European Council may by a decision amend all or part of the provisions of Part Three of the TFEU (where most of the fundamental provisions on the EMU are stipulated) deciding by unanimity after consulting the European Parliament and the Commission, as well as the ECB in the case of "*institutional changes in the monetary area*". On this Article, see Herrnfeld (2019), pp. 408–410.

6.3.2 Objective and Field of Application

(1) The SSMR conferred upon the ECB specific tasks *"concerning policies relating to the prudential supervision of credit institutions"*, a phrase carried over *verbatim* from **Article 127(6) TFEU** (and some other categories of supervised entities, as further discussed below[88]) with a view to *first*, contributing to the safety and soundness of credit institutions and the stability of the financial system within the EU and each Member State and *second*, preventing regulatory arbitrage, fully taking into account and caring for the unity and integrity of the internal market based on equal treatment of credit institutions.[89] This ECB objective is apparently different from the primary objective of the Eurosystem under the TFEU, i.e., maintaining price stability.[90]

(2) As regards the field of application in relation to Member States, a distinction must be made between two categories:

> The *first* category comprises **'participating Member States'**, meaning both the Member States whose currency is the euro (in the SSM-FR also called 'euro area participating Member States') *and* those with a derogation that have established a close cooperation in accordance with **Article 7** (in the SSM-FR defined as 'participating Member States in close cooperation'), also referred to as 'non-euro area participating Member States'.[91]
>
> The *second* category comprises **'non-participating Member States'**, which do not meet the above criteria ('non-euro area Member States' in the SSM-FR terminology).[92]

6.3.3 The System of Rules

The Commission's 2012 proposals on the new EU institutional architecture for financial prudential supervision in the context of the BU revolved around four key elements: *first*, conferring specific tasks on the ECB for the microprudential supervision of credit institutions (and some types of holding

---

[88] See Chapter 8 below, under 8.2.2.

[89] SSMR, Article 1, first sub-paragraph. The institutions referred to in (the above-mentioned) Article 2(5) CRD IV are also excluded from the supervisory tasks conferred on the ECB. The SSMR does not confer on the ECB any supervisory tasks relating to the prudential supervision of CCPs (*ibid.*, Article 1, second sub-paragraph). On these provisions of Article 1, see Ohler (2022), pp. 12–13.

[90] See Chapter 4 above, under 4.1.4.

[91] SSMR, Article 2, point (1) and SSM-FR, Article 2, point (15). The term 'Member States with a derogation' also includes those which opted out of the EMU, i.e., currently (only) Denmark, according to the provisions of and the conditions laid down in (the above-mentioned) Protocol (No 16).

[92] SSM-FR, Article 2, point (13).

companies), passed on from NCAs, *and* establishing the SSM in relation to the *exercise* of these tasks; *second*, specifying the financial firms, mainly credit institutions, with regard to which these specific tasks should be conferred on the ECB; *third*, incorporating the SSM within the ESFS, without, in principle, touching upon the tasks of the EBA and those of other components of the ESFS; and *finally*, creating 'Chinese walls' within the ECB to ensure the effective separation of its monetary policy and other tasks from its supervisory ones in order to prevent the eventuality of conflicts of interest arising from concurrently pursuing these two objectives.[93] All these elements were echoed by the Council (under the influence of the European Parliament) when adopting the SSMR.[94]

6.3.4 Review by the Commission

By **31 December 2015**, and every 3 years thereafter, the Commission must publish a Report on the application of the SSMR, with a special emphasis on monitoring its potential impact on the smooth functioning of the internal market. This Report, which should indicatively evaluate 14 aspects, be forwarded to the co-legislators and be accompanied by proposals, as appropriate,[95] was submitted on **11 October 2017**.[96] It briefly analyses the central aspects of the SSMR and its application, listing the main findings and is accompanied by a Commission Working Document,[97] which gives more insight in relation to the topics discussed. Given the early stage of the SSM, not all the aspects listed in the Commission's review mandate enshrined in **Article 32** could be assessed to the same level of detail. Due to the scope of the review mandate, the Report focused on the legislative, institutional and procedural framework of the SSM.[98]

---

[93] SSMR, Article 25; on this Article, see Chapter 8 below, under 8.5.2.

[94] In this respect, noteworthy is also recital (44): "*Nothing in this Regulation should alter in any way the current framework regulating the change of legal form of subsidiaries or branches and the application of such framework or be understood or applied as providing incentives in favour of such change. In this respect, the responsibility of competent authorities of non-participating Member States should be fully respected, so that those authorities continue to enjoy sufficient supervisory tools and powers over credit institutions operating in their territory in order to have the capacity to fulfil this responsibility and effectively safeguard financial stability and public interest. Moreover, in order to assist those competent authorities in fulfilling their responsibilities, timely information on a change of legal form of subsidiaries or branches should be provided to depositors and to the competent authorities.*"

[95] *Ibid.*, Article 32.

[96] COM/2017/591 final.

[97] At: https://ec.europa.eu/info/sites/info/files/171011-ssm-review-report-staff-working-document_en.pdf.

[98] See on this Gortsos (2022a).

6.3.5 Other Related Legal Acts and Agreements

6.3.5.1 Regulation (EU) No 1022/2013 of the Co-Legislators

In the prospect of conferring supervisory tasks upon the ECB, it was deemed necessary to introduce amendments to certain provisions of the EBAR to bring the EBA's functions in line with the ECB's function as a supervisory authority over credit institutions. These circumstances encouraged the adoption by the co-legislators on 22 October 2013 of **Regulation (EU) No 1022/2013**. As already just noted,[99] this was drafted in parallel and adopted concurrently with the SSMR (hence the term **'twin' Regulations**) and amended the EBAR on several aspects.[100]

6.3.5.2 The SSM 'Framework Regulation'

The ECB was required to adopt and make public a framework to organise the practical modalities of implementation of **Article 6 SSMR**. On the basis of **Article 6(7)**, the ECB thus adopted on 16 April 2014 the **SSM-FR** (Regulation (EU) No 468/2014),[101] which entered into force on 15 May 2014,[102] is in force without any subsequent amendment and does not confer additional supervisory tasks on the ECB.[103]

The SSM-FR must be read in conjunction with the **Rules of Procedure of the ECB** and those of the **ECB Supervisory Board**,[104] in particular with regard to decision-making within the SSM, including the procedure applying between the Supervisory Board and the **GC** as regards non-objection by the latter and other relevant ECB legal acts.[105]

Box 6.4 The structure of the SSM Framework Regulation (SSM-FR)

The SSM-FR contains **153 Articles structured in 12 Parts,** and its subject matter is to lay down rules on the following aspects[106]:

first, the framework referred to in **Article 6(7) SSMR**, i.e., the organisation of the practical arrangements for implementing **Article 6** on cooperation within the SSM;

---

[99] See above, under 6.3.1.

[100] These aspects are further analysed in Chapter 7.

[101] On this Regulation as a source of ECB administrative procedural law, see Lackhoff (2017).

[102] SSM-FR, Article 153.

[103] *Ibid.*, Article 1(2).

[104] On both these Rules of Procedure, see Chapter 8 below, under 8.1.2.

[105] SSM-FR, Article 1(3) with reference to Article 26(8) SSMR.

[106] *Ibid.*, Article 1(1).

> *second*, cooperation and exchange of information between the ECB and NCAs within the SSM regarding the procedures relating to significant and less significant supervised entities, including common procedures applying to authorisations to take up the business of credit institutions, withdrawals of such authorisations, and the assessment of acquisitions and disposals of qualifying holdings;
> *third*, the procedures relating to: cooperation between the ECB and NCAs or NDAs regarding macroprudential tasks and tools within the meaning of **Article 5**; the operation of close cooperation within the meaning of **Article 7**; cooperation between the ECB and NCAs regarding **Articles 10–13**, *inter alia* on certain aspects relating to supervisory reporting; and the adoption of supervisory Decisions addressed to supervised entities and other persons;
> *fourth*, the linguistic arrangements between the ECB and NCAs, as well as between the ECB and supervised entities and other persons; and
> *fifth*, the procedures applicable to the ECB's and NCAs' sanctioning powers within the SSM in relation to the tasks conferred on the ECB by the SSMR.

6.3.5.3 Other ECB Legal Acts: General Overview

The framework governing the SSM is further specified in other legal acts of the ECB's GC, containing provisions on the detailed operational arrangements for the implementation of the ECB supervisory tasks. These legal acts can be classified into two categories: the *first* contains those pertaining to the operation of the internal bodies established within the ECB pursuant to the SSMR (i.e., the Supervisory Board, the Administrative Board of Review (ABoR) and the Mediation Panel) and of the Ethics Committee. The *second* category contains numerous acts (in the form of Regulations, Decisions, Guidelines and Recommendations), which govern various other aspects of the SSM, including (but not limited to) the comprehensive assessment conducted in 2014; the close cooperation procedure, the ECB powers to impose sanctions; the provision of supervisory data to the ECB; the separation of monetary and supervisory functions; supervisory fees; reporting of supervisory financial information; and public access to ECB documents.[107]

---

[107] ECB Decision (EU) 2015/529 of 21 January 2015 "amending Decision ECB/2004/3 on public access to European Central Bank documents" (ECB/2015/1) (OJ L 84, 28 March 2015, pp. 64–66). All other legal acts are further discussed in Chapter 8. For a detailed overview of the ECB legal acts adopted in the period 2014–2015, see Gortsos (2015a), pp. 77–83. Some of these legal acts are presented in Chapter 8, where the institutional and (main) substantive aspects of the SSMR are analysed.

6.3.5.4 The Interinstitutional Agreement with the European Parliament and the Memorandum of Understanding (MoU) with the Council

(1) The SSMR provides that an agreement should be concluded between the European Parliament and the ECB on the detailed modalities of organising discussions between the Chair of the ECB's Supervisory Board and the Chair and Vice-Chairs of the European Parliament's competent committee (Committee on Economic and Monetary Affairs, hereinafter '**ECON**') "*with a view to ensuring full confidentiality in accordance with the confidentiality obligations imposed on the ECB as a competent authority*". In addition, the ECB and the Parliament should conclude appropriate arrangements on the practical modalities of the exercise of democratic accountability and oversight over the exercise of the ECB supervisory, covering, *inter alia*, access to information, cooperation in investigations and information on the selection procedure of the Supervisory Board's Chair.[108] On the basis of these provisions, the two institutions signed in October 2013 an **Interinstitutional Agreement** "on the practical modalities of the exercise of democratic accountability and oversight over the exercise of the tasks conferred on the [ECB] within the framework of the [SSM]" **(2013/694/EU)** (hereinafter the '**EP-ECB Interinstitutional Agreement**'),[109] which entered into force on 7 November 2013.

(2) Two months later, the Council and the ECB signed a **Memorandum of Understanding** ('**MoU**') "on the cooperation on procedures related to the [SSM]" (hereinafter the '**Council-ECB MoU**'),[110] which entered into force on 12 December 2013.[111]

---

[108] SSMR, Article 20(8), second sentence and (9), second and third sentences.

[109] OJ L 320, 30 November 2013, pp. 1–6. The two institutions must carry out periodically an assessment of the practical implementation of this Agreement (*ibid.*, Section VI).

[110] At: https://op.europa.eu/en/publication-detail/-/publication/021e8fcb-96ac-11ea-aac4-01aa75ed71a1/language-en.

[111] The key institutional aspects of the SSMR are presented in detail in Chapter 8 and its substantive provisions in Volume II. For a detailed analysis of this legislative act, see Gortsos (2015a) and Lackhoff (2017). Several aspects of this Regulation (and its proposal) are also analysed in D'Ambrosio (2013), Deutsche Bundesbank (2013), pp. 26–36, Ferran and Babis (2013), Ferrarini and Chiarella (2013), Huber and von Pföstl (2013), Tröger (2013), Verhelst (2013), Brescia Morra (2014), Dietz (2014), Gandrud and Hallenberg (2014), Masciandro and Nieto (2014), Thiele (2014), pp. 519–525, Wymeersch (2014), Wissink *et al*. (2014), Binder (2015a), Alexander (2015), pp. 163–175, Lackhoff und Grünewald (2015) (on the impact on Switzerland) Grundmann (2016), pp. 47–64, Ohler (2020) and Wymeersch (2020). See also the individual contributions in D'Ambrosio (2020, editor), pp. 23–283 and in Binder, Gortsos, Lackhoff and Ohler (2022, editors)).

6.4 THE BANK RECOVERY AND RESOLUTION DIRECTIVE (BRRD)

6.4.1 General Aspects

(1) The Bank Recovery and Resolution Directive (2014/59/EU, **BRRD**) was adopted by the co-legislators on 15 May 2014 in accordance with **Article 289 TFEU** with full respect of the principles of subsidiarity and proportionality.[112] Its legal basis is **Article 114 TFEU**, it was published in the *OJ* on 12 June 2014 and entered into force on 2 July of the same year.[113] It is addressed to all EU Member States[114] and is also of relevance to the non-EU EEA Member States. Most of its provisions apply from **1 January 2015**, except for those on the application of the bail-in tool, which apply from **1 January 2016**.[115]

(2) The BRRD is in force (**by December 2022**) following seven amendment procedures; the most important are those introduced by (the abovementioned) **Directive (EU) 2017/2399** as regards the ranking of unsecured debt instruments in insolvency hierarchy, the **BRRD II** and **Regulation (EU) 2022/2036** (which also amended the CRR, as just noted).[116] It will be further modified by virtue of the legislative acts to be adopted upon the proposals to be submitted by the Commission following its **2021** consultative document on the "Review of the crisis management and deposit insurance framework".[117]

6.4.2 Objective and Field of Application

(1) The BRRD lays down rules and procedures relating to the recovery and resolution of several groups of entities. These include *primarily* 'institutions' established in the EU, i.e., credit institutions and investment firms (unlike the CRR and the CRD IV, which, as already mentioned, no longer apply to investment firms).[118] The field of application also covers: financial institutions established in the EU, which are a subsidiary of a credit institution, of an

---

[112] BRRD, recital (131).

[113] Article 124 on amendments to the CRD IV that entered into force on 1 January 2015 (*ibid.*, Article 131).

[114] *Ibid.*, Article 132.

[115] *Ibid.*, Article 130(1), second and third sub-paragraphs.

[116] Other amendments were introduced by the following legislative acts of the co-legislators: Directive (EU) 2017/1132 of 14 June 2017 "relating to certain aspects of company law (…)" (OJ L 169, 30 June 2017, pp. 46–127); as well as the IFD, Directive (EU) 2019/2162 and Article 93 of Regulation (EU) 2021/23 (on all these, see Chapter 5 above, under 5.2.2). The current consolidated version is available at: https://eur-lex.europa.eu/legal-content/EN/TXT/?uri=CELEX%3A02014L0059-20221114.

[117] See Chapter 5 above, under 5.4.1.

[118] Pursuant to the amendment introduced by Article 63, point (1) IFD, the term 'investment firm' is defined with reference to Article 4(1), point (22) IFR, provided it is

investment firm or of a holding company referred to below and are covered by the supervision of the parent undertaking on a consolidated basis pursuant to **Articles 6–17 CRR**; financial holding companies, mixed financial holding companies and mixed-activity holding companies established in the EU; parent financial holding companies in a Member State, Union parent financial holding companies, parent mixed financial holding companies in a Member State, *and* Union parent mixed financial holding companies; as well as branches of institutions established outside the EU pursuant to the conditions laid down in **Articles 93–98**.[119]

(2) In accordance with the proportionality principle, when establishing and applying the requirements under the BRRD and using the different tools at their disposal in relation to an entity, **NRAs** and NCAs must take account of the nature of its business; its shareholding structure and legal form; its risk profile, size and legal status; its interconnectedness to other institutions or the financial system in general; the scope and complexity of its activities; its membership of an institutional protection scheme (**'IPS'**) meeting the requirements of **Article 113(7)**[120] or other cooperative mutual solidarity systems under **Article 113(6) CRR**; and whether it exercises any investment services or activities as defined in **Article 4(1), point (2) MiFID II**.[121]

'National resolution authority' (NRA) means[122] a public administrative authority (or authorities) designated by Member States, entrusted with public administrative powers, and empowered to apply the resolution tools and exercise the resolution powers. It may be an NCB, a competent ministry, another public administrative authority or authorities entrusted with public administrative powers or, *exceptionally*, the NCA.[123]

(3) Since the BRRD is based on the principle of minimum harmonisation, Member States may adopt or maintain rules that are stricter or additional to those laid down therein and in the delegated and implementing acts adopted by the Commission on its basis (a practice known as 'gold-plating') provided

---

subject to the initial capital requirement laid down in Article 9(1) IFD (BRRD, Article 2(1), amended point (3)).

[119] *Ibid.*, Article 1(1), first sub-paragraph. After the amendment by Article 93 of Regulation (EU) 2021/23, the BRRD does not apply to CCPs that are also authorised in accordance with Article 14 EMIR. On the definition of all these entities, see Table 6.3.

[120] On this CRR Article, see below, under 6.6.2.

[121] BRRD, Article 1(1), second sub-paragraph.

[122] *Ibid.*, Article 2(1), point (18) with reference to Article 3(1)–(2) and (3), first and second sentences.

[123] Member States must have in place adequate 'structural arrangements' to ensure operational independence and avoid conflicts of interest between the functions of supervision pursuant to the CRR and the CRD IV or the other functions of the relevant authority and those of the NRA, without prejudice to the exchange of information and cooperation obligations as required by Article 3(4) (*ibid.*, Article 3(3), third and fourth sentences).

that such stricter or additional rules are of general application and do not conflict with the above acts.[124]

6.4.3 The System of Rules

(1) In accordance with the 'three-pillar system' established by the BRRD, its key provisions govern three closely interrelated aspects (Titles II–V): *first*, preparatory measures, including recovery planning, resolution planning (also called 'living wills'), resolvability and intra-group financial support (**Articles 4–26**), of particular importance in the context of preparation, even though not systematically included therein, are also the rules on the application of the MREL and the TLAC in accordance with **Articles 45–45m**; *second*, early intervention measures (**Articles 27–30**); and *third*, resolution action (**Articles 31–44** and **46–86**) and cross-border group resolution (**Articles 87–92**). In addition, **Articles 99–109** (Title VII) govern national resolution financing arrangements, which Member States should put in place under **Article 100(1)**; **Articles 110–114** (Title VIII) refer to the penalties' regime, and **Article 115** specifies the Commission's power to adopt delegated acts.

(2) According to the sequential order of the above pillars, preparatory measures are taken first (either by NRAs or by NCAs in the case of recovery planning); then, NCAs (and not NRAs) are granted powers to intervene early before an institution's financial position has deteriorated to such an extent (the 'failing or likely to fail' condition) that resolution action by NRAs would be required.[125] The above is classified as either 'crisis prevention' or 'crisis management' measures[126]:

> 'Crisis prevention measure' means the exercise of powers pertaining to direct removal of deficiencies or impediments to recoverability (under **Article 6(6)**), *or* to addressing or removing impediments to resolvability (**Article 17 or 18**); the application of an early intervention measure (**Article 27**); the appointment of a temporary administrator (**Article 29**); or the exercise of the write-down or conversion powers (**Article 59**).[127]
>
> 'Crisis management measure' means a resolution action *or* the appointment of a special manager under **Article 35** or a person under either **Article 51(2)** or under **Article 72(1)**.

---

[124] *Ibid.*, Article 1(2). On the practice of gold-plating in general, see Weatherill (2006), pp. 42–49.

[125] The resolution conditions are discussed in detail in Volume II.

[126] BRRD, Article 2(1), points (101) and (102), respectively.

[127] It is noteworthy that even though Article 59 is included in the third pillar, the exercise of the write-down or conversion power is considered to be a crisis prevention measure.

6.4.4   Other Aspects

6.4.4.1   Reports of the Commission

By 1 June 2018, the Commission should have reviewed the implementation of the BRRD and have submitted a Report to the co-legislators assessing, *inter alia*, the need for any amendments regarding minimising divergences at national level, on the basis of the EBA Report referred to in **Articles 4(7) and 45(19)**, and the functioning and efficiency of the role conferred on the EBA, including carrying out of mediation. Given the Commission's obligation to review the application of the resolution framework under the SRMR by December 2018, it was deemed appropriate to carry out the review jointly.[128] Moreover, however, it was necessary to wait for the adoption of the 2016 "legislative banking package", which amended some important elements of the resolution framework, and particularly the rules concerning the MREL.[129] Hence, the joint Report was published on **30 April 2019**.[130]

6.4.4.2   The Role of the EBA—The EBA Resolution Committee (ResCo)

(1) For the purposes of the BRRD, NCAs and NRAs must cooperate with the EBA in accordance with its statutory Regulation and, without delay, provide it with all information necessary to carry out its duties pursuant to **Article 35 EBAR**. For the same purposes, the EBA must cooperate with the EIOPA and the ESMA within the framework of the ESAs 'Joint Committee' (**Article 54**).[131]

(2) By its Decision of 22 January 2020, the EBA established a "Standing Committee on Resolution" ('**ResCo**').[132] This EBA internal committee is composed of a chairperson and the heads of the NRAs of each Member State (which are its members). The resolution authorities of the non-EU EEA States represented in the **Board of Supervisors** ('**BoS**') the SRB, the Commission, the ESRB, the ECB (SSM) and the other ESAs have observer status.[133] Its mandate consists in the preparation of **decisions** to be taken in accordance with **Article 44 EBAR** in matters relating to the tasks conferred by the BRRD upon NRAs; in accordance with **Article 38(1)**, the EBA must ensure that no such decision impinges in any way on the fiscal responsibilities of Member States. In fulfilling its mandate, the ResCo must, *inter alia*,

---

[128] SRMR, Article 94(1), first sentence and 94(2)–(3).

[129] Commission Report (2019), Section I, p. 2.

[130] COM/2019/213 final. For details, see Gortsos (2022b), pp. 1209–1219.

[131] BRRD, Articles 128 and 127, second sub-paragraph, respectively. On the Joint Committee, see Chapter 7 below, under 7.1.2.

[132] EBA/DC/2020/310, at: https://eba.europa.eu/about-us/organisation/resolution-committee. This Decision was adopted pursuant to Article 41 EBAR, is based on Article 127 BRRD (first and third sub-paragraphs) and entered into force on the date of its adoption in accordance with Article 10 of said Decision.

[133] *Ibid.*, Articles 4 (points (11) and (13)) and 15. On the BoS, see Chapter 7 below, under 7.2.3.

promote, develop and coordinate the methodology for drafting resolution plans, as well as methods for the resolution of failing credit institutions and investment firms.[134] Since, according to the BRRD, the EBA must ensure 'structural separation' between the ResCo and other functions entrusted to the EBA; the ResCo has responsibility to adopt certain specified decisions relating to resolution matters, subject, however, to the responsibility of the BoS to approve or reject the related proposals pursuant to the majority required under **Article 44(1) EBAR**.[135]

6.5 THE SRM REGULATION (SRMR)

6.5.1 General Aspects

(1) The Single Resolution Mechanism Regulation [(EU) No 806/2014, **SRMR**] was adopted by the co-legislators on 15 July 2014 (two months after the BRRD) by the ordinary legislative procedure. Its legal basis is **Article 114 TFEU**; it was published in the *OJ* on 30 July 2014, entered into force on 19 August of the same year and is binding in its entirety and directly applicable to all Member States.[136]

(2) In principle, the SRMR is applicable from **1 January 2016**. From this date onwards, the SRF is also considered to be the participating Member States' resolution financing arrangement in accordance with **Articles 99–109 BRRD**.[137] This is totally consistent with the architecture of the SRMR and the SRF Agreement, which, provide that *first*, the contributions raised at national level in accordance with the BRRD and the SRMR will be transferred to the SRF (allocated, during the initial period, to different 'compartments' corresponding to each Contracting Party),[138] and *second*, the compartments, use of which is already subject to progressive mutualisation, will cease to exist at the end of the initial period.[139] *Exceptionally*, several Articles apply

---

[134] *Ibid.*, Article 2, points (1)–(2).

[135] *Ibid.*, Article 3; see also recital (5). The BRRD is further analysed in Volume II. For a comprehensive overview of its provisions, see Haentjens (2017) and World Bank Group (2017). On various aspects of this Directive, see also Gandrud and Hallenberg (2013), Conlon and Cotter (2014a) and (2014b), Grünewald (2014), pp. 82–116, Huber and Merc (2014), Psaroudakis (2014), Binder (2015a) and (2015b) (on resolution planning), Kleftouri (2015), pp. 166–181 and Stephanou (2016).

[136] SRMR, Article 99(1) and last sentence.

[137] *Ibid.*, Articles 99(2) and 96. It could have applied later, depending on the date on which the SRF Agreement would have entered into force, after its ratification by participating Member States, in accordance with Article 99(6). This was not necessary, however, since the conditions for the transfer of contributions to the SRF were met by end-November 2015 (see also below).

[138] SRMR, Article 67(1), second sentence and SRF Agreement, Article 1(1), points (a) and (b), first sentence.

[139] SRF Agreement, Article 1(1), point (b), second sentence.

from **19 August 2014**[140] and **Articles 69(5), 70(6)** and **71(3)** empowering the Commission to adopt delegated acts and **Article 70(7)** empowering the Council to adopt implementing acts with regard to various aspects of the SRF apply from **1 November 2014**. The rules on the SRB's powers to collect information and cooperate with NRAs for the elaboration of resolution plans pursuant to **Articles 8–9** and all 'other related provisions' apply from **1 January 2015**.[141]

(3) The SRMR is in force as amended by the SRMR II, the IFR and Article 94 of **Regulation (EU) 2021/23**.[142] Like the BRRD, it will be further modified by virtue of the legislative acts to be adopted upon the proposals to be submitted by the Commission following its **2021** consultative document on the "Review of the crisis management and deposit insurance framework" and by the 2021 legislative banking package.

6.5.2 *Objective and Field of Application*

(1) As already mentioned,[143] the objective of the SRMR is to lay down uniform rules and a uniform procedure for the resolution of the categories of entities referred to in **Article 2** which are established in the participating Member States (see just below). These uniform rules and this uniform procedure must be applied within the SRM framework.[144]

(2) The SRMR applies to the following types of entities (hereinafter referred to as **'designated entities'**)[145]: *first*, credit institutions established in participating Member States; *second*, parent undertakings (including financial holding companies and mixed financial holding companies) established in participating Member States, if they are subject to consolidated supervision carried out by the ECB in accordance with **Article 4(1), point (g) SSMR**[146];

---

[140] Articles 1–4 and 6, Article 30 on the obligation to cooperate and on information exchange within the SRM, several Articles on the SRB (42–48), its two sessions (50(1)(a)–(b) and (g)–(p), 50(3), 51, 52(1) and (4) and 53(1)–(2)), its Chair (56) and its financial provisions (57–59), and those containing other and final provisions (80–84, 87–95 and 97–98).

[141] *Ibid.*, Articles 99(3)–(5). As 'other related provisions' should be considered Articles 10 on the assessment of resolvability, 11 on simplified obligations for certain institutions and 12 on the determination of the MREL. Articles 8–12 are duly analysed in Volume II.

[142] The current consolidated version, which does not contain Regulation (EU) 2021/23, is available at: https://eur-lex.europa.eu/legal-content/EN/TXT/?uri=CELEX%3A0 2014R0806-20210626.

[143] See Chapter 4 above, under 4.4.4.

[144] SRMR, Article 1.

[145] *Ibid.*, Article 2. After the amendment by Article 94 of Regulation (EU) 2021/23, the SRMR does not apply to CCPs that are also authorised in accordance with Article 14 EMIR.

[146] Article 4 SSMR is discussed in Chapter 8 below and in more detail in Volume II.

and *third*, investment firms and financial institutions established in participating Member States, if covered by the consolidated supervision of the parent undertaking carried out by the ECB in accordance with **Article 4(1), point (g) SSMR** as well.

For the purposes of the SRMR, **'participating Member States'** are those within the meaning of **Article 2, point (1) SSMR**,[147] namely those whose currency is the euro *and* those with a derogation which have established a close cooperation in accordance with **Article 7 SSMR**.[148] If a close cooperation between a Member State and the ECB is suspended or terminated in accordance with **Article 7 SSMR**, entities established therein cease to be covered by the SRMR from the date of application of the suspending or terminating Decision.[149]

6.5.3 The System of Rules

The **'three-pillar system'** of the BRRD is embedded (albeit with some differentiations) in this legislative act as well: **'resolution planning'** (only) constitutes the *first one* (**Articles 8–12**), **'early intervention'** is the *second pillar* (**Article 13**) and the *third pillar* covers **'resolution'** (**Articles 14–29**). Its other provisions refer *mainly* to the cooperation arrangements within the SRM and with third countries (**Articles 30–33**); the SRB's investigatory and sanctioning powers (**Articles 34–41**); the institutional framework governing the SRB (**Articles 42–56** and **80–92**); its budget (**Articles 57–66**); the SRF (**Articles 67–79**); and the power conferred on the Commission subject to specific conditions (according to standard practice) to adopt delegated acts (**Article 93**).

6.5.4 Relation to the BRRD—Applicable EU and National Law

6.5.4.1 Relation to the BRRD

(1) As already noted, the BRRD lays down the substantive rules pertaining to the resolution of designated entities and groups, while the SRMR *mainly* contains rules on the procedure for resolution planning with regard to, early intervention in, and resolution of such entities and groups by the SRB, the Commission and the Council, or by the NRAs, within the SRM. The SRMR is based on the BRRD and makes such a continuous reference to its provisions that the analysis of the latter is indispensable for the understanding of the

---

[147] SRMR, Article 4(1).

[148] On this Article, see Chapter 8 below, under 8.2.3.

[149] The SRMR continues to apply to resolution proceedings which were ongoing on the date of application of such a Decision. In agreement with the Member State concerned, the SRB must decide (within three months after the date of adoption of the terminating decision) on the modalities for the recoupment of contributions which that Member State transferred to the SRF (SRMR, Article 4(2)–(4)). Recoupments are calculated pursuant to Article 4(3).

former. It is also noted that several aspects covered by the BRRD are not, for various reasons, dealt with in the SRMR. These include *mainly* the following: recovery planning (**Articles 5–9 BRRD**) and intra-group financial support (**Articles 19–26**); government financial stabilisation tools ('**GFSTs**', **Articles 56–58**); resolution powers (**Articles 63–72**); cross-border group resolution (**Articles 87–92**); and the ranking of deposits in insolvency hierarchy (**Article 108**).[150]

(2) On the relationship between the two legal acts, **Article 5(1)** SRMR provides that if, in accordance with the SRMR, the SRB performs tasks and exercises powers which, under the BRRD, are to be performed or exercised by NRAs, for the application of both the SRMR and the BRRD, the SRB is considered to be the '**relevant NRA**', or in the case of a cross-border group resolution, the 'relevant group-level resolution authority' ('**GLRA**').

In terms of definitions[151]: '**relevant NRA**' means the NRA of a participating Member State in which an entity or a group's entity is established; and '**group-level resolution authority**' (GLRA) means the NRA in a participating Member State in which the institution or parent undertaking subject to consolidated supervision (at the highest level of consolidation within participating Member States pursuant to **Article 111 CRD IV**) is established.

6.5.4.2 Applicable EU and National Law
If, according to the **SRMR**, the SRB performs tasks and exercises powers, which, under the BRRD, are to be performed or exercised by the NRA, the latter is considered to be the relevant NRA (or, for cross-border group, the relevant GLRA).[152] The SRB, the Council, the Commission and the NRAs are fully embedded into the system of the resolution framework adopted by EU institutions and further developed by the EBA. In particular[153]:

> *First*, decisions taken by the SRB, the Council, the Commission and (where relevant) the NRAs, are subject to and must be compliant with the relevant EU financial law and in particular any legislative and non-legislative acts, including delegated and implementing acts.
> *Second*, applicable to the SRB, the Council and the Commission are also the following rules: they are subject to the binding RTSs and ITSs developed by the EBA and adopted by the Commission in accordance with **Articles 10–15 EBAR**; they must make every effort to comply with any EBA's Guidelines and Recommendations relating to tasks to be performed by them; if they do not or do not intend to comply with

---

[150] On Articles 5–9 and 19–26, 63–72 and 87–92, see Haentjens (2017), pp. 210–213, 256–272 and 285–296. The GFSTs and the ranking of deposits in insolvency hierarchy are further discussed in Volume II. On the former, see also Gortsos (2016).

[151] SRMR, Article 3(1), points (4) and (27), respectively.

[152] *Ibid.*, Article 5(1).

[153] *Ibid.*, Article 5(2).

such soft law instruments, the EBA must be informed thereof in accordance with **Article 16(3) EBAR**[154]; and they must cooperate with the EBA in the application of **Article 25 EBAR** on recovery and resolution procedures, and **Article 30** on peer reviews of competent authorities.[155] *Finally*, the SRB is also subject to any EBA Decisions in accordance with **Article 19 EBAR** on the settlement of disagreements between competent authorities in cross-border situations (referred to as **'binding mediation'**), where the BRRD provides for such Decisions.[156]

6.5.5 The SRF Agreement

6.5.5.1 General Aspects

Even though (as already mentioned) the SRF was established by the SRMR, its use was contingent upon the entry into force of the Intergovernmental Agreement No 8457/14 (**SRF Agreement**).[157] Pursuant to this Agreement, the Contracting Parties made two commitments to support the effective operation and functioning of the SRF.[158] The *first* is the obligation to transfer gradually the contributions raised at national level to the SRF. The *second* commitment is to allocate, during a (transitional) 'initial period', these contributions to different 'compartments' corresponding to each Contracting Party. This period started on **1 January 2016** (i.e., the date of entry into force of the SRF Agreement) and will lapse on the date when the SRF reaches the target level provided for in **Article 68 SRMR**, but no later than **end-2023** (i.e., 8 years after the date of the Agreement's application).[159] The use of the compartments is subject to 'progressive mutualisation'; they will cease to exist at the end of the initial period.

---

[154] To the same effect, see also Article 6, point (c) CRD IV.

[155] On these Articles, see Wymeersch (2012), pp. 286 and 280–281, respectively; see also Chapter 7 below.

[156] The key institutional aspects of the SRMR are presented in detail in Chapter 9 below and its substantive provisions in Volume II. On this legislative act, see Eckhardt (2013), Gandrud and Hallenberg (2013), Gros (2013), Gordon and Ringe (2014), European Central Bank (2014b), Louis (2014), Ignatowski and Korte (2014), Alexander (2015), pp. 175–186, Carmassi (2015), Hadjiemmanuil (2015), pp. 16–18, Wiggins, Tente and Metrick (2014), Wiggins, Wedow and Metrick (2015), Zavvos and Kaltsouni (2015), pp. 2–35, Dermine (2016), Stephanou (2016) and the individual contributions in Binder, Gortsos, Lackhoff and Ohler (2022, editors)).

[157] SRMR, Article 77, first sub-paragraph.

[158] SRF Agreement, Article 1(1), points (a) and (b) respectively; see also recital (9). For the purposes of the Agreement, applicable are the definitions set out in Article 3 SRMR (*ibid.*, Article 2(3)).

[159] See also Article 3(1), point (37) SRMR and recital (12) SRF Agreement.

(2) The Agreement mainly applies to the Contracting Parties participating in the BU.[160] It is confined to the **specific** elements concerning the SRF which remain within the competence of Member States and is designed as complementary to the BRRD and the SRMR and as supportive and intrinsically linked to the establishment of the internal market in financial services.[161] It is subject to ratification, approval or acceptance by the Contracting Parties pursuant to national constitutional requirements. The respective instruments must be deposited with the Council's General Secretariat (**'Depositary'**), which must then notify accordingly the other Contracting Parties.[162] The Agreement entered into force on **1 January 2016**[163] and applies thereafter to the Contracting Parties that participate in the BU and have deposited their respective instruments.[164]

---

[160] SRF Agreement, Article 1(2). The phrasing is not fully accurate (hence the addition of the term 'mainly') since certain provisions also apply to non-participating Member States; see Article 12(1), discussed below.

[161] *Ibid.*, recital (11). The Contracting Parties' intention was to preserve a level playing field and minimise the overall cost of resolution to taxpayers. When designing the contributions to the SRF and their tax treatment, they also undertook to consider the overall burden on the respective banking sectors (*ibid.*, recital (10)).

[162] *Ibid.*, Article 11(1); the Agreement should be ratified by all participating Member States, which was the case by December 2015, except for Luxembourg (recital (14)). Declaration No. 2 contained in the Agreement's Annex on "Declarations of intent by the Contracting Parties and observers of the Intergovernmental Conference that are members of the Council to be deposited with the SRF Agreement" notes that: "*The signatories (...) declare that they will strive to complete its process of ratification in accordance with their respective national legal requirements in due time to permit the SRM to be fully operational by 1 January 2016.*".

[163] *Ibid.*, Article 11(2).

[164] *Ibid.*, Article 12(2), first sentence (Articles 12(2), second sentence and 12(3) do not apply as the Agreement entered into force on 1 January 2016 and participating Member States had ratified it). The Contracting Parties that have deposited their respective instruments but were not participating in the BU by 1 January 2016 could be part of the 'special agreement' referred to in Article 14(2) for the purposes of submitting to the CJEU any dispute concerning the interpretation and enforcement of Article 15 on compensation (see below). The Agreement applies to them as from the date when the decision abrogating their derogation (as defined in Article 139(1) TFEU) or their exemption (as referred to in Protocol (No 16) on Denmark) takes effect, or in the absence thereof as from the date of entry into force of the ECB Decision on close cooperation referred to in Article 7(2) SSMR. This was the case for Bulgaria and Croatia, which joined in 2020 (see below in Chapter 8, under 8.2.3). Subject to Article 8, which governs the transfer to the SRF by those Contracting Parties, the Agreement will cease to apply to them from the date of its termination pursuant to Article 7(8) SSMR (*ibid.*, Article 12(4)).

6.5.5.2 Other Provisions

Accession: The Agreement is open to accession by Member States other than the Contracting Parties (currently only Sweden), with full rights and obligations in line with those of the Contracting Parties. Accession will become effective upon depositing the instrument of accession with the Depositary.[165]

Consistency and relationship with EU law: As already noted, the SRF Agreement is an instrument of public international law.[166] Hence, the rights and obligations laid down therein are subject to the principle of reciprocity, i.e., their equivalent performance by all Contracting Parties, and the breach by any of them of its obligation to transfer the contributions towards the SRF entails the exclusion of the entities authorised in their territory from access thereto.[167] The Contracting Parties recognised that in such a case the only legal consequence would be the exclusion of the one having committed the breach, upon determination and declaration by the SRB and the Court of Justice of the European Union (**'CJEU'**)[168] from financing under the SRF. They must apply and interpret the Agreement in conformity with **Article 4(3) TEU** on the 'principle of sincere cooperation',[169] as well as with the BRRD and the SRMR, ensuring that financial resources are uniformly channelled to the SRF to guarantee its proper functioning. The Agreement applies insofar as it is compatible with EU law and does not encroach upon the EU competences to act in the field of the internal market.[170]

Dispute settlement: If a Contracting Party either disagrees with another on the interpretation of any provision of the **SRF Agreement** or considers that another has failed to comply with its obligations thereunder, it may bring the matter before the CJEU, the judgement of which is binding on the parties to the proceedings. A Contracting Party for which the Court finds that it has failed to comply with its obligations must take the necessary measures within a period set by the CJEU. In case of non-compliance, the use of its compartments, as laid down in **Article 5(1), point (b)**, is ruled out in relation to institutions established and authorised in its territory. The above provisions

---

[165] The other Contracting Parties must be notified accordingly. Upon authentication by them, the Agreement's text must be deposited in the Depositary's archive as the authentic text (*ibid.*, Article 13; see also recital (15)).

[166] See details in Fabbrini (2014) and Louis (2014).

[167] SRF Agreement, recital (20). For a general overview of the principle of reciprocity in public international law, see Paris and Ghei (2003).

[168] The CJEU, a Treaty-based institution (TEU, Article 13(1), second sub-paragraph, fifth indent), is governed by Articles 251–281 TFEU. In accordance with the last above TFEU Article, its Statute is laid down in Protocol (No 3) (Consolidated version, OJ C 202, 7 June 2016, pp. 210–229); see on this, by means of mere indication, Schwarze und Wunderlich (2019).

[169] Article 4(3) TEU provides that Member States must, *inter alia*, facilitate the achievement of the EU's tasks and refrain from any measure which could jeopardise the attainment of its objectives (third sub-paragraph); for an analysis, see Guastaferro (2018), pp. 354–386, Lenz (2019) and (in detail) Hatje (2019), pp. 69–91.

[170] SRF Agreement, Article 2(1)–(2); see also recital (8).

constitute a **'special agreement'** between the Contracting Parties within the meaning of **Article 273 TFEU**.[171]

Contracting Parties whose currency is not the euro and have ratified the Agreement are *ipso facto* parties to this special agreement for the purpose of submitting to the CJEU any dispute concerning the interpretation and enforcement of **Article 15 SRF Agreement** (discussed just below) on the compensation of non-participating Member States for non-contractual liability and costs related thereto. Such a Member State which has not ratified the SRF Agreement may become as well party to this special agreement for that same purpose by notifying the Depositary of its intention, becoming party to it upon communication of its notification to the Contracting Parties by the Depositary.[172]

Non-participating Member States' compensation: The Contracting Parties committed to reimburse with interest non-participating Member States jointly and promptly for amounts they have paid in own resources, corresponding to the use of the EU general budget, in cases of non-contractual liability and costs related thereto, in respect of the exercise of powers by EU institutions under the SRMR.[173] The amount deemed to have been contributed is determined *pro rata* on the basis of its respective gross national income, as determined in accordance with secondary EU law.[174] The compensation costs must be distributed among participating Member States *pro rata* as well on the basis of the weight of the respective gross national income.[175] Each participating Member State's liability under this arrangement is thus separate

---

[171] *Ibid.*, Article 14(1)–(2). For a commentary of this TFEU Article, see Borchardt (2019), pp. 2753–2754 and Schwarze und Wunderlich (2019).

[172] *Ibid.*, Article 14(3).

[173] *Ibid.*, Article 15(1); see also recital (21), first sentence.

[174] See Article 2(7) of Council Decision 2007/436/EC, Euratom of 7 June 2007 "on the system of the European Communities' own resources" (OJ L 163, 23 June 2007, pp. 17–21).

[175] SRF Agreement, Article 15(2)–(3). These Member States must be reimbursed of the amounts corresponding to the payments from the EU budget to settle the non-contractual liability and the related costs following the adoption of the associated amending budget on the dates of the accounts' entries referred to in secondary EU law (see Article 9(1) of Council Regulation (EC, Euratom) No 1150/2000 of 22 May 2000 "implementing Decision 2007/436/EC, Euratom (…)", OJ L 130, 31 May 2000, pp. 1–12). Any interest must be calculated pursuant to the provisions on interest for amounts made available belatedly applicable to the EU's own resources, and amounts must be converted between national currencies and the euro at an exchange rate determined in accordance with Article 10(3), point (1) of that Regulation. Reimbursement actions by the Contracting Parties must be coordinated by the Commission pursuant to the above criteria (SRF Agreement, Article 15(4)–(5)).

and individual and not joint and several and must respond only for its part of the reimbursement obligation pursuant to the Agreement.[176]

6.6 THE DEPOSIT GUARANTEE SCHEMES DIRECTIVE (DGSD)

6.6.1 General Aspects

(1) The Deposit Guarantee Schemes Directive (2014/49/EU, **DGSD**) was adopted by the co-legislators on 16 April 2014 by the ordinary legislative procedure and with full respect of the EU principles of subsidiarity and proportionality.[177] It is based on a Commission proposal, acting pursuant to Article 12(1) of Directive 94/19/EC, which it repealed with effect from 4 July 2015.[178]

(2) The DGSD, which is in force without any amendment (only two Corrigenda),[179] was published in the *OJ* on 12 June 2014 and entered into force on 3 July of the same year.[180] It is addressed to all EU Member States[181] and is also of relevance to the non-EU EEA Member States. Its provisions apply from **4 July 2015** either directly or by transposition into Member States' legislation.[182] *Exceptionally*, the deadline for compliance with the transitional provision of **Article 8(4)** on the repayment of 'appropriate amounts' by DGSs was **31 May 2016**.[183]

(3) The Directive's legal basis is **Article 53(1) TFEU**, which, as already mentioned,[184] refers to the right of establishment and the freedom to provide services, as well as to the coordination of the national provisions concerning the taking-up and pursuit of activities as self-employed persons. In this respect, **recital (3)** makes the following considerations:

---

[176] *Ibid.*, recital (21), second sentence. The other provisions of the SRF Agreement are discussed in Volume II. On the SRF Agreement, see indicatively Burke (2015), Hadjiemmanuil (2015), pp. 26–29, Zavvos and Kaltsouni (2015), pp. 36–49 and Gortsos (2022b), pp. 1080–1088.

[177] DGSD, recital (54).

[178] *Ibid.*, Article 21, first sub-paragraph; see also recital (56). The ECB also delivered its Opinion on the proposed Directive in 2011 by virtue of Articles 127(4) and 282(5) TFEU (OJ C 99, 31 March 2011, pp. 1–7). The main points of this Opinion are discussed in Volume II (see, however, also below).

[179] At: https://eur-lex.europa.eu/legal-content/EN/TXT/?uri=CELEX%3A02014L0049-20140702.

[180] DGSD, Article 22, first sub-paragraph.

[181] *Ibid.*, Article 23.

[182] *Ibid.*, Articles 22, second sub-paragraph and 20(1), first sub-paragraph, first sentence, respectively. This combination constitutes, in the author's opinion, a 'hybrid' institutional element, given the direct applicability of some of its articles as if it were a Regulation.

[183] *Ibid.*, Article 20(1), second sub-paragraph.

[184] See above, under 6.2.1.

[The Directive] constitutes an essential instrument for the achievement of the internal market from the point of view of the freedom of establishment and the freedom to provide financial services in the field of credit institutions (…) [and] from the point of view of (…) increasing the stability of the banking system and the protection of depositors.

6.6.2 Objective and Field of Application

6.6.2.1 Objective

(1) The DGSD lays down rules and procedures on the establishment and functioning of national DGSs in Member States.[185] In terms of harmonisation to enhance the stability of the banking system and the protection of depositors, the DGSD has a threefold aim. The *first* is broadening the perimeter of aspects covered by harmonisation. Since its adoption and entry into force, the **1994 Directive** harmonised several aspects of the functioning of DGSs, but this harmonisation was partial, excluding (most importantly) funding arrangements for DGSs. The *second* aim is enhancing harmonisation in aspects already covered by it, the most notable example being the tightened information requirements imposed on credit institutions concerning the scope of deposit protection granted through relevant DGSs. Finally, the *third* aim is moving from minimum to maximum harmonisation regarding eligibility criteria and coverage levels for deposit guarantee; **recital (6)** is explicit on this. The ultimate objective is laid down in **recital (7)**:

> As a result of this Directive, depositors will benefit from significantly improved access to DGSs, thanks to a broadened and clarified scope of coverage, faster repayment periods, improved information and robust funding requirements. This will improve consumer confidence in financial stability throughout the internal market.

(2) The Directive provides that DGSs should serve four functions.[186] Their **primary function** is that of the 'paybox' for depositors,[187] which under the Directive 94/19/EC was the exclusive one. The DGSD goes, however, beyond the pure 'paybox' function of DGSs[188]: *first*, it provides that DGSs should also assist with the financing of the resolution of credit institutions in accordance with the BRRD[189]; *second*, it lays down that Member States can, at their national discretion, allow a DGS to use, under specific conditions, its available financial means for the adoption of 'alternative measures'

---

[185] DGSD, Article 1(1).
[186] On this aspect, see also Chapter 1 above, under 1.3.4.
[187] DGSD, Article 11(1); see also recital (14).
[188] *Ibid.*, Article 11(2)–(6).
[189] On this aspect, which is further analysed in Volume II, see Gortsos (2019).

to prevent the failure of a credit institution; and *finally*, the fourth function of DGSs under the DGSD is the financing of measures to preserve the access of depositors to covered deposits in the context of national insolvency proceedings.

6.6.3 DGSs and Credit Institutions Covered by the Field of Application

In contrast to the **1994 Directive**, which applied only to pre-defined DGSs, the scope of the DGSD is wider, covering three types of DGSs and the credit institutions affiliated to them[190]: the *first* is **'statutory DGSs'** set up by law and (usually) administered by a public entity; the *second* is **'contractual DGSs'** to the extent that they are officially recognised as DGSs, i.e., they comply with the relevant requirements of the DGSD[191]; and the *third* is **IPSs**, also to the extent that they are officially recognised as DGSs. An IPS is a contractual or statutory liability arrangement among credit institutions and other financial firms, which protects its members, by ensuring their liquidity and solvency to avoid bankruptcy, where necessary, through mutual bail-out arrangements, hence indirectly resulting in a maximum protection of depositors. It may be officially recognised as a DGS if it fulfils the criteria laid down in **Article 113(7) CRR** (presented in **Box 6.5** just below) and complies with the requirements set out in the DGSD.[192]

Box 6.5 The Conditions Set Out in Article 113(7) CRR in Relation to IPSs

This CRR Article sets out nine criteria which must be cumulatively fulfilled for an IPS to be officially recognised: **(i)** its members are institutions, financial institutions or ancillary services undertakings subject to appropriate prudential requirements, established in the same Member State, and there is no current or foreseen material practical or legal impediment to the prompt transfer of own funds or repayment of liabilities among members; **(ii)** the IPS is able to grant the support necessary under its commitment from funds readily available to it; **(iii)** it has suitable and uniformly defined systems in place for monitoring and classifying risk, in order to obtain a complete overview of the risk situations in all the individual members and the IPS as a whole, with corresponding abilities to exert influence; those systems must suitably monitor defaulted exposures, as these are defined in **Article 178(1) CRR** on 'obligors'

---

[190] DGSD, Article 1(2), points (a)–(d), respectively. In its Opinion (CON/2011/12), the ECB consented to this extension (par. 4).

[191] *Ibid.*, Article 4(2), first sub-paragraph.

[192] *Ibid.*, Articles 2(1), point (2) and 4(2), second sub-paragraph; see also recital (17).

default'; **(iv)** the IPS conducts its own risk review which is communicated to the individual members; **(v)** the adequacy of the systems referred to in points (iii) and (iv) is approved and monitored at regular intervals by the relevant competent authority; **(vi)** the IPS draws up and publishes on an annual basis either a consolidated report, concerning the IPS as a whole, comprising the balance sheet, the profit-and-loss account, the situation report and the risk report; or a report, concerning the IPS as a whole, comprising the aggregated balance sheet, the aggregated profit-and-loss account, the situation report and the risk report; **(vii)** IPS's members give advance notice of at least twenty-four months if they wish to end the institutional protection scheme; **(viii)** the multiple use of elements eligible for the calculation of own funds ('multiple gearing') and any inappropriate creation of own funds between IPS members is eliminated; and **(ix)** the IPS is based on a broad membership of credit institutions of a predominantly homogeneous business profile (such as cooperative or savings banks).

Both contractual DGSs and IPSs are subject to State aid rules under **Articles 107–109 TFEU**[193] (as further discussed in **Box 6.6**).

Box 6.6 The Tercas case

(1) Of importance in this respect is the case-law on the *Tercas* case.[194] Banca Tercas, an Italian credit institution, was placed under special administration in 2012 due to irregularities identified by Banca d'Italia (its supervisory authority). When, in 2013, another Italian bank, Banca Popolare di Bari (**'BPdB'**), expressed an interest in the subscription of additional capital in Banca Tercas, the conditions it imposed were that Banca Tercas should be audited and that its deficit should be covered

---

[193] *Ibid.*, recital (18), second sentence. Classification of a measure as 'State aid' for the purposes of Article 107(1) TFEU requires four conditions to be satisfied: that there is an intervention by the State or through State resources; the intervention is liable to affect trade between Member States; it confers a selective advantage on the beneficiary; and it distorts or threatens to distort competition. See "European Commission Notice on the notion of state aid within the meaning of Article 107 of the [TFEU]" (C/2010/5950 final).

[194] For a detailed perusal of the case's background, including the specificities of Italian law, see Boccuzzi (2022), pp. 39–51.

by one of the Italian DGSs, Fondo Interbancario di Tutela dei Depositi ('**FITD**').[195] After the FITD intervened in 2014 for the benefit of Banca Tercas and decided to cover its negative equity and to grant it certain guarantees (measures were approved by the Banca d'Italia), by its decision of 23 December 2015, the Commission found that this intervention of the FITD constituted unlawful State aid granted by Italy to that credit institution and ordered its recovery.[196]

(2) With its judgement of 19 March 2019 in Joined **Cases T-98/16**, *Italian Republic v Commission*, **T-196/16**, *[BPdB] v Commission* and **T-198/16**, *[FITD] v Commission*[197]), the General Court annulled the Commission's decision, arguing that the latter wrongly had classified as state aid under **Article 107(1) TFEU** the measures adopted for the benefit of Banca Tercas by the FITD.[198] The General Court recalled that State aid must cumulatively meet two separate conditions: *first*, being attributable to the State; and *second*, being granted "through State resources" in accordance with **Article 107(1)**, and considered that these conditions were not met, since the FITD autonomously decided to intervene for the benefit of Banca Tercas. Under Italian law, the public mandate given to the FITD only applies where a member credit institution is subject to compulsory liquidation, which was not the case and, hence, its intervention was not under a public mandate.

(3) Furthermore, the Court stated that the FITD, as a private entity, is acting "*on behalf of and in the interests of the members of the consortium*" subject to its statutes. According to the General Court, the Commission did not prove that the funds granted to Banca Tercas were controlled by Italian public authorities. Even though it claimed that the contributions used by the FITD to finance the intervention were mandatory, since credit institutions are required to belong to a DGS under the DGSD, the General Court's position was that the impossibility to dissociate credit institutions from the FITD is irrelevant and that the

---

[195] The FITD is a consortium of credit institutions operating in Italy. It is governed by private law and acts as a mutual benefit body, having the power to adopt measures for the benefit of its members: *first*, in the form of a statutory guarantee of deposits if one of those has been placed under compulsory liquidation ('mandatory intervention'); and *second*, on a voluntary basis, in accordance with its statute, if it is possible by means of such intervention to reduce the burden that its members may have to bear as a result of guaranteeing deposits ('voluntary intervention', including by way of support or preventive intervention).

[196] Commission Decision (EU) 2016/1208 of 23 December 2015 "on State aid granted by Italy to the bank Tercas" (Case SA.39451 (2015/C) (ex 2015/NN)), OJ 2016 L 203, pp. 1–34.

[197] ECLI:EU:T:2019:167.

intervention for the benefit of Banca Tercas was in accordance with the FITD statutes.

(4) With its judgement of 2 March 2021 in **Case C-425/19 P, European Commission v Italian Republic, [BPdB], Banca d'Italia and [FITD]**,[199] the **CJEU** (Grand Chamber) dismissed the appeal brought by the Commission against the General Court's judgement.[200] The CJEU confirmed that the General Court rightly found that the Commission had erred in law in taking the view that the Italian authorities had exercised substantial public control in establishing the measures adopted by the FITD for the benefit of Banca Tercas and that those measures do not constitute State aid because they are not imputable to the Italian State.[201]

6.6.3.1 DGSs Excluded from the Field of Application

Excluded from the Directive's field of application are contractual DGSs (including schemes offering additional protection to the coverage level laid down in **Article 6(1)**) and IPSs, to the extent that both are not officially recognised as DGSs. However, for the sake of depositors' protection, such schemes must have in place adequate financial means or relevant financing arrangements to fulfil their obligations and are also subject to the provisions on advertising and depositor information.[202]

6.6.4 The System of Rules

The DGSD is a blend of rules maintained from the 1994 Directive and of new ones. In particular, as regards *elements of continuity*, DGSs remain national, Member States are not liable for the funding adequacy thereof (their responsibility being confined to the establishment and official recognition of at least

---

[198] See Nicolaides (2020), p. 29 *et seq*.

[199] ECLI:EU:C:2021:154.

[200] The Commission appealed on 29 May 2019 against the judgement delivered on 19 March 2019 by the General Court in Case T-98/16, T-196/16 and T-198/16, Italy and Others v Commission (OJ C 238, 15 July 2019, pp. 13–14), seeking to set this judgement aside, by which the General Court annulled its (above-mentioned) 2015 Decision (EU) 2016/1208. For the broader impact of the CJEU's judgement, see Bodellini (2021), pp. 366–369.

[201] The CJEU essentially recognised that, unlike a public undertaking, a private consortium of credit institutions possesses a fundamental decision-making autonomy and, as a result, the evidence to prove imputability on the basis of control or a dominant influence on the private entity is subject to an even more stringent requirement for it to be sufficiently probative; see Quigley (2022), p. 42.

[202] DGSD, Article 1(3), first and second sub-paragraphs (the second with reference to Articles 16(5) and 16(7)).

one DGS in their territory), the 'mandatory membership rule' for credit institutions and the fact that DGSs are activated if a credit institution's deposits become 'unavailable'. In addition, the key 'paybox function' of DGSs has been retained but ranks first among four functions that those should or may serve. *Elements of change* include (*inter alia*) the rules adopted on the supervision of DGSs by designated authorities with regard to their operation, the introduction of provisions on the financing of DGSs (in that respect, *ex-ante* financing as a rule, although *ex-post* financing arrangements, including borrowing between DGSs, are also provided for), the fixing of the level of coverage at 100,000 euro (minimum *and* maximum) and the gradual reduction of the repayment period from twenty to seven working days at the latest by end-2023. Of particular interest is the fact that DGSs may be called upon to contribute to the financing of the resolution of credit institutions.[203]

6.6.5 Other Aspects: Commission and EBA Reports

(1) By **3 July 2019**, the Commission should submit a Report, and, if appropriate, a legislative proposal to the **co-legislators** setting out how DGSs operating in the EU may "*cooperate through a European scheme*" to prevent risks arising from cross-border activities and protect deposits from such risks.[204] By the same date, the Commission should also submit a Report on the progress towards the DGSD's implementation addressing several aspects, such as the adequacy of the current coverage level for depositors and the 'target level' on the basis of covered deposits (with an assessment of the appropriateness of the percentage set, taking into account past failures of credit institutions in the EU); and the impact of 'alternative measures' (pursuant to **Article 11(3)**) on the protection of depositors and consistency with the 'orderly winding-up proceedings' in the banking sector.[205]

(2) In supporting the Commission in preparing its Report, the EBA published three Opinions outlining some proposals for consideration: the first of 8 August 2019 "on the eligibility of deposits, coverage level and cooperation between [DGSs]" (**EBA-Op-2019-10**); the second of 30 October 2019 "on [DGS] payouts" (**EBA-Op-2019-14**); and the third of 23 January 2020 "on

---

[203] All these provisions are further analysed in Volume II.

[204] DGSD, Article 19(5). This prospect was already embedded in the 2010 Commission Report to the co-legislators accompanying the proposed Directive (COM/2010/369 final).

[205] *Ibid.*, Article 19(6), first sub-paragraph. The term 'orderly winding-up proceeding' is not defined in the DGSD, which includes no further reference. One can either refer to the term 'winding-up proceedings' in Directive 2001/24/EC or consider that it as an alternative to the term 'normal insolvency proceedings', which is used in Article 9(2) and is defined with reference to Article 2(1), point (47) BRRD.

[DGS] funding and uses of deposit guarantee scheme funds" (**EBA/OP/ 2020/02**).[206]

(3) Among all its other competences and obligations, the EBA should submit, **by 3 July 2019** (as well), a Report to the Commission on '**calculation models**' and their relevance to the commercial risk of DGS members, duly taking account of the risk profiles of various business models[207] (Table 6.1)

Table 6.1 Addressees of and date by which the main provisions of the key legal sources pertaining to the Banking Union (BU) are applicable

Legal act	Member States	Start of (full) application
A. Authorisation—prudential supervision—prudential regulation		
Regulation (EU) No 1024/2013 (SSMR)	Participating Member States	4 November 2014
SSM Framework Regulation (SSM-FR)	Participating Member States	15 May 2014
Regulation 575/2013 (CRR)	All Member States	1 January 2014
Directive 2013/36/EU (CRD IV)	All Member States	1 January 2014
B. Recovery and resolution		
Regulation (EU) No 806/2014 (SRMR)	Participating Member States	1 January 2016
Intergovernmental Agreement on the SRF	Contracting Parties	1 January 2016
Directive 2014/59/EU (BRRD)	All Member States	1 January 2015
C. Deposit guarantee		
Directive 2014/49/EU (DGSD)	All Member States	4 July 2015

---

[206] At: https://www.eba.europa.eu/sites/default/documents/files/documents/10180/2622242/324e89ec-3523-4c5b-bd4f-e415367212bb/EBA%20Opinion%20on%20the%20eligibility%20of%20deposits%20coverage%20level%20and%20cooperation%20between%20DGSs.pdf.

[207] DGSD, Article 19(6), second sub-paragraph.

6.7 The Directive on the Reorganisation and Winding-Up of Credit Institutions

6.7.1 General Aspects

(1) Directive 2001/24/EC "on the reorganisation and winding-up of credit institutions" was adopted by the co-legislators on 4 April 2001 and remains in force, as amended by **Article 117 BRRD**[208]; the creation of the BU has not (yet) opened any prospect of amending it further. Its legal basis is **Article 47(2) TEC** (Article 53(1) TFEU); it is addressed to Member States, was published in the *OJ* on 5 May 2001, entered into force on that date and applies since 5 May 2004.[209]

In terms of definitions[210]: **'winding-up proceedings'** means collective proceedings opened and monitored by the administrative or judicial authorities of a Member State with the aim of realising assets under the supervision of those authorities, including where the proceedings are terminated by a composition or other, similar measure; and **'reorganisation measures'** means measures intended to preserve or restore the financial situation of a credit institution or an investment firm and which could affect third parties' pre-existing rights, including measures involving the possibility of a suspension of payments, suspension of enforcement measures or reduction of claims, as well as the application of the resolution tools and the exercise of resolution powers set out in the BRRD.

6.7.2 Objective and Field of Application

(1) This legislative act does not provide for a minimum harmonisation of national reorganisation measures and winding-up proceedings; the reason is that bank insolvency laws vary across Member States in terms of both type of procedure (judicial or administrative) and available measures. It merely adopted the principle of their mutual recognition. Pursuant to this principle, the administrative or judicial authorities of the home Member State which are responsible for winding-up are alone empowered to decide on the opening of winding-up proceedings concerning a credit institution, including its branches established in other Member States. A decision to open winding-up proceedings taken by these authorities must be recognised, without further formality, within the territory of all other Member States and is effective therein when

---

[208] The current consolidated version is available at: https://eur-lex.europa.eu/legal-content/EN/TXT/?uri=CELEX%3A02001L0024-20140702.

[209] Directive 2001/24/EC, Articles 34–36.

[210] *Ibid.*, Article 2, point (9) and point (7), as amended by Article 117, point (2) BRRD.

the decision is effective in the Member State where the proceedings are opened.[211]

(2) The Directive applies to credit institutions and their branches established in Member States other than those in which they have their head offices. Its provisions concerning the branches of a credit institution having a head office outside the EU apply only where that institution has branches in at least two Member States. It also applies to investment firms as defined in **Article 4(1), point (2) CRR** and their branches located in Member States other than those in which they have their head offices. In the event of application of the resolution tools and exercise of the resolution powers provided for in the BRRD, it also applies to the financial institutions, firms and parent undertakings falling within the scope of the BRRD.[212]

6.7.3 Other Key Provisions

(1) The Directive established a duty of the administrative or judicial authorities of the home Member State to inform the competent (supervisory) authorities of the host Member State of their decision to open winding-up proceedings, including the practical effects which such proceedings may have. This information must be communicated, without delay and by any available means, if possible before the proceedings are opened, or otherwise immediately thereafter, through the competent (supervisory) authorities of the home Member State. The competent authorities of the home Member State must be consulted in the most appropriate form before any voluntary winding-up decision is taken by a credit institution. The decision of a credit institution's governing body for voluntary winding-up does not preclude the adoption of a reorganisation measure or the opening of winding-up proceedings by the administrative or judicial authorities of the home Member State.[213]

(2) If the opening of winding-up proceedings is decided upon in respect of a credit institution in the absence, or following the failure, of reorganisation measures, the authorisation of the institution must be withdrawn (activating the repayment procedure of national DGSs). This withdrawal does not prevent the person or persons entrusted with the winding-up from carrying on some of the credit institution's activities to the extent that is necessary or appropriate for the purposes of winding-up. Upon national discretion, such activities

---

[211] *Ibid.*, Article 9(1). On the operation of the principle of mutual recognition see, by means of mere indication, Weatherill (2016), pp. 258 and 267. For a detailed (recent) study on the differences between bank insolvency laws in the EU, see European Commission (2019).

[212] *Ibid.*, Article 1(1)–(4). Articles 4 and 7 do not apply where Article 83 BRRD is applicable, and Article 33 does not apply where Article 84 BRRD is applicable.

[213] *Ibid.*, Articles 10–11.

Table 6.2 The legal basis of the legislative acts which constitute the sources of EU banking law

Legislative act	Legal basis
CRR	Article 114 TFEU
CRD IV	Article 53(1) TFEU
SSMR	Article 127(6) TFEU
BRRD	Article 114 TFEU
SRMR	Article 114 TFEU
DGSD	Article 53(1) TFEU
CIWUD	Article 47(2) TEC (Article 53(1) TFEU)

must be carried on with the consent, and under the supervision, of the competent authorities of that Member State.[214] The Directive also established special provisions with respect to ensuring the principle of equal treatment of creditors and in the context of winding-up proceedings[215] (Tables 6.2, 6.3 and 6.4)

---

[214] *Ibid.*, Article 12.

[215] *Ibid.*, Articles 13–32. This Directive is analysed in Peters (2011) and Wessels (2017), who uses the abbreviation 'CIWUD' (Credit Institutions Winding-Up Directive). In relation to specific Slovenian reorganisation measures (under the national law having translated that legislative act) and their implementation, see the judgements of the Court (Grand Chamber) of 19 July 2016 in Case C-526/14, *Tadej Kotnik and Others v Državni zbor Republike Slovenije* (ECLI:EU:C:2016:570, the '*Kotnik* case'); of 17 December 2020 in Case C-316/19, *European Commission v Republic of Slovenia* (ECLI:EU:C:2020:1030); and (most recently) of 13 September 2022 in Case C-45/21, *Banka Slovenije* (Central Bank of Slovenia) (ECLI:EU:C:2022:670). The wider importance of this Court judgement on specific aspects relating to EU State aid law and banking regulation is discussed in Volume II.

Table 6.3 Definition of regulated/supervised entities and groups

Entity	Definition
Credit institution	An undertaking the business of which is any of the following: (a) take deposits or other repayable funds from the public and grant credits for its own account; (b) carry out, under conditions, any of the activities referred to in points (3) and (6) of Section A of Annex I to the MiFID II, but it is not a commodity and emission allowance dealer, a collective investment undertaking or an insurance undertaking
Investment firm	An investment firm as defined in Article 4(1), point (1) (in principle, any legal person whose regular occupation or business is the provision of one or more 'investment services' to third parties, and/or the performance of one or more 'investment activities' on a professional basis), which is authorised thereunder; credit institutions are excluded
Financial institution	An undertaking other than an institution or a pure industrial holding company, the principal activity of which is to acquire holdings or to pursue one or more of the activities listed in points (2)–(12) and (15) of Annex I to the CRD IV; *included* are investment firms, financial holding companies, mixed financial holding companies, investment holding companies, payment institutions within the meaning of the PSD II and asset management companies; *excluded* are insurance holding companies and mixed-activity insurance holding companies as defined in of Article 212(1), points (f) and (g), respectively, of the Solvency II Directive
Asset management company	An asset management company as defined in Article 2, point (5) FICOD I *or* an AIFM as defined in Article 4(1), point (b) AIMFD, including, unless otherwise provided, third-country entities that carry out similar activities and that are subject to the laws of a third country which applies supervisory and regulatory requirements at least equivalent to those applied in the EU
Institution	(a) A credit institution authorised under Article 8 CRD IV (b) an undertaking as referred to in point Article 4(1), point (1)(b) CRR, point (1)(b) (that is also covered by the new definition of credit institution), which by end-2019 was carrying out activities as investment firm, authorised under MiFID II, and should have applied for authorisation in accordance with Article 8 CRD IV by 27 December 2020 (**CRD IV**, Article 8a (3))
Parent undertaking	In principle, a parent undertaking within the meaning of Article 22(1)–(5) of the Accounting Directive (2013/34/EU) for the purposes of Section II of Chapters 3 and 4 of Title VII and Title VIII of the CRD IV and Part Five of the CRR, it also means a parent undertaking within the meaning of Article 22(1) of the Accounting Directive *and* any undertaking which effectively exercises a dominant influence over another undertaking

(continued)

Table 6.3 (continued)

Entity	Definition
Subsidiary	In principle, a subsidiary undertaking within the meaning of Article 22(1)–(5) of the Accounting Directive; subsidiaries of subsidiaries are considered to be subsidiaries of the original parent undertaking
Branch	A place of business which forms a legally dependent part of an institution and carries out directly all or some of the transactions inherent in the business of institutions
Financial holding company	A financial institution (as parent undertaking) which is not a mixed financial holding company; its subsidiaries are exclusively or mainly institutions or financial institutions, where at least one of them is an institution and where more than 50% of the financial institution's equity, consolidated assets, revenues, personnel or other indicator considered relevant by the competent authority are associated with subsidiaries that are institutions or financial institutions
Mixed financial holding company	A parent undertaking which is not a credit institution, an insurance undertaking, a reinsurance undertaking, an investment firm, an asset management company or an alternative investment fund manager (i.e., a regulated entity); along with its subsidiaries—at least one of which is a regulated entity which has its registered office in the EU—and other entities, it constitutes a financial conglomerate (according to FICOD I)
Mixed-activity holding company	A parent undertaking, other than a financial holding company or an institution or a mixed financial holding company, the subsidiaries of which include at least one institution
Parent institution in a Member State	An institution in a Member State which has an institution, a financial institution or an ancillary services undertaking as a subsidiary or which holds a participation in an institution, financial institution or ancillary services undertaking; It is not itself a subsidiary of another institution authorised in the same Member State, or of a financial holding company or mixed financial holding company set up in the same Member State;
Ancillary services undertaking	An undertaking the principal activity of which consists of owning or managing property, managing data-processing services, or a similar activity which is ancillary to the principal activity of one or more institutions;
Parent credit institution in a Member State	A parent institution in a Member State that is a credit institution
Parent financial holding company in a Member State	A financial holding company; it is *not* itself a subsidiary of an institution authorised in the same Member State, or of a financial holding company or mixed financial holding company set up in the same Member State

(continued)

Table 6.3 (continued)

Entity	Definition
Parent mixed financial holding company in a Member State	A mixed financial holding company; it is *not* itself a subsidiary of an institution authorised in the same Member State, or of a financial holding company or mixed financial holding company set up in that same Member State
Union (or EU) parent institution	A parent institution in a Member State; it is *not* a subsidiary of another institution authorised in any Member State, or of a financial holding company or mixed financial holding company set up in any Member State
Union (or EU) parent financial holding company	A parent financial holding company in a Member State; it is *not* a subsidiary of an institution authorised in any Member State, or of another financial holding company or mixed financial holding company set up in any Member State
Union (or EU) parent mixed financial holding company	A parent mixed financial holding company in a Member State; it is *not* a subsidiary of an institution authorised in any Member State or of another financial holding company or mixed financial holding company set up in any Member State
Systemically important institution	An EU parent institution, an EU parent financial holding company, an EU parent mixed financial holding company, or an institution the failure or malfunction of which could lead to systemic risk

Table 6.4 Definition of national supervisory and resolution authorities

National competent authority (NCA)	A public authority or body officially recognised by national law, which is empowered by national law to supervise institutions as part of the supervisory system in operation in the Member State concerned
National designated authority (NDA)	(1) According to **Article 458 CRR** on macroprudential or systemic risk identified at the level of a Member State, this must designate the authority in charge of the application of this Article; this authority is either the NCA or the NDA (2) In **Article 136(1) CRD IV**, each Member State must designate a public authority or body (the **'NDA'**) responsible for setting the appropriate CCyB rate
National resolution authority (NRA)	A public administrative authority (or authorities) designated by Member States, entrusted with public administrative powers, and empowered to apply the resolution tools and exercise the resolution powers; it may be a NCB; a competent ministry; another public administrative authority (or authorities) entrusted with public administrative powers; or *exceptionally*, the competent authority (NCA) for the purposes of the CRR and the CRD IV

Excursus: The Emergency Liquidity Assistance (ELA) Mechanism[216]

Introductory Remarks—Documentation

The provision of central bank last-resort lending to solvent credit institutions established in the euro area and exposed to liquidity problems, which is different from (but related to) the monetary policy of the ECB within the Eurosystem, is not governed by any hard law provisions under EU primary and/or secondary law (taking into account the 'constructive ambiguity' dimension of LLR[217]).[218] This aspect was not *explicitly* addressed neither in the TEC (and then in the TFEU) nor in the **ESCB/ECB Statute**. However, according to Smits (1997):

> The absence of lender-of-last-resort (LOLR) support from the text of the ESCB Statute does not make the authority of the ECB to grant it, or to authorize the provision of such support by NCBs, questionable. It is submitted that, under Article 18.1, second indent,[219] the capacity of the ECB and the NCBs to act as lenders of last resort is subsumed.[220]

In this respect, two alternative, diametrically opposed views were put forward: under the **'decentralised approach'**, this power should belong to the NCBs of the Member States whose currency is the euro, while under the **'centralised approach'**, the ECB should be the competent authority, assisted by the **NCBs**. With regard to this issue, the following is pointed out:

> *First*, in case of a generalised crisis in the euro area which would affect the liquidity position of every credit institution operating in the euro area,

---

[216] This Excursus is based on Gortsos (2020), pp. 388–399 (adjusted and fully updated).

[217] On this aspect, see Chapter 1 above, under 1.3.2.

[218] Buiter and Rahbari (2012) have tabled the proposal that the ECB should also act as an LLR for sovereigns in the euro area. From a legal point of view, this would be well beyond the powers conferred upon the ECB by the Treaties and, in the author's view, would be in conflict with Article 123 TFEU on the prohibition of monetary government financing. On this TFEU Article, see, by means of mere indication, Hattenberger (2019).

[219] Article 18.1 reads as follows: "*In order to achieve the objectives of the ESCB and to carry out its tasks, the ECB and the [NCBs] may operate in the financial markets by buying and selling outright (spot and forward) or under repurchase agreement and by lending or borrowing claims and marketable instruments whether in euro or other currencies, as well as precious metals, and conduct credit operations with credit institutions and other market participants, with lending being based on adequate collateral.*"

[220] Smits (1997), p. 269, with reference to Louis (1995), p. 59; see also Lastra (2015), at p. 378. This author fully supports this view and has made proposals for the ECB becoming the LLR for (at least) the significant credit institutions under its direct supervision within the SSM; see Gortsos (2015b) and (2020), pp. 441–445; see also Dietz (2019) (all with extensive further references).

there is a general consensus that the ECB should intervene by means of monetary policy operations,[221] including *in extremis* also non-standard ones.[222] This was the case during both the GFC and the euro area fiscal crisis.[223]

Second, apart from the fact that lending of last resort should, in principle, only be provided to solvent credit institutions, lending to insolvent credit institutions also stumbles on the provisions regarding the prohibition of State aid under **Articles 107–108 TFEU**.[224]

Third, this lending may violate (the just above-mentioned) **Article 123 TFEU**.[225] In such a case, monetary government financing may be effected indirectly if the credit institution uses the liquidity provided to buy government securities. Indirect monetary financing may also be affected if a credit institution is insolvent, since in such a case the central bank enters into government activities (which it is in any event not allowed to engage in), releasing the government from any expenditure incurred due to capital injections to it.

(2) The procedural arrangements governing the provision of such liquidity assistance under the Emergency Liquidity Assistance (**ELA**) mechanism were already laid down since January 1999, but only became public on **17 October 2013** when the ECB issued a relevant Communication.[226] On **19 February 2014**, the ECB's GC approved certain technical specifications on these procedures, the content of which was included in its new Communication ('ECB

---

[221] According to Article 2, point (32) of the ECB Guideline (EU) 2015/510 of 19 December 2014 "on the implementation of the Eurosystem monetary policy framework (General Documentation Guideline) (ECB/2014/60) (recast)" (OJ L 91, 2 April 2015, pp. 3–135, as in force), monetary policy operations include open market operations and standing facilities. On the framework governing these operations, see Smits (1997), pp. 223–288, Papathanassiou (2001), pp. 73–120, European Central Bank (2011), pp. 93–116, as well as Gortsos (2020), pp. 391–399 and (2023) (as an update of the former).

[222] See Padoa-Schioppa (2000), p. 28, Lastra (2000), p. 205 and Schoenmaker (2000), pp. 218–219.

[223] See European Central Bank (2010) and Claeys (2014).

[224] On the compliance of last-resort lending with EU State aid rules, see Smits (1997), pp. 270–271 and Lastra (2015), pp. 380–382.

[225] See European Central Bank (2007b), p. 80. Pursuant to Article 123(1) TFEU, ECB purchases of Member States' sovereign bonds in the primary market (that is, upon their issuance) are prohibited.

[226] At: https://www.ecb.europa.eu/pub/pdf/other/elaprocedures.el.pdf. The sole reference of the ECB to the ELA mechanism until the issuance of this Communication is found in European Central Bank (2007a).

Communication (2014)').[227] Since **May 2017**, the procedural arrangements are laid down in its "Agreement on emergency liquidity assistance"[228] (hereinafter the '**ECB Agreement (2017)**', further analysed below).[229]

(3) The procedures referred to therein relate to the actions necessitated by the ECB's GC, and data to be provided to the ECB, in order for it to be in a position to assess, whether the provision of emergency liquidity by NCBs to individual credit institutions interferes with the objectives and tasks of the Eurosystem pursuant to **Article 14.4 ESCB/ECB Statute**. This Article reads as follows:

> [NCBs] may perform functions other than those specified in this Statute unless the [GC] finds, by a majority of two thirds of the votes cast, that these interfere with the objectives and tasks of the ESCB. Such functions shall be performed on the responsibility and liability of [NCBs] and shall not be regarded as being part of the functions of the ESCB.[230]

Amidst the euro area fiscal crisis and given its negative impact on the banking sector of several Member States, last-resort lending to credit institutions established in euro area Member States was repeatedly activated: in the 2010–2013 period, by Ireland, Greece and Cyprus; in 2014, by Portugal; and in 2015, by Greece again.[231]

Scope of Application of the ECB Agreement (2017)—Definition of 'Emergency Liquidity Assistance'

(1) The **ECB Agreement (2017)** presents a definition of the ELA and describes the allocation of responsibilities, costs and risks for ELA operations, as well as a framework for the provision and exchange of information, as well as the control of liquidity effects to prevent any provision of ELA from interfering with the objectives and tasks of the ESCB.[232] In addition, the Agreement, which should have been reviewed in 2019 at the latest,[233]

---

[227] See European Central Bank (2014c). This Communication is analysed in Gortsos (2015b), pp. 58–63.

[228] At: https://www.ecb.europa.eu/mopo/ela/html/index.en.html.

[229] The Communications and the Agreement do not constitute ECB legal acts and are not legally binding. They merely register the ECB's procedural practices; nevertheless, it is expected that the NCBs comply with them.

[230] This Article is analysed in Smits (1997), pp. 99–101.

[231] For a brief presentation and critical evaluation of the ELA, see also Papadia (2014).

[232] ECB Agreement (2017), Section 1.1, first sentence.

[233] *Ibid.*, Section 9.

acknowledges that the provision of ELA must be in compliance with the prohibition of monetary financing (**TFEU, Article 123**).[234]

(2) In principle, euro area credit institutions may draw liquidity from central banks in two alternative ways: either, as a rule, in the context of monetary policy operations or, exceptionally, *via* the ELA. For the purposes of the **ECB Agreement (2017)**, ELA occurs when:

> (a) a Eurosystem NCB provides central bank money **and/or** (b) any other assistance that may lead to an increase in central bank money to a financial institution or a group of financial institutions facing liquidity problems, where, in either case, such operation is not part of the single monetary policy."[235]

(3) The provision of ELA is not considered part of the single monetary policy in the euro area. Even though in both cases the central bank provides liquidity to the banking system, in the case of monetary policy actions the objective is not to ensure the stability of the financial system, but to maintain price stability. The liquidity granted is not of an emergency nature, is rather permanent and is provided to the banking system as a whole and not to individual credit institutions. Although there is no doubt that the provision of ELA has an impact on total liquidity in an economy, the ECB has the ability to sterilise this through appropriate monetary policy operations:

> The impact of an ELA intervention on aggregate liquidity conditions in the euro area can be managed in a manner consistent with the maintenance of the appropriate single monetary policy stance.[236]

Allocation of Responsibilities, Costs and Risks

ELA is provided under the *main* responsibility of the NCB concerned[237] (and at its sole discretion), on condition, however, that the ECB has not prohibited it (as discussed just below). Hence, it is not the ECB itself that provides ELA. The NCB concerned (or a third party acting as a guarantor) incurs any costs and risks that may arise from the provision of ELA.[238] Accordingly, the

---

[234] *Ibid.*, Section 1.1, second sentence.

[235] *Ibid.*, Section 1.2.

[236] European Central Bank (2007a), p. 81. By means of a 'sterilised intervention', central banks conduct appropriate open market operations (which are a key instrument for the implementation of monetary policy) in order to ensure that ELA provision does not have an impact on the monetary basis and money supply, and does not affect its monetary policy strategy.

[237] ECB Agreement (2017), Section 2.1. On the conditions for this mechanism's compliance with EU state aid law, see paras 62–64 of the Commission's 2013 Banking Communication (2013/C 216/01).

[238] *Ibid.*, Section 2.2.

Situations Where ELA May be Limited or Prohibited

NCBs may provide ELA unless the GC finds, pursuant to **Article 14.4 ESCB/ECB Statute**, that this interferes with the ESCB objectives and tasks.[240] In relation to that aspect, the ECB Agreement (2017) also provides for the following: *first*, the violation of the prohibition of monetary financing under **Article 123 TFEU** may constitute such an interference with the objectives and tasks of the Eurosystem. The provision of ELA as notified under **Sections 3.2(b) and 3.3** is, therefore, assessed *ex-ante* as regards compliance with the prohibition of monetary financing; *second*, ELA transactions akin to an overdraft facility or any other type of credit facility for the State, in particular, any financing of the public sector's obligations *vis-à-vis* third parties, or the central bank *de facto* taking over a state task, violate the prohibition of monetary financing; and *finally*, ELA provision to insolvent institutions and institutions for which insolvency proceedings have been initiated according to national laws violates the prohibition of monetary financing.[241]

The ELA Solvency Criterion for Credit Institutions

In principle, the solvency of credit institutions is being assessed by the authorities competent for their microprudential supervision (i.e., in the euro area the ECB for 'significant' credit institutions and the NCAs for 'less significant' ones). The **ECB Agreement (2017)** provides explicitly that a credit institution is considered solvent for ELA purposes if either of the following conditions is met: *first*, its CET1, Tier 1 and total capital ratios, as reported (under the CRR) on an individual and consolidated basis, comply with the minimum regulatory capital levels (namely 4.5%, 6% or 8%, respectively); or

---

[239] As a common practice, NCBs borrow their funds from other NCBs within the Eurosystem. In any case, pursuant to Article 26.3 ESCB/ECB Statute, the ECB's Executive Board draws up, for analytical and operational purposes, an ESCB consolidated balance sheet, comprising those assets and liabilities of the NCBs that fall within the ESCB. In addition, on the legal basis (mainly) of Article 26.4 ESCB/ECB Statute, the ECB adopted Guideline ECB/2010/20 "on the legal framework for accounting and financial reporting in the [ESCB]" (OJ L 35, 9 February 2011, pp. 31–68) requiring the elaboration of this consolidated balance sheet. Since 2015, the consolidated balance sheet is published together with the ECB Annual Accounts. In this consolidated balance sheet ELA features on the assets side under item 6 titled "Other claims on euro area credit institutions".

[240] ECB Agreement (2017), Section 5.1. This has been the case in Greece in June 2015, which had as a consequence the imposition of a "bank holiday" and of intrusive capital controls (by virtue of Article 65(1), point (b) TFEU); see on this, by means of mere indication, Hadjiemmanuil (2020), pp. 1348–1354.

[241] ECB Agreement (2017), Sections 5.2–5.4.

second, if this condition is not met, there is a credible prospect of recapitalisation by which the above minimum regulatory capital levels would be restored within 24 weeks after the end of the reference quarter of the data that showed that the credit institution does not comply with these standards; in duly justified, exceptional cases the GC may decide to prolong this **'grace period'**.[242]

Duration and Pricing of ELA

(1) The provision of ELA may only exceed twelve months following a non-objection by the GC requested by the Governor of the NCB concerned at the latest once the provision of ELA exceeds 10 months. If this period is exceeded, this Governor must justify the further provision of ELA in a letter to the ECB President on a monthly basis; the GC may impose additional requirements and conditions.[243]

(2) The penalty interest rate charged to the institution receiving ELA is variable[244]: while in the case of ELA euro-denominated reverse transactions NCBs should in principle apply a minimum rate equal to the Eurosystem's marginal lending facility rate[245] plus 100 basis points, irrespective of the net cost of relevant guarantees and other costs of collateral, in the case of euro-denominated intraday ELA reverse transactions, they should in principle apply a minimum rate equal to 1% *per annum*.

Flow of Information, Control of Liquidity Effects and Monetary Policy: The Main Framework

(1) In order to ensure that ELA operations do not interfere with the single monetary policy of the Eurosystem, the ECB would have to be informed or consulted as laid down in **Section 3.2**. This information should allow a smooth sterilisation of any undesired liquidity effects and an assessment of any systemic implications.[246]

(2) The information must be provided by the NCB concerned. If it is provided by the institution receiving ELA, such NCB must ensure that the information is provided by the institution to the NCB and passed on by the NCB to

---

[242] *Ibid.*, Section 4.

[243] *Ibid.*, Section 6.

[244] *Ibid.*, Sections 7.1–7.3.

[245] On this facility and on that rate, see Gortsos (2023), pp. 33–35.

[246] The information obligations set out in the Agreement are additional and without prejudice to any other information obligations that apply under the legal framework in force (ECB Agreement (2017), Section 3.1).

the ECB without undue delay. Regardless of the size or nature of ELA operations, the information to be provided consists at least of five elements.[247] *First*, NCBs should always inform the ECB of the details of any ELA operation, at the latest, within two business days after the operation has been carried out. The information needs to include, at least, nine specific elements. After the initial notification, further relevant information should be provided on an ongoing basis until the ELA is repaid and information on all above-mentioned elements that has not been provided *ex-ante* must be provided *ex-post*. Relevant information must be updated daily; by means of *exception*, **collateral valuation changes** should only be updated when other information changes are reported or upon an ECB request. *Second*, the institution receiving ELA must provide a **funding plan** within two months following the first provision of ELA and update it on a quarterly basis until the ELA is repaid.[248] *Third*, such an institution must also provide monthly up-to-date information on the precise level of its **regulatory capital ratios** (i.e., CET1, Tier 1 and total capital ratios) as well as the **leverage ratio,** as reported under the CRR, both on an individual and on a consolidated basis, within two months after the end of each reference month. *Fourth*, an institution receiving ELA and being in breach of own funds requirements under the CRR must submit a **recapitalisation plan** to the ECB for assessment within a timeframe determined by the GC. *Finally*, if ELA is provided for a period exceeding six months, the Governor of the NCB concerned must address a letter to the ECB President outlining the intended exit strategy; for as long as the institution is receiving ELA it must update the exit strategy in case of changes to the exit plan.

Specific Cases

Size of ELA operations exceeding a threshold of 500 million euro: If the size of ELA operations envisaged by one or more NCBs for a given financial institution or group exceeds this threshold, the NCB (s) involved must inform the Executive Board at the earliest possible time prior to the extension of assistance about the nature of the problem, the instruments to be used and the liquidity implications of the assistance. This information will then be provided by the Executive Board to the GC. The size of ELA operations should be determined as the best possible estimate of the total cumulative amount of assistance needed to resolve the liquidity crisis, considering the financial institution or group on a consolidated basis and including its foreign branches in other euro area Member States.[249]

---

[247] *Ibid.*, Section 3.2 (a).

[248] The funding plan must be provided in line with the funding plan procedure approved by the GC on 25 September 2015.

[249] ECB Agreement (2017), Section 3.2 (b).

Size of ELA operations exceeding a threshold of two billion euro: In addition to the above, where the size of ELA operations envisaged by one or more NCBs for a given financial institution or a given group thereof **exceeds a threshold of two billion euro**, based on all information available, the Executive Board must decide in a timely manner whether the issue needs to be addressed by the GC. If the Executive Board concludes that there is a risk that the respective ELA interferes with the single monetary policy of the Eurosystem, it must request the GC to *take a position at short notice*. NCBs are allowed to undertake the planned ELA operations, unless the GC decides to prohibit their execution, on the grounds that they interfere with the single monetary policy of the Eurosystem, within 24 hours of the notification by the NCBs. At the request of the NCB concerned, and in order either to expedite ELA operations in the case of particular urgency or to avoid potential systemic implications, the GC may decide not to prohibit potential future ELA operations to deal with the same problem up to a certain ceiling and within a short pre-specified period of time, which may be extended by a subsequent decision. Such a ceiling may also refer to several financial institutions and/or several groups thereof at the same time.[250] The GC decision must be taken by a majority vote of two thirds.[251]

ELA operations concerning banking groups with presence in several euro area Member States: For ELA operations concerning a banking group with branches and subsidiaries in several euro area Member States, the NCBs concerned must establish **'central bank networks'** to facilitate their cooperation. The coordination must be entrusted to the NCB of the Member State where the parent of the banking group is established. The ECB in its monetary policy function and the Eurosystem will be involved in accordance with their responsibilities. As appropriate, these **networks** must closely cooperate with the colleges of supervisors or the SSM in matters of common interest.[252]

Liquidity arrangements with non-Eurosystem NCBs: An NCB intending to enter into a **'liquidity arrangement'** with a non-Eurosystem NCB (or

---

[250] The request must be submitted by the NCB to the ECB at least three business days before the GC meeting at which it is to be considered, together with all available *ex-ante* information on the elements listed under points 1–9 of Section 3.2(a) (see just above) under the conditions set out therein. If the threshold refers concurrently to several financial firms or several groups thereof, the information should be provided on a bank-by-bank basis, and a projection—covering, in principle, the period up to the next regular GC meeting—of the funding gap for each individual bank that is to receive ELA on the basis of an expected and a stress scenario.

[251] If immediate action is necessary to avoid systemic implications, the NCB can undertake an overnight operation while the GC's decision is pending. The Executive Board must be informed immediately about any such operation. The above does not apply to operations defined in Section 1.2(b) that have contractual safeguards in place ensuring that the financial firm or the group cannot use the assistance received as collateral for Eurosystem credit operations, subject to adequate monitoring by the lending NCB *and* any GC decision under Article 14.4 ESCB/ECB Statute (*ibid.*, Section 3.3).

[252] *Ibid.*, Section 3.4.

monetary authority) to facilitate the provision of emergency euro or foreign currency liquidity to a financial institution or a group of financial institutions operating within or outside the euro area must notify in advance the GC thereof, through the Executive Board.[253]

Communication on ELA

It is at the discretion of NCBs to communicate publicly about the aggregate provision of ELA in their country if they deem it necessary. In such a case, the NCB must notify in advance the GC with regard to the intended communication plan and content, including a communication proposal.[254] The communication, nevertheless, should not refer to any GC's assessment or decision, but may contain information on the ELA ceiling (including the duration of its applicability) to which the GC did not object, the actual amount of ELA provided by the NCB on average over a recent period of time, and relevant context information, if deemed helpful to facilitate a proper perception by the public. The GC may object to the proposed communication plan and content in view of the potential broader confidence and financial stability implications for the euro area[255] (Table 6.5)

---

[253] The information to be provided should be, to the extent available, the same as laid down in Sections 3.1 and 3.2, point (a), including the name of the NCB's counterparty to the arrangement (i.e., the non-Eurosystem NCB or monetary authority). As regards principles and procedures for the assessment of these arrangements, applicable are *mutatis mutandis* Sections 3.2, point (b) and 3.3 above (*ibid.*, Section 3.5).

[254] *Ibid.*, Sections 8.1–8.2.

[255] *Ibid.*, Sections 8.3, points (a)–(c) and 8.4.

Table 6.5 The partial Europeanisation of the 'bank safety net' (even) within the Banking Union (BU)

Financial policy instruments	Scope of application	Level of action (italics *denotes national elements*)
Granting and withdrawal of authorisation, as well as approval and disposal of acquisition of qualified holdings	Participating Member States	**ECB** within the SSM (for both significant and less significant credit institutions)
Macroprudential oversight	EU Member States	**ESRB** Recommendations and Warnings for the EU financial system as a whole and, within the SSM, ECB power to object to and top up national capital buffers *National macroprudential authorities for monitoring and assessing systemic risk in their jurisdictions*
Microprudential supervision	Participating Member States	**ECB** within the SSM (for significant credit institutions, in relation to its specific supervisory tasks conferred) *NCAs within the SSM (for less significant credit institutions)* *NCAs (for significant and less significant credit institutions, in relation to any task not included in the specific supervisory tasks conferred on the ECB)*
Recovery planning and early intervention	Participating Member States	**ECB** within the SSM (for significant credit institutions) *NCAs within the SSM (for less significant credit institutions)*
Resolution planning, assessment of resolvability and resolution	Participating Member States	**SRB** within the SRM (for significant credit institutions) *NRAs within the SRM (for less significant credit institutions)*
Winding up	EU Member States	*National administrative or judicial authorities*
Deposit guarantee	EU Member States	*National DGSs*
Last-resort lending (ELA)	Euro area Member States	*NCBs-members of the Eurosystem*

Secondary Sources

A

Alexander, K. (2015): European Banking Union: A Legal and Institutional Analysis of the Single Supervisory Mechanism and the Single Resolution Mechanism, *European Law Review*, Issue 2, pp. 154–187

Alexander, K. (2016): The ECB and Banking Supervision: Does Single Supervisory Mechanism Provide an Effective Regulatory Framework?, in Andenas, M. and G. Deipenbrock (2016, editors): *Regulating and Supervising European Financial Markets – More Risks than Achievements*, Springer International Publishing, Switzerland, pp. 253–276

B

Binder, J.-H. (2015a): The European Banking Union – Rationale and Key Policy Issues, in Binder, J.-H. and Ch.V. Gortsos (2015): *Banking Union: A Compendium*, Verlag C.H. Beck, München – Hart, Oxford – Nomos Verlagsgesellschaft, Baden-Baden

Binder, J.-H. (2015b): Resolution Planning and Structural Bank Reform within the Banking Union, in Castaneda, J., Karamichailidou, G., Mayes, D. and G. Wood (2015b, editors): *European Banking Union. Prospects and challenges*, Routledge (also available at: https://ssrn.com/abstract=2540038)

Binder, J.-H., Gortsos, Ch.V., Lackhoff, K. and Ch. Ohler (2022, editors): *Brussels Commentary on the Banking Union*, Verlag C.H. Beck, München – Hart Publishing, Oxford – Nomos Verlagsgesellschaft, Baden-Baden

Boccuzzi, G. (2022): *Banking Crises in Italy: An Application and Evaluation of the European Framework*, Palgrave Macmillan

Bodellini, M. (2021): The Optional Measures of Deposit Guarantee Schemes: Towards a New Bank Crisis Management Paradigm?, *European Journal of Legal Studies*, Volume 13, Issue 1, pp. 341–376

Borchardt, K.D. (2019): Kommentar zum Artikel 273 AEUV, in Lenz, C.O. und K.D. Borchardt (2019, Hrsg.): *EU-Verträge: Kommentar*, 6. Auflage, Bundesanzeiger Verlag, Köln – Linde Verlag, Wien, pp. 2753–2754

Brescia Morra, C. (2014): *From the Single Supervisory Mechanism to the Banking Union. The Role of the ECB and the EBA*, Working Paper No 2, Luiss Guido Carli School of European Political Economy, Luiss University Press, Italy

Buiter, W.H. and Eb. Rahbari (2012): The ECB as Lender of Last Resort for Sovereigns in the Eurozone, *Journal of Common Market Studies, Special Issue: The JCMS Annual Review of the European Union in 2011*, Volume 50, Issue Supplement 2, pp. 6–35 (also available as Area CEPR Discussion Paper No. DP8974, May, at: https://ssrn.com/abstract=2066345)

Burke, J.V. (2015): *Building a Bank Resolution Fund Over Time: When Should Each Individual Bank Contribute?*, available at: https://ssrn.com/abstract=2535722

C

Carmassi, J. (2015): *New Rules for Bank Crisis Resolution in the European Union and the United States*, Istein Istituto Einaudi Regulatory Brief No 3, February

Claeys, G. (2014): *The (Not so) Unconventional Monetary Policy of the European Central Bank Since 2008*, European Parliament, Directorate General for Internal Policies, IP/A/ECON/2–14–02, June, available at: https://www.europarl.europa.eu/studies

Conlon, T. and J. Cotter (2014a): *Eurozone Bank Resolution and Bail-In Intervention, Triggers and Writedowns,* Prepared for the Conference: European Banking Union: Prospects and Challenges University of Buckingham, 21–22 November

Conlon, T. and J. Cotter (2014b): Anatomy of a Bail-in, *Journal of Financial Stability*, Volume 15, December, pp. 257–263

D

D'Ambrosio, R. (2020, editor): *Law and Practice of the Banking Union and of Its Governing Institutions (Cases and Materials)*, Quaderni di Ricerca Giuridica, Banca d'Italia, Numero 88, April

D'Ambrosio, R. (2013): *Due Process and Safeguards of the Persons Subject to SSM Supervisory and Sanctioning Proceedings*, Quaderni di Ricerca Giuridica, Banca d'Italia, Numero 74, Dicembre

Dermine, J. (2016): The Single Resolution Mechanism in the European Union: Good Intentions and Unintended Evil, *Monetary Economics Today*, Festschrift in Honour of Ernst Baltensperger, INSEAD Working Paper No. 2016/69/FIN (also available at: https://ssrn.com/abstract=2838793)

Deutsche Bundesbank (2013): Fortschritte auf dem Weg zur europäischen Bankenunion, *Geschäftsbericht*, pp. 23–41

Dietz, S.-A. (2019): The ECB as Lender of Last Resort in the Eurozone? An Analysis of an Optimal Institutional Design of Emergency Liquidity Assistance Competence Within the Context of the Banking Union, *Maastricht Journal of European & International Law*, Volume 26, Issue 5, available at: https://doi.org/10.1177/1023263X19855628

Dietz, Th. (2014): *On the Single Supervisory Mechanism*, Journal of Risk Management in Financial Institutions, Volume 7, pp. 221–225

E

Eckhardt, Ph. (2013): Bankenabwicklungsmechanismus mit Mängeln, *die Bank, Zeitschrift für Bankpolitik und Praxis*, pp. 35–37

European Central Bank (2014a): *Aggregate Report on the Comprehensive Assessment*, October, available at: https://www.bankingsupervision.europa.eu/banking/comprehensive/html/index.en.html

European Central Bank (2014b): The Single Resolution Mechanism: The Second Pillar of Banking Union, in European Central Bank (2014): *Financial Integration in Europe*, April, available at: https://www.ecb.europa.eu/home/html/search.en.html?q=financial%20integration, Chapter 2: European Institutional Reform, pp. 37–47

European Central Bank (2014c): *ELA Procedures (the Procedures Underlying the Governing Council's Role Pursuant to Article 14.4 of the Statute of the European System of Central Banks and of the European Central Bank with Regard to the Provision of ELA to Individual Credit Institutions)*, October, available at: https://www.ecb.europa.eu/mopo/ela/html/index.en.html

European Central Bank (2011): *The Monetary Policy of the ECB*, European Central Bank, Frankfurt

European Central Bank (2010): The ECB's Monetary Policy Stance During the Financial Crisis, *ECB Monthly Bulletin*, January, pp. 63–71

European Central Bank (2007a): The EU Arrangements for Financial Crisis Management, *Monthly Bulletin*, February, pp. 73–84

European Central Bank (2007b): *Financial Integration in Europe*, European Central Bank, March

European Commission (2019): *Study on the Differences Between Bank Insolvency Laws and on Their Potential Harmonisation*, November, available at: https://finance.ec.europa.eu/system/files/2020-06/191106-study-bank-insolvency_en.pdf

F

Fabbrini, F. (2014): On Banks, Courts and International Law: The Intergovernmental Agreement on the Single Resolution Fund in Context, *Maastricht Journal of European & International Law*, Volume 21, Issue 3, pp. 444–463

Ferran, E. and V. Babis (2013): *The European Single Supervisory Mechanism*, Legal Studies Research Paper Series, University of Cambridge, Faculty of Law, Paper No. 10/2013, March, available at: https://www.law.cam.ac.uk/ssrn

Ferrarini, G. and L. Chiarella (2013): *Common Banking Supervision in the Eurozone: Strengths and Weaknesses*, European Corporate Governance Institute, Working Paper Series in Law No 223/2013, August

G

Gandrud, C. and M. Hallerberg (2014): *Supervisory Transparency in the European Banking Union*, Bruegel Policy Contribution, Issue 01, January

Gandrud, C. and M. Hallerberg (2013): *Who Decides? Resolving Failed Banks in a European Framework*, Bruegel Policy Contribution Paper No 16, November

Gordon, N.J and W.G. Ringe (2014): *Bank Resolution in the European Banking Union: A Transatlantic Perspective on What It Would Take*, Columbia Law and Economics Working Paper No. 465

Gortsos, Ch.V. (2023): *Legal Aspects of the Single Monetary Policy in the Euro Area: From the Establishment of the Eurosystem to the Pandemic Crisis and the Current Inflation Crisis*, Fifth fully updated edition, available at: https://ssrn.com/abstract=3819726

Gortsos, Ch.V. (2022a): Commentary on Article 32 SSMR, in Binder, J.-H., Gortsos, Ch.V, Ohler, C. and K. Lackhoff (2022, editors), Verlag C.H. Beck, München – Hart Publishing, Oxford – Nomos Verlagsgesellschaft, Baden-Baden, pp. 428–445

Gortsos, Ch.V. (2022b): Commentary on Articles 67–74 and 94 SRMR, in Binder, J.-H., Gortsos, Ch.V, Ohler, C. and K. Lackhoff (2022, editors), Verlag C.H. Beck, München – Hart Publishing, Oxford – Nomos Verlagsgesellschaft, Baden-Baden pp. 1079–1088 and 1209–1219

Gortsos, Ch.V. (2020): *European Central Banking Law – The Role of the European Central Bank and National Central Banks under European Law*, Palgrave Macmillan Studies in Banking and Financial Institutions, Palgrave Macmillan, Cham – Switzerland

Gortsos, Ch.V. (2019): *The Role of Deposit Guarantee Schemes (DGSs) in Resolution Financing*, European Banking Institute Working Paper Series, No. 37, available at: https://ssrn.com/abstract=3361750

Gortsos, Ch.V. (2016): *A Poisonous (?) Mix: Bail-Out of Credit Institutions Combined with Bail-In of Their Liabilities Under the BRRD – The Use of 'Government Financial Stabilisation Tools' (GFSTs)*, Paper presented at the Workshop of the Financial and Monetary Law Working Group of the European University Institute (Florence, 12 October), available at: https://ssrn.com/abstract=2876508

Gortsos, Ch.V. (2015a): *The Single Supervisory Mechanism (SSM): Legal Aspects of the First Pillar of the European Banking Union*, Nomiki Bibliothiki – European Public Law Organisation (EPLO), Athens

Gortsos, Ch.V. (2015b): Last-resort Lending to Solvent Credit Institutionsin in the Euro Area: A Detailed Presentation of the Emergency Liquidity Assistance (ELA) Mechanism, in: *ECB Legal Conference 2015 – From Monetary Union to Banking Union, on the Way to Capital Markets Union: New Opportunities for European Integration*, European Central Bank (December 2015), pp. 53–76 (also available at: https://ssrn.com/abstract=2688953)

Gros, D. (2013): *The Bank Resolution Compromise: Incomplete, But Workable?* CEPS Commentary, 19 December

Grundmann, S. (2016): *Bankvertragsrecht*, in Staub: Handelsgesetzbuch – Grosskommentar, herausgegeben von C.-W. Canaris, M. Habersack, C. Schäfer, Zehnter Band, Erster Teilband, 5., neu bearbeitete Auflage, De Gruyter, Berlin/Boston

Grünewald, S.N. (2014): *The Resolution of Cross-Border Banking Crises in the European Union – A Legal Study from the Perspective of Burden Sharing*, International Banking and Finance Law Series, Volume 23, Wolters Kluwer Law & Business, Kluwer Law International, The Netherlands

Guastaferro, B. (2018): Sincere Cooperation and Respect for National Identities, in Schütze, R. and T. Tridimas (2018, editors): *Oxford Principles European Union Law – Volume I: The European Union Legal Order*, Oxford University Press, Oxford, Part II: Constitutional Foundations, Chapter 11, pp. 350–383

H

Hadjiemmanuil, Ch. (2020): The Euro Area in Crisis: 2008–2018, in Amtenbrink, F. and Ch. Herrmann (2020, editors): *Oxford Handbook on the EU Law of Economic and Monetary Union*, Oxford University Press, Oxford, Chapter 40, pp. 1253–1362 (also published in LSE Law, Society and Economy Working Papers 12/2019, available at: https://ssrn.com/abstract=3413000)

Hadjiemmanuil, Ch. (2015): *Bank Resolution Financing in the Banking Union*, LSE Law, Society and Economy Working Papers 6/2015, available at: https://ssrn.com/abstract=2575372

Hadjiemmanuil, Ch. (2006): Financial Services, in Chalmers, D., Hadjiemmanuil, Ch., Monti, G. and A. Tomkins (2006, editors): *European Union Law*, Cambridge University Press, Cambridge, New York, Melbourne, Madrid, Cape Town, Singapore, São Paolo, Chapter 18, pp. 781–829

Haentjens, M. (2017): Selected Commentary on the Bank Recovery and Resolution Directive, in Moss, G., Wessels, B. and M. Haentjens (2017, editors): *EU Banking and Insurance Insolvency*, Chapter IV, Second edition, Oxford University Press, Oxford, pp. 177–318

Hatje, A. (2019): Kommentar zum Artikel 4 EUV, in Schwarze, J., Becker, U., Hatje, A. und J. Schoo (2019, Hrsg.): *EU-Kommentar*, 4. Auflage, Nomos Verlagsgesellschaft, Baden-Baden, pp. 59–91

Hattenberger, D. (2019): Kommentar zum Artikel 123 AEUV, in Schwarze, J., Becker, U., Hatje, A. und J. Schoo (2019, Hrsg.): *EU-Kommentar*, 4. Auflage, Nomos Verlagsgesellschaft, Baden-Baden, pp. 1998–2002

Herrnfeld, H.-H. (2019): Kommentar zum Artikel 48 EUV, in Becker, U., Hatje, A. Schoo, J. und J. Schwarze (2019, Herausgeber): *EU-Kommentar*, 4. Auflage, Nomos Verlagsgesellschaft, Baden-Baden, pp. 402–415

Huber, D. and G. Merc (2014): *The Banking Recovery and Resolution Directive and the EU's Crisis Management Framework: Principles, Interplay with the Comprehensive Assessment and the Consequences for Recapitalizing Credit Institutions in Crisis Situations*, Financial Stability Report 28, December, pp. 75–90

Huber, D. and E. von Pföstl (2013): *The Single Supervisory Mechanism within the Banking Union – Novel Features and Implications for Austrian Supervisors and Supervised Entities*, Financial Stability Report 25, June, pp. 52–56

I-K

Ignatowski, M. and J. Korte (2014): *Resolution Threats and Bank Discipline – What Europe Can Learn for the Single Resolution Mechanism from U.S. Experience*, House of Finance SAFE (Sustainable Architecture for Finance in Europe), Policy Letter No 33, May

Kleftouri, N. (2015): *Deposit Protection and Bank Resolution*, Oxford University Press, Oxford

Knecht, M. (2019): Kommentar zum Artikel 8 GRC, in Schwarze, J., Becker, U., Hatje, A. und J. Schoo (2019, Hrsg.): *EU-Kommentar*, 4. Auflage, Nomos Verlagsgesellschaft, Baden-Baden, pp. 3390–3394

L

Lackhoff, K. (2017): *Single Supervisory Mechanism: A Practitioner's Guide*, Verlag C.H. Beck, München – Hart Publishing, Oxford – Nomos Verlagsgesellschaft, Baden-Baden

Lackhoff, K. und S. Grünewald (2015): Die Bankenunion und Ihre Auswirkungen auf den Drittstaat Schweiz – 1. Teil: Der Einheitliche Aufsichtsmechanismus, *Gesellschafts- und Kapitalmarktrecht*, 2, Dike Verlag, Zürich/St. Gallen, pp. 190–205

Lastra, R.M. (2015): *International Financial and Monetary Law*, second edition, Oxford University Press, United Kingdom

Lastra, R.M. (2013): Banking Union and Single Market: Conflict or Companionship?, *Fordham International Law Journal*, Volume 36, pp. 1189–1223

Lastra, R. M. (2000): The Role of the European Central Bank with Regard to Financial Stability and Lender of Last Resort Operations, in Goodhart, C.A.E. (2000, editor): *Which Lender of Last Resort for Europe?*, Chapter 5, Central Banking Publications, London, pp. 197–212

Lastra, R.M. and J.V. Louis (2013): European Economic and Monetary Union: History, Trends, and Prospects, *Yearbook of Economic Law*, pp. 1–150

Lenz, C.O. (2019): Kommentar zum Artikel 4 EUV, in Lenz, C.O. und K.D. Borchardt (2019, Hrsg.): *EU-Verträge: Kommentar*, 6. Auflage, Bundesanzeiger Verlag, Köln – Linde Verlag, Wien, pp. 15–24

Louis J.-V. (2014) : La difficile naissance du mécanisme européen de résolution des banques, *Cahiers de droit européen*, 2014/1, pp. 7–20

Louis, J.-V. (2009): L'Union européenne et sa monnaie, in Commentaire J. Megret: *Integration des marchés financiers*, 3ᵉ édition, Institut d' Etudes Européennes, Editions de l' Université de Bruxelles, Bruxelles

Louis, J.-V. (1995): *L'Union économique et monétaire*, in Commentaire Mégret: Le Droit de la CEE, 2e édition, Etudes Européennes, Editions de l' Université de Bruxelles, Volume 6, Bruxelles

M-Q

Masciandaro, D. and M. Nieto (2014): *Governance of the Single Supervisory Mechanism: Some Reflections*, BAFFI Center on International Markets, Money and Regulation Research Paper Series No. 2014–149, Bocconi University, Italy

Nicolaides, P. (2020): The Corona Virus Can Infect Banks Too: The Applicability of the EU Banking and State Aid Regimes, *European State Aid Law Quarterly*, Volume 19, Issue 1, pp. 29–38

Ohler, Ch. (2022): Commentary on Article 1 SSMR, in Binder, J.-H., Gortsos, Ch.V., Lackhoff, K. and Ch. Ohler (2022, editors): *Brussels Commentary on the Banking Union*, Verlag C.H. Beck, München – Hart Publishing, Oxford – Nomos Verlagsgesellschaft, Baden-Baden, pp. 1–13

Ohler, Ch. (2020): Banking Supervision, in Amtenbrink, F. and Ch. Herrmann (2020, editors): *The EU Law of Economic and Monetary Union*, Oxford University Press, Oxford, Chapter 37, pp. 1103–1144

Padoa-Schioppa, T. (2000): EMU and Banking Supervision, in Goodhart, C.A.E. (2000, editor): *Which Lender of Last Resort for Europe?*, Chapter 1, Central Banking Publications, London, pp. 13–29

Papadia, F. (2014): Lending of Last Resort? A European Perspective, in Bank for International Settlements (2014): *Re-thinking the Lender of Last Resort*, BIS Papers No 79, September, pp. 93–96

Papathanassiou, Ch. (2001): Das Europäische System der Zentralbanken und die Europäische Zentralbank, in Schimansky, H., Bunte, H.-J. und H.-J. Lwowski (2001, Herausgeber): *Bankrechts-Handbuch*, Verlag C.H.Beck, München, Band III, 24. Kapitel, § 134, pp. 4529–4554

Paris, F. and N. Ghei (2003): The Role of Reciprocity in International Law, *Cornell International Law Journal*, Volume 36, No. 1, article 4, available at: https://scholarship.law.cornell.edu/cilj/vol36/iss1/4

Peters, G. (2011): Developments in the EU, in Lastra, R.M. (2011, editor): *Cross-Border Bank Insolvency*, Oxford University Press, Oxford – New York, Chapter 6, pp. 128–160

Psaroudakis, G. (2014): Das Recht der Bankenrestrukturierung in Zeiten der Wirtschaftskrise, in Hopt, K.J. und D. Tzouganatos (2014, Hrsg.): *Das Europäische Wirtschaftsrecht vor neuen Herausforderungen: Beiträge aus Deutschland und Griechenland*, Mohr Siebeck, Tübingen, pp. 41–76

Quigley, C. (2022): *European State Aid Law and Policy (and UK Subsidy Control)*, Hart Publishing, Oxford

S

Schoenmaker, D. (2000): What Kind of Financial Stability for Europe?, in Goodhart, C.A.E. (2000, editor): *Which Lender of Last Resort for Europe?*, Chapter 6, Central Banking Publications, London, pp. 213–223

Schlag, M. (2019): Kommentar zum Artikel 52 AEUV, in Schwarze, J., Becker, U., Hatje, A. und J. Schoo (2019, Hrsg.): *EU-Kommentar*, 4. Auflage, Nomos Verlagsgesellschaft, Baden-Baden, pp. 935–945

Schwarze, J. und Ph. Voet van Vormizeele (2019): Kommentar zum Artikel 16 GRC, in Schwarze, J., Becker, U., Hatje, A. und J. Schoo (2019, Hrsg.): *EU-Kommentar*, 4. Auflage, Nomos Verlagsgesellschaft, Baden-Baden, pp. 3412–3413

Schwarze, J. und N. Wunderlich (2019): Kommentar zum Artikel 273 AEUV, in Schwarze, J., Becker, U., Hatje, A. und J. Schoo (2019, Hrsg.): *EU-Kommentar*, 4. Auflage, Nomos Verlagsgesellschaft, Baden-Baden, pp. 2957–2959

Smits, R. (1997): *The European Central Bank – Institutional Aspects*, Kluwer Law International, The Hague

Stephanou, C.A. (2016): Le nouveau droit européen en matière de redressement et de résolution bancaire, in *Commemorative Volume for Leonidas Georgakopoulos*, Bank of Greece, Centre for Culture, Research and Documentation, Athens, Volume II, pp. 923–944

T

Thiele, Al. (2014): *Finanzaufsicht*, Jus Publicum 229, Mohr Siebeck, Tübingen

Tröger, H. T. (2013): *The Single Supervisory Mechanism – Panacea or Quack Banking Regulation?*, SAFE Working Paper Series No. 27, 19 October 2013, available at: https://www.wipol.uni-bonn.de/lehrveranstaltungen-1/lawecon-workshop/archive/dateien/troeger2013/at_download/file

V-W & Z

Van Rijn, M. (2022): *Judicial Protection for Banks Under the Single Rulebook and the Single Supervisory Mechanism*, Radboud Business Law Institute, Series law of business and finance, Volume 22, Wolters Kluwer Nederland B.V.

Verhelst, S. (2013): *Assessing the Single Supervisory Mechanism: Passing the Point of No Return for Europe's Banking Union*, Egmont Paper 58, Academia Press for Egmont – The Royal Institute for International Relations, Brussels, June, available at: https://www.egmontinstitute.be/paperegm/ep58.pdf

Voet van Vormizeele, Ph. (2019): Kommentar zum Artikel 47 GRC, in Schwarze, J., Becker, U., Hatje, A. und J. Schoo (2019, Hrsg.): *EU-Kommentar*, 4. Auflage, Nomos Verlagsgesellschaft, Baden-Baden, pp. 3518–3523

Weatherill, S. (2016): *Cases and Materials on EU Law*, 12th edition, Oxford University Press, Oxford

Weatherill, S. (2006): Supply of and Demand for Internal Market Regulation: Strategies, Preferences and Interpretation, in Shuibhne (2006, editor): *Regulating the Internal Market*, Edward Elgar Publishing, Cheltenham, UK, Chapter 2, pp. 29–60

Wessels, B. (2017): Commentary on Directive 2001/24/EC on the Reorganisation and Winding-up of Credit Institutions, in Moss, G., Wessels, B. and M. Haentjens

(2017, editors): *EU Banking and Insurance Insolvency*, Chapter II, Second edition, Oxford University Press, Oxford, pp. 61–117

Wiggins, R., Tente, N. and A. Metrick (2014): *European Banking Union D: Cross-Border Resolution – Dexia Group*, Yale Program on Financial Stability CCase Study 2014, November

Wiggins, R., Wedow, M. and A. Metrick (2015): *European Banking Union B: The Single Resolution Mechanism*, Yale Program on Financial Stability Case Study 2014, November 2014 (revised March 2015)

Wissink, L., Duijkersloot, T. and R. Widdershoven (2014): *Shifts in Competences between Member States and the EU in the New Supervisory System for Credit Institutions and their Consequences for Judicial Protection*, Utrecht Law Review, Volume 10, pp. 92–115

World Bank Group (2017): *Understanding Bank Recovery and Resolution in the EU: A Guidebook to the BRRD*, World Bank Group, Finance & Markets, Financial Sector Advisory Center (FinSAC), available at: https://pubdocs.worldbank.org/en/609571482207234996/FinSAC-BRRD-Guidebook.pdf

Wymeersch, Ed. (2020): The Single Supervisory Mechanism for Banking Supervision: Institutional Aspects, in Busch, D. and G. Ferrarini (2020, editors): *European Banking Union*, second edition, Oxford University Press, Oxford, Chapter 4, pp. 145–191

Wymeersch, Ed. (2014): *The Single Supervisory Mechanism or "SSM", Part one of the Banking Union*, Working Paper Research No 255, National Bank of Belgium, Brussels

Wymeersch, Ed. (2012): The European Financial Supervisory Authorities or ESAs, in Wymeersch, Ed., Hopt, K.J. and G. Ferrarini (2012, editors): *Financial Regulation and Supervision – A Post-Crisis Analysis*, Oxford University Press, Oxford, Chapter 9, pp. 232–317

Zavvos, G. and S. Kaltsouni (2015): The Single Resolution Mechanism in the European Banking Union: Legal Foundation, Governance Structure and Financing, in Haentjens, M. and B. Wessels (2015, editors): *Research Handbook on Crisis Management in the Banking Sector*, Edward Elgar Publishing Ltd., Cheltenham, UK (also available at: https://ssrn.com/abstract=2531907)

PART III

European Banking Regulation (Law): Key Institutional Elements

CHAPTER 7

The European Banking Authority (EBA) and Its (Significant) Role in the Law-Making Process

7.1 THE EUROPEAN SUPERVISORY AUTHORITIES (ESAs) AS THE FIRST PILLAR OF THE ESFS AND THEIR JOINT COMMITTEE

7.1.1 The ESAs as Mainly Regulatory Authorities and the Asymmetry in EU Financial Supervision

(1) As already discussed in **Chapter 4**,[1] the ESFS was created in 2010 for the entire EU (i.e., not only for the euro area) with the main objective:

> to ensure that the rules applicable to the financial sector are adequately implemented to preserve financial stability, and to ensure confidence in the financial system, and effective and sufficient protection for the customers and consumers of financial services.[2]

The ESFS, which applies to all EU Member States, consists of the ESRB, the three ESAs, their Joint Committee,[3] as well as the NCAs in the three main sectors of the EU financial system and the ECB with regard to its supervisory tasks within the SSM.[4] Its *first pillar*, the ESAs, are *mainly* regulatory authorities composed of national supervisory authorities (and the ECB), one of their main tasks being to contribute to the "*establishment of high-quality common regulatory and supervisory standards and practices*", i.e., to the

---

[1] See Chapter 4 above, under 4.3.1.
[2] EBAR/ESMAR/EIOPAR, Article 2(1), second sentence.
[3] See just below, under 7.1.2.
[4] EBAR/ESMAR/EIOPAR, Article 2(2), points (a)–(f), respectively.

development of the 'single rulebook'.[5] Hence, the creation of the ESFS did not, literally speaking, lead to the creation of financial supervisory authorities at EU level. However, in the cases laid down in **Articles 17–19** of their founding Regulations, the ESAs have (partly) the right to substitute NCAs if those fail to comply with Commission's formal opinions or ESAs' decisions (indirect supervisory tasks and related powers).[6]

(2) By way of exception, the ESMA *directly* supervises all credit rating agencies under the **Credit Rating Agencies Regulation**, all trade repositories and third-country CCPs under the **EMIR**, all securitisation repositories under the **STS Securitisation Regulation**, certain data reporting service providers under the **MiFIR**, and administrators of EU critical benchmarks and recognised third-country administrators under the **Benchmark Regulation** (all as in force).[7]

Box 7.1 The short selling case

(1) The powers of the ESAs, as EU agencies,[8] are delimited, shaped and amenable to judicial review in light of the *Meroni* doctrine. It was the European Court of Justice (now CJEU) which laid down the core principles governing the relations between EU institutions and EU agencies, in its seminal 1958 *Meroni* judgement,[9] which became so firmly entrenched in EU jurisprudence that it was considered a doctrine and was consistently applied thereafter. It makes a distinction between, on the one hand, a delegation which involves clearly defined executive powers the exercise of which can, therefore, be subject to strict review in the light of objective criteria determined by the delegating authority and, on the other hand, *a discretionary power*, implying a wide margin of discretion which may, according to the use made of it, make possible the execution of actual economic policy.

---

[5] On the content and judicial review of the single rulebook, see details in Van Rijn (2022), pp. 61–312 and 319–328.

[6] See further below, under 7.3.3.

[7] See at: https://www.esma.europa.eu/supervision/supervision. On this aspect, see further Busch and Gortsos (2022), pp. 12–13, with further references. For the role of the ESMA as an 'important driver in EU supervisory governance', see Howell (2017); on its role in supervisory convergence, see Moloney (2018), Chapter 4 (II). For a comparative analysis of the enforcement styles of EU agencies, including the ESMA, see Joosen and Zhelyazkova (2022).

[8] On EU agencies, see, by means of mere indication, Chiti (2018).

[9] Judgement of the Court of 13 June 1958 in joint Cases C-9/56 and C-10/56, *Meroni & Co., Industrie Metallurgische, SpA v High Authority of the European Coal and Steel Community*, ECLI:EU:C:1958:7.

Under the *Meroni* doctrine, "*a delegation of the first kind cannot appreciably alter the consequences involved in the exercise of the powers concerned, whereas a delegation of the second kind since it replaces the choices of the delegator by the choices of the delegate, brings about an actual transfer of responsibility*" (the "non-delegation principle").[10] Thus, an institution may only delegate clearly defined executive powers subject to strict control in light of objective criteria determined by the delegating authority. This judgement was later elaborated by a subsequent ruling in 1981 (Case 98/90 *Romano v INAMI*),[11] which specified that an institution may not empower an agency to adopt normative acts, i.e., acts of general application having the force of law (the *Romano* doctrine).

(2) In its judgement of 22 January 2014 in **Case 270/12**,[12] the CJEU modernised the *Meroni* doctrine by applying the *Meroni* jurisprudence to the specificities of ESMA's direct intervention powers, which prompted an action for annulment by the UK before the Court, *inter alia*, on grounds derived from the *Meroni* and *Romano* jurisprudence. This '*short selling* case' arose in relation to the ESMA's direct powers (in accordance with **Article 28 of the Short Selling Regulation (EU) No 236/2012** (see **Chapter 4 above, under 4.3.2**) to intervene in capital markets in exceptional circumstances, i.e., in order to address a threat to the orderly functioning and integrity of financial markets or to the stability of the whole or part of the financial system in the EU in case there are cross-border implications, if NCAs have either not taken measures to address the threat or the measures taken do not adequately address the threat.

In more detail, the CJEU considered that the system of ESMA intervention falls within the scope of Article 114 TFEU and ruled that any conferral of implementing powers needs to be clearly defined by the empowering act, and the exercise of the relevant powers must be effectively controlled by the delegating authority ('political control') and be subject to legal review ('judicial control'). As the purpose of the doctrine is the protection of EU institutional balance, political responsibility cannot be conferred upon executive bodies. The CJEU's reasoning was that given the detailed delineation of the powers of intervention available to ESMA, those powers do not imply that ESMA is vested with

---

[10] *Ibid.*, note 152.

[11] Judgement of the Court of 14 May 1981 in Case 98/90, *Giuseppe Romano v Institut National d'assurance Maladie*, ECLI:EU:C:1981:104.

[12] Judgement of the Court (Grand Chamber) of 22 January 2014 in Case 270/12, *United Kingdom of Great Britain and Northern Ireland v European Parliament and Council of the European Union*, ECLI:EU:C:2014:18.

> a "very large measure of discretion" incompatible with the EU Treaties. It accepted that ESMA's margin of discretion was circumscribed by various conditions and criteria, notably the requirement to consult the ESRB and the temporary nature of the measures authorised, and that the two kinds of measure which ESMA may take are strictly limited to those set out in **Article 9(5)** of its founding Regulation. The CJEU also considered that "specific professional and technical expertise" can provide grounds for delegating powers that can be exercised in special circumstances, in which cases there is no question of administrative discretion.[13]
>
> Given the incremental evolution of ESAs and in the absence of clear and precise legal basis in the Treaties to explicitly legitimise the delegation of decision-making powers to EU decentralised agencies, this decision has provided a modern, more flexible approach to the *Meroni* doctrine governing the process of EU agencification over the past decades.[14]

(3) Such direct supervisory powers have not been conferred (yet at least) either to the EBA (since, in relation to the credit institutions established in the Member States participating in the SSM, specific supervisory tasks have been conferred upon the ECB)[15] nor to the EIOPA,[16] even after the ESAs' founding Regulations were amended in 2019. Accordingly, the design of the EU institutional architecture relating to microprudential supervision in the three main sectors of the financial system is quite asymmetric (as presented in **Table 7.1** just below).

---

[13] *Ibid.*, paragraphs 46–50.

[14] For a thorough analysis of the *Meroni* doctrine and the legal limits to "agencification", see, by means of mere indication, Chamon (2016), p. 134 *et seq*. On the short selling case and this judgement, see, by means of mere indication, Repasi (2014), Bergström (2015), Gortsos and Lagaria (2020) and Salerno (2022), pp. 109–110.

[15] However, upon the adoption and entry into force of the MiCAR (see Chapter 5 above, under 5.4.4), the power will be conferred upon the EBA to directly supervise the issuers of asset-referenced tokens that have been classified as significant, and, in the case of e-money token that has been classified as significant, to be responsible for their issuers' compliance with specific requirements (Article 98).

[16] The Commission's proposal of 29 June 2017 (COM/2017/343 final) to place providers of PEPPs under the direct supervision of EIOPA was not adopted by the co-legislators in Regulation (EU) 2019/1238 of 20 June 2019 (discussed in Chapter 5 above, under 5.2.2).

Table 7.1 The asymmetry in EU institutional architecture in relation to prudential supervision in the three main sectors of the financial system

	Banking sector[17]	Capital markets sector	Insurance sector
EU level supervision	ECB (Article 127(6) TFEU): (a) 'significant' credit institutions in participating Member States in relation to the specific tasks set out in Articles 4(1) and 5(2) SSMR (b) certain categories of 'significant' holding companies in participating Member States	ESMA (Article 114 TFEU) (a) CRAs (b) trade repositories (c) data reporting service providers (d) administrators of key benchmarks	–
National supervision	(a) 'significant' credit institutions in participating Member States in relation to tasks not earmarked as specific (b) 'less significant' credit institutions in participating Member States (c) other categories of holding companies in participating Member States (d) all credit institutions in member-states with a derogation (e) electronic money and payment institutions	All other regulated entities providing services on capital markets	(a) insurance and reinsurance undertakings (b) insurance intermediaries

7.1.2 The Joint Committee

Apart from the ESAs, the ESRB and the competent supervisory authorities in the three main sectors of the EU financial system (including the ECB for the banking sector[18]), the ESFS also comprises the Joint Committee.[19] This is one of the joint bodies of the ESAs,[20] established by their founding Regulations,[21] governed by their **Articles 54–57** and composed of the ESAs' Chairpersons and those of any Sub-Committee established pursuant to Article 57. Observer status is granted to the ESAs' Executive Directors, as well as a Commission and an ESRB representative. The Joint Committee has its own rules of procedure.[22] Its Chairperson is appointed on an annual rotational basis from among the ESAs' Chairpersons and in that capacity is also the second Vice-Chair of

---

[17] As further discussed in Chapter 8 below.
[18] See further below, under 7.2.1.
[19] EBAR/ESMAR/EIOPAR, Article 2(2), point (e).
[20] The other is the Board of Appeal, further discussed below, under 7.4.4.
[21] EBAR/ESMAR/EIOPAR, Article 54(1).
[22] Revised Rules of Procedure of 13 July 2022 (JC 2022 30, at: https://www.eba.europa.eu/about-us/legal-framework/eba-regulation-and-institutional-framework).

the ESRB.[23] The Joint Committee serves as a forum for regular and close cooperation among the ESAs to ensure cross-sectoral consistency (considering sectoral specificities) in the fields of financial conglomerates[24] and prudential consolidation; accounting and auditing; prudential analyses of cross-sectoral developments, risks and vulnerabilities for financial stability; retail investment products; cybersecurity; exchange of information and best practices with the ESRB and among the ESAs.[25]

7.2 Founding Regulation, Legal Status, Scope of Action, Objective and Bodies of the EBA

7.2.1 Founding Regulation, Legal Status, Scope of Action and Objective

(1) The EBA, which forms part of the ESAs, was established (as a successor to the CEBS) by virtue of **Regulation 1093/2010** of the co-legislators (**EBAR**) on 1 January 2011.[26] The EBAR is in force as repeatedly amended, most importantly (and as already noted): *first*, by **Regulation (EU) No 1022/ 2013** as regards the conferral of specific tasks on the ECB within the SSM[27]; and *second*, by Article 1 of **Regulation (EU) 2019/2175**.[28]

---

[23] EBAR/ESMAR/EIOPAR, Article 55(1)–(4).

[24] Article 56 contains specific provisions on this aspect. On 22 December 2022, the ESAs published the most updated list of financial conglomerates in the EU (at: https:// www.eba.europa.eu/esas-publish-list-financial-conglomerates-2022).

[25] *Ibid.*, Article 54(2). On the Joint Committee, see further Wymeersch (2012), pp. 288–292.

[26] EBAR, Articles 1(1), 2(1), first sentence and 82, third-sub-paragraph. On the EBA (and in some cases the ESAs in general), see Louis (2010), Gortsos (2011), Tridimas (2011), pp. 801–803, Di Noia and Furlò (2012), Ferran (2012), Wymeersch (2012) and (2014), Moloney (2014), pp. 907–941, Thiele (2014), pp. 494–519, Haar (2015), Chiu (2016), Chiu and Wilson (2019), pp. 291–300, Vuarlot-Dignac and Siracusa (2019) (with emphasis on the ESMA), and in more detail Schemmel (2018) and Enoch (2021). See also the publications in the EBA Staff Paper Series (at: https://www.eba.europa.eu/about-us/staff-papers).

[27] The amendments introduced by this Regulation to the EBAR refer to four aspects: the relationship between the ECB and the EBA; new tasks and powers of the EBA; amendments to its pre-existing tasks and powers; and amendments to the EBA's governance. See on this Schammo (2014), Wymeersch (2014) and Capiello (2015).

[28] The EIOPAR and the ESMAR were also amended by Articles 2–3 of that Regulation. The EBAR has also been amended by Directive 2014/17/EU on credit agreements for consumers relating to residential immovable property (see Chapter 4 above, under 4.3.2), the BRRD and the SRMR, the PSD II, Regulation (EU) 2018/1717 of the co-legislators of 14 November 2018 "amending [the EBAR] as regards the location of the seat of the [EBA]" (OJ L 291, 16 November 2018, pp. 1–2) (see just below), and the IFR. The current consolidated version is available at: https://eur-lex.europa.eu/legal-content/EN/ TXT/?uri=CELEX%3A02010R1093-20210626.

It is also noted that on 20 July 2021 the Commission submitted a Proposal for a Regulation of the co-legislators "establishing an Authority for Anti-Money Laundering and Countering the Financing of Terrorism and amending [the ESAs Regulations]" (COM/2021/421 final). As of December 2022, this legislative act had not been adopted;

(2) The EBA has its seat in **Paris** (since June 2019).[29] As already noted[30] and like all ESAs, it is an agency, a **'Union body'** with legal personality and, thus, enjoys the most extensive legal capacity accorded to legal persons under each Member State's national law.[31]

(3) The EBA's scope of action was wide from its establishment and has been further extended after the amendment of its founding Regulation in 2019[32]:

> *First*, it must act within the powers conferred upon it pursuant to **Articles 8–9 EBAR**, within the scope of specific, exhaustively listed, legislative acts (referred to in **Article 1(2)**[33]), including all legal acts based thereon (i.e., delegated and implementing acts) (hereinafter the **'relevant legislative acts'**), and of any other legally binding EU legal act conferring powers on it, as well as in accordance with the SSMR.
> *Second*, it must act within the powers conferred by the EBAR and within the scope of the third **AML Directive** [(EU) 2015/849] and of the **'Funds Transfers Regulation'**[34] to the extent that those apply to 'financial sector operators'[35] and the competent authorities that supervise them. Exclusively for that purpose, it can carry out the tasks conferred by any legally binding EU act on the EIOPA or on the ESMA, while consulting them and keeping them informed of its activities concerning any entity which is a financial sector operation under the EIOPAR or the ESMAR.
> *Third*, it must act in the field of activities of credit institutions, financial conglomerates, investment firms, as well as payment and e-money institutions in relation to issues not directly covered by the relevant legislative

---

on the progress, see at: https://finance.ec.europa.eu/publications/anti-money-laundering-and-countering-financing-terrorism-legislative-package_en.

[29] EBAR, Article 7; this was a by-product of the UK's withdrawal from the EU since the initial seat was in London. The ESMA is also located in Paris (ab initio), while the EIOPA has its seat in Frankfurt.

[30] See just above, under 7.1.1.

[31] EBAR, Article 5(1)–(2); on this aspect, see also below, under 7.4.5.

[32] *Ibid.*, Article 1(2)–(3).

[33] The list of this Article includes, *inter alia*, the SSMR, CRR, the CRD IV, the DGSD, the PSD II and the FICOD I; the BRRD is not included therein, even though repeated reference is made to it in other Articles.

[34] Regulation (EU) 2015/847 of the co-legislators of 20 May 2015 "on information accompanying transfers of funds (…)", OJ L 141, 5 June 2015, pp. 1–18.

[35] 'Financial sector operator' means an entity as referred to in Article 2 of the third AML Directive, which is either a 'financial institution' as defined in Article 4(1) EBAR or EIOPAR or a 'financial market participant' as defined in Article 4, point (1) ESMAR (EBAR, Article 4, point (1a)). The term 'financial institution' is defined in the EBAR (ibid., Article 4, point (1a) as any undertaking that is subject to regulation and supervision pursuant to any of the legislative acts referred to in Article 1(2), including (apparently) credit institutions. This definition is broader than that in Article 4(1), point (26) CRD IV (as already discussed).

acts, including matters of corporate governance, auditing and financial reporting, taking into account sustainable business models and the integration of **'ESG-related factors'**,[36] to the extent necessary to ensure the effective and consistent application of those acts.

The provisions of the EBAR are without prejudice to the powers of the Commission, in particular pursuant to **Article 258 TFEU**, to ensure Member States' compliance with EU law.[37]

(4) It is also noted that the term 'competent authorities' is defined broadly in this legislative act, to include those which are competent in relation to each of the relevant legislative acts. *Inter alia*[38]: *first*, the ECB is included in the definition of this term along with the NCAs[39]; *second*, regarding the BRRD and the SRMR the term (also) includes the NRAs, the SRB, the Council and the Commission when taking actions under Article 18 SRMR (on the resolution procedure), except where they exercise discretionary powers or make policy choices; and *third*, regarding DGSs, 'competent authorities' means the bodies which administer them pursuant to the DGSD or, where their operation is administered by a private company, the public authority supervising them pursuant to that legislative act, and relevant administrative authorities as referred to therein.[40]

7.2.2 Objective

(1) The EBA's objective consists in protecting the public interest by contributing to the stability and effectiveness of the financial system (in the short-, medium- and long-term) for the EU economy, its citizens and its businesses. In this respect, it must contribute to the following: improving better the functioning of the internal market, including, in particular, a sound, effective and consistent level of regulation and supervision; ensuring financial markets' integrity, transparency, efficiency and orderly functioning; strengthening international supervisory coordination; preventing regulatory arbitrage and promoting equal conditions of competition; ensuring that credit and other risks are appropriately regulated and supervised; enhancing customer protection; enhancing supervisory convergence across the internal market;

---

[36] For the EBA's ESG mandate and the changing nature of EU financial regulation, see Colaert (2022).

[37] EBAR, Article 1(4); on Article 258 TFEU, see Schwarze und Wunderlich (2019) and Schima (2019).

[38] *Ibid.*, Article 4, points (2)(i), (iv) and (v), respectively.

[39] Accordingly, Articles 18–19 (on the EBA's actions in 'emergency situations' and its 'mediation powers' between competent authorities in cross-border situations, further discussed below) were amended to take into account that the ECB is also a competent authority.

[40] On this aspect, see details in Volume II.

and preventing the use of the financial system for the purposes of money laundering and terrorist financing. For these purposes, it must contribute to the consistent, efficient and effective application of the relevant legislative acts, foster supervisory convergence and provide Opinions to the European Parliament, the Council and the Commission.[41]

(2) The content and form of its actions and measures (Guidelines, Recommendations, Opinions, questions and answers ('**Q&As**'), as well as draft RTSs and ITSs), must fully respect the applicable provisions of the EBAR and of the relevant legislative acts. To the extent permitted and relevant under those provisions, its actions and measures must, in accordance with the principle of proportionality, take due account of the nature, scale and complexity of the risks inherent in the business of a financial institution, undertaking, other subject or financial activity affected by its actions and measures.[42] As an integral part thereof, the EBA should establish a Committee advising it as to how, in full compliance with applicable rules, its actions and measures should take account of specific differences prevailing in the sector, pertaining to the nature, scale and complexity of risks, to business models and practice, as well as to the size of financial institutions and of markets to the extent that such factors are relevant under the rules considered.[43]

7.2.3 Bodies

7.2.3.1 The Board of Supervisors[44]

Composition and tasks: The EBA's governance is structured around the following five bodies: a Board of Supervisors (**BoS**), a Management Board, a Chairperson, an Executive Director and a Board of Appeal ('**BoA**') (which, like the Joint Committee, is a joint body of the ESAs).[45] Its 'strategic' governing body is the **BoS**, which has been assigned the tasks laid down in **Article 43 EBAR**. It is composed of a Chairperson, the heads of the NCAs from each Member State (be they NCBs or other independent administrative authorities[46]) and one representative each from the Commission, the ESRB, the ESMA, the EIOPA and the ECB's Supervisory Board (not necessarily a

---

[41] EBAR, Article 1(5), first and second sub-paragraphs. In this respect, the EBA.

[42] *Ibid.*, Article 1(5), fifth sub-paragraph.

[43] *Ibid.*, Article 1(6).

[44] The rules governing this organ are laid down in Articles 40–43, 43a and 44; these were extensively amended by Regulation (EU) No 1022/2013 and then by Regulation (EU) 2019/2175.

[45] EBAR, Article 6. As just noted, the Board of Appeal is discussed below, under 7.4.4.

[46] NCBs which are not NCAs are not represented in the BoS; cooperation between all NCBs of EU Member States takes place only within the Banking Supervision Committee (BSC) of the ESCB.

member of that Board or a person employed by the ECB[47]). The opposite, however, does not apply; the EBA is not represented in the ECB's Supervisory Board, not even under observer status.

Only the Chairperson (in principle) and the heads of NCAs have voting rights (as further discussed below). It is noted the ECB representative's position is subordinated to that of the NCAs-members of the BoS.[48] For the purposes of acting within the scope of the BBRD, the Chair of the SRB is an observer to the BoS.[49]

Internal committees and independent panels: Either on its own initiative or at the request of the Chairperson, the BoS may establish internal committees for specific tasks attributed to it; upon request from the Management Board or from the Chairperson, the BoS may also establish internal committees for specific tasks attributed to the Management Board.[50] *Furthermore*, for the purposes of **Articles 17** and **19** (on the breach of EU law and on binding mediation, respectively[51]), the Chairperson shall propose a Decision to convene independent panels, to be adopted by the BoS, consisting of himself/ herself and six other members.[52] The panels or the Chairperson shall propose Decisions pursuant to the above Articles, except on matters concerning the prevention of the use of the financial system for the purpose of money laundering or terrorist financing, for final adoption by the BoS.[53] *Finally*, for the purposes of conducting the inquiry provided for in **Article**

---

[47] Article 13o (1)–(2) of the Rules of Procedure of the ECB clarifies that the ECB representative is appointed (and revoked) by the ECB President on a proposal by the Supervisory Board and that the above-mentioned accompanying representative is nominated by the ECB President.

[48] As Wymeersch (2014), at p. 67, correctly pointed out: "*(...) So will the ECB [be] represented on the Board of Supervisors of the EBA, but without a vote, where all national supervisors – including those of non-participating states – still have a vote*".

[49] EBAR, Article 40(6), third sub-paragraph. Decisions on specific matters related to the resolution of credit institutions and investment firms have been delegated by the BoS to the Resolution Committee (ResCo); on this Committee, see Chapter 6 above, under 6.4.4.

[50] EBAR, Article 41(1).

[51] See below, under 7.3.2.

[52] This is without prejudice to the role of the Standing Committee on anti-money laundering and countering terrorist financing ('AMLSC'), which was (newly) established by virtue of Article 9a(7) EBAR to coordinate measures and prepare draft decisions to be taken by the BoS in relation to such matters. This is composed of a Chairperson and high-level representatives of all AML/CFT competent authorities (57 in total). Among them, one competent authority from each Member State is designated as a member with voting rights (27 in total), while the others are Members without voting rights (30 in total). The AMLSC also includes observers from the EIOPA, the ESMA, the SSM Supervisory Board, the Commission, the EEA EFTA countries represented in the BoS and the EFTA Surveillance Authority.

[53] *Ibid.*, Article 41(2)–(3) and (5), first sentence.

22(4), first sub-paragraph,[54] the Chairperson *may* propose a Decision to launch the inquiry and a decision to convene an independent panel, to be also adopted by the BoS, consisting of the Chairperson and six other members as well. This panel shall present the outcome of the inquiry conducted pursuant to Article 22(4) to the BoS.[55]

Upon request from one or more competent authorities, the European Parliament, the Council or the Commission or on its own initiative, the EBA may conduct an inquiry into a particular type of financial institution or type of product or type of conduct in order to assess potential threats to the stability of the financial system or to the protection of customers or consumers.

Decision-making: In relation to the decision-making process in the BoS the principle of simple majority (each voting member having one vote) prevails with the following exceptions, which reflect the need to keep a balance between participating and non-participating Member States[56]:

> *First*, with regard to the acts specified in **Articles 10–16 EBAR** (on the development of draft RTSs and ITSs and the adoption of Guidelines and Recommendations) and measures and decisions adopted under **Article 9(5), third sub-paragraph** (on the prohibition or restriction of certain financial activities), the BoS takes decisions by a dual majority: a qualified majority (as defined in Article 16(4) TEU and in Article 3 of **Protocol No (36)**) of its members, including at least a simple majority of its members from competent authorities of participating Member States, *and* a simple majority of its members from competent authorities of non-participating Member States. In this case, the Chairperson has no voting rights.[57]
>
> *Second*, as regards decisions adopted under **Article 18(3)–(4)** (on action in emergency situations), the BoS shall take decisions by a simple majority of its voting members, but in this case a simple majority of its members from both groups of competent authorities is required. *Similarly*, with regard to decisions in accordance with **Articles 17** and **19**, the decision proposed by the independent panel is also adopted by a dual majority of the voting members of the BoS, but a simple majority of its members from both groups of competent authorities is required as well. By way

---

[54] This inquiry may be conducted by the EBA, upon request from one or more competent authorities, the European Parliament, the Council or the Commission, or on its own initiative, into a particular type of financial institution or type of product or type of conduct in order to assess potential threats to the stability of the financial system or to the protection of customers or consumers.

[55] EBAR, Article 41(4) and (5), second sentence.

[56] On the ECB's relationship with the EBA after the establishment of the SSM in particular with regard to non-participating Member States, see Guarracino (2013) and Schammo (2014).

[57] EBAR, Article 44(1), first-third sub-paragraphs.

of exception, from the date when the voting members from competent authorities of non-participating Member States are four or less, the decision proposed by the panel must be adopted by a simple majority of BoS voting members, including at least one vote from those members.[58]

Attendance of meetings: The non-voting members and the observers are not allowed to attend any discussions within the BoS relating to individual financial institutions, unless otherwise provided for in **Article 75(3)**[59] or in the relevant legislative acts. The ECB representative may exceptionally, like the EBA's Executive Director, attend such discussions.[60]

7.2.3.2 Management Board—Chairperson—Executive Director
The EBA's 'operational' management body is the **Management Board**,[61] composed of the EBA Chairperson, and six other BoS members, elected by and from its voting members.[62] Its tasks are laid down in **Article 47**. The **Chairperson** is a full-time independent professional, appointed by the BoS and representing the EBA.[63] He/she is selected based on merit, skills, knowledge of financial institutions and markets, and of experience relevant to financial regulation and supervision, following an open selection procedure, which must respect the principle of gender balance and shall be published in the OJ. His/her term of office shall be 5 years and may be extended once. His/her tasks include preparing the work of the BoS, convening and chairing its meetings, setting the agenda and chairing the meetings of the Management Board, as well as inviting the Management Board to consider setting up a **Coordination Group** in accordance with **Article 45b**.[64] Finally, the

---

[58] *Ibid.*, Article 44(1), fifth sub-paragraph and (3b). On Articles 17–19, see also further below, under 7.3.

[59] Article 75(1)–(2) governs the participation in the EBA's work of third countries which have concluded agreements with the EU whereby they have adopted and are applying EU law in the areas of the EBA's competence pursuant to Article 1(2), and the EBA cooperation with these countries. In accordance with Article 75(3), reference to which is made in several EBAR Articles as discussed below, the nature, scope and procedural aspects of the involvement of these countries in the EBA work, relating to financial contributions and to staff and their potential representation, as an observer, on the BoS should be specified in bilateral arrangements.

[60] *Ibid.*, Article 44(4). In discussions not relating to such institutions, he/she may be accompanied by another ECB representative (again not necessarily a person employed by the ECB) with expertise on central banking tasks. According to the review close of Article 81a, the Commission must review and report to the European Parliament, the European Council and the Council on the overall operation of the voting arrangements in Articles 41 and 44, taking into account any experience gained in the application of the EBAR.

[61] The rules governing this body are laid down in Articles 45, 45a, 45b and 46–47.

[62] *Ibid.*, Article 45(1), first sub-paragraph.

[63] *Ibid.*, Articles 5(3), 48(1), first sub-paragraph and 48(2), first sub-paragraph.

[64] *Ibid.*, Articles 48(1), second-fourth sub-paragraphs, 48(2), first sub-paragraph and 48(3). Coordination Groups are set up by the Management Board on 'defined topics' for

Executive Director, a full-time (as well) independent professional in charge of managing the EBA, is appointed by the BoS as well upon confirmation by the European Parliament. *Inter alia*, he/she is in charge of the EBA's management and the preparation of the Management Board's work.[65]

7.3 TASKS AND POWERS OF THE EBA

7.3.1 The Structure of Chapter II of the EBA Regulation

(1) In order to fulfil its objective, specific tasks and powers have been conferred upon the EBA; these are laid down in Chapter II (**Articles 8–39**), which is structured as follows: **Article 8(1) EBAR** contains an exhaustive (without prejudice to Article 9) list of the tasks conferred upon the EBA; **Articles 10–39** offer a qualified description of the tasks under Article 8[66]; **Article 8(2)** features an exhaustive list of all regulatory and other powers conferred on the EBA to fulfil these tasks; and finally, **Article 9** refers to its task and powers relating to consumer protection and financial services.

(2) In the exercise of its tasks, the EBA must pay particular attention to any systemic risk posed by financial institutions whose failure may impair the operation of the financial system or the real economy.[67] *In addition*, when carrying out its tasks, it must use the full powers available to it, take fully into account the different types, business models and sizes of financial institutions (with due regard to the objective to ensure the safety and soundness of financial institutions), as well as take account of technological innovation, innovative and sustainable business models and the integration of ESG-related factors.[68] *Furthermore*, when carrying out its tasks and exercising its powers, it must act based on and within the limits of the legislative framework and have due regard to the principle of proportionality, where relevant, and better which there may be a need to coordinate having regard to specific market developments (*ibid.*, Article 45b (1)).

[65] *Ibid.*, Articles 51 and 53.

[66] Since Regulation (EU) No 1022/2013 had conferred upon the EBA four new tasks, Wymeersch (2014) correctly remarked (at p. 68) that in order to meet its enhanced tasks the EBA will have to be endowed with additional human and financial resources. This applies *a fortiori* after the amendments introduced in 2019.

[67] EBAR, Article 1(5), third sub-paragraph. 'Systemic risk' is defined in the ESRBR (Article 2, point (c)) to mean a risk of disruption in the financial system with the potential to have serious negative consequences for the internal market and the real economy; all types of financial firms, markets and infrastructure may be potentially systemically important to some degree. On the concept of systemic risk, see also Chapter 1 above, under 1.2.5.

[68] EBAR, Article 8(1a). In relation to the integration of ESG factors, see De Smet (2023), pp. 286–290, with extensive further references.

regulation, including the results of cost-benefit analyses in accordance with the EBAR.[69]

7.3.2 The EBA's Tasks According to Article 8(1) EBA Regulation

7.3.2.1 Establishment of Common Regulatory and Supervisory Standards and Practices—Development of European Handbooks (Points (a), (aa) and (ab))

(1) The first (and, in the author's opinion, predominant) task is the contribution to the *"establishment of high-quality common regulatory and supervisory standards and practices"*, in particular by developing draft RTSs and ITSs, Guidelines, Recommendations and other measures based on the relevant legislative acts, including Opinions. This aspect is discussed in more detail further below.[70]

(2) Related is its task to develop and keep updated a legally non-binding **"European supervisory handbook"** on the supervision of financial institutions in the EU, which sets out supervisory best practices for methodologies and processes,[71] by taking into account, *inter alia*, changing business practices and models. In addition, it must develop and keep updated a **"European resolution handbook"** on the resolution of financial institutions in the EU, also setting out best practices and high-quality methodologies and processes for resolution, taking into account the work of the SRB, changing business practices and models, as well as the size of financial institutions and markets.[72]

7.3.2.2 Consistent Application of Legally Binding EU Acts (Point (b))

Equally important is the task of contributing to the *"consistent application of legally binding EU acts"*. This task is executed by various means:

(1) The EBA must contribute to the creation of a "common supervisory culture" among competent authorities. This aspect is further regulated by **Article 29 EBAR**, on the basis of which it has adopted, since 2021 a

---

[69] The open public consultations referred to in Articles 10 and 15–16a must be conducted as widely as possible to ensure an inclusive approach towards all interested parties (*ibid.*, Article 8(3)).

[70] See below, under 7.5. An innovative element, introduced by the 2019 amendment of the EBAR, is the attribution to the EBA of the power to promote convergence of the SREP referred to in Article 97 CRD IV to bring about strong EU supervisory standards (*ibid.*, Article 20a).

[71] See on this Wymeersch (2014), pp. 67–68. As a matter of fact, there are several modules of this supervisory handbook on specific supervisory aspects, as further discussed in the following Chapters, as appropriate. This handbook is different from the ECB's "Guide to banking supervision", which is addressed to supervised entities in participating Member States.

[72] In this case as well, there are several modules of the handbook on specific resolution aspects, as also further discussed in the following Chapters, as appropriate.

European Supervisory Examination Programme ('**ESEP**') and a European Resolution Examination Programme ('**EREP**'). While the former is part of an annual cycle and contributes to enhancing supervisory convergence in the EU by providing common directions and focus areas for supervisory authorities to shape their prudential supervisory priorities and respective practices, the latter is aimed at shaping resolution authorities' work priorities and respective practices and identifies key topics for resolution attention across the EU.[73]

(2) The EBA must also prevent financial institutions from resorting to "supervisory arbitrage", i.e., opting for the Member State with the comparatively most favourable prudential supervisory regime for their establishment; fostering and monitoring supervisory independence; as well as ensuring efficient and consistent prudential supervision of financial institutions, and a coherent functioning of colleges of supervisors. The latter aspect is further regulated by **Article 21 EBAR**.

(3) Finally, it must ensure the following: consistent, efficient and effective application of the relevant legislative acts (to avoid breach of EU law); the taking of action in emergency situations, namely in case of adverse developments, which may seriously jeopardise the orderly functioning and integrity of financial markets or the stability of the financial system; as well as mediation and settlement of disagreements, assisting the settlement of disputes between competent authorities in cross-border situations ('**binding mediation**').[74] This dimension is further governed by **Articles 17–19**, respectively.[75]

Article 17, in particular, on the "breach of Union law", is a critical element of EBA's governance arrangements supporting the delivery of its task discussed herein. In relation to this Article, the following is noted:

> *First*, the procedure laid down there in is (only) activated if an NCA has not applied the relevant legislative acts or has applied them in a way which appears to be a breach of Union law.[76] The entities who have standing to request (but no power to force) the EBA to initiate an investigation are explicitly (and exhaustively) listed in Article 17(2): one

---

[73] The ESEP and the EREP for 2023, adopted on 27 October 2022 (EBA/REP/2022/28 and EBA/REP/2022/27, respectively), are available at: https://www.eba.europa.eu/eba-sets-examination-programme-priorities-prudential-supervisors-2023 and https://www.eba.europa.eu/eba-sets-examination-programme-priorities-resolution-authorities-2023.

[74] The settlement of disagreements between competent authorities across sectors is a task assigned to the Joint Committee (*ibid.*, Article 20).

[75] On Articles 17–19 (in their initial phrasing), see Wymeersch (2012), pp. 255–271 and (2014), pp. 70–72. It is further noted that, pursuant to Article 17a (1) EBAR, the EBA must have in place dedicated reporting channels for receiving and handling information provided by a natural or legal person reporting on actual or potential breaches, abuse of law or non-application of EU law. Specific safeguards relating to Articles 18–19 and the decision-making procedures in relation to all three Articles (17–19) are laid down in Articles 38–39.

[76] *Ibid.*, Article 17(1).

or more NCAs, the European Parliament, the Council, the Commission and the Banking Stakeholder Group ('**BSG**')[77]; natural and legal persons are not listed therein. However, the EBA has also a "own-initiative jurisdiction" to initiate an investigation "*including when this is based on well substantiated information from natural or legal persons*". In this respect, it is endowed with discretionary powers to initiate (or refuse to initiate) an investigation by outlining "*how it intends to proceed with the case and, where appropriate, investigate the alleged breach or non-application of Union law*".[78]

Second, on 22 January 2020, the BoS adopted a Decision "concerning Rules of Procedure for investigation of breach of Union law".[79] According to recital (2) of these Rules, "*although initiating investigations remains within the EBA's discretion, for reasons of transparency and legal certainty, these rules (…) set out factors, criteria and other related matters to be taken into account in relation to requests to initiate investigations that are received from third parties or, to the extent relevant, to EBA own initiative investigations*". Furthermore, it is expressly specified that "*the EBA shall respond to a Request by outlining how it intends to proceed with the case and, if appropriate, investigate the alleged breach of or non-application of Union law, in accordance with these Rules of Procedure*".[80] Hence, and in conjunction with recital (2), the EBA is committed to outlining how it intends to proceed, regardless of who initiates a request for action.

7.3.2.3 Assessment of Market Developments—'Stress Tests' (Points (f) and (g))

The monitoring and assessment of market developments in the field of its competence, including (if relevant) developments relating to trends in credit, in particular, to households and SMEs and in innovative financial services duly considering developments relating to ESG-related factors, as well as the undertaking of market analyses to inform the discharge of its functions are

---

[77] This group was established pursuant to Article 37 to help facilitate consultation with stakeholders in areas relevant to its tasks. It is composed of thirty members representing EU financial institutions, employees' representatives of EU financial institutions, consumers, users of banking services and representatives of SMEs, and also participated in by four independent top-ranking academics. On its workings, see at: https://www.eba.europa.eu/about-us/organisation/banking-stakeholder-group. Periodically, the BSG publishes own-initiatives papers on various issues; see, e.g., its recent (24 March 2022) "BSG own-initiative paper on non-bank lending" (BSG 2022 011, at: https://www.eba.europa.eu/sites/default/documents/files/document_library/1029857/EBA%20BSG%20OIP%20on%20non-bank%20lending.pdf).

[78] EBAR, Article 17(2), first subparagraph, as amended by Regulation (EU) No 2019/2175.

[79] EBA/DC/2020/312. This Decision was adopted on the basis of Articles 17 and 41(4) EBAR, repealed a previous one of 23 December 2016 and is in force as amended on 3 December 2021 (EBA/DC/2021/419).

[80] EBA Rules of Procedure, Article 2(4).

additional tasks.[81] A specific aspect in this context is the initiation and coordination of Europe-wide assessments of the resilience of financial institutions to adverse market developments ("stress tests").[82] In that respect, the EBA must consider, at least annually, whether the carrying out of such stress tests is appropriate, inform the European Parliament, the Council and the Commission of its reasoning, and, if considered appropriate, disclose the results for each participating financial institution.[83] Furthermore, it must develop, in cooperation with the ESRB: *first*, common methodologies for: assessing the effect of economic scenarios on financial institutions' financial position taking into account, *inter alia*, risks arising from adverse environmental developments; identifying the financial institutions to be included in the EU-wide stress tests; assessing the effect of particular products or distribution processes on financial institutions; asset evaluation for the purpose of stress-testing; and assessing the effect of environmental risks on the financial stability of financial institutions; *second*, common approaches to communication on the outcomes of those assessments of the resilience of financial institutions.[84]

> **Box 7.2 The EBA methodology for its 2023 EU-wide stress test**
>
> On 4 November 2022, the EBA published the (final) methodology, draft templates and template guidance its 2023 EU-wide stress test, which will last from end-January (with the publication of the macroeconomic scenarios) to end-July (with the publication of the results).[85] The methodology is based on the lessons from the 2021 exercise and covers all risk areas (credit, market, counterparty and operational risk). The focus is assessing the impact of adverse shocks on credit institutions' solvency. In this respect:
>
> (a) The key element of continuity is reliance mainly on a constrained "bottom-up approach".
> (b) Elements of change include: *first*, projections on net fee and commission income ('**NFCI**') will be based on a top-down

---

[81] These aspects are further governed by Article 32(1) EBAR.

[82] For recent research on stress tests, see Konietschke *et al.* (2022). For "green" stress tests, see, by means of mere indication, Reinders *et al.* (2020). See also the EBA Report of 21 May 2021 "Mapping climate risk: Main findings from the EU-wide pilot exercise" (EBA/Rep/2021/11), which aims to map credit institutions' exposures to climate risk and provide an insight into the green estimation efforts they had carried out (at: https://www.eba.europa.eu/eba-publishes-results-eu-wide-pilot-exercise-climate-risk).

[83] EBAR, Article 22(1a).

[84] *Ibid.*, Article 32(2).

[85] At: https://www.eba.europa.eu/eba-publishes-methodology-and-draft-templates-2023-eu-wide-stress-test.

> model, as a first step of revising the EU-wide stress test framework towards a hybrid (bottom-up and top-down) approach; and *second*, the sample coverage has been increased by adding an additional 26 credit institutions compared to the 2021 exercise; and *third*, further proportionality has been introduced into the methodology.
>
> This exercise will assess EU banks' resilience to an adverse economic shock and inform the 2023 SREP.[86]

7.3.2.4 Tasks Relating to the Promotion of Several Aspects on Financial Stability (Point (i))

The EBA is called upon to promote the following: the consistent and coherent functioning of colleges of supervisors[87]; the identification, monitoring, assessment and measurement of systemic risk[88]; and the development and coordination of recovery and resolution plans, providing a high level of protection to depositors and investors throughout the EU and developing methods for the resolution of failing financial institutions and an assessment of the need for appropriate financing instruments, with a view to fostering cooperation between competent authorities involved in the crisis management concerning cross-border institutions that may pose a systemic risk.[89] *Furthermore*, pursuant to **Article 26 EBAR** on the "European system of deposit guarantee schemes", the EBA has the task to contribute to the strengthening of the European system of national DGSs by acting under the powers conferred to it by the EBAR in order to ensure the correct application of the DGSD with the aim of ensuring that national DGSs are adequately funded by

---

[86] The EBA stress test will cover fifty-seven of the euro area's largest credit institutions (with broadly 75% of the euro area's banking assets). In parallel, the ECB will conduct its own stress test for another forty-two medium-sized credit institutions under its remit.

[87] It is noteworthy that his aspect, governed by Article 21 EBAR, is also referred to in point (b) of Article 8(1), as already noted.

[88] This aspect is governed by Articles 22–24. Article 22(1) in particular provides that the EBA must duly consider systemic risk (as defined in the ESRBR, as just noted above) and address any risk of disruption in financial services that is caused by an impairment of all or parts of the financial system and has the potential to have serious negative consequences for internal market and the real economy. It must consider, as appropriate, the monitoring and assessment of systemic risk as developed by the ESRB and itself and respond to ESRB Warnings and Recommendations in accordance with Article 17 ESRBR.

[89] This aspect is governed by Article 25 EBAR. *Inter alia*, the EBA may organise and conduct peer reviews of the exchange of information and of the joint activities of the SRB and of non-participating Member States' NRAs in the resolution of cross-border groups, by developing methods to allow for objective assessment and comparison (ibid., Article 25(1a), inserted by Article 95 SRMR). Related is also Article 27 EBAR on the "European system of bank resolution and funding arrangements".

contributions from credit institutions and provide a high level of protection to all depositors in a harmonised framework throughout the EU.[90]

7.3.2.5 Tasks Relating to AML (Point (l))

A new EBA task is the contribution to the prevention of the use of the financial system for the purposes of money laundering and terrorist financing, including by promoting consistent, efficient and effective application of the relevant legislative acts referred to in Article 1(2) of the three founding Regulations. This task is further specified by more detailed provisions in **Articles 9a and 9b** (the latter referring to the request for investigation in that respect).

7.3.2.6 Other Tasks

In addition to the above-mentioned, the EBA is called upon to stimulate and facilitate the delegation of tasks and responsibilities among competent authorities, as well as to conduct peer reviews thereof and, in that context and with a view to strengthening consistency in supervisory results, issue Guidelines and Recommendations and identify best practices.[91] It must *also* closely cooperate with the ESRB, in particular by providing the latter with the necessary information for the achievement of its tasks, and by ensuring a proper follow-up to its Warnings and Recommendations.[92]

Furthermore, its tasks include the fostering of depositor, consumer and investor protection, in particular regarding shortcomings in a cross-border context and taking related risks into account, while a new task is the contribution to the establishment of a "common EU financial data strategy".[93] *In addition*, it has to publish on its website and regularly update information relating to its field of activities, in particular on registered financial institutions, to ensure easy access to information by the public, as well as all RTSs, ITSs, Guidelines, Recommendations and Q&As for each relevant legislative act, including overviews that concern the state of play of ongoing work and the planned timing of the adoption of draft RTSs and ITSs[94] *Finally*, it is responsible for the fulfilment of any other tasks set out in the EBAR or in other legislative acts, including its general coordination role between competent authorities and its international relations (including equivalence assessments) (Table 7.2).[95]

---

[90] In this respect it has the power to develop RTSs and ITSs pursuant to Articles 10–15 EBAR and adopt Guidelines and Recommendations applying to DGSs pursuant to Article 16 (ibid., Article 26(1)–(3)).

[91] *Ibid.*, Article 8(1), points (c) and (e); these aspects are governed by Articles 28 and 30, respectively.

[92] *Ibid.*, Article 8(1), point (d); this aspect is governed by Article 36.

[93] *Ibid.*, Article 8(1), points (h) and (ia).

[94] *Ibid.*, Article 8(1), points (k) and (ka).

[95] *Ibid.*, Article 8(1), point (j); these aspects are governed by Articles 31 and 33, respectively. Furthermore, pursuant to Article 31a, the ESAs must jointly establish a system

Table 7.2 The relation between Article 8(1) EBAR (on the EBA's tasks) and other provisions of the EBAR

Article 8(1) EBAR	Other EBAR provisions (in numerical order)
Contribution to the prevention of the use of the financial system for the purposes of money laundering and terrorist financing	**Article 9a**: Special tasks related to preventing and countering money laundering and terrorist financing **Article 9b**: Request for investigation related to the prevention and countering of money laundering and of terrorist financing
Establishment of high-quality common regulatory and supervisory standards and practices	**Articles 10–14**: Regulatory technical standards (RTSs) **Article 15**: Implementing technical standards (ITSs) **Article 16**: Guidelines and Recommendations **Article 16a**: Opinions
Ensuring consistent, efficient and effective application of the relevant legislative acts	**Article 17**: Breach of Union law
Ensuring the taking of action in emergency situations	**Article 18**: Action in emergency situations
Assisting 'binding mediation'	**Article 19**: Settlement of disagreement between competent authorities in cross-border situations
Promoting the convergence of the SREP (Article 97 CRD IV) to bring about strong EU supervisory standards	**Article 20a**: Convergence of supervisory review process
Ensuring a coherent functioning of colleges of supervisors	**Article 21**: Colleges of supervisors
Promoting the identification, monitoring, assessment and measurement of systemic risk	**Articles 22–24**: General provisions on systemic risk; identification and measurement of systemic risk; and permanent capacity to respond to systemic risks
Promoting the development and coordination of recovery and resolution plans	**Article 25**: Recovery and resolution procedures **Article 27**: European system of bank resolution and funding arrangements
Contribution to the strengthening of the European system of national DGSs	**Article 26**: European system of deposit guarantee schemes
Stimulation and facilitation of the delegation of tasks and responsibilities among competent authorities	**Article 28**: Delegation of tasks and responsibilities
Creation of a common supervisory culture among competent authorities	**Article 29**: Common supervisory culture (basis for adoption of European Supervisory Examination Programmes (ESEP) and European Resolution Examination Programmes (EREP))
Conduct of peer reviews of competent authorities	**Article 30**: Peer reviews of competent authorities

(continued)

Table 7.2 (continued)

Assumption of a general coordination role between competent authorities	**Article 31**: Coordination function **Article 31a**: Information exchange on fitness and propriety
Assessment of market developments—stress tests	**Article 32**: Assessment of market developments, including stress tests (see also **Article 22(1a)**)
Development of contacts and entering into administrative arrangements with various financial authorities, international organisations and third-country administrations	**Article 33**: International relations including equivalence
Close cooperation with the ESRB	**Article 36**: Relationship with the ESRB

7.3.3 The EBA's Powers Under Article 8(2) EBA Regulation

Extensive powers have been assigned to the EBA to carry out its above-mentioned tasks. These powers can be grouped as follows:

(1) The first group covers the EBA's regulatory powers, which include the development of draft RTSs and ITSs, the issuance of Guidelines and Recommendations,[96] as well as the issuance of Recommendations, as laid down in **Article 29a**[97] and Warnings pursuant to **Article 9(3)**.[98]

(2) In the cases laid down in (the already discussed[99]) **Articles 17–19**, the EBA has the following specific powers:

> *First*, in the event of a breach of Union law it may, not later than two months from initiating its investigation under Article 17(2), issue a Recommendation addressed to the competent authority concerned setting out the action necessary to comply with Union law.[100]

for the exchange of information relevant to the assessment of the fitness and propriety of holders of qualifying holdings, directors and key function holders of financial market participant by competent authorities.

[96] *Ibid.*, Article 8(2), points (a)–(c); these powers are discussed in detail under 7.5.2–7.5.4.

[97] According to this Article, at least every three years, the EBA must identify up to two priorities of EU-wide relevance reflecting future developments and trends, factoring in contributions received from competent authorities, existing work by EU institutions, as well as ESRB analyses, Warnings and Recommendations.

[98] EBAR, Article 8(2), points (ca) and (da).

[99] See just above, under 7.3.1 when discussing Article 8(1), point (b) on the consistent application of legally binding EU acts.

[100] EBAR, Article 8(2), point (d), with reference to Article 17(3). Before issuing such a Recommendation, the EBA must engage with the competent authority concerned, where it considers such engagement appropriate in order to resolve a breach of Union law, to reach agreement on actions necessary for the competent authority to comply with Union law (*ibid.*, Article 17(2a)). On the actions and inactions of the ESAs in relation to the investigation of breaches of EU law, see Schammo (2018).

Second, in two cases, the EBA may take individual Decisions addressed to competent authorities.[101] *On the one hand*, in emergency situations under Article 18, if the Council has adopted a decision pursuant to Article 18(2) and, exceptionally, if coordinated action by competent authorities is necessary to respond to adverse developments which may seriously jeopardise the orderly functioning and integrity of financial markets or the stability of the EU financial system or customer and consumer protection, the individual decision shall require competent authorities to take the necessary action in accordance with the relevant legislative acts to address any such developments by ensuring that financial institutions and competent authorities satisfy the requirements laid down in those legislative acts. *On the one hand*, in the case of binding mediation under Article 19, if the competent authorities concerned fail to reach an agreement within the conciliation phase referred to in Article 19(2), the individual decision shall require those authorities to take specific action, or to refrain from certain action, in order to settle the matter, and to ensure compliance with EU law.[102] In these cases, the EBA has (under conditions) the right to **substitute competent authorities**.[103]

Furthermore, in specific cases concerning directly applicable EU law, it may also take individual Decisions addressed to financial institutions.[104]

(3) The EBA has also the power to issue Opinions addressed to the European Parliament, the Council or the Commission on all issues related to its area of competence, either upon a request from these institutions or on its own initiative.[105] In this respect, **recital (45)** refers to the EBA as an *"independent advisory body to the European Parliament, the Council, and the Commission"*. Furthermore, it has the power to issue Q&As.[106]

(4) In exceptional circumstances, the EBA has the power to take action in accordance with **Article 9c**, if it considers that the application of one of the relevant legislative acts, or of any delegated or implementing acts based thereon is liable to raise significant issues for any of the following reasons: it considers that provisions contained in such act may directly conflict with another relevant act; where the act is one of the relevant legislative acts, the absence of delegated or implementing acts that would complement or specify

---

[101] *Ibid.*, Article 8(2), point (e), with reference to Articles 18(3) and 19(3), respectively.

[102] This decision shall be binding on the competent authorities concerned and may require them to revoke or amend a decision they have adopted or to make use of the powers which they have under the relevant EU law.

[103] In the author's opinion, up to end-2022, this was the sole genuine EBA's supervisory task (albeit indirect), exercised without prejudice to the relevant Commission's powers under (the above-mentioned) Article 258 TFEU.

[104] EBAR, Article 8(2), point (f), with reference to Articles 17(6), 18(4) and 19(4).

[105] *Ibid.*, Article 8(2), point (g), with reference to Article 16a.

[106] *Ibid.*, Article 8(2), point (ga), with reference to Article 16b.

that act would raise legitimate doubts concerning the legal consequences flowing from the legislative act or its proper application; or the absence of Guidelines and Recommendations pursuant to Article 16 would raise practical difficulties concerning the application of the relevant legislative act.[107]

(5) *Finally*, the EBA's powers also include the following: collection of the necessary information concerning financial institutions; development of common methodologies for assessing the effect of product characteristics and distribution processes on the financial position of institutions and on consumer protection; and provision of a centrally accessible database of registered financial institutions in the field of its competence, if specified in the relevant legislative acts.[108]

7.3.4 The EBA's Task and Powers Relating to Consumer Protection and Financial Activities Under Article 9 EBA Regulation

(1) In accordance with **Article 9(1) EBAR**, the EBA's tasks also include "*promoting transparency, simplicity and fairness in the market for consumer financial products or services across the internal market*". To fulfil this task, the EBA collects, analyses and reports on consumer trends; undertakes in-depth thematic reviews of market conduct, building a common understanding of market practices in order to identify potential problems and analyse their impact; develops retail risk indicators for the timely identification of potential causes of consumer harm; reviews and coordinates financial literacy and education initiatives by competent authorities and develops training standards for the financial system; contributes to the development of common disclosure rules and to a level playing field in the internal market where consumers and other users of financial services have fair access to financial services and products; fosters further developments in terms of regulation and supervision which could facilitate deeper harmonisation and integration at the EU level; and coordinates mystery shopping activities of competent authorities, if applicable.

---

[107] *Ibid.*, Article 8(2), point (gb).

[108] *Ibid.*, Article 8(2), points (h) (with reference to Article 35) and (i)–(j). Pursuant to Article 35(7a), when the EBA requests information directly from relevant financial institutions, holding companies or branches thereof and/or non-regulated operational entities within a financial group or conglomerate that are significant to the financial activities of the relevant financial institutions, and the addressees of such a request do not provide it promptly and without undue delay with clear, accurate and complete information, it must inform the ECB and the NCAs in the Member States concerned, which, subject to national law, must cooperate with the EBA to ensuring full access to the information and verify it.

(2) In that respect, the EBA's obligations and powers are as follows[109]:

First, it must monitor new and existing financial activities and may adopt Guidelines and Recommendations with a view to promoting the safety and soundness of markets, and convergence and effectiveness of regulatory and supervisory practices. It may also issue Warnings if a financial activity poses a serious threat to the objectives laid down in Article 1(5). *Second*, it should establish a "Committee on consumer protection and financial innovation", with the participation of all relevant competent authorities, including the ECB, and authorities responsible for enhancing consumer protection, achieving a coordinated approach to the regulatory and supervisory treatment of new or innovative financial activities, and providing advice to be presented to the European Parliament, the Council and the Commission.[110] The ESAs' **"Consumer Protection and Financial Innovation Sub-Committee"** was created on **20 December 2021**. Its task consists in assisting the Joint Committee to ensure the necessary degree of cross-sectoral consistency among ESAs in relation to matters pertaining to consumer protection and financial innovation as covered under its work programme.
Third, it may "*temporarily prohibit or restrict the marketing, distribution or sale of certain financial products, instruments or activities*" that have the potential to cause significant financial damage to customers or consumers, or threaten the orderly functioning and integrity of financial markets or the stability of the EU financial system in the cases specified, and under the conditions laid down in the relevant legislative acts, or (if so required) in the case of emergency situations (pursuant to **Article 18**). It may also "*assess the need to prohibit or restrict certain types of financial activity*", and if there is such a need, it must inform the Commission in order to facilitate the adoption of any such prohibition or restriction.

Accordingly, the EBA does not only address the issue-area of protecting consumers' financial interests but also that of promoting their right to training (namely two of the three pillars of EU policy on protecting consumers pursuant to **Article 169 TFEU**[111]).

---

[109] *Ibid.*, Article 9(2)–(5).
[110] *Ibid.*, Article 9(4).
[111] On this TFEU Article, see, by means of mere indication, Strumpf (2019).

7.4 The EBA's Integration Within the EU Institutional Framework

7.4.1 Introductory Remarks

On the basis of the above-mentioned, it is evident that the EBA has been endowed with a significant range of tasks and powers. Hence, it was deemed necessary to lay down provisions ensuring its integration in the EU institutional framework, providing for the independence of the EBA, its bodies and their members, the EBA's accountability *vis-à-vis* EU institutions and other bodies, as well as the judicial review of the EBA's Decisions and its liability. With a view to ensuring transparency of its operation, the EBA is also subject to the EU legislation on combatting fraud, corruption and other illegal activities, privileges and immunities, processing of personal data and access to documents.[112]

7.4.2 Independence

The institutional independence of the EBA is principally premised on the general clause of **Article 1(5)**, which reads as follows:

> When carrying out its tasks, the [EBA] must act independently and objectively and in a non-discriminatory and transparent manner, in the interests of the Union as a whole and shall respect, where relevant, the principle of proportionality.[113]

The institutional independence of BoS members is anchored in the EBAR as well. In particular, **Article 42** provides (in a wording almost identical to that of **Articles 130 TFEU** and **7 ESCB/ECB Statute**) that when carrying out the tasks conferred upon them, these members must act independently and objectively in the sole interest of the EU as a whole and neither seek nor take instructions from the EU institutions or bodies, any government or any other public or private body. Furthermore, neither Member States, the EU institutions or bodies nor any other public or private body shall seek to influence them in the performance of their tasks.[114] Similar rules govern the

---

[112] EBAR, Articles 66–67 and 71–72. For more general remarks on the place of EBA in the institutional design, see Ferran (2012) and Payne (2020). Article 73 governs the language arrangements and Article 74 the Headquarters Agreement with the French authorities (at: https://www.eba.europa.eu/sites/default/documents/files/documents/10180/2613666/d6cdbf39-6cef-490f-b057-ce3955194147/Seating%20Agreement%20EBA.pdf?retry=1).

[113] *Ibid.*, Article 1(5), fourth sub-paragraph, first sentence. This is an important element of its overall independence, notably in the context of performing its task of organising and conducting 'peer reviews' of NCAs and of its general coordinating role in accordance with Articles 30–31; see Louis (2010), at p. 155.

[114] *Ibid.*, Article 42(1)–(2).

institutional independence of the members of the Management Board and of the BoA, the Chairperson and the Executive Director.[115]

(2) The EBA's financial independence is also (at least partially) ensured, since the revenues of its 'autonomous' budget consist of obligatory contributions from the NCAs, any fees paid to it in the cases specified in EU law, but also of a subsidy from the EU (entered in the General Budget—Commission Section).[116]

(3) The EBAR also contains specific rules in relation to the personal independence of the Chairperson, the Executive Director and the members of the BoA. In particular[117]: *first*, on the Chairperson, there are two provisions. *On the one hand*, if he/she no longer fulfils the conditions referring to his/her (just above-mentioned) institutional independence (Article 49) or has been found guilty of serious misconduct, the Council may, acting on a proposal from the Commission and approved by the European Parliament, adopt a Decision to remove him/her from office. *On the other hand*, he/she may be removed from office on serious grounds (only) by the European Parliament following a Council Decision, adopted after consulting the BoS (which appointed him/her). *Second*, the Executive Director may be removed from office only upon a decision of the BoS (without further specification of the conditions that should be met). *Third*, the members of the BoA may be removed upon a decision of the Management Board (after consulting the BoS) only if found guilty of serious misconduct.

(4) Finally, it can reasonably be argued that the EBA's operational independence is also granted based on the above in relation to the powers assigned to it to fulfil its tasks and its objective.

7.4.3   Accountability

(1) As a general principle it is provided that *"the Authority shall be accountable and act with integrity and shall ensure that all stakeholders are treated*

---

[115] *Ibid.*, Articles 46, 59(1) and (6), 49 and 52, respectively.

[116] *Ibid.*, Article 62(1) and recital (59). For this purpose, the EBA is considered a "European body" in accordance with Regulation (EU, Euratom) 2018/1046 of the co-legislators of 18 July 2018 "on the financial rules applicable to the general budget of the Union (…) (OJ L 193, 30 July 2018, pp. 1–222)"; this repealed, with effect from 3 August 2018, Regulation (EU, Euratom) No 966/2012 of the same institutions of 25 October 2012 (OJ L 298, 26 October 2012, pp. 1–96). Articles 62(2)–(4) and 63–65 EBAR contain further rules on the budget's structure, establishment, implementation and control, as well as on the financial rules applicable to the EBA.

[117] *Ibid.*, Articles 48(2), second sub-paragraph and (5), 51(5) and 58(5), respectively.

fairly".[118] This is further specified by the following rules laid down in **Article 3 EBAR**[119]:

> *First*, the EBA is accountable to the European Parliament and to the Council[120]; in accordance with **Article 226 TFEU**,[121] it must fully cooperate with the European Parliament during any investigation carried out under that Article and reply orally or in writing to any question addressed to it by the European Parliament or by the Council within five weeks of its receipt; *furthermore*, without prejudice to confidentiality obligations arising from its participation in **international fora**, the EBA must inform the European Parliament upon request about its contribution to a united, common, consistent and effective representation of the EU's interests therein.
> *Second*, the BoS must adopt an Annual Report on the EBA's activities, including on the performance of the Chairperson's duties, transmit it to the European Parliament, the Council, the Commission, the ECA and the European Economic and Social Committee and make it public.[122]
> *Third*, the Chairperson must participate in a hearing before the European Parliament (at least annually) on the EBA's performance and, upon request, make a statement before the institution and answer any questions from its members; *furthermore*, he/she must report, in writing, on the EBA's activities to the European Parliament when requested and at least 15 days before making the above-mentioned statement (in addition to the information referred to in **Articles 11–18, 20 and 33**, the report must include any relevant information requested by the European Parliament on an *ad hoc* basis); *finally*, upon request, he/she must also hold confidential oral discussions behind closed doors with the Chair, Vice-Chairs and Coordinators of the European Parliament's competent committee (**ECON**), with due respect (by all) to the professional secrecy requirements.

(2) For the sake of transparency of BoS decisions, within six weeks of each of its meetings, the EBA must also, at least, provide the European Parliament with a comprehensive record of its proceedings that enables a full understanding of the discussions, including an annotated list of decisions. Such

---

[118] *Ibid.*, Article 1(5), fourth sub-paragraph, second sentence.

[119] *Ibid.*, Article 3(1)–(9).

[120] Article 3(1), second sentence clarifies that the ECB is accountable to these EU institutions with regard to the exercise of its supervisory tasks under the SSMR; see also Chapter 8 below, under 8.4.2.

[121] On this Article, see the analysis in Schoo (2019a).

[122] See also Article 43(5) EBAR.

record shall not reflect discussions within the BoS relating to individual financial institutions, unless otherwise provided for in Article 75(3) or in the relevant legislative acts.[123]

7.4.4 Appeals—Judicial Review of EBA Decisions

7.4.4.1 Board of Appeal (BoA)

(1) As already mentioned,[124] the BoA is one of the EBA's bodies—a joint body of the ESAs (like the Joint Committee), established by Article 58(1) of their founding Regulations and governed by **Articles 58–60** and its Rules of Procedure.[125] The BoA, which a form of administrative pre-litigation review mechanism (like the Appeal Panel in the SRM[126]), is fully independent, composed of six members and six alternates, who shall be individuals of high repute with a proven record of relevant knowledge of EU law and international professional experience, to a sufficiently high level in the fields of relating to the financial system; excluded are current staff of the competent authorities or other national or EU institutions or bodies involved in the ESAs' activities and members of the BSG. The BoA should *collectively* have sufficient legal expertise to provide expert legal advice on the legality of the ESAs' exercise of its powers. Two members and two alternates are appointed by the Management Board of each ESA, according to a specific procedure, for a term of five years, which is extendable once; the President is designated by BoA.[127]

In terms of personal independence, members can be removed during his/her term of office, unless he/she has been found guilty of serious misconduct and the Management Board takes a Decision to that effect after consulting the BoS. They are also independent in making their decisions, not bound by any instructions, and they must undertake to act independently and in the public interest.[128]

(3) Appeals can be lodged by any natural or legal person, including competent authorities against an EBA (or ESMA/EIOPA) Decision referred to in Articles 17–19 or taken by it in accordance with the relevant legislative acts, which

---

[123] This applies notwithstanding Article 70 EBAR on the obligation of professional secrecy (*ibid.*, Article 3(1)–(9)). On Article 75(3), see above, under 7.2.3, on the attendance of meetings.

[124] See above, under 7.2.3 as well.

[125] EBAR/ESMAR/EIOPAR, Article 60(6). Its currently into force Rules of Procedure of 25.02.2020 (BoA 2020 01) are available at: https://www.esma.europa.eu/sites/default/files/library/boa_rules_of_procedure_2020.pdf.

[126] See Chapter 9, under 9.5.

[127] *Ibid.*, Article 58(2)–(4). Article 58(6)–(8) contains procedural and administrative rules. The BoA Secretariat rotates on an annual basis; in 2022, it was managed by the EIOPA, in 2023 it will be managed by the EBA.

[128] *Ibid.*, Articles 58(5) and 59(1), first and second sentences and (6), first sentence. Article 59 contains further provisions relating to the avoidance of conflicts of interest.

is either addressed to that person or is of direct and individual concern to it.[129] Hence, the BoA is responsible for deciding on appeals only against *specific* Decisions of the ESAs; otherwise, appeals are inadmissible.[130] If an appeal is admissible, the BoA examines whether it is well-founded and, following a specific procedure, may confirm the Decision of the competent body of the ESA, or remit the case to it, in which case the BoA's Decision is binding and an amended Decision regarding the case concerned must be adopted. The BoA's decisions must be reasoned, be made public by the relevant ESA[131] and can be appealed to the CJEU as set out in **Article 61(1)**.[132]

7.4.4.2 Actions Before the Court of Justice of the European Union (CJEU)

Proceedings may be brought before the CJEU, in accordance with **Article 263 TFEU**, contesting a BoA Decision or, if there is no right of appeal, by the EBA. Such proceedings may be instituted by Member States, EU institutions and any natural or legal person. If the EBA is under an obligation to act but fails to take a Decision, proceedings for failure to act may be brought before the CJEU in accordance with **Article 265 TFEU**. In both cases, the EBA is required to take the necessary measures to comply with the Court's judgement.[133]

---

[129] *Ibid.*, Articles 60(1). Article 60(2) contains administrative provisions, while Article 60(3) sets out that appeals lodged do not have suspensive effect, unless the BoA considers that circumstances so require.

[130] On the admissibility of Appeals relevant are the judgements of the General Court (Third Chamber) of 9 September 2015 in Case T-660/14, *SV Capital OÜ v [EBA]* (ECLI:EU:T:2015:608) and of the Court (First Chamber) of 14 December 2016 in Case C-577/15 P, *SV Capital OÜ v [EBA]* (ECLI:EU:C:2016:947, the '*SV Capital* case'), as well as the Order of the General Court of 10 August 2021 in Case T-760/20, *Stasys Jakeliūnas v. ESMA* (ECLI:EU:T:2021:512).

[131] EBAR/ESMAR/EIOPAR, Articles 60(4)–(5) and (7).

[132] An inventory of the decisions taken by the BoA (its most recent of July 2022) is available at: https://www.eba.europa.eu/about-us/organisation/joint-board-of-appeal/decisions. On the BoA's work, see Blair (2012), Wymeersch (2012), pp. 292–297, Chiu and Wilson (2019), pp. 304–306, Van Rijn (2022), pp. 313–317, and in detail Lamandini and Ramos Muñoz (2020), pp. 122–124, 128–134 and 145–160 discussing lessons drawn from the first years of experience of its operation, including some of the cases decided by it and the inherent weaknesses in this form of *quasi*-judicial protection.

[133] EBAR, Articles 60–61. About Article 263 TFEU and the procedure, see, among many others, Craig and de Búrca (2020), Chapters 15 and 16, as well as Lenaerts, Maselis and Gutman (2014), pp. 253–417. On Article 265 TFEU, see Lenaerts, Maselis, and Gutman (2014), pp. 419–440. On the more general question of whether more judicial review is always a positive step forward, see Arnull (2015). Another related (and disputable) question is whether recourse to an administrative review panel (such as the above-mentioned BoA) should be made mandatory prior to initiating judicial proceedings before the Court.

7.4.5 Liability

(1) In the case of non-contractual liability, the EBA must make good any damage caused by it or by its staff in the performance of their duties in accordance with the general principles common to the laws of the Member States.[134] In this respect it is noted that EU financial authorities (in general) can only be successfully held liable in relation to acts or omissions in the performance of their duties if the following (additional) four conditions are met on a cumulative basis: *first*, there is a sufficiently serious breach of a rule of EU law; *second*, the rule of EU law infringed must be intended to confer rights on individuals; *third*, there exists actual and certain damage; and *fourth*, a direct causal link is established between the breach of the obligation and the damage sustained by claimant.[135] The CJEU has jurisdiction in any dispute over the remedying of such damage.[136]

(2) The personal financial liability and disciplinary liability of EBA staff towards the EBA is governed by the relevant provisions applying to the EBA staff.[137]

---

[134] EBAR, Article 69(1), first sentence, which sets up a liability regime replicating Article 340, second sub-paragraph TFEU.

[135] See on this Almhofer (2021), pp. 22–244 (discussed under the perspective of the ECB within the SSM and the SRB within the SRM) and Busch and Gortsos (2022), pp. 32–51, both with extensive further references to the relevant jurisprudence of the Court and to secondary sources. *Inter alia*, key judgements in this respect are:

> *first*, the judgement of the Court of 19 November 1991 in joint Cases C-6/90 and C-9/90, *Andrea Francovich and Danila Bonifaci and others v Italian Republic* (ECLI:EU:C:1991:428, the '*Francovich* case'), which developed the *Francovich* liability doctrine that may require disregarding a national statutory limitation of supervisory liability to cases of intentional relevant harm;
> *second*, the judgement of the Court (sitting as a full Court) of 12 October 2004 in Case C-222/02, *Peter Paul, Cornelia Sonnen-Lütte, Christel Mörkens v Bundesrepublik Deutschland* (ECLI:EU:C:2004:606, the '*Peter Paul* case'), which refused to apply *Francovich* type Member State liability to the obligations incumbent on them to exercise prudential supervision over credit institutions pursuant to the EU legal acts of that time; and
> *third*, the (most recent) judgement of the Court (Fifth Chamber) of 4 October 2018 in Case C-571/16, *Nikalay Kantarev v Balgarska Narodna Banka* (ECLI:EU:C:2018:807, the '*Kantarev* case'), which is relevant for the liability of NCBs and NCAs for incorrect application of EU law and focuses on the scope of the *Francovich* liability doctrine.

[136] EBAR, Article 69(1), second sentence, which sets up a liability regime replicating Article 340, fourth sub-paragraph TFEU. This aspect is further discussed below in relation to the liability of the ECB and NCAs within the SSM (see Chapter 8, under 8.6.2) and, in more detail, in relation to the liability of the SRB and NRAs within the SRM (see Chapter 9, under 9.6.2).

[137] EBAR, Article 69(2).

7.5 The Law-Making Process and EBA's Role Therein

7.5.1 The TFEU Provisions and Their Application to EU Financial Law

7.5.1.1 The TFEU Provisions

Legal acts and soft law instruments: The legal acts which constitute the sources of EU banking (and in general EU financial) law are currently adopted pursuant to the TFEU provisions. The Treaty contains legal instruments and soft law (non-legal) instruments.[138] In particular, **Article 288** (first sentence) **TFEU** stipulates the following: "*To exercise the Union's competences the institutions shall adopt regulations, directives, decisions, recommendations and opinions*". The legal nature of these legal instruments is as follows[139]:

First, Regulations, Directives and Decisions are the key legal instruments: Regulations have general application, are binding in their entirety and directly applicable in all Member States; Directives are binding as to the result to be achieved by Member States to which they are addressed but leave to national discretion the choice of form and methods; and Decisions are binding in their entirety and binding only on those to whom they are addressed (if specified).

Second, Recommendations, as defined in **Article 292**,[140] and Opinions are soft law instruments and have no binding force.

Hierarchy of norms: According to the hierarchy of norms instituted by the Lisbon Treaty, the constituent Treaties sit at the *first tier*, along with the **2000 Charter of Fundamental Rights of the European Union**[141] (hereinafter the '**Charter**', or '**CFR**').[142] Since the entry into force of the Lisbon Treaty, the

---

[138] On the definition and content of European soft law, see MacCormick (1989) and Trubek *et al.* (2005). On the content of soft law in international financial law, see Chapter 2 above, under 2.4.2.

[139] TFEU, Article 288, second-fifth sentences. See on this Craig and de Búrca (2020), pp. 136–140 and Klamert and Loewenthal (2019).

[140] In principle, Recommendations are adopted by the Council, acting either on a proposal of the Commission in all cases where the Treaties so provide, or unanimously in those areas in which unanimity is required for the adoption of an EU act (TFEU, Article 292, second and third sentences). Recommendations may also be adopted by the Commission and the ECB in the specific cases stipulated in the Treaties (*ibid.*, fourth sentence).

[141] See Craig and de Búrca (2020), pp. 141–142.

[142] Even though initially it did not have any binding legal effect, on 1 December 2009, with the entry into force of the Treaty of Lisbon, the Charter became legally binding on the EU institutions and on national governments, and, according to the Article 6(1), first sub-paragraph TEU, has the same legal value as the EU Treaties. The Charter was initially solemnly proclaimed at the Nice European Council on 7 December 2000 by the European Parliament, the Council, and the Commission (OJ C 364, 18 Decembr 2000, pp. 1–22).

Charter is regularly taken into consideration in judgements of the CJEU.[143] The *second tier* in the hierarchy of norms is occupied by the 'general principles of law', which can be used for the interpretation of Treaties' Articles.[144] Regulations, Directives and Decisions may take the form of 'legislative acts', as defined in **Article 289**, 'delegated acts', as defined in **Article 290**, and 'implementing acts', as defined in **Article 291**, constituting the *third tier* in the hierarchy of norms.[145]

7.5.1.2 Application to EU Banking, Capital Markets and Insurance Law

The (legally binding) acts which constitute the sources of the three main branches of EU financial law (EU banking, capital markets and insurance law), except for those of the ECB on EU banking supervision,[146] are adopted at three levels, according to the terminology of the 'Lamfalussy process',[147] and at the first two levels in accordance with the above TFEU Articles. For a summary of the law-making procedure relating to the legal acts constituting the sources of the three main branches of EU financial law (EU banking, capital markets and insurance law), see **Tables 7.3 and 7.4 below**.

'Level 1': legislative acts (Article 289 TFEU): At 'Level 1', legislative acts, as defined in **Article 289(3) TFEU**, are those adopted by either the ordinary legislative procedure or the special legislative procedure: *On the one hand*, pursuant to **Article 289(1) TFEU**,[148] the ordinary legislative procedure consists in the adoption by the co-legislators of a Regulation, Directive or Decision on a proposal from the Commission in accordance with **Article 294 TFEU**. The practice of EU institutions to mainly issue Directives, rather than Regulations is founded on **Article 5 TEU** and **Protocol (No 2)** "on

---

It is currently in force (Consolidated version, OJ C 202, 7 June 2016, pp. 389–405) as adapted on 12 December 2007 in the context of the Lisbon Treaty negotiations (OJ C 303, 14 December 2007, pp. 1–17), and is supplemented by the "Explanations relating to the Charter of Fundamental Rights" (OJ C 303, 14 December 2007, pp. 17–35). It is noted that the CJEU, shortly after 2009 when the Charter became binding, declared that "*[t]he applicability of [EU] law entails applicability of the fundamental rights guaranteed by the Charter*", demonstrating thus the broad scope of application of this piece of primary law. See the Judgement of the Court (Grand Chamber) of 26 February 2013 in Case C-617/10, *Åklagaren v Hans Åkerberg Fransson*, ECLI: EU:C:2013:105.

[143] At: https://ec.europa.eu/justice/fundamental-rights/charter/index_en.htm.

[144] See Craig and de Búrca (2020), pp. 142–144.

[145] *Ibid.*, pp. 113–120. On the hierarchy of norms within the EU legal order more generally, see, by means of mere indication, Weatherill (2016), Chapter 4 and Barnard and Peers (2020), Chapter 9.

[146] See Chapter 8 below, under 8.3.1.

[147] See Table 4.1 above.

[148] On Article 289 TFEU in general, see Loewenthal (2019a).

the application of the principles of subsidiarity and proportionality".[149] This approach prevailed due to Member State pressures to preserve the principle of subsidiarity and use the form of legal acts (namely Directives) which would provide them with the greatest possible flexibility during the transposition of European law provisions into their national legal orders. *On the other hand*, **Article 289(2) TFEU** provides that the special legislative procedure consists in the adoption of Regulations, Directives or Decisions either by the European Parliament with the participation of the Council or *vice versa*.[150] As a rule, these acts are adopted upon a proposal of the Commission pursuant to **Article 17(2) TEU**.[151] By way of exception, **Article 289(4) TFEU** lays down a *lex specialis*, according to which:

> In the specific cases provided for by the Treaties, legislative acts may be adopted on the initiative of a group of Member States or of the European Parliament, on a recommendation from the [ECB] or at the request of the Court of Justice or the European Investment Bank.

'Level 2': delegated and implementing acts (Articles 290 and 291 TFEU, respectively): At 'Level 2', the Commission may be empowered by a 'Level 1' legislative act to adopt delegated acts and implementing acts, in accordance with **Articles 290** and **291 TFEU**, respectively. These acts are (usually) adopted on the basis of draft RTSs and ITSs developed by the ESAs.[152]

'Level 3': Recommendations and Guidelines: At 'Level 3', the EBA, the ESMA and the EIOPA have the power to adopt Recommendations and Guidelines.[153]

---

[149] OJ C 202, 7 June 2016, pp. 206–209. On these two principles, see, by means of mere indication, Lienbacher (2019) and Craig and de Búrca (2020), pp. 125–133 and 583–591, respectively.

[150] As already noted in Chapter 6, under 6.3.1), the Regulations adopted by virtue of Article 127(6) TFEU are a manifest example. On both these procedures, see Craig (2010), pp. 252–253, Schoo (2019b), pp. 3029–3034 and Craig and de Búrca (2020), pp. 144–145.

On a related matter, and by way of reminder, in accordance with Article 48(7) TEU, which was introduced by the Treaty of Lisbon, where the TFEU provides for legislative acts to be adopted by the Council in accordance with a special legislative procedure, the European Council may adopt a decision allowing for the adoption of such acts in accordance with the ordinary legislative procedure. For such a decision to be adopted, the European Council shall act by unanimity after obtaining the consent of the European Parliament, which shall be given by a majority of its component members.

[151] On this Article, see Nemitz (2019), pp. 256–258.

[152] See further just below, under 7.5.2 and 7.5.3.

[153] This aspect is further discussed below, under 7.5.4.

7.5.2 Delegated Acts and Regulatory Technical Standards (RTSs)

7.5.2.1 The Provisions of Article 290 TFEU

(1) The second category of legal acts under the TFEU comprises the delegated acts[154]; the power to adopt them is conferred on the Commission. These are (non-legislative) acts of general application, adopted by the Commission upon fulfilment of the following conditions: *first*, the power to adopt such acts is delegated to the Commission by means of a legislative act; and *second*, they supplement or amend certain 'non-essential' elements of a given legislative act.[155] Accordingly, a legislative act may delegate to the Commission the power to adopt such acts, including *ex-ante* and *ex-post* restrictions on this delegation without following the Comitology procedure.[156]

(2) The content of legislative acts, by which the power is delegated to the Commission to adopt such delegated acts, must contain the following elements: *first*, the objectives, content, scope and duration of the delegation of power must be explicitly defined in the legislative act; the essential elements of an area are reserved for the legislative act and, hence, are not the subject of a delegation of power.[157] *Second*, the legislative act must explicitly (as well) lay down the conditions to which the delegation is subject. These conditions may be the following: either the ability of the European Parliament or the Council (each acting separately) to decide to revoke the delegation; or the provision that the delegated act may enter into force only if the European Parliament or the Council have not expressed an objection within a period set by the legislative act.[158]

7.5.2.2 The Provisions of the EBAR

(1) Particularly as regards the provisions of EU financial law, in **Declaration 39** concerning provisions of the Treaties,[159] the Commission states its intention to "*continue to consult experts appointed by the Member States in the preparation of draft delegated acts in the financial services area, in accordance with its established practice*". In this respect, **recital (22) EBAR** considers the following:

> There is a need to introduce an effective instrument to establish harmonised [RTSs] in financial services to ensure, also through a single rulebook, a level playing field and adequate protection of depositors, investors and consumers

---

[154] TFEU, Article 290(3).

[155] *Ibid.*, Article 290(1), first sub-paragraph.

[156] On the Comitology procedure, see details in the *Excursus* below.

[157] TFEU, Article 290(1), second sub-paragraph.

[158] *Ibid.*, Article 290(2), first sub-paragraph, points (a) and (b), respectively. For more details on Article 290, see Craig (2010), pp. 57–64 and 253–254, Schoo (2019b), pp. 3034–3042 and Craig and de Búrca (2020), pp. 145–147.

[159] OJ C 326, 26 November 2012, p. 350.

across the Union. As a body with highly specialised expertise, it is efficient and appropriate to entrust the Authority, in areas defined by Union law, with the elaboration of draft [RTSs], which do not involve policy choices.

According then to **Article 10**, where the co-legislators delegate by a relevant legislative act power to the Commission to adopt RTSs by means of delegated acts[160] pursuant to **Article 290 TFEU** in order to ensure consistent harmonisation in the areas *specifically* set out in that act, the EBA may develop draft RTSs after having conducted open public consultations on them and, in principle, a cost-benefit analysis, and after having requested the BSG's advice.[161] It must define the content of its draft RTSs on the basis of the restrictions set out in **Article 290 TFEU**, as further qualified in **Article 10 EBAR**. These standards are technical in nature, do not imply strategic decisions or policy choices, and their content is delimited by the legislative acts on which they are based[162]; they shall be adopted by means of Regulations or Decisions.[163]

(2) The exercise and revocation of the delegation and the objections to RTSs by the co-legislators are governed by **Articles 11–13 EBAR**.[164] According to standard practice in the field of EU banking law,[165] this power is subject to the following conditions: (a) the conferral of power is for an indeterminate period of time from the relevant dates referred to in specific Articles of the legislative act; (b) the delegation of power may be revoked at any time by the European Parliament or the Council by a decision putting an end to the

---

[160] On the basis of this wording, it is not excluded that a legislative act can empower the Commission to adopt a delegated act without RTSs; see, e.g., Article 2(2) BRRD.

[161] The EBA must submit its draft RTSs to the Commission for adoption and concurrently forward them for information to the co-legislators (EBAR, Article 10(1), first and third sub-paragraphs). Even though in most cases the wording of the legislative acts is that the EBA "shall develop" RTSs, it cannot be excluded that it is merely given the discretion ("may develop"); see, e.g., Article 27(5) BRRD.

[162] *Ibid.*, Article 10(1), second sub-paragraph.

[163] *Ibid.*, Article 10(4), first sentence. The Commission must decide whether to adopt or not a draft RTS within three months of its receipt; it may adopt it partly only, or with amendments, where the EU interests so require. In such cases, it must send the draft RTS back to the EBA, explaining why it does not adopt it or the reasons for its amendments and setting a six-week period to the EBA to amend it based on the proposed amendments and resubmit it in the form of a formal opinion to the Commission. If, on the expiry of that period, the EBA has not submitted an amended draft RTS or has submitted a draft that is not amended in a way consistent with the Commission's proposed amendments, the latter may adopt the RTS with the amendments it considers relevant or reject it. In any case, the Commission may not change the content of a draft RTS prepared by the EBA without prior coordination with it (*ibid.*, Article 10(1), fourth—seventh sub-paragraphs). Articles 10(2)–(3) and 14 contain further specific rules on these aspects.

[164] There provisions are consistent with Article 290(2), first sub-paragraph, points (a) and (b). On Articles 10–14 (as these were initially in force), see Gortsos (2011), pp. 34–35 and Wymeersch (2012), pp. 249–254.

[165] See Articles 462 CRR, 148 CRD IV, 115 BRRD, 93 SRMR and 18 DGSD. The SSMR does not provide for the adoption of delegated acts.

delegation specified therein, taking effect the day following the publication of the decision in the *OJ* or at a later date specified therein, and not affecting the validity of any delegated acts in force; (c) upon its adoption, the Commission must notify the delegated act simultaneously to the European Parliament and the Council; (d) a delegated act can enter into force only if no objection has been expressed either by the European Parliament or the Council within a period of (usually) three months (extendable by another three months) of its notification to these institutions, or if, before the expiry of that period, both these institutions have informed the Commission that they do not object[166]; and (e) the Commission may not adopt delegated acts, if the scrutiny time of the European Parliament is reduced through recess to less than five months, including any extension.

7.5.3 Implementing Acts and Implementing Technical Standards (ITSs)

7.5.3.1 The Provisions of Article 291 TFEU

According to **Article 291(1) TFEU**,[167] Member States must adopt "*all measures of national law necessary to implement legally binding Union acts*". If it is deemed that uniform conditions for the implementation of legally binding acts are needed, the Commission or, in "duly justified specific cases" and in the cases provided for in **Articles 24** and **26 TEU**,[168] the Council are entitled to issue implementing acts,[169] based on 'implementing powers' conferred on them by means of the above legally binding acts.[170] For the purposes of implementing the latter, the **co-legislators**, deciding by means of a Regulation by the ordinary legislative procedure, should lay down in advance the rules and general principles concerning mechanisms for control by Member States of the Commission's exercise of implementing powers.[171] This is the legal basis for the Comitology procedure, which continues to apply only under **Article 291 TFEU** for the adoption of implementing acts in accordance with the provisions of **Regulation (EU) No 182/2011** of the **co-legislators** of 16 February 2011 "laying down the rules and general principles concerning mechanisms for control by Member States of the Commission's exercise of implementing powers", as discussed in detail in the ***Excursus*** **below**.

---

[166] This is consistent with Article 290(2), first sub-paragraph, point (b).
[167] On this Article, see Loewenthal (2019b).
[168] Both these Articles refer to the common EU foreign and security policy.
[169] TFEU, Article 291(4).
[170] *Ibid.*, Article 291(2).
[171] *Ibid.*, Article 291(3). On Article 291 TFEU, see Craig (2010), pp. 64–66 and 254–255, Schoo (2019b), pp. 3042–3046 and Craig and de Búrca (2020), pp. 148–152.

7.5.3.2 The Provisions of the EBAR

According to **Article 15 EBAR**, where the co-legislators confer by a relevant legislative act power on the Commission to adopt ITSs by means of implementing acts pursuant to **Article 291 TFEU** in the areas *specifically* set out in that act, the EBA may develop draft ITSs after having conducted open public consultations on them and, in principle, a cost-benefit analysis, and after having requested the BSG's advice. These standards, like the RTSs, are technical in nature and do not imply strategic decisions or policy choices; unlike the RTSs, their content is to determine the conditions of application of the legislative acts on which they are based. ITSs shall be adopted by means of Regulations or Decisions as well.[172] They have been broadly used to provide for common templates and instructions, mainly for reporting purposes.[173]

7.5.4 EBA Recommendations and Guidelines

7.5.4.1 The Provisions of the EBAR

(1) According to **Article 16 EBAR**, the EBA shall issue Recommendations and Guidelines in accordance with the powers conferred upon it by the relevant legislative acts. Their objectives are to establish consistent, efficient and effective supervisory practices within the ESFS and to ensure the common, uniform and consistent application of EU law; their addressees are either competent authorities or financial institutions (as defined in the EBAR).[174] If appropriate, the EBA must conduct open public consultations on them and, in principle, a cost-benefit analysis, and request the BSG's advice; its decision not to conduct open public consultations or not to request such an advice must be reasoned. Guidelines and Recommendations should not merely refer to, or reproduce, elements of legislative acts and, to avoid any duplication, before issuing a new Guideline of Recommendation, the EBA must first review existing ones.[175]

(2) Guidelines and Recommendations forming part of European 'soft' law[176] do not have a legally binding character. Competent authorities and

---

[172] EBAR, Article 15(1), first sub-paragraph. The content of the provisions of the following sub-paragraphs is, *mutatis mutandis*, identical to that of Article 10(1), fourth – seventh sub-paragraphs.

[173] On Article 15 (as initially in force), see Wymeersch (2012), pp. 254–255.

[174] EBAR, Article 16(1). The legislative act may provide that Guidelines should be issued in close cooperation with the ESRB; see, e.g., Article 5(7) BRRD.

[175] *Ibid.*, Article 16(2) and (2a).

[176] On this matter, see the Judgement of the Court (Second Chamber) of 13 December 1989 in Case C-322/88, *Salvatore Grimaldi v Fonds des maladies professionnelles* (ECLI:EU:C:1989:646, the '*Grimaldi* case'), discussing the effects of Recommendations of EU agencies, and in particular whether those are binding for national courts, which can apply by analogy to all acts of European soft law. See also the 2007 European Parliament's Report "on institutional and legal implications of the use of 'soft law' instruments" (A6-0259/2007 final, 28 June 2007).

financial firms must, however, make every effort to comply with their provisions according to the **"comply or explain" principle**.[177] In case of compliance, competent authorities should incorporate these Guidelines and Recommendations into their supervisory practices, as appropriate. Lacking compliance, an explanation must be offered to the EBA providing accounting for the approach taken by the competent authority or the financial firm, respectively, fostering in this way accountability. **Article 16(3)** reads in this respect as follows:

> Within **2 months** of the issuance of a guideline or recommendation, each competent authority must confirm whether it complies or intends to comply with that guideline or recommendation. In the event that a competent authority does not comply or does not intend to comply, it must inform the [EBA], stating its reasons.

The EBA must publish the fact that a competent authority does not or does not intend to comply with a Guideline or Recommendation and may also decide, on a case-by-case basis, to publish the reasons provided by the competent authority for non-compliance. Financial institutions must also clearly and in detail report, if required by a Guideline or Recommendation, whether they do comply with that.[178]

7.5.4.2 Relevant case law

On **15 July 2021**, the CJEU (Grand Chamber) issued a judgement in **Case C-911/19** *Fédération Bancaire Française (FBF) v Autorité de contrôle prudentiel et de résolution (ACPR)*, relating to the EBA Guidelines of 22 March 2016 (**EBA/GL/2015/18**) on product governance for retail banking products.[179] This case relates to the limitations of the EBA's power to

---

[177] On the compliance of the ECB with EBA Guidelines and Recommendations, see at: https://www.bankingsupervision.europa.eu/legalframework/regulatory/compliance/html/index.en.html. On the 'comply or explain' principle, which is broadly used in the field of corporate governance codes resulting from self-regulation and also in Recommendations of the Commission, the ECB and/or the EBA, see, by means of mere indication, Bianchi *et al.* (2010), Andersson (2011), pp. 91–105 and Keay (2012).

[178] The Annual Report (see above, under 7.4.3) must contain information on the Guidelines and Recommendations issued (EBAR, Article 16(4). On ESAs' Guidelines and Recommendations (as initially in force), see Wymeersch (2012), pp. 276–277.

[179] These Guidelines deal with the establishment of product oversight and governance arrangements for manufacturers and distributors; refer to internal processes, functions and strategies aimed at designing products, bringing them to the market and reviewing them over their life cycle; establish procedures relevant for ensuring the interests, objectives and characteristics of the target market are met; but do not deal with the suitability of products for individual consumers. On product intervention, see Colaert (2019).

adopt, soft law, non-binding acts (such as Guidelines), and to the relationship between the direct and indirect judicial review by the CJEU as to their potential annulment.

> **Box 7.3 The *FBF v ACPR* case**
>
> (1) In September 2017, the French supervisory Authority (Autorité de contrôle prudentiel et de resolution, **ACPR**) publicly confirmed its compliance with the above-mentioned EBA Guidelines. The relevant notification of the ACPR, which was published on the EBA website, in line with **Article 16(3) EBAR**, was challenged before the French Conseil d'État by the French Banking Federation (Fédération Bancaire Française, '**FBF**'), claiming that the EBA did not have the competence to adopt these Guidelines. The Conseil d'État referred to the CJEU, for a preliminary ruling, three questions about the justiciability and validity of the EBA Guidelines, including questions relating to the applicability in this case of **Articles 263** and **267 TFEU**.
>
> (2) According to the Opinion of Advocate General Bobek of 15 April 2021 in that case,[180] these EBA Guidelines should be considered invalid because their subject matter and content do not fall within the relevant legislative acts (as discussed above). Furthermore, he expressed the views that it is not possible to use the action for annulment under **Article 263 TFEU** to obtain a declaration of invalidity of soft law instruments; that **Article 267 TFEU** allows for the submission of a request for a preliminary ruling on the assessment of the validity (also) of EU non-binding EU acts; and that a professional federation (like the FBF) is not precluded from challenging Guidelines addressed to the members whose interests it protects, even if those do not concern it directly and individually.[181]

---

[180] ECLI:EU:C:2021:294. It is interesting to note that the Introduction of this Opinion (paragraph 1) includes a quote from Game of Thrones: "*As a line from Game of Thrones has it, 'what is dead may never die'. Thus, perhaps with the exception of White Walkers, what is dead also cannot be killed. However, can something that has never been alive (or rather never came into existence as a binding EU-law act) be annulled (or rather declared invalid) by the Court of Justice on a preliminary ruling? Alternatively, can the Court provide (binding) interpretation of a non-binding EU measure?*". See also Annunziata (2021), p. 2 and Kyriazis (2021).

[181] On the questions which acts are reviewable under Article 263 and which under Article 267 TFEU, see Lenaerts, Maselis and Gutman (2014), pp. 257–274 and 456–468, respectively. These Articles are further discussed below in Chapter 8, under 8.6.1 and in Chapter 9, under 9.6.1.

(3) In its judgement exactly three months later (15 July 2021),[182] the Grand Chamber of the Court came to following conclusions:

> *First*, unlike the Advocate General's Opinion, the Guidelines on product governance are valid, since their adoption falls within the general competences of the EBA and its institutional activity.
>
> *Second*, and most importantly, it clarifies the system of judicial review of non-legally binding acts by confirming that, **even though the Guidelines cannot be subject to an action for annulment under Article 263** since they are legally non-binding, NCAs and financial institutions must follow the 'comply or explain' principle, and the Guidelines **can be subject to judicial review by the Court under Article 267 TFEU**.
>
> *Third*, it also clarifies that under EU law there is no requirement that the admissibility before a national court of a plea of illegality directed against an EU act should be conditioned on that act being of direct and individual concern to the person relying on that plea.[183]

7.5.5 Concluding Remarks

All in all, the new legislative process enables the adoption of rules by EU institutions with the more active involvement of supervisory authorities, through the EBA and the other ESAs, which *de facto* have the technical know-how in the subject matters.[184] As a matter of fact, the role of their legally non-binding acts, such as their Recommendations and Guidelines, is steadily increasing.

It is also noted that, pursuant to the amendments introduced to the EBAR by **Regulation 2019/2175**, the perimeter of non-binding acts that the EBA (and the other ESAs) may adopt has been widened. In particular, the EBA may, upon a request from the European Parliament, the Council or the Commission, provide legally non-binding Opinions to them on all issues

---

[182] ECLI:EU:C:2021:599.

[183] On this quite important (case and) judgement, see, by means of mere indication, Annunziata (2021), Chamon and De Arriba-Sellier (2021) and Busch and Gortsos (2022), pp. 37–38. In this respect it is also noted that, on 22 July 2022, the Conseil d'État rejected by a new decision another challenge of (among others) the FBF to another set of EBA Guidelines, namely those of 29 May 2020 on loan origination and monitoring (EBA/GL/2020/06) and the ACPR's compliance with them. This decision (no 449898) is available at: https://www.conseil-etat.fr/fr/arianeweb/CE/decision/2022-07-22/449898.

[184] The EBA RTSs, ITSs and Guidelines are available at: https://eba.europa.eu/regulation-and-policy/single-rulebook; related Q&As are available at: https://eba.europa.eu/single-rule-book-qa.

related to its area of competence, as well as technical advice to them in the areas set out in the relevant legislative; it may also, at the request of one of the NCAs concerned provide Opinions on the assessments referred to in **Article 22 CRD IV** (on the acquisition of a qualifying holding in a credit institution).[185] Furthermore, the EBA shall provide non-binding answers to questions relating to the practical application or implementation of the provisions of relevant legislative acts, associated delegated and implementing acts, and Guidelines and Recommendations, adopted pursuant to these acts, submitted by any natural or legal person, including competent authorities and EU institutions and bodies. Questions that require the interpretation of EU law must be forwarded to the Commission; any answers provided by the latter shall be published by the EBA.[186]

Excursus: The Comitology Procedure: A Closer Look[187]

Introductory Remarks

As already noted,[188] the Comitology procedure applies after the entry into force of the Lisbon Treaty only for the adoption of implementing acts under **Article 291 TFEU**. It is governed by **Regulation (EU) No 182/2011** of the co-legislators of 16 February 2011 "laying down the rules and general principles concerning mechanisms for control by Member States of the Commission's exercise of implementing powers".[189] This legislative act was adopted on the basis of **Article 291(3) TFEU**, entered into force on 1 March of the same year, repealed **Council Decision 1999/468/EC** (as in force, at that time, after its amendment by **Council Decision 2006/512/EC**[190]) and is binding in its entirety and directly applicable in all Member

---

[185] EBAR, Article 16a (1)–(4).

[186] *Ibid*, Article 16b (1)–(5).

[187] This Section is based (albeit with several differentiations) on Gortsos (2016).

[188] See above, under 7.5.3.

[189] OJ L 55, 28 February 2011, pp. 13–20. On the comitology procedure before the entry into force of the TFEU, see, by means of mere indication, Blumann (1988), Bradley (1992) and Savino (2005). On the comitology procedure post-Lisbon, see, by means of mere indication, Craig (2016).

[190] The effects of Article 5a of that Decision, on the regulatory procedure with scrutiny, were maintained for the purposes of basic acts referring thereto (*ibid.*, Article 12; see also recital (21)). If a basic act adopted before the entry into force of the Regulation provided for the exercise of implementing powers by the Commission in accordance with that Decision, applicable were the rules laid down in Article 13 (for a summary see Table 7.3 below). As a transitional arrangement, the Regulation did not affect pending procedures, in which a Committee had already delivered its opinion in accordance with that Decision (*ibid.*, Article 14).

States.¹⁹¹ It lays down the rules and general principles governing the mechanisms applying where a legally binding EU act (a 'basic act') identifies the need for uniform conditions of implementation and requires that the adoption of implementing acts by the Commission should be subject to Member States' control.¹⁹² Taking into account the nature or the impact of the implementing act required, a basic act may provide for the application of any of the following procedures: either the **'examination'** or the **'advisory procedure'**.¹⁹³ Before discussing them in turn, reference is made to the Committees which play an important role therein.

The 'Committees'

*Common Provisions*¹⁹⁴

(1) When the Commission adopts implementing acts under **Article 291 TFEU**, it is assisted by a 'Committee' composed of Member States' representatives and is chaired by a representative of the Commission who is not allowed to take part in the Committee vote.¹⁹⁵ As already discussed,¹⁹⁶ there are three such Committees established under the Lamfalussy process for each of the three main sectors of the financial system: the European Banking Committee (**EBC**), the European Securities Committee (**ESC**) and the European Insurance and Occupational Pensions Committee (**EIOPC**). Even though the rules of the Regulation equally apply to all Committees, the following discussion will focus on the EBC (unless otherwise necessary).

(2) The 'normal' operating procedure for the EBC is the following¹⁹⁷: *first*, the draft implementing act to be adopted by the EBC is submitted to it by the Chair, who, except in duly justified cases, must convene a meeting not less than fourteen days from the date of submission to the Committee of the draft implementing act and of the draft agenda. The EBC must deliver its opinion on the draft implementing act within a time limit laid down by the Chair based on the urgency of the matter.¹⁹⁸ *Second*, until the opinion is delivered, if EBC members suggest amendments, the Chair *may* present an amended version of the draft implementing act, endeavouring to find solutions commanding the widest possible consensus and inform the EBC how the discussions and

---

[191] Regulation (EU) No 182/2011, Article 16.
[192] *Ibid.*, Article 1.
[193] *Ibid.*, Article 2(1); see also recital (8).
[194] These provisions apply to all procedures referred to in Articles 4–8, as discussed below (*ibid.*, Article 3(1)).
[195] *Ibid.*, Article 3(2); see also recital (6).
[196] See Chapter 4 above, under 4.2.3.
[197] Regulation (EU) No 182/2011, Article 3(3)–(4), respectively.
[198] Time limits must be proportionate and afford the EBC members early and effective opportunities to examine the draft implementing act and express their views.

suggestions for amendments have been considered (in particular as regards suggestions largely supported within the Committee).

(3) In duly justified (usually urgent) cases, the Chair may obtain the EBC's opinion by written procedure,[199] sending to its members the draft implementing act and laying down a time limit for delivery of an opinion according to the urgency of the matter. Any member not opposing the draft or not explicitly abstaining from voting thereon before the expiry of the time limit is deemed to have tacitly agreed to it. Unless otherwise provided in the basic act, the written procedure is terminated without result, within the above time limit, upon the Chair's decision or a member's request. In this case, the Chair must convene an EBC meeting within a reasonable time.[200]

Rules of Procedure and Register of Committee Proceedings
The EBC Rules of Procedure are adopted, on the proposal of its Chair, by a simple majority of its members; these rules must be based on 'standard rules' drawn up by the Commission (following consultation with Member States) and be published in the *OJ*.[201] The Commission is required to keep a register of (all) Committees proceedings containing information on several aspects[202] and publish an Annual Report on the Committees' work.[203]

---

[199] According to recital (9), to simplify further the procedures, common procedural rules should apply to the Committees, including the key provisions relating to their functioning and the possibility of delivering an opinion by written procedure.

[200] *Ibid.*, Article 3(5). In any case, the EBC's opinion must be recorded in the minutes, and its members have the right to ask for their position to be recorded therein. The minutes must be sent by the Chair to the members without delay (*ibid.*, Article 3(6)).

[201] Applicable to the EBC are the principles and conditions on public access to documents and the rules on data protection as applied to the Commission (*ibid.*, Article 9(1)–(2)). Public access to information must be ensured in accordance with Regulation (EC) No 1049/2001 of the co-legislators of 30 May 2001 "regarding public access to European Parliament, Council and Commission documents" (OJ L 145, 31 May 2001, pp. 43–48). This legal act is based on Article 15(3) TFEU, according to which citizens and residents of EU countries have a right of access to documents of the European Parliament, the Council and the Commission.

[202] This includes, *inter alia*, a list of Committees; the agendas of their meetings and the summary records; the draft implementing acts on which the Committees are asked to deliver an opinion; the voting results; as well as the final draft implementing acts following delivery of the opinion and their adoption by the Commission.

[203] *Ibid.*, Article 10(1)–(2); see also recital (20). The co-legislators have access to this information in accordance with the applicable rules on a regular basis (*ibid.*, recital (17)). In addition,
   the Commission must make available to them the documents referred to in Article 10(1), points (b), (d) and (f) and inform them of the availability of such documents. The references of all documents referred to in Article 10(1) and the information referred to point (h) thereof must be made public in the register (*ibid.*, Articles 10(3)–(5)).

The Examination Procedure

General Provisions

The examination procedure applies for adopting implementing acts of 'general scope'.[204] It must ensure that the Commission will not adopt implementing acts if those are not in accordance with the opinion of the EBC, except in very exceptional circumstances where they may apply for a limited period of time. It must also ensure that the Commission can review these draft implementing acts if no opinion is delivered by the EBC, taking into account the views expressed within the EBC.[205] Under this procedure, the EBC must deliver its opinion by the qualified majority set out in **Article 16(4) TEU**[206] and, if applicable, **Article 238(3) TFEU**, for acts to be adopted on a proposal from the Commission.[207] Depending on the content of the EBC opinion delivered, the Commission can take any of the following courses of action in relation to the draft implementing act:

(I) **Positive opinion**: in the case of a positive opinion, the Commission must adopt it.[208]

(II) **Negative opinion**: If a negative opinion is delivered, the Commission cannot, in principle, adopt it. However, without prejudice to **Article 7**, if an implementing act is deemed necessary, the EBC Chair may either submit an amended version within two months of delivery of the negative opinion or submit to the Appeal Committee the draft implementing act within one month of such delivery for further deliberation.[209]

(III) **No opinion**: If no opinion is delivered, the Commission may *in principle* adopt the draft implementing act; in case it does not adopt it, the EBC Chair may submit to the Committee an amended version.[210]

---

[204] It also applies to specific implementing acts with a potentially important impact, such as those relating to programmes with substantial budgetary implications, the common agricultural and common fisheries policies, the environment, security and safety (or protection of the health or safety) of humans, animals or plants, the common commercial policy and taxation (*ibid.*, Article 2(2); see also recital (11), first sentence).

[205] *Ibid.*, recital (11), second and third sentences.

[206] See also Article 3 of Protocol No (36) attached to the Treaties "on transitional provisions" (Consolidated version, OJ C 202, 7 June 2016, pp. 322–326).

[207] The votes of Member States' representatives within the EBC shall be weighted in the manner set out in those Articles (Regulation (EU) No 182/2011, Article 5(1)).

[208] *Ibid.*, Article 5(2). On this, the European Parliament, the Council, and the Commission made the following Statement (attached to the Regulation): "*Article 5(2) of the Regulation requires the Commission to adopt a draft implementing act where the committee delivers a positive opinion. This provision does not preclude that Commission may, as is the current practice, in very exceptional cases, take into consideration new circumstances that have arisen after the vote and decide not to adopt a draft implementing act, after having duly informed the committee and the legislator*".

[209] *Ibid.*, Article 5(3); the Appeal Committee is discussed just below.

[210] *Ibid.*, Article 5(4), first sub-paragraph.

Exceptionally, and without prejudice to **Article 7** (in this case as well), the Commission is not allowed to adopt the draft implementing act in any of the following cases: the act concerns, *inter alia*, financial services; the basic act provides that this draft may not be adopted without the delivery of an opinion; *or* a simple majority of the EBC members opposes it.[211] However, if it is deemed that an implementing act is necessary, the EBC Chair may either submit an amended version of that act within two months of the vote or submit the draft implementing act within one month of the vote to the Appeal Committee for further deliberation.[212]

The Appeal Committee

Common provisions: Where applicable, the mechanism for the control by Member States of the Commission's exercise of implementing powers includes referral to an 'Appeal Committee', which should meet the appropriate level, adopts its own rules of procedure by a simple majority of its members, on a proposal from the Commission, and is chaired by a representative of the latter.[213]

Referral to the Appeal Committee: Whenever a case is referred to it, the Appeal Committee must deliver its opinion by qualified majority (pursuant to **Article 5(1)** above). Until its delivery, any of its members may suggest amendments to the draft implementing act and its Chair may decide whether to modify it or not.[214] Depending on the Appeal Committee's Opinion, the Commission must act as follows: in the case of a positive Opinion, it must adopt the draft implementing act; if no Opinion is delivered, it *may* adopt it; and if a negative Opinion is delivered, it shall not adopt it.[215]

---

[211] *Ibid.*, Article 5(4), second sub-paragraph.

[212] *Ibid.*, Article 5(4), third sub-paragraph. Derogating provisions from Article 5(4) apply in the case of draft 'definitive anti-dumping or countervailing measures' (*ibid.*, Article 5(5)). The above-mentioned Article 7 provides that, by way of derogation from Articles 5(3) and 5(4), second sub-paragraph, the Commission may adopt a draft implementing act if its adoption without delay is necessary to avoid creating either a significant disruption of the markets in the area of agriculture, or a risk for the EU financial interests within the meaning of Article 325(3) TFEU. In this case, the Commission must immediately submit the adopted implementing act to the Appeal Committee; if the latter delivers a negative opinion on the adopted act, the Commission must repeal it immediately; if it delivers a positive opinion or no opinion is delivered, the act remains in force.

[213] Except in duly justified cases, if the Appeal Committee is seized, it must meet at the earliest fourteen days and at the latest six weeks after the referral date. The EBC Opinion must be delivered within two months of that date notwithstanding Article 3(3). To enable Member States and the Commission to ensure an appropriate level of representation the Chair must closely cooperate with the members in setting meeting dates (*ibid.*, Article 3(7)).

[214] The Chair must endeavour to find solutions under the same conditions as those provided in Article 3(4) above for the Chair of the EBC (*ibid.*, Article 6(1)–(2)).

[215] *Ibid.*, Article 6(3). A derogating provision applies for the adoption of 'definitive multilateral safeguard measures' (*ibid.*, Article 6(4)).

The Advisory Procedure

The advisory procedure applies, in principle, for the adoption of implementing acts other than those of 'general scope' or specific implementing acts with a potentially important impact as referred to in **Article 2(2)**; it may, however, also apply to such implementing acts, albeit in duly justified cases only. Under this procedure, the EBC must deliver its opinion (if necessary) by taking a vote (by a simple majority of its members) and decide on the adoption of the draft implementing act, duly taking into account the conclusions drawn from the discussions within the EBC and the opinion delivered.[216]

Immediately Applicable Implementing Acts

By way of derogation from **Articles 4–5** on the two above-mentioned procedures, a basic act may provide that on "*duly justified imperative grounds of urgency*" immediately applicable implementing acts can be adopted pursuant to **Article 8**. In this case, and unless otherwise provided in the basic act, the Commission *may* adopt an implementing act, which applies immediately and remains in force for a period not exceeding six months. At the latest 14 days after its adoption, the EBC Chair must submit it to the Committee to obtain its opinion. If under the examination procedure the EBC delivers a negative opinion, the Commission must immediately repeal the implementing act.[217]

Right of Scrutiny for the Co-legislators

If a basic act is adopted by the ordinary legislative procedure, either the European Parliament or the Council may at any time indicate to the Commission that, in its view, a draft implementing act exceeds the implementing powers provided for in the basic act. In such a case, the Commission must review that act, taking account of the positions expressed, and inform the European Parliament or the Council whether it intends to maintain, amend or withdraw it[218] (Table 7.5).

---

[216] *Ibid.*, Article 4(1)–(2).

[217] *Ibid.*, Article 8(1)–(4); see also recital (16). This procedure always applies when the Commission adopts 'provisional anti-dumping or countervailing measures' after consulting or, in cases of extreme urgency, after informing the Member States (*ibid.*, Article 8(5)).

[218] *Ibid.*, Article 11, see also recital (18).

Table 7.3 Equivalence between Articles in Decision 1999/648/EC and in Regulation 182/2011

Decision 1999/648/EC	Regulation 182/2011
Article 3: advisory procedure	Article 4: advisory procedure
Article 4: management procedure	Article 5: examination procedure (except for Article 5(4), second and third sub-paragraphs)
Article 5: regulatory procedure	Article 5: examination procedure
Article 5a: regulatory procedure with scrutiny	Article 5: examination procedure
Article 6: safeguard procedure	Article 8: immediately applicable implementing acts

Table 7.4 Procedure for the adoption of legal acts which constitute the sources of European financial law after the entry into operation of the ESFS([a])

	Level 1 ([a]): legally binding acts	Level 2([a]): legally binding acts		Level 3 ([a]): non-legally binding acts (soft law)
Type of legal act	Legislative acts falling within the ESAs' scope of action (Article 289 TFEU)	RTSs by means of delegated acts (Article 290 TFEU)	ITSs by means of implementing acts (Article 291 TFEU)	Guidelines and Recommendations (ESAs founding Regulations)
Body issuing the legal act	European Parliament and Council (by the ordinary legislative procedure)	European Commission	European Commission	EBA/ESMA/EIOPA (depending on the scope of action)
The role of the ESAs and the Committees	EBC/ESC/EIOPC[b] (as advisory committees) EBA/ESMA/EIOPA (as opinion-giving bodies)	EBA/ESMA/EIOPA (elaborating draft RTSs)	EBA/ESMA/EIOPA (elaborating draft ITSs) EBC/ESC/EIOPC (as regulatory committees)[c]	

[a]Reference to these "3 levels" mirrors the wording used (without any explicit legal basis) in the Lamfalussy Report
[b]European Banking Committee, European Securities Committee, European Insurance and Occupational Pensions Committee
[c]According to the Comitology procedure (**Regulation (EU) No 182/2011**)
Note The ECB must be consulted on any proposed EU legal act according to **Article 127(4) TFEU**

Table 7.5 The four levels of the making and enforcement of public international and European financial law: a comparative view

Levels	International financial law (multinational law)	European financial law (supranational law)
Level of political decision-making	G7, G10, G20	European Council
Level of adoption of rules	Standard-setting bodies (international financial standards—soft law) *No authority to issue legal acts of hard law and create binding rules*	European Parliament and Council (legal acts by the ordinary legislative procedure—hard law) European Commission (delegated and implementing acts in the form of technical standards—hard law) EBA—ESMA—EIOPA (guidelines—soft law)[a]
Level of coordination	Financial Stability Board (FSB)	Joint Committee (common organ of EBA—ESMA—EIOPA)
Level of enforcement	1. peer group pressure exerted within the international financial fora (including the FSB) 2. 'Assessment Programs' conducted by these fora 3. 'thematic' and 'country peer reviews' conducted by the FSB 4. the IMF's Financial Sector Assessment Programme (the 'FSAP') as part of its regulatory authority	European Commission (for hard law) EBA—ESMA—EIOPA (for soft law)

[a] Mainly for European (EU) banking law, capital markets law and insurance law

SECONDARY SOURCES

A-B

Almhofer, M. (2021): The Liability of Authorities in Supervisory and Resolution Activities, in Zilioli, Ch. and K.-Ph. Wojcik (2021, editors): *Judicial Review in the European Banking Union*, Edward Elgar Publisher, Cheltenham, UK – Northampton, MA, USA, Chapter 14, pp. 221–234

Andersson, J. (2011): Evolution of Company Law, Corporate Governance Codes and the Principle of Comply or Explain – A Critical Review, in Birkmose, H., Neville, M. and K.E. Sørensen (2011, editors): *The European Market in Transition*, Kluwer Law International, pp. 91–105

Annunziata, F. (2021): *The Remains of the Day: EU Financial Agencies, Soft Law and the Relics of Meroni*, European Banking Institute Working Paper Series, No. 106, November, available at: https://ssrn.com/abstract=3966980

Arnull, A. (2015): Judicial Review in the European Union, in Arnull, A. and D. Chalmers (2015, editors), *The Oxford Handbook of European Union Law*, Oxford University Press, Oxford, Chapter 15

Barnard, C. and S. Peers (2020): *European Union Law*, 3rd edition, Oxford University Press, Oxford

Bergström, C.F. (2015): Shaping the New System for Delegation of Powers to EU Agencies: United Kingdom v. European Parliament and Council (Short Selling), *Common Market Law Review*, Volume 52, pp. 219–242

Bianchi, M., Ciavarella, An., Novembre, V. and R. Signoretti (2010): *Comply or Explain? Investor Protection Through Corporate Governance Codes*, ECGI Finance Working Paper No 278/2010, available at: https://ssrn.com/abstract=1581350

Blair, Sir W. (2012): *Board of Appeal of the European Supervisory Authorities*, University of Oslo Faculty of Law Research Paper No. 2012–30, available at: https://ssrn.com/abstract=2159206

Blumann, C. (1988): Le pouvoir exécutif de la Commission à la lumière de l'Acte unique Européen, *Revue Trimestrielle de Droit Européen*, no. 24, Janv. – Mars, Paris, pp. 23–59

Bradley, K. (1992): Comitology and the Law: Through a Glass, Darkly, *Common Market Law Review*, Volume 29, pp. 693–721

Busch, D. and Ch.V. Gortsos (2022): Liability of the European Central Bank, the Single Resolution Board and the ESAs (ESMA, EBA and EIOPA), in Busch, D., Gortsos, Ch.V. and G. McMeel (2022, editors): *Liability of Financial Supervisors and Resolution Authorities*, Chapter 2, pp. 9–54

C-D

Capiello, S. (2015): *The EBA and the Banking Union*, in Grundmann, S. and J.-H. Binder (2015, editors): The Banking Union and the Creation of Duties, *European Business Organisation Law Review*, Springer – Asser Press, pp. 421–437

Chamon, M. (2016): *EU Agencies: Legal and Political Limits to the Transformation of the EU Administration*, Oxford University Press, Oxford

Chamon, M. and N. De Arriba-Sellier (2021): *FBF*: On the Justiciability of Soft Law and Broadening the Discretion of EU Agencies, *European Constitutional Law Review*, Volume 18, Issue 2, pp. 286–314 (also available at: https://doi.org/10.1017/S157401962200013X)

Chiti, Ed. (2018): Decentralised Implementation: European Agencies, in Schütze, R. and T. Tridimas (2018, editors): *Oxford Principles European Union Law – Volume I: The European Union Legal Order*, Oxford University Press, Oxford, Part IV: Legislative and Executive Governance, Chapter 23, pp. 748–776

Chiu, I.H-Y. (2016): Power and Accountability in the EU Financial Regulatory Architecture: Examining Inter-Agency Relations, Agency Independence and Accountability, in Andenas, M. and G. Deipenbrock (2016, editors): *Regulating and Supervising European Financial Markets – More Risks Than Achievements*, Springer International Publishing, Switzerland, pp. 67–101

Chiu, I.H-Y. and J. Wilson (2019): *Banking Law and Regulation*, Oxford University Press, Oxford

Colaert, V. (2022): The Changing Nature of Financial Regulation: Sustainable Finance as a New EU Policy Objective, *Common Market Law Review*, Volume 59, pp. 1669–1710

Colaert, V. (2019): Product Intervention: A Cross-Sectoral Analysis', in Colaert, V., Busch, D. and T. Incalza (2019, editors): *European Financial Regulation: Levelling the Cross-Sectoral Playing Field*, Hart Publishing, Oxford, Chapter 16, pp. 395–402

Craig, P. (2016): Comitology, Rulemaking, and the Lisbon Settlement: Tensions and Strains, in Bergström, C.-F. and D. Ritleng (2016, editors), *Rulemaking by the European Commission: The New System for Delegation of Powers*, Oxford University Press, Oxford, Chapter 9, pp. 173–202

Craig, P. (2010): *The Lisbon Treaty: Law, Politics and Treaty Reform*, Oxford University Press, Oxford – New York

Craig, P. and G. de Búrca (2020): *EU Law: Texts, Cases, and Materials*, Seventh edition, Oxford University Press, Oxford – New York

De Smet, J. (2023): Sustainability and Systemic Risk in EU Banking Regulation, in Böffel, L. and J. Schürger (2023, editors): *Digitalisation, Sustainability, and the Banking and Capital Markets Union*, EBI Studies in Banking and Capital Markets Law, Palgrave Macmillan, Cham – Switzerland, Chapter 9, pp. 273–294

Di Noia, C. and M.Ch. Furlò (2012): The New Structure of Financial Supervision in Europe: What's Next, in Wymeersch, Ed., Hopt, K.J. and G. Ferrarini (2012, editors): *Financial Regulation and Supervision – A Post-Crisis Analysis*, Oxford University Press, Oxford, Chapter 7, pp. 172–192

E-H & J

Enoch, Ch. (2021): *Europe Beyond the Euro: Building Protection for Europe's Economies in the Times of Risks*, St Antony's Series (Series Editors Healey D. and L. Payne), Palgrave Macmillan, Cham – Switzerland

Ferran, E. (2012): Understanding the New Institutional Architecture of EU Financial Market Supervision, in Wymeersch, Ed., Hopt, K.J. and G. Ferrarini (2012, editors): *Financial Regulation and Supervision – A Post-Crisis Analysis*, Oxford University Press, Oxford, Chapter 5, pp. 111–158

Gortsos, Ch.V. (2016): *The 'Comitology Procedure' Under the European Parliament and Council Regulation (EU) No 182/2011 and its Importance for EU Banking Law*, available at: https://ssrn.com/abstract=2716026

Gortsos, Ch.V. (2011): *The European Banking Authority within the European System of Financial Supervision*, ECEFIL Working Paper Series, No. 1, August, available at: https://www.ecefil.eu//UplFiles/wps/wps2011-1.pdf

Gortsos, Ch.V. and K. Lagaria (2020): The European Supervisory Authorities (ESAs) as "Direct" Supervisors in the EU Financial System, in Chryssochoou, D., Hatzopoulos, V. and A. Passas (2020, editors): *European Governance in Times of Uncertainty/ Gouvernance Européenne en temps incertains – Liber Amicorum Prof. Constantin Stephanou*, Nomiki Bibliothiki, Athens, Chapter 10, pp. 231–245 (also in European Banking Institute Working Paper Series, No. 57, available at: https://ssrn.com/abstract=3534775)

Guarracino, F. (2013): Role and Powers of the European Central Bank and of the European Banking Authority in the Perspective of the Forthcoming Single Supervisory Mechanism, *Law and Economics Yearly Review*, Volume 2, Part 1, pp. 184–210 (also available at: https://ssrn.com/abstract=2319136)

Haar, B. (2015): Organising Regional Systems: The EU Example, in Moloney, N., Ferran, E. and J. Payne (2015, editors): *The Oxford Handbook of Financial Regulation*, Oxford University Press, United Kingdom, Chapter 6, pp. 157–187

Howell, E. (2017): The Evolution of ESMA and Direct Supervision: Are There Implications for EU Supervisory Governance? *Common Market Law Review*, pp. 1027–1057

Joosen, R. and A. Zhelyazkova (2022): How Do Supranational Regulators Keep Companies in Line? An Analysis of the Enforcement Styles of EU Agencies, *Journal of Common Market Studies*, Volume 60, Issue 4, pp. 983–1000

K-L-M-N

Keay, An. (2012): *Accountability and the Corporate Governance Framework: From Cadbury to the UK Corporate Governance Code*, Working Paper, available at: https://ssrn.com/abstract=2143171

Klamert, M. and P.-J. Loewenthal (2019): Commentary on Article 288 TFEU, in Kellerbauer, M., Klamert, M. and J. Tomkin (2019, editors): *The EU Treaties and the Charter of Fundamental Rights: A Commentary*, Oxford University Press, Oxford, pp. 1895–1910

Konietschke, P., Ongena, S.R.G. and A. Ponte Marques (2022): *Stress Tests and Capital Requirement Disclosures: Do They Impact Banks' Lending and Risk-Taking Decisions?*, Swiss Finance Institute Research Paper No. 60, July, available at: https://ssrn.com/abstract=4182633

Kyriazis, D. (2021): EBA and Game of Thrones: A Match Made in Luxembourg, *European Law Blog*, May 5, available at: https://europeanlawblog.eu/2021/05/05/eba-and-game-of-thrones-a-match-made-in-luxembourg

Lamandini, M. and D.R. Muñoz (2020): Law and Practice of Financial Appeal Bodies (ESAs' Board of Appeal, SRB Appeal Panel): A View from the Inside, *Common Market Law Review*, Volume 57, Issue 1, pp. 119–160

Lenaerts, K., Maselis, Ig. and K. Gutman K (2014): *EU Procedural Law*, Oxford European Union Law Library, Oxford University Press, Oxford

Lienbacher, G. (2019): Kommentar zum Artikel 5 EUV, in Becker, U., Hatje, A. Schoo, J. und J. Schwarze (2019, Herausgeber): *EU-Kommentar*, 4. Auflage, Nomos Verlagsgesellschaft, Baden-Baden, pp. 91–124

Louis, J.V. (2010): The Implementation of the Larosière Report: A Progress Report, in Giovanoli, M. and D. Devos (2010, editors): *International Monetary and Financial Law: The Global Crisis*, Oxford University Press, Oxford – New York, Chapter 7, pp. 305–328

Loewenthal, P.-J. (2019a): Commentary on Article 289 TFEU, in Kellerbauer, M., Klamert, M. and J. Tomkin (2019a, editors): *The EU Treaties and the Charter of Fundamental Rights: A Commentary*, Oxford University Press, Oxford, pp. 1911–1916

Loewenthal, P-J. (2019b): Commentary on Article 291 TFEU, in Kellerbauer, M., Klamert, M. and J. Tomkin (2019b, editors): *The EU Treaties and the Charter of Fundamental Rights: A Commentary*, Oxford University Press, Oxford, pp. 1925–1932

MacCormick, D.N. (1989): Spontaneous Order and the Rule of Law: Some Problems, *Ratio Juris*, Volume 2, no. 1, March, pp. 41–54

Moloney, N. (2018): *The Age of ESMA – Governing EU Financial Markets*, Hart Publishing, Oxford

Moloney, N. (2014): *EU Securities and Financial Markets Regulation*, Oxford European Union Law Library, Third edition, Oxford University Press, Oxford

Nemitz, P.F (2019): Kommentar zum Artikel 17 EUV, in Becker, U., Hatje, A. Schoo, J. und J. Schwarze (2019, Herausgeber): *EU-Kommentar*, 4. Auflage, Nomos Verlagsgesellschaft, Baden-Baden, pp. 235–274

P-R-S

Payne, J. (2020): The Institutional Design of Financial Supervision and Financial Stability, in Amtenbrink, F. and Ch. Herrmann (2020, editors): *Oxford Handbook on the EU Law of Economic and Monetary Union*, Oxford University Press, Oxford, Chapter 20, pp. 568–570

Reinders, H., Schoenmaker, D. M. Van Dijk (2020): A Finance Approach to Climate Stress Testing, *Journal of International Money and Finance*, Volume 131, pp. 1–19 (also available at: https://ssrn.com/abstract=3573107)

Repasi, R. (2014): *Assessment of the Judgment of the European Court of Justice in Case C-270/12, United Kingdom vs Council and European Parliament – Impact of This Judgment on the Proposal of the SRM Regulation*, European Parliament, 23 January, available at: https://www.sven-giegold.de/wp-content/uploads/2014/01/Assessment-ECJ-Case-C-270-12-and-relevance-for-the-SRM1.pdf

Salerno, M.E. (2022): The Approximation of National Banking Law in the European Banking Union, in Gimigliano, G. and V. Cattelan (2022, editors): *Money Law, Capital, and the Changing Identity of the European Union*, Hart Publishing, Oxford

Savino, M. (2005): *The Constitutional Legitimacy of the EU Committees*, Cahiers Européens, no. 3, Centre d' Etudes Européennes

Schammo, P. (2018): Actions and Inactions in the Investigation of Breaches of Union Law by the European Supervisory Authorities, *Common Market Law Review*, Volume 55, pp. 1423–1455

Schammo, P. (2014): *Differentiated Integration and the Single Supervisory Mechanism: Which Way Forward for the European Banking Authority?*, available at: https://ssrn.com/abstract=2514720

Schemmel, J. (2018): *Europäische Finanzmarktverwaltung: Dogmatik und Legitimation der Handlungsinstrumente von EBA, EIOPA und ESMA*, Studien zum Regulierungsrecht, Mohr Siebeck, Tübingen

Schima, B. (2019): Commentary on Article 258 TFEU, in Kellerbauer, M., Klamert M. and J. Tomkin (2019, editors): *The EU Treaties and the Charter of Fundamental Rights: A Commentary*, Oxford University Press, Oxford, pp. 1773–1784

Schoo, J. (2019a): Kommentar zum Artikel 226 AEUV, in Schwarze, J., Becker, U., Hatje, A. und J. Schoo (2019, Hrsg.): *EU-Kommentar*, 4. Auflage, Nomos Verlagsgesellschaft, Baden-Baden, pp. 2710–2716

Schoo, J. (2019b): Kommentar zu den Artikeln 289–291 AEUV, in Becker, U., Hatje, A. Schoo, J. und J. Schwarze (2019, Herausgeber): *EU-Kommentar*, 4. Auflage, Nomos Verlagsgesellschaft, Baden-Baden, pp. 3029–3046

Schwarze, J. und N. Wunderlich (2019): Kommentar zu den Artikeln 258 und 281 AEUV, in Schwarze, J., Becker, U., Hatje, A. und J. Schoo (2019, Hrsg.): *EU-Kommentar*, 4. Auflage, Nomos Verlagsgesellschaft, Baden-Baden, pp. 2822–2836 and 2985–2989

Strumpf, C. (2019): Kommentar zum Artikel 169 AEUV, in Schwarze, J., Becker, U., Hatje, A. und J. Schoo (2019, Hrsg.): *EU-Kommentar*, 4. Auflage, Nomos Verlagsgesellschaft, Baden-Baden, pp. 2311–2329

T & V-W

Thiele, Al. (2014): *Finanzaufsicht*, Jus Publicum 229, Mohr Siebeck, Tübingen

Tridimas, T. (2011): EU Financial Regulation: Federalization, Crisis Management, and Law Reform, in Craig, P.P. and G. de Búrca (2011, editors): *The Evolution of EU Law*, 2nd edition, Oxford University Press, Oxford – New York, pp. 783–804

Trubek, D.M., Cottrell, P. and M. Nance (2005): *"Soft Law", "Hard Law", and European Integration: Toward a Theory of Hybridity*, University of Wisconsin Law School, Legal Studies Research Paper Series, no. 1002

Van Rijn, M. (2022): *Judicial Protection for Banks Under the Single Rulebook and the Single Supervisory Mechanism*, Radboud Business Law Institute, Series Law of Business and Finance, Volume 22, Wolters Kluwer Nederland B.V.

Vuarlot-Dignac, S. and E. Siracusa (2019): The European System of Financial Supervision and in Particular the European Securities and Markets Authority, in Fabbrini, F. and M. Ventoruzzo (2019, editors): *Research Handbook on EU Economic Law*, Edward Elgar Publishing, Cheltenham, UK – Northampton, MA, USA, Chapter 14, pp. 397–433

Weatherill, S. (2016): *Law and Values in the European Union*, Oxford University Press, Oxford

Wymeersch, Ed.O. (2014): *The Single Supervisory Mechanism or "SSM", Part One of the Banking Union*, Working Paper Research No 255, National Bank of Belgium, Brussels

Wymeersch, Ed.O. (2012): The European Financial Supervisory Authorities or ESAs, in Wymeersch, Ed.O., Hopt, K.J. and G. Ferrarini (2012, editors): *Financial Regulation and Supervision – A Post-Crisis Analysis*, Oxford University Press, Oxford, Chapter 9, pp. 232–317

Wymeersch, Ed.O., Hopt, K.J. and G. Ferrarini (2012, editors): *Financial Regulation and Supervision – A Post-Crisis Analysis*, Oxford University Press, Oxford

CHAPTER 8

The Single Supervisory Mechanism (SSM)

8.1 THE EUROPEAN CENTRAL BANK (ECB) AS A SUPERVISORY AUTHORITY WITHIN THE SSM

8.1.1 The Specific Supervisory Tasks Conferred on the ECB

(1) The specific supervisory tasks conferred upon the ECB by virtue of the SSMR (the ECB **'supervisory tasks'**) are carried out, since November 2014, within the SSM. This mechanism is neither an authority nor an agency, has no legal personality and is defined as the 'system of financial supervision' composed of the ECB and the NCAs of participating Member States (including those with a derogation which have established a 'close cooperation' according to Article 7 SSMR) as described in **Article 6**.[1] Thus, the SSM has a different institutional architecture from the Eurosystem, since members of the latter are the ECB and (exclusively) the NCBs of the Member States whose currency is the euro, operating under the principle of decentralisation.[2]

(2) As already noted,[3] the SSMR confers on the ECB an extensive range of **'specific tasks'** in relation to credit institutions and other supervised entities incorporated in participating Member States, which cover principal areas of

---

[1] SSMR, Article 2, point (9), and Article 6(1), first sentence. Carletti, Dell'Ariccia and Marquez (2016) (correctly) use the term "hub and spokes" supervisory regime.

[2] TFEU, Article 282(1), second sentence and ESCB/ECB Statute, Article 1, first sub-paragraph, second sentence. On this principle, see Priego and Conlledo (2015), who describe it as "one of the essential defining features of the ESCB's legal framework". See also Krauskopf and Steven (2009), pp. 1159–1161. It is noted that NCAs, unlike NCBs, are not referred to in the Treaties.

[3] See Box 6.3 in Chapter 6 above.

microprudential, and specific areas of macroprudential regulation, as "exclusively" set out in **Articles 4(1)** and **5(2)**, respectively.[4] The ECB has been assigned these tasks under the CRR, the CRD IV and the BRRD (namely its provisions on recovery planning and early intervention measures[5]). In this respect, the SSMR sets out the following general principles:

> *first*, when carrying out its tasks under the SSMR, and without prejudice to the objective of ensuring the safety and soundness of credit institutions, the ECB must have full regard to the different types, business models and sizes of credit institutions, as well as the systemic benefits of diversity in the banking industry of the EU;
> *second*, no ECB action, proposal or policy should, directly or indirectly, discriminate against any Member State or group of Member States as a venue for the provision of banking or financial services in any currency; and
> *third*, the provisions of the SSMR are without prejudice to the responsibilities and related powers of the NCAs of participating Member States to carry out supervisory tasks not conferred on the ECB, as well as to the responsibilities and related powers of the NCAs or NDAs of participating Member States to apply macroprudential tools not foreseen in relevant acts of European banking law (in particular in the CRR and the CRD IV).[6]

Supervisory tasks not included in the list of these 'specific tasks' have not been conferred on the ECB; they fall within NCA competences. These include, *inter alia*, the power to receive notifications from credit institutions in relation to the right of establishment and the freedom to provide services; carrying out day-to-day verifications of credit institutions; and the exercise of the function of a competent authority over credit institutions in relation to markets in financial instruments, the prevention of the use of the financial system for the purpose of money laundering and terrorist financing, as well as consumer protection.[7]

---

[4] These Articles are discussed in detail in Volume II. For an early analysis of the limits of the SSM, see Ferrarini (2015).

[5] BRRD, Articles 5–9 and 27–30, respectively; all already noted, these provisions are included in its 'crisis prevention' regime.

[6] SSMR, Article 1, third-sixth sub-paragraphs and recital (17); see Ohler (2022), pp. 1–13.

[7] *Ibid.*, recital (28). As regards credit institutions established in non-participating Member States, which have opened branches or provide cross-border services (without establishment) in a participating Member State pursuant to Articles 35–39 CRD IV, the ECB must carry out its supervisory tasks (within the scope of Article 4(1)) if the national authorities are competent as *host Member State supervisors* pursuant to Articles 40–46 CRD IV (*ibid.*, Article 4(2)); see Lackhoff and Witte (2022), pp. 64–66. For a comparison between the SSM and the Anti-Money Laundering framework, see Lo Schiavo (2022).

It is noted that, when examining the operational efficiency of the ECB's management under **Article 27.2 ESCB/ECB Statute**, the **ECA** (governed by **Articles 285–287 TFEU**[8]) must, *inter alia*, take also into account the ECB supervisory tasks.[9]

8.1.2 Organisational Principles: The New Governance Structure

8.1.2.1 General Overview

The organisational principles (or more accurately aspects) of the SSM are laid down in Chapter IV (Articles 19–31 SSMR). They can be classified into 5 groups: the *first* contains **Articles 24–26** on the Supervisory Board, the Mediation Panel and the Administrative Board of Review ('**ABoR**'), which constitute new elements in the ECB governance structure, as well as rules on the internal structure of the ECB regarding its supervisory tasks and the composition of Eurosystem/ESCB Committees; the *second* comprises three Articles on independence: **Article 19** on the institutional independence of the ECB and the NCAs, and **Articles 28–30** on the ECB's financial independence; the *third* group contains **Articles 20–21** on the accountability of the ECB *vis-à-vis* the European Parliament, the Council and the national parliaments of participating Member States; *fourth*, **Article 22** deals with the aspect of due process for adopting supervisory Decisions; finally, the *fifth* group includes the Articles referring to the reporting of violations (**Article 23**); the professional secrecy of Supervisory Board members and ECB staff when carrying out the ECB supervisory tasks and the exchange of information (**Article 27**); and the exchange and secondment of staff, under the responsibility of the ECB, with and among NCAs (**Article 31**).[10]

8.1.2.2 The Supervisory Board
Introductory Remarks
The 'planning and execution' of the ECB supervisory tasks have been assigned to the Supervisory Board.[11] The functioning of this *internal body* is mainly governed by **Article 26 SSMR** and several Articles of the SSM-FR; two ECB Decisions of 2014, the first amending the Rules of Procedure of the ECB (hereinafter the '**ECB Rules of Procedure**')[12] and the second on the

---

[8] On the ECA and these TFEU Articles, see Kennedy (2018), Lienbacher (2019), and Craig and de Búrca (2020), pp. 96–97.

[9] SSMR, Article 20(7).

[10] The provisions of these SSMR Articles are further detailed in the SSM-FR, several ECB legal acts and the EP-ECB Interinstitutional Agreement, as discussed below. For a detailed overview of the SSM's institutional aspects, see Wymeersch (2020).

[11] SSMR, Article 26(1), first sub-paragraph, first sentence; see also recital (67). For a detailed analysis of Article 26, see Gruber (2022), pp. 354–381.

[12] ECB Decision 2014/179/EU of 22 January "amending Decision ECB/2004/2 adopting the Rules of Procedure of the ECB" (ECB/2014/1) (OJ L 95, 29.3.2014,

appointment of representatives of the ECB to the Supervisory Board[13]; and the **Rules of Procedure of the Supervisory Board** supplementing the ECB Rules of Procedure.[14] Also applicable are the following: the 2022 **Code of Conduct for high-level ECB Officials** (further discussed below); the provisions of **Section II** of the EP-ECB Interinstitutional Agreement on the selection procedures for the Supervisory Board members; and the provisions of Section II of the MoU between the Council and the ECB (the '**Council-ECB MoU**') on the procedure for the selection and appointment of the Supervisory Board's Chair.

The Supervisory Board is not an ECB Decision-making body, like the GC and the Executive Committee; this would have required an amendment to **Article 282(2) TFEU**. The **ECB Rules of Procedure** clarify that any tasks of the Supervisory Board shall be without prejudice to the competences of the ECB Decision-making bodies.[15]

Composition

The Supervisory Board is composed of a Chair and a Vice-Chair, four ECB representatives appointed by its GC, and one representative of the NCA in each participating Member State; all have to act in the interest of the EU (which, *mutatis mutandis*, mirrors the composition of the GC). In those (participating) Member States where the NCA is not the NCB,[16] the Supervisory Board member may decide to bring a representative from the NCB; however, for the purposes of voting (further discussed below), the representatives of each Member State's authorities are cumulatively considered as one member.[17] A representative of the Commission may participate, as an observer, in the meetings of the Supervisory Board upon invitation, albeit without access to confidential information relating to individual institutions.[18] Furthermore, for the purposes of the SRMR, the ECB may invite the SRB

---

pp. 56–63); its legal basis are Articles 25(2) and 26(12) SSMR. The new Articles 13a–13o of the ECB Rules of Procedure explicitly refer to the supervisory tasks of the ECB and Article 17a to its legal instruments related to these tasks. The ECB Rules of Procedure have been subsequently further amended; the current consolidated version is available at: https://eur-lex.europa.eu/legal-content/EN/TXT/?uri=CELEX%3A02004D0002-20160924.

[13] ECB Decision 2014/427/EU of 6 February "on the appointment of representatives of the ECB to the Supervisory Board" (ECB/2014/4) (OJ L 196, 3.7.2014, pp. 38–39), adopted on the basis of Article 26(1)–(2) and (5) SSMR.

[14] OJ L 182, 21.6.2014, pp. 56–63; these were adopted on the basis of Article 26(12) SSMR.

[15] ECB Rules of Procedure, Article 13a, second sentence.

[16] See Table 8.1 below.

[17] SSMR, Article 26(1); see also recital (68).

[18] *Ibid.*, Article 26(11). An EBA representative is not listed in this Article, as was provided for in the Commission's proposal. However, in accordance with recital (70), second and third sentences the perimeter of observers can be wider: "*In order to ensure full coordination with the activities of EBA and with the prudential policies of the Union, the Supervisory Board should be able to invite EBA and the Commission as observers. The*

Chair to participate as an observer in the Supervisory Board; this, however, is noted provided for in the SSMR but in the SRMR.[19]

Appointment of the Chair and the Vice-Chair—selection Procedures

The SSMR provisions: The Chair and the Vice-Chair are appointed by an implementing Decision of the Council acting by qualified majority, without taking into account the vote of its members which are non-participating Member States. This Decision is adopted upon an ECB proposal, submitted, after hearing the Supervisory Board, to the European Parliament for approval. The appointments must respect the principles of gender balance, experience and qualification.

The Chair is chosen on the basis of an open selection procedure—on which the European Parliament and the Council must be kept duly informed—from among individuals of recognised standing and experience in banking and financial matters which are not GC members. To allow for an appropriate rotation, the Chair's term of office is confined to five years and cannot be renewed. Once appointed, he/she shall be a full-time professional, not allowed to hold any offices at NCAs. The Vice-Chair is chosen from among the members of the ECB Executive Board.[20]

The provisions of Section II of the EP-ECB Interinstitutional Agreement: The above provisions of the SSMR are further specified in **Section II** of the EP-ECB Interinstitutional Agreement as follows:

> *First*, the ECB must specify and make public the criteria for the Chair's selection, including the balance of skills, knowledge of financial institutions and markets and experience in financial supervision and macroprudential oversight. In specifying these criteria, it must aim at the highest professional standards and consider the need to safeguard the EU interest and diversity in the Supervisory Board's composition. The European Parliament's competent Committee (**ECON**) must be informed two weeks before the GC publishes the vacancy notice of the selection criteria, the specific job profile and the open selection procedure to be applied for the Chair's selection. It must also be informed of the composition of the pool of applicants for the position and of the method for screening the pool of applicants to draw up a shortlist of candidates.

Chair of the European Resolution Authority, once established, should participate as observer in the meetings of the Supervisory Board".

[19] SRMR, Article 30(4); see also Chapter 9 below, under 9.2.3. On the composition of the Supervisory Board as of December 2022, see at: https://www.ecb.europa.eu/ecb/orga/decisions/ssm/html/index.en.html. There is no information therein as to current status of observers.

[20] SSMR, Article 26(2)–(3); see also recital (69).

Furthermore, this shortlist must be provided by the ECB to the ECON at least three weeks before it submits its proposal for the Chair's appointment. The ECON may submit questions to the ECB on the selection criteria and candidate shortlist within a week from receiving it and the ECB must respond to those in writing within two weeks. The European Parliament must decide on the approval of the candidate proposed by the ECB for Chair and Vice-Chair through a vote in the ECON and in the plenary within six weeks of the proposal. If the proposal for the Chair is not approved, the ECB may decide to draw on the pool of candidates that originally applied for the position, or to re-initiate the selection process.

The provisions of Section II of the Council-ECB Memorandum of Understanding (MoU): The SSMR provisions regarding the selection and appointment of the Chair are also further specified in the Council-ECB MoU. *Inter alia*, it provides that the Council must be informed by the GC two weeks before the latter publishes the vacancy notice of the details of the open selection procedure to be applied for the selection, as well as of the composition of the pool of applicants for the Chair's position and the method for screening the pool of applicants to draw up a shortlist of candidates. This shortlist must be provided by the ECB to the Council at least three weeks before it submits its formal proposal for the Chair's appointment to the European Parliament for approval.[21]

Removal

For the sake of his/her personal independence, the Chair may be removed from office only under two conditions: if he/she no longer fulfils the conditions required for the performance of his/her duties *or* has been guilty of serious misconduct. The relevant implementing Decision is adopted by the Council (acting by qualified majority, without taking into account the vote of its members which are non-participating Member States) following an ECB proposal approved by the European Parliament. The Vice-Chair may be removed from office, if he/she compulsorily retires as a member of the Executive Board,[22] the material conditions being the same as those for the removal of the Chair. The relevant implementing Decision is taken, in this case as well, by the Council and under the same procedural conditions. For these purposes, the European Parliament or the Council may inform the ECB that they consider the conditions for the removal of the Chair or Vice-Chair

---

[21] Council-ECB MoU, Section II, first-fifth points.

[22] In accordance with Article 11.4 ESCB/ECB Statute: "*If a member of the Executive Board no longer fulfils the conditions required for the performance of his duties or if he has been guilty of serious misconduct, the Court of Justice may, on application by the GC or the Executive Board, compulsorily retire him*".

from office to be fulfilled, to which the ECB must respond in writing within four weeks.[23]

Appointment and Removal of the Four ECB Representatives
The appointment and removal of the four representatives of the ECB as members of the Supervisory Board are governed by the following rules[24]:

> *First*, they are appointed by the GC from among persons of recognised standing and experience in banking and financial matters. Their term of office is five years and not renewable.[25]
>
> *Second*, in accordance with the terms and conditions of their employment, which are set out in a contract with the ECB and are fixed by the GC on a proposal from the Executive Board, they must perform their duties on a full-time or part-time basis, are not allowed to perform any duty for an NCA and may not be engaged in any occupation, whether gainful or not, unless authorised by the GC. No authorisation may be given for activities which are liable *or* may be perceived to give rise to a conflict of interest with their positions as Supervisory Board members, especially if directly related to the ECB monetary policy tasks.[26]
>
> *Third*, if any ECB representative no longer fulfils the conditions required for the performance of his/her duties or if he/she has been guilty of serious misconduct, the GC may, on application of the Executive Board and after having heard him/her, decide his/her removal from office. Any vacancy is filled by the appointment of a new representative.

Supporting Structures: The Steering Committee and the Secretariat
The Steering Committee: The Supervisory Board must set up from among its members a Steering Committee, in accordance with **Article 9** of its Rules of Procedure, to support its activities. This Committee is chaired by the Supervisory Board' Chair or, in his/her absence, the Vice-Chair and has no decision-making powers. Its composition, consisting of no more than ten members (including the Chair, the Vice-Chair and one additional representative from the ECB), must ensure a fair balance and rotation between NCAs. The Steering Committee must execute its tasks in the interest of the EU and work in full transparency with the Supervisory Board.[27]

---

[23] SSMR, Article 26(4), first-third sub-paragraphs, EP-ECB Interinstitutional Agreement, Section II, eight-tenth point and (on the last aspect) Council-ECB MoU, Section II, sixth point.

[24] ECB Decision 2014/427/EU, Article 1(1)–(6).

[25] Exceptionally, the term of office of the four ECB representatives for the initial appointment was between three and five years.

[26] On this latter aspect, see also SSMR, Article 26(5), first sentence.

[27] *Ibid.*, Article 26(10). Chapter II of the Rules of Procedure of the Supervisory Board further specifies the SSMR provisions on the Steering Committee's mandate (Article 10)

The Secretariat: The activities of the Supervisory Board are supported by a Secretariat. Secretary of the Supervisory Board (and of the Steering Committee) is appointed a member of the ECB staff, who is responsible for assisting the Chair or, in his/her absence, the Vice-Chair in preparing the Supervisory Board meetings and for drafting their proceedings.[28]

Provisions on Decision-Making
In principle, Decisions of the Supervisory Board are taken by a simple majority of its members, with each member (including the ECB representatives) having one vote. In case of a draw, the Chair has a casting vote. *Exceptionally*, Regulations under **Article 4(3)**[29] are adopted by qualified majority of its members (in accordance with **Article 16(4) TEU**); in this case, each ECB representative has a vote equal to the median vote of the other members.[30]

Duties
General provisions: Since responsible for taking Decisions is ultimately the GC, without prejudice to **Article 6 SSMR** (on cooperation within the SSM), the Supervisory Board must carry out preparatory works regarding the ECB supervisory tasks and propose to the GC complete draft Decisions for adoption, which concurrently must be transmitted to the NCAs of the Member States concerned. The GC has the power either to adopt a draft Decision or to object to it under the following conditions: *first*, a draft Decision is deemed to have been adopted unless the GC objects within a period not exceeding a maximum period of ten working days (the '**no-objection procedure**'); in emergency situations, this period may not exceed 48 hours; *second*, if the GC objects to a draft Decision (e.g., by asking for amendments), its decision must be in writing and reasoned, in particular "*stating monetary policy concerns*".[31]

---

and composition and on the appointment of its members (Article 11) and contains specific provisions about its meetings (Article 12).

[28] SSMR, Article 26(9) and ECB Rules of Procedure, Article 13 m (3)–(4).

[29] See below, under 8.3.1.

[30] SSMR, Article 26(5), second sentence, (6) and (7). The voting modalities in this case are further specified in Article 13c and in the Annex of the ECB Rules of Procedure. Chapter I (Articles 2–8) of the Rules of Procedure of the Supervisory Board contains detailed provisions about its operation (convening of, attendance at and organisation of meetings, access to information, voting rules, action in emergency situations and delegation of power). In addition, pursuant to Article 13f (first sentence) of the ECB Rules of Procedure, the meetings must be normally held at the ECB premises.

[31] SSMR, Article 26(8), first-third and fifth-sixth sentences. The reference to "monetary policy concerns" is a clear indication of the concern not to undermine the objective(s) of monetary policy (which is further regulated by Article 25 setting out the principle of separation between the monetary policy and supervision functions of the ECB, due to the difference of their objectives; see below, under 8.5.2). Since, however, the sixth sentence makes an indicative reference ("in particular"), the GC may also raise objections relating to supervisory concerns; see Gruber (2022), pp. 377–378 with reference to Ohler (2015).

Provisions pertaining to non-euro area participating Member States: If a non-euro area participating Member State (which is not represented in the GC) disagrees with a Supervisory Board's draft Decision, applicable is the procedure set out in **Article 7(8) SSMR**, which may lead, *in extremis*, to the Member State concerned requesting the ECB to terminate the close cooperation. If a Decision is amended following an objection by the GC, the non-euro area participating Member State may notify the ECB of its reasoned disagreement with the objection. In such a case, applicable is the procedure set out in **Article 7(7)**, which may, also *in extremis*, lead to the suspension or termination of the close cooperation, upon an ECB initiative this time.[32]

The Code of Conduct for Supervisory Board Members as High-Level ECB Officials

(1) The GC should establish and publish a Code of Conduct for the ECB staff and management involved in banking supervision concerning (in particular) conflicts of interest.[33] This was adopted on 12 November 2014[34]; its provisions were then included in the single **"Code of Conduct for high-level ECB Officials"** of 5 December 2018,[35] which entered into force on 1 January 2019 and was repealed (in **2022**, with effect from 1 January 2023) by a new Single Code.[36] This primarily applies to the so-called "members", namely the members of the GC and of the Supervisory Board when exercising their functions as members of a high-level ECB body, to the members of the Executive Board, to members of the GC and of the Supervisory Board when acting as members of the Steering Committee and the Mediation Panel, where applicable, as well as to representatives of NCBs, where the NCA is not the NCB, participating in meetings of the Supervisory Board.[37] The high-level Ethics Committee[38] is mandated to advise the members of high-level ECB

---

[32] *Ibid.*, Article 26(8), fourth and seventh sentences and recital (72).

[33] *Ibid.*, Article 19(3). Pursuant to Section IV of the EP-ECB Interinstitutional Agreement, before adopting this Code, the ECB should inform the ECON on its main elements, and upon written request of the latter inform the Parliament in writing on its implementation and the need for updates.

[34] OJ C 93, 20.3.2015, pp. 2–7.

[35] OJ C 89, 8.3.2019, pp. 2–9.

[36] Code of Conduct for high-level ECB officials, 2022/C 478/03, OJ C 478, 16.12.2022, pp. 3–14.

[37] 'High-level ECB bodies' means the GC, the Executive Board and the Supervisory Board (Code of Conduct, Article 1.1). The Code also applies to persons replacing the members in meetings of the GC or the Supervisory Board (the "alternates") in the performance of their duties and responsibilities relating to these high-level bodies where explicitly provided for in the Code (*ibid.*, Article 1.2). The Code is without prejudice to stricter ethical rules applicable to members and alternates by virtue of national law (*ibid.*, Article 2.2).

[38] The establishment and the Rules of Procedure of this Committee are governed by ECB Decision (EU) 2015/433 of 17 December 2014 (ECB/2014/59) (OJ L 70, 14.3.2015, pp. 58–60); the principles are laid down in ECB Guideline (EU) 2015/856

bodies on any doubt relating to the provisions laid down in the Code or their practical application.[39]

(2) In accordance with Article 3, which sets out the basic principles, Members and alternates must carry out their duties and responsibilities in strict compliance with the Treaty, the ESCB/ECB Statute, the SSMR, the ECB Rules of Procedure and the Rules of Procedure of the Supervisory Board. In carrying them out they must observe the highest standards of ethical conduct and integrity; are expected to act honestly, independently and impartially, with discretion and without regard to self-interest; be mindful of the importance of their duties and responsibilities; take into account the public character of their functions; and conduct themselves in a way that inspires ethical conduct within the Eurosystem, the ESCB and the SSM, and maintains and promotes public trust in the ECB. **Articles 4–18** set specific standards of ethical conduct relating to professional secrecy, the separation of the supervisory function from the monetary policy function, independence and conflicts of interest.[40]

8.1.2.3 Internal Structure of the ECB with Regard to Its Supervisory Tasks and New Composition of Eurosystem/ESCB Committees: The Provisions of the ECB Rules of Procedure

Competent in respect of the ECB's internal structure and staff is the Executive Board.[41] This competence also covers the ECB's supervisory tasks; on such internal structure, the Executive Board must consult the Supervisory Board's Chair and Vice-Chair. In agreement with the Executive Board, the Supervisory Board may establish and dissolve 'temporary' sub-structures (working groups or task forces) to assist in the work regarding the supervisory tasks and report to it.[42] When assisting the ECB Decision-making bodies with its supervisory tasks, the Eurosystem/ESCB Committees must include one member from the NCB and one from the NCA of each participating Member State.[43]

---

of 12 March 2015 (ECB/2015/12) (OJ L 135, 2.6.2015, pp. 29–34). The former was adopted by virtue of Article 9a of the ECB Rules of Procedure and the latter by virtue of Article 6(1) and (7) SSMR.

[39] *Ibid.*, Article 1.6.

[40] The provisions relating to separation are further discussed under 8.5.2 below; on those relating to independence and conflicts of interest, see below, under 8.4.1.

[41] ECB Rules of Procedure, Articles 10–11.

[42] *Ibid.*, Article 13 m (1)–(2); paragraphs 3 and 4 refer to the Secretariat.

[43] *Ibid.*, Article 9.4 (as amended).

8.2 Division of Tasks Within the SSM and Cooperation Arrangements

8.2.1 The Two Components of the SSM

8.2.1.1 The ECB as the Main Actor

The SSMR introduced a 'vertical' transfer, from the Member States to the EU level, of specific tasks concerning policies relevant to the microprudential supervision of credit institutions with a view (as already noted in **Chapter 6**) to contributing to the safety and soundness of credit institutions and the stability of the financial system within the EU and each Member State.[44] Hence, as of 4 November 2014, the scope of the tasks of the ECB, which has legal personality according to **Article 282(3)**, first sentence **TFEU**, has been further broadened, consisting of:

first, the ECB's 'basic tasks' within the Eurosystem, as set out in **Article 127(2) TFEU**[45];

second, the other ECB tasks set out in the TFEU and the ESCB/ECB Statute;

third, the 'specific tasks' conferred on the ECB under **Article 2 of Council Regulation (EU) No 1096/2010** on the macroprudential oversight of the EU financial system in the context of the functioning of the ESRB; and

finally, the supervisory tasks conferred on the ECB by the SSMR.[46]

(2) Applicable to the ECB are (also) the following legislative acts[47]: *first*, by virtue of **Article 342 TFEU, Council Regulation No 1** (as in force) determining the languages to be used by the EEC[48]; *second*, with regard to the processing of personal data by the ECB for the purposes of the SSMR, two co-legislators' legislative acts[49]; and *third*, the co-legislators' **Regulation** concerning investigations conducted by the European Anti-Fraud Office

---

[44] See Chapter 6 above, under 6.3.2 (1).

[45] See Chapter 4 above, under 4.1.4.

[46] For a comprehensive analysis of the role of the ECB within the Eurosystem, the SSM and the other systems and mechanisms where it participates, see Lamandini, Ramos and Solana (2017) and Gortsos (2020), both with extensive further references. See also Lastra and Alexander (2020).

[47] SSMR, recitals (62) and (81)–(82).

[48] OJ 17, 6.10.1958, p. 385. On this TFEU Article and on that Council Regulation, see Gortsos (2022b).

[49] Regulation (EU) 2016/679 of 27 April 2016 "on the protection of natural persons with regard to the processing of personal data and on the free movement of such data (...) (General Data Protection Regulation)" (OJ L 119, 4.5.2016, pp. 1–88) ('GDPR'), and Regulation (EC) No 45/2001 of 18 December 2000 "on the protection of individuals with regard to the processing of personal data by the Community institutions and bodies and on the free movement of such data" (OJ L 8, 12.1.2001, pp. 1–22).

(widely known after the French acronym '**OLAF**'—Office Européen de Lutte Antifraude).[50]

8.2.1.2 The National Competent Authorities (NCAs)

NCAs are defined[51] to mean the authorities designated as such by the participating Member States in accordance with the CRR and the CRD IV. In most participating Member States these are their NCB[52]; however, seven[53] participating Member States have assigned by national law microprudential banking supervision to independent administrative authorities other than the NCB to separate monetary policy from banking supervisory tasks (see Table 8.1 just below).

8.2.2 The Regulatory Perimeter

8.2.2.1 The Perimeter in Respect of Different Types of Financial Firms

The assignment to the ECB of specific tasks in relation to the microprudential supervision of financial firms exclusively covers *first*, credit institutions[54]; *second*, 'financial holding companies', in the context of the conduct of consolidated supervision of banking groups; and *third*, 'mixed financial holding companies', in the context of the conduct of supplementary supervision on financial conglomerates. All these types of financial firms are included in the definition of the term '**supervised entities**'. This term also includes branches established in a participating Member State by a credit institution incorporated in a non-participating Member State, and CCPs that qualify as credit institutions under the CRD IV, without prejudice to their supervision by relevant national authorities under the EMIR.[55]

---

[50] The OLAF was established by virtue of Commission Decision 1999/352/EC, ECSC, Euratom of 28 April 1999 (OJ L 136, 31.5.1999, pp. 20–22). Of relevance is also Regulation (EU, Euratom) No 883/2013 of 11 September 2013 "concerning investigations conducted by the European Anti-Fraud Office (OLAF) and repealing Regulation (EC) No 1073/1999 (...)" (OJ L 248, 18.9.2013, pp. 1–22). On the basis of the repealed Regulation, the ECB adopted on 3 June 2004 Decision 2004/525/EC "concerning the terms and conditions for [OLAF] investigations of the [ECB] in relation to the prevention of fraud, corruption and any other illegal activities detrimental to the European Communities' financial interests and amending the Conditions of Employment for Staff of the [ECB]" (ECB/2004/11) (OJ L 230, 30.6.2004, pp. 56–60).

[51] SSMR, Article 2, point (2).

[52] See in this respect also the second sentence in Article 2, point (9) SSM-FR.

[53] As of 1 January 2023, the number is reduced to six, since the Latvian NCB (Latvijas Banka) is becoming the financial market supervisor (and resolution authority) in that Member State.

[54] As already noted in Chapter 6 (under 6.3.2 (1)), exempted are the credit institutions which are also exempted from the field of application of Article 2(5) CRD IV.

[55] SSM-FR, Article 2, point (20); see also Chapter 6 above, under 6.3.2 (1).

Table 8.1 National competent authorities (NCAs)—members of the Single Supervisory Mechanism (SSM)

Member state	NCA (NCB: national central bank)
Austria	Österreichische Finanzmarktaufsicht—FMA
Belgium	Nationale Bank van België/Banque Nationale de Belgique (**NCB**)
Bulgaria	Bulgarian National Bank (**NCB**)
Croatia	Hrvatska narodna banka (Croatian National Bank) (**NCB**)
Cyprus	Central Bank of Cyprus (**NCB**)
Estonia	Finantsinspektsioon
Finland	Finanssivalvonta—FIVA (Financial Stability Authority)
France	Banque de France (**NCB**)[56]
Germany	Bundesanstalt für Finanzdienstleistungsaufsicht—BaFin
Greece	Τράπεζα της Ελλάδος (Bank of Greece) (**NCB**)
Ireland	Central Bank of Ireland/Banc Ceannais na hÉireann (**NCB**)
Italy	Banca d'Italia (**NCB**)
Latvia	Finanšu un kapitāla tirgus komisija (Financial and Capital Market Commission)
	Latvijas Banka (**NCB**) (as of 1 January 2023)
Lithuania	Lietuvos bankas (**NCB**)
Luxembourg	Commission de Surveillance du Secteur Financier—CSSF
Malta	Malta Financial Services Authority—MFSA
Netherlands	De Nederlandsche Bank (**NCB**)
Portugal	Banco de Portugal (**NCB**)
Slovakia	Národná banka Slovenska (**NCB**)
Slovenia	Banka Slovenije (**NCB**)
Spain	Banco de España (**NCB**)

8.2.2.2 The Perimeter in Respect of Member States

The scope of the SSMR covers mainly and in principle credit institutions and other supervised entities incorporated in euro area Member States. Specific provisions apply also to branches established in participating Member States by credit institutions incorporated (and authorised) in non-participating Member States, and to credit institutions and other supervised entities incorporated in Member States with a derogation, which have established a 'close cooperation' according to **Article 7**.[57]

---

[56] It is noted that, even though in France the supervisory authority for the banking (and the insurance) sector is the ACPR, which is also representing France in the Basel Committee (see Chapter 3 above, under 3.1.4), in the Supervisory Board the national representative comes from the Banque de France, to which the ACPR is operationally attached.

[57] See further below, under 8.2.3.

8.2.2.3 The Perimeter in Respect of Credit Institutions and Other Supervised Entities

The SSMR established a 'two-tier system' with regard to the distribution of powers within the SSM, distinguishing between **'significant' and 'less significant'** supervised entities (for an overview of all relevant definitions, see Box 8.1 just below).[58] The provisions of **Article 6 SSMR** in this respect are further specified in the detailed provisions of **Articles 39–72 SSM-FR** (Part IV).

> **Box 8.1 Essential definitions regarding 'significant' and 'less significant supervised entities**[59]
>
> **'Significant supervised entity'**: a significant supervised entity in a euro area Member State, and a significant supervised entity in a non-euro area participating Member State.
>
> **'Significant supervised entity in a euro area Member State'**: a supervised entity established in a euro area Member State which has this status pursuant to an ECB Decision based on Article 6(4) SSMR, or on Article 6(5), point (b).
>
> **'Significant supervised entity in a participating non-euro area Member State'**: a supervised entity established in a non-euro area participating Member State which has the status of a significant supervised entity pursuant to an ECB Decision based on the same above (under (2)) Articles of the SSMR.
>
> **'Supervised group'**: any of the following:
>
> (a) a group whose parent undertaking is a credit institution or financial holding company with its head office in a participating Member State;
>
> (b) a group whose parent undertaking is a mixed financial holding company with its head office in a participating Member State, provided that the coordinator of the financial conglomerate, within the meaning of FICOD I, is an authority competent for the supervision of credit institutions and is also the coordinator in its function as supervisor of credit institutions.

---

[58] It is noted that the term 'significant credit institution', which is legally defined, is close, but not equivalent, to the more generic term SIFI (as discussed in Chapters 1 and 2 above).

[59] SSM-FR, Article 2, points (16), (17), (18), (21), (22) and (23), respectively.

> (c) supervised entities each having their head office in the same participating Member State, provided that they are permanently affiliated to a central body which supervises them under the conditions laid down in Article 10 CRR and is established in the same participating Member State.
>
> **'Significant supervised group'**: a supervised group which has this status following an ECB Decision based on Article 6(4) SSMR, or on Article 6(5), point (b).
> **'Less significant supervised group'**: a supervised group which does not have the status of a significant supervised group within the meaning of Article 6(4) SSMR.

(2) A supervised entity can be classified as significant on the basis of any of the following criteria[60]: *first*, its size (**'size criterion'**), if the total value of its assets exceeds 30 billion euro; *second*, its importance for the EU economy or the economy of a participating Member State (**'economic importance criterion'**); *third*, its significance with regard to cross-border activities (**'cross-border activities criterion'**), if it has established banking subsidiaries in more than one participating Member States, and its cross-border assets or liabilities represent a significant part of its total assets or liabilities; *fourth*, a request for or the receipt of *direct* public financial assistance from the EFSF or (henceforth) the ESM[61] (**'direct public financial assistance criterion'**); and *fifth*, the fact that it is one of the three most significant credit institutions (or groups) in each participating Member State.[62]

Supervised entities not meeting the above criteria are considered 'less significant' and are classified as such. These continue to be supervised directly by NCAs, within the framework of the SSM.[63] Significant supervised entities are directly supervised by the ECB, unless their supervision by NCAs is justified by **'particular circumstances'**.[64] Such circumstances exist if there are "*specific and factual circumstances*" leading to the classification of a significant supervised entity as less significant, taking into account the objectives and principles of the SSMR and, in particular, the need to ensure the consistent application of high supervisory standards.[65]

---

[60] SSMR, Article 6(4), second sub-paragraph and SSM-FR, Article 39(3).

[61] On the EFSF and the ESM, see Chapter 5 above, under 5.1.5.

[62] SSMR, Articles 6(4), first sub-paragraph.

[63] Applicable in this case are Articles 6(5)–(6) SSMR and 96–100 SSM-FR.

[64] SSM-FR, Article 39(4).

[65] Based on the list set up by the ECB on 4 September 2014, five credit institutions were classified as less significant under such circumstances (see at: https://www.bankingsupervision.europa.eu/banking/list/who/html/index.en.html).

(3) The ECB may also, on its own initiative or upon a request by an NCA, directly supervise a less significant supervised entity or group under a Decision adopted pursuant to **Article 6(5), point (b) SSMR** to the effect that it will directly exercise itself all relevant powers referred to in **Article 6(4)**. Such an entity or group is then classified as a significant supervised one.[66]

> **Box 8.2 The *Landeskreditbank Baden-Württemberg—Förderbank v ECB* case**
>
> (1) Of significant importance in this context is the judgment of the General Court of 16 May 2017 in **Case T-122/15**, *Landeskreditbank Baden-Württemberg—Förderbank v European Central Bank*.[67] This German credit institution, which is an investment and development bank and a legal person governed by public law and wholly owned by the German State (Land) of Baden-Württemberg, was classified by the ECB as significant on the basis of the size criterion, since the value of its assets exceeded 30 billion euro by virtue of Article 6(4) SSMR.[68] Accordingly, it became subject to direct supervision by the ECB.
>
> (2) The bank brought before the General Court an action for the annulment of the contested ECB Decision, putting forward five pleas in law: *first*, infringement of Article 6(4) SSMR and Article 70 of the SSM Framework Regulation in the choice of criteria applied by the ECB; *second*, manifest errors of assessment of the facts; *third*, infringement of the obligation to state reasons; *fourth*, misuse of powers arising from

---

[66] SSM-FR, Article 39(5). Specific provisions apply in respect of branches of credit institutions incorporated in non-participating Member States and of subsidiaries of credit institutions incorporated in non-participating Member States and third countries; on the procedure for classifying supervised entities as significant and for determining their significance; as well as on the beginning and end of direct supervision by the ECB, including the reasons for ending such direct supervision (*ibid.*, Articles 41–47). Article 6 SSMR and the related provisions of the SSM-FR related are discussed in more detail in Volume II. On Article 6(4)–(6), see Gortsos (2022a), pp. 104–133 (with extensive further references) and in particular on Article 6(5), point (b), pp. 127–131.

[67] ECLI:EU:T:2017:337.

[68] The initial ECB Decision was taken on 1 September 2014. In its Opinion of 20 November 2014, the ABOR found this Decision lawful and on 5 January 2015 the ECB adopted Decision ECB/SSM/15/1 ('the contested decision'), which repealed and replaced the decision of 1 September 2014, while maintaining the applicant's classification as a significant entity; see CJEU Decision, paras 4–7.

the ECB's failure to exercise its discretion[69]; and *fifth*, infringement by the ECB of its obligation to take into consideration all the relevant circumstances of the case.

(3) In its judgment, the General Court rejected all five pleas (the fifth as unfounded) and, accordingly, dismissed the action brought by the Landeskreditbank in its entirety.[70] The first plea was rejected, *inter alia*, on the basis that, under the relevant provisions of the SSMR and the SSM Framework Regulation, a credit institution must be classified as a 'significant entity' and therefore become subject to the direct supervision of the ECB, *inter alia*, where the value of its assets exceeds 30 billion euros. Its classification as significant may be avoided only if there are 'particular circumstances' entailing that the direct prudential supervision by NCA is *better able* to attain the objective of financial stability protection and to ensure the consistent application of high supervisory standards. In this context, the Court highlighted the following[71]:

> "The exercise by NCAs of direct prudential supervision of LSIs is overseen by the ECB, which, under Article 6(5)(a) and (b) [SSMR], has the competence to communicate to those authorities 'regulations, guidelines or general instructions to national competent authorities, according to which the tasks defined in Article are performed' and, moreover, to remove authority from a national authority and to decide to exercise directly itself all the relevant powers for one or more credit institutions".

(4) Most importantly, when discussing the first plea, the General Court pointed out that, from the examination of the interaction between Article 4(1) and Article 6 SSMR, it is apparent that:

> "The logic of the relationship between them consists in allowing the exclusive competences delegated to the ECB to be implemented within a "decentralised framework", rather than having a distribution of competences between the ECB and the NCAs in the performance of the tasks referred to in Article 4(1)."

Similarly, under Article 6(4), second sub-paragraph, the ECB has exclusive competence for determining the 'particular circumstances' in which direct supervision of an entity which should fall solely under its supervision might instead be under the supervision of an NCA. According to the Court, this finding is supported by the reading of recitals (15), (28)

---

[69] For a more general and comprehensive overview of EU Courts' review of administrative discretion, see Mendes (2016).

[70] CJEU Decision, paras 100, 112, 136, 142 and 150, respectively.

[71] *Ibid.*, par. 24.

and (38)–(40), noting that the arrangement of the latter suggests that direct prudential supervision by the NCAs under the SSM was envisaged by the Council as "*a mechanism of assistance to the ECB rather than the exercise of autonomous competence*".[72]

It also noted that the ECB retains important prerogatives even when NCAs perform the supervisory tasks laid down in Article 4(1), points (b) and (d)–(i) SSMR, the existence of which is indicative of the subordinate nature of the intervention by the national authorities in the performance of those tasks (with further analysis of the provisions of Article 6(5)). Furthermore, it considers that the competences conferred on the ECB are also evident from the comparison of the provisions allowing for adjustments to the criterion for distribution of the roles between the ECB and the NCAs relating to the size of the supervised entity (comparing Article 6(5), point (b) to Article 6(4), second subparagraph).[73] On the basis of the above, the Court concluded that the Council has delegated to the ECB exclusive competence in respect of the tasks laid down in Article 4(1) SSMR and in addition:

"*The sole purpose of Article 6 is to enable decentralised implementation under the SSM of that competence by the [NCAs], under the control of the ECB, in respect of the less significant entities and in respect of the tasks listed in Article 4(1)(b) and (d) to (i), whilst conferring on the ECB exclusive competence for determining the content of the concept of 'particular circumstances' within the meaning of Article 6(4), second subparagraph, which was implemented through the adoption of Articles 70 and 71 of the SSM Framework Regulation*".[74]

(5) The General Count also rejected the second plea, in which the Landeskreditbank claimed that it should, *inter alia*, have been classified as a 'less significant' entity, because the objectives of the SSMR (namely ensuring financial stability, the safety and solidity of credit institutions and the protection of depositors) would be *sufficiently* achieved by being supervised by the German NCA (BaFin), given its low-risk profile by virtue of the practical impossibility of its finding itself in a situation of insolvency. In this respect, the Court noted that the applicant credit institution did not argue that the German authorities would be better able to attain these objectives than the ECB.[75]

---

[72] *Ibid.*, paras 54–58.

[73] *Ibid.*, paras 59–61 and 62, respectively.

[74] *Ibid.*, par. 63.

[75] *Ibid.*, paras 101–111. On this judgement, see Tröger (2017), Annunziata (2018) and (2019), pp. 3–13, Chiti (2019), pp. 129–130, Montemaggi (2020), Riso (2021) and Rosas (2021); on its interpretation by the German constitutional Court, see its judgement

8.2.3 Cooperation Arrangements

8.2.3.1 Cooperation Within the SSM

The ECB supervisory tasks must be exercised, according to **Article 6**, within the framework of the SSM, which consists of the ECB and the NCAs of the participating Member States, and the ECB has been assigned the responsibility for its *"effective and consistent functioning"*.[76] The ECB and the NCAs are subject to a 'duty of cooperation in good faith' and an obligation to exchange information.[77] The ECB is responsible for the direct prudential supervision of significant supervised entities and groups in participating Member States[78] according to the procedures set out in the SSM-FR, in particular in respect of the tasks and the composition of **JSTs**. Specific rules govern the role of NCAs in assisting the ECB, the exchange of information and compliance with fit-and-proper requirements for managers.[79] With regard to less significant supervised entities (and taking into account the rules of the SSM-FR) the ECB has also been granted a wide range of powers, even though, in principle, these are under the direct supervision of NCAs.[80]

8.2.3.2 'Close Cooperation' Between the ECB and the Competent Authorities of Member States with a Derogation

(1) Credit institutions and other supervised entities and groups incorporated in a non-participating Member State may become subject to the supervisory

---

of 30 July 2019 (2 BvR 1685/14, 2 BvR 2631/14) (at: https://www.bundesverfassungsgericht.de/SharedDocs/Entscheidungen/DE/2019/07/rs20190730_2bvr16851.html;jsessionid=4BB0A89EFCA84FFFBE41EE3FC025115C.1_cid392). It is noted that, with its judgement of 8 May 2019 in Case C-450/17 P (ECLI:EU:C:2019:372), the Court (First Chamber) dismissed in its entirety the appeal brought on 26 July 2017 by *Landeskreditbank Baden-Württemberg—Förderbank*, seeking to have set aside the above judgement of the General Court.

For legal standing in BU cases before the CJEU, see Simoncini (2020). On the judicial review in the SSM in general as of 2021, see the contributions in Zilioli and Wojcik (2021, editors) at pp. 235–365 (some of which are discussed in this Chapter) and in particular Lehmann (2021), on jurisdiction, *locus standi* and the circulation of judgments in the BU, as well as van Rijn (2022), pp. 417–591. Several other related judgements of the Court are further discussed in Volume II.

[76] The creation of the SSM (and the SRM0 can thus be viewed, within the EU's multi-level system of governance, through the lens of the "integrated administration", which is a form of cooperation among national and supranational administrations. See on this Hofmann and Turk (2007). On this integrated administration and the mismatches in jurisdiction, see Simoncini (2021).

[77] SSMR, Article 6(1) and (2), first sub-paragraph, and SSM-FR, Articles 20–21. See on this Gortsos (2022a), pp. 98–100 and 102–103.

[78] SSM-FR, Article 39(4).

[79] *Ibid.*, Articles 89–94.

[80] The rules governing the JSTs (Articles 3–6 SSM-FR), and all the other aspects referred to in this paragraph are further analysed in Volume II. See on this Della Negra and Lo Schiavo (2022).

authority of the ECB under the provisions of the SSMR once a 'close cooperation', as provided for in **Article 7**, has been established. The close cooperation between the ECB and the NCA of a non-euro area participating Member State is established by an ECB Decision if the requirements laid down in **Article 7(2)** are met; the ECB may, to that end, address Instructions to the NCA or the NDA of the participating Member State whose currency is not the euro.[81] This procedure is also governed by **Articles 106–119 SSM-FR** and by **ECB Decision 2014/434/EU**,[82] **Article 4** of which refers to the assessment by the ECB of a request to that effect.

(2) Upon the establishment of a close cooperation, the ECB may carry out its specific tasks in relation to supervised entities and groups established in the relevant non-euro area participating Member State in accordance with **Article 6 thereof**.[83] The first two Member States which resorted to Article 7 and joined the SSM (and the SRM) since October 2020 are Bulgaria and Croatia.[84]

(3) The ECB may decide to issue a Warning to a non-euro area participating Member State that the close cooperation will be suspended or terminated if it deems that the conditions set out in **Article 7(2), points (a)–(c)** are no longer met by that Member State, or the NCA does not act in accordance with the obligation referred to in **point (c)**. If no decisive corrective action has been taken by the Member State concerned within fifteen days after the notification of such a Warning, the ECB may decide to suspend or terminate a close cooperation.[85]

---

[81] SSMR, Article 7(1).

[82] Decision 2014/434/EU of 31 January 2014 "on the close cooperation with the [NCAs] of participating Member States whose currency is not the euro" (ECB/2014/5), OJ L 198, 5.7.2014, pp. 7–13. The current consolidated version of that Decision is available at: https://eur-lex.europa.eu/legal-content/EN/TXT/?uri=CELEX%3A02014D0445-20210101. For possible lessons on close cooperation within the SSM that can be learned by drawing from the framework governing the ESAs, see Moloney (2019).

[83] SSMR, Article 7(1), first sub-paragraph and SSM-FR, Article 107(1).

[84] At: https://www.bankingsupervision.europa.eu/press/pr/date/2020/html/ssm.pr200710~ae2abe1f23.en.html and https://www.bankingsupervision.europa.eu/press/pr/date/2020/html/ssm.pr200710_1~ead3942902.en.html, respectively. On 12 July 2022, the Council formally approved the accession of Croatia to the euro area as of 1 January 2023; Croatia thus becomes its 20th Member State (see Council Decision (EU) 2022/1211 of 12 July 2022 "on the adoption by Croatia of the euro on 1 January 2023", adopted on the basis of Article 140(2) TFEU (OJ L 187, 14.7.2022, pp. 31–34). It also determined a Croatian kuna conversion rate of 7.53450 per euro. Hence, as of 1 January 2023, Article 7 does not apply to Croatia.

[85] SSMR, Article 7(5). The Member State may also terminate the close cooperation under the conditions set out in Article 7(6)–7(9).

Box 8.3 The application of other provisions of the SSM-FR on close cooperation
Articles 109–115 and 117 SSM-FR provide that its other provisions also apply, *mutatis mutandis*, when a close cooperation is established, as follows:

(1) The provisions of **Part II** (Articles 3–18) on the organisation of the SSM and **Part VI** (Articles 89–95) on the procedures for the supervision of significant supervised entities apply to significant supervised entities and significant supervised groups established in non-euro area participating Member States in accordance with **Article 115(2)–(5)**. In addition, **Article 116** lays down specific procedural rules on decisions that NCAs may adopt, only upon the ECB's instructions, in respect of significant supervised entities and significant supervised groups in such a case.
(2) The only provisions of **Part III** (Articles 19–38) which apply to NCAs of non-euro area participating Member States are those of **Article 23** on the language regime (**Article 109**).
(3) The provisions of **Part IV** (Articles 39–72) on the determination of the status of supervised entities or supervised groups as significant or less significant apply in respect of supervised entities and supervised groups in non-euro area participating Member States in accordance with **Article 110(2)–(3)**.
(4) The provisions of **Part V** (Articles 73–88) on 'common procedures' apply in respect of supervised entities and supervised groups in non-euro area participating Member States, subject to **Article 111(2)–(4)**. These common procedures refer to the granting and withdrawal of authorisation of credit institutions, and the assessment of notifications of the acquisition and disposal of qualifying holdings in credit institutions.
(5) The provisions of **Part VII** (Articles 96–100) on the procedures for the supervision of less significant supervised entities apply to less significant supervised entities and less significant supervised groups in non-euro area participating Member States in accordance with **Article 117(2)–(3)**.
(6) The provisions of Part **VIII** (Articles 101–105) on cooperation between the ECB, the competent and designated national authorities with regard to macroprudential tasks and tools apply in respect of supervised entities and supervised groups in non-euro area participating Member States (**Article 112**).
(7) The provisions of **Part X** (Articles 120–137) on administrative penalties apply in respect of supervised entities and supervised

> groups in non-euro area participating Member States, subject to **Article 113(2)–(3)**.
>
> (8) Finally, the provisions of **Part XI** (Articles 138–146) relating to cooperation with regard to **Articles 10–13 SSMR** apply in respect of supervised entities and supervised groups in non-euro area participating Member States subject to the provisions of **Article 114(2)–(4)**.[86]

8.2.3.3 Cooperation Outside the SSM and the ESFS

Cooperation with competent authorities of non-participating Member States: The SSMR imposes on the ECB to closely cooperate with the competent authorities of non-participating Member States. To that end, it must conclude with them an **MoU** describing, in general terms, the modalities of this cooperation in the performance of their supervisory tasks under EU banking law in relation to supervised entities, as well as an MoU with the competent authorities of non-participating Member States which are home to at least one **G-SII**. Each MoU must be reviewed on a regular basis and be published, subject to appropriate treatment of confidential information.[87]

Cooperation with the SRB and NRAs: The ECB must also closely cooperate with the SRB and NRAs, *inter alia*, in the preparation of resolution plans (according to **Articles 10–14 BRRD**) in particular in the context of the cross-border crisis management groups, and the resolution colleges established for this purpose.[88]

Cooperation with public financial assistance facilities: Finally, the ECB must closely cooperate with public financial assistance facilities, including the EFSF and the ESM, in particular if such a facility has granted or is likely to provide, directly or indirectly, financial assistance to a supervised entity.[89] This cooperation requirement is subject to **Articles 1, 4** and **6**[90]; accordingly, the ECB's objectives and specific tasks and the principles on the cooperation within the SSM should not be compromised.

---

[86] For a detailed analysis of Article 7, see Ohler (2022), pp. 133–141; on the judicial review of ECB Instructions under this Article, see Pizzolla (2021), pp. 345–361.

[87] SSMR, Article 3(6); see also recitals (14) and (42), first and second sentences.

[88] *Ibid.*, Article 3(4); see also recital (27), third and fourth sentences.

[89] According to Article 6(4) (fourth sub-paragraph), any supervised entity for which direct public financial assistance has been requested or which has received such assistance from the EFSF, or the ESM is classified as significant and comes under the direct supervision of the ECB; see also above, under 8.2.2.

[90] *Ibid.*, Article 3(5).

8.2.3.4 In Particular: The SSM as Part of the European System of Financial Supervision (ESFS)

As already noted, the SSMR and (its twin) **Regulation (EU) No 1022/2013** were aimed at incorporating the SSM within the ESFS and, thus, in 2014 the ECB became a part of the ESFS as regards its supervisory tasks.[91] In this respect,

> it is called upon to closely cooperate with the ESAs, the ESRB and the other authorities forming part of the ESFS, which ensure an adequate level of regulation and supervision in the EU, i.e., the NCAs, as specified in the EU legal acts referred to in **Article 1(2) EBAR**. *In addition,* the ECB must carry out its supervisory tasks without prejudice to the competence and the tasks of the ESAs and the ESRB and, in particular, it is not permitted to take on the EBA's tasks. *Furthermore,* and as also already noted, for the purposes of the SSMR, the ECB participates in the EBA's BoS with a representative nominated by the Supervisory Board. *Finally,* if necessary, it must enter into MoUs with Member States' national authorities responsible for markets in financial instruments[92]; for the sake of accountability and transparency, such MoUs must be made available to the European Parliament, the Council and the NCAs of all Member States.[93]

8.2.3.5 International Cooperation

In relation to its supervisory tasks, the ECB may develop contacts and enter into administrative arrangements with supervisory authorities, international organisations[94] and the administrations of third countries. This is without prejudice to the respective competences of the Member States and the other EU institutions and bodies, including the EBA, while appropriate coordination with the EBA is a prerequisite. It is specifically provided that such arrangements do not create legal obligations in respect of the EU and its Member States.[95]

---

[91] EBAR, Article 2(2), point (f), as amended by Article 1, point (2), of Regulation (EU) No 1022/2013; see also Chapter 7 above, under 7.1.1.

[92] These are designated in accordance with Article 67 MIFID II and are also part of the ESFS (through the ESMA). The Regulation does not specify any criteria on the basis of which to assess this necessity; nevertheless, from the phrasing of the relevant provision it can be concluded that it is up to the ECB to take the initiative.

[93] SSMR, Article 3(1)–(3) and recitals (31) and (33). Article 3 is analysed in Kaufhold (2022), pp. 23–27.

[94] In the author's view, the use of the term "international organisations" is not appropriate, since it could be read as excluding cooperation with international financial fora, such as the FSB and the BCBS. In line with Article 138 TFEU, it should be "international organisations and conferences". However, this wording has not prevented the SSM from already becoming a member of international fora.

[95] SSMR, Article 8 (and recital (80)); on this Article, see details in Ohler (2022), pp. 141–146.

8.3 Powers of the ECB and the NCAs

8.3.1 Regulatory Powers

8.3.1.1 Substantive Provisions: Article 4(3) SSMR—A First Reading

For the purpose of carrying out its tasks under the SSMR and with the objective of ensuring high standards of supervision, the ECB must apply *first*, all relevant legal acts which constitute sources of European banking law, i.e., co-legislators' legislative acts (**Article 289 TFEU**), as well as Commission delegated and implementing acts (**Articles 290–291 TFEU**) based on EBA's draft RTSs and ITSs (**Articles 10–15 EBAR**); and *second*, to the extent that this EU law is composed of Directives or Regulations, it must apply the *national legislation* either transposing those Directives or implementing Member States' options available under those Regulations; hence, the ECB is called upon to apply not only uniform EU law but also national law that incorporates EU banking law (namely, the CRD IV and the BRRD) that may vary among participating Member States.[96]

> To that effect, the ECB has been granted the power to adopt **Guidelines and Recommendations** and take **Decisions**. This regulatory power is subject to and must be compliant with the relevant EU banking law, including any legislative and non-legislative acts.[97] In particular, the ECB is subject to the following: **Articles 10–15 EBAR** on the RTSs and ITSs developed by the EBA and then adopted by the Commission in the form of delegated and implementing acts; **Article 16 EBAR** on EBA Guidelines and Recommendations; and the EBAR provisions on the European supervisory handbook. If deemed necessary, it must contribute to the development of draft RTSs and ITSs or draw the EBA's attention to a potential need to submit to the Commission draft standards amending existing ones. The ECB may also adopt (by qualified majority) **Regulations**[98] to the extent necessary in order to organise or specify the modalities for carrying out its tasks. Before adopting a Regulation, it

---

[96] *Ibid.*, Article 4(3), first sub-paragraph (reference to which is made in several other SSMR Articles); see also recital (34). According to Sarmiento (2022): *"As a result, an EU institution becomes the 'interpreter' and 'enforcer' of national law – but of a national law that is very closely connected to EU law"*. On this very important provision of the SSMR, which concerns the application of national law by the ECB within the SSM and is discussed, *inter alia*, also through the lens of the Crédit Agricole cases and the *Corneli v ECB* case (to be developed in Volume II), see (also) Boucon and Jaros (2017), Kornezov (2017), Annunziata (2019), pp. 16–28, D'Ambrosio (2020), pp. 131–138, Gagliardi and Wissink (2020), Gortsos (2021) and Lackhoff and Witte (2022), pp. 71–76.

[97] According to recital (34), last sentence: *"The ECB should, when adopting guidelines or recommendations or when taking decisions, base itself on, and act in accordance with, the relevant binding Union law"*. Its power to adopt them is based on Article 132(1) TFEU (carried over *verbatim* in Article 34 ESCB/ECB Statute), whereas the power to adopt Guidelines is based on Articles 12.1 ESCB/ECB Statute.

[98] See above, under 8.1.2 (on decision-making in the Supervisory Board).

must, for the sake of transparency, conduct open public consultations and conduct a related costs-benefit analysis, unless such consultations and such analysis are disproportionate in relation to the scope and impact of the Regulation concerned or the urgency of the matter (to be justified).[99]

In addition, with regard to less significant credit institutions, the ECB has the power to issue **Regulations, Guidelines or general Instructions** to NCAs, relating to the performance by them of the tasks defined in Article 4(1), excluding points (a) and (c) on the common procedures and the adoption of supervisory Decisions. Such Instructions may refer to the specific powers set out in **Article 16(2)** for groups or categories of credit institutions for the purposes of ensuring the consistency of supervisory outcomes within the SSM.[100]

8.3.1.2 Procedural Provisions

Unless otherwise provided for in Regulations adopted by the ECB pursuant to the SSMR, applicable to the legal instruments related to its supervisory tasks, namely ECB Guidelines, Instructions and Decisions, is **Article 17a** of the **ECB Rules of Procedure**. According to this Article,[101] **ECB Guidelines** relating to its supervisory tasks in accordance with **Articles 4(3) and 6(5), point (a) SSMR** (as discussed above), are adopted by the GC, signed on its behalf by the President and then notified to NCAs by various means; the same procedure applies to reasoned **ECB Instructions** related to its supervisory tasks under **Article 6(5), point (a)**, which must state the reasons on which they are based.[102] **ECB Decisions** regarding supervised entities and entities having applied for authorisation to take up the business of credit institutions

---

[99] SSMR, Article 4(3), second-fourth sub-paragraphs (see Lackhoff and Witte (2022), pp. 76–85). Section V of the EP-ECB Interinstitutional Agreement provides that the ECB must duly inform the ECON of the procedures it has instituted for adopting Regulations, Decisions, Guidelines and Recommendations, which are subject to public consultation under Article 4(3) SSMR. In particular, it must inform it of the principles and kinds of indicators or information used in elaborating acts and policy recommendations aimed at enhancing transparency and policy consistency; transmit to the ECON the draft acts before the public consultation procedure's beginning, and, if the European Parliament submits comments, informally exchange views with it on such comments in parallel with the open public consultations; send to the ECON the adopted act; and regularly inform the European Parliament in writing about the need to update the adopted acts.

[100] SSMR, Article 6(5), point (a). The acts adopted by the ECB do not, in principle, create any rights or impose any obligations in non-participating Member States; recital (50) is explicit on this. On a taxonomy of ECB instruments available for banking supervision, see Bax and Witte (2019); on the judicial control of its regulatory powers in the framework of the SSM, see De Gregorio Merino (2021), pp. 340–343.

[101] ECB Rules of Procedure, Article 17a (1)–(4).

[102] This procedure also applies to reasoned ECB Instructions related to Article 6(3) on the responsibility of NCAs to assist the ECB; Article 7(1) and (4) on the establishment of a close cooperation; Article 9(1) on the ECB supervisory and investigatory powers; and Article 30(5) on the right of NCAs to levy supervisory fees.

under **Article 14 SSMR** are adopted by the GC, signed on its behalf by the President and then notified to the persons to whom they are addressed.

8.3.1.3 Due Process for Adopting Supervisory Decisions[103]
ECB Supervisory Procedures
General principles and rules:[104] Any ECB supervisory procedure initiated in accordance with **Articles 4** (but not 5) and **14–18** SSMR must be carried out in accordance with **Article 22 SSMR** and **Articles 25–32 SSRM-FR** (which do not apply to procedures carried out by the ABoR). Parties to an ECB supervisory procedure are those making an application, and those to which the ECB intends to address or has already addressed a supervisory Decision; NCAs are exempted. A party may be represented by its legal or statutory representatives or by any other representative empowered by written mandate to take actions relating to that procedure. If an ECB supervisory procedure is initiated *ex officio*, the ECB must in principle determine the facts relevant for adopting its final Decision and, in its assessment, take account of all relevant circumstances; subject to EU law, a party must participate in an ECB supervisory procedure and provide assistance to clarify the facts. In procedures initiated at a party's request, the ECB may limit its determination of the facts to requesting it to provide the relevant factual information.[105]

Right to be heard: Before taking supervisory Decisions according to **Articles 4** and **14–18 SSMR**, the ECB must, in principle, give the persons subject of the proceedings the right to be heard. *Exceptionally*, if urgent action is needed to prevent significant damage to the financial system, it may adopt a 'provisional Decision' and give the persons concerned the opportunity to be heard as soon as possible thereafter.[106] The **SSM-FR** is more detailed on this.[107] It provides that, before adopting a supervisory Decision addressed to a party whose rights would be adversely affected, the ECB must give it the opportunity to comment in writing on the facts, objections and legal grounds relevant to that Decision (in a meeting if deemed appropriate). The relevant

---

[103] For more details on this aspect, see D'Ambrosio (2013) and Kaufhold (2022), pp. 307–318.

[104] SSM-FR, Articles 25–30.

[105] The ECB must make use of evidence as it deems appropriate to ascertain the facts of a case and, subject to EU law, the parties must assist it in this respect. If deemed necessary, it may also hear witnesses and experts; when an expert is appointed, the ECB must define his/her task in an agreement and set a time-limit for the submission of the relevant report. The ECB may require that the persons mentioned in Article 11(1) SSMR attend as witnesses in its offices or in any other place determined by it. If such a person is a legal person, it is the natural persons representing it who are obliged to attend.

[106] SSMR, Article 22(1); see also recital (54). See on this Article 41(2), point (a) of the Charter, analysed in Voet van Vormizeele (2019).

[107] SSM-FR, Article 31(1)–(5), which explicitly does not apply to Articles 10–13 SSMR on investigatory powers; on these Articles, see below, under 8.3.2.

ECB notification must mention the material content of the intended supervisory Decision, as well as the material facts, objections and legal grounds on which the ECB intends to base it.

Furthermore (by specifying the (above-mentioned SSMR provision), the SSM-FR provides that, in principle, the party must be given the opportunity to provide its comments within an (extendable) time-limit of two weeks following receipt of a statement setting out the facts, objections and legal grounds on which the ECB intends to base its supervisory Decision.[108] However, in cases of urgency and in order to prevent significant damage to the financial system, the ECB may exceptionally adopt a (provisional) supervisory Decision addressed to a party whose rights would be adversely affected without giving it the opportunity to comment on the relevant facts, objections and legal grounds prior to its adoption. In this case, the party must be given the opportunity to comment in writing, without undue delay, after its adoption.[109]

Right of access to ECB's files: The rights of defence of the persons concerned must be fully respected in the proceedings. These are entitled to have access to the ECB's files (except for confidential information), subject to the legitimate interest of other persons in the protection of their business secrets.[110] NCAs must forward to the ECB, without undue delay, any request received relating to the access to files relevant with its supervisory procedures. The files consist of all documents obtained, produced or assembled by the ECB during the supervisory procedure, irrespective of the storage medium. The ECB or NCAs cannot be prevented from disclosing or using the information necessary to prove an infringement.[111]

ECB Supervisory Decisions

ECB supervisory Decisions must be reasoned, be accompanied by a statement of reasons, which should contain the material facts and the legal reasons on

---

[108] Under particular circumstances and in the situations covered by Articles 14–15 SSMR and 120–137 SSM-FR (on the common procedures), the ECB may shorten the time-limit to three working days.

[109] These provisions do not apply to ECB supervisory procedures relating to administrative penalties pursuant to Article 18 SSMR (SSM-FR, Article 31(6)); on this SSMR Article, see below, under 8.3.5.

[110] SSMR, Article 22(2), first sub-paragraph; see also recital (59), which refers to (the above-mentioned) Article 15(3) TFEU, the second sub-paragraph of which refers to the above-mentioned Regulation (EC) No 1049/2001. To the best of the author's knowledge, this Regulation has not yet been amended to accommodate the provisions introduced by the SSMR. See also recital (63) SSMR, according to which: "*When determining whether the right of access to the file by persons concerned should be limited, the ECB should respect the fundamental rights and observe the principles recognised in the Charter (...), in particular the right to an effective remedy and to a fair trial*". This right is governed by (the above-mentioned) Article 47 of the Charter. For further analysis of this Article 47, see Krommendijk (2016) and Lock and Denis (2019).

[111] SSM-FR, Article 32(1)–(5).

which they are based, and be based only on facts and objections on which the parties concerned have been able to comment (subject to the above-mentioned **Article 31(4) SSM-FR** on provisional supervisory Decisions).[112] The ECB *may* decide that the application of a supervisory Decision has a suspensory effect either by stating it in the Decision, or on request of its addressee, in cases other than a request for review by the ABoR; this applies without prejudice to **Articles 278 TFEU** and **24(8) SSMR**.[113]

8.3.2 Investigatory Powers

8.3.2.1 General Overview

Articles 9–13 SSMR detail the ECB's investigatory powers, which are distinct from its specific and other supervisory powers under **Articles 14–16**.[114] In particular, **Article 9** contains some general principles on the powers of the ECB and their exercise, and the following **Articles 10–13** deal particularly with the investigatory powers of the ECB, including requests for the provision of information, the conduct of general investigations and the conduct of on-site inspections. Several provisions of these Articles are further specified in **Articles 138–139** and **141–146 SSM-FR** (Part XI). **Article 138** on the "cooperation between the ECB and NCAs as regards the powers referred to in Articles 10-13 SSMR" stipulates that these provisions apply to significant supervised entities, and to less significant supervised entities if the ECB decides, pursuant to **Article 6(5), point (d) SSMR**, to make use of the powers referred to in Articles 10–13 with respect to them. This is, however, without prejudice to the competence of NCAs to directly supervise less significant entities pursuant to **Article 6(6)**.[115]

8.3.2.2 Powers of the ECB and Their Exercise

(1) For the purposes of carrying out its supervisory tasks in accordance with **Articles 4((1)–(2)** *and* **5(2) SSMR**, the ECB is considered to be the NCA or (as appropriate) NDA in participating Member States, as stipulated in EU banking law; it also has all the powers and obligations set out in the SSMR, in particular, those in **Articles 10–18** and those which NCAs and NDAs have pursuant to EU banking law, unless otherwise provided for in the SSMR. Accordingly, the ECB is a fully-fledged competent and designated authority. The ECB may also request, by way of Instructions, NCAs and NDAs to make

---

[112] SSMR, Article 22(2), second sub-paragraph and SSM-FR, Article 33(1)–(3).

[113] SSM-FR, Article 34. Detailed provisions on the ways in which the ECB must notify its supervisory Decisions to the parties concerned are laid down in Article 35. On Article 278 TFEU, see Schwarze und Voet van Vormizeele (2019), pp. 2971–2979; On Article 24(8) SSRM, see below, under 8.5.1.

[114] See below, under 8.3.3.

[115] For a detailed analysis of Article 9, see Gruber (2022), pp. 14–147; on Articles 10–13, see Segoin (2021) and Lackhoff and Prokop (2022).

use of their powers under the following three conditions: it is necessary to carry out its tasks under the SSMR (in general); the conditions set out in national law are met; and the SSMR does not confer such powers on the ECB. The national authorities must fully inform the ECB about the exercise of such powers.[116] Their acts remain national acts.

(2) The ECB must exercise these powers in accordance with the legal acts referred to in **Article 4(3), first sub-paragraph**, as already discussed,[117] except with regard to credit institutions established in non-euro area participating Member States that have established a close cooperation, where the ECB must exercise its powers pursuant to **Article 7**. Furthermore, the ECB must closely cooperate with NCAs in the exercise of their respective supervisory and investigatory powers.[118]

8.3.2.3 *The Specific Investigatory Powers*[119]
Requests for the Provision of Information
(1) In order to carry out its supervisory tasks, the ECB has the right to require from specifically designated persons the provision of information. This is without prejudice to its powers under **Article 9(1)** and subject to the conditions set out in EU banking law and **Article 4** (on the tasks conferred upon it).[120] This requirement covers both *ad hoc* requests and those for the provision of information '**at recurring intervals**' and '**in specified formats**' for supervisory and related statistical purposes.

This rule is further specified in the **SSM-FR** as follows: *first*, the ECB must take account of information already available to NCAs before requiring the provision of information. It must then specify the information concerned and a reasonable time-limit within which it should be provided, as well as make available to the relevant NCA a copy of any information received from

---

[116] SSMR, Article 9(1); see also recital (45). On the legal review of ECB Instructions under this Article, see Hernández Saseta (2021).

[117] See above, under 8.3.1.

[118] SSMR, Article 9(2)–(3); on Article 7, see above, under 8.2.3.

[119] According to Article 138 SSM-FR, Articles 10–13 SSMR and 139–146 SSM-FR apply to significant, as well as to less significant supervised entities if the ECB decides, pursuant to Article 6(5), point (d) SSMR, to make use of the powers referred to in Articles 10–13 SSMR with respect to them, without prejudice to NCAs' competence to supervise those directly pursuant to Article 6(6) SSMR.

[120] SSMR, Article 10(1). The designated persons are the following: significant supervised entities (i.e., credit institutions, financial holding companies and mixed financial holding companies) established in participating Member States; as well as persons 'belonging' to these entities and third parties to whom these have outsourced functions or activities (see also recital (49)). The ECB is responsible for ensuring compliance with relevant EU law imposing requirements on credit institutions in the field of reporting to competent authorities. For this purpose, it has the tasks and powers regarding significant supervised entities as laid down in the relevant EU law on supervisory reporting, while NCAs have the tasks and powers regarding less significant supervised entities as laid down in relevant EU law on reporting to competent authorities (SSM-FR, Article 140(1)–(2)).

the legal or natural person to whom the request for information has been addressed.[121] *Second*, if the ECB requires legal or natural persons designated in **Article 10(1) SSMR** to provide information at recurring intervals, each supervised entity must communicate to its relevant NCA the information to be reported on a regular basis in accordance with relevant EU law. The ECB must organise the processes relating to collection and quality review of data reported by supervised entities subject to, and in compliance with relevant EU law and EBA ITSs.[122] *Third*, with regard to its power to require information to be provided at recurring intervals and 'in specified formats', it may require supervised entities to report *additional* supervisory information (if it considers that this is necessary to carry out its supervisory tasks) and specify in particular the categories of information to be reported, as well as the processes, formats, frequencies and time-limits for provision of the information concerned.[123]

(2) Since the provision of the information requested to the ECB is not deemed to be in breach of professional secrecy, the designated persons have a duty to supply it. The information obtained directly from these persons must be made available by the ECB to the NCAs concerned.[124]

Conduct of Investigations
(1) In order to carry out its supervisory tasks and subject to other conditions set out in EU banking law, the ECB has the power to conduct all necessary investigations of any person designated in **Article 10(1)**, established or located in a participating Member State. In this respect, it has the following rights: require the submission of documents by these persons; examine their books and records and take copies or extracts therefrom; obtain from them (or their representatives and staff) written or oral explanations; as well as interview any other consenting person for the purpose of collecting information relating to the subject matter of an investigation.[125]

(2) Each investigation must be conducted on the basis of an **ECB Decision**.[126] If a person obstructs its conduct, the NCA of the participating

---

[121] SSM-FR, Article 139; see also recital (47), second sentence SSMR.

[122] SSM-FR, Article 140(3)–(4).

[123] *Ibid.*, Article 141. Based on this Article (as well as on several other Articles of the SSMR and the SSM-FR) the ECB adopted on 17 March 2015 Regulation (EU) 2015/534 "on reporting of supervisory financial information" (ECB/2015/13), OJ L 86, 31.3.2015, pp. 13–151 (in force, as amended three times).

[124] SSMR, Article 10(2)–(3). In EU banking law, professional secrecy is governed by Article 53 CRD IV. Recital (48) SSMR considers the following on protection against self-incrimination: "*Legal profession privilege is a fundamental principle of Union law, protecting the confidentiality of communications between natural or legal persons and their advisors, in accordance with the conditions laid down in the case-law of the Court of Justice of the European Union (CJEU)*".

[125] *Ibid.*, Article 11(1).

[126] This Decision must specify, *inter alia*, the ECB intention to exercise the powers laid down in Article 11(1) SSMR, and the fact that any obstruction of the investigation by the

Member State where the relevant premises are located must afford, in compliance with national law, the 'necessary assistance' for the exercise of the above-mentioned rights. This includes, in the cases referred to in **Articles 12–13** (see just below), facilitating the ECB's access to the business premises of the legal persons designated in **Article 10(1)**.[127]

In Particular: On-Site Inspections
The provisions of the SSMR: In order to carry out its supervisory tasks and subject to other conditions set out in EU banking law, the ECB may, according to **Article 13** (see just below) and subject to prior notification to the NCA concerned, conduct all necessary on-site inspections at the business premises of the legal persons designated in **Article 10(1)**, and any other undertaking included in consolidated supervision (including any branches (not only significant) and subsidiaries in non-participating Member States), in the cases where the ECB is the consolidating supervisor (pursuant to **Article 4(1), point (g)**). Any on-site inspection must be conducted on the basis of an **ECB investigation Decision** and may be carried out without prior announcement to those legal persons, if the proper conduct and efficiency of the inspection so require.[128]

If an on-site inspection provided for in **Article 12(1)–(2)** or the assistance by an NCA provided for in **Article 12(5)** requires authorisation by a judicial authority under national law, such authorisation has to be applied for by the ECB. In such a case, the national judicial authority ('**NJA**') must control the authenticity of the ECB Decision and, having regard to the subject matter of the inspection, the potential arbitrariness and non-proportionality of the envisaged coercive measures. In its control of the proportionality of the coercive measures, the NJA may ask the ECB for detailed explanations, in particular relating to the grounds the ECB has for suspecting that an infringement of the legal acts referred to in **Article 4(3), first sub-paragraph**, has taken place; the seriousness of the suspected infringement; and the nature of the involvement of the person subject to the coercive measures.

However, this judicial review is bounded. The NJA is not allowed to review the necessity for the inspection or demand to be provided with the information on the ECB's file, since the lawfulness of the ECB Decision is subject to review only by the CJEU.[129]

---

person being investigated constitutes a breach of an ECB Decision, within the meaning of Article 18(7) on periodic penalty payments, without prejudice to national law as provided for in Article 11(2) (see just below) (SSM-FR, Article 142).

[127] SSMR, Article 11(2).

[128] The officials of and other persons authorised by the ECB to conduct on-site inspections may enter any business premises and land of the legal persons subject to its Decision and have all powers stipulated in Article 11(1) on general investigation (*ibid.*, Article 12(1)–(3)). Article 12(4)–(5) sets out specific assistance obligations.

[129] *Ibid.*, Article 13(1)–(2). On the review of ECB legal acts by the CJEU, see below, under 8.6.1.

The provisions of the SSM-FR: This Regulation lays down specific rules in relation to four aspects relating to on-site inspections[130]:

ECB Decision to conduct an on-site inspection: The ECB must appoint 'on-site inspection teams' to conduct all necessary on-site inspections on the premises of a legal person designated in **Article 10(1) SSMR**. Without prejudice to **Article 142 SSM-FR** and pursuant to **Article 12(3) SSMR**, the relevant ECB Decision must specify the on-site inspection's subject matter and the purpose and the fact that any obstruction to that by the legal person subject to it constitutes a breach of an ECB Decision within the meaning of **Article 18(7)** (without prejudice to national law as provided for in **Article 11(2)**) If the on-site inspection follows an investigation conducted on the basis of an ECB Decision (as discussed) and the purpose and scope of this inspection and this investigation are identical, the officials and other persons authorised by the ECB and by an NCA must be granted access to the business premises and land of the legal person subject to the investigation on the basis of the same decision pursuant to **Article 12(2)** and **(4) SSMR**, and without prejudice to **Article 13**.

Establishment and composition of on-site inspection teams: The establishment and composition of such teams, with the involvement of NCAs in accordance with **Article 12 SSMR**, is a duty imposed on the ECB, which must designate its head from among ECB and NCA staff members. The ECB and NCAs must consult with one another and agree on the use of NCA resources regarding these teams.

Procedure and notification of an on-site inspection: The ECB must notify the legal person subject to an on-site inspection of the ECB Decision referred to in **Article 143(2)** above and the identity of the members of the on-site inspection team, at least five working days before the start of the on-site inspection. It must also notify of such an inspection the NCA of the Member State where this is to be conducted at least one week before notifying the legal person subject to that inspection. If required by the proper conduct and efficiency of the inspection, the ECB may carry out an on-site inspection even without notifying the supervised entity concerned beforehand. In this case, the NCA must be notified as soon as possible before the start of such an inspection.

Conduct of on-site inspections: The persons carrying out the on-site inspection must follow the instructions of the head of the on-site inspection team. In the case of an inspection relating to a significant supervised entity, responsible for the coordination between the on-site inspection

---

[130] SSM-FR, Articles 143(1)–(3), 144(1)–(3), 145(1)–(2) and 146(1)–(2), respectively.

team, and the joint supervisory team (JST) in charge of the supervision of that entity according to the provisions of **Article 3(2), point (d) SSM-FR,** is the head of the on-site inspection team.

8.3.3 Supervisory Powers

Articles 14–15 refer to the 'specific supervisory powers' with regard to the 'common procedures', namely the authorisation of credit institutions and the assessment of acquisitions of qualifying holdings in them; these are further specified in **Articles 73–88 SSM-FR**. *Furthermore*, for the purposes of carrying out its tasks according to **Article 4(1) SSMR**, and without prejudice to other powers conferred on it, the ECB was given extensive specific supervisory powers under the circumstances laid down in **Article 16(1)**. In particular, it may require any supervised entity established in participating Member States to take the necessary measures at an early stage to address relevant problems, if any of the following three conditions is met: that entity does not meet the requirements of the legal acts of **Article 4(3)**; the ECB has evidence that the entity is likely to breach the requirements of these legal acts within the next twelve months; or the governance arrangements, strategies, processes and mechanisms implemented by the entity and the own funds and liquidity held by it do not ensure a sound management and coverage of risks.[131]

8.3.4 Powers of Host Authorities and Cooperation on Consolidated Supervision

The procedures set out in EU banking law for credit institutions intending to establish branches or to exercise the freedom to provide services by carrying out their activities within the territory of another Member State, as well as the related competences of home and host Member States[132] apply among participating Member States only for the purposes of the tasks not conferred upon the ECB under **Article 4**. The provisions of EU banking law on the cooperation between NCAs from different Member States for the conduct of consolidated supervision[133] do not apply to the extent that the ECB is

---

[131] All these aspects are further discussed and analysed in Volume II, including the Judgement of the Court (Grand Chamber) of 19 December 2018 in Case C-219/17, *Silvio Berlusconi and Finanziaria d'investimento Fininvest SpA (Fininvest) v Banca d'Italia and Istituto per la Vigilanza Sulle Assicurazioni (IVASS)* (ECLI:EU:C:2018:1023, the '*Berlusconi* case'), which dealt with the legal review of acts adopted under Article 15 SSMR. On Articles 14–15, see details in Gurlit (2022); on Article 16, see Gortsos (2022a), pp. 236–251. For the duty of care as a judicial review tool in the SSM composite procedures, see Budinská and Tegelaar (2023).

[132] CRD IV, Articles 33–46.

[133] *Ibid.*, Articles 111–118; All these CRD IV Articles are discussed in detail in Volume II.

the only competent authority involved.[134] In fulfilling its tasks under **Articles 4–5 SSMR**, the ECB must respect a 'fair balance' between all participating Member States according to **Article 6(8)**[135] and in its relationship with non-participating Member States it must respect the balance between home and host Member States as established in EU banking law.[136]

8.3.5 Administrative Penalties

8.3.5.1 An Overview of the Legal Framework

In addition to its general powers to impose sanctions in the exercise of its other tasks governed by a Council Regulation and an ECB Regulation, both of 1999,[137] the ECB has been granted specific powers to impose administrative penalties on supervised entities in two cases of breaches related to its supervisory tasks: *first*, breach of regulatory requirements under directly applicable EU legal acts; and *second*, breach of ECB legal acts. In addition, procedures for cooperation between the ECB and NCAs have been instituted with regard to other cases of breaches of EU banking law. To adapt the EU legal framework on ECB sanction-imposing powers to the functioning of the SSM, on **16 April 2014** the GC adopted an **ECB Regulation** amending its 1999 Regulation on its powers to impose sanctions, while, on 27 January 2015, the 1999 Council Regulation was also amended.[138]

---

[134] SSMR, Article 17(1) and (2), respectively; see also recitals (51)–(52).

[135] According to this Article, when the ECB is assisted by NCAs or NDAs for exercising its tasks under the SSMR, both the ECB and NCAs must comply with the provisions set out in EU banking law in relation to the allocation of responsibilities and cooperation between competent authorities from different Member States.

[136] SSMR, Article 17(3). The rules of Article 17 are further detailed by Articles 8–17 SSM-FR.

[137] Council Regulation (EC) No 2532/98 of November 1998 "concerning the powers of the [ECB] to impose sanctions" (OJ L 318, 27.11.1998, pp. 4–7) and ECB Regulation (EC) No 2157/1999 of 23 September 1999 "on the powers of the [ECB] to impose sanctions" (ECB/1999/4) (OJ L 264, 12.10.1999, pp. 21–26), adopted on the basis of Article 6(2) of the Council Regulation.

[138] Council Regulation (EU) 2015/159 "amending Council Regulation (EC) No 2532/98 concerning the powers of the [ECB] to impose sanctions" (OJ L 27, 3.2.2015, pp. 1–6) and ECB Regulation (EU) No 469/2014 "amending Regulation (EC) No 2157/1999 on the powers of the [ECB] to impose sanctions (ECB/1999/4)" (ECB/2014/18) (OJ L 141, 14.5.2014, pp. 51–53). *Inter alia*, the amendments to the ECB Regulation were aimed at clarifying that its provisions do not apply to the sanctions that may be imposed by the ECB in the exercise of its supervisory tasks, since those are covered exclusively by Article 18 SSMR. Council Regulation (EU) 2015/159 aimed at bringing Council Regulation (EC) No 2532/98 in line with Article 18 SSMR, in particular with regard to the upper limits of sanctions imposed by the ECB in the exercise of its supervisory tasks (new Article 4a); the specific procedural rules for sanctions imposed by the ECB in the exercise of its supervisory tasks (new Article 4b); and the specific time-limits for administrative penalties imposed by the ECB in the exercise of its supervisory tasks (new Article 4c). These new Articles were inserted by Article 1(5) of Council Regulation (EU) 2015/159.

The relevant (very complex, indeed) framework is governed by **Article 18** SSMR, **Articles 120–137 SSM-FR** (Part X) and the above-mentioned (Council and ECB) Regulations. For a summary, including the division of competences between the ECB and NCAs, see Table 8.2 below.

Table 8.2 The powers of the ECB and NCAs to impose administrative penalties

1. Breach of directly applicable EU legal acts (EU Regulations)	
Significant supervised entities	(a) The ECB may impose **administrative pecuniary penalties** (Article 18(1) SSMR) (b) The ECB may ask NCAs to impose **non-pecuniary penalties** (Article 134(1) SSM-FR)
Less significant supervised entities	Only NCAs can impose penalties (notification to the ECB)
Natural persons in significant supervised entities	(a) The ECB may ask NCAs to impose **non-pecuniary and/or pecuniary penalties** (Article 134(1) SSM-FR) (b) An NCA may ask the ECB to request it to open proceedings (Article 134(2) SSM-FR)
Natural persons in less significant supervised entities	Only NCAs can impose penalties
2. Breach of national legislation (including breach of national rules transposing EU Directives)	
Significant supervised entities	(a) The ECB may ask NCAs to impose **pecuniary penalties** (Article 18(5) SSMR) and/or **non-pecuniary penalties** (Article 134(1) SSM-FR) (b) An NCA may ask the ECB to request it to open proceedings (Article 134(2) SSM-FR)
Less significant supervised entities	Only NCAs can impose penalties (notification to the ECB)
Natural persons in significant supervised entities	(a) The ECB may ask NCAs to impose **administrative penalties or measures** (Article 18(5) SSMR), as well as **non-pecuniary or pecuniary penalties** (Article 134(1) SSM-FR) (b) An NCA may ask the ECB to request it to open proceedings (Article 134(2) SSM-FR)
Natural persons in less significant supervised entities	Only NCAs can impose penalties
3. Breach of ECB legal acts (Regulations and Decisions) (Article 18(7) SSMR)	
Significant supervised entities	The ECB may impose **fines and periodic penalty payments**
Less significant supervised entities	The ECB may impose **fines and periodic penalty payments** only if its legal acts impose obligations on such entities *vis-à-vis* the ECB

8.3.5.2 Breach of Regulatory Requirements Under EU Banking Law (Other Than ECB Regulations): Conditions for Imposition of penalties—the Penalties

(1) The ECB can impose administrative pecuniary penalties on significant supervised entities in the case of breach of a requirement under directly applicable EU legal acts which constitute sources of EU banking law, i.e., the CRR and the RTSs/ITSs adopted in the form of Regulations, and in relation to which such sanctions are available to NCAs under the provisions of relevant EU banking law, i.e., **Article 67 CRD IV**. Hence, the ECB does not have the power under **Article 18(1) SSRM** to impose such sanctions if a significant supervised entity breaches a requirement under the national law which transposed the CRD IV. The breach may have occurred either intentionally or negligently.[139]

(2) The penalties that the ECB can impose in this case are the following: up to twice the amount of the profits gained or losses avoided because of the breach, if those can be determined; up to 10% of the total annual turnover, as defined in EU banking law, of a legal person in the preceding business year, or such other pecuniary sanctions as may be provided for in EU banking law.[140] The penalties applied must be effective, proportionate and dissuasive. In determining whether to impose a penalty and its appropriateness, the ECB must closely cooperate with NCAs pursuant to **Article 9(2)**.[141]

8.3.5.3 Breach of ECB Legal Acts: Substantive and Procedural Rules

(1) In case of breaches of its Regulations or supervisory Decisions, the ECB may also impose sanctions in the form of fines and periodic penalty payments, in accordance with **Council Regulation (EC) No 2532/98** (as in force).[142] They can be imposed if there is a failure to comply with obligations under ECB

---

[139] SSMR, Article 18(1); see also recitals (36), third sentence and (53). The application of Article 18(1) only to significant supervised entities can be deduced from Article 134 SSM-FR.

[140] If the legal person is a subsidiary of a parent undertaking, the relevant total annual turnover referred to above is the total annual turnover resulting from the consolidated account of the ultimate parent undertaking in the preceding business year (SSMR, Article 18(1)–(2)). The total annual turnover is the annual turnover, as defined in Article 67 CRD IV, of a supervised entity according to its most recent available annual financial accounts. If the supervised entity that has committed the breach belongs to a supervised group, the relevant total annual turnover is that resulting from the most recent available consolidated annual financial accounts of the supervised group (SSM-FR, Article 128).

[141] SSMR, Article 18(3). These provisions apply *mutatis mutandis* in respect of supervised entities and groups in participating Member States under the 'close cooperation' regime (SSM-FR, Article 113. On the procedural rules applying in this case, see Article 18(4) SSMR (with reference to the procedures contained in Article 4b of Council Regulation (EC) No 2532/98, as appropriate) and Article 121(1) SSM-FR. Furthermore, the cooperation between the ECB and NCAs is governed by Article 18(5) SSMR and Articles 134–135 SSM-FR.

[142] SSMR, Article 18(7); see also recital (36), first and second sentences.

Regulations or supervisory Decisions either by significant supervised entities, or by less significant ones, if the relevant ECB legal acts impose obligations on them *vis-à-vis* the ECB.[143]

The procedural rules applicable to periodic penalty payments are laid down in **Article 129 SSM-FR**; they complement those laid down in the **Council Regulation** and must be applied in accordance with **Article 25–26 SSMR** on mediation and on the Supervisory Board.[144] After an infringement procedure has been carried out by the ECB, the Supervisory Board must propose to the GC a complete draft Decision to impose a sanction on the entity concerned pursuant to the procedure laid down in **Article 26(8) SSMR**. A hearing regarding the alleged infringement committed by the undertaking concerned must precede the submission by the Supervisory Board of the complete draft Decision. The supervised entity concerned has the right to request a review by the ABoR of the Decision taken by the GC, in accordance with the procedure laid down in **Article 24 SSMR**.[145]

(2) In case of a continuing breach of an ECB Regulation or supervisory Decision, the ECB may impose a periodic penalty payment with a view to enforcing compliance of the persons concerned (by application of **Articles 22 SSMR and 25–35 SSM-FR**). Such a payment must be effective and proportionate and be calculated for each day of infringement until the person concerned becomes compliant. The upper limits for such payments are specified in the **Council Regulation**.[146] In addition, the relevant period must begin on the date stipulated in the Decision imposing the periodic penalty payment, the earliest date stipulated being that on which the person concerned is notified in writing of the ECB's reasons for imposing the periodic penalty payment. A periodic penalty payment may be imposed for periods that may not exceed a period of six months following the date specified in the Decision imposing the penalty payment.[147]

---

[143] The latter is the only case in which the ECB can impose administrative penalties to a less significant supervised entity (SSM-FR, Article 122).

[144] *Ibid.*, Article 121(2). It is worth noting that the ECB's Executive Committee is not involved in the process.

[145] Council Regulation (EC) No 2532/98, Article 4b (2)–(3); see also recital (10) of that Regulation.

[146] According to recital (9) of Council Regulation 2015/159, for the sake of consistency in the treatment of equally serious infringements, the upper limit of a fine that the ECB may impose on an entity for failure to comply with an ECB Regulation or Decision in the supervisory field should not differ from that it may impose on it for a breach of directly applicable EU law. According to Article 4a (1), the upper limit is twice the amount of the profits gained or losses avoided because of the infringement if these can be determined, or 10% of the total annual turnover of the entity, and the upper limit of periodic penalty payments is 5% of the average daily turnover per day of infringement.

[147] SSM-FR, Article 129. Common provisions applying to administrative penalties imposed by the ECB on supervisory entities either under Article 18(1) or under Article 18(7) SSMR and concerning time-limits, publication of Decisions, exchange of information

8.4 Independence and Accountability

8.4.1 Aspects of Independence

8.4.1.1 Introductory Remarks[148]

The independence of the ECB (and of the NCBs-members of the ESCB[149]) in relation to the basic tasks of the ECB within the Eurosystem under **Article 127(2) TFEU** is one of the major attributes of its functioning since its establishment on 1 June 1998 and is embodied in the TFEU and the ESCB/ECB Statute.[150] In particular: institutional independence is anchored in **Article 130 TFEU** (carried over *verbatim* in Article 7 ESCB/ECB Statute); operational independence is stipulated in **Articles 17–24 ESCB/ECB Statute** on the ESCB's monetary functions and operations; personal independence is governed by **Article 283(2)**, second and third sub-paragraphs **TFEU** (Article 11.2 ESCB/ECB Statute) and by **Articles 11.4 and 14.2 ESCB/ECB Statute** (the former on the members of the Executive Board and later on the NCB Governors which are GC members); and financial independence is covered by **Articles 282(3)**, third sentence **TFEU** (*"[the ECB] shall be independent (...) in the management of its finances"*) and **28.2 ESCB/ECB Statute** providing that the sole subscribers to and holders of the capital of the ECB are the NCBs-members of the ESCB.[151]

(2) All these aspects of independence also apply to the ECB function as a supervisory authority.[152] In particular, institutional independence is governed by **Article 19** SSMR; operational independence is guaranteed by **Articles 9–18** laying down the ECB's necessary powers to fulfil its objectives and

---

with the EBA, criminal offences and proceeds from penalties are laid down in Articles 130–132 and 136–137 SSM-FR. For a more detailed analysis of Article 18, see Papathanassiou (2022); see also D'Ambrosio (2021).

[148] On the notion of central banks' independence, see the seminal work of Eijffinger and De Haan (1996). See also Lastra and Goodhart (2017) and Louis (2023), Section D, discussing the widely extended phenomenon of populism and its impact on independence.

[149] An NCB's independence is also one of the 'legal' convergence criteria for entering the EMU (TFEU, Article 141(1), with reference to Articles 130–131).

[150] Accordingly, any modification of the relevant provisions would require an amendment of the TFEU and of the ESCB/ECB Statute. On the basis of empirical evidence, it is concluded that the degree of independence of the ECB is higher than that of the US Federal Reserve System and the Deutsche Bundesbank; see De Grauwe (2020), pp. 174–175, with reference to Bini-Smaghi and Gros (2000), pp. 118–143 and De Haan and Eijffinger (2016).

[151] See on this indicatively Smits (1997), pp. 152–169, Louis (2009), pp. 173–177 and Gortsos (2020), pp. 266–269. According to Judgment of the Court of 10 July 2003 in Case C-11/00, *Commission of the European Communities v [ECB]* (ECLI:EU:C:2003:395), this independence does neither separate the ECB from the EU nor does it exempt it from the application of EU law.

[152] This aspect of independence is also included in the "Core principles for effective banking supervision" of the Basel Committee (Principle 2, pp. 22–24); see Chapter 2 above, under 2.4.3.

its supervisory tasks; personal independence is governed by (the above-mentioned) **Article 26(3)–(4)**; and financial independence is stipulated in **Articles 28–30**.[153]

8.4.1.2 Institutional Independence
(1) In relation to institutional independence, the SSMR provides that when carrying out their tasks under the SSMR, the ECB and the NCAs acting within the SSM must act independently. Furthermore (in a wording, *mutatis mutandis*, identical to that of **Article 42 EBAR**[154] and similar to Article 130 TFEU), Supervisory Board and Steering Committee members must act independently and objectively in the interest of the EU as a whole and neither seek nor take instructions from the EU's institutions or bodies, from any government of a Member State or from any other public or private body. On a reciprocal basis, EU institutions, bodies, offices and agencies, as well as the governments of the Member States and any other bodies must respect that independence.[155]

(2) These rules are repeated in the **Code of Conduct for high-level ECB Officials** for Supervisory Board members and alternates, adding that they must act independently and objectively in the interest of the EU as a whole "*regardless of national or personal interest*".[156] This Code, however, also contains detailed rules pertaining to the avoidance of **conflicts of interest**. The general principle is laid down in Article 11,[157] which provides that members and alternates must avoid any situation which could give rise to concerns of conflict of interest[158] and may not use their involvement in a decision-making process, or the professional information they possess, to gain personal advantage of any kind. *Furthermore*, they must disclose in writing, without undue delay, to the Supervisory Board's Chair and to the **Ethics Committee** any situation that may raise conflict of interest concerns, and

---

[153] For an overview of the SSMR provisions and in general of the independence of the ECB (also) within the SSM, see more details in De La Parra (2015), Louis (2015), Fromage, Tuori and Dermine (2019), Amtenbrink (2022), pp. 277–288, Thiele (2022) and Louis (2023), Section B.

[154] See Chapter 7 above, under 7.4.2.

[155] SSMR, Article 19(1)–(2); see also recital (75).

[156] Code of Conduct for high-level ECB Officials, Article 6, with reference to Articles 130 TFEU, 7 ESCB/ECB Statute and 19(1) SSMR.

[157] *Ibid.*, Article 11.1–11.2. More detailed rules relating to conflicts of interest are laid down in Articles 12–18 on gainful occupational activity of a spouse or partner; gifts and hospitality; awards, honours and decorations; invitations to events; private financial transactions; post-employment; and non-compliance (the latter applying to the violation of all rules laid down in the Code).

[158] Such a concern arises when these persons have personal interests that may influence, or may be perceived as influencing, the "*impartial and objective carrying out of their duties and responsibilities*" (extending, but not limited to their direct family members, spouses, or partners); a conflict of interest does not exist where a member is only concerned as part of the general public or a broad class of persons.

recuse themselves from taking part in any discussions, deliberations or votes in relation to any such situation and shall not be provided with any related documentation.

8.4.1.3 Financial Independence
Financial Resources—Budget
The ECB is responsible for devoting the necessary financial (and human) resources to the exercise of its supervisory tasks.[159] As part of its independence in the management of its finances, any expenditure arising from the discharge of these task is covered by its budget, separately identifiable therein; the ECB must report in detail in its Annual Report[160] on the budget for these tasks.[161]

Annual Supervisory Fees
Scope of application: The ECB can levy annual supervisory fees on (significant and less significant) supervised entities established in participating Member States and on branches established in such a Member State by supervised entities established in a non-participating one. These must *exclusively* cover the ECB expenditure in relation to its supervisory tasks under **Articles 4–6 SSMR**.[162]

Level of fees: The amount of the fee levied on a supervised entity or branch is calculated in accordance with the modalities defined, and published in advance, by the ECB.[163] In the case of consolidated supervision, it must be calculated at the highest level of consolidation within participating Member States, be allocated to the supervised entities established therein and included in the consolidated supervision, and be based on objective criteria relating to the importance and risk profile of the supervised entity concerned, including its RWAs. The basis for calculating the fee for a given calendar year is the expenditure relating to the supervision of supervised entities and branches in that year. The ECB may require advance payments in respect of the fee, based on a reasonable estimate, and must communicate, *on the one hand*, with NCAs before deciding on the final fee level in order to ensure that supervision remains "*cost-effective and reasonable*" for the supervised entities and branches concerned and, *on the other hand*, to the latter the basis for the calculation of the fee.[164]

---

[159] *Ibid.*, Article 28.

[160] See below, under 8.4.2.

[161] SSMR, Article 29(1) and (2), first sentence. On Articles 28 (including on human resources) and 29, see details in Almhofer (2022).

[162] *Ibid.*, Article 30(1); see also recital (77).

[163] Before defining these modalities, the ECB must conduct open public consultations, analyse the potential related costs and benefits and publish the results of both (*ibid.*, Article 30(2)).

[164] *Ibid.*, Article 30(3).

Other provisions: The ECB must report on the levying of annual supervisory fees in accordance with **Article 20**.[165] NCAs continue to have the right to levy fees under their national law to the extent that supervisory tasks have not been conferred on the ECB, or in respect of costs of cooperation with and assistance to the ECB and acting on its Instructions, pursuant to EU banking law and subject to the arrangements on the SSMR implementation, including **Articles 6** and **12** (as discussed above).[166]

8.4.1.4 The Provisions of the ECB Supervisory Fees Regulation (SFR) and of ECB Decision (EU) 2019/2158

(1) The ECB **"Supervisory Fees Regulation"**[167] ('**SFR**') sets out the arrangements for calculating the total amount of the annual supervisory fees to be levied in respect of supervised entities and groups for each fee period; the methodology and criteria for calculating the fee to be borne by each supervised entity and group; and the procedure for the collection by the ECB of the fees. Their total amount encompasses the annual supervisory fee in respect of each significant and less significant supervised entity or group and must be calculated by the ECB at the highest level of consolidation within the participating Member States.[168]

(2) ECB Decision (EU) 2019/2158[169] applies to 'fee debtors' and NCAs. It lays down the methodology and the procedures for the determination and collection of data regarding the fee factors used for the calculation of the annual supervisory fees to be levied in respect of supervised entities and groups under the above-mentioned Regulation, and for the submission of the 'fee factors' by the fee debtors referred to in its Article 10(3), point (bd), as well as procedures for the submission of such data by NCAs to the ECB.[170]

---

[165] See below, under 8.4.2.

[166] SSMR, Article 30(4)–(5).

[167] ECB Regulation (EU) No 1163/2014 of 22 October 2014 "on supervisory fees (ECB/2014/41)" (OJ L 311, 31.10.2014, pp. 23–31). Its legal basis are Articles 4(3), second sub-paragraph, 30 and 33(2), second sub-paragraph SSMR; it is in force as amended by ECB Regulation (EU) 2019/2155 of 5 December 2019 (ECB/2019/37) (OJ L 327, 17.12.2019, pp. 70–74); the current consolidated version is available at: https://eur-lex.europa.eu/eli/reg/2014/1163/2020-01-01.

[168] SFR, Article 1(1)–(2). 'Annual supervisory fee' means the fee payable in respect of each supervised entity and each supervised group as calculated in accordance with the arrangements set out in Article 10(6) (*ibid.*, Article 2, point (1)).

[169] "ECB Decision (EU) 2019/2158 of 5 December 2019 (ECB/2019/38)" (OJ L 327, 17.12.2019, pp. 99–107), which as of 1 January 2020 repealed ECB Decision (EU) 2015/530 of 11 February 2015 (ECB/2015/7) (OJ L 84, 28.3.2015, pp. 67–72). Its legal basis are Articles 4(3), second sub-paragraph and 30 SSMR.

[170] Pursuant to Article 2 (points (3) and (4)) SFR, 'fee debtor' means the fee-paying credit institution or fee-paying branch determined in accordance with Article 4 and to which the fee notice is addressed; and 'fee factors' means the data related to a supervised entity or group defined in Article 10(3), point (a) which are used to calculate the annual

8.4.2 Accountability of the ECB vis-à-vis EU Institutions and National Parliaments

8.4.2.1 Accountability vis-à-vis EU Institutions

Introductory Remarks

(1) The ECB's accountability *vis-à-vis EU* towards EU institutions in relation to its basic tasks within the Eurosystem under **Article 127(2) TFEU** is laid down in **Article 284(3) TFEU** (carried over in **Article 15.3 ESCB/ECB Statute**)[171]; relevant is also **Article 284(1)–(2) TFEU** on mutual participation in meetings. Pursuant to **Article 26.2 ESCB/ECB Statute**, its annual accounts, as approved by the GC, must be published.[172]

(2) The ECB is accountable to the European Parliament and to the Council for the implementation of the SSMR as well, and notably in an enhanced way.[173] The rules are laid down in **Article 20 SSMR**, complemented by specific provisions in Sections I-II of the EP-ECB Interinstitutional Agreement and in Section I of the Council-ECB MOU. Furthermore, pursuant to **Article 29(2)**, the ECB annual accounts must include the income and expenses related to its supervisory tasks (the supervisory section is audited in line with **Article 27.1 ESCB/ECB Statute**[174]).[175]

---

supervisory fee. On Article 30 SRMR, the SFR and ECB Decision (EU) 2019/2158, see Zagouras (2022).

[171] Unlike the case of its independence, the accountability of the ECB is less developed if compared to the US Federal Reserve System; see De Grauwe (2020), p. 175, with reference to Buiter (1999) and Eijffinger and De Haan (2000), Chapter 2. The argument is based on the fact that the Statutes of the Federal Reserve can be amended by US Congress by a simple majority, while the amendment of the TFEU requires unanimity by all Member States (Article 48 TFEU) and, hence, the role of the European Parliament is weaker than that of the US Congress.

[172] See on this indicatively Smits (1997), pp. 169–178, and Louis (2009), pp. 190–196. For an assessment of the BU's accountability system in practice, see Lamandini and Ramos Muñoz (2022a).

[173] SSMR, Article 20(1); see also recital (55), which lays down the following considerations: "*The conferral of supervisory tasks implies a significant responsibility for the ECB to safeguard financial stability in the Union and to use its supervisory powers in the most effective and proportionate way. Any shift of supervisory powers from the Member State to the Union level should be balanced by appropriate transparency and accountability requirements. The ECB should therefore be accountable for the exercise of those tasks towards the European Parliament and the Council as democratically legitimised institutions (...). Any reporting obligations should be subject to the relevant professional secrecy requirements*". As already noted in Chapter 2 above, under 2.4.3, Banking supervisors' accountability is also included (in the same Principle 2 governing their independence) in the "Core principles for effective banking supervision" of the BCBS (see).

[174] According to this Article, the accounts of the ECB and of the NCBs are audited by independent external auditors and approved by the Council following a GC's Recommendation. Auditors are fully empowered to examine all books and accounts of the ECB and the NCBs and obtain full information about their transactions.

[175] The literature on the accountability of the ECB (also) in the SSM is vast. See, by means of indication, Athanassiou (2011), Božina Beroš (2019), Fromage (2019), Fromage,

Specific Provisions
Annual Report: The ECB must submit to the European Parliament (hereinafter in this sub-section the **'EP'**), the Council, the Commission and the Eurogroup an Annual Report on the execution of its tasks under the SSMR. This is adopted by the GC on a proposal from the Supervisory Board,[176] whose Chair must present it in public to the EP and to the Eurogroup in the presence of representatives from any non-euro area participating Member State.[177] The Annual Report must be submitted to the EP in all EU official languages, be published on the SSM website, and cover, *inter alia*, the following fields: execution of supervisory tasks and separation between those and monetary policy tasks; sharing of tasks with NCAs and cooperation with other relevant authorities; evolution of supervisory structure and staffing, including the number and national composition of seconded experts; implementation of the **Code of Conduct**; calculation method and amount of supervisory fees; budget for supervisory tasks; and experience with reporting of violations. Concurrently, the ECB must submit the Annual Report also to the Council and the Eurogroup, covering all the above-mentioned fields and containing an annex listing the legal instruments adopted by the ECB pursuant to **Article 4(3) SSMR**, and publish them on its website.[178]

The ECB must also publish in its website the supervisory fees and an explanation of their calculation,[179] as well as its **"Guide to banking supervision"**, which was published for the first time in September 2014 and applies as subsequently updated.[180]

Hearings and confidential oral discussions: The Supervisory Board's Chair may, at the request of the Eurogroup, be heard by it on the execution of the ECB supervisory tasks in the presence of representatives from any non-euro area participating Member State. Furthermore, at the request of the EP, he/she must participate in a hearing on the execution of these tasks by the ECON and, upon request, hold confidential oral discussions (*"behind closed doors"*) with the ECON's Chair and Vice-Chairs concerning these tasks, where such discussions are required for the exercise of the EP's powers under

---

Tuori and Dermine (2019), Lamandini and Ramos Muñoz (2020b), Markakis (2020), Smits (2019) and (2020), Akbik (2022) (on lessons learned for the Monetary Dialogues), Amtenbrink (2022), pp. 288-302, Amtenbrink and Markakis (2022) and Louis (2023), Section C. See also Lastra (2020), on a comparative analysis with the BoE.

[176] ECB Rules of Procedure, Article 13n.

[177] SSMR, Article 20(2)-(3).

[178] EP-ECB Interinstitutional Agreement, Section I, para. 1.

[179] At: https://www.bankingsupervision.europa.eu/organisation/fees/html/index.en.html.

[180] At: https://www.bankingsupervision.europa.eu/press/publications/html/index.en.html. These requirements are set out in Section I, para. 4 of the EP-ECB Interinstitutional Agreement.

the TFEU.[181] The **Council-ECB MoU** further specifies that the Supervisory Board's Chair must participate in two exchanges of views per year and may be invited to additional '*ad-hoc* exchanges of views' on supervisory issues with the Eurogroup in relation to any aspect of the SSM activity and functioning.[182]

Responding to questions: The ECB must reply, orally or in writing, to questions put to it by the EP or by the Eurogroup, in the presence of representatives from any non-euro area participating Member State.[183] The questions put by the EP and the Eurogroup must be replied as promptly as possible, and in any event within five weeks of their submission to the ECB, while those put by the Eurogroup must also be communicated to the representatives from any non-euro area participating Member State.[184]

Access to information and safeguarding of ECB classified information and documents: The ECON must be provided with, at least, a comprehensive and meaningful record of the Supervisory Board's proceedings enabling an understanding of the discussions. If the GC objects against a draft Decision of the Supervisory Board pursuant to **Article 26(8) SSMR**,[185] the ECB President must inform the ECON's Chair of the reasons for such an objection subject to confidentiality requirements. In general, the EP must implement safeguards and measures corresponding to the level of sensitivity of the ECB information or documents and inform accordingly the ECB; in any case, information or documents disclosed can only be used for the purpose for which they have been provided and non-confidential information relating to the winding-up of a credit institution may be disclosed only *ex-post* once any restrictions on the provision of information resulting from confidentiality requirements cease to apply. The ECB must also seek its consent to any disclosure to additional persons or institutions, and its cooperation in any judicial, administrative or other proceedings in which access to such information or documents are sought.[186]

Investigations: When **Committee of Inquiry** pursuant to **Article 226 TFEU** is set up by the EP, the ECB must assist it in carrying out its tasks pursuant to the principle of 'sincere cooperation'.[187] It must also cooperate sincerely with any EP investigation within the same framework applying to

---

[181] SSMR, Article 20(4)–(5) and (8), first sentence. Section I, para. 2 of the EP-ECB Interinstitutional Agreement contains very detailed additional provisions in this respect.

[182] Council-ECB MoU, Section I, para. 2.

[183] SSMR, Article 20(6).

[184] EP-ECB Interinstitutional Agreement, Section I, para. 3 and Council-ECB MoU, Section I, para. 3.

[185] See above, under 8.1.2 (on the duties of the Supervisory Board).

[186] EP-ECB Interinstitutional Agreement, Section I, paras 4 and 5.

[187] SSMR, Article 20(9), first sentence and recital (57). This obligation is identical to that imposed to EBA (see Chapter 7 above, under 7.4.3). The Committee of Inquiry is governed by Decision 95/167/EC of the European Parliament, the Council and the Commission of 19 April 1995 "on the detailed provisions governing the exercise of the European Parliament's right of inquiry", as in force (OJ L 113, 19.5.1995, pp. 1–4).

Committees of Inquiry and under the same confidentiality protection set out in the Agreement for oral confidential meetings. All recipients of information provided to the EP in the context of investigations are subject to confidentiality requirements equivalent to those applying to the Supervisory Board members and to the ECB supervisory staff. The EP and the ECB must agree on the measures to be applied to ensure the protection of information.[188]

8.4.2.2 Accountability vis-à-vis National Parliaments
The ECB is also accountable to the national parliaments of participating Member States in relation to its specific supervisory tasks within the SSM (an obligation not applying in relation to its basic tasks within the Eurosystem). In this respect, the following is set out[189]: *first*, when submitting the Report provided for in **Article 20(2)**, the ECB must simultaneously forward it directly to these national parliaments, which may address to the ECB their reasoned observations on it; and *second*, the national parliaments may, through their own procedures, request the ECB to reply in writing to any observations or questions submitted to it respect of its functions under the SSMR; they may also invite the Chair or a member of the Supervisory Board to participate in an exchange of views in relation to the prudential supervision of credit institutions in that Member State with an NCA representative. These provisions are without prejudice to the accountability of NCAs to national parliaments in accordance with national law for the performance of tasks not conferred on the ECB thereby and activities carried out by national parliaments in accordance with **Article 6**.

8.5   THE ADMINISTRATIVE BOARD OF REVIEW (ABoR) AND THE MEDIATION PANEL

8.5.1   The ABoR

8.5.1.1   Establishment and Composition
(1) The Administrative Board of Review (**ABoR**) should be established for "*carrying out an internal administrative review of the Decisions taken by the ECB in the exercise of its powers under [the SSMR]*" after a request for review. The scope of this review pertains to the 'procedural and substantive

---

[188] If the protection of a public interest recognised in the ECB Decision 2004/258/EC of 4 March 2004 "on public access to [ECB] documents (ECB/2004/3)" (OJ L 80, 18.3.2004, pp. 42–44) requires preserving confidentiality, the EP must ensure it and not divulge the content of any such information. The rights and obligations of EU institutions and bodies, as laid down in Decision 95/167/EC, apply *mutatis mutandis* to the ECB (EP-ECB Interinstitutional Agreement, Section III).

[189] *Ibid.*, Article 21(1)–(4); see also recital (56).

conformity' of ECB Decisions with the SSMR.[190] The ABoR operating rules are laid down in its **Decision** of 14 April 2014[191] supplementing the ECB Rules of Procedure[192] Its operation is without prejudice to the right to bring proceedings before the CJEU in accordance with the Treaties.[193]

(2) The ABoR is composed of five members and two alternates appointed by the GC, which must be of high repute, be nationals from Member States and have a proven record of relevant knowledge and professional experience, including supervisory experience, to a sufficiently high level in the field of financial services. Their term of office is five years, which may be extended once. Excluded are existing staff members of the ECB and of competent authorities or other national/EU institutions, bodies, offices and agencies involved in the supervisory tasks under the SSMR. Members are not bound by any instructions and must act independently and in the public interest.[194]

8.5.1.2 Request for the Review of a Decision—Review and Decision-Making Process

(1) Any natural or legal person to whom a Decision of the ECB under the SSMR is addressed or a Decision is of direct and individual concern may request its review.[195] The ABoR must adopt an Opinion on the review, which is not binding either on the Supervisory Board or on the GC, and propose

---

[190] *Ibid.*, Article 24(1); see also recital (64). This is comparable to the BoA of the ESAs and the Appeal Panel of the SRB under Article 85 SRMR, albeit with significant differences (see, respectively, Chapter 7 above, under 7.4.4, and Chapter 9 below, under 9.5). See on this Lamandini and Ramos Muñoz (2020c).

[191] Decision 2014/360/EU "concerning the establishment of an [ABoR] and its Operating Rules (ECB/2014/16)" (OJ L 175, 14.6.2014, pp. 47–53); its legal basis is Article 24(10) SSMR, and it is in force as amended by Decision (EU) 2019/1378 of 9 August 2019 (ECB/2019/27) (OJ L 224, 28.8.2019, pp. 9–11). The current consolidated version is available at: https://eur-lex.europa.eu/legal-content/EN/TXT/?uri=CELEX%3A02014D0016%2801%29-20190917.

[192] *Ibid.*, Article 1, first sentence.

[193] SSMR, Article 24(11) and Decision ECB/2014/16, Article 19. An ABoR review is optional, prior to the initiation of proceedings before the CJEU, for persons to whom an ECB Decision under the SSMR is addressed, or to whom it is of direct and individual concern (Decision 2014/360/EU, recital (4)).

[194] *Mutatis mutandis*, these requirements are almost identical to those for the members of the ESAs' BoA (see Chapter 7 above, under 7.4.4). Since the resources and expertise of the ABoR must be sufficient to assess the exercise of the ECB powers under the SSMR, the latter must provide it with appropriate support, including legal expertise, to assist in this assessment (SSMR, Article 24(2), and Decision 2014/360/EU, Articles 3–4 and 6). Members and alternates are subject to the professional secrecy requirements laid down in Article 37 ESCB/ECB Statute even after their duties have ceased. Documents drawn up or held by the ABoR constitute ECB documents and are classified and handled pursuant to Article 23.3 ECB Rules of Procedure (Decision 2014/360/EU, Article 22(1) and (3)).

[195] SSMR, Article 24(5) and Decision 2014/360/EU, Article 7(1). Submission of the notice of review does not have suspensory effect on the application of the contested Decision, unless the GC, upon a proposal by the ABoR, decides to suspend its application provided, however, that the request for review is admissible and the Decision's immediate

whether the initial Decision should be abrogated, be replaced with a Decision of identical content, or be replaced with an amended one, containing proposals for the necessary amendments.[196]

(2) The ABoR review is confined to the examination of the grounds relied on by the applicant, as set out in the notice of review.[197] It must determine whether and to what extent the request for review is admissible before examining whether it is legally founded; if the request for review is deemed, wholly or partly inadmissible, this assessment must be recorded in its Opinion.[198] The latter must be adopted within a time period appropriate to the urgency of the matter (and not later than two months from the date of receipt of the notice of review) and propose whether the initial Decision should be abrogated, be replaced with a Decision of identical content or be replaced with an amended one, containing proposals for the necessary amendments. The Opinion, which is not binding either on the Supervisory Board or on the GC,[199] must be adopted in writing by a majority of at least three ABoR members, be reasoned, and be sent to the Supervisory Board without delay.[200]

(3) Taking into account and assessing the ABoR's Opinion, the Supervisory Board must promptly submit a new draft Decision to the GC; its assessment therein is not confined to the examination of the grounds relied upon by the applicant. This can, again, either abrogate the initial Decision, replace it with a Decision of identical content (in both cases, it must be submitted to the

---

application is deemed to cause irreparable damage (SSMR, Article 24(8), and Decision 2014/360/EU, Article 9(1)–(2)).

[196] SSMR, Article 24(7), first sentence and Decision 2014/360/EU, Article 16(1)–(2) and (5). The applicant's right of defence must be fully respected, including the right of access to the ECB's documents, subject to the legitimate interest of legal and natural persons other than the applicant, in the protection of their business secrets. This right does not extend to confidential information, including internal documents of the ECB or an NCA, and correspondence between the ECB and an NCA or between NCAs (*ibid.*, Article 20(1)–(4)).

[197] SSMR, Article 24(1), second sentence, and Decision 2014/360/EU, Article 10(1)–(2).

[198] Decision 2014/360/EU, Article 11(1). Articles 11(2) to 15 contain further procedural provisions.

[199] Lamandini and Ramos Muñoz (2020c), at p. 127, correctly point out that this is a distinctive feature of the ABoR, if compared to the ESAs' BoA (see Chapter 7 above, under 7.4.4) and the SRB's Appeal Panel (see Chapter 9 below, under 9.5), which take decisions, making it thus "*more an internal administrative feature than a quasi-judicial body*".

[200] SSMR, Article 24(3) and (7), first–second sentences, and Decision 2014/360/EU, Article 16(1)–(5). The ABoR's opinions are taken into account by the CJEU. By means of mere indication, see para. 125 of the above-mentioned (in Box 8.2) General Court's judgement of 16 May 2017 in Case T-122/15 (*Landeskreditbank Baden-Württemberg—Förderbank v European Central Bank*), according to which: "*In the present case, the [ABoR's] Opinion is part of the context of which the contested decision forms a part and may, therefore, be taken into account for the purpose of determining whether that decision contained a sufficient statement of reasons as referred to in the case-law (...)*".

GC within twenty working days of receipt of the ABoR Opinion) or replace it with an amended one (in this case, within ten working days). The new draft Decision is deemed adopted unless the GC objects within a period of ten working days. The ABoR's Opinion, the new draft Decision submitted by the Supervisory Board and the Decision adopted by the GC must be reasoned and be notified to the parties.[201]

8.5.2 Creation of 'Chinese Walls'—The Mediation Panel

8.5.2.1 Creation of Chinese Walls

(1) Article 25 SSMR lays down the principle of separation between the monetary policy and supervision functions of the ECB, due to the difference of their objectives, by creating 'Chinese walls' within it, by imposing on it two obligations: *first*, when carrying out its supervisory tasks, to *"pursue exclusively the objectives set therein"*[202] (as set out in **Article 1** (first sub-paragraph) **SSMR**[203]); and *second*, to carry them out 'separately' from both its tasks relating to the definition and implementation of the single monetary policy (**Article 127(2), first indent TFEU**) and its other tasks.[204] The second leg of the separation principle is further specified: *first*, for the sake of accountability, the ECB must report to the European Parliament and to the Council regarding its compliance with this provision; *second*, the ongoing monitoring of the solvency of its monetary policy counterparties should not be altered; and

---

[201] SSMR, Article 24(7), second-fourth sentences and (9) and Decision 2014/360/EU, Articles 17–18. In December 2022, the ECB published a document titled: "Administrative Board of Review: Eight years of experience reviewing ECB supervisory decisions", which sets out the ABoR review procedure and presents the major issues and questions faced by it from September 2014 to September 2022 (see at: https://www.bankingsupervision.europa.eu/ecb/pub/pdf/ssm.aborreview202212~ce9fb4e503.en.pdf). For more details on the ABoR, see Brescia Morra *et al.* (2017), Lackhoff (2017), pp. 237–250, Brescia Morra (2019), Pizzolla (2021), pp. 362–365, Smits (2022) and Van Rijn (2022), pp. 414–416. On the role of independent panels of administrative review in general, see Blair (2019).

[202] SSMR, Article 25(1); see also recital (65).

[203] See Chapter 6 above, under 6.3.2.

[204] SSMR, Article 25(2), first sub-paragraph, first-third sentences. The 'other tasks' referred to, apart from the specific tasks relating to the ESRB, contain the ECB's other basic tasks within the Eurosystem as set out in Article 127(2), second to fourth indents TFEU, as well the other (non-basic) ECB tasks set out, e.g., in Article 128 TFEU (in relation to euro banknotes and coins) and in Article 127(5) TFEU (on its contribution to financial stability, as already discussed). See also Article 13 k.1–2 of the ECB Rules of Procedure, which was inserted by ECB Decision 2014/179/EU to adjust the internal organisation of the ECB and its decision-making bodies to the new requirements arising from the SSMR and clarify the interaction of the bodies involved in the process of preparing and adopting supervisory Decisions.

third, the staff involved in carrying out its supervisory tasks must be organisationally separated from, and subject to, separate reporting lines from the staff involved in carrying out the other tasks conferred on the ECB.[205]

(2) In order to comply with the above rules, the ECB adopted and made public in 2014 a **Decision** on the implementation of separation between its monetary policy and supervision functions,[206] which governs the organisational separation, professional secrecy, access to information between policy functions and classification, and the exchange of confidential information between its two '**policy functions**'. In this respect, the **Code of Conduct for high-level ECB Officials** provides that members and alternates must respect the separation of the ECB's supervisory tasks from its tasks relating to monetary policy, as well as other tasks, and comply with any rules adopted by the ECB pursuant to **Article 25(3) SSMR**. *In addition*, in carrying out their duties and responsibilities, Supervisory Board members and their alternates must consider the objectives of the SSMR and not interfere with the ECB's non-supervisory tasks, while duly respecting the specific duties and responsibilities of the Supervisory Board's Vice-Chair.[207]

(3) The ECB should also ensure that the GC's operation is completely differentiated as regards monetary and supervisory functions (including strictly separated meetings and agendas).[208] In this respect, the **ECB Rules of Procedure** provide for the following: *first*, the GC meetings regarding the supervisory tasks must take place separately from its regular meetings and have separate agendas. *Second*, on a proposal from the Supervisory Board, the Executive Board must draw up a provisional agenda and send it, together with the relevant documents prepared by the Supervisory Board, to the members of the GC and other authorised participants at least eight days before the relevant meeting. Exceptionally, in case of emergency the Executive Board must act appropriately having regard to the circumstances. *Third*, the GC must consult with the Governors of the NCBs of the non-area participating Member States before objecting to any draft Decision prepared by the Supervisory Board that is addressed to **NCAs** in respect of credit institutions established in such Member States. The same applies if the NCAs concerned inform the GC of their reasoned disagreement with such a draft decision. *Finally*, in principle the general provisions pertaining to GC meetings[209] also apply to GC meetings as far as the ECB's supervisory tasks are concerned.[210]

---

[205] SSMR, Article 25(2), first sub-paragraph, fourth-fifth sentences and second sub-paragraph and recital (66).

[206] ECB Decision 2014/723/EU of 17 September 2014 (ECB/2014/39), OJ L 300, 18.10.2014, pp. 57–62; its legal basis is Article 25(3).

[207] Code of Conduct for high-level ECB Officials, Article 5.1–5.2.

[208] SSMR, Article 25(4).

[209] ECB Rules of Procedure, Articles 2–5a.

[210] *Ibid.*, Article 13 l.1–13 l.4, respectively, (inserted by ECB Decision 2014/179/EU). The ECB established a structure of four Directorates-General for the performance

8.5.2.2 The Mediation Panel

The ECB should also establish a 'Mediation Panel' tasked with the resolution of differences of views on the part of NCAs of interested participating Member States regarding an objection of the GC to a draft Decision by the Supervisory Board. It is composed of one member per participating Member State, chosen by the members of the GC and the Supervisory Board deciding by simple majority.[211] Its setting up and its Rules of Procedure are governed by an **ECB Regulation**[212] on membership, internal organisation, the mediation procedure, confidentiality and professional secrecy.[213]

8.6 INSTITUTIONAL SAFEGUARDS AND LIABILITY

8.6.1 Institutional Safeguards

8.6.1.1 Audits by the European Court of Auditors (ECA)

The ECB is subject to the audit of the ECA, since the European Parliament and the Council may request the ECA to examine any other relevant matters falling within their competence as set out in **Article 287(4) TFEU**.[214]

---

of supervisory tasks and a Secretariat to the Supervisory Board, functionally reporting to its Chair and Vice Chair (ECB Decision 2014/723/EU, recital (11), third sentence; see also recital (O) of the EP-ECB Interinstitutional Agreement and recital (G) of the Council-ECB MoU).

[211] SSMR, Article 25(5), first-third sentences; see also recital (73).

[212] ECB Regulation (EU) No 673/2014 (ECB/2014/26) of 2 June 2014, OJ L 179, 19.6.2014, pp. 72–76; its legal basis is Article 25(5), fourth sentence SSRM.

[213] For more details on Article 25, including on the Mediation Panel, see Gortsos (2022a), pp. 341–354.

[214] *Ibid.*, Article 92(5). In particular, in accordance with the second sub-paragraph of Article 287(4), the ECA may, at any time, submit observations, particularly in the form of special reports, on specific questions and deliver opinions at the request of one of the other EU institutions. These special Reports set out the results of the ECA's performance and compliance audits of specific budgetary areas or management topics; these audit tasks are designed to be of maximum impact by considering the risks to performance or compliance, the level of income or spending involved, forthcoming developments and political and public interest. See on this Lienbacher (2019), pp. 3008–3009.

8.6.1.2 Actions Before the Court of Justice of the European Union (CJEU)

Judicial proceedings before the CJEU against Decisions of the ECB can be based either on **Article 263** or **Article 265 TFEU**.[215] In particular, in accordance with **recital (60) SSMR**:

> "*Pursuant to Article 263 TFEU, the CJEU is to review the legality of acts of, inter alia, the ECB, other than recommendations and opinions, intended to produce legal effects vis-à-vis third parties.*"[216]

On the other hand, **Article 265 TFEU** explicitly provides that proceedings for failure to act may be brought before the CJEU if the ECB were to fail to act in infringement of the Treaties.[217]

8.6.2 Liability

The SSMR does not contain any provisions on the contractual and/or non-contractual liability of the ECB within the SSM. However, **recital (61)** considers the following:

> "*In accordance with Article 340 TFEU,*[218] *the ECB should, in accordance with the general principles common to the laws of the Member States, make good any damage caused by it or by its servants in the performance of their duties. This should be without prejudice to the liability of [NCAs] to make good any damage caused by them or by their servants in the performance of their duties in accordance with national legislation.*"[219]

---

[215] For more details in relation to Article 263 TFEU, on the review of the legality of acts adopted by EU institutions, bodies, offices and agencies and on actions for their annulment, see, by means of mere indication, see Craig and de Búrca (2020), pp. 609–614, Borchardt (2019), pp. 2636–2670 and more analytically Schwarze und Voet van Vormizeele (2019), pp. 2856–2892. The judicial control of the ECB's legal acts is also governed by Article 35 ESCB/ECB Statute (see on this Smits (1997), pp. 106–110). On the role of judicial review as a mechanism of accountability, see Bell (2019), pp. 8–12. On Article 265 TFEU, see Craig and de Búrca (2020), pp. 558–571, Borchardt (2019), pp. 2673–2683 and Schwarze und Voet van Vormizeele (2019), pp. 2895–2908. On the procedures under Articles 263 and 265 TFEU, see Lenaerts, Maselis and Gutman (2014), pp. 253–417 and 419–440, respectively.

[216] SSMR, Article 13(1)–(2).

[217] For a regularly updated inventory of actions against ECB Decisions, see the EBI website at: https://ebi-europa.eu/publications/eu-cases-or-jurisprudence. On the judicial review of decisions taken pursuant to the SSMR, see also various contributions in Zilioli and Wojcik (2021, editors); see also Tridimas (2022).

[218] Reference it made to the third sub-paragraph of Article 340, which specifically applies to the ECB.

[219] For details see D'Ambrosio (2015).

The four above-mentioned conditions for the ECB to be successfully held liable in relation to acts or omissions in the performance of its duties apply in this case as well.[220] An important issue relating to supervisory liability within the SSM (and the SRM as well[221]) is that the judicial review of acts adopted by the ECB and by NCAs is likely to be governed by different procedural rules, since the NCAs' review will take place according to national laws, while for the ECB EU law will apply. This discrepancy could give rise to undesirable differences in outcomes across jurisdictions.[222] (Table 8.3)

---

[220] See Chapter 7 above, under 7.4.5. On the liability of NCAs within the SSM, see Almhofer (2021), pp. 230–232.

[221] See Chapter 9 below, under 9.6.2.

[222] On this aspect, see Busch and Gortsos (2022), pp. 506–507.

Table 8.3 ECB Legal acts on the Single Supervisory Mechanism (SSM)—other than the SSM-FR

Legal basis (SSMR or other)	Subject matter	Legal act	Entry into force
A. Legal acts pertaining to the operation of the bodies and Committees established by the SSMR			
Article 26(1)–(2) and (5)	Supervisory Board (appointment of ECB representatives)	Decision 2014/427/EU (ECB/2014/4)	6 February 2014
Article 26(12)	Supervisory Board	Rules of Procedure	1 April 2014
Rules of Procedure of the Supervisory Board, Article 13e	Supervisory Board	Code of Conduct[223]	13 November 2014
Article 24(10)	ABoR	Decision 2014/360/EU (ECB/2014/16)	15 June 2014
Article 25(5), fourth sentence	Mediation Panel	Regulation (EU) No 673/2014 (ECB/2014/26)	20 June 2014
ECB Rules of Procedure, Article 9a	Ethics Committee	Decision (EU) 2015/433 (ECB/2014/59)	15 March 2015
Article 6(1) and (7)		Guideline (EU) 2015/856 (ECB/2015/12)	18 March 2016

(continued)

[223] Since 2019, this has been included in the Code of Conduct for high-level ECB Officials (as in force).

Table 8.3 (continued)

Legal basis (SSMR or other)	Subject matter	Legal act	Entry into force
B. Legal acts pertaining to other aspects of the SSM			
Articles 25(2) and 26 (12)	Amended ECB Rules of Procedure	Decision 2014/179/EU (ECB/2014/1)	24 January 2014
Articles 4(3) and 33(3)–(4)	'Comprehensive assessment'	Decision 2014/123/EU (ECB/2014/3)	6 February 2014
Article 7	'Close cooperation'	Decision 2014/434/EU (ECB/2014/5)	27 February 2014
Article 18	Sanctions	Regulation (EU) No 469/2014 (ECB/2014/18)	15 May 2014
Article 6(2)	Provision to the ECB of supervisory data	Decision 2014/477/EU (ECB/2014/29)	19 July 2014
Article 25(1)–(3)	Separation between monetary policy and supervision functions	Decision 2014/723/EU (ECB/2014/39)	18 October 2014
Articles 4(3), second sub-paragraph, 30, and 33(2), second sub-paragraph	Supervisory fees	Regulation (EU) No 1163/2014 (ECB/2014/41) (as in force)	1 November 2014
Articles 4(3), second sub-paragraph and 30	Supervisory fees	ECB Decision (EU) 2019/2158 (ECB/2019/38)	29 March 2015
Articles 4(1) and (3), 6(2) and (5), point (d) and 10, and SSM-FR, Articles 21(1) and 140–141	Reporting of supervisory financial information	Regulation (EU) 2015/534 (ECB/2015/13)	1 April 2015
ESCB/ECB Statute, Article 12.3 & ECB Rules of Procedure, Article 23	Public access to ECB documents	Decision (EU) 2015/529 (ECB/2015/1)	29 March 2015

Secondary Sources

A-B-C

Akbik, Ad. (2022): *SSM Accountability: Lessons Learned for the Monetary Dialogues*, Banking Union Scrutiny, In-depth Analysis, European Parliament, Economic Governance Support Unit, July, available at: https://www.europarl.europa.eu/RegData/etudes/IDAN/2022/699545/IPOL_IDA(2022)699545_EN.pdf

Almhofer, M. (2022): Commentary on Articles 28–29 SSMR, in Binder, J.-H., Gortsos, Ch.V., Lackhoff, K. and Ch. Ohler (2022, editors): *Brussels Commentary on the Banking Union*, Verlag C.H. Beck, München – Hart Publishing, Oxford – Nomos Verlagsgesellschaft, Baden-Baden, pp. 404–412

Almhofer, M. (2021): The Liability of Authorities in Supervisory and Resolution Activities, in Zilioli, Ch. and K.-Ph. Wojcik (2021, editors): *Judicial Review in the European Banking Union*, Edward Elgar Publisher, Cheltenham, UK – Northampton, MA, USA, Chapter 14, pp. 221–234

Amtenbrink, F. (2022): Commentary on Articles 19 and SSMR, in Binder, J.-H., Gortsos, Ch.V., Lackhoff, K. and Ch. Ohler (2022, editors): *Brussels Commentary on the Banking Union*, Verlag C.H. Beck, München – Hart Publishing, Oxford – Nomos Verlagsgesellschaft, Baden-Baden, pp. 277–302

Amtenbrink, F. and M. Markakis (2022): The Legitimacy and Accountability of the ECB at the Age of Twenty, in Beukers, T., Fromage, D. and G. Monti (2022, editors): *The New European Central Bank: Taking Stock and Looking Ahead*, Oxford University Press, Oxford, Chapter 11

Annunziata, F. (2019): Fostering Centralization of EU Banking Supervision Through Case-Law: The European Court of Justice and the Role of the European Central Bank, *Bocconi Legal Studies Research Papers*, No. 3372346, April, available at: https://ssrn.com/abstract=3372346

Annunziata, F. (2018): European Banking Supervision in the Age of the ECB: Landeskreditbank Baden-Württemberg – Förderbank v. ECB, *Bocconi Legal Studies Research Papers*, No. 3139567, also available at: https://ssrn.com/abstract=3139 2567

Athanassiou, Ph. (2011): *Financial Sector Supervisors' Accountability: A European Perspective*, European Central Bank, Legal Working Paper Series, No 12, 18 August (also available at: https://papers.ssrn.com/abstract=1807174)

Bax, R. and A. Witte (2019): The Taxonomy of ECB Instruments Available for Banking Supervision, *ECB Economic Bulletin*, Issue 6, available at: https://www.ecb.europa.eu/pub/economic-bulletin/html/eb201906.en.html

Bell, J. (2019): Judicial Review in the Administrative State, in de Poorter, J., Ballin, E.H. and S. Lavrijssen (2019, editors): *Judicial Review of Administrative Discretion in the Administrative State*, Springer – Asser Press, Chapter 1, pp. 3–26

Bini-Smaghi, L. and D. Gros (2000): *Open Issues in Central Banking*, Palgrave Macmillan London

Blair, W. (2019): The ABoR and the Role of Independent Panels of Administrative Review: An Introduction, in *Building Bridges: Central banking law in an interconnected world*, ECB E-Book, pp. 333–334

Brescia Morra, C. (2019): Nature and Role of the ABoR, in: *Building Bridges: Central Banking Law in An Interconnected World*, ECB E-Book, pp. 335–349

Brescia Morra, C., Smits, R. and A. Magliari (2017): The Administrative Board of Review of the European Central Bank: Experience After 2 Years, *European Business Organisation Law Review (EBOR)*, Volume 18(3), September (The European Banking Union in Action), Springer – Asser Press, pp. 567–589

Borchardt, K.D. (2019): Kommentar zu den Artikeln 263 und 265 AEUV, in Lenz, C.O. und K.D. Borchardt (2019, Hrsg.): *EU-Verträge: Kommentar*, 6. Auflage, Bundesanzeiger Verlag, Köln – Linde Verlag, Wien, pp. 2636–2670 and 2673–2683

Boucon L. and D. Jaros (2017): The Application of National Law by the European Central Bank within the EU Banking Union's Single Supervisory Mechanism: A New Mode of European Integration, *European Journal of Legal Studies*, Volume 10, pp. 155 *et seq.*

Božina Beroš, M. (2019): The ECB's Accountability Within the SSM Framework: Mind the (transparency) Gap, *Maastricht Journal of European and Comparative Law*, Volume 26, Issue 1 (Special issue: "The CB's Accountability in a multilevel European order"), available at: https://doi.org/10.1177/1023263X18822790

Budinská, B. and J. Tegelaar (2023): Duty of Care as a Judicial Review Tool for SSM Composite Procedures, in Böffel, L. and J. Schürger (2023, editors): *Digitalisation, Sustainability, and the Banking and Capital Markets Union*, EBI Studies in Banking and Capital Markets Law, Palgrave Macmillan, Cham – Switzerland, pp. 329–351

Buiter (1999): Alice in Wonderland, *Journal of Common Market Studies*, Volume 37(2), pp. 181–209

Busch, D. and Ch.V. Gortsos (2022): Liability of the European Central Bank, the Single Resolution Board and the ESAs (ESMA, EBA and EIOPA), in Busch, D., Gortsos, Ch.V. and G. McMeel (2022, editors): *Liability of Financial Supervisors and Resolution Authorities*, Chapter 2, pp. 9–54

Busch, D., McMeel, G. and Ch.V. Gortsos (2022): Comparative Law Evaluation, in Busch, D., Gortsos, Ch.V. and G. McMeel (2022, editors): *Liability of Financial Supervisors and Resolution Authorities*, Chapter 17, pp. 463–512

Carletti, El., Dell'Ariccia, G. and R.S. Marquez (2016): *Supervisory Incentives in a Banking Union*, IMF Working Paper No. 16/186, September, available at: https://ssrn.com/abstract=2882624

Chiti, M.P. (2019): The European Banking Union in the Case Law of the Court of Justice of the European Union, in Chiti, M.P. and V. Santoro (2019, editors): *The Palgrave Handbook of European Banking Union Law*, Palgrave – Macmillan, USA, Chapter 6, pp. 105–134

Craig, P. and G. de Búrca (2020): *EU Law: Texts, Cases, and Materials*, Seventh edition, Oxford University Press, Oxford – New York

D

D'Ambrosio, R. (2021): The Legal Review of SSM Administrative Sanctions, in Zilioli, Ch. and K.-Ph. Wojcik (2021, editors): *Judicial Review in the European Banking Union*, Edward Elgar Publisher, Cheltenham, UK – Northampton, MA, USA, Chapter 19, pp. 316–332

D'Ambrosio, R. (2020): The Application of National Law by the ECB, in D'Ambrosio, R. (2020, editor): *Law and Practice of the Banking Union and of its governing Institutions (Cases and Materials)*, Quaderni di Ricerca Giuridica, Banca d'Italia, Numero 88, April, Part One, Chapter II, pp. pp. 131–138

D'Ambrosio, R. (2015): *The ECB and NCA liability within the Single Supervisory Mechanism*, Quaderni di Ricerca Giuridica, Banca d'Italia, Numero 78, Gennaio, available at: https://www.bancaditalia.it/pubblicazioni/quaderni-giuridici/2015-0078/QRG-78.pdf

D'Ambrosio, R. (2013): *Due Process and Safeguards of the Persons Subject to SSM Supervisory and Sanctioning Proceedings*, Quaderni di Ricerca Giuridica, Banca d'Italia, Numero 74, Dicembre

De Grauwe, P. (2020): *Economics of Monetary Union*, 13th Edition, Oxford University Press, Oxford – New York

De Gregorio Merino, Al. (2021): The ECB's Regulatory Powers, Their Scope and Their Judicial Review, in Zilioli, Ch. and K.-Ph. Wojcik (2021, editors): *Judicial Review in the European Banking Union*, Edward Elgar Publisher, Cheltenham, UK – Northampton, MA, USA, Chapter 20, pp. 333–344

De Haan, J. and S.C.W. Eijffinger (2016): *The Politics of Central Bank Independence*, De Nederlandsche Bank Working Paper No. 539, December, available at: https://ssrn.com/abstract=2888836

De La Parra, S. (2015): La BCE entre indépendance et responsabilité, in Allemand, F. (2015, editor): *L'Union économique et monétaire: origine, fonctionnement et futur*, CVCE, Coll. European Integration Studies (also available at: https://webintra.cvce.eu/obj/la_bce_entre_independance_et_responsabilite-fr-47ac1c44-2de8-4a11-9544-088a74d38353.html)

Della Negra, F. and G. Lo Schiavo (2022): The Relationship Between the ECB and the National competent Authorities in the Single Supervisory Mechanism: Problems and Perspectives, in Beukers, T., Fromage, D. and G. Monti (2022, editors): *The New European Central Bank: Taking Stock and Looking Ahead*, Oxford University Press, Oxford, Chapter 8

E-F

Eijffinger, S. and J. De Haan (2000): *European Monetary and Fiscal Policy*, Oxford University Press, Oxford

Eijffinger, S. and J. Haan (1996): *The Political Economy of Central-Bank Independence*, Special Papers in International Economics, No. 19, May

Ferrarini, G. (2015): Single Supervision and the Governance of Banking Markets: Will the SSM Deliver the Expected Benefits? *European Business Organization Law Review*, Volume 16, pp. 513–537

Fromage, D. (2019): Guaranteeing the ECB's Democratic Accountability in the Post-Banking Union Era: An Ever More Difficult Task? *Maastricht Journal of European and Comparative Law*, Volume 26, Issue 1 (Special issue: "The CB's accountability in a multilevel European order"), available at: https://doi.org/10.1177/1023263X18822788

Fromage, D., Tuori, Kl. and P. Dermine (2019): ECB independence and accountability today: towards a (necessary) redefinition? *Maastricht Journal of European and Comparative Law*, Volume 26, Issue 1 (Special issue: "The ECB's Accountability in a Multilevel European order"), available at: https://doi.org/10.1177/1023263X19827819

G-H

Gagliardi, En. and L. Wissink (2020): Ensuring Effective Judicial Protection in Case of ECB Decisions Based on National Law, *Review of European Administrative Law*, Issue 1 (also available at: https://ssrn.com/abstract=3522363)

Gortsos, Ch.V. (2022a): Commentary on Articles 6, 16 and 25 SSMR, in Binder, J.-H., Gortsos, Ch.V., Lackhoff, K. and Ch. Ohler (2022, editors): *Brussels Commentary on the Banking Union*, Verlag C.H. Beck, München – Hart Publishing, Oxford – Nomos Verlagsgesellschaft, Baden-Baden, pp. 92–133, 236–251 and 341–354

Gortsos, Ch.V. (2022b): Commentary on Article 81 SRMR, in Binder, J.-H., Gortsos, Ch.V., Lackhoff, K. and Ch. Ohler (2022, editors): *Brussels Commentary on the Banking Union*, Verlag C.H. Beck, München – Hart Publishing, Oxford – Nomos Verlagsgesellschaft, Baden-Baden, pp. 1150–1153

Gortsos, Ch.V. (2021): The Crédit Agricole Cases: Banking Corporate Governance and Application of National Law by the ECB, in Zilioli, Ch. and K.-Ph. Wojcik (2021, editors): *Judicial Review in the European Banking Union*, Edward Elgar Publisher, Cheltenham, UK – Northampton, MA, USA, Chapter 31, pp. 510–520

Gortsos, Ch.V. (2020): *European Central Banking Law – The Role of the European Central Bank and National Central Banks under European Law*, Palgrave Macmillan Studies in Banking and Financial Institutions, Palgrave Macmillan, Cham – Switzerland

Gruber, G. (2022): Commentary on Articles 9 and 26 SSMR, in Binder, J.-H., Gortsos, Ch.V., Lackhoff, K. and Ch. Ohler (2022, editors): *Brussels Commentary on the Banking Union*, Verlag C.H. Beck, München – Hart Publishing, Oxford – Nomos Verlagsgesellschaft, Baden-Baden, pp. 146–157 and 354–381

Gurlit, El. (2022): Commentary on Articles 14–15 SSMR, in Binder, J.-H., Gortsos, Ch.V., Lackhoff, K. and Ch. Ohler (2022, editors): *Brussels Commentary on the Banking Union*, Verlag C.H. Beck, München – Hart Publishing, Oxford – Nomos Verlagsgesellschaft, Baden-Baden, pp. 189–234

Hernández Saseta, C. (2021): The Legal Review of ECB Instructions Under Article 9 SSM Regulation, in Zilioli, Ch. and K.-Ph. Wojcik (2021, editors): *Judicial Review in the European Banking Union*, Edward Elgar Publisher, Cheltenham, UK – Northampton, MA, USA, Chapter 18, pp. 304–315

Hofmann, H.C.H. and Al. Turk (2007): The Development of Integrated Administration in the EU and its Consequences, *European Law Journal*, Volume 13, Issue 2, March, pp. 253–271, available at: https://ssrn.com/abstract=973954

K

Kaufhold, A.-K. (2022): Commentary on Articles 3 and 22 SSMR, in Binder, J.-H., Gortsos, Ch.V., Lackhoff, K. and Ch. Ohler (2022, editors): *Brussels Commentary on the Banking Union*, Verlag C.H. Beck, München – Hart Publishing, Oxford – Nomos Verlagsgesellschaft, Baden-Baden, pp. 23–37 and 307–318

Kennedy, T. (2018): The Court of Auditors, in Schütze, R. and T. Tridimas (2018, editors): *Oxford Principles European Union Law – Volume I: The European Union Legal Order*, Oxford University Press, Oxford, Part III: Institutional Framework, Chapter 20, pp. 651–686

Kornezov, A. (2017): The Application of National Law by the ECB—A Maze of (Un)answered Questions, *ESCB Legal Conference 2016*, January, pp. 270–282 (also available at: https://www.ecb.europa.eu/pub/pdf/other/escblegalconferenc e2016_201702.en.pdf?6f2cc599a5c8486e2cd5345a2610325d)

Krauskopf, B. and C. Steven (2009): The Institutional Framework of the European System of Central Banks: Legal Issues in the Practice of the First Ten Years of its Existence, *Common Market Law Review*, Volume 46, pp. 1143–1175

Krommendijk, J. (2016): Is There Light on the Horizon? The Distinction Between "Rewe Effectiveness" and the Principle of Effective Judicial Protection in Article 47 of the Charter after Orizzonte, *Common Market Law Review*, Volume 53, Issue 5, pp. 1395–1418

L-M

Lackhoff, K. and M. Prokop (2022): Commentary on Articles 10–13 SSMR, in Binder, J.-H., Gortsos, Ch.V., Lackhoff, K. and Ch. Ohler (2022, editors): *Brussels Commentary on the Banking Union*, Verlag C.H. Beck, München – Hart Publishing, Oxford – Nomos Verlagsgesellschaft, Baden-Baden, pp. 158–189

Lackhoff, K. and A. Witte (2022): Commentary on Article 4 SSMR, in Binder, J.-H., Gortsos, Ch.V., Lackhoff, K. and Ch. Ohler (2022, editors): *Brussels Commentary on the Banking Union*, Verlag C.H. Beck, München – Hart Publishing, Oxford – Nomos Verlagsgesellschaft, Baden-Baden, pp. 37–85

Lackhoff, K. (2017): *Single Supervisory Mechanism: A Practitioner's Guide*, Verlag C.H. Beck, München – Hart Publishing, Oxford – Nomos Verlagsgesellschaft, Baden-Baden

Lamandini, M., and D.R. Muñoz (2022a): Banking Union's Accountability System in Practice: A Health Check-Up to Europe's Financial Heart, *European Law Journal*, pp. 1–31

Lamandini, M. and D.R. Muñoz (2020b): *SSM and the SRB Accountability at European level: What Room for Improvements?* Banking Union Scrutiny, In-depth Analysis, European Parliament, Economic Governance Support Unit, April, available at: https://beta.op.europa.eu/en/publication-detail/-/publication/ 5dbbd54d-44cc-11eb-b59f-01aa75ed71a1/language-en/format-PDF/source-200 399137

Lamandini, M. and D.R. Muñoz (2020c): Law and Practice of Financial Appeal Bodies (ESAs' Board of Appeal, SRB Appeal Panel): A View from the Inside, *Common Market Law Review*, Volume 57, Issue 1, pp. 119–160

Lamandini, M., Muñoz, D.R. and J. Solana (2017): The European Central Bank (ECB) as a Catalyst for Change in EU Law. Part 1: The ECB's Mandates, *Columbia Journal of European Law*, Volume 23, Issue 2, pp. 199–263

Lastra, R.M. (2020): *Accountability Mechanisms of the Bank of England and of the European Central Bank*, Monetary Dialogue Papers, European Parliament, September, available at: https://www.europarl.europa.eu/cmsdata/211623/1_L ASTRA-final.pdf

Lastra, R.M. and K. Alexander (2020): *The ECB's Mandate: Perspectives on Sustainability and Solidarity*, Study for the Committee on Economic and Monetary Affairs, Policy Department for Economic, Scientific and Quality of Life Policies, European Parliament, available at: https://www.europarl.europa.eu/RegData/etudes/ IDAN/2020/648813/IPOL_IDA(2020)648813_EN.pdf

Lastra, R.M. and C. Goodhart (2017): Populism and Central Bank Independence, *Open Economies Review 29*, pp. 49–68, available at: https://doi.org/10.1007/s11079-017-9447-y

Lehmann, M. (2021): Banking Union, in Zilioli, Ch. and K.-Ph. Wojcik (2021, editors): *Judicial review in the European Banking Union*, Edward Elgar Publisher, Cheltenham, UK – Northampton, MA, USA, Chapter 6, pp. 77–96

Lenaerts, K., Maselis, Ig. and K. Gutman (2014): *EU Procedural Law*, Oxford European Union Law Library, Oxford University Press, Oxford

Lienbacher, G. (2019): Kommentar zum Artikel 285–287 AEUV, in Becker, U., Hatje, A. Schoo, J. und J. Schwarze (2019, Herausgeber): *EU-Kommentar*, 4. Auflage, Nomos Verlagsgesellschaft, Baden-Baden, pp. 2992–3010

Lo Schiavo, G. (2022): The Single Supervisory Mechanism (SSM) and the EU Anti-Money Laundering Framework Compared: Governance, Rules, Challenges and Opportunities, *Journal of Banking Regulation*, Volume 23, pp. 91–105

Lock, T. and M. Denis (2019): Commentary on Article 47 CFR, in Kellerbauer M., Klamert M., and Tomkin J. (2019, editors): *The EU Treaties and the Charter of Fundamental Rights: A Commentary*, Oxford University Press, New York, pp. 2214–2226

Louis, J.V. (2023): Independence and Accountability of Central Banking, in Blair, W., Zilioli, Ch. and Ch.V. Gortsos (2023, editors), *International Monetary and Banking Law in the post COVID-19 World*, Chapter 17, Oxford University Press, Oxford

Louis, J.-V. (2015): BCE – Indépendance et responsabilité, *Mélanges en l'honneur du professeur Catherine Flaesch-Mougin*

Louis, J.-V. (2009): L'Union européenne et sa monnaie, in Commentaire J. Megret: *Integration des marchés financiers*, 3e édition, Institut d' Etudes Européennes, Editions de l' Université de Bruxelles, Bruxelles

Markakis, M. (2020): *Accountability in the Economic and Monetary Union: Foundations, Policy, and Governance*, Oxford Studies in European Law, Oxford University Press, Oxford

Mendes, J. (2016): Discretion, Care and Public Interests in the EU Administration: Probing the Limits of Law, *Common Market Law Review*, Volume 53, pp. 419–452

Moloney, N. (2019): Close Cooperation: The SSM Institutional Framework and Lessons from the ESAs, in *Building Bridges: Central Banking Law in an interconnected world*, ECB E-Book, pp. 296–313

Montemaggi, St. (2020): Judgements of the General Court and of the ECJ on the Landeskreditbank (General Court, T-122/15 and ECJ, C-450/17 P, in D'Ambrosio, R. (2020, editor): *Law and Practice of the Banking Union and of its governing Institutions (Cases and Materials)*, Quaderni di Ricerca Giuridica, Banca d'Italia, Numero 88, April, Part One, Chapter V.B, pp. 217–229

O-P-Q-R

Ohler, Ch. (2022): Commentary on Articles 1 and 7–8 SSMR, in Binder, J.-H., Gortsos, Ch.V., Lackhoff, K. and Ch. Ohler (2022, editors): *Brussels Commentary on the Banking Union*, Verlag C.H. Beck, München – Hart Publishing, Oxford – Nomos Verlagsgesellschaft, Baden-Baden, pp. 1–13 and 133–146

Ohler, Ch. (2015): *Bankenaufsicht und Geldpolitik in der Währungsunion*, Verlag C.H. Beck, München

Papathanassiou, Ch. (2022): Commentary on Article 18 SSMR, in Binder, J.-H., Gortsos, Ch.V., Lackhoff, K. and Ch. Ohler (2022, editors): *Brussels Commentary on the Banking Union*, Verlag C.H. Beck, München – Hart Publishing, Oxford – Nomos Verlagsgesellschaft, Baden-Baden, pp. 264–277

Pizzolla, Ag. (2021): Close Cooperation and Aspects of Judicial Review, in Zilioli, Ch. and K.-Ph. Wojcik (2021, editors): *Judicial Review in the European Banking Union*, Edward Elgar Publisher, Cheltenham, UK – Northampton, MA, USA, Chapter 21, pp. 345–365

Priego, F.-J. and F. Conlledo (2015): TheRole of the Decentralisation Principle in the Legal Construction of the European System of Central Banks, in *Legal Aspects of the European System of Central Banks*, ECB E-Book, pp. 189–198

Riso, A.L. (2021): A Prime for the SSM Before the Court: The *L-Bank* Case, in Zilioli, Ch. and K.-Ph. Wojcik (2021, editors): *Judicial Review in the European Banking Union*, Edward Elgar Publisher, Cheltenham, UK – Northampton, MA, USA, Chapter 29, pp. 494–503

Rosas, A. (2021): EMU in the Case Law of Union Courts: A General Overview and Some Observations, *European Papers*, Volume 6, Issue 3, pp. 1397–1414

S-T

Sarmiento, D. (2022): Setting the Limits of Implementation of national law by EU Institutions: The *Corneli v ECB* case (T-502/19), EU Law Live, Op-Ed, 24 October, available at: https://eulawlive.com/op-ed-setting-the-limits-of-implementation-of-national-law-by-eu-institutions-the-corneli-v-ecb-case-t-502-19-by-daniel-sarmiento

Schwarze, J. und Ph. Voet van Vormizeele (2019): Kommentar zu den Artikeln 263, 265 und 278 AEUV, in Schwarze, J., Becker, U., Hatje, A. und J. Schoo (2019, Hrsg.): *EU-Kommentar*, 4. Auflage, Nomos Verlagsgesellschaft, Baden-Baden, pp. 2856–2892, 2895–2904 and 2971–2979

Segoin, D. (2021): The Investigatory Powers, Including On-Site Inspections, of the ECB, and Their Judicial Control, in Zilioli, Ch. and K.-Ph. Wojcik (2021, editors): *Judicial Review in the European Banking Union*, Edward Elgar Publisher, Cheltenham, UK – Northampton, MA, USA, Chapter 17, pp. 285–303

Simoncini, M. (2021): Challenges of Justice in the European Banking Union: Administrative Integration and Mismatches in Jurisdiction, *Yearbook of European Law*, Volume 40, pp. 310–334

Simoncini, M. (2020): Different Shades of Legal Standing and the Right to Judicial Protection of Private Parties in the Banking Union: Trasta Komercbanka, *Common Market Law Review*, Volume 57, pp. 1867–1886

Smits, R. (2022): Commentary on Article 24 SSMR, in Binder, J.-H., Gortsos, Ch.V., Lackhoff, K. and Ch. Ohler (2022, editors): *Brussels Commentary on the Banking Union*, Verlag C.H. Beck, München – Hart Publishing, Oxford – Nomos Verlagsgesellschaft, Baden-Baden, pp. 321–341

Smits, R. (2020): *SSM and the SRB Accountability at European Level: Room for Improvements?* Banking Union Scrutiny, In-Depth Analysis, European Parliament, Economic Governance Support Unit, April, available at: https://www.europarl.europa.eu/RegData/etudes/STUD/2020/645726/IPOL_STU(2020)645726_EN.pdf

Smits, R. (2019): Accountability of the European Central Bank, *Ars Aequi*, January, available at: https://www.speakersacademy.com/wp-content/uploads/2018/06/Accountability-of-the-European-Central-Bank.pdf, pp. 27–37

Smits, R. (1997): *The European Central Bank – Institutional Aspects*, Kluwer Law International, The Hague

Thiele, Al. (2022): The Independence of the ECB: Justification, Challenges and Possible Threats, in Beukers, T., Fromage, D. and G. Monti (2022, editors): *The New European Central Bank: Taking Stock and Looking Ahead*, Oxford University Press, Oxford, Chapter 10

Tridimas, T. (2022): The ECB and the Court of Justice: Old Toolbox, New Problems, in Beukers, T., Fromage, D. and G. Monti (2022, editors): *The New European Central Bank: Taking Stock and Looking Ahead*, Oxford University Press, Oxford, Chapter 12

Tröger, T.H. (2017): *How Not To Do Banking Law in the 21st Century – The Judgement of the European General Court (EGC) in the Case T-122/15 Landeskreditbank Baden-Württemberg – Förderbank v European Central Bank (ECB)*, Oxford Business Law Blog, 16 June, available at: https://www.law.ox.ac.uk/business-law-blog/blog/2017/06/how-not-do-banking-law-21st-century-judgement-european-general-court

V-W & Z

Van Rijn, M. (2022): *Judicial Protection for Banks Under the single rulebook and the Single Supervisory Mechanism*, Radboud Business Law Institute, Series law of business and finance, Volume 22, Wolters Kluwer Nederland B.V.

Voet van Vormizeele, Ph. (2019): Kommentar zum Artikel 41 GRC, in Schwarze, J., Becker, U., Hatje, A. und J. Schoo (2019, Hrsg.): *EU-Kommentar*, 4. Auflage, Nomos Verlagsgesellschaft, Baden-Baden, pp. 3503–3507

Wymeersch, Ed. (2020): The Single Supervisory Mechanism for Banking Supervision: Institutional Aspects, in Busch, D. and G. Ferrarini (2020, editors): *European Banking Union*, second edition, Oxford University Press, Oxford, Chapter 4, pp. 145–191

Zagouras, G. (2022): Commentary on Article 30 SSMR, in Binder, J.-H., Gortsos, Ch.V., Lackhoff, K. and Ch. Ohler (2022, editors): *Brussels Commentary on the Banking Union*, Verlag C.H. Beck, München – Hart Publishing, Oxford – Nomos Verlagsgesellschaft, Baden-Baden, pp. 413–421

Zilioli, Ch. And K.-Ph. Wojcik (2021, editors): *Judicial Review in the European Banking Union*, Edward Elgar Publisher, Cheltenham, UK – Northampton, MA, USA

CHAPTER 9

The Single Resolution Mechanism (SRM)

9.1 THE SINGLE RESOLUTION BOARD

9.1.1 Legal Status

As already noted,[1] the SRB was established by the SRMR and became fully operational on 1 January 2015.[2] Unlike the ECB (which, as also already noted, is a Treaty-based EU institution), it belongs to the EU **decentralised agencies** with a specific structure corresponding to its specific tasks serving the public interest, which departs from the model of all other EU agencies in order to ensure a swift and effective decision-making process in resolution.[3] The SRB has legal personality.[4] Hence, it enjoys in each Member State (including non-participating ones) the most extensive legal capacity accorded to legal persons under national law (*inter alia*, the right to acquire or dispose of movable and immovable property and the right to be a party to legal proceedings) and is represented by its Chair. It must act in compliance with EU law and in particular (since it is not an EU institution and does not have

---

[1] See above in Chapter 6, under 6.5.1.

[2] SRMR, Articles 42(1), first sentence (and 98(1). Article 98(2)–(3) provides that the Commission was responsible for the SRB's establishment and initial operation, until the latter had the operational capacity to implement its own budget and lays down the powers of its interim Chair, which were not activated (see also recital (119)).

[3] *Ibid.*, Article 42(1), second sentence; see also recital (31), first sentence. On the clash between public interest and property rights in banking resolution, see, by means of mere indication, Anastopoulou (2023), with extensive further references.

[4] *Ibid.*, Article 42(1), third sentence.

the power to take final binding Decisions) with Council and Commission decisions, pursuant to the SRMR.[5]

9.1.2 Seat—Headquarters Agreement and Operating Conditions

The SRB, whose seat is located in Brussels,[6] should have concluded with Belgium a Headquarters Agreement after obtaining the approval in its Plenary Session and not later than 20 August 2016. This should lay down the necessary arrangements concerning the accommodation to be provided for the SRB in Belgium, the facilities to be made available by that Member State, and the specific rules applicable therein to the SRB's Chair, its members in its Plenary Session, its staff and members of their families. Belgium, as the country in which the SRB has its seat, must also provide the best possible conditions to ensure the proper functioning of the SRB "*including multilingual, European-oriented schooling and appropriate transport connections*".[7]

9.1.3 Composition and Governance

9.1.3.1 General Overview

(1) In order to ensure that due account is taken of all relevant interests at stake in resolution procedures, the SRB is composed of the following: *first*, a Chair and a Vice-Chair, responsible for carrying out the Chair's functions under the SRMR in his/her absence or reasonable impediment; *second*, four further full-time members (hereinafter '**the further full-time members**'); and *finally*, a member appointed by each participating Member State, representing their NRAs (if in a participating Member State there are more than one NRA (e.g., one for credit institutions and their groups and one for investment firms and their groups), a second representative may participate as observer, albeit without voting rights). Each member, including the Chair, has one vote. In addition, the Commission and the ECB also designate a representative each, entitled to participate in the meetings of the SRB's Plenary and Executive Sessions as '**permanent observers**' and to have access to all documents.[8]

The SRB's administrative and management structure comprises a Plenary Session, an Executive Session, the Chair (all discussed below) and a Secretariat

---

[5] *Ibid.*, Articles 42(2)–(3) and 44. On the compliance of SRB decisions with EU law, see also Article 5(2), first sub-paragraph; on Article 42, see Ohler (2022). For the peculiar legal features of the SRB, see Ruccia (2021).

[6] *Ibid.*, Article 48.

[7] *Ibid.*, Article 97(1)–(2). To the best of the author's knowledge, as of December 2022, this Agreement was not publicly available.

[8] *Ibid.*, Article 43(3)–(4); see also recital (31), second sentence.

providing administrative and technical support on the performing of the tasks of the SRB.[9]

On the basis of **Article 83(3)**, the SRB established 'internal resolution teams' ('**IRTs**') composed of its own staff and staff of the NRAs, as well as observers from non-participating Member States' resolution authorities; it has also appointed coordinators of those teams from its own staff, which may be invited, pursuant to **Article 51(3) SRMR**, as observers to attend the meetings of its Executive Session.[10] The establishment, scope of activities and composition of IRTs, as well as the role of IRTs coordinators and sub-coordinators are governed by **Articles 24–26 of a Board Decision** of 17 December 2018.[11] The SRB may also establish 'internal committees' to provide it with advice and guidance on the discharge of its functions.[12]

9.1.3.2 The SRB's Plenary Session
Composition and Tasks
(1) Plenary Sessions are participated in by the Chair, the further full-time members (which are the 'permanent members') and an appointed representative of the NRA from each participating Member State.[13] The SRB may invite observers, if relevant, in addition to the permanent ones appointed by the Commission and the ECB (which, as just noted, participate as 'permanent observers), to participate in the Plenary Session's meetings on an ad hoc basis, including an EBA representative, in particular when matters are discussed for which, in accordance with the BRRD, the EBA is required to develop RTS or ITSs or issue Guidelines'.[14] Other observers, such as a representative of

---

[9] SRMR, Article 43(5) and recital (32), first sentence and Rules of Procedure of the Board in its Plenary Session, Article 13.

[10] The members appointed by the respective Member States participate in accordance with Article 53(3)–(4) (*ibid.*, Article 83(4)); Article 53(3)–(4) is discussed further below in this Section. The IRTs resemble to the JSTs in the SSM framework.

[11] Decision SRB/PS/2018/15 "establishing the framework for the practical arrangements for the cooperation within the [SRM] between the [SRB and [NRAs])". The tasks of IRTs are extensive and their assistance is of primary importance in the phase of preparation for resolution, since they are the main forum in which the Board and NRAs cooperate in performing resolution activities (resolution planning and preparation of resolution schemes). Most importantly, they assist in performing the assessment of entities' and/or groups' recovery plans; in defining the need for information, formulating the request of information and performing the analysis of submissions from the entities and groups; and in drawing up such plans (*ibid.*, Article 24(4), points (a)–(c)).

[12] SRMR, Article 84. On Articles 83(3)–(4) and 84, see Gortsos (2022), pp. 1158–1163.

[13] SRMR, Article 49, with reference to Article 43(1), and Rules of Procedure of the Board in its Plenary Session, Article 1(2)–(3). On the participation of non-euro area Member States in the SRM, see Binder (2019). For lessons learned from the non-euro area Member States joining the SRM as regards multilevel cooperation, especially in the EU resolution of cross-border bank groups, see Smoleńska (2022).

[14] SRMR, Article 51(3) and recital (35), first sentence and Rules of Procedure of the Board in its Plenary Session, Article 1(7).

the ESM, should, if appropriate, also be invited to attend.[15] The Chair may also invite representatives of non-participating Member States' NRAs or other authorities and bodies, wherever appropriate, to participate on an ad hoc basis as observers.[16]

The SRB in this Session has a wide range of resolution and managerial tasks (see Box 9.1 just below) and, when taking Decisions, it must act pursuant to the general principles laid down in **Article 6** and the resolution objectives set out in **Article 14**.[17]

Box 9.1 Tasks of the SRB in its Plenary Session

A. Key tasks[18]

(1) The SRB in its Plenary Session must adopt: its own **Rules of Procedure** and those of the Executive Session[19]; by 30 November each year, the SRB **Annual Work Programme** for the following year, based on a draft by the Chair, which must then be transmitted for information to the European Parliament, the Council, the Commission and the ECB; the SRB **Annual Report**, which must contain detailed explanations on the implementation of the budget; the **Financial Regulations** applicable to the SRB in accordance with **Article 64**[20]; an anti-fraud strategy, proportionate to fraud risks, under a cost–benefit analysis; rules for the prevention and management of conflicts of interest for its members[21]; and the framework provided for in **Article 31(1)** to organise the practical arrangements for the cooperation between the SRB and NRAs.[22]

(2) It must also adopt *and monitor* the SRB annual budget, approve its final accounts and give discharge to the Chair.

---

[15] SRMR, recital (35), third-fifth sentences.

[16] Rules of Procedure of the Board in its Plenary Session, Article 1(8).

[17] SRMR, Article 50(2), first sub-paragraph.

[18] *Ibid.*, Article 50(1), points (k), (a), (g), (h), (i), (j), (q) and (b), respectively.

[19] These Rules of Procedure, which have just been referred to, supplement the SRMR (Article 1(1) of both SRB Decisions). They were firstly adopted on 29 April 2015 by SRB Decisions and entered into force on the same date (SRB/PS/2015/9 and SRB/PS/2015/8, respectively) and then replaced, with effect from 1 July 2020, by new SRB Decisions of 24 June 2020 documents (SRB/PS/2020/15 and SRB/PS/2020/14, respectively).

[20] On the Annual Report and the Financial Regulations, see below, under 9.4.

[21] This aspect is governed by the Code of Conduct of the SRB; see under 9.4 below.

[22] On this aspect, see under 9.2.3 below.

B. Tasks relating to the SRF[23]

(1) The SRB in its Plenary Session must decide on the use of the SRF, if its support in a specific resolution action is required above the threshold of five billion euro for which the weighting of liquidity support is 0.5.[24] In this case, the draft resolution scheme prepared by the Executive Session is deemed to be adopted, unless within three hours from its submission at least one Plenary Session member has called a meeting of that Session; in the latter case, the Decision on the resolution scheme must be taken by the Plenary Session.

(2) Once, the net accumulated use of the SRF in the last consecutive twelve months reaches the threshold of five billion euro, it must evaluate the application of resolution tools, in particular the use of the SRF, and provide guidance to the Executive Session (*inter alia*, differentiating, if appropriate, between liquidity and other forms of support), which the latter must follow in subsequent resolution Decisions. Guidance should also focus on ensuring the non-discriminatory application of resolution tools, avoiding a depletion of the SRF and differentiating appropriately between no-risk or low-risk liquidity and other forms of support.

(3) If SRF support is required exceeding the threshold of five billion euro, it must decide on the necessity to raise extraordinary *ex-post* contributions, voluntary borrowing between financing arrangements, resort to alternative financing means and the mutualisation of national financing arrangements.

(4) It must decide on the SRF's investments.[25]

C. Other tasks[26]

(1) The SRB in its Plenary Session must exercise with respect to the staff of the SRB the **'appointing authority powers'** conferred by the Staff Regulations on the Appointing Authority *and* by the Conditions

---

[23] SRMR, Articles 50(1), points (c) (in conjunction with Article 50(2), second subparagraph) and (d)–(f), respectively.

[24] Recital (33), fifth sentence considers that, if liquidity support involves no or significantly less risk than other forms of support (e.g., in the case of a short-term, one-off extension of credit to solvent institutions against adequate collateral of high quality), it is justified to give such a form of support a lower weight of only 0.5.

[25] Articles 71–74 and 78–79 governing these aspects are analysed in Volume II. On Articles 71–74, see Gortsos (2022), pp. 1109–1122; on Articles 75 and 79, see Psaroudakis (2022), pp. 1123–1129 and 1140–1141.

[26] SRMR, Article 50(1), points (l)–(p), respectively, (point (m) in conjunction with Article 50(3)).

of Employment of Other Servants of the EU, pursuant to **Council Regulation (EEC, Euratom, ECSC) No 259/68** of 29 February 1968[27] "laying down the Staff Regulations of Officials and the Conditions of Employment of Other Servants of the European Communities and instituting special measures temporarily applicable to officials of the Commission" ('**Staff Regulations**').

(2) Pursuant to **Article 110** of these Regulations, it must adopt *first*, a Decision delegating to the Chair relevant appointing authority powers and establishing the conditions under which the delegation of powers can be suspended[28]; and *second*, appropriate implementing rules for giving effect to the Staff Regulations and the Conditions of Employment.

(3) It must appoint an Accounting Officer, subject to the Staff Regulations, who must be functionally independent in the performance of his/her duties.

(4) It must ensure the adequate follow-up to findings and recommendations arising from internal or external audit reports and evaluations, as well as from OLAF investigations.

(5) It must take Decisions on the establishment and adjustment, if necessary, of the SRB's internal structures.

Meetings and Decision-Making Process
(1) The Chair convenes and chairs the meetings of the Plenary Session (in accordance with **Article 56(2), point (a)**). The SRB in its Plenary Session must hold at least two ordinary meetings annually. In addition, it meets on the initiative of the Chair or at the request of at least one-third (1/3) of its members. If the Commission's representative requests the Chair to convene a meeting of the Plenary Session and the Chair decides not to convene it in due time, he/she must provide reasons in writing. The secretariat of the Plenary Session is provided by the SRB.[29] The Vice-Chair is entitled to attend the meetings of the Plenary Session. Where more than one NRA is established in a participating Member State, only the representative of one authority may participate as member, while the representative of the other authority shall

---

[27] OJ L 56, 4.3.1968, pp. 1–7.

[28] In exceptional circumstances, the SRB in this session may decide to temporarily suspend the delegation of the appointing authority powers to the Chair and any sub-delegation by the latter and either exercise them itself or delegate them to one of its members or to a staff member other than the Chair (*ibid.*, Article 50(3)).

[29] SRMR, Article 51(1)–(2) and (4).

be allowed to participate to the meetings of the Plenary Session as observer without exercising any voting rights.[30]

(2) In principle, the SRB in its Plenary Session takes decisions by a simple majority of its members. By way of derogation, the following rules apply: *First*, decisions regarding the use of the SRF in accordance with **Article 50(1), points (c)–(d)**, are taken by a simple majority as well, representing (however) at least 30% of contributions. The same applies to decisions on the mutualisation of national financing arrangements (in accordance with **Article 78**) *limited to the use* of the financial means available in the SRF. *Second*, decisions on the raising of *ex-post* contributions, on voluntary borrowing between financing arrangements and on alternative financing means (in accordance with **Articles 71–74**) are taken by a majority of two thirds (2/3) of SRB members representing at least 50% of contributions during the eight-year initial period until the SRF is fully mutualised, and, from then on, a majority of two thirds (2/3) of SRB members representing at least 30% of contributions. The same applies to decisions on the mutualisation of national financing arrangements (in accordance with **Article 78**) *exceeding the use* of the financial means available in the SRF.[31]

9.1.3.3   *The SRB's Executive Session*
Composition and Tasks

(1) In accordance with the SRMR, the SRB in its Executive Session is composed of the Chair, the (four) further full-time members and the permanent observers appointed by the Commission and the ECB. SRB members appointed by each participating Member State, representing their NRAs, participate in the SRB's Executive Session according to the following: *first*, when deliberating on a designated entity or group established only in one participating Member State, the member appointed by that Member State must participate in the deliberations and in the decision-making process (by application of the rules laid down in **Article 55(1)**); *second*, when deliberating on a cross-border group, the member appointed by the Member State in which the GLRA is situated, and the members appointed by the Member States in which a subsidiary or entity covered by consolidated supervision is

---

[30] Rules of Procedure of the Board in its Plenary Session, Article 1(5)–(6).

[31] In all cases, each member has one vote and in the event of a tie the Chair has a casting vote (SRMR, Article 52(1)–(4)). Articles 2–10 of the Rules of Procedure establish more detailed provisions, including voting arrangements, in particular the circumstances in which a member may represent another member, including, where appropriate, rules governing quorums. It is also noted that, in accordance with Article 13, the Plenary Session may establish, amend and dissolve Plenary Session substructures, which shall advise its members or the Vice-Chair in the discharge of their duties. On a proposal from the Chair, the Plenary Session shall adopt, amend or revoke the mandates of these substructures and appoint their Chairpersons, which must regularly report on the ongoing work of the substructures to the Executive and the Plenary Sessions, as appropriate. Articles 49–52 SRMR are further analysed in Heinz (2022), pp. 975–997.

established must also participate in the decision-making process; in this case applicable are the rules laid down in **Article 55(2)**.[32]

The Rules of Procedure of the Board in its Executive Session provide that the Executive Session may be convened in two formats: in an extended composition and in a restricted one (see Box 9.2 just below).

Box 9.2 Composition of the two formats of the SRB Executive Session

Format	Composition
Extended Executive Session	This is composed of: (i) the Chair and the further full-time members (the 'permanent members'); (ii) when deliberating on an individual designated entity or a group of such entities established in a participating Member State, the appointed representative of the NRA therein; and (iii) when deliberating on a cross-border group, the appointed representative of the GLRA, as well as the appointed representative of the NRA of each Member State where a subsidiary or entity covered by consolidated supervision is established Hence, its composition depends on the individual entity or group in issue
Restricted Executive Session	This is composed of the Chair and the further full-time members. The Vice-Chair participates therein as a non-voting member but carries out the functions of the Chair in his/her absence[33]

If relevant, the SRB in its Executive Session may invite at its meetings observers in addition to the permanent ones, including an EBA representative, in particular when matters are discussed for which, in accordance with the BRRD, the EBA is required to develop RTS or ITSs or issue Guidelines, and, on an *ad hoc* basis, NRAs of non-participating Member States, when deliberating on a group having subsidiaries or significant branches therein.[34]

---

[32] SRMR, Article 53(1), first and second sub-paragraphs and (2)–(4). On Article 55(1)–(2), see just below when discussing the decision-making process.

[33] Rules of Procedure of the Board in its Executive Session, Article 1(2)–(5). The Restricted Executive Session may establish, amend and dissolve Executive Session substructures advising its members or the Vice-Chair in the discharge of their duties. On a proposal from the Chair, the Executive Session shall adopt, amend or revoke the mandates of these substructures and appoint their Chairpersons, which must regularly report on the ongoing work of the substructures to the Executive Session (*ibid*, Article 13).

[34] SRMR, Article 53(1), third sub-paragraph and Rules of Procedure of the Board in its Executive Session, Article 1(6), (9) and (11).

(2) Since the composition of participants in the decision-making process of the SRB in its Executive Session varies depending on the Member State where the relevant institution or group operates, the Chair and the further full-time members must ensure that resolution Decisions and actions, in particular with regard to the use of the SRF, across the different formations of the Executive Session are coherent, appropriate and proportionate.[35] Its tasks are presented in Box 9.3 just below.

Box 9.3 Tasks of the SRB in its Executive Session

(1) The SRB's tasks in its Executive Session consist in preparing the decisions to be adopted by its Plenary Session and taking the decisions to fully implement the SRMR, unless otherwise provided therein.[36] In exercising these tasks it must undertake the following[37]:

first, at the phase of preparation for resolution (due to the institution-specific nature of the information contained therein), prepare, assess and approve resolution plans for designated entities and groups (pursuant to **Articles 8** and **10–11**), apply simplified obligations to certain entities and groups (**Article 11**), and determine their MREL (**Article 12**)[38];

second, provide the Commission, as early as possible, with a resolution scheme (**Article 18**) accompanied by all relevant information, allowing in due time the Commission to assess and decide *or*, where appropriate, propose a decision to the Council (**Article 18(7)**); and

third, decide upon the SRB's part II of the budget on the SRF (**Article 60**).

---

[35] SRMR, Article 53(5); see also recital (34).

[36] *Ibid.*, Article 54(1); see also recital (33), first sentence.

[37] *Ibid.*, Article 54(2), points (a)–(e); see also recital (33), following sentences.

[38] In this context, it is worth noting that the MREL requirement contains two components: the *first* is the loss absorption amount ('LAA'), which equals to the amount of losses to be covered, and should facilitate the recapitalisation of a credit institution (or of part thereof) or its placing under normal bankruptcy proceedings and avoid the resort to a bail-out with public funds (aiming thus to make shareholders/creditors contribute to the absorption of losses); and the *second* is the recapitalisation amount ('RCA'), which is the amount required to enhance a credit institution's capital basis (since the LAA may not be sufficient) and, as a rule, is not required if a credit institution were to be placed under normal bankruptcy proceedings.

> (2) In cases of urgency, it may take certain provisional decisions on behalf of the SRB in its Plenary Session, in particular on administrative management matters, including budgetary ones and must keep the latter informed of its decisions on resolution.[39]

Meetings and Decision-Making Process
The SRB in this Session must meet as often as necessary. Meetings are convened by the Chair on his/her own initiative or at any member's request and are chaired by him/her.[40] With regard to the decision-making process, when deliberating on an individual entity or a group established only in one participating Member State, the Chair and the further full-time members may take a decision by a simple majority if all members referred to in **Article 53(1)** and **(3)** are not able to reach a joint agreement by consensus within a deadline set by the Chair. Equally, when deliberating on a cross-border group, if all members referred to in **Article 53(1)** and **(4)** are not able to reach a joint agreement by consensus within a deadline set by the Chair, the latter and the further full-time members may take a decision by a simple majority.[41] Like in the case of the Plenary Session, the Vice-Chair is entitled to attend the meetings of the Executive Session and, where more than one NRA is established in a participating Member State, only the representative of one authority may participate as member, while the representative of the other authority shall be allowed to participate to the meetings of the Executive Session as observer without exercising any voting rights.[42]

9.1.3.4 The Chair

The SRB is chaired by a full-time Chair who is responsible for preparing its work, in its Plenary and Executive Sessions, as well as convening and chairing its meetings. He/she is also responsible for all staff members and matters of day-to-day administration; the establishment of a draft SRB budget and its implementation; the SRB's management and the implementation of its annual work programme; and the preparation of a draft of the Annual Report.[43] In the performance of these tasks, the Chair is assisted by a "dedicated staff", as

---

[39] SRMR, Article 54(3)–(4).

[40] *Ibid.*, Article 53(1), first sub-paragraph, second sentence and second sub-paragraph.

[41] In the event of a tie, the Chair has a casting vote (*ibid.*, Article 55(1)–(3)).

[42] Rules of Procedure of the Board in its Executive Session, Article 1(7)–(8). The meetings and the decision-making process are also governed by the (more detailed) provisions of Articles 2–10 of the Rules of Procedure. Articles 53–55 SRMR are further analysed in Heinz (2022), pp. 997–1010.

[43] On the budget and the Annual Report, see below, under 9.4.

well as by the Vice-Chair, who must carry out the functions of the Chair in his/her absence or reasonable impediment.[44]

9.1.3.5 Appointment and Removal of the Chair, the Vice-Chair and the Other Full-Time SRB Members

Appointment

The provisions of the SRMR: Taking into account the SRB's tasks, the Chair, the Vice-Chair and the further full-time members are appointed on the basis of merit, skills, knowledge of banking and financial matters and of experience relevant to financial supervision, regulation, as well as bank restructuring, insolvency and resolution. They must be chosen on the basis of an open selection procedure, respecting the principles of gender balance, experience and qualification. The European Parliament and the Council must be kept duly informed at every stage of the procedure in a timely manner. All these members may not hold office at national, EU or international level; their term of office is five years and not renewable[45] and they remain in office until their successors are appointed.[46]

As regards the appointment procedure, the Commission, after hearing the SRB in its Plenary Session, must provide the European Parliament with a shortlist of candidates for the positions of these members and inform accordingly the Council. It must also submit a proposal for the appointment of these members to the European Parliament for approval. Upon approval, the Council, acting by qualified majority, must adopt an Implementing Decision to appoint these members.[47]

The provisions of the Interinstitutional Agreement between the European Parliament and the SRB: On 16 December 2015, the European Parliament (hereinafter in this Sub-section the **'EP'**) and the SRB signed an **Interinstitutional Agreement** "on the practical modalities of the exercise of democratic accountability and oversight over the exercise of the tasks conferred on the (...) Board within the framework of the [SRM]"[48] (hereinafter the **'EP-SRB Agreement'**). According to this Agreement, in their respective roles in the

---

[44] SRMR, Article 56(1)–(3). It is noted that the Vice-Chair is not an SRB member in accordance with Article 43 (see above in Section A, under 3). As already mentioned in Chapter 7 above (under 7.2.3), for the purpose of acting within the scope of the BRRD, the Chair is an observer to the EBA's Board of Supervisors (*ibid.*, Article 95, point (3) adding a new sub-paragraph to Article 40(6) EBAR).

[45] *Exceptionally*, the term of office of the first Chair was three years, renewable once for a 5-year period; as a matter of fact, the term of the first Chair, Elke König, was renewed (and expired in 2022). A Chair whose term of office has been extended may not participate in a selection procedure for the same post at the end of the overall period.

[46] SRMR, Article 56(4)–(8).

[47] Apparently, for the appointment of the first members of the SRB, the Commission provided the candidates' shortlist without hearing the SRB (*ibid.*, Article 56(6); see also recital (31), fifth to seventh sentences).

[48] OJ L 339, 24.12.2015, pp. 58–65.

selection procedure, the EP and the SRB should aim at the highest professional standards and must take into account the need to safeguard the EU interests as a whole and diversity in the composition of the SRB. In particular:

> *first*, to the extent that the SRB has been involved, it must keep the ECON duly and in a timely manner informed of all stages of the selection procedure, such as concerning the publication of the vacancy notice, the selection criteria and the specific job profile, the composition of the pool of applicants, as well as of the method by which the pool of applicants is screened in order to draw up a shortlist of at least two candidates for each of the positions of Chair, Vice-Chair and the further full-time members of the SRB;
> *second*, when the Commission provides the EP with a shortlist of candidates pursuant to **Article 56(6) SRMR** above, the ECON may consult the SRB concerning the shortlisted candidates;
> *third*, when the Commission submits for approval to the EP its proposals for SRB members, the ECON may, in the context of a public hearing, consult the SRB on the proposed candidates; and
> *finally*, the EP must inform the SRB of its decision on the approval of each candidate proposed by the Commission, including the outcome of a vote in the ECON and the EP's plenary.[49]

Removal

In terms of personal independence, the Chair, the Vice-Chair and the further full-time members may be removed from their office *only* if they no longer fulfil the conditions required for the performance of their duties or have been guilty of serious misconduct.[50] The removal is effected by a Council Implementing Decision (adopted in this case as well by qualified majority) on a proposal from the Commission and approved by the European Parliament. For this purpose, the European Parliament or the Council may inform the Commission that it considers the conditions for the removal of any member from office to be fulfilled, to which the Commission must respond.[51] When the European Parliament informs the Commission about its consideration on the fulfilment of the conditions for removing from office of any SRB member it may also inform the SRB thereof.[52]

---

[49] The EP must aim to take that decision within six weeks of the date of receipt of the proposal from the Commission concerning the candidates (EP-SRB Agreement, Section II (1)–(4)).

[50] The same conditions apply regarding the removal of the Chair of the ECB Supervisory Board in the context of the SSM (SSMR, Article 26(4), first sub-para).

[51] SRMR, Article 56(9).

[52] EP-SRB Agreement, Section II (5). Article 56 is further analysed in Heinz (2022), pp. 1010–1016.

9.2 General Principles Governing the Operation of the SRM, Division of Tasks Within the SRM and Cooperation Arrangements

9.2.1 General Principles Governing the Operation of the SRM

Article 6 SRMR lays down six general principles governing the operation of the SRM[53]:

> *First*, according to the **principle of non-discrimination**, no action, proposal or policy of the SRB, the Council, the Commission or an NRA may discriminate against entities, depositors, investors or other creditors established in the EU on grounds of nationality or place of business.[54]
>
> *Second*, any action, proposal or policy of the SRB, the Council, the Commission or an NRA must be undertaken with full regard and duty of care for the unity and integrity of the internal market.[55]
>
> *Third*, according to the **principle of due consideration to the resolution objectives** and other specific factors, when making decisions or taking action which may have an impact in more than one Member State (in particular when taking decisions concerning groups established in several Member States), due consideration must be given both to the resolution objectives referred to in **Article 14 SRMR**[56] and to the following factors: (a) the interests of the Member States where a group operates, and in particular the impact of any decision or action or inaction on financial stability, fiscal resources, the economy, financing arrangements, the DGS or the ICS of any of those Member States and the SRF; (b) the objectives of balancing the interests of the Member States involved and of avoiding unfairly prejudicing or protecting a Member State's interests; and (c) the need to minimise a negative impact for any

---

[53] On this Article, see details in Binder (2022), pp. 497–506. More generally on the SRM, see Bruzzone, Cassella and Micossi (2017).

[54] SRMR, Article 6(1). The term 'depositor' is defined, with reference to Article 2(1), point (6) DGSD, to mean the holder or, in the case of a joint account, each of the holders, of a deposit The term 'investor' is defined with reference to Article 1(4) of Directive 97/9/EC on investor compensation schemes, according to which investor means any person who has entrusted money or instruments to an investment firm in connection with investment business (*ibid.*, Article 3(1), points (53) and (54), respectively).

[55] *Ibid.*, Article 6(2).

[56] The resolution objectives laid down in Article 14(2), first sub-paragraph are five: ensure the continuity of 'critical functions', as defined in Article 2(1), point (35) BRRD; avoid significant adverse effects on financial stability, by preventing contagion, including to market infrastructures and by maintaining market discipline; protect public funds by minimising reliance on extraordinary public financial support; protect depositors covered by the DGSD and investors covered by the ICSD; as well as protect client funds and client assets. These same objectives are laid down in Article 31 BRRD. This SRMR Article and the critical functions are further discussed in detail in Volume II. For details on Article 14, see Binder (2022), pp. 619–630.

part of a group of which a designated entity subject to resolution is a member.[57] The SRB, the Council and the Commission must balance these factors with the resolution objectives as appropriate to the nature and circumstances of each case and comply with the decisions made by the Commission under **Article 107 TFEU** and **Article 19 SRMR** on State aid and SRF aid.[58]

Fourth, when making decisions or taking actions regarding entities or groups established in a participating and in a non-participating Member State, into consideration must be taken possible negative effects on non-participating Member States, including on entities established therein.[59]

Fifth, according to the **principle of 'fiscal neutrality'**, Decisions or actions of the SRB, the Council or the Commission may neither require Member States to provide 'extraordinary public financial support' nor impinge on their budgetary sovereignty and fiscal responsibilities.[60]

Finally, when the SRB takes a Decision addressed to an NRA, the latter has the right to further specify the measures taken.[61]

9.2.2 Division of Tasks Within the SRM

9.2.2.1 The SRB

(1) The SRB is responsible for the effective and consistent functioning of the SRM, like the ECB for the SSM. Subject to **Article 31(1)** on the cooperation within the SRM,[62] it is also responsible for drawing up the resolution plans and adopting all resolution Decisions relating to the following categories of entities and groups: *first*, the designated entities that are not part of a group; *second*, groups which are either classified as significant in accordance with **Article 6(4) SSMR**, or in relation to which the ECB has decided, in accordance with **Article 6(5), point (b) SSMR**, to directly exercise all of the

---

[57] SRMR, Article 6(3).

[58] *Ibid.*, Article 6(5). Article 19 is discussed in detail in Volume II. On Article 107 TFEU, see (out of a vast existing literature) Craig and de Búrca (2020), pp. 1164–1167 (with extensive references to case law), Bailey and John (2018, editors) and Bär-Bouyssière (2019). See also Grünewald (2014), pp. 122–129, as to its applicability to bank resolution.

[59] SRMR, Article 6(4).

[60] *Ibid.*, Article 6(6). 'Extraordinary public financial support' means (*ibid.*, Article 3(1), point (29)) State aid within the meaning of Article 107(1) TFEU, or any other public financial support at supra-national level, which, if provided at national level, would constitute State aid, and which is provided to preserve or restore the viability, liquidity or solvency of a designated entity or of a group of which such an entity forms a part. On State aid granted to credit institutions after the BRRD and the SRMR, see, by means of mere indication, Rosaria Miserendino (2018).

[61] SRMR, Article 6(7).

[62] On this aspect, see just below, under 9.3.2.

relevant powers (classified as significant as well); and *third*, other cross-border groups.[63]

(2) If necessary, in order to ensure the consistent application of high resolution standards under the SRMR, the SRB may issue a Warning to the relevant NRA, within the appropriate timeframe having regard to the urgency of the circumstances, if it considers that the draft Decision with regard to any entity or group referred to in **Article 7(3)** does not comply with the SRMR or with its general Instructions. It may also decide, at any time, to directly exercise all relevant powers under the SRMR with regard to any such entity or group, in particular, if the above Warning has not been appropriately addressed. The SRB may take such a Decision either on its own initiative, after consulting the NRA concerned, or upon a request from the latter.[64]

(3) Participating Member States may also decide that the SRB exercises all relevant powers and responsibilities conferred on it by the SRMR in relation to entities and groups, other than those referred to in **Article 7(2)**, established in their territory.[65]

9.2.2.2   The National Resolution Authorities (NRAs)
NRAs retain significant tasks and powers within the SRM. In particular, they must perform, and are responsible for, specific tasks with regard to entities and groups other than those referred to in **Article 7(2)**. This is without prejudice to the responsibilities of the SRB for the tasks conferred on it by the SRMR. The tasks assigned to NRAs are following[66]: *first*, at the phase of preparation and in accordance with **Articles 8–12**, adopt resolution plans, carry out an assessment of resolvability, apply simplified obligations or waive the obligation to draft a resolution plan and determine the **MREL**; *second*, adopt measures during early intervention in accordance with **Article 13(3)**; *third*, adopt resolution Decisions and apply resolution tools in accordance with the relevant procedures and safeguards, provided that the resolution action does not require any use of the SRF and is financed exclusively by the write-down and conversion of 'relevant capital instruments' and by resolution tools and/or by the DGS; if the resolution action requires the use of the SRF, the resolution

---

[63] SRMR, Article 7(1)–(2). These are the 'entities and groups referred to in Article 7(2)'.

[64] *Ibid.*, Article 7(4), points (a) and (b), respectively.

[65] In such a case, the following provisions do not apply: Article 7(3)–(4) on NRAs' tasks within the SRM; Articles 9 and 12(2) on resolution plans drawn up and the MREL determined by NRAs; and Article 31(1) on cooperation within the SRM (*ibid.*, Article 7(4), points (a) and (b), respectively).

[66] *Ibid.*, Article 7(3), first and second sub-paragraphs.

scheme must be adopted by the SRB; and *finally*, write-down or convert 'relevant capital instruments' in accordance with **Article 21** and the cooperation procedure laid down in **Article 31**.[67]

(2) When adopting a resolution Decision, NRAs must consider and follow the resolution plan, unless they assess, taking into account the case's circumstances, that the resolution objectives can be achieved more effectively by taking actions not provided for in the resolution plan. When performing these tasks, they must apply the relevant SRMR provisions; exercise the powers conferred on them under the national law transposing the BRRD; inform the SRB of the measures to be taken, closely coordinate with it when taking them and submit to it the resolution plans and any updates thereof accompanied by a reasoned assessment of the resolvability of the entity or group concerned[68] (Table 9.1).

9.2.3 Cooperation Arrangements

9.2.3.1 Obligation to Cooperate and Information Exchange Within the SRM and with the ESAs

The obligation to respect the principle of sincere cooperation by virtue of **Article 4(3) TEU**[69] and the regime of information exchange within the SRM are governed by the following rules[70]:

> *First*, the SRB must inform the Commission of any action taken to prepare for resolution; with regard to any information received from the SRB, the Council and the Commission, members and staff are subject to the professional secrecy requirements set out in **Article 88 SRMR**.[71]
>
> *Second*, in the exercise of their respective responsibilities under the SRMR, the SRB, the Council, the Commission, the ECB, the NRAs and the NCAs must at each stage (resolution planning, early intervention and resolution) closely cooperate and provide each other with all information necessary for the performance of their tasks.[72]

---

[67] The term 'relevant capital instruments' is defined in Article 3(1), point (51). All these aspects are further discussed in detail in Volume II.

[68] *Ibid.*, Article 7(3), third-sixth sub-paragraphs. Any references to the SRB in the Articles enumerated exhaustively in these sub-paragraphs must be read as references to NRAs regard to groups and entities other than those referred to in Article 7(2). Article 7 is discussed in detail in Wojcik (2022).

[69] *Ibid.*, recital (88).

[70] *Ibid.*, Article 30(1)–(6), respectively.

[71] On this SRMR Article, see Gortsos (2022), pp. 1187–1190. In this respect, on 1 August 2019, the SRB and the Commission signed an MoU "in respect of certain elements of cooperation and information exchange pursuant to the [SRMR]" (at: https://www.srb.europa.eu/system/files/media/document/mou_between_the_ec_and_the_srb.pdf).

[72] See also recital (89), third sentence SRMR.

Table 9.1 National resolution authorities (NRAs)—members of the Single Resolution Mechanism (SRM)

Member State	National resolution authority
Austria	Österreichische Finanzmarktaufsicht—FMA
Belgium	Nationale Bank van België/Banque Nationale de Belgique
Bulgaria	Bulgarian National Bank
Croatia	Hrvatska narodna banka (Croatian National Bank)
Cyprus	Central Bank of Cyprus
Estonia	Finantsinspektsioon (Estonian Financial Supervision Authority)
Finland	Financial Stability Authority
France	Autorité de contrôle prudentiel et de résolution (ACPR)
Germany	Bundesanstalt für Finanzdienstleistungsaufsicht—BaFin
Greece	Τράπεζα της Ελλάδος (Bank of Greece—Resolution Unit)
Ireland	Central Bank of Ireland/Banc Ceannais na hÉireann
Italy	Banca d'Italia—Resolution and crisis management Unit
Latvia	Finanšu un kapitāla tirgus komisija (Financial and Capital Market Commission)
	Latvijas Banka (as of 1 January 2023)
Lithuania	Lietuvos bankas (Bank of Lithuania)
Luxembourg	Commission de Surveillance du Secteur Financier—CSSF
Malta	Malta Financial Services Authorities—MFSA
Netherlands	De Nederlandsche Bank (DNB)—Resolution Division
Portugal	Banco de Portugal
Slovakia	Slovak Resolution Council
Slovenia	Banka Slovenije
Spain	Fondo de Resolución Ordenada Bancaria (FROB)

Third, the ECB or the NCAs must transmit to the SRB and to the NRAs the group financial support agreements authorised and any changes thereto.[73]

Fourth, for the purposes of the SRMR, the ECB may invite the SRB Chair to participate as an observer in its Supervisory Board; if deemed appropriate, the SRB may appoint another representative to replace the Chair for that purpose.[74] For the same purpose, it is entitled to appoint a representative to participate in the **ResCo** of the EBA.[75]

Fifth, the SRB must endeavour to closely cooperate with any public financial assistance facility (e.g., the ESM), in the extraordinary circumstances

---

[73] As already noted, the group financial support agreements are governed by Articles 19–26 BRRD.

[74] By error, in the text of the SRMR reference is made to Article 19 SSMR which governs the institutional independence of the ECB and the NCAs within the SSM.

[75] This Committee was discussed in Chapter 6 above, under 6.4.4.

set out in **Article 27(9)**[76] or when such a facility has granted (or is likely to grant) direct or indirect financial assistance to entities established in a participating Member State.[77]

Furthermore, to enhance the effectiveness of the SRM, the SRB must also closely cooperate with the EBA, and, where appropriate, with the ESRB, the EIOPA, the ESMA and the other authorities which constitute the ESFS.[78]

(2) On **22 December 2015**, the SRB and the ECB concluded an MoU "in respect of cooperation and information exchange" (hereinafter the '**SRB-ECB MoU**'),[79] which has been published, subject to the requirements of professional secrecy, on their websites.[80] Its provisions *on cooperation* govern institutional representation, communication between the Participants and external communication, general arrangements for cooperation, cooperation relating to other activities, as well as cooperation with regard to non-participating Member States and with third-country authorities.[81]

9.2.3.2 Cooperation Within the SRM
(1) For the effective management of the resolution process of failing credit institutions and other entities, the SRB must perform its tasks within the SRM in close cooperation with the NRAs not only for the implementation of its resolution Decisions, but also prior to their adoption, at the stage of resolution planning and/or during the phase of early intervention. In addition, in cooperation with the NRAs, it should approve and publish a framework to organise the practical arrangements for the cooperation between the SRB and NRAs.[82]

---

[76] Article 27(9) SRMR refers to the conditions for seeking alternative financing sources when the bail-in resolution toll is applied; see on this Hadjiemmanuil (2022), p. 840.

[77] See also recital (89), last sentence.

[78] *Ibid*, recital (89), first–second sentences.

[79] At: https://eur-lex.europa.eu/legal-content/EN/TXT/PDF/?uri=IMMC:MOU/2018/0530l&from=EN. It is in force as recently (19 December 2022) updated (at: https://www.srb.europa.eu/en/content/srb-and-european-central-bank-revise-memorandum-understanding. Its legal basis are Articles 30(7), first sentence SRMR (see also recital (54), first sentence) and 34(5) (see below, under 9.3.1). On Article 30, see details in Hadjiemmanuil (2022), pp. 881–895. Pursuant to paragraph 4 SRB-ECB MoU, the MoU is a 'statement of intent' and does not create, directly or indirectly any enforceable rights; hence, its Participants must endeavour to fulfil their responsibilities thereunder 'on a best-effort basis'. *Furthermore*, it does not modify or supersede any EU law or any national laws nor does it affect any provisions under other multilateral or bilateral agreements in force and applicable to the Participants. *In addition*, it does not authorise or prohibit a Participant from taking measures (other than those identified therein) to obtain information necessary to ensure compliance with relevant EU law.

[80] SRMR, Article 30(7), second sentence and recital (54), second sentence and SRB-ECB MoU, par. 18.

[81] SRB-ECB MoU, paras 5–6, 8–9 and 11–12, respectively.

[82] SRMR, Article 31(1), first sub-paragraph; see also recital (89), fourth and fifth sentences.

This framework was established by an SRB Decision of 28 June 2016 (**SRB/PS/2016/07**) (the "Cooperation Framework Agreement", '**COFRA**'); it is in force as amended in December 2018[83] to further clarify the division of responsibilities among them.

(2) In order to ensure the effective and consistent application of these requirements, the SRB has the following powers: *first*, to issue Guidelines and general Instructions addressed to NRAs on the performance of their tasks and the adoption of SRB resolution Decisions; *second*, to exercise, at any time, its investigatory powers[84]; *third*, to request, on an ad hoc or continuous basis, information from NRAs on the performance of their tasks in accordance with **Article 7(3)**[85]; and *finally*, upon receipt of draft Decisions from NRAs, to express its views and indicate their elements not complying with the SRMR or with its general Instructions. *In addition*, for the purposes of evaluating resolution plans, the SRB may request NRAs to submit all information necessary, as obtained by them pursuant to **Articles 11** and **13(1) BRRD** (without prejudice to its investigatory powers).[86]

9.2.3.3 Consultation of, and Cooperation with, Non-participating Member States and Third Countries

As the SRB has replaced participating Member States' NRAs in their resolution Decisions, it must also replace them for the purposes of cooperation with non-participating Member States. Furthermore, since many EU credit institutions operate internationally, an effective resolution mechanism needs to set out principles of cooperation with the relevant third-country authorities; support to third-country authorities should be provided in accordance with the rules set out in **Article 88 BRRD**.[87] Based on these considerations, the following has been established[88]: *First*, for the purposes of consultation and cooperation with non-participating Member States or third countries pursuant to **Articles 7–8, 12–13, 16, 18, 55 and 88–92 BRRD**, if a group includes entities established both in participating Member States and in non-participating Member States or in third countries, the NRAs of the former are represented by the SRB. This is without prejudice to any approval by the Council or the Commission required under the SRMR. *Furthermore*, if a group includes entities established in participating Member States and subsidiaries established,

---

[83] SRB Decision of 17 December 2018 (SRB/PS/2018/15).

[84] See below, under 9.3.1.

[85] See above, under 9.2.2.

[86] SRMR, Article 31(1), second and third sub-paragraphs. Pursuant to Article 31(2), the relations between the NRAs of participating Member States are governed by the relevant provisions of the SRMR and not by Articles 13(4)–(10) and 88–92 BRRD. The same applies to a joint Decision and any other Decision taken in accordance with Article 45(9)–(13) BRRD. Article 31 is further analysed in Hadjiemmanoil (2022), pp. 895–918.

[87] SRMR, recitals (91) and (92), first and second sentences, respectively.

[88] *Ibid.*, Article 32(1).

or significant branches located, in non-participating Member States, the SRB must communicate any plans, decisions or measures referred to in **Articles 8** and **10–13** relevant to the group to the competent authorities and/or the resolution authorities of the non-participating Member State concerned, as appropriate.

(2) The conclusion of MoUs is also provided for in this respect, which must be regularly reviewed and be published subject to the requirements of professional secrecy.[89] In particular, the SRB, the ECB and the resolution and competent authorities of non-participating Member States must conclude MoUs describing in general terms the way of their cooperation in the performance of their tasks under the BRRD and clarifying, *inter alia*, the consultation relating to SRB Decisions that have effect on subsidiaries established or branches located in these Member States if the parent undertaking is established in a participating one. *Furthermore*, and without prejudice to the above, the SRB must conclude an MoU concerning cooperation and information exchange in resolution with the resolution authority of each non-participating Member State (designated as such in accordance with Article 3(1) BRRD) which is home to at least one **G-SII**.[90]

(3) The SRB is also empowered to conclude, on behalf of the NRAs of participating Member States, non-binding cooperation arrangements in line with the **"EBA framework cooperation arrangements"** referred to in **Article 97(2) BRRD** (notifying accordingly the EBA).[91]

9.2.3.4   Recognition and Enforcement of Third-Country Resolution Proceedings

Detailed procedural rules govern the recognition and enforcement of third-country resolution proceedings, unless (and until) an international agreement as referred to in **Article 93(1) BRRD** enters into force with one or more

---

[89] *Ibid.*, Article 32(3).

[90] *Ibid.*, Article 32(2); see also recital (38). An agreement of the second type was signed on 16 December 2016 with the Swedish National Debt Office (Riksgälden, 'SNDO'), the Swedish resolution authority (at: https://www.srb.europa.eu/system/files/media/document/memorandum_of_understanding_between_the_srb_and_riksgaldskontoret.pdf).

[91] *Ibid.*, Article 32(4). As of December 2022, the SRB had concluded fourteen bilateral cooperation arrangements with third-country banking resolution authorities in order to facilitate resolution planning, the implementation of resolution decisions for cross-border entities and the exchange of information (including with the US Federal Deposit Insurance Corporation ('FDIC') and the Canada Deposit Insurance Corporation ('CDIC') in September 2017; the BoE in April 2019; and the Swiss Financial Market Supervisory Authority ('FINMA') in October 2021). Their legal basis is Article 97(4) BRRD in conjunction with Article 5(1) SRMR; their minimum content is specified in Article 97(3) BRRD and covers, *inter alia*, the development of resolution plans, the assessment of resolvability and the application of powers to address or remove impediments thereto. A repository of these cooperation arrangements is available at: https://srb.europa.eu/en/content/european-co-operation. On Article 97(2)–(4) BRRD, see Haentjens (2017a), pp. 300–301; on Article 32 SRMR, see Psaroudakis (2022), pp. 918–921.

relevant third countries.[92] They will apply following the entry into force of such an international agreement with the relevant third country to the extent that recognition and enforcement of third-country resolution proceedings is not governed by it.[93] In particular:

> *First*, upon due assessment, the SRB must issue a Recommendation addressed to NRAs on the recognition and enforcement of resolution proceedings conducted by third-country resolution authorities in relation to a third-country institution or parent undertaking with one or more Union subsidiaries[94] established in one or more participating Member States, *or* with assets, rights or liabilities located therein or governed by their laws.[95] Prior to its assessment, it must have consulted the NRAs and, if a **"European Resolution College"** is established pursuant to **Article 89 BRRD**,[96] the resolution authorities of non-participating Member States. It must also give due consideration to the interests of each participating Member State where a third-country institution or parent undertaking operates and, in particular, to the potential impact of the recognition and enforcement of the third-country resolution proceedings on other parts of the group and the financial stability in those Member States.[97]
>
> *Second*, the SRB may recommend the refusal of the recognition or enforcement of the above-mentioned resolution proceedings if it considers that *any* of the following conditions is met: (a) the third-country resolution proceedings would have an adverse effect on financial stability in a participating Member State; (b) creditors, including depositors located or payable therein, would not receive the same treatment as third-country creditors and depositors with similar legal rights under the third-country home resolution proceedings; (c) recognition or enforcement of the third-country resolution proceedings would have material fiscal implications for the participating Member State; or (d) the effects

---

[92] On this BRRD Article, see Haentjens (2017a), pp. 296–298.

[93] SRMR, Article 33(1).

[94] 'Union subsidiary' means an institution which is established in a Member State, and which is a subsidiary of a third-country institution or a third-country parent undertaking (BRRD, Article 2(1), point (84)).

[95] This is required to ensure a coherent approach *vis-à-vis* third countries and avoid the taking of divergent decisions in the participating Member States with respect to the recognition of resolution proceedings conducted in third countries in relation to such institutions or parent undertakings (SRMR, recital (92) third sentence).

[96] These colleges are further discussed in Volume II.

[97] SRMR, Article 33(2).

of such recognition or enforcement would be contrary to the national law of the participating Member State.[98]

NRAs must implement the SRB Recommendation and ask for the recognition or enforcement of the resolution proceedings in their respective territories or explain in a reasoned statement to the SRB why they cannot implement it. Resolution powers in relation to third-country entities must be exercised by NRAs, if relevant, on the basis of **Article 94(4) BRRD**.[99]

9.3 Powers of the SRB and the NRAs

9.3.1 Investigatory Powers

9.3.1.1 General Overview

For the purpose of performing its tasks under the SRMR, the SRB was given investigatory powers. The regime governing these powers is, *mutatis mutandis*, similar to that of the ECB under **Articles 10–13 SSMR**[100] and covers the following: powers to request information; conduct investigations; and conduct on-site inspections, including the necessary authorisation by a judiciary authority.[101]

9.3.1.2 Requests for Information

(1) The SRB may require the designated entities, their employees and/or third parties to whom functions or activities have been outsourced to provide all information necessary to perform its tasks, either through the NRAs or directly (after informing them), making full use of the information available to the ECB and the NCAs.[102] The entities and persons referred to above have a duty to supply the information requested, since this is not deemed to infringe the professional secrecy requirements. The information obtained directly by the SRB must be made available to the NRAs concerned. The SRB has the power to obtain, on an ad hoc or on a continuous basis, any information necessary for the exercise of its functions, in particular on capital, liquidity, assets and liabilities concerning any institution under its remit.[103]

---

[98] *Ibid.*, Article 33(3).

[99] *Ibid.*, Article 33(4)–(5). On Article 94(4) BRRD, see Haentjens (2017a), pp. 298–299; on Article 33 SRMR, see Psaroudakis (2022), pp. 921–927.

[100] See Chapter 8 above, under 8.3.2.

[101] On the considerations regarding the SRB's investigation powers, see recital (93) SRMR.

[102] NCAs or the ECB and NRAs must cooperate with the SRB to verify whether the information requested is already available (wholly or partly) and, in a positive case, provide it to the SRB (*ibid.*, Article 34(6)).

[103] *Ibid.*, Article 34(1)–(4); see also recital (94).

(2) In relation to *information exchange*, the **SRB-ECB MoU**, which was adopted on the basis of **Article 34(5) SRMR** as well,[104] governs the general arrangements for information exchange; the exchange of information related to the close cooperation between the ECB and the NCAs of Member States with a derogation; the permissible use of information and the confidentiality regime; data protection; and the exchange of general information relating to their respective fields of competence, *inter alia* in the context of training, conferences and workshops ('knowledge exchange').[105]

9.3.1.3 General Investigations

Subject to any other conditions laid down in relevant EU law, the SRB may, either through the NRAs or directly after informing them, conduct all necessary investigations of any legal or natural person referred to in **Article 34(1)** above that is established or located in participating Member States. To that end, it may require from these persons the submission of documents; examine their books and records and take copies or extracts therefrom; obtain written or oral explanations from those persons, their representatives or their staff; and interview any other consenting natural or legal person. Investigations are launched on the basis of an SRB Decision. If a person obstructs their conduct, the NRAs of the participating Member State where the relevant premises are located must afford, under national law, the necessary assistance including facilitating the access by the SRB to the business premises of these persons to facilitate the exercise of those rights.[106]

9.3.1.4 On-Site Inspections—Authorisation by a Judicial Authority

(1) Subject to other conditions laid down in relevant EU law, the SRB may conduct all necessary on-site inspections at the business premises of the natural or legal persons referred to in **Article 34(1)** above; the legal persons are subject to on-site inspections on the basis of an SRB Decision. Inspections must be conducted in accordance with **Article 37 SRMR** below and subject to prior notification to the NRAs and the relevant NCAs concerned (and, if appropriate, in cooperation with them). *Exceptionally*, if required for its proper conduct and efficiency, an inspection may be carried out without prior announcement to the above-mentioned legal persons.[107]

(2) Persons authorised by the SRB to conduct an on-site inspection may enter any business premises and land of the legal persons, subject to an SRB investigation Decision pursuant to **Article 35(2)**, and have the powers set out in **Article 35(1)**. Officials of, and other accompanying persons authorised or appointed by, the NRAs of the Member States where the inspection is to be

---

[104] See under 9.2.3 above.
[105] SRB-ECB MoU, paras 7, 10 and 13–15, respectively.
[106] SRMR, Article 35(1)–(2).
[107] *Ibid.*, Article 36(1) and (3).

conducted must, under the SRB's supervision and coordination, actively assist the persons authorised by the SRB, enjoying the same powers, and have the right to participate in the on-site inspections. If the persons authorised by the SRB find that a person opposes an inspection, the NRAs of the participating Member States concerned must afford the necessary assistance pursuant to national law, including, to the extent necessary, the sealing of any business premises and books or records. If that power is not available to these NRAs, the SRB must request the necessary assistance of other national authorities.[108]

(3) If an on-site inspection or the assistance provided for in **Article 36(5)** above requires authorisation by a judicial authority in accordance with national rules, such authorisation must be applied for. In such a case, the NJA must control the SRB Decision's authenticity and that the coercive measures envisaged are neither arbitrary nor excessive, taking into account the inspection's subject matter. The lawfulness of the SRB Decision is subject to review only by the CJEU.[109]

9.3.2 Power to Impose Fines and Periodic Penalty Payments

9.3.2.1 Fines: Conditions for Imposition—Amount of Fines
(1) The SRB must take a Decision imposing a fine if it finds that a designated entity has intentionally or negligently committed any of the following infringements: does not supply the information requested (in accordance with **Article 34**); does not submit to a general investigation or an on-site inspection (**Articles 35–36**); *or* does not comply with an SRB Decision addressed to it (**Article 29**).[110] In the case of other infringements, the SRB may recommend to NRAs to take action to ensure the imposition of appropriate penalties in accordance with **Articles 110–114 BRRD** and any relevant national legislation.[111]

(2) The basic amount of the fines must be a percentage of the total annual net turnover of the entity in the preceding business year (including the gross income consisting of interest receivable and similar income, income from shares and other variable or fixed-yield securities, and commissions or fees

---

[108] *Ibid.*, Article 36(2) and (4)–(5).

[109] In controlling the proportionality of the coercive measures, the NJA may ask the SRB for detailed explanations, in particular relating to the grounds it has for suspecting that an infringement of its resolution Decisions under Article 29 (discussed in Volume II) has taken place, the seriousness of the suspected infringement and the nature of the involvement of the person subject to the coercive measures. However, it is not allowed to review the necessity for the inspection or demand to be provided with the information on the SRB's file (*ibid.*, Article 37(1)–(2)). On Articles 34–37, see more details in Kerlin (2021) and Lackhoff and Prokop (2022).

[110] An infringement is considered to have been committed 'intentionally' if objective factors demonstrate that the entity, its management body, or its senior management acted deliberately to commit it (*ibid.*, Article 38(1)–(2); see also recital (95)).

[111] *Ibid.*, Article 38(8).

receivable pursuant to **Article 316 CRR**), under the following limitations: for the two first above-mentioned infringements, the basic amount must range between 0,05% and 0,15%; for the third infringement it must range between 0,25% and 0,5%.[112] These basic amounts are adjusted, if necessary, by the SRB by taking into account specific **'aggravating or mitigating factors'** in accordance with specific **'adjustment coefficients'**.[113]

Both the **mitigating and the aggravating coefficients** must be applied *one by one* to the basic amount; on the other, if more than one mitigating coefficient is applicable, the difference between the basic amount and the amount resulting from the application of each individual mitigating coefficient must be subtracted from the basic amount, while if more than one aggravating coefficient is applicable, the difference between the basic amount and the amount resulting from the application of each individual aggravating coefficient must be added to the basic amount.[114] In any case, the fines applied may not exceed 1% of the annual turnover of the entity concerned in the preceding business year, unless the entity has directly or indirectly benefited financially from the infringement and the profits gained or the losses avoided accordingly are determinable; in such a case, the fine must be at least equal to that financial benefit.[115]

Box 9.4 Aggravating and mitigating factors—adjustment coefficients

A. Aggravating factors (Article 38(5), Points (a)–(F), Respectively)

(1) the infringement has been committed intentionally;
(2) it has been committed repeatedly;
(3) it has been committed over a period exceeding three months;
(4) it has revealed systemic weaknesses in the organisation of the entity, in particular in its procedures, management systems or internal controls;
(5) no remedial action has been taken since its identification;
(6) the entity's senior management has not cooperated with the SRB in carrying out its investigations.

B. Adjustment coefficients linked to aggravating factors (Article 38(9), first sub-paragraph, points (a)–(f), respectively).

---

[112] *Ibid.*, Article 38(3), first sub-paragraph. In Member States with a derogation this basic amount must be the corresponding value in the national currency on 19 August 2014. Details are set out in the second sub-paragraph.

[113] This is consistent with the consideration in recital (95), first sentence, according to which the fines imposed should be 'proportionate and dissuasive'.

[114] *Ibid.*, Article 38(4).

[115] *Ibid.*, Article 38(7), first and second sub-paragraphs. If an act or omission constitutes more than one infringement, only the higher fine applies (*ibid.*, Article 38(7), third sub-paragraph).

(1) the infringement was committed repeatedly: for every repetition, applicable a coefficient of 1.1;
(2) it was committed over a period exceeding three months: applicable a coefficient of 1.5;
(3) it has revealed systemic weaknesses in the entity's organisation, *inter alia* in its procedures, management systems or internal controls: applicable a coefficient of 2.2;
(4) it was committed intentionally: applicable a coefficient of 2;
(5) no remedial action has been taken since its identification: applicable a coefficient of 1.7;
(6) the entity's senior management has not cooperated with the SRB in carrying out its investigations: applicable a coefficient of 1.5.

C. Mitigating factors (Article 38(6), points (a)–(d), respectively).
(1) the infringement has been committed over a period of less than ten working days;
(2) the entity's senior management can demonstrate all measures necessary to prevent it were taken;
(3) the entity has brought it quickly, effectively and completely to the SRB's attention;
(4) the entity has voluntarily taken measures to ensure that a similar infringement cannot be committed in the future.

D. Adjustment coefficients linked to mitigating factors (Article 38(9), second sub-paragraph, points (a)–(d), respectively).
(1) the infringement was committed over a period of less than ten working days: applicable a coefficient of 0.9;
(2) the entity's senior management can demonstrate that all measures necessary to prevent it have been taken: applicable a coefficient of 0.7;
(3) the entity brought it quickly, effectively and completely to the SRB's attention: applicable a coefficient of 0.4;
(4) the entity has voluntarily taken measures to ensure that a similar infringement cannot be committed in the future: applicable a coefficient of 0.6.

9.3.2.2 Periodic Penalty Payments: Conditions for Imposition—Amount of Payment

The SRB must, by a Decision, impose a periodic penalty payment on a designated entity to compel it to comply with a Decision adopted pursuant to **Article 34**, or on a person referred to in Articles 34(1), 35(1) and 36(1), respectively, to supply complete information required, to submit to an investigation or to submit to an on-site inspection ordered. The payment must meet the following requirements: it should be effective and proportionate; be imposed on a daily basis until the designated entity or the person concerned complies with the relevant SRB Decisions; be 0.1% of the average daily turnover in the preceding business year; and be calculated from the date stipulated in the Decision imposing it. A periodic penalty payment may be imposed for a period of no more than six months following the notification of the SRB Decision.[116]

9.3.2.3 Right to Be Heard and Right of Access to SRB's Files

On the basis of the **'principle of due process'**, the following rules have been adopted: *first*, before taking any Decision imposing a fine and/or periodic penalty payment under (the just above-mentioned) **Articles 38** or **39**, the SRB must grant the natural or legal persons subject to the proceedings the right to be heard on its findings. Its Decision must be based only on findings on which these persons concerned have had the opportunity to comment.[117] *Second*, the right of defence of the natural or legal persons concerned must also be fully complied with during the proceedings. These persons are entitled to have access to the SRB's file, subject to the legitimate interest of other persons in the protection of their business secrets, except for confidential information or internal preparatory SRB documents.

9.3.2.4 Publication, Nature and Enforcement and Allocation of Fines and Periodic Penalty Payments

(1) SRB Decisions imposing fines and periodic penalty payments under **Articles 38(1)–39(1)** must be published, unless this would endanger the resolution of the entity concerned. Under any of the following circumstances, the publication must be on an anonymous basis: the information published contains personal data and, following an obligatory prior assessment, their publication is considered to be disproportionate; publication would jeopardise either the stability of financial markets or an ongoing criminal investigation; or publication would cause, if that can be determined, disproportionate damage to the natural or legal persons involved. Alternatively, the publication of the data in question may be postponed for a reasonable period if it is foreseeable that the reasons for anonymous publication will cease to exist within that period.[118]

(2) Fines and periodic penalty payments imposed pursuant to **Articles 38–39** are of an administrative nature and enforceable, enforcement governed by the applicable procedural rules in force in the participating Member State where it is carried out. The order for the Decision's enforcement must be appended to it only by verification of its authenticity by the authority designated for that purpose by the government of each participating Member State; this must be

---

[116] *Ibid.*, Article 39(1)–(4); see also recital (95).

[117] *Ibid.*, Article 40(1)–(2).

[118] The SRB must inform the EBA of all fines and periodic penalty payments imposed under Articles 38–39 and provide information on the appeal status and outcome thereof. (*ibid.*, Article 41(1)).

notified to the SRB and the CJEU. Upon completion of these formalities, the party concerned may proceed to enforcement in accordance with national law, by bringing the matter directly before the competent body. Enforcement may be suspended only by a decision of the CJEU, even though the courts of the participating Member State concerned have jurisdiction over complaints on irregularities in its implementation.[119] The amounts of the fines and periodic penalty payments are allocated to the SRF.[120]

9.4 Independence and Accountability

9.4.1 Independence

9.4.1.1 General Overview

The SRMR contains specific provisions on the independence of the SRB and the NRAs. In particular, their institutional independence is governed by **Article 47 SRMR**; the SRB's financial independence is stipulated in **Articles 57–65** (on these two aspects, see below); its operational independence is guaranteed by **Articles 8–16** and **28–41**, which lay down its necessary powers in order to fulfil its objectives; finally, the personal independence of its full-time members (including the Chair) is governed by **Article 56** (as already discussed).[121]

9.4.1.2 Institutional Independence

Institutional independence is governed by **Article 47 SRMR** and **Article 4 of the "Code of Conduct of the SRB"**,[122] which provide the following[123]:

> *First*, when performing the tasks conferred on them by the SRMR, SRB members and their alternates, as well as the NRAs must act independently, in the general interest and in accordance with the general principles laid down in **Article 6** and the resolution objectives set out

---

[119] *Ibid.*, Article 41(2)-(3).

[120] *Ibid.*, Article 41(4). On Articles 38–41, see more details in Papathanassiou (2022); on the judicial review of fines and penalty payments set by the SRB, see Flynn (2021).

[121] See above, under 9.1.3.

[122] This was adopted by Decision SRB/PS/2020/16 of 24 June 2020, which is based on Article 50(1), point (j) and repealed the Code of Conduct for Members of the Plenary Session and Executive Session of the SRB (SRB/PS/2015/13) of 25 November 2015. Different is the "SRB Ethics and Compliance Framework" adopted by Decision SRB/CH/2020/17 of 27 October 2020 on the basis of (*inter alia*) Article 82(1) on the staff, which repealed Decision SRB/PS/2015/12 "Code of Ethics and good administrative behaviour for staff of the [SRB]".

[123] The provisions of the SRMR apply to both the SRB and the NRAs, while those of the Code only to SRB members and other participants, including alternates, in accordance with Article 1 on its scope of application.

in **Article 14**.[124] The SRB should have the capacity to deal with large groups, act swiftly and impartially and ensure that appropriate account is taken of financial stability in the EU and of the internal market.[125]

Second, in the deliberations and decision-making processes within the SRB, the Chair, the Vice-Chair and the further full-time members must express their own views and vote independently, and they must perform their tasks in conformity with the Decisions of the SRB, the Council and the Commission. In acting independently and objectively in the interest of the EU, they must and neither seek nor take instructions from EU institutions or bodies, any Member State's government or any other public or private body; *vice versa*, neither the Member States and the EU institutions or bodies nor any other public or private body may seek to influence them.[126] SRB members and their alternates must carry out the tasks conferred upon them free from any interference (in particular from industry) that would affect their independence.[127]

Third, SRB members must abstain from any professional activities and resign from any position that could hinder their independence or present them with the possibility of using privileged information.[128]

Finally, in accordance with the **Staff Regulations**, after leaving service, the Chair, the Vice-Chair and the further full-time members continue to be bound by the duty to behave with integrity and discretion as regards the acceptance of certain appointments or benefits.[129]

9.4.1.3 *Financial Independence*
Resources—General Provisions on the SRB's Budget and Establishment Plan
(1) Devoting the necessary financial (and human) resources to the performance of the tasks conferred upon it is a responsibility of the SRB; the funding of its budget or its resolution activities may under no circumstances engage the budgetary liability of the Member States.[130] In view of its mission and the resolution objectives, which include, *inter alia*, the protection of public funds,

---

[124] SRMR, Article 47(1) (see also recital (39), first sentence) and Code of Conduct, Article 4(1).

[125] SRMR, recital (39), second and third sentences.

[126] SRMR, Article 47(2)–(3) and Code of Conduct, Article 4(2)–(3). The phrasing in the last sentence is, *mutatis mutandis*, identical to the equivalent provisions in the EBAR and the SSMR, as discussed in Chapters 7 and 8 above.

[127] Code of Conduct, Article 4(4). *Inter alia*, Article 8 governs in detail the related issue of cooling-off periods.

[128] *Ibid.*, Article 4(5); see also Article 56(5), second sub-paragraph SRMR.

[129] SRMR, Article 47(4). This Article is further discussed in Amtenbrink (2022), pp. 968–973.

[130] Article 57(1)–(2), respectively. The provision in Article 61(1) is, *mutatis mutandis*, identical to that of Article 28 SSMR (see Chapter 8 above, under 8.4.1).

its functioning should be financed by contributions paid by the designated entities established in the participating Member States.[131] In order thus to guarantee its (full autonomy and) independence, the SRB has an autonomous budget, which is not part of the EU budget, must be balanced in terms of revenue and expenditure and comprises two parts: **Part I** for the SRB's administration and **Part II** for the SRF[132]:

The *revenues of Part I* consist of the annual contributions necessary to cover the annual estimated administrative expenditure; its *expenditure* covers staff, remuneration, administrative, infrastructure, professional training and operational expenses; this is without prejudice to NRAs' right to levy fees in order to cover their administrative expenditures, including expenditures for cooperating with and assisting the SRB.[133]

On the other hand, the *revenues of Part II* consist of *first*, contributions paid by institutions established in the participating Member States; *second*, loans received either from other resolution financing arrangements in non-participating Member States or from financial institutions or other third parties; *third*, returns on the investments of the amounts held in the SRF; and *finally*, any part of the expenses incurred for the purposes of **Article 76** which is recovered in the resolution proceedings. Its *expenditure* consists of the expenses for the purposes of **Article 76**, investments pursuant to **Article 75** and interest paid on loans received either from financial institutions or other third parties, or from resolution financing arrangements in non-participating Member States.[134]

(2) A draft budget, including a statement of estimates of the revenue and expenditure for the following year together with the establishment plan, is drawn up by the Chair, by 15 February each year, and submitted to the SRB for adoption. By 31 March then, the SRB in its Plenary Session can, if necessary, adjust this draft and must adopt the final budget and the establishment plan.[135]

Internal Audit and Control

The internal audit function set up within the SRB is performed in compliance with the international standards adopted by the **IFAC**.[136] The internal

---

[131] *Ibid.*, recital (41).

[132] *Ibid.*, Article 58; see also recital (97).

[133] *Ibid.*, Article 59(1)–(3), respectively; see also recital (98).

[134] *Ibid.*, Article 60(1)–(2), respectively; the related Articles 69–76 are discussed in Volume II.

[135] *Ibid.*, Article 61(1) and (2), respectively. The 2023 budget and establishment plan were adopted by Decision SRB/PS/2022/13 of 28 September 2022 (at: https://www.srb.europa.eu/system/files/media/document/2022-12-12_SRB-PS-2022-13-SRB-Decision-on-Budget-and-Establishment-Plan-2023.pdf).

[136] On this international financial forum, see Chapter 3 above, under 3.3.3.

auditor, appointed by the SRB, is responsible for verifying the proper operation of the budget implementation systems and the budgetary procedures and for advising the SRB on dealing with risks by issuing independent opinions on the quality of management and control systems and recommendations for improvements. Internal control systems and procedures suitable for performing the internal auditor's tasks must be put in place by the SRB.[137]

Implementation of the Budget, Presentation of Accounts and Discharge

The implementation of the budget, which is the responsibility of the Chair in his capacity as "authorising officer",[138] the presentation of accounts and the discharge of the Chair in respect of the budget implementation are governed by the following rules:

(1) The SRB **Accounting Officer** must send, by 1 March of the following financial year, the SRB provisional accounts, accompanied by the Report on budgetary and financial management during the financial year, to the ECA for observations and, by 31 March of that financial year, submit this Report to the SRB members, the European Parliament, the Council and the Commission. By the same date, the Chair must also transmit to the European Parliament, the Council and the Commission the provisional accounts for the preceding financial year. Upon receipt of the ECA's observations on these accounts, the Chair, acting in his/her responsibility, must draw up the SRB's final accounts and send them to the SRB in its Plenary Session for approval.[139]

(2) Following approval by the SRB, the Chair must, by 1 July each year, send the final accounts for the preceding financial year to the European Parliament, the Council, the Commission and the ECA; if observations are received from the ECA, the Chair must reply by 30 September. The final accounts are published in the *OJ* by 15 November each year. The Chair must also submit to the European Parliament or to the Council, at their request, any information relating to the accounts, subject to professional secrecy requirements. The SRB, in its Plenary Session, is competent to give discharge to the Chair in respect of the budget implementation.[140]

Adoption of Financial Regulations

Article 64 SRMR imposes on the SRB to adopt, after consulting the ECA and the Commission, internal financial rules specifying the detailed procedure for establishing and implementing the SRB's budget in accordance with (the just above-mentioned) **Articles 61** and **63**. These **'SRB Financial Regulations'** should be based, to the extent compatible with the SRB's particular

---

[137] SRMR, Article 62.
[138] *Ibid.*, Article 63(1).
[139] *Ibid.*, Article 63(2)–(4).
[140] *Ibid.*, Article 63(5)–(9).

nature, on the **'General Financial Regulation'** adopted (for bodies set up under the TFEU) in accordance with Article 70 of (the above-mentioned) Regulation (EU, Euratom) 2018/1046.[141]

Contributions to the Administrative Expenditures of the SRB
The designated entities must contribute to Part I of the SRB's budget in accordance with the SRMR and the Commission's delegated act adopted on the basis of **Article 65(5) SRMR**.[142] The amounts of contributions must be fixed at a level ensuring that revenue in respect thereof is in principle sufficient for the balancing of Part I of the SRB's budget each year. The SRB must determine and raise, in accordance with these delegated acts, the contributions due by each designated entity in a Decision addressed to it and apply any rules ensuring that these are paid fully in a timely manner. The amounts raised can only be used for the purposes of the SRMR.[143]

9.4.2 Accountability

9.4.2.1 Accountability Vis-À-Vis EU Institutions
The Provisions of the SRM Regulation
For reasons of transparency and democratic control and to safeguard the rights of the EU, the SRB is accountable to the European Parliament (hereinafter in this section, the **'EP'**), the Council and the Commission for the implementation of the SRMR.[144] This accountability requirement is governed by the following rules: *First*, the SRB must submit an **Annual Report** to the EP, the national parliaments of participating Member States (in accordance with **Article 46**, discussed below), the Council, the Commission and the ECA on the performance of its tasks under the SRMR. Subject to the requirements of professional secrecy that Report must be published on its website and the

---

[141] See Chapter 7 above, under 7.4.2. The first Financial Regulation was adopted on 25 March 2015 (see at: https://www.srb.europa.eu/en/system/files?file=media/document/2015-srb-financial-regulation_en.pdf).

[142] Commission Delegated Regulation (EU) 2017/2361 of 14 September 2017 "on the final system of contributions to the administrative expenditures of the [SRB]" (OJ L 337, 19.12.2017, pp. 6–14), which is in force as amended on 11 February 2021 by Delegated Regulation (EU) 2021/517 (OJ L 104, 25.3.2021, pp. 30–33). It is noted that the 2017 Regulation repealed Delegated Regulation (EU) No 1310/2014 (OJ L 354, 11.12.2014, pp. 1–5), which had been adopted on 8 October 2014, since its legal basis (Article 65(5)) is among those which, by way of derogation, apply from 19 August 2014. The current consolidated version is available at: https://eur-lex.europa.eu/legal-content/EN/TXT/?uri=CELEX%3A02017R2361-20210326.

[143] SRMR, Article 65(1)–(4). The above-mentioned Delegated Regulation determines the type of these contributions and the matters for which they are due, how their amount is calculated and the way in which they are to be paid; it also specifies registration, accounting, reporting and other rules necessary to ensure that these contributions are fully paid in a timely manner.

[144] *Ibid.*, Article 45(1); see also recital (42), third sentence.

Chair must present it in public to the EP and to the Council.¹⁴⁵ *In addition*, the SRB must reply, orally or in writing, to questions addressed to it by the EP or by the Council, pursuant to its own procedures and in any event within five weeks of receipt of a question. It must also cooperate with the EP during investigations, subject to **Article 226 TFEU** (see on this further below) and the Regulations referred to therein.¹⁴⁶ *Third*, at the request of the EP, the Chair must, at least on an annual basis, participate in a hearing by the ECON on the performance of the SRB's resolution tasks. He/she may also be heard by the Council, at its request, on the performance of these tasks. In addition, upon request, the Chair must hold confidential oral discussions with the Chair and the Vice-Chairs of the ECON if such discussions are required for the exercise of its powers under the TFEU.¹⁴⁷

The Provisions of the EP-SRB Agreement
Reports and other disclosures: The SRB Annual Report, which must be submitted to the EP and be presented by the SRB Chair to it at a public hearing, must be made available on a confidential basis to the EP seven working days in advance of the public hearing and of its publication on the SRB website and include a detailed explanation of nine specific aspects.¹⁴⁸ *In addition*, depending on the resolution tools applied, the SRB must publish the total amount of losses borne by the different classes of creditors where bail-in was applied, the amount and sources of funding used in the resolution process, and the proceeds of any sales of business units or assets.¹⁴⁹

Ordinary public hearings, ad hoc exchanges of views and special confidential meetings: At the request of the ECON, the Chair must participate in *ordinary public hearings* on the execution of the resolution tasks conferred on the SRB, including a discussion on the SRF; two hearings must be held annually. He/she may also be invited to additional *ad hoc* exchanges of views

---

¹⁴⁵ *Ibid.*, Article 45(2)–(3). The (last published) 2021 Annual Report is available at: https://www.srb.europa.eu/system/files/media/document/27-06-2022_SRB-Annual-Report-2021.pdf.

¹⁴⁶ *Ibid.*, Article 45(6) and (8), first sentence.

¹⁴⁷ *Ibid.*, Article 45(4)–(5) and (7).

¹⁴⁸ Pursuant to Section I (1) of the EP-SRB Agreement, these include: execution of the tasks conferred on the SRB by the SRMR; sharing of tasks with NRAs; cooperation with other national or EU relevant authorities, with any public financial assistance facility as provided for in Article 30(6) SRMR and with third countries, including recognition and assessment of third-country resolution proceedings; evolution of the SRB's structure and staffing, including the number and the national composition of seconded national experts; implementation of the Code of Conduct referred to in Section IV of the Agreement; amounts of administrative contributions raised in accordance with Article 65 SRMR; implementation of the budget for resolution tasks; and application of the provisions on the SRF.

¹⁴⁹ *Ibid.*, Section I (4).

with the ECON on issues within the SRB's responsibility.[150] Discussions in *special confidential meetings* involve the exchange of confidential information regarding the execution of resolution tasks. With a few exceptions, only the SRB Chair and the ECON Chair and Vice-Chairs may attend such meetings. All participants therein are subject to confidentiality requirements equivalent to those applying to the members of the SRB and to its staff.[151]

Responding to questions: The SRB must reply in writing to written questions put to it by the EP at the latest within five weeks of their transmission. Both the SRB and the EP must dedicate a specific section of their websites for these Q&As.[152]

Access to information: At the latest within six weeks from the date of an Executive or Plenary Session, the SRB must provide the ECON with a comprehensive record of its proceedings, enabling an understanding of the discussions. *Furthermore*, in the event of the resolution of an entity, non-confidential information relating to it must be disclosed *ex-post*, once any restrictions on the provision of relevant information resulting from confidentiality requirements have ceased to apply. Such information must include a suitably consolidated balance sheet valued according to the principles set out in the SRMR at the time the decision to resolve the entity was taken, clearly showing the net asset value of the entity and the value of the classes of assets and liabilities.

If **Article 19 SRMR** on State aid and SRF aid applies,[153] non-confidential information relating to the exchanges between the Commission and the SRB, as well as the Annual Reports referred to in **Article 19(6)** must be disclosed *ex-post* by the SRB to the ECON. The SRB must also publish on its website general guidelines regarding its resolution practices. The EP must apply appropriate safeguards and measures corresponding to the level of classification of SRB information or documents and inform the SRB thereof. On the other hand, the SRB must inform the EP of the measures taken and the acts adopted to apply the security principles contained in the Commission security rules referred to in **Article 91 SRMR**, including information on the procedures for

---

[150] Applicable to the SRB is the 'principle of openness' of EU institutions, bodies, offices and agencies as set out in Article 15(1) TFEU.

[151] Ordinary public hearings, ad hoc exchanges of views and special confidential meetings may cover all aspects of the activity and functioning of the SRM. Persons employed by the EP or by the SRB may not disclose to any unauthorised person or to the public information relating to the tasks conferred on the SRB by the SRMR and acquired by application of the EP-SRB Agreement, even after their employment has ended or they have left such employment, unless that information has already been made public or is accessible to the public (EP-SRB Agreement, Section I (2)).

[152] *Ibid.*, Section I (3).

[153] This Article is analysed in Volume II.

classifying information and the treatment of classified information.[154] In accordance with the (above-mentioned) **Regulation (EC) No 1049/2001**,[155] the EP must consult the SRB for the assessment of any request addressed to it to access an SRB document submitted to it. The EP and the SRB must keep each other informed on the initiation and outcome of any judicial, administrative or other proceedings in which access to SRB documents submitted to the EP is sought. The SRB may request that the EP maintains a list of persons having access to classified SRB information and SRB documents disclosed.[156]

Investigations: When the EP sets up a **Committee of Inquiry** (pursuant to **Article 226 TFEU**), the SRB must assist it in carrying out its tasks in accordance with the principle of sincere cooperation, in particular in relation to any investigation referred to in **Article 45(8) SRMR** within the same framework that applies to committees of inquiry and under the same confidentiality protection as foreseen in the Agreement for special confidential meetings. All recipients of information provided to the EP in the context of investigations are subject to confidentiality requirements equivalent to those applying to the members of the SRB. The EP and the SRB must agree on the measures to be applied to ensure the protection of such information. The EP must have regard to the public or private interests governing the right of access to EP, Council and Commission documents recognised in (the just above-mentioned) **Regulation (EC) No 1049/2001**, which are involved in information and documents submitted by the SRB in the context of a Committee of Inquiry.[157]

Code of Conduct: Before adopting the Code of Conduct by its Plenary Session,[158] the SRB should inform the ECON of its main elements. Upon written request of the ECON, the SRB must inform the EP in writing of its implementation and about the need for its updating.[159]

Adoption of acts by the SRB: The SRB must duly inform the ECON of its procedures for the adoption of its acts (i.e., Decisions, Guidelines, Instructions, Recommendations and Warnings) and, in particular, of the principles and types of indicators or information generally used in developing them, with a view to enhancing transparency and policy consistency. In addition, it must, before launching a public consultation procedure on draft acts, submit them

---

[154] The SRB must also inform the EP of the practical implementation of its internal security rules, including classification carried out during the year of the usual types of information handled by it and the treatment of classified information. When classifying information for which it is the originator, the SRB must ensure the application of appropriate classification levels in line with its internal security rules, taking due account of the need for the EP to be able to access classified documents for the effective exercise of its competences and prerogatives.

[155] See the *Excursus* in Chapter 7 above.

[156] EP-SRB Agreement, Section I (4).

[157] *Ibid.*, Section III.

[158] See above, under 9.4.1 (on institutional independence).

[159] EP-SRB Agreement, Section IV.

to the ECON, send it also the adopted acts and regularly inform the EP in writing about any need for updates.[160]

9.4.2.2 *Accountability* vis-à-vis *National Parliaments*

For the same reasons as in the case of the SRB and by analogy to the provisions of the SSMR,[161] the national parliaments of participating Member State or their competent committee have (also) the right to obtain information about the activities of, and to engage in a dialogue with, the SRB. In particular: *first*, by means of their own procedures, they may request the SRB to reply (and the latter is obliged to do so in writing) to any observations or questions in respect of its functions. *Second*, taking into account the potential impact that resolution actions may have on public finances, institutions, their customers and employees, as well as the markets in those Member States, they may invite the Chair (and the Chair is obliged to accept) to participate in an exchange of views in relation to the resolution of designated entities in that Member State together with an NRA representative. *Finally*, the Annual Report must be submitted by the SRB directly to these national parliaments, which may address their reasoned observations thereon. The SRB must reply orally or in writing to any observations or questions addressed to it, in accordance with its own procedures.[162]

9.5 The Appeal Panel

(1) On **18 December 2015**, the SRB established, by virtue of **Article 85(1) SRMR**, the Appeal Panel for the purposes of deciding on appeals submitted. This Panel, which adopted and made public its Rules of Procedure in 2016,[163] is composed of five individuals of high repute from the Member States (including non-participating ones), with a proven record of relevant knowledge and professional experience (including on resolution) to a sufficiently high level in the field of banking or other financial services. Excluded are the current SRB staff, and current staff of resolution authorities or other national or EU institutions, bodies, offices and agencies involved in performing the tasks conferred upon the SRB. These members and two

---

[160] *Ibid.*, Section V.

[161] See Chapter 8 above, under 8.4.2.

[162] These provisions are without prejudice to the accountability of NRAs to their national parliaments, in accordance with national law, for the performance of tasks not conferred upon the SRB, the Council or the Commission, and the activities carried out by them pursuant to Article 7(3) SRMR (Article 46(1)–(4); see also recitals (42), fourth sentence and (43)). On the accountability of the SRB, see details in Lamandini and Ramos Muñoz (2020a), Smits (2020) and Amtenbrink (2022), pp. 955–968.

[163] These Rules of Procedure were adopted by virtue of Article 85(10) SRMR and are available at: https://srb.europa.eu/sites/srbsite/files/2016rules_of_procedure_of_srb_appealpanel.pdf.

alternates are appointed by the SRB for a term of five years, extendable once.[164]

(2) Any natural or legal person, including NRAs, may appeal against specific SRB Decisions if those are either addressed or are of direct and individual concern to it. The Decisions against which an appeal can be submitted are confined to those which *first*, address or remove impediments to resolvability in accordance with **Article 10(10)**; apply simplified obligations in relation to the drafting of resolution plans or waive the obligation to draft such plans in accordance with **Article 11**; and determine the MREL; *second*, impose fines and periodic penalty payments in accordance with **Articles 38–41**; *third*, raise contributions to the SRB's administrative expenditures in accordance with **Article 65(3)** or raise extraordinary *ex-post* contributions in accordance with **Article 71**; and *finally*, grant or deny access to documents under the "public access to documents framework" in accordance with **Article 90(3)**.[165]

(3) Appeals, accompanied by a statement of grounds, must be filed in writing at the Appeal Panel within six weeks of the date of notification of the Decision to the person concerned, or in the absence of a notification, of the day on which it came to its knowledge. An appeal does not have suspensive effect unless the Panel considers that circumstances so require. If the appeal is admissible, the Panel must, subject to a specific procedure, examine whether it is well founded and then it may confirm the SRB Decision or remit the case to the latter. The SRB is bound by the Panel's decision and must adopt an amended Decision regarding the case concerned.[166]

9.6 Institutional Safeguards and Liability

9.6.1 Institutional Safeguards

9.6.1.1 Audits by the European Court of Auditors (ECA)

The SRB is subject to the ECA's audit. The latter is required, within six months of the end of the relevant period, to produce an Annual Report, starting on **1 April each year**, examining whether sufficient regard was given to economy, efficiency and effectiveness in the SRF's use (with a view to minimising that use) and whether the assessment of SRF aid was efficient and rigorous. *In addition*, following consideration of the SRB final accounts

---

[164] *Ibid.*, Article 85(2), first and third sentences.

[165] *Ibid.*, Article 85(3), first sub-paragraph. On Article 90(3), see Gortsos (2022), p. 1198.

[166] *Ibid.*, Article 85(3), second sub-paragraph, (4), (6) and (9). A thematic register of the Appeal Panel is available at: https://www.srb.europa.eu/en/cases/thematic-register-search. On the work of this Panel, which in terms of functions is similar to ESAs' Board of Appeal (as discussed in Chapter 7 above, under 7.4.4), see Lamandini and Ramos Muñoz (2021) (viewing it as an administrative pre-litigation review mechanism) and (2020b), pp. 124–126 and 134–160 (also discussing some of the cases decided by it, and the inherent weaknesses in this form of *quasi*-judicial protection).

(pursuant to **Article 63 SRMR**), the ECA must prepare a Report on its findings by **1 December** following each financial year, reporting on any contingent liabilities arising as a result of the performance of the tasks conferred on the SRB, the Council, or the Commission. Both these Reports[167] must be sent to the SRB, the European Parliament, the Council and the Commission and be made public without delay. In this respect, the ECA has the power to obtain from the SRB, the Council and the Commission any information relevant for performing its tasks and those must provide it with any information requested. *Finally*, the European Parliament and the Council may also request the ECA to examine any other relevant matters falling within their competence as set out in **Article 287(4) TFEU**.[168]

9.6.1.2 Actions Before the Court of Justice of the European Union (CJEU)

Judicial proceedings before the CJEU against Decisions of the SRB can be based either on **Article 263** or **Article 265 TFEU**.[169] In particular:

First, in accordance with **Article 263 TFEU**, the CJEU has jurisdiction to review the legality of Decisions adopted by the SRB, the Council and the Commission. Hence, proceeding may be brought before the Court in accordance with this TFEU Article contesting a decision taken either by the Appeal Panel or by the SRB if there is no right of appeal to the Appeal Panel (e.g., a decision concerning resolution action in respect of a credit institution or another designated entity).[170] Such proceedings may be instituted by Member States, EU institutions, as well as any natural or legal person if the SRB's or the Appeal Panel's Decision is either addressed or is of direct and individual concern to them.

Second, if the SRB fails to take a Decision despite its obligation to act, proceedings for failure to act may also be brought before the CJEU in accordance with **Article 265 TFEU**.

In both cases, the SRB must take the necessary measures to comply with the Court's judgement.[171]

---

[167] On the use of reports, and especially "special reports", by the ECA in discharge of its duties, see Stephenson (2015).

[168] Within two months of the date on which each such Report is made pubic the Commission must provide a detailed written response to be made public (SRMR, Article 92).

[169] See Chapter 8 above, under 8.6.1.

[170] SRMR, Article 86(1) and recital (120), second sentence.

[171] *Ibid.*, Article 86(2)–(4). According to Kaufhold (2022), at pp. 1175–1178 these provisions are of a pure declaratory nature. For the legal consequences following the annulment of an EU act under Article 263 TFEU, see Lenaerts, Maselis and Gutman (2014), pp. 411–418, and for those following a finding of a failure to act by the EU under Article 265 TFEU, see Lenaerts, Maselis and Gutman (2014), pp. 439–440.

It is also noted that, since the CJEU has, in accordance with **Article 267 TFEU**, competence to give preliminary rulings upon request of NJAs on the validity and interpretation of acts of EU institutions, bodies or agencies, these authorities are competent, in accordance with their national law, to review the legality of decisions adopted by NRAs of the participating Member States in the exercise of the powers conferred on them by the SRMR.[172]

As of **December 2022**, judicial proceedings against the SRB concerned, *inter alia*, Decisions on *ex-ante* contributions to the SRF, the SRB's June 2017 Decision on the resolution of Banco Popular Español and its February 2018 Decisions regarding the winding up of ABLV Bank, AS and its subsidiary in Luxembourg.[173]

9.6.2   Liability

9.6.2.1   Introductory Remarks

The SRB' liability is governed by **Article 87 SRMR**, which sets up a liability regime replicating **Article 340 TFEU** (and, in one case, **Article 272**), and **Article 41(3) of the Charter**, which lays down the right to compensation as one of the principles of good administration.[174] It is thus (like just above-mentioned Article 86) mainly of a declaratory nature, reflecting a typical feature of enabling regulations for EU agencies, which contain provisions identical to those in **Article 340 TFEU**.[175] An exception constitutes **Article 87(4) SRMR**.

9.6.2.2   Non-contractual Liability

(1) The CJEU has jurisdiction to determine the non-contractual liability of the SRB, the Council and the Commission.[176] In this respect, the SRMR sets out that the SRB must, in accordance with the general principles governing

---

[172] SRMR, recital (120), third and fourth sentences. On Article 267 TFEU, see Craig and de Búrca (2020), pp. 497–502, and more analytically Lenaerts, Maselis and Gutman (2014), pp. 456–479, Borchardt (2019), pp. 2687–2730, and Schwarze und Voet van Vormizeele (2019), pp. 2908–2939.

[173] Most of these cases are discussed, as appropriate, in Volume II. For a regularly updated inventory of actions against SRB Decisions, see the EBI website at: https://ebi-europa.eu/publications/eu-cases-or-jurisprudence, under Sect. 9.3. On the judicial review of decisions taken pursuant to the SRMR, see also various contributions in Zilioli and Wojcik (2021, editors). On the judicial review of resolution actions in accordance with Articles 85–86 BRRD, see Haentjens (2017b).

[174] Since (as already noted under 9.1.1 above) the SRB has legal personality, it can itself be the party against whom claims may be asserted. On Article 41(3) of the Charter, see Voet van Vormizeele (2019); see also Arons (2020), para. 84.

[175] See Kaufhold (2022), p. 1179, with due reference to Article 21 of Council Regulation (EC) No 58/2003 of 19 December 2002 "laying down the statute for executive agencies to be entrusted with certain tasks in the management of Community programmes" (OJ L 11, 16.1.2003, pp. 1–8).

[176] SRMR, recital (120), second sentence.

the liability of Member States' public authorities, restore any damage caused by it or by its staff in the performance of their duties, in particular their resolution functions including acts and omissions in support of foreign resolution proceedings.[177]

Furthermore, the distinctive element introduced by the (just above-mentioned **Article 87(4)**) is that the SRB is obliged to compensate an NRA for damages which the latter has been ordered to pay by a national court, or which it has undertaken, in agreement with the SRB, to pay under an amicable settlement, resulting from an act or omission committed by that NRA in the course of any resolution of designated entities and groups. Hence, it is recognised that all measures taken during the resolution of an institution under the SRB's remit ultimately go back to its resolution Decision, even if the NRA might have had discretion when deciding upon the mode of application and the SRB would thus not be liable pursuant to **Article 87(3) SRMR**. In order to disincentivise the NRA to disregard decisions of the SRB (e.g., for protecting national interests to the detriment of the EU), this obligation does not apply if the act or omission constituted an infringement (committed intentionally or with manifest and serious error of judgement) of the SRMR, another provision of EU law or a Decision of the SRB, the Council or the Commission.[178]

The conditions for the SRB to be successfully held liable in relation to acts or omissions in the performance of its duties are equal to those applying to the EBA and the ECB within the SSM.[179] Just like in the case of the SSM,[180] the issue arises that, in general, the judicial review of acts adopted by the SRB and by NRAs is likely to be governed by different procedural rules (EU law in the case of the SRB and national laws for NRAs).[181]

(2) The CJEU has jurisdiction in any dispute relating to both the SRB's non-contractually liability and its obligation to compensate NRAs.[182] In accordance with **Article 267 TFEU**, the CJEU is also competent to give preliminary rulings, when NJAs exercise their own competence, in accordance with their national law, to determine the non-contractual liability of NRAs of

---

[177] *Ibid.*, Article 87(3) and recital (120), second sentence; for more details on this provision, see Kaufhold (2022), pp. 1181–1184.

[178] This paragraph of Article 87 expresses and further develops the division of responsibilities within the SRM; see details in Busch and Gortsos (2022), pp. 508–509 and Kaufhold (2022), p. 1189–1190.

[179] See above Chapter 7, under 7.4.5 and Chapter 8, under 8.6.2. On the liability of NRAs within the SRM, see Almhofer (2021), pp. 230–232.

[180] See Chapter 8 above, under 8.6.2.

[181] See Busch and Gortsos (2022), pp. 507–508.

[182] Proceedings in matters arising from such a liability is barred after a period of five years from the occurrence of the event giving rise thereto (*ibid.*, Article 87(5)).

the participating Member States in the exercise of the powers conferred on them by the SRMR.[183]

(3) Regarding the use of the EU budget for the purposes of liability claims connected to the performance of tasks under the SRMR, it is noted that participating Member States have committed to reimburse each non-participating Member State for the amount corresponding to the use of the general EU budget *"in cases of non-contractual liability and costs related thereto, in respect of the exercise of powers by the [EU] institutions under the [SRMR]"*.[184]

9.6.2.3 Contractual Liability—Personal Liability of the Staff

The SRB's contractual liability is governed by the law applicable to the contract in question[185]; the CJEU has jurisdiction to give judgement according to any arbitration clause contained in such a contract.[186] The personal liability of SRB staff towards the agency is governed by the provisions laid down in the Staff Regulations or the Conditions of Employment (in accordance with **Council Regulation (EEC, Euratom, ECSC) No 259/68** of 29 February 1968[187]) applicable to them.[188]

Secondary Sources

A–D

Almhofer, M. (2021): The Liability of Authorities in Supervisory and Resolution Activities, in Zilioli, Ch. and K.-Ph. Wojcik (2021, editors): *Judicial Review in the European Banking Union*, Edward Elgar Publisher, Cheltenham, UK – Northampton, MA, USA, Chapter 14, pp. 221–234

Amtenbrink, F. (2022): Commentary on Article 45–46 and 47 SRMR, in Binder, J.-H., Gortsos, Ch.V., Lackhoff, K. and Ch. Ohler (2022, editors): *Brussels Commentary on the Banking Union*, Verlag C.H. Beck, München – Hart Publishing, Oxford – Nomos Verlagsgesellschaft, Baden-Baden, pp. 955–968 and 968–973

Anastopoulou, E. (2023): Game of Thrones—The Clash Between Public Interest and Property Rights in Banking Resolution, in Böffel, L. and J. Schürger (2023, editors): *Digitalisation, Sustainability, and the Banking and Capital Markets*

---

[183] *Ibid.*, recital (120), third and fourth sentences.

[184] SRMR, recital (99) and SRF Agreement, Article 15(1). The narrow wording used in the Agreement referring only to "institutions" of the EU makes it questionable whether this provision also covers compensation for damages caused by unlawful conduct of the SRB.

[185] This provision repeats *verbatim* the general rule on the contractual liability of the EU under Article 340, first sub-paragraph TFEU.

[186] SRMR, Article 87(1)–(2); for more details, see Kaufhold (2022), pp. 1180–1181.

[187] See under 9.1.3 above.

[188] SRMR, Article 87(6), which replicates Article 340, fourth sub-paragraph TFEU. On the basis of this provision, the SRB's staff members cannot be held personally liable towards private individuals for damage caused in the course of the performance of their duties; for more details, see Kaufhold (2022), pp. 1186–1187.

Union, EBI Studies in Banking and Capital Markets Law, Palgrave Macmillan, Cham – Switzerland, Chapter 12, pp. 353–375

Arons, T.M.C. (2020): Judicial Protection of Supervised Credit Institutions in the European Banking Union, in Busch, D. and G. Ferrarini (2020, editors): *European Banking Union*, Second edition, Oxford University Press, Oxford, Chapter 3, pp. 93–141

Bär-Bouyssière, B. (2019): Kommentar zum Artikel 107 AEUV, in Becker, U., Hatje, A. Schoo, J. und J. Schwarze (2019, Herausgeber): *EU-Kommentar*, 4. Auflage, Nomos Verlagsgesellshaft, Baden-Baden, pp. 1501–1702

Bailey, D. and L.E. John (2018, editors): *Bellamy & Child – European Union Law of Competition*, Eighth edition, Oxford University Press, Oxford

Binder, J.-H. (2022): Commentary on Articles 6 and 14 SRMR, in Binder, J.-H., Gortsos, Ch.V., Lackhoff, K. and Ch. Ohler (2022, editors): *Brussels Commentary on the Banking Union*, Verlag C.H. Beck, München – Hart Publishing, Oxford – Nomos Verlagsgesellschaft, Baden-Baden, pp. 497–506 and 619–630

Binder, J.-H. (2019): Participation of Non-euro Area Member States in the SRM: Centralised Decision-Making, Decentralised Implementation – Shared Responsibilities, in *Building Bridges: Central Banking Law in an Interconnected World*, ECB E-Book, pp. 314–330

Borchardt, K.D. (2019): Kommentar zum Artikel 267 AEUV, in Lenz, C.O. und K.D. Borchardt (2019, Hrsg.): *EU-Verträge: Kommentar*, 6. Auflage, Bundesanzeiger Verlag, Köln – Linde Verlag, Wien, pp. 2687–2730

Bruzzone, G., Cassella, M., & S. Micossi (2017): The New Regulatory Framework for Bank Resolution, in Laprévote F-C., Joanna Gray, and Francesco de Cecco (2017, editors): *Research Handbook on State Aid in the Banking Sector*, Edward Elgar Publishing, pp. 505–537

Busch, D. and Ch.V. Gortsos (2022): Liability of the European Central Bank, the Single Resolution Board and the ESAs (ESMA, EBA and EIOPA), in Busch, D., Gortsos, Ch.V. and G. McMeel (2022, editors): *Liability of Financial Supervisors and Resolution Authorities*, Chapter 2, pp. 9–54

Busch, D., McMeel, G. and Ch.V. Gortsos (2022): Comparative Law Evaluation, in Busch, D., Gortsos, Ch.V. and G. McMeel (2022, editors): *Liability of Financial Supervisors and Resolution Authorities*, Chapter 17, pp. 463–512

Craig, P. and G. de Búrca (2020): *EU Law: Texts, Cases, and Materials*, Seventh edition, Oxford University Press, Oxford – New York

F–H

Flynn, L. (2021): The Judicial Review of Fines and Penalty Payments Set by the SRB, in Zilioli, Ch. and K.-Ph. Wojcik (2021, editors): *Judicial Review in the European Banking Union*, Edward Elgar Publisher, Cheltenham, UK – Northampton, MA, USA, Chapter 25, pp. 429–442

Gortsos, Ch.V. (2022): Commentary on Articles 71–74, 83–84 88 and 90 SRMR, in Binder, J.-H., Gortsos, Ch.V., Lackhoff, K. and Ch. Ohler (2022, editors): *Brussels Commentary on the Banking Union*, Verlag C.H. Beck, München – Hart Publishing, Oxford – Nomos Verlagsgesellschaft, Baden-Baden, pp. 1109–1122, 1156–1163 1187–1190 and 1195–1198

Grünewald, S.N. (2014): *The Resolution of Cross-Border Banking Crises in the European Union – A Legal Study from the Perspective of Burden Sharing*, International

Banking and Finance Law Series, Volume 23, Wolters Kluwer Law & Business, Kluwer Law International, The Netherlands

Hadjiemmanuil, Ch. (2022): Commentary on Articles 27 and 30–31 SRMR, in Binder, J.-H., Gortsos, Ch.V., Lackhoff, K. and Ch. Ohler (2022, editors): *Brussels Commentary on the Banking Union*, Verlag C.H. Beck, München – Hart Publishing, Oxford – Nomos Verlagsgesellschaft, Baden-Baden, pp. 767–847 and 881–918

Haentjens, M. (2017a): Selected Commentary on the Bank Recovery and Resolution Directive, in Moss, G., Wessels, B. and M. Haentjens (2017, editors): *EU Banking and Insurance Insolvency*, Chapter IV, Second edition, Oxford University Press, Oxford, pp. 177–318

Haetjens, M. (2017b): Judicial Review of Resolution Action, in World Bank (2017): *Understanding Bank Recovery and Resolution in the EU: A Guidebook to the BRRD*, World Bank Group, Washington, DC, available at: https://pubdocs.worldbank.org/en/609571482207234996/FinSAC-BRRD-Guidebook.pdf, Chapter 23, pp. 159–163

Heinz, J. (2022): Commentary on Articles 48–56 SRMR, in Binder, J.-H., Gortsos, Ch.V., Lackhoff, K. and Ch. Ohler (2022, editors): *Brussels Commentary on the Banking Union*, Verlag C.H. Beck, München – Hart Publishing, Oxford – Nomos Verlagsgesellschaft, Baden-Baden, pp. 973–1016

K–L

Kaufhold, A.-K. (2022): Commentary on Articles 86–87 SRMR, in Binder, J.-H., Gortsos, Ch.V., Lackhoff, K. and Ch. Ohler (2022, editors): *Brussels Commentary on the Banking Union*, Verlag C.H. Beck, München – Hart Publishing, Oxford – Nomos Verlagsgesellschaft, Baden-Baden, pp. 1173–1178 and 1178–1187

Kerlin, J. (2021): The Procedure to Exercise Investigatory Powers, Including On-Site Inspections, by the SRB and their Judicial Control, in Zilioli, Ch. and K.-Ph. Wojcik (2021, editors): *Judicial Review in the European Banking Union*, Edward Elgar Publisher, Cheltenham, UK – Northampton, MA, USA, Chapter 24, pp. 416–428

Lackhoff, K. and M. Prokop (2022): Commentary on Articles 34–37 SRMR, in Binder, J.-H., Gortsos, Ch.V., Lackhoff, K. and Ch. Ohler (2022, editors): *Brussels Commentary on the Banking Union*, Verlag C.H. Beck, München – Hart Publishing, Oxford – Nomos Verlagsgesellschaft, Baden-Baden, pp. 927–941

Lamandini, M. and D.R. Muñoz (2021): Administrative Pre-litigation Review Mechanism in the SRM: The SRM Appeal Panel, in Zilioli, Ch. and K.-Ph. Wojcik (2021, editors): *Judicial Review in the European Banking Union*, Edward Elgar Publisher, Cheltenham, UK – Northampton, MA, USA, Chapter 4, pp. 44–58

Lamandini, M. and D.R. Muñoz (2020a): *SSM and the SRB Accountability at European Level: What Room for Improvements?* Banking Union Scrutiny, In-depth Analysis, European Parliament, Economic Governance Support Unit, April, available at: https://beta.op.europa.eu/en/publication-detail/-/publication/5dbbd54d-44cc-11eb-b59f-01aa75ed71a1/language-en/format-PDF/source-200399137

Lamandini, M. and D.R. Muñoz (2020b): Law and Practice of Financial Appeal Bodies (ESAs' Board of Appeal, SRB Appeal Panel): A View from the Inside, *Common Market Law Review*, Volume 57, Issue 1, pp. 119–160

Lenaerts, K., Maselis, Ig. and K. Gutman (2014): *EU Procedural Law*, Oxford European Union Law Library, Oxford University Press, Oxford

Lock, T. and M. Denis (2019): Article 47 CFR, in Kellerbauer M., Klamert M. and J. Tomkin (2019, editors): *The EU Treaties and the Charter of Fundamental Rights: A Commentary*, Oxford University Press, New York, pp. 2214–2226

O–P & R

Ohler, Ch. (2022): Commentary on Article 42 SRMR, in Binder, J.-H., Gortsos, Ch.V., Lackhoff, K. and Ch. Ohler (2022, editors): *Brussels Commentary on the Banking Union*, Verlag C.H. Beck, München – Hart Publishing, Oxford – Nomos Verlagsgesellschaft, Baden-Baden, pp. 950–953

Papathanassiou, Ch. (2022): Commentary on Articles 38–41 SRMR, in Binder, J.-H., Gortsos, Ch.V., Lackhoff, K. and Ch. Ohler (2022, editors): *Brussels Commentary on the Banking Union*, Verlag C.H. Beck, München – Hart Publishing, Oxford – Nomos Verlagsgesellschaft, Baden-Baden, pp. 941–950

Psaroudakis, G. (2022): Commentary on Articles 32–33, 75 and 78 SRMR, in Binder, J.-H., Gortsos, Ch.V., Lackhoff, K. and Ch. Ohler (2022, editors): *Brussels Commentary on the Banking Union*, Verlag C.H. Beck, München – Hart Publishing, Oxford – Nomos Verlagsgesellschaft, Baden-Baden, pp. 918–927, 1123–1129 and 1140–1141

Rosaria Miserendino, M. (2018): State Aid for the Banking Sector: What Has Changed After the New BRRD and SRM Regulation, *European State Aid Law Quarterly*, pp. 204 et seq.

Ruccia, N. (2021): The Single Resolution Board: Salient Features, Peculiarities and Paradoxes, in Pollak, J. and Slominski, P. (2021, editors): *The Role of EU Agencies in the Eurozone and Migration Crisis*, Palgrave Macmillan, Cham – Switzerland, pp. 103–125

S

Schwarze, J. und Ph. Voet van Vormizeele (2019): Kommentar zum Artikel 267 AEUV, in Schwarze, J., Becker, U., Hatje, A. und J. Schoo (2019, Hrsg.): *EU-Kommentar*, 4. Auflage, Nomos Verlagsgesellschaft, Baden-Baden, pp. 2908–2939

Smits, R. (2020): *SSM and the SRB accountability at European level: Room for Improvements?*, Banking Union Scrutiny, In-depth Analysis, European Parliament, Economic Governance Support Unit, April, available at: https://www.europarl.europa.eu/RegData/etudes/STUD/2020/645726/IPOL_STU(2020)645726_EN.pdf

Smoleńska, A. (2022): Multilevel Cooperation in the EU Resolution of Cross-Border Bank Groups: Lessons from the Non-euro Area Member States Joining the Single Resolution Mechanism (SRM), *Journal of Banking Regulation*, Volume 23, Issue 1, pp. 42–53

Stephenson, P. (2015): Reconciling Audit and Evaluation?: The Shift to Performance and Effectiveness at the European Court of Auditors, *European Journal of Risk Regulation*, Volume 6, Issue 1, pp. 79–89

V–W & Z

Voet van Vormizeele, Ph. (2019): Kommentar zum Artikel 41 GRC, in Schwarze, J., Becker, U., Hatje, A. und J. Schoo (2019, Hrsg.): *EU-Kommentar*, 4. Auflage, Nomos Verlagsgesellschaft, Baden-Baden, pp. 3503–3507

Wojcik, K.-Ph. (2022): Commentary on Article 7 SRMR, in Binder, J.-H., Gortsos, Ch.V., Lackhoff, K. and Ch. Ohler (2022, editors): *Brussels Commentary on the Banking Union*, Verlag C.H. Beck, München – Hart Publishing, Oxford – Nomos Verlagsgesellschaft, Baden-Baden, pp. 506–517

Zilioli, Ch. And K.-Ph. Wojcik (2021, editors): *Judicial Review in the European Banking Union*, Edward Elgar Publisher, Cheltenham, UK – Northampton, MA, USA

INDEX

A

ABLV Bank, AS, 537
Accountability, 37, 58, 119, 121, 122, 128, 140, 141, 146, 161, 187, 244, 335, 408, 420, 439, 459, 478, 481, 484, 487, 509, 526, 530, 534
Accountability *vis-à-vis* national parliaments, 481, 534
Accounting Directive, 301, 302, 359, 360
Action in emergency situations, 393, 397, 402, 444
Action plan, 110, 186, 274, 282, 289, 300, 301
Act or explain, 232
Adjustment coefficients, 523, 524
Administrative authorities, 25, 38, 50, 109, 143, 164, 170–172, 184, 203, 337, 361, 390, 391, 448
Administrative Board of Review (ABoR), 334, 439, 452, 462, 464, 473, 481–484, 489
Administrative expenditures, 528, 530, 535
Administrative pecuniary penalties, 471, 472
Administrative penalties, 463, 470, 471, 473
Advanced economies, 10, 13, 37, 91–93, 97, 100, 107, 113, 116, 127, 129, 187. *See also* economically developed countries

Adverse selection, 10
Advisory procedure, 424, 428, 429
Aggravating factors, 523
Allsopp Report, 162
Alternative Investment Fund (AIF), 7, 98, 238, 360
Alternative Investment Fund Manager (AIFM), 359
Alternative Investment Fund Managers Directive (AIFMD), 238, 239, 285
Alternative measures, 28, 349, 354
American International Group Inc. (AIG), 99, 239
Ancillary services undertaking, 350, 360
Annual report, 193, 409, 420, 425, 476, 479, 502, 508, 530–532, 534, 535
Anti-Money Laundering (AML), 388, 392
Anti-Money Laundering Directives/ AML Directives, 220, 223, 234, 389
Anti-Money Laundering Standing Committee (AMLSC), 392
Appeal Committee, 426, 427
Appeal Panel, 410, 482, 483, 534–536
Article IV consultations (IMF), 123, 129, 248
Artificial intelligence, 306
Asia/Pacific Group on Money Laundering (APG), 192
Asian crisis, 92, 96, 97, 124

© The Editor(s) (if applicable) and The Author(s), under exclusive license to Springer Nature Switzerland AG 2023
C. V. Gortsos, *The European Banking Regulation Handbook, Volume I*, https://doi.org/10.1007/978-3-031-32859-6

546　INDEX

Asset Management Company (AMC), 359, 360
Asset (or market) liquidity risk, 28
Asset separation tool, 46, 53
Asymmetric/asymmetry, 19, 213, 284, 386, 387
Audit(s), 36, 188, 486, 504, 528, 535
Authorisation, 12, 15, 23–25, 32, 37, 38, 49, 53, 57, 61, 87, 165, 206, 238, 241, 246, 249, 286, 323, 334, 355, 357, 359, 443, 461, 467, 469, 520–522
Autorité de Contrôle Prudentiel et de Résolution (ACPR), 170, 171, 420–422, 449, 515

B

Bail-in, 53, 55, 61, 144, 277, 336, 516, 531
Balance of payments, 91, 106, 123
Balance sheet, 28, 29, 33, 34, 41, 46, 50, 52, 123, 284, 351, 366, 532
Banca d'Italia, 351, 352, 449, 515
Banca Popolare di Bari (BPdB), 351
Banco Ambrosiano, 133
Banco Ambrosiano Holding S.A., 95, 133
Banco Popular Español, 537
Bank-based systems, 7
Bank for International Settlements (BIS), 40–42, 44, 47, 48, 64, 85, 100, 106, 108, 110, 112–114, 117, 118, 132, 162, 168, 172, 176, 180, 189–191, 193–195, 306
Bank holiday, 366
Banking book, 9, 141, 273
Banking Communication, 365
Banking crisis/crises, 22, 24, 44, 46, 49, 50, 56, 94, 99, 162, 163
Banking intermediation, 3, 8, 28
Banking panic(s), 20, 21, 46, 56, 57
Banking sector, 3, 14, 19, 20, 22, 24, 44, 45, 49, 61, 89, 109, 149, 167, 169, 214, 217, 222, 228, 235, 236, 243, 244, 250, 290, 293, 296, 306, 345, 354, 364, 387
Banking Stakeholder Group (BSG), 398, 410, 417, 419

Banking Supervision Committee (BSC), 222, 230, 391
Banking system, 3, 5, 8, 10, 14, 20, 21, 23, 25, 32, 36, 40, 46, 49, 54–56, 87, 91, 95, 98, 99, 101, 102, 104, 127, 134, 135, 162, 163, 165, 166, 168, 174, 175, 206, 234, 236, 284, 299, 300, 304, 349, 365
Banking Union (BU), 205, 213, 246–248, 253, 355, 371
Banknotes, 4, 209, 212
Bank of Commerce and Credit International (BCCI), 95
Bank of England (BoE), 39, 170–172, 189, 190, 479, 518
Bank Recovery and Resolution Directive (BRRD), 234, 249, 250, 252, 253, 270, 298–300, 321, 325, 336–346, 349, 354–358, 388–390, 417, 419, 438, 458, 460, 501, 506, 509, 511, 512, 514, 515, 517–520, 522, 537
Bank Recovery and Resolution Directive No II (BRRD II), 271, 336
Bank run(s), 21, 56, 59, 61
Bank safety net, 14, 19, 23–25, 32, 48, 56, 63, 87, 146, 231, 244, 371
Barings Bank, 95
Basel Committee on Banking Supervision (BCBS), 14, 26, 28, 30, 33, 36, 41, 44, 45, 47, 92, 94, 95, 102, 109, 111, 114, 117, 132–136, 140, 161, 162, 164–169, 172–181, 183, 185, 186, 215, 217, 219, 223, 234, 274, 293, 299, 306, 319, 320, 459, 478
Basel Concordats, 133, 217
Basel Consultative Group (BCG), 172, 174, 175, 180
Basel Framework, 135, 306
Basel I capital adequacy framework, 135
Basel II capital adequacy framework, 135, 175
Basel III impact, 101, 290
Basel III Monitoring Reports, 179
Basel III regulatory framework, 45, 101, 133–135, 178, 179, 271, 291, 317, 323, 326
Basel IV Regulatory Framework, 134
Basel process, 110, 112, 114, 189

INDEX 547

Basic tasks, 211, 213, 330, 447, 474, 478, 481, 484
BCBS-FSI High Level Meetings, 180
Behaviour/behavioural, 10, 11, 21, 32, 45, 48, 174, 240, 526
Benchmark, 240, 288, 301
Benchmarks regulation, 240
Berlusconi case, 469
Binding mediation, 344, 392, 397, 402, 404
Blunden Committee, 162
Board of Appeal (BoA), 391, 408, 410, 411, 482, 483
Board of Appeal (ESAs), 410
Board of Supervisors (BoS, EBA), 339, 391, 392, 509
Bottom-up approach, 399
Branch, 3, 42, 60, 86–90, 121, 131, 165, 167, 184, 188, 203, 205–208, 213, 214, 216, 218, 220, 223, 226, 240, 322, 332, 337, 356, 357, 360, 368, 369, 405, 414, 438, 448, 449, 452, 467, 469, 476, 477, 506, 518
Breach of ECB legal acts, 470–472
Breach of Union law, 397, 398, 402, 403
Bretton Woods agreement, 122
Bretton Woods system, 91–93, 123, 161, 165
Bridge institution tool, 53
Budget, 99, 120, 146, 342, 347, 408, 476, 479, 499, 502, 507, 508, 527–531, 539
Building-blocks approach, 29
Bundesanstalt für Finanzdienstleistungsaufsicht (BaFin), 170, 191, 449, 515
Bundesverfassungsgericht (BVerfG), 275
Business day, 368, 369

C

Calculation models, 355
Canada Deposit Insurance Corporation (CDIC), 518
Capital Adequacy Directive (CAD), 219
Capital adequacy ratio(s), 33, 34, 43, 44, 63, 219

Capital Conservation Buffer (CCB), 43, 44, 134, 292, 326
Capital controls, 56, 366
Capital Markets Recovery Package, 298
Capital Markets Union (CMU), 270, 281–284, 287, 289, 300
Capital Requirements Directive No I (CRD I), 226
Capital Requirements Directive No IV (CRD IV), 207, 247–249, 252, 253, 270, 271, 273, 285, 291–293, 299, 303, 319–327, 331, 336, 337, 343, 344, 355, 358, 359, 361, 389, 396, 402, 417, 423, 438, 448, 460, 466, 469, 472
Capital Requirements Directive No V (CRD V), 271, 303, 325
Capital Requirements Regulation (575/2013) (CRR), 247, 317
Capital Requirements Regulation no. II (CRR II), 271, 294, 303, 318, 319, 324
Caribbean Financial Action Task Force (CFATF), 192
Case law, 233, 420, 512
Ceiling, 61, 277, 278, 369, 370
Central Bank Digital Currency (CBDC), 306
Central Banking law, 213
Central bank money solution, 49
Central bank(s), 9, 17, 23, 25, 37–39, 42, 48, 49
Central CounterParties (CCPs), 44, 143, 148, 239, 271, 286, 319, 331, 337, 341, 384, 448
Central, Eastern and Southeastern Europe (CESEE), 292
Centralised approach, 362
Central Securities Depositories Regulation (CSDR), 239
Central Securities Depository (CSD), 239
Channels of transmission, 64
Charter of Fundamental Rights (CFR), 413
Charter of Fundamental Rights of the European Union (Charter), 413
Chinese walls, 332, 484
Climate change, 31, 128, 136, 289, 303

548   INDEX

Climate-related financial risks, 31, 136, 137, 174, 302
Close cooperation, 167, 180, 232, 246, 329–331, 334, 342, 345, 388, 403, 419, 437, 445, 449, 455–457, 461, 465, 472, 490, 516, 521
CMU Action Plan, 282–284, 287, 300, 301
Code of Conduct, 445, 479, 489, 502, 527, 531, 533
Code of Conduct for high-level ECB Officials, 440, 445, 475, 485, 489
Code of Good Practices on Fiscal Transparency, 139
Code of Good Practices on Transparency in Monetary and Financial Policies, 139, 146
Coins, 4, 209, 484
Co-insurance, 59, 251
Co-insurance phase, 251, 280
Collateral, 27, 41, 47, 50, 51, 144, 148, 195, 303, 367, 369, 503
Collateral/liquidity channel, 64
Collateralised Loan Obligations (CLOs), 175, 298
Comitology, 221
Comitology procedure, 223, 416, 418, 423, 429
Commission Announcement, 244
Committee of European Banking Supervisors (CEBS), 222, 223, 229, 230, 388
Committee of European Insurance and Occupational Pensions Supervisors (CEIOPS), 222, 223, 229, 230
Committee of European Securities Regulators (CESR), 222, 223, 229, 230
Committee of Inquiry (European Parliament), 480, 533
Committee on Payment and Settlement Systems (CPSS), 16, 17, 109, 117, 148, 162, 163, 188
Committee on Payments and Markets Infrastructures (CPMI), 26, 109, 111, 113, 114, 118, 132, 139, 148, 185, 188, 189
Committee on the Global Financial System (CGFS), 22, 35, 41–43, 64, 100, 109, 111, 113, 114, 117, 118, 132, 189, 193, 194
Common backstop, 269, 276–280
Common currency, 209, 212
Common Equity Tier 1 (CET1), 44, 292
Common EU financial data strategy, 401
Compendium of Standards and Codes, 118, 133, 137
Compensation, 17, 54, 59, 61, 62, 88, 185, 207, 220, 273, 345, 347, 511, 539
Compliance, 11, 23, 31, 36–38, 42, 123, 125, 131, 142, 144–147, 178, 183, 211, 285, 321, 324, 326, 346, 348, 363, 365, 366, 386, 390, 391, 404, 420–422, 446, 455, 465–467, 473, 484, 486, 499, 500, 516, 528
Comply or explain, 295, 301, 420, 422
Comprehensive surveillance review, 130
Conditions for resolution, 52, 53, 57
Conduct of business (COB), 38, 240, 298
Conduct regulation, 38
Conference of Insurance Supervisors (CIS), 230
Conflicts of interest, 39, 332, 337, 410, 445, 446, 475, 502
Consolidated basis, 16, 88, 187, 208, 217, 219, 326, 327, 337, 366, 368
Consolidated Supervision Directive, 217, 219
Constructive ambiguity, 51, 88, 206, 362
Consumer protection, 16, 116, 122, 214, 224, 235, 236, 306, 395, 404–406, 438
Consumer Protection and Financial Innovation Sub-Committee (EBA), 406
Contagion, 12, 16, 20, 22, 33, 41, 45, 52, 127, 129, 236, 277, 511
Continental Illinois (Bank), 62, 95
Contractual DGSs, 350, 351, 353
Contractual liability, 539
Contribution to resolution financing function, 57
conventional monetary policy, 291
Convergence criteria, 209, 474

INDEX 549

Conversion, 22, 46, 53, 338, 456, 513
Cooke Committee, 162
Cooperation arrangements, 342, 447, 455, 511, 514, 518
Cooperation Framework Agreement (COFRA), 517
Core Principles (CPs), 47, 58, 62, 139–142, 145, 146, 149, 177, 182, 384, 474, 478
Core Principles for Effective Banking Supervision, 47, 133, 140, 149, 178
Core Principles for Islamic Financial Regulation, 149
Core Principles Methodology, 140
Corporate governance, 33, 98, 112, 116, 125, 132, 136, 139, 141, 147, 148, 390, 420
Corporate Sustainability Reporting Directive (CSRD), 301
Cost-benefit analysis, 417, 419, 502
Council-ECB MoU, 335, 440, 442, 443, 478, 480, 486
Council of Europe Committee of Experts on the Evaluation of Anti-Money Laundering Measures and the Financing of Terrorism (MONEYVAL), 192
Countercyclical Capital Buffer (CCyB), 36, 43, 44, 134, 135, 292, 293, 326, 361
Counterparty Credit Risk (CCR), 27, 271
Counterparty risk, 219, 323
Country Assistance Strategies (CASs), 131
Country peer reviews, 122, 430
Country risk, 27, 94
Court of Justice of the European Union (CJEU), 233, 240, 273, 345–347, 353, 384–386, 411, 412, 414, 420, 421, 452, 453, 455, 466, 467, 482, 483, 487, 522, 526, 536–539
Coverage level, 59, 61–63, 236, 349, 353, 354
Credit institution, 55, 99, 133, 140, 144, 145, 171, 205–208, 212, 214, 216–220, 224–226, 228, 234, 235, 237, 241, 242, 244, 246–251, 270–274, 276, 277, 280, 284, 290–296, 298, 299, 302–304, 306, 318, 321–323, 325, 326, 328, 330–334, 336, 340, 341, 349–354, 356, 357, 359, 360, 362–367, 386, 387, 389, 392, 399–401, 412, 423, 437, 438, 447–455, 457, 461, 465, 469, 477, 480, 481, 485, 500, 507, 512, 516, 517, 536
Credit Institutions Winding-Up Directive (CIWUD), 358
Credit Rating Agencies Regulation, 238, 384
Credit Rating Agency (CRA), 185
Credit risk, 7–9, 27, 44, 95, 135, 141, 147, 195, 226, 272, 274, 319, 323, 324
Credit risk mitigation, 323
Credit risk transformation, 9
Credit Valuation Adjustment (CVA), 27, 323
Crisis-legislation hypothesis, 92
Crisis management, 23, 46, 49, 51, 52, 63, 121, 141, 142, 146, 189, 277, 299, 336, 338, 341, 400, 515
Crisis Management Groups (CMGs), 143, 458
Crisis management measure(s), 25, 338
Crisis prevention, 23, 45, 46, 338, 438
Crisis prevention measure(s), 23, 25, 45, 338
Critical functions, 52, 53, 103, 249, 511
Cross-border activities criterion, 451
Cross-border financial transactions, 90, 91, 93
Cross-border Payments in Euro Regulation, 225
Cross-sectional dimension (of systemic risk), 22, 41, 43, 44
Crowdfunding, 4, 286
Crowdfunding service, 4, 286
Crowdfunding service provider, 286
CRR quick fix, 294, 318
Crypto-assets, 4, 305, 306
Cyber risk(s), 26, 128, 136, 190
Cybersecurity, 388

D

Daisy chain, 300

Damage, 23, 47, 231, 273, 406, 412, 462, 463, 483, 487, 525, 538, 539
Data protection, 3, 425, 521
Debt instruments, 4–7, 28, 29, 240, 270, 274, 336
Decentralised agencies, 386, 499
Decentralised approach, 362
Decentralised finance (DeFi), 4, 13
Decentralised management, 217, 223, 227
Declaration, 346, 421
Deficit, 243, 351
Deglobalisation, 196
de Larosière, Jacques, 40, 228
de Larosière Report, 228, 232
Delegated act(s), 289, 301, 338, 341, 342, 414–418, 429, 530
Delimitation, 48, 85, 86, 88, 90, 209
Deposit guarantee, 23, 25, 47, 50, 56–58, 61, 63, 87, 111, 132, 139, 167, 177, 181, 182, 206, 349, 355, 371
Deposit Guarantee Scheme (DGS), 22, 24, 25, 53, 56–63, 220, 244, 250–252, 349, 350, 352, 354, 355, 511, 513
Deposit Guarantee Schemes Directive (1994), 220
Deposit Guarantee Schemes Directive (DGSD), 182, 252, 253, 299, 348–350, 352–355, 358, 389, 390, 400, 417, 511
Deposit insurance, 23, 110, 145, 146, 181–184, 299, 336, 341
Deposit Insurance Fund, 55
Deposit Insurance Scheme (DIS), 182, 183
Deposit protection, 23, 59, 182, 236, 349
Deposit protection scheme(s), 167, 182
Derivatives, 4, 5, 7, 15, 22, 24, 27, 29, 43, 44, 94, 98, 104, 135, 143, 189, 195, 207, 239, 240, 284
Designated entity/entities, 341, 342, 505–507, 512, 520, 522, 524, 528, 530, 534, 536, 538
Designated group(s), 505–507, 512, 538

Detailed Assessments Report (DAR), 131
Deutsche Bundesbank, 117, 170, 474
Dexia Bank, 99
Dichotomy, 51, 54
Digital finance, 304
Digital finance package, 304
Digital finance strategy, 304, 305
Digital operational resilience, 305
Digital Operational Resilience Act (DORA), 305
Digital Stored-value Product (DSP), 58
Direct financing, 4, 6, 7, 13
Direct public financial assistance criterion, 451
Direct Recapitalisation Instrument (DRI), 247, 276, 277, 328
Disclosure of information, 146, 185
Disclosure requirements, 271, 286, 302, 303, 319
Dispute(s), 273, 345, 347, 397, 412, 538
Dispute settlement, 19, 346
Disruption(s), 22, 45, 52, 136, 143, 295, 305, 395, 400, 427
Distance Marketing of Consumer Financial Services Directive, 225
Distributed Ledger Technology (DLT), 304–306
Distributed Ledger Technology Regulation (DLTR), 304
Dividend(s), 44, 294, 295, 297
Division of tasks, 447, 511, 512
Domestic Systemically Important Banks (D-SIBs), 43, 179
Due process, 181, 439, 462

E

Early intervention, 23, 25, 46–48, 57, 338, 342, 371, 438, 513, 514, 516
Early warning, 132
Eastern and Southern Africa Anti-Money Laundering Group (ESAAMLG), 192
EBA Guidelines, 248, 249, 274, 275, 420–422, 460
EBA Recommendations, 419
ECB Agreement (2017), 364–368

ECB decision, 328, 330, 334, 345, 439, 440, 443, 445, 446, 450–452, 456, 461, 466–468, 477, 481, 482, 484–487, 490
ECB Guidelines, 211, 363, 445, 461
ECB Instructions, 461
ECB Regulations, 253, 470, 473, 477, 486
ECB Rules of Procedure, 439, 440, 444, 446, 461, 479, 482, 484, 485, 489, 490
ECB supervisory Decisions, 463, 484
ECB supervisory procedures, 462, 463
ECON (European Parliament), 409, 441, 442, 445, 461, 479, 480, 510, 531–534
Economically developed countries, 10, 166. *See also* Advanced economies
Economically developing countries, 96, 107, 117
Economically less developed countries, 10, 107
Economic and Financial Affairs Council (ECOFIN), 214
Economic and Monetary Affairs Committee (ECON), 335
Economic and Monetary Union (EMU), 209–213, 215, 241–243, 250, 269, 270, 280, 283, 284, 330, 331, 474
Economic Consultive Committee (ECC), 114
Economic growth, 40, 44, 97, 116, 231, 287, 291
Economic importance criterion, 451
Economic interests, 17, 214
Economic transplants, 203
Economic union, 213, 215
EFTA Surveillance Authority (ESA), 232, 392, 410, 411
Elements of change, 354, 399
Elements of continuity, 353
Emergency Liquidity Assistance (ELA), 49, 212, 363–370
Emerging Market Economies (EMEs), 10, 91, 107, 113, 116, 127, 129, 130, 165, 194
EMIR REFIT, 285
E-money Institutions Directive, 225, 236

EMU reflection paper, 280
enhanced General Data Dissemination Standard (e-GDDS), 147
Enhanced General Data Dissemination System, 139, 147
Environmental factors, 31
Environmental materiality side, 31
Environmental risks, 26, 30, 31, 287, 399
Environmental, Social and Governance (ESG), 30, 31, 287, 288, 303, 304, 390, 395, 398
EP-ECB Interinstitutional Agreement, 335, 439–441, 443, 445, 461, 478–481, 486
Equities, 4–7, 14, 22, 27, 29, 94, 190, 194, 352, 360
Equivalence, 176, 204, 401, 403, 429
ESCB/ECB Statute, 210–212, 232, 241–243, 277, 329, 362, 364, 366, 369, 407, 437, 439, 442, 446, 447, 460, 474, 475, 478, 482, 487
ESG factors, 31
ESG risks, 300, 302–304
Ethics Committee, 334, 445, 475, 489
EU agencies, 384, 419, 499, 537
EU financial law, 204–209, 214–216, 218, 220, 223, 225–227, 240, 305, 343, 413, 414, 416
EU Green Bond Standard (EUGBS), 302
EU law, 45, 134, 204, 207, 209, 210, 213, 214, 226, 243, 252, 279, 299, 319, 346, 347, 390, 392, 394, 397, 403, 404, 408, 410, 412, 419, 422, 423, 460, 462, 465, 466, 473, 474, 488, 499, 500, 516, 521, 538
EurAsian Group (EAG), 192
Euro, 9, 49, 62, 93, 164, 171, 172, 196, 205, 211, 212, 215, 220, 221, 223, 235, 236, 242, 244–246, 248, 272, 275–278, 283, 284, 292, 295, 322, 330, 342, 347, 354, 362–368, 370, 371, 383, 400, 449, 451, 452, 456, 503
Euro banknotes, 484
Euro coins, 212
Eurogroup, 106, 211, 243, 278, 279, 281, 479, 480

552   INDEX

Eurogroup Report to Leaders on EMU deepening, 280
European Bank for Reconstruction and Development (EBRD), 182, 228
European Banking Authority Regulation (EBAR), 229, 236, 248, 296, 329, 333, 339, 340, 343, 344, 383, 387–405, 407–412, 416, 417, 419–423, 459, 460, 509, 527
European Banking Committee (EBC), 222, 223, 424–429
European Banking Institute (EBI), 298, 487, 537
European Coal and Steel Community (ECSC), 448
European Court of Auditors (ECA), 287, 409, 439, 486, 529, 530, 535, 536
European Crowdfunding Service Providers Regulation (ECSPR), 286
European Deposit Insurance and Resolution Authority (EDIRA), 245, 246
European Deposit Insurance Fund (EDIF), 250, 281
European Deposit Insurance Scheme (EDIS), 182, 246, 250, 251, 253, 269, 278, 280, 281, 299
European Economic Area (EEA), 205–207, 324, 336, 339, 348, 392
European (EU) banking law, 205, 206, 214, 430
European (EU) capital markets law, 207
European (EU) central banking law, 213
European (EU) financial conglomerates law, 208
European (EU) insurance law, 208
European (EU) monetary law, 89, 209
European (EU) payment and settlement systems law, 205
European Financial Stability Facility (EFSF), 276, 451, 458
European Forum of Deposit Insurers (EFDI), 182, 252
European Free Trade Association (EFTA), 205
European Insurance and Occupational Pensions Authority (EIOPA), 229, 230

European Insurance and Occupational Pensions Authority Regulation (EIOPAR), 383, 387–389, 410, 411
European Insurance and Occupational Pensions Committee (EIOPC), 222, 223, 424, 429
European Investment Bank (EIB), 281, 415
Europeanisation/europeanised, 229, 231, 244, 371
European Long-Term Investment Funds Regulation (ELTIFR), 239
European Market Infrastructure Regulation (EMIR), 239, 284, 286, 337, 341, 384
European Monetary Fund (EMF), 275–278
European resolution college, 519
European Resolution Examination Programme (EREP), 397, 402
European resolution handbook, 396
European Securities and Markets Authority (ESMA), 229, 230, 238, 292, 298, 339, 384–389, 391, 392, 410, 415, 430, 459, 516
European Securities and Markets Authority Regulation (ESMAR), 383, 387–389, 410, 411
European Securities Committee (ESC), 222, 223, 424, 429
European Social Entrepreneurship Funds Regulation (EuSEFR), 239
European Stability Mechanism (ESM), 49, 247, 275–280, 328, 451, 458, 502, 515
European Supervisory Authorities (ESAs), 228, 229, 231, 232, 238, 284, 317, 339, 383, 384, 386–389, 391, 406, 410, 411, 415, 422, 429
European Supervisory Examination Programme (ESEP), 397, 402
European supervisory handbook, 396, 460
European Systemic Risk Board (ESRB), 228, 230–233, 270, 272, 292, 297, 324, 339, 371, 383, 386–388, 391, 399, 401, 403, 447, 459, 516

INDEX   553

European Systemic Risk Board
    Regulation (ESRBR), 230–233,
    395, 400
European system of bank resolution and
    funding arrangements, 400, 402
European system of deposit guarantee
    schemes, 400, 402
European System of Financial
    Supervision (ESFS), 212, 213, 228,
    230, 332, 383, 384, 387, 419, 429,
    458, 459, 516
European Venture Capital Funds
    Regulation (EuVeCaR), 239
Euro Summit, 273, 278–281
Eurosystem, 201, 210–213, 215, 242,
    243, 277, 291, 303, 330, 331,
    362–364, 366, 367, 369, 370, 437,
    439, 446, 447, 474, 478, 481, 484
Eurosystem credit operations, 369
Eurosystem Ethics Framework, 211
Event risk, 29
Examination procedure, 426, 428, 429
Exchange of information, 113, 183,
    185, 217, 334, 337, 364, 388, 400,
    403, 439, 455, 473, 518, 521
Executive Board, 125, 129–131, 276,
    281, 366, 368–370, 441–443, 445,
    446, 474, 485
Executive Session (SRB), 500–503,
    505–508, 526
Expected Credit Loss (ECL), 104, 294
Experts, 109, 125, 174, 227, 327, 410,
    416, 462, 479, 531
Explanations relating to the Charter of
    Fundamental Rights, 414
Exposure at Default (EAD), 27
Extraordinary public financial support,
    511, 512

F
Failing or likely to fail (FOLF), 23, 53,
    338
Failure management function, 46, 57
FATF Recommendations, 147, 234
FATF-Style Regional Body (FSRB), 192
FBF v ACPR case, 421
Federal Constitutional Court (FCC),
    275

Federal Deposit Insurance Corporation
    (FDIC), 61, 171, 518
Federal Reserve System, 171, 188, 193,
    211, 474, 478
Fédération Bancaire Française (FBF),
    420–422
Financial Action Task Force (FATF),
    107, 110, 116, 132, 139, 178, 192,
    193, 234, 305
Financial Action Task Force on Money
    Laundering in South America
    (GAFISUD), 192
Financial Collateral Arrangements
    Directive, 224
Financial Conduct Authority (FCA), 39
Financial conglomerate, 15, 37, 38, 88,
    109, 111, 117, 132, 191, 205, 208,
    360, 388, 389, 448, 450
Financial Conglomerates Directive No I
    (FICOD I), 226
Financial Conglomerates Directive No II
    (FICOD II), 226
Financial contracts law, 204
Financial crisis/crises, 13, 20, 26, 35,
    64, 96, 98–100, 107, 109, 127,
    130, 141, 165, 249, 290
Financial development, 129–131
Financial developmental module (World
    Bank), 129
Financial enforcement, 11
Financial firm, 3, 4, 6, 8, 10–12, 15–18,
    22, 31, 32, 35, 37, 38, 40–42, 48,
    58, 87, 89, 91, 93–99, 117, 118,
    131, 142, 172, 196, 203–208, 214,
    223, 225, 227, 228, 245, 250, 330,
    332, 350, 369, 395, 420, 448
Financial group, 15, 405
Financial holding company/companies,
    219, 271, 319, 321, 326, 327, 337,
    341, 359–361, 448, 450, 465
Financial inclusion, 14, 58, 110, 111,
    190
Financial independence, 408, 439,
    474–476, 526, 527
Financial institution, 118, 120, 121,
    128, 138, 143, 189, 190, 192, 206,
    207, 216, 233, 245, 250, 297, 326,
    330, 336, 342, 350, 357, 359, 360,
    365, 368–370, 389, 391, 393–401,

404, 405, 410, 419, 420, 422, 441, 528
Financial Intelligence Unit (FIU), 192
Financial intermediaries, 7–9, 38, 93, 94, 298
Financial intermediation, 4, 7
Financial literacy, 18, 116, 405
Financial Market Infrastructures (FMIs), 143, 148, 184
Financial materiality side, 31
Financial oversight, 11, 15
Financial Policy Committee (FPC), 39
Financial policy objectives, 10, 14, 16, 25, 35, 203, 204
Financial regulation(s), 3, 4, 10, 11, 13, 14, 16, 17, 35, 92, 102, 138, 223, 227, 229, 284, 323, 390, 394, 502, 530
Financial Regulations (SRB), 502, 529
Financial resources, 32, 233, 346, 395, 476
Financial risk(s), 10, 13, 26, 31, 32, 94, 165, 174
Financial Sector Assessment (FSA), 125, 130
Financial Sector Assessment Program (FSAP), 122, 124, 129, 430
Financial Services Action Plan (FSAP), 223, 224
Financial Services and Markets Act (FSMA), 14, 39
Financial stability, 4, 12–14, 16, 23, 32, 38–40, 42, 44, 46, 47, 52, 56, 60, 63, 64, 97, 100, 102, 103, 105, 113, 116, 117, 119, 121, 123, 124, 128–130, 136, 142, 145, 167–169, 175, 184, 189, 193–196, 212, 213, 215, 231, 235, 242, 270, 276, 290, 291, 295–297, 299, 303, 322, 323, 349, 370, 388, 399, 400, 453, 454, 484, 511, 519, 527
Financial Stability Board (FSB), 8, 12, 24, 30, 40–42, 44, 54, 55, 100, 102–104, 108, 113, 114, 116, 118–122, 125, 132, 133, 136, 137, 139, 142–144, 161, 167, 177–179, 181, 183, 185–190, 192, 193, 196, 232, 234, 270, 290, 302, 305, 430, 459

Financial Stability Forum (FSF), 92, 97, 100, 107, 116–118, 137, 181
Financial Stability Institute (FSI), 47, 180, 191
Financial stability module (IMF), 129, 130
Financial supervision, 11, 171, 172, 228, 437, 441, 509
Financial system, 3, 4, 8, 10–17, 22–24, 30, 33, 35, 37–43, 45, 47–49, 51, 55, 56, 64, 85, 86, 88, 89, 91–95, 97–99, 101–103, 105–107, 109, 111, 112, 114, 116–118, 120, 121, 124–132, 137, 138, 140, 146, 161, 167, 171, 177, 180, 191–194, 196, 202, 203, 208, 212, 214, 215, 217, 221, 223, 227–232, 234, 236, 241, 242, 244, 249, 257, 292, 295, 297, 299, 301, 302, 320, 325, 331, 337, 365, 371, 383, 385–387, 390–393, 395, 397, 400–402, 404–406, 410, 424, 438, 447, 462, 463
Financial System Stability Assessment (FSSA), 130, 131
Financial Technology (FinTech), 36, 58, 128
Financial Union, 204, 250, 270
Fines, 11, 471, 472, 522, 523, 525, 526, 535
First Banking Directive, 206, 216–218
First pillar, 165, 224, 232, 244, 273, 302, 383
Fiscal crisis in the euro area, 64, 215, 234, 243, 273, 290
Fiscal discipline, 213
Fit-and-proper, 32, 455
Five Presidents Report, 250
Fixed exchange rates, 91, 93, 106, 161, 164
Fondo Interbancario di Tutela dei Depositi (FITD), 352
Forbearance, 47, 274
Forborne exposures (FBEs), 274
Foreign exchange crisis, 24, 100
Foreign exchange risk, 26, 29, 30, 219
Foreign reserves, 211
Fortis Bank, 99
Forum of European Securities Commissions (FESCO), 222, 230

INDEX 555

Forward-looking approach, 47, 296
Fourth pillar, 101, 165
Francovich liability doctrine, 412
Francovich liability doctrine, 412
Freedom(s), 204, 206–208, 216, 218, 324, 325, 327, 348, 349, 438, 469
FSB Assessment Methodology, 144
Full insurance, 251
Full integration approach, 38, 171, 172
Functional approach, 87, 171, 172, 204, 205, 209, 228
Functional or 'twin peaks' approach, 38, 40
Fundamental, 137, 204, 306, 330, 353, 463, 466
Funding (or liability) liquidity risk, 28
Funds Transfers Regulation, 389

G
G7, 92, 96, 105–108, 111, 117, 132, 192, 305, 430
G7 Fundamental Elements for Threat-Led Penetration Testing (G7FE-TLPT), 305
G10, 92, 105, 106, 113, 123, 132, 162, 163, 168, 169, 189, 193, 430
G20, 33, 92, 97, 100, 102, 105–108, 110, 117, 118, 120, 122, 132, 136, 137, 147, 148, 168, 169, 178, 185, 188, 189, 191, 193, 303, 430
G20 Summit(s), 108, 110, 132
General Agreement on Trade and Tariffs (GATT), 91
General Agreement on Trade in Services (GATS), 96, 114, 115, 131, 133, 138, 167
General Arrangements to Borrow (GAB), 106
General Board, 232, 233, 296
General Data Protection Regulation (GDPR), 447
General instructions, 461, 513, 517
Generally Accepted Accounting Principles (GAAP), 187
Glass-Steagall Act, 24
Global (bank) Stress Test (IMF) (GST), 128
Global bank stress testing approach, 128

Global Economy Meeting (GEM), 113, 114, 189, 193
Global Financial Crisis (GFC), 7, 12, 24, 28, 33, 34, 37, 39, 41, 42, 48, 62, 92, 97, 98, 101, 102, 108, 127, 130, 140, 142, 145, 146, 148, 177, 194, 196, 212, 215, 227, 228, 233–237, 239, 242, 245, 273, 290, 363
Global financial reforms, 101, 102, 178
Global Partnership for Financial Inclusion (GPFI), 14, 110, 111
Global public good, 13
Global Systemically Important Bank(s) (G-SIBs), 104, 144, 179, 270
Global Systemically Important Financial Institutions (G-SIFIs), 143
Global Systemically Important Institution(s) (G-SIIs), 292, 300, 319–321
Governing Council (GC), 211
Government Financial Stabilisation Tools (GFSTs), 343
Grace period, 367
'Greek alphabet' risks, 29
Green bonds, 301, 302
Green Deal, 301
Green Paper, 235, 282
Greenwashing, 288
Grimaldi case, 419
Gross Domestic Product (GDP), 113, 243
Groupe de Contact (GdC), 222, 230
Group-Level Resolution Authority (GLRA), 343, 505, 506
Group of Governors and Heads of Supervision (GHOS), 113, 114, 134, 162, 169, 173, 175, 176
Growth and Emerging Markets Committee (GEMC), 185
G-SII buffer, 293, 325, 326
Guidelines, 33, 121, 124, 137, 139, 141, 167–169, 173, 176–178, 211, 278, 294, 303, 324, 334, 343, 391, 393, 396, 401–403, 405, 406, 415, 419–423, 429, 430, 453, 460, 501, 506, 517, 532, 533
Guide to banking supervision, 396, 479

Gulf Cooperation Council (GCC), 111, 192

H
Hague Convention, 112
Harmonisation, 139, 140, 167, 177, 201, 203, 204, 208, 217, 223, 224, 227, 229, 245, 249, 253, 274, 349, 405, 417
Headquarters Agreement, 112, 407, 500
Hedge funds, 7, 98, 235
Herstatt Bank, 92, 95, 133, 162, 163
Herstatt risk, 162
Hierarchy of norms, 413, 414
High – level Expert Group on Sustainable finance (HLEG), 287
High Level Securities Supervisors Committee (HLSSC), 222, 230
High-quality liquid assets (HQLA), 34, 134
High resolution standards, 513
Home bias, 273
Homogeneous financial activities, 15
Horizontal, 3, 15, 37, 112, 214
Host authorities, 144, 177, 469

I
IADI Core Principles for Effective Deposit Insurance Systems, 47, 133, 139, 145, 252
IFRS 9, 270, 292, 294, 318
Impediment(s), 46, 53, 296, 338, 350, 500, 509, 518, 535
Impediments to recoverability, 338
Implementation lag, 39
Implementation of monetary policy, 50, 365
Implementing act, 245, 247, 249, 253, 317, 337, 341, 343, 389, 404, 414, 415, 418, 419, 423–430, 460
Implementing Technical Standards (ITSs), 274, 317, 324, 343, 391, 393, 396, 401–403, 415, 418, 419, 422, 429, 460, 466, 472, 501, 506
Income risk, 26, 28, 29
Independence, 37, 141, 146, 397, 407, 439, 446, 474–476, 478, 526–528
Industrial organisation theory approach, 11
Inflation, 92, 211, 215, 231
Informational channel, 20
Information and Communication Technology (ICT), 305
Information asymmetry/asymmetries, 7, 10, 16–21, 214
Infrastructure(s), 4, 13–15, 26, 44, 52, 86, 95, 111, 122, 128, 130, 138, 139, 142, 220, 239, 281, 282, 284, 304, 320, 395, 511, 528
Initial period, 340, 344, 505
Insolvency, 12, 14, 17, 21, 23, 28, 32, 44–46, 49, 51, 52, 54, 56, 57, 62, 99, 112, 139, 147, 165–167, 249, 270, 285, 297, 336, 343, 350, 354, 356, 357, 366, 509
Insolvency and Creditor Rights' (Standard) (ICR), 139, 147
Institutional balance, 385
Institutional independence, 407, 408, 439, 474, 475, 515, 526, 533
Institutional protection scheme (IPS), 337, 350, 351
Institutional safeguards, 486, 535
Institutions for Occupational Retirement Provision Directive No I (IORPD I), 226, 241
Institutions for Occupational Retirement Provision Directive No II (IORPD II), 241
Institutions for Occupational Retirement Provisions (IORP), 226, 241
Insurance Core Principles, 149, 190
Insurance Distribution Directive (IDD), 241
Insurance holding companies, 359
Insurance Mediation Directive (IMD), 225
Insurance policyholders, 15, 208
Insurance regulation, 190
Insurance undertaking(s), 8, 15, 24, 99, 171, 208, 226, 239, 241, 272, 284, 322, 330, 359, 360
Interest rate income risk, 26
Inter-Governmental Action Group against Money Laundering in West Africa (GIABA), 192

INDEX 557

Intergovernmental Agreement, 344
Interinstitutional Agreement, 247, 329, 335, 509
Interinstitutional Agreement between the European Parliament and the SRB, 509
Internal Capital Adequacy Assessment Process (ICAAP), 326
Internal Liquidity Adequacy Assessment Process (ILAAP), 327
Internal market, 231, 289, 331, 332, 345, 346, 390, 405, 511, 527
International Accounting Standards Board (IASB), 110, 111, 117, 118, 139, 177, 186, 187, 270
International Association of Deposit Insurers (IADI), 96, 102, 110, 111, 113, 114, 139, 145, 146, 167, 177, 181–183
International Association of Insurance Supervisors (IAIS), 102, 109, 111, 113, 114, 117, 118, 149, 181, 190, 191, 223
International Chamber of Commerce (ICC), 90
International Conferences of Banking Supervisors (ICBS), 180
International cooperation, 86, 95, 108, 116, 163, 166, 181, 183, 192, 193, 196, 233, 459
International Court of Justice, 138
International Federation of Accountants (IFAC), 110, 111, 132, 139, 188, 528
International Financial Reporting Standard (IFRS), 139, 186, 187
International forum/fora, 91, 96, 97, 110, 116, 188
International Institute for the Unification of Private Law (UNIDROIT), 90
International Monetary Fund (IMF), 49, 85, 91, 106–108, 117, 118, 121–125, 128–131, 138, 182, 191
International Network on Financial Education (INFE), 18
International Organisation of Securities Commissions (IOSCO), 102, 109, 111, 117, 118, 139, 148, 149, 181, 184–186, 189, 191, 215, 223, 234, 237, 238
International Standards on Auditing (ISA), 139, 188
International Sustainability Standards Board (ISSB), 187
International Swaps and Derivatives Association (ISDA), 90
intra-group financial support agreements, 25
Investigatory power(s), 464, 465, 517, 520
Investment firms, 6, 15, 16, 37, 87, 109, 166, 205, 208, 219, 234, 244, 249, 285, 298, 321, 325, 336, 340, 342, 357, 359, 389, 500
Investment Firms Directive (IFD), 285
Investment Firms Regulation (IFR), 285
Investment services, 6, 15–17, 24, 88, 207, 220, 234, 237, 337, 359
Investment Services Directive (ISD), 219
Investor compensation, 17
Investor Compensation Scheme/system (ICS), 17
Investor Compensation Schemes Directive (ICSD), 220
Investor protection, 16, 37, 88, 185, 240, 298, 401
Islamic banking, 149
Islamic Financial Services Board (IFSB), 149, 183
Istituto per la Vigilanza Sulle Assicurazioni (IVASS), 469

J
Joint Committee (of the ESAs), 228, 339, 383, 387, 391, 406, 410
Joint Supervisory Team (JST), 295, 469
Judicial authority, 25, 467, 522
Judicial control, 385
Judicial review, 384, 407, 421, 422, 467, 488, 538

K
Kantarev case, 412
Key Attributes Assessment Methodology for the Banking Sector, 143

Key Attributes of Effective Resolution Regimes for Financial Institutions, 54, 133, 139, 142, 167, 234, 250
Key Information Document (KID), 240
Key Standards for Sound Financial Systems, 133, 137, 178, 183
Kotnik case, 358

L

Lamfalussy, Alexandre, 221–223, 230
Lamfalussy Committee, 221, 229
Lamfalussy process, 221, 414, 424
Lamfalussy Report (1990), 221, 229
Lamfalussy Report (2001), 221
*Landeskreditbank Baden-Württemberg – Förderbank v ECB*case, 452
Large exposures, 33, 175, 219, 271, 319, 324
Large Exposures Directive, 219
Large-value, 10, 17, 93, 189, 224
Lato sensu, 204
Lean against the financial cycle, 41
Legacy NPLs, 273
Legal acts, 87, 204, 205, 215–218, 221, 223, 226, 237, 247, 253, 271, 333, 334, 343, 413, 415, 459, 460, 465, 467, 469, 470, 472, 473
Legal instrument(s), 302, 413, 461, 479
Legally binding, 86, 122, 140, 389, 414, 418, 422
Legally significant, 140
Legal person, 4, 32, 359, 389, 398, 410, 411, 467
Legal personality, 164, 182, 231, 277, 389, 437, 447, 499
Legal status, 337, 388, 499
Legal Theory of Finance (LTF), 13, 97
Legislative act, 215, 235, 236, 238, 240, 270, 278, 285, 294, 321, 389, 401, 404, 405, 415–417, 423, 447
Legislative banking package, 269, 270, 299, 304, 318, 319, 325, 339, 341
Lehman Brothers, 239
Lender of last resort (for sovereign states), 51, 64, 123, 212, 242, 277
Lending of last resort (LLR), 25, 48, 50, 64, 363

Less significant supervised entity/ entities, 452, 477
Less significant supervised group, 452, 477
Level 1, 414, 415
Level 2, 415, 429
Level 3, 415, 429
Leverage, 8, 13, 98, 175, 179, 194, 271, 318, 319, 324
Leverage ratio, 33, 34, 175, 179, 271, 318, 368
Liability, 112, 347, 350, 407, 412, 488, 537
Liikanen, Erkki, 235
Liquidation, 47, 51, 52, 54, 60, 62, 96, 147, 167, 352
Liquidity, 8, 16, 21, 26, 28, 32, 47–49, 55, 64, 101, 134, 145, 290, 292, 297, 350, 363–365, 370, 520
Liquidity Coverage Ratio (LCR), 34, 134, 135, 179, 292
Liquidity crises, 49, 55, 64
Liquidity crisis management, 49
Liquidity position, 28, 362
Liquidity risk, 27, 28, 32, 49, 96, 98, 134, 135, 148, 286, 297, 319
Listing Particulars Directive, 224
London Interbank Offer Rate (LIBOR), 102
Loss Absorption Amount (LAA), 507
Loss Given Default (LGD), 27
Loss minimiser mandate, 57
Low Carbon Benchmarks Regulation, 288

M

Macroeconomic failure, 99
Macroeconomic integration, 201, 202
Macroeconomic policies, 63, 96, 112, 125, 139, 142, 146, 201
Macrofinancial, 44, 195, 281
Macro Prudential Indicator (MPI), 126
Macroprudential oversight, 23, 42, 87, 194, 206, 212, 215, 230–232, 292, 371, 441, 447
Macroprudential policies, 25, 35, 40–42, 44, 64, 98, 195, 212, 231, 292, 293

INDEX 559

Macroprudential policy measures, 42
Macroprudential regulation, 6, 12, 15, 23, 45, 87, 101, 109, 133, 140, 165, 176, 190, 206, 249, 291, 323, 326, 438
Macroprudential supervision, 42
Macroprudential tool(s), 438
Management Board (EBA), 391, 392, 394, 395, 408, 410
Managers of Micro, Small and Medium-sized Enterprises (MSME), 18
Mandatory membership, 57, 58, 354
Marginal lending facility, 367
Market-based financing, 300
Market-based system, 7
Market discipline, 12, 19, 56, 59, 63, 142, 511
Market failure(s), 10, 19, 21, 34, 273
Market Maker of Last Resort (MMLR), 100
Market risk framework, 104, 134, 135, 179, 319
Market risks, 26, 27, 29, 63, 94, 134, 135, 141, 219, 226, 271, 293, 318, 319, 323
Markets Abuse Directive No II (MAD II), 237, 238
Markets Abuse Regulation (MAR), 237, 238
Markets in Crypto-Assets Regulation (MiCAR), 305, 306, 386
Markets in Financial Instruments Directive No I (MiFID I), 224, 237
Markets in Financial Instruments Directive No II (MiFID II), 237, 240, 286, 298, 322, 337, 359, 459
Markets in Financial Instruments Regulation (MiFIR), 237, 384
Material conditions, 442
Material facts, 463
Materiality, 31, 302
Maturity transformation, 10, 28
Maximum harmonisation, 349
Mediation Panel, 334, 439, 445, 481, 484, 486, 489
Member jurisdiction assessments, 179

Member States whose currency is the euro, 210, 211, 213, 246, 277, 329, 331, 362, 437
Member States with a derogation, 209, 210, 242, 329, 331, 449, 455, 521
Memorandum of Understanding (MoU), 247, 277, 335, 440, 442, 458, 514, 516, 518
Meroni doctrine, 328, 384–386
Methodology, 126, 128–130, 140, 142, 149, 179, 320, 340, 399, 400, 477
Microeconomic integration, 201, 202, 209
Microprudential regulation, 15, 32, 42, 44, 51, 95, 98, 109, 148, 149, 166, 225, 249
Microprudential supervision, 11, 12, 15, 23, 33, 36–40, 87, 98, 109, 140, 148, 149, 190, 241, 326, 327, 330, 331, 366, 371, 386, 447, 448
Middle East and North Africa Financial Action Task Force (MENAFATF), 192
Minimum harmonisation, 203, 216, 225, 250, 337, 356
Minimum Requirement (for own funds and) Eligible Liabilities (MREL), 176, 270
Mitigating factors, 523, 524
Mixed-activity holding company/companies, 360
Mixed-activity insurance holding companies, 359
Mixed financial holding company/companies, 320, 321, 360, 361, 450
Modified sectoral approach, 38, 171
Monetary authority, 25, 38, 39, 48, 170, 212, 242, 370
Monetary policy, 17, 22, 24, 37–40, 49–51, 64, 89, 100, 101, 125, 146, 195, 196, 209–213, 215, 223, 225, 291, 303, 329, 330, 332, 362, 363, 365, 367, 369, 443, 444, 446, 448, 479, 484, 485, 490
Monetary system, 24, 89, 91, 123, 164
Monetary union, 168, 196, 209, 210, 213

560   INDEX

Money laundering, 59, 60, 89, 110, 111, 132, 139, 192, 193, 214, 234, 305, 325, 391, 392, 401, 402, 438
Money Market Fund (MMF), 235
Money Market Funds Regulation (MMFR), 239
Moral hazard, 10, 12, 19, 51, 59, 61, 63, 145, 250
Multilateral Memorandum of Understanding (MmoU), 185
Multilateral Trading Facility (MTF), 6

N

National Central Bank (NCB), 109, 112, 169–172, 210, 337, 361, 365, 367–370, 440, 445, 446, 448, 449, 474
National Competent Authority (NCA), 228, 320, 321, 337, 361, 383, 397, 438, 440, 443, 445, 446, 449, 452–454, 456, 464–468, 471, 481, 483
National Designated Authority (NDA), 293, 320, 361, 456, 464
National Judicial Authority (NJA), 467, 522
National law, 49, 62, 164, 169, 177, 203, 212, 271, 321, 324, 346, 358, 361, 366, 389, 405, 418, 445, 448, 460, 465, 467, 468, 472, 477, 481, 488, 499, 514, 516, 520–522, 526, 534, 537, 538
National legislation, 6, 59, 203, 213, 460, 471, 487, 522
National parliaments, 439, 478, 481, 530, 534
National Resolution Authority (NRA), 248, 337, 343, 361, 500, 501, 504, 506, 508, 511–513, 515, 534, 538
Natural person, 447, 462, 466, 471, 483, 521
Negative financial integration, 202, 204
Net Fee and Commission Income (NFCI), 399
Net Stable Funding Ratio (NSFR), 34, 179, 271
Network for Greening the Financial System (NGFS), 30

New Arrangements to Borrow (NAB), 106
New International Financial Architecture (NIFA), 85, 96, 196
New Sustainable Finance Strategy, 300–303
No creditor worse off (NCWO), 54–56, 62, 143
Non-Bank Financial Intermediation (NBFI), 102, 103
Non-contractual liability, 231, 273, 347, 412, 487, 537–539
Non-euro area participating Member State(s), 331, 445, 456–458, 465, 479, 480
Non-Financial Reporting Directive (NFRD), 301
Non-legislative, 294, 300, 343, 416, 460
Non-participating Member State(s), 331, 345, 347, 393, 394, 400, 438, 441, 442, 448, 449, 452, 455, 458, 461, 467, 470, 501, 502, 506, 512, 516–519, 528, 539
Non-pecuniary penalties, 471
Non-Performing Exposure (NPE), 273, 275
Non-Performing Loan (NPL), 46, 273
Non-regulated market, 6
Non-systematic risk, 29
Non-voting member(s), 394, 506
No-objection procedure, 444
NPL Action Plan, 297

O

Objectives and Principles of Securities Regulation, 15, 16, 148, 149, 186
Observer(s), 106, 108, 114, 168, 169, 172, 173, 175, 180, 182, 190–192, 339, 345, 387, 392, 394, 440, 441, 500–502, 505, 506, 508, 509, 515
Office Européen de Lutte Antifraude (European Anti-Fraud Office) (OLAF), 448, 504
Offshore financial centres, 3
On-site inspection(s), 464, 467–469, 520–522, 524
Open market operations, 50, 363, 365

INDEX   561

Operational independence, 58, 145, 337, 408, 474, 526
Operational risk, 26, 31, 136, 141, 148, 175, 226, 319, 323
Opinion, 35, 52, 214, 215, 242, 323, 348, 350, 354, 384, 391, 396, 402, 404, 413, 417, 421–429, 452, 482–484, 486, 529
Organisation for Economic Co-operation and Development (OECD), 18, 91, 102, 106, 110, 116–118, 132, 138, 139, 147, 192
O-SII buffer, 326
Other Systemically Important Institution (O-SII), 292, 293, 320, 321
Over-regulation, 35
Oversight of payment and settlement systems, 16, 17, 44
Over-the-counter (OTC) derivatives, 5
Own funds, 4, 5, 9, 28, 34, 46, 218, 251, 270, 271, 318, 319, 321, 323, 350, 351, 469
Own Funds Directive, 218
Own funds requirements, 285, 291, 318, 319, 368

P
Packaged Retail and Insurance-based Investment Product(s) (PRIIP), 240
Pandemic crisis, 92, 100, 101, 103, 105, 128, 134, 174, 175, 186, 215, 290–292, 295–301, 318, 325
Pan-European Personal Pension Product (PEPP), 285
Parent Committees, 191
Parent company/companies, 37, 218
Parent credit institution in a Member State, 360
Parent financial holding company in a Member State, 321, 360, 361
Parent institution in a Member State, 321, 360, 361
Parent mixed financial holding company in a Member State, 361
Parent undertaking, 165, 337, 341–343, 357, 359, 360, 450, 472, 518, 519
Participating Member States, 246, 248, 272, 276, 277, 331, 332, 340–343, 345, 347, 355, 371, 387, 393, 396, 437–440, 446, 448–451, 455, 456, 460, 464–467, 469, 470, 472, 476, 477, 481, 485, 486, 500, 501, 504–506, 508, 513, 516, 517, 519, 521, 522, 525, 528, 530, 534, 537, 539
Participating Member States in close cooperation, 331
Particular circumstances, 451, 453, 454, 463
Paybox, 46, 57, 349
Paybox 'plus' mandate, 57
Paybox mandate (of DGSs), 57, 62
Payment and settlement systems, 16, 17, 52, 88, 91, 94, 109, 137, 139, 163, 189, 207, 208, 213
Payment institution(s), 359, 387
Payment Services Directive No II (PSD II), 236, 359, 388, 389
Payment Services Directive (PSD), 225
Payment systems, 17, 22, 125, 127, 143, 148, 189, 208, 212, 306
Payout, 54, 57, 60–62, 236, 280, 354
Payout (or paybox) function, 25, 57, 58, 61, 349, 354
Periodic penalty payments, 467, 471–473, 522, 524–526, 535
Personal independence, 408, 410, 442, 474, 475, 510, 526
Personal liability, 539
Peter Paul case, 412
Physical risks, 31, 304
Pillar 1, 270, 299, 323, 326
Pillar 2, 270, 299, 326
Pillar 2 Guidance (P2G), 292
Pillar 2 Requirements (P2R), 292
Pillar 3, 271, 300, 324
Pillar 3 disclosure requirements, 104, 134, 135, 319
Plenary Session (SRB), 500–505, 507–509, 528, 529, 532, 533
Policy and Standards Group (PSG), 174, 175
Policy Development Group (PDG), 175
Policy function(s), 485
Policy objective(s), 3, 11–13, 16–19, 34, 56, 59, 86, 88, 107, 108, 116, 145, 165, 168, 202, 208, 209

Political risk, 26
Position risk, 9, 26, 29, 219
Positive financial integration, 203–205
Post-FSAP, 227
Preparation for resolution, 25, 501, 507
Preparatory measures, 338
Price-based prudential tools, 43
Price stability, 39, 49, 97, 211, 212, 242, 331, 365
PRIIPS Regulation, 240
Primary law, 206, 414
Primary market, 5, 9, 207, 363
Principle of decentralisation, 437
Principle of due consideration to the resolution objectives, 511
Principle of fiscal neutrality, 512
Principle of non-discrimination, 511
Principle of proportionality, 391, 395, 407
Principle of separation, 168, 171, 444, 484
Principle of subsidiarity, 210, 415
Principles for Financial Market Infrastructures, 139, 148, 189
Principles of Corporate Governance (G20/OECD), 33, 139, 147, 148
Private money solution, 49
Private Sector Involvement (PSI), 272
Probability of Default (PD), 27
Procyclicality, 35, 41, 43, 194
Professional Accountancy Organisation (PAO), 188
Professional networks, 109
Professional secrecy, 409, 439, 446, 466, 482, 485, 486, 514, 516, 518, 520, 529, 530
Prospectus Directive, 224
Prudential backstop, 294
Prudential Regulation Authority (PRA), 14, 170
Prudential supervision, 38, 58, 63, 94, 133, 166, 170, 171, 191, 206, 208, 212, 215, 223, 225, 228, 229, 232, 233, 236, 241, 242, 244, 246, 247, 253, 285, 325, 326, 328, 330, 331, 355, 387, 397, 412, 453–455, 481
Public choice theory, 11, 35
Public disclosure of information, 33, 324

Public financial assistance facilities, 52, 458
Public interest, 173, 332, 390, 410, 481, 482, 486, 499
Public interest approach, 11, 35
Public international banking law, 86–88, 133, 140, 217, 245
Public international capital markets law, 86–88, 188
Public international financial conglomerates, 87, 88, 191
Public international financial law, 54, 55, 85–88, 90, 92, 95–97, 99, 105, 108, 110, 112, 122, 131–133, 138, 140, 205, 207, 215, 233, 252
Public international insurance law, 87, 88, 190
Public international monetary law, 85, 88, 89
Public international payment and settlement systems law, 87, 88, 188
Pure information contagion, 22

Q
Qualified majority, 393, 426, 427, 441, 442, 444, 460, 509, 510
Qualifying holding(s), 325, 334, 403, 423, 457, 469
Quantity-based prudential tools, 43
Quasi-judicial, 411, 535
Questions and Answers (Q&As), 391

R
Reaction lag, 39
Recapitalisation, 23, 144, 270, 271, 298, 328, 367, 507
Recapitalisation Amount (RCA), 507
Recapitalisation of banks by public funds, 25
Recognition lag, 39
Recommendations, 12, 30, 105, 114, 120, 121, 131, 139, 141, 169, 176, 181, 185, 189, 192, 194, 218, 228, 229, 231, 232, 235, 287, 294, 295, 297, 305, 334, 343, 371, 391, 393, 396, 400–403, 405, 406, 413, 415, 419, 420, 422, 423, 429, 460, 461, 478, 487, 504, 519, 520, 529, 533

Recovery and Resilience Facility (RRF), 291
Recovery planning, 45, 338, 343, 371, 438
Recurring intervals, 465, 466
Reform agenda, 233, 269
Reg-tech, 11
Regulated market, 5–7, 116, 187, 188, 207, 208, 224, 283
Regulatory arbitrage, 25, 35, 36, 62, 89, 98, 191, 214, 331, 390
Regulatory capture, 35
Regulatory Consistency Assessment Programme (RCAP), 122, 178, 179, 293
Regulatory failure, 34, 39, 272
Regulatory Fitness and Performance Programme (REFIT), 285
Regulatory powers, 37, 403, 460, 461
Regulatory Technical Standards (RTSs), 317, 324, 343, 391, 393, 396, 401–403, 415–417, 419, 422, 429, 460, 472
Reimbursement, 22, 57, 60, 145, 347, 348
Reinsurance phase, 280
Reinsurance undertaking(s), 15, 88, 109, 190, 208, 240, 241, 360, 387
Relevant capital instruments, 513, 514
Relevant legislative acts, 389–391, 394, 396, 397, 401, 402, 404–406, 410, 417, 419, 421, 423
Reorganisation measures, 46, 225, 356–358
Repayable amount, 59, 60
Reports on the Observance of Standards and Codes (ROSCs), 125, 146
Reputational risk, 26, 32
Reserve Bank, 114, 171, 189, 193
Resilience, 35, 36, 39, 41, 101, 102, 104, 125, 134, 136, 174, 175, 195, 196, 235, 250, 270, 282, 300, 302–304, 399, 400
Resolution action, 23, 51, 54, 62, 144, 338, 503, 513, 534, 536, 537
Resolution authorities, 23, 24, 48, 49, 51–55, 60, 62, 63, 120, 248, 296, 339, 361, 397, 501, 518, 519, 534

Resolution financing, 54, 62, 338, 340, 528
Resolution framework(s), 15, 54, 55, 61, 144, 295, 300, 339, 343
Resolution fund, 25, 54, 55, 244, 248
Resolution planning, 25, 45, 46, 53, 143, 291, 295, 296, 338, 342, 371, 501, 514, 516, 518
Resolution Planning Cycle (RPC), 296
Resolution strategy, 52, 53, 300
Resolution tool(s), 51, 53–55, 62, 145, 277, 337, 356, 357, 361, 503, 513, 531
Resolvability, 23, 46, 52, 53, 296, 338, 371, 535
Resolvability assessment, 52, 53, 143
Reverse transactions, 367
Right of access, 60, 425, 463, 483, 525, 533
Right to be heard, 462, 525
Right to compensation, 54, 61, 537
Risk arising from open positions in commodities, 29, 30
Risk-benefit analysis, 34
Risk management, 11, 33, 57, 94, 131, 136, 137, 141, 287, 303, 304
Risk minimiser mandate, 57
Risk reduction measures, 269, 280, 281
Risks and Vulnerabilities Assessment Group (RVG), 174, 175
Risk sharing, 7, 269
Risk-Weighted Assets (RWAs), 33, 43, 44, 476
Romano doctrine, 385
Rules of Procedure of the Supervisory Board, 440, 443, 444, 446, 489

S

Sale of business tool, 53
Sanctioning powers, 37, 141, 334, 342
Sanctions, 11, 37, 238, 326, 334, 470, 472, 490
Scenario analyses, 36
Seat, 99, 108, 110–112, 118, 161, 162, 181, 184, 186, 188, 190–193, 231, 252, 388, 389, 500
Secondary law, 207, 213, 362

564   INDEX

Secondary markets, 5, 9, 16, 19, 28, 207, 297
Second Banking Directive, 218, 219
Second Consolidated Supervision Directive, 219
Second pillar, 96, 165, 224, 244, 296, 299, 342
Secretariat, 113, 119, 173, 176, 178, 181, 190, 232, 233, 345, 410, 444, 446, 486, 500, 504
Sectoral approach, 37, 171, 172, 208, 229, 231
Sector-specific, 3, 33, 109, 143, 208
Securities and Exchange Commission (SEC), 187
Securities clearing and settlement systems, 17, 189
Securities Financing Transaction (SFT), 235
Securities Financing Transactions Regulation (SFTR), 240
Securities regulation, 125, 149, 185, 186
Securitisation, 19, 98, 175, 235, 284, 318, 323, 384
Separation, 38, 330, 332, 334, 446, 479, 484, 485, 490
Settlement risk, 26, 94, 162, 189, 219, 319, 323
Seven-day payout target, 60
Shadow banking, 8, 235
Short selling, 239, 298
Short selling case, 384–386
Short Selling Regulation, 239
Signal information contagion, 22
Significant credit institution(s), 362, 371, 450, 451, 461
Significant supervised entities, 294, 295, 334, 450, 451, 455, 457, 464, 465, 468, 471–473
Significant supervised entity in a euro area Member State, 450
Significant supervised entity in a non-euro area participating Member State, 450, 457
Significant supervised group, 294, 457
Simple, Transparent and Standardised (STS), 284
Single currency, 209, 221

Single economic area, 201, 202
Single Euro Payments Area (SEPA), 236
Single European Act (SEA), 217
Single market, 201, 204, 217, 230, 245, 284, 300, 306, 325
Single Resolution Board (SRB), 121, 122, 143, 244, 248, 251, 269, 275–278, 291, 295, 296, 339, 341–344, 346, 371, 390, 392, 396, 400, 412, 440, 458, 482, 483, 499–539
Single Resolution Fund (SRF), 244, 248, 251, 253, 269, 275, 277, 279, 340–342, 344–348, 355, 503, 505, 507, 511, 513, 526, 528, 531, 535, 537, 539
Single Resolution Mechanism Regulation no. II (SRMR II), 271, 341
Single Resolution Mechanism Regulation (SRMR), 248, 340
Single Resolution Mechanism (SRM), 246, 248, 515
Single rulebook, 245, 247, 249, 252, 253, 269, 273, 299, 323, 384, 416
Single Supervisory Mechanism Regulation (SSMR), 246, 247, 327–329, 331–335, 341, 345, 355, 358, 387, 389, 409, 417, 437–444, 446–456, 458–470, 472, 473, 475–487, 489, 510, 515, 527, 534
Single Supervisory Mechanism (SSM), 169–171, 212, 229, 244, 246, 247, 328, 449, 489
Size criterion, 451, 452
Size transformation, 9
Small-Medium Enterprise (SME), 101
Small-value payment systems, 17
Social and Structural Reviews (SSRs), 131
Soft law, 85, 122, 139, 294, 344, 413, 419, 421, 429, 430
Solidarity, 213, 291, 337
Solvency crises, 25, 55
Solvency crisis management, 23, 49
Solvency criterion, 366
Solvency II (Directive), 240, 241, 284, 359
Solvency Ratio Directive, 218

Sound practices, 167–169, 173, 176–178
Sovereign Bond-Backed Securities (SBBSs), 269, 272, 273
Sovereign crisis management mechanism, 275
Special agreement, 122, 345, 347
Special Data Dissemination Standard (SDDS), 139, 147
Special purpose vehicle (SPV), 26, 286
Special resolution regime (SRR), 52
Specific tasks, 171, 212, 213, 229, 230, 232, 233, 244, 246, 328, 330–332, 387, 388, 392, 395, 437, 438, 447, 448, 456, 458, 484, 499, 513
Spill-over effects, 10, 14, 15, 20, 21, 23, 42, 52, 62, 94, 102, 128, 144, 291
Spill-over mechanism, 63
SRB-ECB MoU, 516, 521
SRF Agreement, 248, 279, 340, 344, 346, 347
SRF aid, 512, 532, 535
SSM Framework Regulation (SSM-FR), 247, 331, 333, 355, 439, 448, 450–457, 462–468, 470, 472–474
Stability and Growth Pact (SGP), 213
Stability of financial systems, 183
Stablecoins, 305
Staff Regulations, 503, 504, 527, 539
Standard-setter(s), 109, 110, 132, 191
Standing Committee on Assessment of Vulnerabilities (SCAV), 120
Standing Committee on Budget and Resources (SCBR), 120
Standing Committee on Resolution (ResCo), 339, 340, 515
Standing Committee on Standards Implementation (SCSI), 120
Standing Committee on Supervisory and Regulatory Cooperation (SCSRC), 120
Standing facilities, 363
State aid, 203, 294, 298, 351–353, 358, 363, 365, 512, 532
Statutory DGSs, 350
Steering committee, 113, 119, 146, 232, 233, 443–445, 475
Strategic management body, 190, 391

Stress test(s), 36, 58, 59, 127, 128, 293, 304, 398–400, 403
Stricto sensu, 26, 203, 204, 245
Structural reform, 234, 235
Structural regulations, 24
Structural systemic risk, 41–43, 45
STS Securitisation Regulation, 284, 384
Subsidiary, 15, 39, 133, 171, 172, 206, 320, 336, 360, 361, 472, 505, 506, 519, 537
Sub-state networks, 109
Supervised entities, 36, 246, 331, 334, 359, 396, 437, 448–452, 455–458, 461, 466, 470, 472, 476, 477
Supervised group, 328, 450, 451, 457, 458, 472, 477
Supervision and Implementation Group (SIG), 175
Supervisory authorities, 6, 23, 30, 32, 33, 36–39, 42, 46–49, 94, 96, 101, 111, 117, 121, 133, 140–142, 146, 149, 163–165, 167–169, 171, 172, 175, 177, 180, 217, 222, 223, 227, 228, 230, 235, 241, 304, 383, 384, 387, 397, 422, 459
Supervisory Board, 290, 333–335, 391, 392, 439–441, 443–446, 449, 459, 460, 473, 475, 479–486, 489, 510, 515
Supervisory college, 121, 322
Supervisory Cooperation Group (SCG), 174, 175
Supervisory failure, 25, 39, 243
Supervisory fees, 334, 461, 476, 477, 479, 490
Supervisory Fess Regulation (SFR), 477, 478
Supervisory powers, 39, 171, 229, 231, 241, 285, 326, 386, 464, 469, 478
Supervisory review and evaluation process (SREP), 292, 304, 326, 327, 396, 400, 402
Supervisory tasks, 38, 124, 229, 247, 329–331, 333, 334, 371, 383, 384, 386, 404, 409, 437–440, 444, 446–448, 455, 458, 459, 461, 464–467, 470, 475–479, 481, 482, 484–486

566 INDEX

Supplementary supervision of financial conglomerates, 88, 208, 226
Sup-tech, 11
Sustainable Development Goals (SDGs), 30
Sustainable finance, 30, 136, 284, 287–290, 301, 302
Sustainable Finance Action Plan (2018), 287
Sustainable Finance Disclosure Regulation (SFDR), 287, 288
Sustainable Finance Strategy, 300
SV Capital case, 411
Swedish National Debt Office (SNDO), 518
Swiss Financial Market Supervisory Authority (FINMA), 170, 518
Systemically Important Banks (SIBs), 134, 141
Systemically Important Financial Institution (SIFI), 450
Systemically Important Financial Sectors (SIFS), 128–130
Systemically Significant Financial Institutions (SSFIs), 12
Systemic risk, 17, 22, 35, 40–43, 45, 96, 97, 117, 118, 121, 128, 141, 149, 231, 232, 272, 292, 320, 325, 361, 395, 400, 402
Systemic risk buffer, 44, 45, 292, 293, 325, 326

T

Takeover Bids Directive, 224
Target fund size, 58
Task Force on Climate-related Financial Disclosures (TCFD), 30, 32, 136
Task Force on Climate-related Financial Risks (TFCR), 174
Task Force on Evaluations (TFE), 174
Taxonomy Regulation (TR), 288–290, 302
Taxpayers' money, 12, 23
Technical Screening Criteria (TSC), 289
Temporary administrator, 338
Tercas case, 351
Thematic assessments, 179
Thematic peer reviews, 122, 430

Third pillar, 101, 165, 225, 245, 300, 304, 338, 342
Three-pillar system, 338, 342
Threshold, 368, 369, 503
Tietmeyer Report, 116, 117
Time dimension (of systemic risk), 22, 35, 41, 43
Too-big-to-be-left-to-fail, 12
Too-big-to-fail (TBTF), 12, 44, 51, 61, 103, 142, 144
Total Loss Absorbing Capital (TLAC), 144, 270, 338
Trading book, 9, 27, 29, 30, 219
Training and Capacity Building Unit (TCBU), 184
Transfer risk, 27, 141
Transitional provisions, 319, 324, 327, 348, 426
Transition risk, 31, 32, 287
Transparency, 16, 58, 88, 89, 98, 112, 119, 121, 125, 127, 129, 137–139, 142, 146–148, 186, 187, 192, 207, 221, 224, 235, 237–239, 286–288, 306, 390, 398, 405, 407, 409, 443, 459, 461, 478, 530, 533
Transparency Directive, 224, 298
Treaties, 90, 133, 209, 210, 246, 328, 330, 362, 413–416, 426, 437, 487
Treaty (establishing the) European Community (TEC), 209, 210, 218, 220, 222, 242, 362
Treaty of Lisbon (Lisbon Treaty), 242, 275, 413–415, 423
Treaty of Maastricht, 209, 210, 218
Treaty of Rome, 216–218
Treaty on European Union (TEU), 210–212, 242, 275, 287, 327, 330, 346, 393, 413–415, 418, 426, 444, 514
Treaty on the Functioning of the European Union (TFEU), 207, 209–213, 229–233, 242, 245, 246, 273, 275, 276, 317, 324, 328–331, 336, 340, 346–348, 351, 352, 356, 358, 362, 363, 365, 366, 385, 387, 390, 404, 406, 407, 409, 411–416, 418, 421, 425, 427, 437, 439, 447, 456, 459, 463, 464, 474, 475, 478,

INDEX 567

480, 484, 487, 512, 530–532, 536, 537, 539
Trilemma, 13, 23
Trilogy, 284, 289, 301, 304, 306
'Twin' crisis, 24, 100
Two-pronged strategy, 142

U
UCITS Directive No IV (2009/65/EC) (UCITS IV), 238, 285
UCITS Directive No V (UCITS V), 238
UCITS Directives no. I (2001, 224
UCITS Directives no. I (2001/107/EC and 2001/108/EC) (UCITS I), 217
UCITS IV Directive, 238
Unanimity, 217, 275, 330, 413, 415, 478
Unavailable, 61, 220, 280, 354
Unconventional monetary policy, 49, 291
Undertakings for Collective Investment in Transferable Securities (UCITS), 7, 16, 217, 222
Union body, 231, 389
Union (or EU) parent financial holding company, 361
Union (or EU) parent institution, 361
Union (or EU) parent mixed financial holding company, 361
United Kingdom (UK), 14, 108, 132, 170, 172, 235, 242, 248
United Nations Commission on International Trade Law (UNCITRAL), 90, 147
United Nations Office on Drugs and Crime (UNODC), 192

United Nations (UN), 30, 122
United States (of America) (US), 7, 12, 24, 48, 61, 62, 92, 93, 95, 97–99, 102, 105, 106, 108, 114, 115, 122, 132, 163, 171, 172, 188, 193, 234
Universal banking model, 24, 207, 220

V
Van Rompuy Report, 215, 243
Virtual Asset Service Provider (VASP), 305
Virtual Networks (BCBS), 173–176
Voting members, 393, 394
Voting rights, 112, 392, 393, 500, 505, 508

W
Warning(s), 231, 232, 371, 400, 401, 403, 406, 456, 513, 533
Washington Consensus, 124
White Paper, 216, 227
White Paper "Financial Services Policy 2005-2010", 227
Winding-up, 15, 25, 87, 166, 167, 206, 225, 226, 356, 357, 480
Winding-up proceedings, 23, 225, 354, 356–358
Withdrawal of authorisation, 325, 371, 457
World Bank, 10, 107, 108, 110, 112, 117, 118, 124, 125, 127–132, 138, 139, 142, 147, 182, 184, 192, 252
World Trade Organization (WTO), 96, 107, 110, 114, 115, 140
Write-down, 46, 53, 338, 513, 514

Printed in the United States
by Baker & Taylor Publisher Services